PHYSICAL

EDUCATION

IN THE

ELEMENTARY SCHOOL

WINIFRED VAN HAGEN
GENEVIE DEXTER
JESSE FEIRING WILLIAMS

CALIFORNIA STATE DEPARTMENT OF EDUCATION
SACRAMENTO, 1951

printed in
CALIFORNIA STATE PRINTING OFFICE
SACRAMENTO   5378 9-54 60M
THIRD PRINTING

FOREWORD

Educators have long recognized the need for a thorough program of physical education during the early years of childhood. These are the years of rapid growth and development when strength and stamina are acquired to form a healthy body. These are the years when posture habits are being formed and fundamental motor skills are being learned to give the individual poise, grace, and bodily efficiency. In these years basic skills may be acquired that will give the individual wholesome recreational habits throughout his lifetime. In his early years, a child's notions of fairness and co-operation and good sportsmanship are shaped by the give-and-take on the playing field. During the elementary school years, boy-girl relationships can be guided into wholesome and healthy channels through coeducational play. In the philosophy of today's schools the whole child is educated—not the mind alone, not the body alone, but the whole personality. Physical education, with its many kinds of activities offered to develop the whole child, has an important place in the program of the elementary school.

The California Physical Education Act of 1917 provided for the organization and supervision of courses in physical education in the public schools of the State. The State Board of Education was required to adopt such rules and regulations as it might deem necessary to carry out the provisions of the act, to appoint a state supervisor of physical education, and to compile a manual in physical education for distribution to teachers. The first State Supervisor of Physical Education, Clark Hetherington, prepared the first *Manual in Physical Education* for the California public schools in 1918. In 1929 this was superseded by a *Manual of Physical Education Activities for the Elementary Schools of the State of California*, prepared by N. P. Neilson, the third State Supervisor of Physical Education, and Winifred Van Hagen, Assistant Supervisor. The *Manual* served as an effective guide to elementary school teachers and supervisors in conducting sound physical education programs. A revised edition of this publication was printed by A. S. Barnes and Company in 1931 for sale and use in other states. The activities presented in the Manual have thus helped boys and girls not only in California but in all states of the nation to acquire useful habits and skills and to develop wholesome attitudes through physical education.

After the *Manual* had been in continuous use for many years, it was thought advisable to select and compile material for a teacher's guide in line with broadened concepts and changed practices of education in general and physical education in particular. The task of preparing the new guide was undertaken by Miss Van Hagen, who commenced the work under the general direction of W. H. Orion, then Chief of the Division of Health and Physical Education, and continued it under the direction of Verne S. Landreth, who succeeded him in 1942. Work on the guide involved endless correspondence with professional leaders and continuous study of recently published material in the field of physical education for elementary school children. From the date of Miss Van Hagen's appointment in 1918 to her retirement in 1948 California has had the benefit of her unfailing enthusiasm and high professional competence. This book is a testimonial to her service and devotion to pupils and teachers in the elementary schools of California.

Miss Van Hagen retired from the State Department of Education in 1948, leaving the manuscript of the guide partially completed. She was succeeded by Genevie Dexter, Consultant in Physical Education, who continued the work, selecting and revising materials for the graded programs of activities and adding up-to-date bibliographical data. In the preparation of the manuscript for publication the State benefitted greatly from the collaboration of an outstanding authority in the field, Dr. Jesse Feiring Williams, Chairman Emeritus, Department of Health and Physical Education, Teachers College, Columbia University, and now a resident of California.

Physical Education in the Elementary School is the result of the work of many of the professional leaders in the state. On a later page a list of acknowledgments is printed as evidence of appreciation to the many persons who have made valuable contributions.

The guide is divided into two parts. Part I, on the characteristics of an adequate physical education program, is written to help teachers, supervisors, and administrators to plan and organize a good program for elementary schools. The basic philosophy of physical education is clearly stated through the discussion of the growth of the elementary school child, his needs, and his ways of acquiring motor skills. Schedules and procedures for setting up ideal programs are discussed. Standards for facilities and equipment are suggested. Desirable types of physical activity are discussed in chapters dealing with body mechanics, games, rhythmical activities, self-testing activities, recreation, and camping. Workable methods of evaluation conclude Part I.

Part II describes activities suitable for physical education in grades 1 through 8. An analysis of skills developed through elementary school physical education introduces this second part. Each chapter contains games, relays (except grades 1 and 2), rhythmical activities, and stunts chosen for one of the eight grades. Graded activities provide experiences that challenge the interest of the child because they parallel his normal growth and development.

The California legal provisions relating to health education, physical education, and recreation in California are given in an appendix. Lists of books, magazines, phonograph records, films, and other materials useful in teaching physical education are also appended.

The material in this book was recommended by the Curriculum Commission to the State Board of Education, which adopted it as a teacher's manual for use in the public elementary schools of the state.

Roy E. Simpson

Superintendent of Public Instruction

ACKNOWLEDGMENTS

The preparation of a book to assist teachers and students to have richer and more satisfying experiences in physical education is a large task. Many individuals in the State of California other than those mentioned in the "Foreword" have given aid and guidance in this project. It is desirable, therefore, to express to them deep appreciation and most sincere thanks for the time and effort they so generously contributed and the encouragement they so uniformly gave. Teachers in service who use this book are indebted in particular to the following persons: Elizabeth Kelley, Professor of Health Education, Fresno State College, Marjorie Miller and Elizabeth Cawthorne, Pomona College, Virginia Covey, Supervisor of Physical Education, Pomona Public Schools, Mrs. Maud Knapp, Director of Physical Education for Women, Stanford University, and Harry A. Applequist, Director of Physical Education, Sacramento Public Schools, each of whom read certain portions or all of the manuscript and gave assistance on many particular sections; to Sarah Davis, Professor Emeritus, University of California, Lucile Grunewald, formerly Associate Professor, Department of Physical Education for Women, University of California at Los Angeles, Claire Colestock, Supervisor of Physical Education, Pasadena Public Schools, and Eleanor Metheny, Professor of Physical Education, University of Southern California, who helped greatly in evaluating the materials on body mechanics; to Herbert R. Stolz, M.D., Deputy Superintendent in Charge of Special Education, State Department of Education, and formerly State Supervisor of Physical Education, Lela J. Beebe, M.D., formerly Director of School Health, Vallejo Unified School District, and Mrs. Ethel Ward, Director of Division of Instruction, Alameda County, for reading and evaluating materials pertaining to health education; to Florence Weeks, formerly Supervisor of Physical Education for Girls, Oakland Public Schools, and Mrs. Violet Richardson Ward, Supervisor of Health and Physical Education, Berkeley Public Schools, for arranging to have a number of teachers try out certain games and give their reactions to them; to Charles W. Bursch, Assistant Division Chief, School Planning, State Department of Education, for reviewing the materials relating to school environment; to Doyt Early, Architect, School Planning, for assistance in the preparation of charts and diagrams; to Edna Roof, a former Supervisor of Physical Education, Los Angeles Public Schools, for aid given in the preparation of the sections on facilities for preschool, kindergarten, and primary grades; to Luella Weed Guthrie, Stanford University, Jane Shurmer and Lola Osborn, Chico State College, and the late Margaret Van Voorhees, formerly Elementary Co-ordinator, San Diego Public Schools, for assistance with certain game materials; to Lloyd E. Webster, Director of Division of Health Education and Physical Education, Los Angeles County, Harold Schoenfeld, Supervisor of Health Education, Physical Education, and Recreation, Alameda County, David Snyder, Supervisor of Physical Education, and Jack M. Capri, Physical Education Co-ordinator, Oakland Public Schools, for reviewing the graded materials and providing supplemental materials; to Mrs. Anna Hermitage for her assistance and advice in the music arrangement; to William Stabler, photographer, Bureau of Audio-Visual Education, State Department of Education, and Long Beach Public Schools for pictures taken at Camp Hi-Hill and on school playgrounds; to San Diego City-County Camp Commission for pictures and materials on camping; to Contra Costa County Superintendent's Office for photographs and Oakland Recreation Department for folk dancing pictures; to Lawton Harris, Assistant Professor of Religious Education, College of the Pacific, Lucile Czarnowski, Associate Supervisor of Physical Education, University of California at Berkeley, Fredericka Moore, Co-ordinator of Corrective Physical Education and Dance, Los Angeles County, for assistance with the material on rhythmical activities; to the National Safety Council, Inc., for poster on "Right and Wrong Way to Lift"; to Richland Elementary School District and to Roger Sturtevant, photographer, San Francisco, for photographs; to Arthur Cobbledick, landscape architect, Eckbo, Royston, and Williams, landscape architects, and Koblik and Fisher, architects, for plans of school grounds and buildings; to Los Angeles Public Schools for drawings relating to safety on the school grounds and for photographs of recreational activities; and to Carson Conrad, Consultant in Community Recreation, California State Department of Education, for assistance in the sections on recreation.

Acknowledgment is made in footnotes throughout the guide to publishers of various copyrighted material who very kindly gave permission to reprint descriptions of games or dances, musical compositions, or other matter.

Because of the many weeks, months, and years it has taken to select, compile, edit, and review the materials in this publication, we regret that it will be impossible to name each person who has made a contribution to the preparation and final publication of these materials. To all such persons we express our appreciation with a hope that each one will join with us in a feeling of mutual satisfaction in a difficult job well done.

VERNE S. LANDRETH
Chief, Bureau of Health Education,
Physical Education, and Recreation

CONTENTS

PART ONE: CHARACTERISTICS OF AN ADEQUATE PHYSICAL EDUCATION PROGRAM

PART TWO: ACTIVITIES FOR PHYSICAL EDUCATION IN GRADES ONE THROUGH EIGHT

APPENDIXES

PART ONE

CHARACTERISTICS OF AN ADEQUATE PHYSICAL EDUCATION PROGRAM

Chapter I
PHYSICAL EDUCATION IN THE SCHOOL CURRICULUM

Physical education is relatively new in the school curriculum, and yet it is an exceedingly old form of education. The first physical educator was probably the parent who taught his son to throw a spear, to climb a tree, to leap a brook, and to perform the many skills that were necessary for survival in the tribal life of uncivilized man. Since those faraway days the social scene has changed tremendously, but the old motor patterns remain. The need to throw a spear has passed, but the need to throw continues; the frequent need to climb a tree is gone, but the urge to climb reappears in every child; the need to leap a brook rarely occurs but the necessity to leap arises again and again.

It is apparent on every hand that the accumulated social inheritance is a staggering load to be acquired by each new generation. When youth had a few skills to learn or one or two legends to memorize, the task of education was simple indeed. Today, the wise selection of instructional materials for the total curriculum is exceedingly difficult. Likewise in physical education, the great wealth of material in physical activities demands careful selection. All motor experiences are physically educative but some are worth more than others in desirable effects produced. It might be said that a good physical education program includes "the sum of man's physical activities, selected as to kind and conducted as to outcomes." [1]

This concept requires that a selection should be made of some of all types of the many physical activities that children might perform in terms of the outcomes that are sought for each child. Children should have experiences in all phases of the physical education program—quiet and active games, individual and team games, tumbling, folk dances, exercises, rhythmical games, apparatus activities, and aquatics—but selection of specific activities should be made on the basis of maturity and ability of each child. For instance, when one desires to develop organic vigor in children, vigorous activities are chosen, or when the specific objective is the development of locomotor skills, free rhythmical activities are selected. Each activity has its own unique purpose. Yet the total physical education program has as its single purpose the development of the whole personality—physical, social, or mental—insofar as physical

---

[1] Jesse Feiring Williams and C. L. Brownell, *The Administration of Health and Physical Education*. Philadelphia: W. B. Saunders Co., 1947 (third edition), p. 20.

education activities may contribute to this end. For physical education is more than physical. It is concerned with emotional responses, personal relationships, mental learnings, and other social, emotional, and esthetic aspects of individual growth. This concern for the total behavior of the individual arises from recognition of the fact that all the experiences of the individual affect the whole person and are not restricted to the overt aspect of behavior.

PURPOSES OF PHYSICAL EDUCATION

A list of the major purposes of physical education includes the following:

1. Development of basic muscular strengths and the co-ordinations used in fundamental skills
2. Development of correct postural habits and the ability to relax
3. Development of mastery of physical powers, with the capacity for sustained effort through the exercise of the large muscles and vigorous play
4. Development of body poise and creativity in motion through enjoyable rhythmical activities
5. Development of sufficient skill in motor activities to provide pleasure and satisfaction
6. Development of the individual's interest in maintaining his own optimum physical, mental, social, and emotional well-being
7. Development of the individual's desire to appreciate and master worthwhile physical recreational skills
8. Development of the social integration of each individual within the group through activities that give opportunity for satisfying experiences
9. Development of emotional stability through frequent and vigorous participation in activities within the capacity of the individual to realize
10. Development of desirable social attitudes inherent in group relationships, such as leadership and followership, subordination of the individual to the welfare of the group, generosity to opponents, tolerance toward playmates of different races or creeds or of different physical abilities
11. Development of a sense of individual and group responsibility for civic behavior on the playground, in the school, and in the community
12. Development of courage, initiative, alertness, self-control, and co-operation in group activities or individual games.

Immediate Outcomes

The many purposes of physical education are not all achieved at one time. Some appear to be served almost daily, while others have a more remote quality. The immediate outcomes to which some progress toward fulfillment may be expected are those relating to the development of motor skills, body efficiency, leadership-followership, the status of the individual within the group, and creativity in motion.

The Development of Motor Skills. It requires years for the child to acquire fully the neuro-muscular co-ordinations needed for the fundamental motor skills, but definite achievement should be made day by day. These fundamental motor skills include those of walking, running, throwing, catching, climbing, jumping, and their various modifications used in locomotion, for safety, and in recreational skills. All of these occur over and over in the games, rhythms, and other activities of the physical education program. To the uninformed, the obvious objective in each of these activities is the achievement of some particular skill, but to the understanding teacher, the development of the fundamental co-ordinations is the principal end in view.

When man depended upon his motor skills to catch animals for food and to defend himself against his enemies, then the role of motor skills

Figure 1. Caught in mid-air by the fast camera lens, this kindergartner exhibits perfect balance as she jumps on a low plank in the school playground.

was very important for his life and safety. Today, because there is less need for him to use his skills in such ways, faulty judgments have been formed concerning the significance of motor skills in modern life. Regardless of the tremendous differences between the life of primitive and modern man, the role of motor skills has not grown less; indeed, its importance has become even greater. These skills not only serve such utilitarian purposes as safety but also are essential for recreation.

The fundamental motor skills are the skills of locomotion. The feat of moving the body from one place to another is a great achievement for the young child. This skill must be analyzed by the teacher before she can teach proper balance and co-ordination. Walking, as well as the more complicated ways of moving such as running, hopping, and jumping, must be taught. Finally, leaping, skipping, galloping, and sliding skills should be mastered by the primary-age child.

Although machines perform most of modern man's work, there still remains the necessity to move about, to lift weights, to carry loads, and to climb. Work that involves lifting, carrying, climbing, and judgment of the speed of moving objects is performed more efficiently by those who have learned in childhood the proper motor co-ordinations. People everywhere climb stairs, yet many do not know the simple skills necessary for graceful, efficient motion. Certain skillful co-ordinations such as those involved in stooping, carrying suitcases, opening windows, and numerous acts of daily life should be taught and learned at school. The skills learned in physical education today are not required as protection against wild animals but they insure somewhat against modern hazards. They teach boys and girls how to fall safely, how to jump and guard against injury, how to maintain balance, and how to judge the speed of moving objects.

As machines are developed to do the work that formerly required so much of his time, man's leisure hours increase. For this leisure many interests compete, but for the great majority of persons in young adult life motor activities predominate. Everywhere the problem of recreation is the acquisition of skill for the activity. Selection of an activity depends largely upon the satisfaction it gives. One gets little satisfaction, however, from an experience in which one is inept. Those who do not sing do not join glee clubs, and those who cannot swim rarely choose to go swimming. A person normally chooses to do those things in which he is skillful. Participation always requires some degree of proficiency. In early childhood the standards of skill are low, but with adolescence the desire for at least average skill becomes important. The teaching of a wide variety of recreational motor skills then takes a large place in the physical education program.

Since many of the problems of youth arise out of their use of leisure time, it is imperative that the school teach those skills that will serve them in wholesome recreation. The social scene can be greatly improved if children, youth, and adults are able to engage in wholesome play during their free hours.

The Development of Body Efficiency. Another immediate purpose of physical education is the development of the child's body efficiency. This includes the proper functioning of the vital organs, correct postures, muscular strength, capacity for sustained activity, and general physical vigor. The realization of this goal depends upon a program chosen to fit the individual's need. Growth in the power of the vital organs results from daily participation in vigorous physical activities. The growth in muscular strength that is sufficient to maintain good postures and adequate for effective participation in the activities of games depends on continual exercise of the large muscles. Growth in functional skills that serve the various motor needs of boys and girls results from frequent practice of those skills.

The Development of Leadership and Followership. The traits of leadership and followership are necessary in citizens of a democracy. Encouraging these basic democratic relationships is one of the major purposes of education in a democracy. The teacher of physical education should exemplify a democratic relationship with pupils by decisions made on the playground and by creating and using opportunities for children to take responsibility.

Figure 2. Climbing and hanging on parallel bars and jumping off them is fun for small children and develops large body muscles.

The responsibility of the teacher is to instruct, to provide leadership, and to supervise children on the playground. Unless supervision is provided, a playground may become a safety hazard, a social menace, and a civic liability. The children's lack of experience in organizing activities and the fact that so many are unskilled and actually lack knowledge of game rules may lead to the development of antisocial situations, if wise leadership is not provided on the school playground. Timid children may be left out of activities because other children fail to accept or recognize them as equals. Aggressive children may dominate playing areas to the detriment of the remaining children. Bullies are apt to cause trouble. Unsportsmanlike behavior could become the order of the day unless there is planned supervision. A school playground during periods before and after school, at recesses, and at the noon hour should never be without the presence of one or more teachers. A teacher assigned to supervise the playground enjoys an opportunity to observe characteristics and interests of the child that never are apparent in the classroom. In this sphere she has an opportunity to direct and help form the child's social attitudes.

The development of leadership abilities and of attitudes that help children to lead and to follow leaders will be facilitated by knowledge of the qualities that good leaders and good followers should possess. To this end it is important for teachers to spend some time in eliciting from children their opinions as to the following points: (1) what to look for in leaders; (2) how to choose leaders; (3) what are the duties of followers; and (4) what are the duties of leaders.

The ability to lead and to follow is developed through practice. Physical education offers innumerable opportunities to develop these qualities. Here are a few suggestions as to ways in which the alert teacher will utilize such opportunities:

1. As children develop socially, assign them to teach games or rhythms. Before the presentation, give help to those assigned if assistance is requested.
2. After instruction and supervision, assign pupils to and hold them responsible for such duties as officiating, scoring, timing, and control of equipment.
3. As the pupils become aware of the responsibilities and skills required in leadership, permit them to choose their own leaders.
4. At appropriate times, stress the importance of having all the pupils follow the leaders they have chosen.

The Development of the Status of the Individual Within the Group. Each child is an individual with varying background and inherited characteristics such as strength, skill, resistance to disease, likes and dislikes, intelligence, educability, memory, and visual and auditory acuity. It is unreasonable, therefore, to expect the same performance from all children. Just as children with impaired hearing should be seated near the front of the room, so those with impaired strength should be protected from the more severe demands of physical effort. The teacher should be able to recognize individual differences, abilities, and limitations of children; to meet, as far as possible, individual needs; and to judge performance in terms of the individual's capacities. An appreciation for individual differences should operate with respect to the gifted individual as well as to the less able.

Every child needs to find his place within a group. Physical education activities, because they are so varied, offer an unusual opportunity to develop each child's potentialities and thus to give him status. While some may be particularly skillful at games, others will have special ability to create rhythms, and still others will show qualities of leadership or initiative. The child who is slow in arithmetic or spelling may find much satisfaction in physical activities. The teacher who is able to recognize these individual potentialities and give them opportunity to develop will contribute greatly to the social integration of each child.

The Development of Creativity in Motion. The fifth immediate purpose of the teacher of physical education is to develop the creative ability of the child. This purpose will be realized largely through the use of rhythmical and dramatic activities. Every child from the kindergarten through all the elementary school grades should be provided with every opportunity to use physical rhythmical patterns to express simple motion, to identify himself with his surroundings, and to communicate ideas. Moreover, it should be recognized that the exercise of this ability relates to the four preceding purposes, since the development of creativity in motion requires motor skill, promotes body efficiency, offers experience in leadership and followership, and contributes very definitely to the establishment of individual status.

THE RELATIONSHIP OF PHYSICAL EDUCATION TO THE SCHOOL HEALTH PROGRAM

Physical education makes a major contribution to the school health program. "Health is a state of complete physical, mental and social well-being and not merely the absence of disease or infirmity." [1] This concept should be fundamental to any well-balanced school program, and in par-

---

[1] From the Preamble of the Constitution of the World Health Organization, 1946. *Yearbook of the United Nations, 1946-47.* Lake Success, New York: United Nations, Department of Public Information, 1947, pages 793-800.

ticular to any physical education program. Health education and physical education have one goal in common—the development of optimum health for each individual child within his capacity for realization. Although physical education activities contribute to the abundant health of the individual, the status of an individual's health is influenced by many other factors. He needs a safe and healthful environment, proper food, enough rest, and the professional services, when required, of physicians, dentists, nurses, nutritionists, and psychologists. While physical education is as necessary to the pupil's well-being as is a good school health program, it should not be assumed that physical education can or should equip pupils with the knowledge of personal and community hygiene and provide all the opportunities necessary for healthful living. A school health program that attempts to meet the health needs of every child requires co-operative planning and working together of many groups. Included in these groups are the school health personnel, civic and lay organizations, voluntary agencies, the medical and dental professions, parents, pupils, and school administrators and teachers. Many communities, in order to insure this co-ordination and co-operation, have developed school health councils.

The Physician and the Physical Education Program

The physical education program should be based on the physical condition of the child. The teacher or administrator of the physical education program must depend upon the school physician for advice as to handicapped or disabled children who are unfit to engage in a full program of physical activities. In some cases the physician will advise modification of the program, and his advice should be followed. However, physicians employed either on a full-time or part-time basis by the school, or family physicians, should have a thorough understanding of the physical vigor involved in various activities in order to make suitable recommendations for individuals requiring special or modified programs. In some cases the physician may recommend exercises for the correction of postural defects, which may be performed during the physical education period.

The physician may advise that children returning to school following a serious illness should be limited in their program until recovery is complete. This limitation applies to both academic tasks and vigorous physical activity. A rest class should be arranged for some children, preferably at a time other than the physical education period. During the physical education period, temporarily handicapped children may study activities being taught, may umpire, keep score, or serve as leaders in activities that do not call for undue strain or physical vigor. At the same time they will be receiving benefit from the sun and fresh air, learning the rules of games, and keeping up with their classmates.

Adjustments in the Physical Education Program for the Individual Child

The school physician may advise regarding physical education programs for underweight and overweight children. A mid-morning lunch may be recommended for underweight children. This should be followed by a rest class, which should come at a time other than the physical education period, since children should not be denied the opportunity to learn games and enjoy happy play with other members of the school. Care should be taken that underweight children who are nervous and fatigue easily do not play too strenuously or carry extra responsibilities in dramatic, musical, or social events; they should be allowed to play in only a part of an intramural play period, and they should be provided tournament play in table games or less strenuous individual and dual games.

Overweight children present as serious a problem, if not a more serious one, than do underweight children. Glandular dysfunction may be the factor that causes the overweight, but often it is simply due to an excessive consumption of high calorie foods. In some overweight children sexual maturity is markedly delayed. Boys and girls of this type should have early medical examination to determine whether normal sexual development is taking place. The physician should recommend treatment for the overweight condition.

Children suffering from overweight cannot be expected to be energetic or to maintain prolonged physical effort. Their overweight condition should not be mistaken for mature growth, nor should size be taken to indicate muscular strength. They may need rest as much as underweight children do. While such children cannot be good performers in many activities they can develop some skill, particularly in nonrunning activities. As compensation, they should be allowed to develop to the utmost any powers of leadership they may possess.

Schools are faced with the problem of what adjustments should be made in the physical education programs for girls during menstruation. For a large majority of girls no adjustment is needed, since the continuation of normal activity at such times is beneficial. Moreover, participating in activity helps to develop the concept that menstruation is not a sickness but a normal biological phenomenon. Some girls, however, have painful menstruation. Exercise immediately preceding the onset of the period is beneficial for some who experience discomfort. All girls who have severe discomfort should have medical advice. Where no family physician is available, the school nurse or school medical adviser may give information regarding facilities for examination and treatment. It may be desirable to assign to a rest class girls who are uncomfortable because of menstrual cramps. Others should be assigned to some activity, perhaps of a less strenuous nature than those normally chosen. Girls should not enter swimming pools during the period, for sanitary reasons.

Co-ordination of Physical Education and Health Education Programs

It is obvious that physical education should be conducted to improve and never to injure the health of children. Since physical education is for the most part an activity program, it logically follows that there is little, if any, opportunity for systematic classroom health instruction. Such classroom instruction should not be regarded as a physical education function. However, through the activity program the physical education teacher may find opportunity for pointing out the need for a healthful amount of exercise, sufficient rest, and such health habits as cleanliness and relaxation.

Some of the health precautions a teacher should remember in connection with physical activity are included in the following list:

1. Guard from overexertion the child who returns to school following an operation or after a serious illness such as a heavy cold, influenza, or contagious disease.
2. See that underweight and overweight children are provided with rest and less strenuous activity as recommended by the physician or school health personnel.
3. Have girls continue activity during menstrual periods unless otherwise advised by a physician. They may, if uncomfortable, be assigned less strenuous activities than those used by the rest of the class, and they should avoid jumping or jarring elements in games.
4. Have activities take place out of doors rather than indoors whenever possible. When playing outdoors, have pupils remove coats and sweaters and keep warm by taking part in vigorous activities. When indoors, see that windows are open as long as children are active enough to keep warm.
5. Encourage pupils to wear low, broad heels.
6. Provide suitable games and tournaments for physically handicapped or temporarily incapacitated pupils. Have them learn the rules of games played by the children, so that they can participate at least as spectators.

Physical Education and Healthful School Living

For safe and healthful school living each school should provide a spacious playground which includes a surfaced area for multiple use and, if climatic conditions permit, a turfed area. Each playground should be equipped with adequate and safe apparatus and facilities, with areas for

Figure 3. Games involving running, throwing, and catching are enjoyed by boys and girls of the intermediate grades.

field games, court games, and individual and dual activities. Indoor space for rhythmical and social activities is essential for a balanced program. Elementary school buildings should include playrooms with shower facilities. Each child should be given an equal opportunity to participate in all phases of a well-rounded program. Such a program is one that is adjusted to the individual needs of every child, so that maximum growth physically, emotionally, and socially is possible.

In organizing the school program, consideration should be given to the levels of maturity of the children with respect to the time of the physical education period, the vigor of the activity, and the length of the activity. It is not a desirable hygienic practice for children to engage in highly competitive play immediately after the noon lunch period or to return to indoor classes perspiring freely and emotionally excited. All physical education activities should contribute toward a maximum health level for each child. An activity that is dangerous, overstimulating, or too vigorous has no place in the school curriculum. If the appropriateness of an activity is in doubt, a physician's advice should be sought.

ATHLETICS AND THE PHYSICAL EDUCATION PROGRAM

The character of the athletic part of the program for boys and girls should reflect the best judgment regarding the effect of strenuous competitive athletics upon young and rapidly growing children. Vigorous activity is decidedly beneficial for children but excessive amounts of activity result in strain and emotional overstimulation.

American football is not recommended by authorities in the field of physical education as suitable for pupils in the first eight grades, either as a physical education activity or as a recreational activity. The general immaturity of pupils in these grades and the fact that their bones are insufficiently developed to withstand hard tackling and blocking makes the game a dangerous one for elementary school pupils. Touch football and flag football should be played in accordance with rules designed for young boys and should be carefully supervised. No tackling or dive blocking should ever be permitted.

In the elementary school, girls may be permitted to take part in almost all activities of the physical education program. They should be taught how to land safely and without jar during game situations or when jumping from heights. They should be trained to fold their arms over their breasts when scrimmage situations develop during the playing of such games as soccer. Activities that involve body contact should not be used, and jumping events (high jump and broad jump) should be omitted from the program for adolescent girls.

Interschool Competition

Boys and girls in the elementary school grades are emotionally immature and easily overstimulated. They are insufficiently developed physically to withstand the strain of interscholastic competition. For these reasons educators have consistently opposed highly organized games to determine school championships for boys and girls below the ninth grade. Such contests are contrary to the best current philosophy and practice in modern education. Aside from the factor of overstimulation, educators feel that interscholastic competition at the elementary school level puts the wrong emphasis on relations between groups. Children's contacts with outside groups should be on a friendly basis in which neighbors play with each other for the fun of the game and in which school loyalty is unimportant. During later school and adult years individuals will have ample opportunity to take part in highly organized competitive sports.

The Representative Assembly of the American Association for Health, Physical Education, and Recreation, a department of the National Education Association, adopted the following resolution in April, 1947:

WHEREAS, elementary school boys and girls are emotionally immature;

WHEREAS, activity for all is the desired standard rather than activity for the few;

WHEREAS, the interest of boys and girls is in playing the game and not in playing other schools unless artificially stimulated to do so;

WHEREAS, small schools may not be able to have satisfactory competition within their own small group; and

WHEREAS, a play or sports-day type of program broadens social horizons:

We therefore recommend: That activity for *all* be stressed in grades one through eight in the elementary school physical education program; that a strong intramural program be developed for grades five through eight; that interschool competition be considered only as a natural outgrowth of a full intramural program; that we go on record as definitely opposed to interscholastic competition for elementary school boys and girls.[1]

Similar recommendations were made by the Society of State Directors of Health, Physical Education, and Recreation. In 1949 this Society, after working for a year with other organizations concerned with athletics in elementary schools, made a report which reaffirmed its strong and unequivocal support of a well-rounded program of instruction in physical education for all children and youth. It emphasized its interest in an interesting, challenging intramural program for boys and girls of upper-elementary and high school grades in as large numbers as possible, but decried any intramural athletic activity which tends to discourage or limit the development of the instructional program. It also encouraged playdays and sports days. The Society's recommendations were expressed as follows:

Highly organized competitive athletic leagues are not desirable for children and youth of elementary and junior age (Grades 1 through 8). Physical education in elementary and junior high school should stress a well-rounded program of instruction for all children, and for as many as possible, an interesting extensive program of intramural competition on a team, dual, and individual sports supplemented by sports days and playdays. In schools where intramural program competition is not possible, sports days and playdays should be given particular emphasis. All athletic competition should be conducted in accordance with the needs, capabilities, and interests of growing children.

All girls' athletic activities should be taught and coached by trained women leaders and refereed by competent certified officials and should be divorced entirely from any interscholastic athletic competition for boys. It is recommended that organized interschool competition for girls be limited and that invitational events chiefly in the form of sports days and playdays, involving mass participation, be emphasized.

Playing seasons which are reasonable in terms of duration and number of content: no pre-season game should be played until participants are well drilled in fundamentals and are in excellent physical condition. Post-season contests are to be discouraged. If any should be considered full thought should be given to the total time devoted to the sport and to other safeguards recommended in this section.

---

[1] "Recommendations from the Seattle Convention Workshops," *Journal of Health and Physical Education*, XVIII (September, 1947), 432.

Competitive Sports for Girls

In 1941 the Board of Managers of the California Congress of Parents and Teachers passed the following resolution condemning competitive sports for girls:

WHEREAS, Certain types of competitive athletics have created unwholesome conditions for girls in that, first, they have emphasized winning the game regardless of the cost to the individual; second, team interest has been placed above individual welfare; and third, that girls have been exploited for selfish ends; and
WHEREAS, We believe athletic activities for girls should be instituted for the values directly inherent in themselves, namely the development of the individual physically, and the encouragement of sportsmanship,
Therefore be it
Resolved, That the Board of Managers of the California Congress condemn the practice of exploiting the girls for commercial and publicity purposes under the guise of competitive sports, and be it further
Resolved, That girls of junior and senior high school age be encouraged to take part in athletics and physical education programs afforded by their schools where adequate physical examinations are given before such participation and where trained direction and supervision is given them.[1]

SAFETY IN THE PHYSICAL EDUCATION PROGRAM

Many of the motor skills taught to children in the elementary school physical education program contribute to safety in work and in play. The effort to develop these safety skills should be paralleled by the effort to promote safety in the school and on the playground. Children must be taught to think in terms of safety for the individual and for members of the group during participation in any activity. Good examples of incorporating safety procedures in the learning situation occur in a stunt program in which safety precautions are a necessary part of performance and in a softball game in which the method of handling the bat and the location of players waiting to bat is a vital factor. It is true that children should and must live adventurously. It is also true that they must be helped to acquire habits of observing basic safety procedures. The acquisition of a constructive attitude and daily attention to safety controls will not only eliminate many accident hazards but will prevent damage to the equipment.

Teachers must be alert and aware of all that is going on in the entire playground group even while they are occupied with a given child or group of children. They must be acutely alive to situations that could cause accidents or endanger children during their play. As playground supervisors, teachers must know what activities are being played, what apparatus is in use, and which supplies are in service. They must be aware of the distribution of the children on the playground and the hazards that might exist or develop. If an accident should occur, a definite proce-

---

[1] As reported in *Journal of Health and Physical Education*, XII (June, 1941), 384.

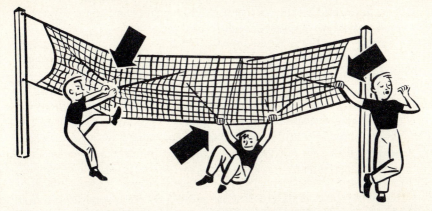

Figure 4. Pupils should be taught respect for playground equipment; hanging on nets should be forbidden.

dure should be followed. Such procedures should be formulated by each school to cover the following points: (1) the giving of first aid; (2) the notification of the parent; (3) the securing of expert assistance if necessary (school nurse or physician); (4) the reporting to the principal and other authorities of all accidents and their causes.

The following list includes safety points that the teacher should keep in mind when supervising the playground or when teaching physical education.[1]

1. Formulating a plan of organization that will provide all children with an opportunity to engage in activities that are challenging and interesting to them. This means that there will be enough equipment, places to play, and leadership for every boy and girl.

Figure 5. In the interests of safety to the child and care for equipment, the pupil must be taught not to climb up and hang from basketball goals.

_____
[1] See also *Education for Safety,* Bulletin of the California State Department of Education, Vol. XVI, No. 5, December, 1947. Sacramento: California State Department of Education, 1947, pp. 76-88.

2. Teaching children the correct use of playground apparatus for maximum safety of themselves and others.

3. Assigning children to game groups with others of their own age, size, and maturity.

4. Forbidding dangerous stunt practices, such as forming high pyramids. The use of apparently big and husky boys and girls as bases for such pyramids may result in permanent injury because of great weight placed on not yet fully developed bones to which the ligaments are attached.

5. Knowing the essentials of first aid and having readily available a first aid kit. The kit should be refilled as supplies are used.

6. Inspection of playground equipment and school playing areas (ground surface) frequently and systematically for safety hazards. Any equipment that needs repair should be removed from use until repairs can be made. Ground areas considered dangerous should be designated out of bounds until the hazard is removed or corrected.

PHYSICAL EDUCATION AND RECREATION [1]

The school has a responsibility to include in the physical education program experiences that will equip pupils to participate in the dance, in sports and games, and in other outdoor activities with at least a fair degree of efficiency. Skills that are learned during the instructional program in physical education can be enjoyed, further developed, and often mastered through participation in the extended curricular program. Supervised playgrounds, playdays, intermural and intramural sports, fun nights, hobby and club periods, school parties and dances, and corecreational activities are to be encouraged as outgrowths of a functional physical education program. The keynote of the extended curricular or school recreation program is participation for all in a great variety of recreational experiences.

Recreational programs should be organized for before school, noontime, after school, Saturday, and vacation periods. It is particularly important, wherever possible, that school playgrounds be supervised during out-of-school periods. In a recent study of recreation services in California public school districts it was found that 196 public school dis-

---

[1] Chapter X is devoted to a discussion of the relation between recreation and physical education.

Figure 6. Boys and girls enjoy swimming and diving together.[1]

tricts participated in support of community recreation programs and that
822 school playgrounds throughout the state were supervised regularly
after school and on Saturdays.[2]

COEDUCATIONAL ACTIVITIES IN PHYSICAL EDUCATION

Normal life situations constantly throw men and women together in
the home, in social gatherings, and in the business world. Many adults,
however, are unhappy and ill at ease in such situations because in their
youth they did not have adequate opportunity to learn the social amenities
and to practice adaptation to social customs. The prevention of such mal-
adjustment in adults lies in the hands of the teachers of America. As the
school prepares young people to enjoy academic pursuits and to achieve
vocational efficiency, so the school must also prepare young people to
take their places courteously, graciously, and successfully in social situations. The ability to adapt easily and gracefully to constantly shifting circumstances entails learning certain accepted social customs and procedures that must be practiced frequently in order that they may become
habitual and thus a real part of the personality of the individual.

Modern apartments and the cramped living quarters of small homes
do not permit the normal neighborhood social gatherings customary in
the earlier history of this country. The social experiences of school life

---

[1] This photograph of the aquatic center in the Richland Elementary School district, Shafter,
California (Kump and Falk, Architects Engineers) is reproduced by permission of the photographer,
Roger Sturtevant, San Francisco.

[2] Carson Conrad, "Recreation Services in California Public School Districts," *California Schools,*
XIX (June, 1948), 178.

should help especially those boys who have no sisters and those girls who have no brothers.

Practice in these social adjustments can be provided through coeducational physical activities. In the lower grades the children normally study and play together, but in the upper elementary grades, and in high school and college, there has been a traditional separation of boys from girls in all physical education activities. Boys have had one section of the playing field, girls another. Custom has even separated them in the use of the gymnasium or auditorium floor when weather conditions have necessitated a program within doors. Yet many of the activities lend themselves very readily to coeducational practice, and the value of some, such as rhythmical activities, is greatly enhanced when they are taught to mixed groups of boys and girls. Administrators and teachers now realize that the physical education program must include at least some activities part of the year for coeducational groups.

ESSENTIALS OF A GOOD PHYSICAL EDUCATION PROGRAM

The scope and purposes of the physical education program have necessarily been discussed in very brief fashion in this chapter. The aim has been, not to give an exhaustive treatment of the subject, but to indicate the trend of opinion among authorities in physical education on specific matters of policy. The short statements that follow are suggested as general characteristics of a good physical education program.

1. A good physical education program develops not merely the muscles and organs, but the whole child, physical, mental, and social.

2. A good physical education program is well co-ordinated with the school health program so that the optimum health of each child is developed.

3. A good physical education program provides the friendly and sociable contacts of playdays and recreational meets in preference to the overstimulation of interschool athletic contests.

4. A good physical education program protects the child from physical hazards in the schoolroom and on the playground.

5. A good physical education program is well co-ordinated with the recreational program of the school and the community.

6. A good physical education program seeks to foster healthy social growth through coeducational activities.

SELECTED REFERENCES [1]

Health Education: A Guide for Teachers in Elementary and Secondary Schools and Institutions for Teacher Education. A Report of the Joint Committee on Health Problems in Education of the National Education Association and the American Medical Association. Washington, D. C.: National Education Association, 1948 (4th revision).

HUGHES, WILLIAM L., AND WILLIAMS, JESSE FEIRING. *Sports, Their Organization and Administration.* New York: A. S. Barnes & Co., 1944.

LAMBERT, CLARA. *Play: A Yardstick of Growth.* New York: Summer Play Schools Committee of the Child Study Association of America, 1938.

LAMBERT, CLARA, AND SHOEMAKER, ROWENA. *Let Them Play: A Primer to Help Children Grow Up.* New York: Play Schools Association, 1943.

LEONARD, FRED EUGENE, AND AFFLECK, GEORGE B. *A Guide to the History of Physical Education.* Philadelphia: Lea & Febiger, 1947 (third edition).

Mental Hygiene in the Classroom. A Report of the Joint Committee on Health in Education and the American Medical Association. Washington, D. C.: Committee for Mental Hygiene, National Education Association, 1939.

NATIONAL RECREATION ASSOCIATION. *Community Sports and Athletics.* New York: A. S. Barnes & Co., 1949.

OBERTEUFFER, DELBERT. *School Health Education.* New York: Harper & Bros., 1949.

The Physically Below-Par Child. Changing Concepts Regarding His Care and Education. New York: National Tuberculosis Association, 1939.

ROGERS, JAMES F. *What Every Teacher Should Know About the Physical Conditions of Her Pupils.* Washington, D. C.: U. S. Office of Education, Federal Security Agency, 1945.

SCHWENDENER, NORMA. *A History of Physical Education in the United States.* New York: A. S. Barnes & Co., 1942.

Solving School Health Problems. The Astoria Demonstration Study, Sponsored by the Department of Health and the Board of Education of New York City, directed by Dorothy Nyswander. New York: Commonwealth Fund, 1942.

WILLIAMS, JESSE FEIRING, AND BROWNELL, CLIFFORD LEE. *The Administration of Health and Physical Education.* Philadelphia: W. B. Saunders Co., 1946.

---

[1] Appendix B also lists reference materials.

Chapter II
THE ELEMENTARY SCHOOL CHILD

It has been pointed out that the main objective of physical education is to contribute in every possible way to the development of the whole personality of the child. In planning and carrying out an adequate program of physical education, school administrators and teachers should be aware of much more than the techniques of teaching certain motor skills and games. They must first of all accept the concepts of the "whole child" and the "total situation," two phrases that express important phases of modern educational philosophy. They must understand the development of the normal child throughout his school life—not only his physical development but his psychological and social growth—in order to plan the physical education program to meet the needs of the individual child.

THE WHOLE CHILD IN THE TOTAL SITUATION

For some time educators have accepted the statement that the whole child goes to school. In this acceptance they have abandoned the older notion of separate body and mind and are committed to the principle of organismic unity. This concept is not difficult to hold, since the evidence to support the idea is overwhelming. But it is not easy to translate the concept into the practical everyday particulars that make up the work of the school. Wholeness of the individual is everywhere accepted by enlightened persons, but separateness of mind and body is too often the expression of school practice.

It is inevitable that this discrepancy should exist. The lag is marked in all lines of social activity in which tradition and custom have any influence. The traditions of the curriculum, of administration, and of teaching compete at many points with the facts about the nature of the child, how learning takes place, and the effect of the environment upon behavior. It is a fact that to the classroom each morning come children with defective eyesight, impaired hearing, diseased tonsils, carious teeth, weak muscles, poor co-ordinations, depressing fears, and physical fatigue. Even the evidence that such defects interfere with learning is often not sufficient to change the traditional attitude that the function of the school concerns only the mental learnings.

As teachers and administrators accept the doctrine that the whole child goes to school, they must translate the general statement into particular actions. These particulars should be directed toward physical, social, and emotional functions as well as intellectual ones. Since the child is a unity, all phases of his development are important.

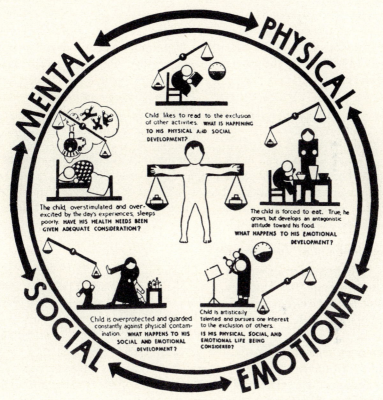

Figure 7. The teacher must recognize that the whole child goes to school.[1]

In recent years another phrase, the total situation, has come into use in educational circles. This concept implies that behavior is an expression of the individual in relation to all the forces of the environment that play upon him. What any child manifests, then, is a composite of his own powers as these are played upon by all of the various acting and interacting forces that surround him. In order to understand the child's behavior, it is necessary to apply the concept of the total situation to all the particular experiences that children have.

[1] From M. E. Breckenridge and E. L. Vincent, *Child Development*. Philadelphia: W. B. Saunders & Co., 1943. By permission.

The principle of reaction and interaction between the individual and his environment is readily accepted, but its translation into efforts to improve the environmental situation is not so easily made. Schools teach art to children and then continue to house them in ugly schoolrooms. Hygiene and sanitation are taught in the classroom, but locker rooms and toilets are allowed to be indescribably filthy. If education is to be realistic, the teacher's faith in the efficacy of classroom recitation must be supplemented by belief in the powerful influence that environmental forces have on the child.

GROWTH AND DEVELOPMENT OF THE ELEMENTARY SCHOOL CHILD

There are a number of facts about the growth and development of the young child that should guide in the education of the young. Several will be discussed in this chapter—the development of vital organs, the skeleton of the young, factors influencing growth, sex differences, and developmental hazards.

Development of Vital Organs

Vitality, a term that denotes the strength of the life force, is manifested through the functioning of the vital organs. These organs are involved in the circulation, respiration, digestion, elimination, innervation, and control of the individual. To develop vitality in a person, it is necessary to develop the functional powers of the heart, lungs, kidneys, digestive tract, endocrine glands, and nervous system. How can these organs and their functional powers be developed? There is only one way. *They are developed by exercise of the large muscles of the trunk and hip joints.* Aside from the influence of heredity, the only source for the development of vitality resides in the activity of the large muscles.

Moreover, there is a strategic time for this large muscle development to occur. Weak children do not usually grow into vigorous adults. The vital organs must be started on their development during the preschool years and the years of elementary schooling. Then is the time to lay the foundation for vitality in later years. Consequently, the young child should be encouraged in vigorous play in which there is running and jumping, climbing and pulling.

The Skeleton of the Young

The skeleton of the individual remains partly cartilage until the early twenties (Figure 8). Consequently, during the school years the skeleton is easily affected by postural patterns, and habits of standing, sitting, and moving are built into the plastic bones. The size and shape of the thorax are determined largely by the opportunities given the child to climb, swing, pull, push, hang, and run. Many of the postural faults of the young child are due to insufficient muscle and may be corrected by development of muscle. Neither admonitions nor shoulder braces can take the place of muscle.

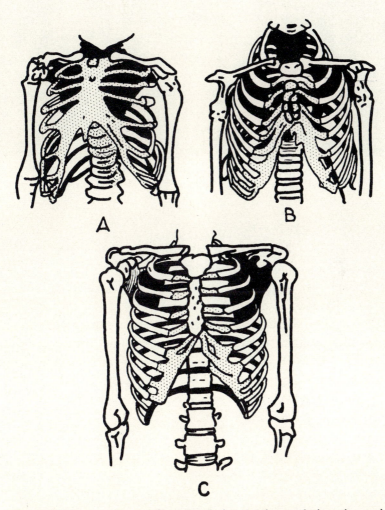

Figure 8. Progressive ossification of the cartilage of the ribs and sternum is shown by dotted portions in the illustrations of (A) a child at birth; (B) child at seven years; (C) adult of thirty years of age.

Figure 9. Every child should have opportunity to engage in some form of vigorous activity.

Factors Influencing Growth

Children in a favorable environment grow larger than those in unfavorable ones. Factors influencing growth are food, sunshine, exercise, sleep, and physical condition. Both quantity and quality of food are important. Diets that are otherwise satisfactory are often lacking in sufficient amounts of proteins, minerals, and vitamins that are essential in a child's diet. Sunshine is useful in stimulating the formation of hemoglobin and vitamin D, which is necessary for proper body functioning and growth, but an excess of sunshine is undesirable. Exercise and rest play a combined role in the promotion of growth. The former stimulates the tissues to heightened functioning and causes a demand for food, and the latter provides for a recovery period in which waste from the cells can be removed and the individual is made ready again for activity. Physical defects interfere with normal growth. Some defects are more serious in this respect than others. Growth acceleration often follows the removal of diseased adenoids and tonsils, and improved nutrition often follows the correction of dental defects. During periods of acute illness growth may be retarded or even stopped.

Sex Differences and the Pattern of Growth

Until the beginning of puberty boys and girls grow at about the same rate and girls can do readily many of the things that appeal to boys (Figure 10). At the onset of puberty, however, there is a change in the

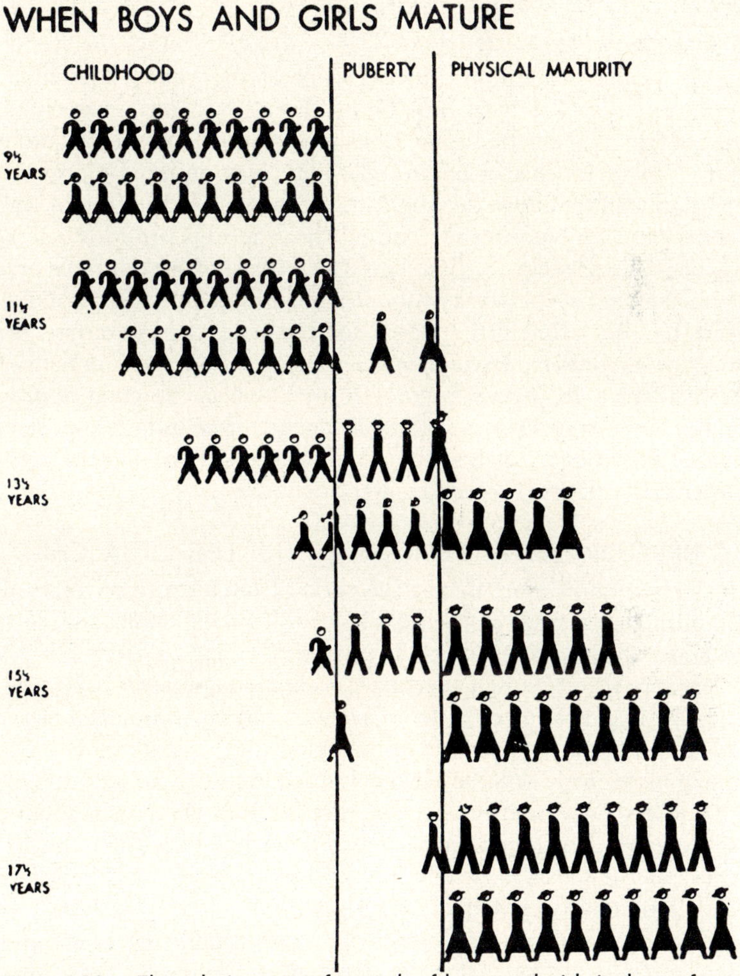

WHEN BOYS AND GIRLS MATURE

Figure 10. The relative rate of growth of boys and girls is shown from childhood to physical maturity.[1]

pattern of growth. The girl begins to broaden at the pelvis and from that time onward is never able to run as easily as the boy. At the same time the boy develops greater muscular strength. The structural changes in the

[1] From M. E. Breckenridge and E. L. Vincent, *Child Development*, Philadelphia: W. B. Saunders & Co., 1943. By permission.

adolescent girl require that the program of physical education for her be different from that for the boy. In these years, it is not desirable for her to engage in activities involving jarring such as high jumping, in apparatus work in which the body is supported by the arms, or in body contact sports such as boxing and wrestling.

Developmental Hazards

The rapid growth and development of the young is attended by certain hazards. Teachers must be on the alert to recognize signs that indicate failure of the organism to maintain its soundness. If the arches of the foot are weakened, pain and disability may ensue. To prevent this condition, children must be taught the proper use of the foot in walking and the need for wearing well-fitting shoes appropriate to the activities in which they participate; girls should be warned of the injurious practice of wearing high heels. Weak abdominal muscles result when the individual spends too much time sitting down and too little time in exercise. Strong abdominal muscles are essential in maintaining the normal functions of the intestinal tract. In the years from 10 to 14 when the child is growing rapidly, heart irregularities may occur but are of no serious importance if physical activities are well selected and well supervised and the pressures of interscholastic sport are not incurred.

DEVELOPMENTAL PERIODS IN THE LIFE OF A CHILD

A child learns more during the period from birth to six years of age than during all the rest of his life. He learns to walk, climb, run, to speak and understand a language, to jump, to throw, and to catch fairly well. He learns to adjust himself acceptably to home requirements. During this period he begins also to adjust to persons and environmental situations outside his home. From then on his education consists of the further refining of the basic skills and habits learned in those first six years of life. The public school enters into the picture for most children at about their fifth year and from then on has a profound influence for good or bad because of the social, academic, physical, recreational, and civic experiences it offers or does not offer.

As the child proceeds through the many stimulating experiences of school, certain phases of his development are evident. These may be grouped in four developmental periods: (1) an exploratory period in which the self is the center of attention; (2) a further exploratory period in which the self in relation to others is the center of attention; (3) a period of rapid growth in which self development is comparable to an ideal or hero as center of attention; and (4) a maturing period in which there is a consolidation and refinement of powers. These periods naturally overlap.

No strict line can be drawn between one and the next. The chart that follows describes the characteristics of the individual at the different stages of his development and points out the implications of each characteristic for the teacher of physical education.

CHARACTERISTICS OF THE CHILD DURING FOUR DEVELOPMENTAL PERIODS AND IMPLICATIONS FOR PHYSICAL EDUCATION *

CHARACTERISTICS OF THE CHILD	IMPLICATIONS FOR PHYSICAL EDUCATION

I. Exploratory Period in Which the Self is the Center of Attention. Ages Approximately 4½ to 7.

1. Gradual growth in weight and height	1. Need for regular weight and height record
2. Disease susceptibility high	2. Need for daily health observation and to teach health conservation
3. Endurance low; heart small	3. Need for frequent periods of relaxation and rest
4. Low visual ability to focus on small, fast-moving objects	4. Need to control physical environment in relation to special senses
5. Bones soft	5. Need to emphasize posture in standing, sitting, and all activity
6. Muscular control more effective with large objects	6. Need to use large objects for muscular control
7. Imitative	7. Need to develop rhythms and dramatizations
8. Marked activity urge	8. Need to encourage interest in running and tag games; also games of low organization
9. Short interest span	9. Need to change activity frequently
10. Individualistic and assertive	10. Need to teach safety for self and others in small groups
11. Indifferent to sex distinctions	11. Need to develop opportunities for varied physical activities for all boys and girls

II. Exploratory Period in Which the Self in Relation to Others is the Center of Attention. Ages Approximately 7 to 10.

1. Gradual growth in weight and height	1. Need for weight and height record
2. Increased resistance to disease	2. Need for daily health observation
3. Endurance improved	3. Need to lengthen periods of activity but relaxation and rest still necessary
4. Eyes functioning properly except in special cases	4. Need to control physical environment with special regard to individual cases
5. Muscular control improving; finer co-ordination possible	5. Need to offer opportunity for finer co-ordinations in all activities

* Adapted from an article by Kay Bishop, "All Out, System-wide Health Program Works Wonders in Santa Barbara," *School Management*, XI (June, 1942), 267, 271-73.

CHARACTERISTICS OF THE CHILD DURING FOUR DEVELOPMENTAL
PERIODS (Continued)

CHARACTERISTICS OF THE CHILD	IMPLICATIONS FOR PHYSICAL EDUCATION
6. Ossification progressing	6. Need to continue postural emphasis in all activities
7. Liking for excitement and adventure	7. Need to continue rhythms and dramatizations
8. Gradual growth in interest span	8. Need to introduce activities that encourage group co-operation
9. Beginning gregarious and co-operative spirit	9. Need to provide opportunity to play in more highly organized games with pupil leadership, planning, and evaluation

III. **Period of Rapid Growth in which Self Development is Comparable to Ideal or Hero as Center of Attention. Ages Approximately 10 to 13.**

1. Rapid growth. Age of puberty. Girls in advance of boys by one or two years. Maturation levels vary between girls and boys and between individuals.	1. Need for records of child growth and knowledge of general habits
2. Endurance decreased	2. Need for daily health observation by first period and core teacher
3. Danger of over-fatigue	3. Need to focus attention on individual students during this period of extreme variation of growth (posture, endurance, emotions, social attitude); need to teach conservation of health
4. Individuals differ in maturation of special sense organs	4. Need to continue attention to physical environment and its contribution to general well-being (individual and group)
5. Great variability in muscular control	5. Need to use many activities in co-operation with special interest area
6. Rapid growth of long bones	6. Need to instruct in techniques of relaxation and good body mechanics
7. Girls interested in personal appearance and in boys	7. Need to teach personal and social hygiene
8. Boys more interested in approbation of other boys than in girls	8. Need to develop standards of behavior and provide activities of interest to both groups
9. Increased interest in competitive activities	9. Need to promote sportsmanship and to develop training rules
10. Establishment of group loyalty; hero worship	10. Need to discuss the function of ideals
11. Decided physical and mental change	11. Need to show sympathetic understanding of problems that arise
12. Increasing power of attention and abstract reasoning	12. Need to provide activities that are challenging to good leadership and followership

Characteristics of the Child During Four Developmental Periods (Continued)

Characteristics of the Child	Implications for Physical Education
IV. Maturing Period in Which There is a Consolidation and Refinement of Powers. Ages Approximately 13 to 16.	
1. Girls' growth more nearly completed; boys still in period of rapid growth	1. Need for inspection of records and knowledge of general health and growth of the child (weight, height, etc.)
2. Physical maturity progressing	2. Need for daily health observation by first period and core teachers
3. Endurance increased	3. Need to focus attention on individual needs of students during this period of extreme variation in growth (posture, endurance, emotions, social attitudes)
4. Individuals differ in maturation of special sense organs	4. Need for continued attention to physical environment and its contribution to general well-being (individual and group)
5. Muscular control. Girls show gradual improvement; boys show noticeable improvement	5. Need for use of many activities in co-operation with special interest area
6. Ossification practically complete	6. Need for postural emphasis
7. Marked development in self-confidence and emotional change	7. Need to promote confidence by successful completion of tasks
8. Interest in opposite sex	8. Need to provide coeducational physical activity
9. Strong combative tendency in boys	9. Need to offer competitive activities
10. Greater powers of attention and reasoning	10. Need to promote sportsmanship
11. Co-operation tempered by consideration of personal interest	11. Need to identify personal and community interests; need for attention to problems in safety, opportunities for recreation, and health conservation

BIOLOGICAL NEED FOR ACTIVITY

Civilization has produced conditions foreign to the nature of man. Over the years the most marked changes in his environment have been the wearing of clothing, the development of forms of work that tax the eyes and small muscles, artificial heat that reduces climatic stimuli, and indoor living with all its attendant shortages in sunshine, fresh air, and physical movement.

Today, science attempts to state the essential biological needs of man and to set forth the conditions that must be fulfilled if civilized living is not to impair the health and vitality of people. In the school, there are standards to maintain so that healthful living can go on. These are not arbitrary, but are well established by experience. Consequently, school administrators and teachers are responsible as educational agents for seeing that the biological needs of children for activity are met by making available facilities and equipment, time, schedule, and leadership.

Effects of Muscular Exercise

Muscular exercise affects the whole body. Exercise not only increases the circulation of blood to the part of the body exercised but increases the circulation throughout the entire body. This increased circulation speeds the transfer of food to the tissues, the removal of wastes, the distribution of the endocrine secretions, and equalizes the water content and heat of the body.

Activity of the large muscles increases the body's requirement for oxygen, thus causing increased respiration with a resulting increase in

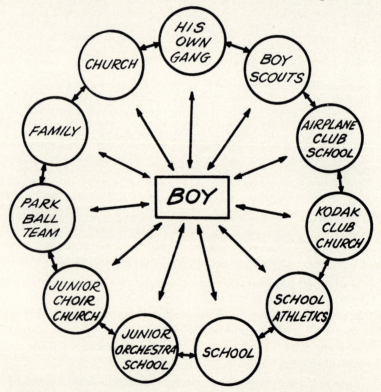

Figure 11. Each individual must make adjustments to all phases of his life.

the rate of oxygenation of the blood, increased rate of elimination of carbon dioxide, and increased oxygen supply to the tissues. During increased activity the respiratory organs respond by frequent and deep respirations. Deep breathing without preceding muscular exercise does not have the same results and is a mistaken practice.

Exercise improves digestion and assimilation. If the musculature of the alimentary canal is flaccid, digestion is retarded and impeded. Peristaltic movements are more vigorous when the muscle tone of the alimentary canal is good. Exercise is essential to keep the muscles in good condition. The constipation resulting from sedentary life is in large part due to inadequate muscular activity.

Exercise of the skeletal muscles strengthens the heart. The best-known way in which some types of weak heart can be made strong is by gradual and increasing amounts of physical work of the skeletal muscles. However, it is imperative that the amount and kind of exercise that a pupil with a weak heart should take should be arranged under the direction of a physician.

Vigorous activity of the large muscles, those covering the trunk and hip joints, is absolutely essential for the growing child. Development of these muscles, especially those of the trunk, is of great importance to health since the trunk muscles must be strong in order to maintain the upright posture necessary for the best position and functioning of the abdominal and pelvic organs.

ABILITIES TO BE DEVELOPED IN THE CHILD

In terms of the whole child and the needs of human society, it is essential that the schools develop in the child certain abilities. First among these is the ability to live as a vigorous organism. It is an essential in education to develop vitality in the individual, since vigor and vitality are forces that motivate all his functions. Whenever a person grows to adulthood without attaining the strength and vigor that he might have known, then he is condemned to live at a level lower than was otherwise possible for him. The development of the ability to apply mental skills is the traditional and well-established function of the schools, and, while it is still an essential, exclusive attention to mental development with a neglect of physical and social development tends to discredit the work of the schools and the professional competence of teachers and administrators.

The ability of the individual to engage in productive work is essential for his own development and is required by his membership in a community of other persons. Respect for the worker, the dignity of labor whether mental or physical, and recognition of his particular contribution have been a part of our American social heritage. It is important for the schools to pass on to each generation such concepts.

As man's hours of work are lessened and his leisure time increases, the manner in which persons, especially young persons, use this free time has great effect on their behavior. Today it is essential in education to teach young people how to use their leisure time in wholesome ways. Hobbies of all kinds, such as recreational reading, music, dramatics, gardening, collecting, handcrafts, and activities necessitating the expenditure of large amounts of physical energy have great leisure time values.

Finally, the child must be helped to become a useful member of a social group. The standards of behavior that each generation passes on to the next are taught in and through the many experiences of children. The modern world with all its conveniences finds its crucial problems arising out of human relationships. Today, as never before, learning how to work, play, and live with each other is an essential in education. Obviously, all the educational forces that can aid in this problem must be utilized.

A well-rounded program of physical education can contribute to the development of all of these abilities. By encouraging the vigorous activity of the large muscles, by correcting postural defects, by giving opportunity for creative and pleasurable motor activities, and by allowing the child to participate in group thinking and group planning, physical education can build up in each child the vigor and the stamina that will enable him to take his place as a healthy member of society.

SELECTED REFERENCES [1]

BRECKENRIDGE, MARIAN E., AND VINCENT, E. LEE. *Child Development*. Philadelphia: W. B. Saunders Co., 1943.

LASALLE, DOROTHY. *Physical Education for the Classroom Teacher*. New York: A. S. Barnes & Co., 1937.

————. *Guidance of Children Through Physical Education*. New York: A. S. Barnes & Co., 1946.

SALT, ELLIS B., AND OTHERS. *Teaching Physical Education in the Elementary School*. New York: A. S. Barnes & Co., 1942.

SEHON, ELIZABETH L., AND OTHERS. *Physical Education Methods for Elementary Schools*. Philadelphia: W. B. Saunders Co., 1948, pp. 24-29.

WILLIAMS, JESSE FEIRING. *Personal Hygiene Applied*. Philadelphia: W. B. Saunders Co., 1946 (eighth edition), pp. 153-91.

————. *The Principles of Physical Education*. Philadelphia: W. B. Saunders Co., 1948 (fifth edition), pp. 51-85.

_____

[1] Appendix B also lists reference materials.

Chapter III

THE TEACHING OF MOTOR SKILLS

The concept of the whole child is important in all education. We teach the whole child, and it is the whole child that learns. But we do not teach the whole child in general. We teach particular skills, we arouse particular interests, and we secure particular responses. It is the particular that has meaning for the learner. The whole child goes to school, but his learning consists of such particulars as climbing a rope, catching a ball, writing letters, and numerous other particulars. The concept of the interrelationship of all aspects of the individual is essential in education; but it should never lead the teacher to neglect of the particular in contemplation of the general good.

IMPORTANT FACTORS IN LEARNING MOTOR SKILLS

The learning of particular skills operates in relation to a number of important factors that are described by the words "readiness, goal, satisfaction, motive, and example."

Readiness and Learning

It is a well-known fact that readiness for an activity is an important factor in learning. When young children are introduced to activities for which they are not ready, either psychologically or physiologically, they learn slowly, haltingly, or not at all. In learning motor skills, the child may not have adequate muscle strength and nerve co-ordinations to perform the act. In such instances, he cannot learn the skills. The principle of readiness suggests, therefore, that the level of the activity should not be above the ability of the individual.

Goals and Learning

It is important for the learner to know what he is trying to accomplish, and the first step in teaching a motor skill is to acquaint the child with the end to be achieved by his action. After each trial, he then has a measure by which he can judge how well he has done and what is still to be accomplished. For example, in archery he knows how well he has done because he has a target.

The goal should be well defined, such as to throw the ball over the plate, to run to a mark, to tag another player, or to jump over a stick.

Moreover, the instruction should be definite. A movement may require a take-off from one foot, thrust of the arms forward and upward, a ducking of the head, or an arching of the trunk. Whatever the immediate or remote goal may be, a clear understanding of what is to be accomplished is an aid in learning. Many children fail to learn to play games well because the teaching has been too general.

Satisfaction and Learning

Learning is facilitated by satisfaction achieved from the effort made. Success tends to give satisfaction and failure dissatisfaction. The measure of success may be the individual's aspiration rather than a reasonable test. When a child attempts a feat that is too difficult for him, he is likely to fail. It is important to keep the experiences within the reasonable limits of the individual's ability.

Motive and Learning

When an individual has an interest and purpose in learning any skill, then he has motive toward the end, and this motivation facilitates learning. At times extrinsic motives are employed to stimulate effort but they are unnecessary when the activity appeals to the purposes of the individual. Motive is often related to need as understood by the pupil. For instance, boys will not be motivated to learn social dancing until there is a social situation that requires it. Most physical education activities carry their own motives.

If awards are used as an artificial means to stimulate effort, and the award, because of its monetary value, becomes of greater importance to contenders than does the pleasure experienced during the competition, the value of the award becomes a liability and actual psychological damage to the contenders may result. If awards are used, none should have a greater than nominal value. The knowledge that one has succeeded and the listing of names of winners on a bulletin board or in a newspaper provides adequate recognition of success.

Example and Learning

Learning is facilitated by imitation of a good example. In motor learning, example is usually a better approach than mere explanation. It is important to present the movement slowly. In teaching complex co-ordinations, it is better that each part of the movement be performed by the teacher or a pupil before it is combined with others into the complete movement. Films and posters also are a means of demonstrating motor skills.

MOTOR DEVELOPMENT AND LEARNING

Children who learn to creep early will usually walk early; they tend to learn motor co-ordinations readily. The child learns through practice, and although the process is slow and his efforts are clumsy, it is the only way. Gains in strength roughly parallel the gains that a child makes in height.

Individuals who show competence in one motor skill are likely to be similarly adept in other motor acts. This does not mean that there exists a quality of general motor ability, but rather that some children are skillful in many movements. The program should always present diversified offerings so that all children can find some activity in which they can succeed. Some children acquire a reputation for awkwardness because they have no opportunity to perform those skills in which they have some competence.

Competition appears to be a factor in the development of motor skill in the young. From the first grade onward, children keep count or make a record of their performances. They are interested in doing as well as another child, or in excelling their own or another's record. However, organized teamwork is not appropriate until the later years of the elementary school. At that time children want to improve for the benefit of the team and the rules and regulations of games become important to them.

Participation in recreational sports in adult years seems to depend to a great degree upon childhood experiences in the learning of games. Nestrick reports that an insignificant number of his subjects participated as adults in activities if they were without experience in them in the years between 6 and 18.[1] About 50 per cent who had childhood experience in game skills still participated as adults, and 29 per cent of those not participating gave lack of knowledge as the reason.

In practically all motor movements the child can profit by direct instruction without suffering a loss in spontaneity or creativeness. An individual may not be conscious how he acquires improved skill; he often stumbles into the right co-ordination without being aware of it. He may be unable to tell others how to do it, nor does he know himself how he does it. Much of motor learning, however, is the learning of a pattern. Practicing the correct pattern is important to gaining motor skill, whether it be pitching a softball, serving a tennis ball, or shooting a basket. When the pattern is faulty, correction of the error may be made by having the pupil analyze the error. In this way he becomes aware of the fault and thus learns to eliminate it.

---

[1] W. V. Nestrick, *Constructional Activities of Adult Males.* New York: Bureau of Publications, Teachers College, Columbia University, 1939.

Plateaus in Motor Learning

The progress a person makes in learning complex motor skills may come to a temporary halt when, although practice continues, he seems to mark time. The curve of learning flattens out and a plateau is reached. (Figure 12.) Such periods of no progress are inherent in the learning process and are only temporary. Sometimes failure to progress is due to

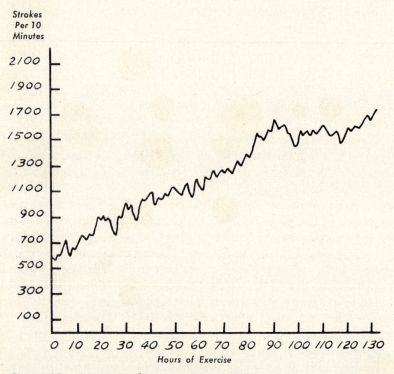

Figure 12. Progress in learning a motor skill is uneven and reaches a plateau.[1]

complexity of the skill that is practiced, the immaturity of the learner, too great length and distribution of the practice periods, fatigue, or competing interests. In some instances, the plateau results from a certain method of working. If the method is changed, the plateau disappears. The plateau may mark the level of achievement that can be attained with the purpose that prevails. If the intent is improved, the plateau disappears. It is the function of the teacher to be aware of all the possibilities that may interfere with learning progress and to be able to suggest a remedy.

---

[1] From Jesse Feiring Williams, *Principles of Physical Education*. Philadelphia: W. B. Saunders, 1948, p. 104. (By permission.)

DESIRED OUTCOMES IN TEACHING MOTOR SKILLS

In the teaching of motor skills the objectives of the teacher fall into three classifications: (1) helping the child to learn motor skills; (2) promoting the child's knowledge in areas associated with motor skills; (3) guiding the child's learning of approved social attitudes through certain motor skills.

Principles of Movement

A number of objectives in teaching motor skills relate to the performance of the movement. It is desirable that young children learn correctly the simple movements of their games and dances. It is the function of the teacher to develop good form in motor skills as well as good form in speech, writing, and drawing. There are five principles of movement that should guide in the performance of physical activities. These are (1) opposition; (2) energy conservation; (3) follow-through; (4) objective focus; and (5) total assembly.

The Principle of Opposition. In all throwing and locomotor movements, the motion of arm and leg should be opposed. Thus, in throwing,

Figure 13. In kicking the soccer ball backwards, this girl exemplifies the principle of opposition. As her right leg swings forward it is accompanied by her left arm.

right-handed children should be taught to move the left foot forward while the right hand makes the throw. Left-handed children should place the right foot forward while throwing with the left hand. Boys learn this co-ordination quite early from parents or older playmates but girls often continue into the high school, unless properly instructed, patterns of throwing that interfere with their ability to play games well. In the same manner, a right-handed child should be taught in catching a ball to have the left foot forward so that he is in position to throw the ball when it is caught. Likewise, in running and walking, the arms and legs should be used in opposition. When the right leg is swung forward, the left arm should accompany it. As children learn this simple co-ordination, they walk and run better.

The Principle of Energy Conservation.   It is undesirable in the performance of activities involving motor skills to employ more energy than is needed for the efficient performance of the movement. This principle is violated by pupils who do not know the correct way of performing an activity.

Children should be taught to make the climbing movements in climbing stairs with an upward and not a downward accent. Here, energy is employed to lift the person upward, not to accent a down beat. Pounding the feet down upon the steps is a waste of energy interfering with the proper performance of the skill.

The Principle of Follow-through.   It has long been known in sports that expert performance depends upon the performer's following through with the body any swinging or striking movement made with the arm or any kicking movement made with the leg. Thus, in batting a ball with the hand as in volleyball, one should continue the force of the movement after the impact of the hand with the ball. In throwing a ball, one should follow through with the body the movement that is started with the arm. It is impossible to perform well such difficult skills as those involved in tennis and golf unless the player has learned how to follow through in his strokes.

The Principle of Objective Focus.   Children learn more rapidly all throwing and batting skills if they learn to keep their eyes fixed on the objective. Sometimes the objective is the ball one is trying to hit or catch; at other times the objective is the target or goal that one is trying to hit with a ball. For example, in pitching horseshoes and throwing a ball, the performer should keep the eyes on the target. In batting a ball and catching a ball, he should keep his eyes on the ball.

The Principle of Total Assembly.   Skill and grace depend on total body movement in an action. Awkwardness is often the product of trying

Figure 14. These boys illustrate the principle of objective focus. In batting and catching they keep their eyes on the ball.

to perform an act with the arms or legs alone when it requires the participation of the total motor mechanism. Thus in running, the whole body should participate and not just the legs. In throwing, the whole body is involved and not just the arm.

The extent to which these principles may be emphasized depends upon the age and development of the individual. Children in the first few grades are not interested particularly in skill, but beginning with the nine-year-old the fundamentals of technique can be stressed. However, the skills of running, throwing, jumping, and similar skills should be taught to the younger children as opportunity occurs.

Associated Knowledge Gained Through Motor Skills

Almost every activity yields some related knowledge. The extent of the associated knowledge is very small in young children but as they grow older the associations increase in importance. For example, in learning to swim, an individual will master the co-ordinations that enable him to keep up in the water and to propel himself through the water. But learning does not stop there. He will be concerned also with buoyancy, air pressure, the hygiene of pools and swimming places, breathing, and numerous other physical, physiological, and hygienic matters. Moreover, since such learning is perceptual in character, it is far more educative than the word-learning which characterizes so much of school experience.

The extent of the associated learnings depends first upon the age of the child; secondly, upon the character of the activity; and thirdly, upon the ability of the teacher to utilize this opportunity for education. Even if the teacher ignores the areas of associated knowledge, the child will acquire some learning, but he will acquire much more learning if the teacher is aware of the opportunity. Thus, children learning to run may develop not only speed and distance running, but acquire numerous associated learnings growing out of the practice of running. One of these might be an understanding of how foods provide the chemical compounds needed in vigorous activities. The playing of some games may open up a rich area of learning about the athletic customs of the ancient Greeks. Likewise, the folk dance opens up rich areas in folkways, national cultures, pageantry, and music. The use of color, the meaning of design, and the role of music in the dance may contribute richly to learning.

Social Attitudes Gained Through Motor Skills

In addition to the technical learnings and associated learnings that grow out of motor experiences, there are always concomitant attitudes that may be as significant as the learning of the skills themselves. In all games, children are concerned with relationships with other children, the teacher, the rules and regulations of the game, the ideals of fair play and sportsmanship, and numerous other things. Learnings in this area are inevitable even though the teacher pays no attention to them. It is important, therefore, for the teacher to utilize the opportunity to inculcate approved social attitudes. Without proper guidance, children may show poor sportsmanship, unfairness, ungenerous behavior, and similar selfish and antisocial characteristics. Even in the kindergarten the matter is important, since the beginning of character formation is connected with these concomitant learnings. A shy and timid child may stay by himself and appear to be very antisocial, but let him learn to climb the ladder and go down the slide with the other children and his social inadequacy soon disappears.

OPPORTUNITIES PROVIDED IN AN ENRICHED PHYSICAL EDUCATION PROGRAM

The use that young persons make of their physical education depends upon all the learnings that surround the experiences they have. If they lack technical skill, they will be poor performers and therefore unlikely

Figure 15. Folkways may be learned through the dances of various countries.

to be willing to participate. The foundation for using leisure time enjoyably and profitably in physical activity must be laid during the years of elementary schooling, since many physical activities learned during school days will provide enjoyment not only then but during adulthood. Among a few to be mentioned are quoits, tennis, shuffleboard, volleyball, handball, table tennis, paddle tennis, archery, croquet, swimming, badminton, and rhythmical activities, including natural and creative rhythms, social dancing, folk games, and dances. The equipment necessary for some of these activities such as badminton, archery, tennis and golf can be carried with one the world over. Not all games require group activity. Some require only one partner. Many other activities such as golf, archery, and fly casting may be practiced alone.

Most boys and girls wish to learn to dance as soon as they become interested in the opposite sex. The courtesies and standards of social dancing can best be taught under supervision in the wholesome surroundings of the school. Other activities of physical education also offer opportunity for the learning of customs and manners. In addition to practicing the techniques of each game, children should learn the social customs and courtesies which belong to each game. Observance of these courtesies makes the game pleasanter and often safer. Thus, in golf, courtesy allows the more rapid players to overtake the slower players, while in archery the observance of courtesies removes the hazards of the sport. Tennis is known as a gentlemen's game in the true sense of the word because of the system of courtesies that have become part of the game over the years.

Experiences that include learning and mastering social customs as part of the game should be an important part of the planned program for all children. Children learn by practicing as do adults. Therefore, there should be definite practice in such amenities as asking a person to be a partner when games are to be played, making introductions, offering a chair to an older person, asking a friend for a dance, and excusing one's self at its conclusion.

SELECTED REFERENCES [1]

ALLEN, BETTY, AND BRIGGS, MITCHELL PIRIE. *Behave Yourself!* Chicago: J. B. Lippincott, 1945 (revised edition).

————. *If You Please!* Chicago: J. B. Lippincott, 1942.

BOYKIN, ELEANOR. *This Way, Please: A Book of Manners.* New York: The Macmillan Co., 1940.

BRECKENRIDGE, MARIAN E., AND VINCENT, E. L. *Child Development.* Philadelphia: W. B. Saunders Co., 1943.

COLESTOCK, CLAIRE, AND LOWMAN, CHARLES LEROY. *Fundamental Exercises for Physical Fitness.* New York: A. S. Barnes & Co., 1943, pp. 1-35; and 185-314.

DUNBAR, FLANDERS. *Emotions and Bodily Changes.* New York: Columbia University Press, 1943 (third edition).

GATES, A. I., AND OTHERS. *Educational Psychology.* New York: The Macmillan Co., 1948 (third edition).

GESELL, ARNOLD, AND OTHERS. *The Child from Five to Ten.* New York: Harper & Bros., 1946.

GOODRICH, LAURENCE B. *Living with Others.* New York: American Book Co., 1939.

McGRADY, M. E. F., AND WHEELER, B. *Manners for Moderns.* New York: E. P. Dutton & Co., 1942.

RATHBONE, JOSEPHINE LANGWORTHY. *Corrective Physical Education.* Philadelphia: W. B. Saunders Co., 1934.

TODD, MABEL E. *The Thinking Body.* New York: P. B. Hoeber, Inc., 1937.

---

[1] Appendix B also lists reference materials.

Chapter IV
PLANNING THE PHYSICAL EDUCATION PROGRAM

In planning the physical education program, the basic philosophy as well as the immediate objectives of physical education should be kept clearly in mind. A knowledge of the physical and social development of the elementary school child and of the learning process in respect to the motor skills is fundamental to such planning. These matters have been discussed in the foregoing chapters. In addition, there should be an understanding of the needs and characteristics of children at the various stages of their development, so that activities may be chosen to fit those needs. The size of the classes and the facilities available will be determining factors in building the program.

The needs of any particular school population can be met by providing opportunity for activity and relaxation, for development of good body mechanics, for learning of recreational skills, for followership education, for the mastery of at least one activity, and for means of self expression. Every child should have experience in the following types of activities: exercises related to body mechanics, tag games and relays, physical activity in small, informal groups, individual games and sports (after the primary grades), team games and sports (with simple team games used before and during intermediate grades), group games, social games, rhythms, folk dancing, social dancing (after primary grades), stunts, tumbling, apparatus play, and swimming (if facilities are available).

Calisthenic (gymnastic) drills are not included in this guide. Such drills are not related to basic interests of childhood. Children never turn to them spontaneously to satisfy their urge for activity. For selected children, however, group exercises have value when used for remedial purposes under the direction of teachers trained in their use. Group exercises are also especially suitable for brief, warm-up activity at the beginning of the instruction period.

Time should not be spent in developing skill in the execution of formation drills while marching, since more active games and rhythmical experiences are greatly to be preferred as stimulants to heart, lungs, and physiological processes in general. Formal marching procedures are not used in everyday situations such as during fire drills, entering or leaving motion picture theaters, churches, or public gatherings. Since this is the case, it is doubtful if any instructional time during school hours should be devoted to the teaching of marching.

FITTING THE PROGRAM TO THE NEEDS OF THE CHILDREN IN THE GROUP

In helping the child to develop through physical activity, an analysis of the characteristics and needs of the child at different ages is necessary. In this connection, teachers must work with and not against nature. Such an analysis may be made in three stages of development: first, of the very young children in kindergarten and the first three grades; second, of the children in the intermediate grades (4, 5, and 6); and third, of the pre-adolescents and adolescents in grades 7 and 8.

Characteristics and Needs of Young Children in Kindergarten and Grades 1, 2, and 3

The needs of young children are well known. A satisfactory program of physical activities that will meet these needs is dependent upon an awareness and an acceptance of these needs by those responsible for the program.[1]

Biological Urge for Action. The need to move and to make noise are essential urges of children in the early grades. Both are necessary for desirable growth. Silence should not be required of children during play and instructional periods. The program should meet the basic urge for action by offering opportunities to develop movements involving the activities of walking, running, jumping, skipping, hopping, sliding, climbing, throwing, catching, kicking, pulling, pushing, hanging, crawling, and carrying. Play equipment should be available to provide opportunities for experimenting with various forms of movement.

Necessity for a Variety of Simple Large Muscle Activities. Muscle groups develop irregularly. The child in the early grades should not be expected to learn complex skills and specific techniques. Small children are interested chiefly in games as games—not in forms used and the ultimate outcome. Emphasis should be placed upon activities involving the large muscles.

The interest of children in these grades is centered largely in activities that require expenditure of energy together with opportunity to move in space. Traditional tag games have great value in satisfying these urges. It should be kept in mind, however, that children at this age tire easily. Hence, their participation in physical education activities should not overtax their endurance. Because of their short interest span they should be given frequent opportunity to change the activity.

---

[1] Help in the preparation of the sections on characteristics and needs of children was given by Dr. Elizabeth Kelley, Fresno State College, Elizabeth Cawthorne and Marjorie Miller, both of Pomona College, Virginia Covey, Pomona Public Schools, and Margaret Van Voorhees, formerly of the Office of the County Superintendent of Schools, San Diego County.

Figure 16. Wagons large enough to load with big wooden building blocks furnish exercise both to the one pulling and the one loading.

Children within the kindergarten and first three grades should not be segregated by sex during any instructional periods. Although some segregation may occur in grade 4, it is not recommended, since activities for boys and girls in this grade level need not be differentiated.

Strong Dramatic Interest. At this age, much time should be spent on dramatization that will give outlet to the curiosity and vivid imagination so characteristic of children in these years. Dramatic activities should emphasize expression rather than form, with no specific aim to develop pronounced creative skill.

Rhythmic Expression Basic. Several periods weekly or, if possible, a daily period should be scheduled for children to take part in the fundamentals of locomotion, in natural rhythms, and in singing games, all accompanied with appropriate music. Children may gain additional rhythmic experiences through the development of rhythm patterns as part of the social studies and music programs.

Concern of Child for Individual Rather Than Group Performance. Children in the first two grades are individualistic in their interests. Such activities as running or tag games are useful in satisfying their desire for individual achievement. The spirit of rivalry should also have legitimate outlets. The challenge of pulling and tussling activities under guidance is valuable. Hauling wagons, hustling boxes and planks, wrestling on the lawn, and performance of very simple stunt activities on the ground and on apparatus are indicative of types of activities to be employed.

Children four and a half to seven years of age enjoy activity in small groups in which their individual activity is more important than the group activity. Kindergarten and first grade teachers should not expect to teach even simple group games to all the children at once, but through planning and opportunity for many varied activities should guide the children in their attainment of many motor skills.[1]

Introduction to Team Activities in Grade 3. Ability to co-operate in group undertakings develops slowly. Until a child is nine years old he is not interested in being a member of a group. Participation in simple lead-up or group games assists in this growth only if the child is mature enough to participate as a group member. Use of group games should result in acquisition of simple skills and an aroused interest that will be the basis for the later perfection of skills and the enjoyment of sports suitable for older children.

Development of Proper Body Alignment. Strong and well co-ordinated back, shoulder, abdominal, leg, and foot muscles are among the important factors in the acquisition and maintenance of good postures. Continuous opportunity for developing these muscle groups is essential. Hanging and pulling, running and throwing activities are particularly valuable. There should be scheduled and supervised opportunity during and following school hours for use of equipment that aids in strengthening these muscle groups.

Specific Skills for Pupils in Kindergarten and Grades 1, 2, and 3

Children should have acquired the following specific skills by the conclusion of the primary grades:

1. Catching and throwing somewhat accurately large balls and bean-bags
2. Running to a given mark and back without stopping
3. Hopping on either foot
4. Skipping using both feet
5. Jumping using both feet
6. Walking successfully a low ledge, low ridge pole, or balance beam
7. Knowing the words, music, and action used when playing singing games
8. Performing simple stunts
9. Knowing how to walk, run, gallop, and skip to music
10. Knowing how to use climbing apparatus for climbing and low horizontal bars for rolling, rolling over, or for hanging

---

[1] *Teachers Guide to Education in Early Childhood* Sacramento: California State Department of Education (in preparation).

Characteristics and Needs of Pupils in Grades 4, 5, and 6

Children in grades 4, 5, and 6 are growing rapidly and developing new needs as they acquire new characteristics. Some of their needs can be met through a well-planned program of physical education.

Need for Vigorous and Sustained Activity. The biological necessity for activity becomes intensified for children in grades 4, 5, and 6. Only through more vigorous activity can increased organic power and muscular development be obtained. Growth needs for many children in these grades are met by means of longer, more vigorous, and more sustained concentration on the more technical aspects of the physical skills and activities that they experienced in the primary grades. Children nine, ten, and eleven years old may drive themselves too hard in play; over-exertion must be avoided.

Increased Perfection of Neuro-muscular Patterns of Co-ordination. As basic co-ordinations are established, greater refinement of execution is desirable. Continued practice is essential for continuous physical growth and assists greatly in obtaining physical and emotional satisfaction. Opportunities should be provided for the following skills and activities:

1. Improved skills and techniques involving the total muscular system

Figure 17.   Walking a plank gives children practice in balance.

2. Rhythm activities, including introduction of folk games and social rhythms
3. Stunt skills and improved play on apparatus
4. Running and tag games that offer speed running for short distances with opportunity for frequent rest
5. Team games that are simple in organization but offer each child an opportunity for vigorous play with rotation of playing positions

Organizing a class into squads is an effective way to supervise children while they practice skills and perfect specialized co-ordinations.

Activities in Coeducational Groups. Boys and girls at the ages of nine, ten, and eleven, for the most part, are able to engage in the same activities together. Unless there are unusual circumstances, almost all activities in the first six grades should be coeducational. Some opportunity may be provided for boys and girls to play separately, but the introduction of units of activity for boys and girls in separate groups is needed only if the class is made up of many early maturing or older boys and girls. It is very important that the program include creative rhythms as well as suitable folk dances in coeducational groups.

At these ages boys and girls are beginning to be interested in individual and dual games, as well as to have a strong interest in activities that possess the team element. When groups are formed for playing in teams, the basis for classifying pupils should be not sex or age but physical maturity. Because of the varying rates of growth, nine-, ten-, and eleven-year-old children differ greatly within each age range. In order to provide equitable playing conditions, therefore, the development and ability of each child should be considered when teams are formed. The teacher may use his own judgment of the child's abilities, or he may use the more objective method of classification based on age, height, and weight discussed in Chapter VII of this guide.

Improvement of Body Mechanics. For continuing improvement of body mechanics, muscle tone must be maintained through exercise, but exhaustion must be avoided. Psychological factors must be recognized. Fear, lack of confidence, and a sense of inferiority produce poor postures. Desire for personal improvement should be encouraged. Employment of supervisors trained in the field of corrective physical education to help teachers in service is a real need in the elementary school field. Such supervisors are much more important for the elementary school than for senior high school and college, since corrections are much more easily made during the child's early years.

Desire for Group Approval. The urge for group approval becomes very strong in this age group and group standards often determine individual behavior. Planning play situations in which the child can gain personal satisfaction as well as secure group approval is important.

Planned Program to Develop Pupil Leadership. The school program must be planned so that all children experience the responsibilities of leadership and followership. Some have innate leadership ability; for others a long training period is necessary to develop it. Opportunity for such training must be given from the beginning of school life, and should be emphasized in the program from the fourth grade on.

Wide Variety of Activities. A planned program that offers widely diversified experiences in many phases of physical activity is all important for children in the intermediate grades. Specialization in any one field is not desirable at these age levels. Recess, noon, and after school hours, and vacation days offer time for continuous growth through the fullest utilization of school play facilities.

Specific Skills for Pupils in Grades 4, 5, and 6

Taking into consideration the needs of children in the intermediate group and the activities suited for them, the teacher may expect children to achieve competence in the following skills:

1. Attaining and maintaining correct postures
2. Knowing how to play individual, and dual games such as paddle tennis, handball, croquet
3. Catching, throwing, and batting small balls with accuracy
4. Handling large balls with increasing accuracy and greater speed
5. Controlling a soccer ball with the foot or feet.
6. Chinning two or more times while grasping bar with back of hand toward face
7. Dancing polka, schottische, two-step, and waltz steps, together with several folk dance patterns based on those steps
8. Knowing how to secure a partner for a game and leaving her graciously at conclusion of activity
9. Knowing the rules of at least one organized game and being able to carry on the game without an adult leader
10. Knowing how to float and to use at least one swimming stroke successfully

Characteristics and Needs of Pupils in Grades 7 and 8

Young people in grades 7 and 8 are fast approaching the age when they must assume many of the responsibilities of adults. The physical education program must prepare pupils for successful social experiences and at the same time give them opportunity to take part in vigorous games. The characteristics of upper grade pupils indicate the need for careful selection of activities.

Importance of Biological Changes. Ossification of bones is well advanced in seventh- and eighth-grade pupils but bones and ligaments are still not strong enough to allow hard body contacts and bearing of heavy weights. American football, boxing, and commando tactics are not desirable activities for boys and girls at these age levels. The growing areas of the upper end of the thigh bone may be permanently injured by heavy pressure, since these areas of growth are still plastic. For this reason forming high pyramids in stunts is undesirable. The heart increases greatly in size during this growth period, with veins and arteries developing much more slowly. The heart, therefore, should not be overtaxed with heavy or too-continuous activity. Soccer, basketball, speed· ball, and long-distance running under pressure need special controls and wise supervision during these years. While many activities are suitable for both boys and girls, some activities, such as wrestling, broad jumping, high jumping, and weight lifting are not desirable for girls.

Continued Supervision of Body Mechanics. The desire of seventh- and eighth-grade pupils to improve body mechanics is apparent and this should be stimulated by verbal encouragement and advice. During these years there is a maturing period in which skill patterns are consolidated and body power and control are refined. The leaders should know the proper techniques for the performance of standard game activities and should recognize and then help students to correct wrong performance patterns.

Importance of Coeducational Activities.[1] Coeducational activities are so important for this age group that several such activities should be scheduled each week. Since swimming instruction is the same for boys and girls, segregation for swimming classes is not necessary, providing a sufficient number of dressing rooms and showers are available for both boys and girls. There should also be no segregation by sex in the upper grades for instruction in rhythmical activities. Equal opportunity should continue for both boys and girls in rhythmical activities: in creative rhythms and folk and square dancing. A well-rounded rhythmical program will provide boys and girls with most of the step patterns and social knowledge necessary for social dancing. It is desirable that both men and women teachers give instruction in social dancing and guidance in the development of social standards. Units of social activities, individual sports, and recreational activities should be part of the coeducational physical education program of the seventh and eighth grades.

---

[1] Further discussion of this subject is found on page 68.

Wise Guidance by Adults. During the seventh and eighth grades there is often an appearance of clumsiness and poor co-ordination caused by the different rates of growth of different parts of the body. Careful consideration for the feelings of children at this age is particularly important. Ridicule or any reference to physical inadequacies must be avoided. Adult leaders must show sympathy for the child's problems and help him to analyze his own needs.

Development of Pupil Leadership. During these early adolescent years evidences of growth in self-confidence become apparent to a marked degree. Opportunity for the development of this quality must be provided through creation of social situations that call for acceptance of responsibility and the carrying through to a conclusion of accepted assignments. Officiating at playdays, swim parties, or tournaments, and leading in squads and games all offer invaluable opportunity for leadership experience. Assignments should include boys and girls on the same committees. In order to emphasize the importance of leadership and the responsibility of pupil committees, a wise teacher will sometimes let a social event fail rather than step in if pupils have repeatedly failed to fulfill the responsibilities given to them.

Playdays as a Form of Interschool Meets. For grades 7 and 8 there should be separate playdays for boys and girls as well as opportunity for coeducational playdays. During these occasions large numbers of pupils have the experience of meeting with pupils from other schools and playing with them in a situation where school rivalries are forgotten and they meet as neighbors, not as opponents. Play is vigorous but the emphasis is upon social outcomes. In the seventh and eighth grades there are thousands of boys unable to qualify for school teams who welcome playdays as a means of meeting young people from other schools. They love to play equally as much as do those who are especially endowed with specific athletic skills.

For upper grade pupils there is great danger of adopting a program of interschool contests and championship team games that eliminates from participation many of the less adept pupils while it overemphasizes specialized techniques for many of the boys and girls. Administrators would do well to eliminate all highly organized and regularly scheduled interschool contests for this age group. The rash enthusiasm of young teachers, the civic pride of townspeople, the desire to raise money for purchase of athletic supplies often put pressure on school administrators to undertake a program that can only be detrimental to the children under their jurisdiction.

Figure 18. Children on a modified program as well as those on an unrestricted one can enjoy horseshoes both at home and at school.

Leisure Time Pursuits. The school must help pupils of this age to use their leisure time wisely and with satisfaction. It should develop in pupils an interest in wholesome physical activities useful for recreation immediately as well as in adult years. High specialization in any one field is not desirable at this period. Although pupils in seventh and eighth grades will enjoy team games, they should also learn numerous individual and dual games as well as take part in parties, picnics, playdays, and excursions which give them an opportunity to live in a social situation.

Modified Programs for Pupils in Grades 7 and 8. Because of the variance in maturity and needs of the individuals in this age group, it is particularly important that physical education activities be selected to suit the needs of each individual. Activities must be modified to provide the best growth and development for each child in his present stage. Many times this will mean a long review of activities supposedly learned in previous grades. Other times it will mean the inclusion of less vigorous activities, such as sitting or quiet games or additional rest for a child.

Specific Skills for Pupils in Grades 7 and 8

Taking into consideration the characteristics and abilities of children in grades 7 and 8, the teacher may expect pupils in these grades to attain the following skills and knowledge:

1. Understanding the principles controlling body mechanics; maintaining correct postural positions at all times
2. Swimming well enough to have confidence in deep water
3. Playing six or seven individual and dual games well enough to be accepted readily by other players
4. Knowing general rules and technical skills used when playing standard national games such as soccer, speed ball, softball, basketball, tennis, volleyball
5. Dancing basic steps used in social dancing such as the waltz, two-step, mazurka, schottische, polka, one-step
6. Dancing a given number of early American dance patterns
7. Dancing a given number of folk game patterns other than American
8. Directing several dual, individual, or team games without adult supervision
9. Contributing to the planning and executing of a social event for boys and girls of own age

ADJUSTING THE ACTIVITIES TO THE CAPACITY OF THE INDIVIDUAL

Authorities in the field of physical education strongly advise that no pupil able to attend a public school be permanently excused from the physical education program because of general organic or nervous weakness, or because of a crippled condition, old or recent injury, or health deficiency; but that all pupils whose physical condition indicates needed adjustments in their academic and physical education programs be assigned temporarily or permanently to some less vigorous forms of activity during their physical education period.

Physicians' Excuses for Children [1]

When a physician recommends that a pupil be excused for a long period of time from the physical education program, the purpose underlying the program, as well as the mildness, severity, or recreational value of the activities taught, should be explained to him. The physician should be asked to co-operate with the school in adjusting the program so that the pupil will not miss certain educational experiences and yet will be protected from a possible unfavorable health situation. The physician should be asked to rescind a blanket recommendation that a pupil be excused from all physical education experiences and to give in its place recommendations for a modified program. He should be asked to recommend the type of activity he favors for his patient and the school should

---

[1] See "The Physician and the Physical Education Program," Chapter I, page 10.

then endeavor to provide that type of activity for that child. When such co-operative understanding prevails, the recommendation of the physician should prove of great assistance to administrators and teachers responsible for arranging the educational programs best suited to meet the individual needs of each child.

All physicians' recommendations should cover only the period of one semester. This practice should lead automatically to a re-examination to determine the physical condition of pupils and to their possible early return to the general school program of physical education.

Physically Handicapped Children

Boys and girls who are physically handicapped should not be denied the thrill of acquiring and perfecting skills in games suited to their particular needs. The experience of team membership, with the responsibility and discipline in good sportsmanship that such membership will entail, and the joy of a contest well played will give them increasing enjoyment in the playing of suitable types of sports and games.

Planning a Modified Program

Those taking a limited physical education program should be assigned individually or by twos, threes, or by squads to rest or to activities and games suitable to their particular needs. This school policy will help decrease the number who try to avoid physical education. Such a policy also insures that these children acquire some beneficial leisure time interests and habits, builds up the morale of the entire school, and creates a favorable attitude on the part of the community toward the physical education program.

Improvement of health and health habits is of first importance for children on a modified physical education program. Therefore, such pupils should be limited as to the academic load carried and the amount of time they may devote to other phases of school life, such as band, orchestra, glee club, school office, dramatics, and school dances. Participation in these activities should be restricted until the pupil's full co-operation in health procedures is gained.

Tournaments and contests for pupils on a limited program should occasionally be arranged. The activities recommended for the tournaments should be those played in a modified program. Such pupils need the emotional and civic discipline that such play opportunities offer, since good sportsmanship can be shown during a checker or horseshoe tournament as well as on a basketball court.

Pupils on limited programs or on a rest program should be graded if grades are given for those participating in the regular vigorous activities. Earnestness of effort, knowledge of rules of games (whether played or not), leadership ability, skill, and the spirit of co-operation shown should be among the determining factors in giving the grade. Pupils who co-operate fully during rest periods and participate intelligently in the regimes outlined for their individual improvement are entitled to a high rating.

The objectives of the recommended program for any pupil or group of pupils temporarily or permanently handicapped are (1) to build up the morale of the individuals who are apt to feel that they are different from other children because of their handicap; (2) to return those on a limited program to the regular program of activities as soon as the handicaps may be removed or the condition improved; (3) to give all such pupils a chance to acquire skill in games, as the pleasure experienced may result in play activities being continued after school days are ended; (4) to help pupils develop attitudes toward their own health problems that will enable them to so organize and engineer their daily living as to conserve their strength and develop emotional stability; and (5) to develop recreational habits that will be constructive, wholesome, and satisfying.

Activities Suggested for a Limited Program

Since the physical limitations and handicaps that call for a limited program vary widely, the choice of activity must be dictated by the individual case. Swimming, for instance, is an activity well suited to many pupils who could not participate in running or team games. Since it is a popular leisure time sport, swimming is very valuable to such pupils, not only physically but socially and psychologically. Other pupils may require very mild forms of exercise or quiet table games. The following list is suggestive of the activities that might be chosen:

Aerial darts	Checkers	Maze
Archery	Chess	Pool (miniature)
Backgammon	Croquet	Quoits
Beanbag games	Darts	Shuffleboard
Bowling	Fly casting	Suction cup dart baseball
Box hockey	Horseshoes	Table croquet
Carom	Lawn bowling	Table shuffleboard

The purchase of special materials and supplies for games and activities that require but little physical effort is quite as essential as is the purchase of playground apparatus and athletic supplies used for generally accepted vigorous games.[1]

---

[1] See "Equipment for Indoor Games," and "Commercial Equipment for Quiet and Social Games," Chapter V, pages 112-14.

Instructional Program for Migratory Groups

Teachers who have pupils from groups of migratory workers should make a special effort to plan a physical education program to meet the needs of these children. Many of these children are undernourished and overworked and games chosen for them should not be of the strenuous type. There are numerous games that tired children may learn and enjoy at school and later play in camps wherever they may be located. For these children, the less strenuous tag games, relays, rhythms, and individual and dual games are especially recommended. Some of the individual and dual games that are popular are paddle tennis, tether ball, deck tennis, horseshoes, and volleyball doubles. Games of low organization, such as Duck on a Rock and Pig in a Hole, have particular value. Instruction in rhythms is important. Many children in these schools have come from other states and can teach their classmates new rhythm patterns. Game boards for simple table games can be made at school and afterwards taken home when the rules for the games have been learned.

Schools have the responsibility for equipping these boys and girls with the knowledge and skills of worth-while recreational physical activities and of encouraging them to carry on these pleasurable experiences while living in their camps.

SELECTING THE ACTIVITIES

With the needs of the particular class and the particular individuals in that class in mind, the teacher selects from the great wealth of physical education activities those that seem most worth while. Examples of games, stunts, relays, or rhythms chosen for the development of some particular skill or because of their specific value or because they fit into a modified program are given in the following charts. Descriptions of the activities may be found in Part II of this guide.

EXAMPLES OF ACTIVITIES SUITABLE FOR PRIMARY GRADES

Type of Activity	Name of Activity	Remarks
Tag Games	Squirrels in Trees	Rapidly moving game played in a circle in groups of three
	Back to Back	Players get partners by hooking elbows
	Flying Dutchman	Running game played in a circle by couples
Ball Games	Beanbag Throwing for Distance	Practice in overhand throwing
	Ring Call Ball	Practice in tossing and catching

EXAMPLES OF ACTIVITIES SUITABLE FOR PRIMARY GRADES (Continued)

Type of Activity	Name of Activity	Remarks
Ball Games	Kick Ball	Team game, involving skills of softball and soccer
Games Played in Classroom	Chase the Animals Around the Corral	Circle game, with practice in object handling
	Numbers Exchange	A semiactive tag game
	The Ocean is Stormy	Involves seat exchange
Relays (Grade 3)	Across the Room	Played in classroom; semiactive
	Stoop and Stretch	Involves body exercise
Stunts (no mat needed)	Fourfooted Walk	Involves body exercise to develop arm strength
	Climb Through the Stick	Develops body flexibility
	Jumping	Develops leg power and technique of landing
	Deep Squat	Develops leg power and balance
Play on Apparatus	Climbing on Apparatus	Develops shoulder muscles and flexibility
	Hang and Drop	Develops arm strength and body balance in landing
	Horizontal Ladder Travel	Develops arm strength and body control
Rhythms	Free Rhythms	Includes skipping, running, hopping
	Identification Rhythms	Pupils represent animals, people, things
	Dramatization Rhythms	Creativity from songs, poems, events
Singing Games and Simple Folk Dances	Looby Loo	Circle game involving singing and pantomime
	A-Hunting We Will Go	A singing line game involving sliding and running
	Cshebogar	A partner circle dance involving skipping and turning
Body Mechanics	Climbing on Apparatus	Develops body strength and flexibility
	Walking Line or Balance Board	Develops good foot posture
	Standing Against Wall	Develops good body posture and balance

EXAMPLES OF ACTIVITIES SUITABLE FOR INTERMEDIATE GRADES

TYPE OF ACTIVITY	NAME OF ACTIVITY	REMARKS
Tag Games	Link Tag	Involves running, co-ordination
	Last Couple Out	Couple formation involving running, dodging
	Club Snatch	Involves running and balancing
Simple Lead-up Games	End Ball	A team game involving throwing
	Hit Pin Baseball	A team game of the softball type involving kicking
	Indian Ball	Involves batting and fielding
Team Games	Long Ball	Involves batting
	Softball	Official game with boys and girls using identical rules
	Nine-Court Basketball	Basketball rules used; game involves guarding, shooting baskets
Individual Games	Pateca	Can be played anywhere; equipment can be purchased or made
	Volley Tether Ball	Played with hands; large ball on a pole
	Paddle Ball	Played against backboard with tennis strokes
	Paddle Tennis	Played on small, surfaced court with tennis strokes
Relays	Toss Over Relay	Involves ball handling
	Shuttle Relays	Involves running
	Skip Rope Relay	Involves skipping
Games Played in Classroom	Poison Seat	A semiactive game
	Screwylouie	A volleyball type game played with a balloon or ball bladder
	Bowling at Indian Clubs	An accuracy game using a softball
Stunts and Tumbling (No mat needed)	Frog Hand Stand or Tip Up	Involves body balance on hands
	Cart Wheel	Develops co-ordination
	Elephant Walk	A stunt for two
Apparatus Play	Skin the Cat	Develops strength and flexibility on bar
	Horizontal Bar Walk	Develops balance and co-ordination
	Travel on Rings or Giant Stride	Develops arm strength
Rhythms	Free Rhythms	Involves basic motor skills
	Identification Rhythms	Usually connected with ideas concerning animals, peoples, and things

EXAMPLES OF ACTIVITIES SUITABLE FOR INTERMEDIATE GRADES
(Continued)

TYPE OF ACTIVITY	NAME OF ACTIVITY	REMARKS
Rhythms	Dramatization Rhythms	Highest form of creative rhythmical expression from everyday and classroom experiences. When repeated to a set pattern a dance is created.
Folk Dances	Bleking	A circle dance of couples involving hopping and turning
	Paw Paw Patch	A line dance of couples involving singing
	Ace of Diamonds	A dance in which couples polka
	Varsovienne	A dance of couples; varsovienne step
	Captain Jinks	A square dance with easy calls and steps
Social Dancing	Two-step	A couple dance; step-together-step
	Schottische	A couple dance involving step, step; step, hop
	Waltz	A couple dance; step, step, together
	Polka	A couple dance; step, together, step, hop
Body Mechanics	Dodging, Stopping, and Starting	Involves balance of body weight; use of feet
	Pull-ups	Aids body alignment; develops shoulder girdle strength
	Class posture check	Teaches children what good posture is; suggestions may be made for better posture

EXAMPLES OF ACTIVITIES SUITABLE FOR UPPER GRADES

TYPE OF ACTIVITY	NAME OF ACTIVITY	REMARKS
Lead-up Games	Football Lead-up Games	Football skills are taught in game situations
	Knock-Out or Freeze-Out	Basketball type of game involving shooting baskets and backboard recovery
	Basket Speed Ball	Speed ball type of game; soccer-basketball review
	Volley Tennis	Volleyball type of game
Team Sports	Basketball	Separate game for boys and girls; use official rules and adapted equipment
	Soccer	Separate game for boys and girls; use official rules and adapted equipment

EXAMPLES OF ACTIVITIES SUITABLE FOR UPPER GRADES (Continued)

TYPE OF ACTIVITY	NAME OF ACTIVITY	REMARKS
Team Sports	Touch Football	A two-hand touch game for boys; on a fumble the ball is dead
	Volleyball	A separate game for boys and girls; use official rules; or mixed recreational game
Individual and Dual Games	Horseshoe Pitching	For boys and girls; use official rules and adapted equipment
	Tennis	For boys and girls; use official rules
	Deck Tennis	Semiactive game for boys and girls
	Shuffleboard	Semiactive game for boys and girls
	Badminton	For boys and girls; use official rules
Relays	Obstacle Relay	Involves dodging
	Jack Rabbit Relay	Involves vigorous exercise; jumping
Games Played in Classroom	Progressive End Ball	Involves throwing at moving target
	Poison Snake	A semiactive game
Stunts and Tumbling	Corkscrew	Develops flexibility
	Chest Stand	Couple stunt; develops body balance
Self-testing Activities	Sit-ups	Develop abdominal strength
	Dashes	Develop endurance
	Distance Throws	Develop strength and co-ordination
	Jumps	Standing jump; running jump; high jump
Rhythms	Dramatizations	Based on ideas, ideals, or emotions
Folk Dances	Waves of Tory	A line dance with square dance steps
	Swing the Man from Arkansas	A square dance
	California Schottische	A progressive dance with couples
	La Raspa	A couple dance, with Bleking step
Social Activities for the Classroom	Labyrinth Tag	Group tag; suitable for small space
	Table Tennis	For boys and girls; official rules
	Rye Waltz	A couple dance; waltz, slide
	School Bowling	Equipment can be made or purchased
	Hello-Goodbye	A double circle mixer
Body Mechanics	Running Posture	Teacher and pupil should check on form
	Skills for Work	Raising windows; picking up objects; lifting; pushing
	Sitting and Standing Posture	Pupil and teacher check on form to correct faulty habits

Group Games with Elements Found in Team Games

Many of the activities used in the primary and intermediate grades, besides being valuable in themselves, are useful in developing the skills used in such highly organized games as softball, basketball, and tennis. For this reason these games are called lead-up games. By learning the skills used in these simple games, the pupil will be enabled to grasp readily the techniques of the highly organized games when he is introduced to them in the higher grades or in high school. The accompanying chart shows skills and activities suitable for use in the various grade levels that are also necessary to the game of basketball. Similar charts may be made for other games as a guide to teaching activities throughout the lower grades.[1] The activities are described in Part II of this guide.

ACTIVITIES USING SKILLS AND TECHNIQUES OF BASKETBALL

GRADES	SKILLS AND TECHNIQUES	ACTIVITIES
Primary	Stopping and starting	Stop and Start Stoop Tag
	Dodging	Cat and Rat Dodge Ball
	Jumping	Jack Be Nimble Jump Jim Crow
	Handling balls	Galloping Lizzie Chase the Animals Around the Corral
	Tossing and catching	Beanbag Ring Throw Sky High Ball
	Overhand throwing	Center Base Boundary Ball
Intermediate	Passing (one or two-hand underarm, bounce, or chest)	Captain Ball Elimination Pass Zigzag Bounce Relay Pass and Change
	Pivoting and guarding	Net Basketball Zone Dodge Ball Center Catch Touch Ball
	Techniques of game organization	Pin Basketball Goal-Hi Basketball

[1] See "Classification of Games by Type in Relation to the More Highly Organized Games to Which They Lead," pages 154-155.

ACTIVITIES USING SKILLS AND TECHNIQUES OF BASKETBALL (Continued)

GRADES	SKILLS AND TECHNIQUES	ACTIVITIES
Intermediate	Team play	Nine-Court Basketball (sixth-grade boys and girls play this together)
Upper	Shooting	Free-throw End Ball Frame Basketball Twenty-one
	Techniques in a game situation	Half-court Basketball Side-line Basketball
	Passing, pivoting, shooting, guarding, team strategy, and officiating	Circle Pass Drills Keep Away (using bounce or dribble, pivot, etc.) Squad pivot and pass Line formation shooting (one line off backboard; two lines, one receiving and shooting, the other recovering and passing; three lines, passing, pivoting, and shooting)
	Official rules of play	Basketball for Boys Basketball for Girls

SCHEDULING OF ACTIVITIES

Programs should be planned for the entire year and the activities listed that will meet the desired objectives in skills, attitudes, and knowledge for a specific group of children. The percentage of time over the period of a school year to be allotted to various physical education activities should be determined. In providing a balanced program in one year, a teacher must take into consideration not only the specific needs of the children, but the availability of apparatus and equipment, the type of weather, the kind of indoor and outdoor facilities, and the particular social studies units to be used. A year's plan must fit into the plans of the other years in school to avoid overlapping or omissions. After all these points are taken into consideration and the various activities are listed, then a detailed plan should be made for a shorter period of time. This period of time may be a season, a month, or a week.

In the kindergarten and primary grades, each day's activity is built upon that of the previous day; usually a complete unit is planned for each day. During a week the teacher may wish to work toward one or two climaxes. Activity will follow naturally from the centers of interest, from dramatic play, and from the physical activity of the previous day. However, the physical activities involving pushing, pulling, and climbing may be climaxed by dramatic play in which the climbing apparatus and the hollow blocks become a fishing boat. The bouncing of balls and throwing at targets may culminate in a new ball game participated in by all the children in small groups.

In the intermediate and upper grades, the complexity of the activities and the longer interest span of the children will make it possible and desirable to use longer units of activity. The length of the unit will depend on the complexity of the activity and the maturity of the children. For example, in learning the game of alley soccer, the class will need many days of relays, simple soccer type game, study of rules, and officiating before a game can be played well enough to provide a feeling of achievement. If rhythmical activities are taught several days in succession, learning takes place more rapidly because new skills build upon skills learned the day before and ensure quick mastery. Opportunity to master fundamental rhythms must be given before the more complicated dance steps are used in a particular dance. Equipment, facilities, and play space can be used to the advantage of all children if planned for a period of time.

After the year's program has been outlined and the monthly or weekly units of activity are scheduled, the teacher should make the daily lesson plans. The presentation of activities, formation, equipment, and means of evaluation should be thought out. The children should be brought into the planning each day by building upon what has gone before.

In the pages that follow, some of the important points in scheduling are discussed in detail; the allotment of time to each type of activity; the factors of repetition and of sustained activity; adjustments of schedule to meet weather changes; and periods of coeducational instruction. In the sample schedules it will be noted that one type of activity is repeated for several days, then another is introduced. This block or unit plan for teaching provides the best teaching situations, facilities, and progression. In schools where this plan seems impractical, like activities should at least follow each other and not be scattered throughout the week. The presentation of different types of activities with entirely new skills every day sets up a difficult learning situation for children.

Percentage of Time Allotment to Types of Activity

As children grow and develop, their capacities and needs change. Consequently, the percentage of time devoted to the various types of activity in the physical education program varies from grade to grade. The following chart suggests the desirable percentages of time over the period of a school year to be spent in the various kinds of activity for the primary, intermediate, and upper grades.

SUGGESTED PERCENTAGE OF PHYSICAL EDUCATION TIME TO BE ALLOTTED TO VARIOUS TYPES OF ACTIVITY EACH YEAR

GRADES	TYPE OF ACTIVITY	PERCENTAGE OF TIME
Primary	Rhythmical activities and body mechanics	50
	Running games and small group play	25
	Apparatus construction play and body mechanics	20
	Stunts	5
Intermediate	Rhythmical activities and body mechanics	35
	Simple games and relays	20
	Running games	15
	Apparatus, stunts, and body mechanics	15
	Team games	10
	Individual and dual games	5
Upper	Rhythmical activities and body mechanics	30
	Team games	20
	Simple games, relays	15
	Individual and dual games	15
	Stunts, tumbling, apparatus, and body mechanics	10
	Track, field, and skill testing activities and body mechanics	10

The Factor of Repetition

Repeated practice periods to perfect specific skills are essential. It is not desirable, however, to use the same activity day after day and week after week. The continuous use of Darebase, Run Sheep Run, softball, or basketball is a typical example of careless leadership and poor teaching. Simple activities can be taught in a few minutes and enjoyed by all. More complex activities need simple games, relays, discusion of rules, and skill drills before the game is enjoyed. Drills are needed at times for the perfection of some motor skills. Slow and unskilled performers should have special attention; the teacher and the more skillful pupils should aid them with encouragement and active assistance.

The Factor of Sustained Activity

Activities calling for long periods of endurance are not suitable for students in elementary grades. However, through the use of play periods in the grades the basis is laid for maintaining in later years sustained effort requiring maximum speed, endurance, and skill. Strength, agility, endurance, and skill are essential to perform hard and active work. Leg, forearm, and hand muscles of children are fairly well developed because of their use during the hours of daily living, but there is specific need to develop through vigorous activity the muscular strength of the side and front abdominal muscles, back muscles, shoulder retractor muscles, and the muscles that control the arches of the feet. This means that performers must not stop at the first sign of fatigue but must continue activities until they are tired. Increased stamina will result when muscular activity is increased beyond the habitual performance rate of the individual but not to the point of exhaustion.

Weather Conditions and Planned Activities

Weather conditions may often be the determining factor in the kind of activities used on a given day. Cold days call for games or activities that busily engage all performers simultaneously. Hot days call for less strenuous games or activities that require the performance of but a few players at a time, with players changing frequently. Instruction must sometimes be carried on indoors. The following places can be used as indoor play areas—gymnasium, playroom, cafeteria, auditorium, unobstructed classrooms, hallways, sidewalks under shelter, kindergarten rooms, basement areas, and the stage of the auditorium. The areas available will determine whether all may play together or whether small separate groups will need to be organized.

When outdoor activities are inadvisable because of heat, cold, dust storms, or rain, it is well for the teacher to have not only lesson plans but also plans for recess and the noon hour made up of indoor activities. Primary grades can carry on indoor programs using rhythms and tag games. Intermediate or upper grades may use a variety of games, relays, stunts, and rhythmical activities, the choice being dependent upon the size of the class and the space available. It is not necessary to abandon the particular unit of activity that is being studied merely because the activity must be carried on indoors. For instance, if the unit of study is volleyball, an indoor game of volleyball may be played in the auditorium or classroom by using an inflated bladder covered with cambric or an old piece of stocking. There are numerous simple games and relays that can be played even in a classroom with fixed desks, using the aisles and sides of the room.

Figure 19. Volleyball is a team game that boys and girls can play together.

Each class should plan and execute activities suitable for a party at home or at school. Excellent indoor games are classified for each grade in Part II of this guide; some recreational games and stunts are described in Chapter X.

Coeducational Instruction [1]

Almost all physical educational activities through the sixth grade can be coeducational. Separation of boys and girls in seventh and eighth grades comes as a result of the introduction of vigorous team sports and the development of individual interests. While it is right that segregation should begin during the seventh and eighth grades, authorities in physical education urge that teachers in the elementary school and in the high school select and organize an activity program in which boys and girls study and play together frequently. In the upper grades not less than the equivalent of two periods a week should provide such opportunity.

Among recommended activities that boys and girls can take part in together in the elementary school are both individual and team games such as bat ball, hit pin baseball, netball and volleyball, field dodge ball, paddle tennis, tether ball, table tennis, handball, nine-court basketball, softball, captain ball, horseshoes, shuffleboard, croquet, and tennis. Other activities which boys and girls can take part in together are social and rhythmical

[1] See Chapter I, pages 19-20 and pages 50 and 52 of this chapter.

games such as those suggested in the section "Programs for Special Occasions," Chapter X, page 258; all rhythmical activities; swimming; and many track and field events. Social occasions such as picnics and skating parties should be planned for boys and girls together when possible.

Sample Schedules

The charts on pages 70 and 71 may be used as guides in setting up weekly schedules of activities for primary, intermediate, and upper grades.

PLANS OF ORGANIZATION OF PHYSICAL EDUCATION PERIODS

In the teaching of physical education it is important to organize procedures and make clear to the children how they can help in planning and in carrying out the plans made. Plans may be made in the classroom and carried out on the playground.

Planning in the Classroom

Preliminary organization of a play period should take place in the classroom. The following procedures may be followed:

1. A grade captain should be chosen. Captains should be elected in grades above the first; captains may possibly be elected in the first grade if pupils seem mature enough.

2. Qualities of leaders should be agreed upon. The teacher should teach squad captains to lead and squad members to follow. She should allow each child, as he develops, the privilege of officiating. In a one- or two-room school, the older pupils can be given opportunity in leadership and can learn more by officiating than by irregular participation.

3. Squads should be chosen; six to eight children in a squad are best; captains should be chosen in rotation, so that each serves for a week.

4. Activities should be scheduled for available space and equipment. A labeled chart of the play area will help the class to understand the procedure.

5. Games should be assigned, selected according to the maturity and interest of the group and based on skills that have been mastered.

6. Equipment should be ready.

7. Each squad should understand the game to be played, the area to be used, and the organization of the particular game or activity.

8. Signals for starting and stopping of play should be agreed upon.

SAMPLE SCHEDULES

Schedule I. A Weekly Schedule For Primary Grades

Grade	Monday	Tuesday	Wednesday	Thursday	Friday
K	Guided play using large toys, hanging and climbing equipment	Guided play	Guided play	Rhythms (skipping, running)	Rhythms
1	Rhythms and dramatizations	Rhythms	Rhythms	Small group activities Running games (tag and "it" games)	Small group activities
2	Running games	Running games	Running games or hanging apparatus	Rhythms or singing games	Rhythms or singing games
3	Relays or running games	Running games	Team or running games or hanging apparatus	Rhythms, creative, singing, and/or simple folk dances	Rhythms

Schedule II. A Weekly Schedule For Intermediate Grades

Grade	Monday	Tuesday	Wednesday	Thursday	Friday
4	Running games or relays or hanging apparatus involving skills of games	Running games, relays, or apparatus play	Simple group games	Simple group games	Simple group games
5	Free and identification rhythms	Dramatization rhythms	Dramatization rhythms	Singing game	Simple folk dance
6	Running game, relay involving skills of games	Continue skills relays and games	Introduce individual or dual game	Individual and dual games	Individual and dual games

SCHEDULE III. A WEEKLY SCHEDULE FOR UPPER GRADES, USING ONE ACTIVITY UNIT THROUGH THE WEEK

GRADES	MONDAY	TUESDAY	WEDNESDAY	THURSDAY	FRIDAY
7	Paddle Tennis 1. Dodging game 2. Batting relay 3. Rules of paddle tennis	Paddle Tennis 1. Explanation and demonstration of serve 2. Practice of serve 3. Return serve	Paddle Tennis 1. Demonstration of forehand and backhand strokes 2. Practice of strokes 3. Practice in keeping ball active	Paddle Tennis 1. Rules of game explained 2. Games played	Paddle Tennis 1. Discussion of practice needed 2. Practice elements of game 3. Play game
8	Volleyball 1. Warm-up relay 2. Review serving 3. Return practice serves	Volleyball 1. Set-up demonstration 2. Set-up relay 3. Play game	Volleyball 1. Review rules and skills 2. Practice, in groups, needed skills 3. Play game	Volleyball 1. Warm-up on needed skills 2. Concentrate on set-up in game	Volleyball 1. Play a full game 2. Evaluate progress at end of period

SCHEDULE IV. A WEEKLY SCHEDULE FOR UPPER GRADES, USING MORE THAN ONE TYPE OF ACTIVITY IN THE WEEK

GRADES	MONDAY	TUESDAY	WEDNESDAY	THURSDAY	FRIDAY
7	Stunts, relays, or skills practice	Team games	Team games	Rhythms; creative, social, or folk	Rhythms
8	Individual and dual games	Individual and dual games	Rhythms: creative, folk or social	Rhythms	Rhythms

Playground Organization

When the class arrives on the playground, it is important to have plans that will help in the conduct of an orderly, efficient, and happy period. The following list suggests effective procedures:

1. Squads should be assigned to play areas, close enough together for supervision, but far enough apart for safety.
   a. Games should be far enough apart so that a batted ball from one game does not go into another game area.
   b. Designated areas should be numbered or named in accordance with the chart prepared in the classroom.
2. Grades can be grouped for play if the number in one grade is too small for the activity chosen.
   a. Grades 1, 2, and 3 can play together.
   b. Grades 4, 5, and 6 can be grouped for most activities, but children should be classified for competition.
3. Beginning not earlier than the sixth grade, boys and girls should be separated for certain activities only when interest and ability are too different.
   a. In team games that have separate sets of rules for girls and boys, boys of several grades may be grouped into one set of playing squads and the girls into another set of squads, providing the players on each squad are of like size and skill.
   b. Simple team games providing skills and techniques for the more highly organized games should be used in the intermediate grades in preference to team games that require segregation.

Suggestions to the Teacher on Organizing the Program

In the classroom and on the playground there are numerous points that will assist the teacher in carrying out the physical education program efficiently and with the maximum benefit to the pupils. A few suggestions on the details of organization follow:

1. Keep a record of activities taught.
2. Seek constantly to improve the equipment.
3. Be resourceful in adapting games to prevailing ground and weather conditions. For instance,
   a. Save indoor games for use on days of inclement weather.
   b. During cold weather use games that require the active participation of many children, such as field dodge ball, progressive dodge ball, Spider and Flies, Duck on the Rock, and Black and White.

c. If regulation balls are not available, use substitutes such as bean-bags, handmade balls, or stuffed leather ball casings.

4. Have pupils study the rules for all new games or activities before undertaking to play the game out of doors. Make explanations as simple and concise as possible. Simple demonstrations are more effective than lengthy explanations.

a. Have children keep rules in a "Games Notebook."

b. Give opportunity for rules of games to be expressed in writing in the intermediate and upper grades.

5. For recess and noon play, use activities studied during the physical education period. For example,

a. Circle running games with instruction may be practiced and played during class and then played in squads or teams in a scheduled noon or extended day period.

b. Kicking skills and elements of kick ball may be learned during class and then scheduled games may be played at noon or after school.

6. Develop respect for game officials. Teach pupils the function of the officials and insist that all show respect for the decisions made.

a. Point out that games go faster and more successfully when all accept without discord the decisions of the referee.

b. Show that professional umpires and referees sometimes make incorrect decisions and that pupils also may be in error some-times, but that players do not show disrespect for the officials.

c. Provide opportunity for class discussions of decisions if there is any doubt concerning the correctness of the interpretations given by the referee. The discussion should occur following the activity period, never on a field of play.

7. Act quickly in starting a game.

8. Whenever possible, use no more than six players to a file for relay races. If the group to play is very large, divide it into smaller units and have each unit play a game by itself. If the number of players makes it advisable, vary the size of the playing courts.

9. Whenever possible, arrange teams so that the players are nearly equal in skill and strength. Designate team memberships by using colored bands, pinnies, or other distinguishing insignia.

10. Organize pupils with poor co-ordination into small squads with plenty of equipment for maximum amount of practice.

11. Watch closely for waning interest and change to a new activity.

12. When using running tag games, start with a game in which all par-ticipate and finish with a game in which players await turns.

13. Emphasize character and sportsmanship values in activities and in social situations that develop. Do not permit certain pupils to monopolize a game location or special playground equipment. Teach children to await their turn when using playground apparatus. Do not tolerate profanity, cheating, or bullying.

14. Have court and game areas properly outlined so that strict obedience to game rules can be effective.

15. Play with the children.

16. Encourage children to center their interest in the contribution made by their own position to the game.

17. Do not curb enthusiasm and spontaneity, but remember that uncontrolled behavior may result in discourtesy and confusion, detracting from the success of the game.

EVALUATION OF THE PROGRAM

Teachers will find it helpful to have some general measure by which they may judge the effectiveness of their plans for physical education. Consideration of the following questions will help the teacher to review the planning in terms of the broad purposes and objectives of physical education.

1. Does the program for the year give attention to the basic needs of the children at their various levels of maturity?

2. Does the program give consideration to change of seasons and interests through the year?

3. Does the schedule include the variety of activities needed in a well-rounded physical education program?

4. Are playdays or demonstrations of the different phases of the physical education program planned for as often as twice a month?

5. Are coeducational classes (for grades 7 and 8) provided about 50 per cent of the time?

6. Are activities included to meet the personal needs of handicapped or temporarily disabled children, and are game materials available for them?

7. Does the program aim to increase the ability of children to manage their own activities?

8. Will the program give frequent opportunity for creative expression on the part of the children?

9. Does the program take into account the factor of individual differences?

Another set of questions will serve as a guide in judging the value of activities in terms of the individual child.

1. Are the child's remediable defects corrected?
2. Is he increasing in height and weight?
3. Does he play with enthusiasm and pleasure?
4. Does he adjust easily from the play period to the quiet activity of the classroom?
5. Is he growing in endurance?
6. Is he growing in arm and shoulder-girdle strength? In upper back strength? In abdominal strength?
7. Is he growing in play skills?
8. Is he growing in emotional stability?
9. Is he growing in a consideration of the rights and feelings of others during play?
10. Is he growing in co-operation?
11. Is he growing in leadership?
12. Is he growing in followership? [1]

SELECTED REFERENCES [2]

LaSalle, Dorothy. *Physical Education for the Classroom Teacher.* New York: A. S. Barnes & Co., 1937.

Sehon, Elizabeth, and Others. *Physical Education Methods for Elementary Schools.* Philadelphia: W. B. Saunders Co., 1948.

Williams, Jesse Feiring, and Brownell, C. L. *The Administration of Health and Physical Education.* Philadelphia: W. B. Saunders Co., 1946 (third edition).

---

[1] Dorothy LaSalle, *Guidance of Children Through Physical Education.* New York: A. S. Barnes & Co., 1946, pp. 141-42. Quoted by permission.

[2] Appendix B also lists reference materials.

Chapter V
FACILITIES, EQUIPMENT, AND SUPPLIES

The playground is an essential part of a school. It is sometimes difficult for parents to understand that play is nature's method of teaching the young many important skills and relationships, but in recent years both the biological and social values of play have been increasingly appreciated. It is now known that the skill of the athlete is the result of years of development. The muscular co-ordinations called for in the vigorous play of young children lay a foundation for those muscular skills that serve so effectively in many ways in later years. The earlier these experiences begin, the better. Moreover, the playground is a great school of citizenship. The Duke of Wellington recognized this fact when he said that the Battle of Waterloo was won on the playing fields of Eton.

Since physical education is a part of the school program, the teaching materials used in physical education classes are an essential part of the equipment of the school. Among such materials are to be listed play areas, outdoor and indoor, playground apparatus, game and athletic equipment and supplies, and teaching tools such as phonographs and records, films, and books. Without adequate materials, teaching procedures will be ineffective and the physical development of the children will not be aided as it should be. The unrealized possibilities of many adults with respect to the skills they possess, the interests they have, and the attitudes they manifest can often be traced to the poor and inadequate play equipment of their school days. Lack of such facilities and equipment may result in deficiencies in human personality, in lessened agility, in awkwardness, and in sedentary habits.

OUTDOOR PLAY SPACE

It is important that school sites provide level, graded, and surfaced areas, fenced for safety, in order to allow for building and landscaping and to permit the simultaneous activities of running and tag games, individual and dual games, team games, rhythmical experiences, and play on apparatus. The standard for elementary school grounds in California provides a minimum site of five acres with an additional acre for each 100 of estimated enrollment. For example, a school population of 200 would need at least seven acres, and a school population of 500 would need at least 10 acres.

Play Area

Children under ten years of age should have an area for play near the classroom, so situated that they will not be interfered with by older boys and girls. In this play area they should be able to have many types of

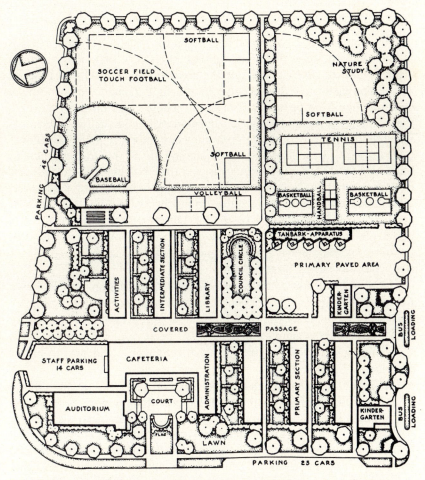

Figure 20.   A plan showing landscaping, layout of buildings, and playing areas suitable for all age levels is that of Sunnyvale Elementary School.[1]

manipulative experiences during which they have opportunity to play with building blocks, boxes, ladders, balance board, wheeled toys, balls, and rhythm instruments. There must be ample space for a large sandbox.

[1] Reproduced by permission of Arthur Cobbledick, Landscape Architect, Menlo Park, California.

Room is needed for the use of tricycles, wagons, and doll buggies, and a large area is essential for playing running games, for dramatic play, singing games, and rhythmical activities. A movable amplifying phonograph that can be regulated in the speed desired or a piano that can be moved about easily is a necessity for the last three activities.

Layout of School Grounds

It is important to prepare and maintain the grounds so that the needs of the children for activity can be met, the safety of children can be insured, and the attractiveness of the area will be an asset and pleasure to the community. It has become increasingly recognized that school grounds should be planned to serve the whole community.[1] Figure 20 shows the layout of the school playground and buildings for an elementary school that is intended to serve the community. The grounds cover twelve acres, of which approximately one and a half acres are given over to buildings. There are large lawn areas about the buildings, and classrooms have individual gardens, mostly lawn with planting strips for class use, surrounded by hedges that require little pruning. Playfields at the rear are fenced off from the rest of the grounds to permit separate use as a public play area during the summer and after school hours. Access is given to toilets and equipment rooms at the ends of the near buildings. Space has been allowed for onsite parking.

Another California elementary school site utilization plan is shown in Figure 21. The plan includes outdoor classrooms, paved and turfed play areas adjacent to the separate buildings, and a large area devoted to playing fields for all types of games.

Another plan for a community-centered school and playground is described in Chapter X.[2]

Fences. A fence is needed on each terraced area and usually around other areas used for play purposes. Probably nothing is more discouraging and annoying to players when a fast game is in progress than the loss of a ball down a sloping area or outside the school grounds. A fence is needed at both ends of tennis and paddle tennis courts and as backstops for softball diamonds. Fences should also separate apparatus areas from other playground areas when the apparatus is concentrated. Most important of all, fencing in most urban neighborhoods provides a safety factor that no school can afford to ignore. The amount and height of the fencing depends entirely on the safety needs of the particular school site.

[1] For a description of beautification of school grounds in Long Beach, see Walter L. Scott, "A Playground Improvement Project," *California Journal of Elementary Education,* IX (August, 1940), 49-54.
[2] See page 257.

Shade Trees and Shrubs. Shade is particularly desirable for school playgrounds and its location is important. Shrubbery should be planted along fences, but outside them. Trees should be planted inside and near fences, never in the middle of open areas where they will interfere with free space essential for games. Trees should provide protection from the sun during the pupils' lunch period and while they are playing table games.

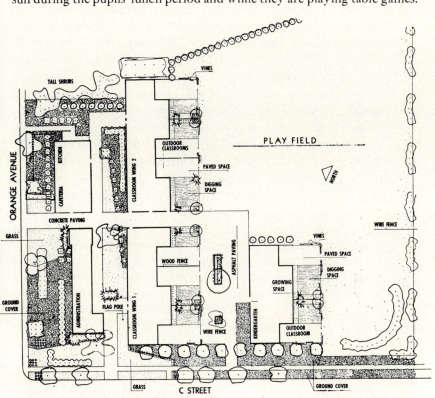

Figure 21. Good relationship of buildings to play areas is shown in the plans for a primary school in South San Francisco.[1]

Trees and shrubs are useful for breaking glare during periods of play. In addition, they help to provide pleasing surroundings in the rear as well as in the front of the school buildings. In too many cases school grounds are beautifully cared for in front, a section that children seldom see or use, while at the rear, where children spend most of their free time, the outlook is dreary, dirty, unsightly, and uninspiring.

[1] Reproduced by permission of Eckbo, Royston & Williams, Landscape Architects. Bamberger & Reid, Architects.

Lawn Areas.   If weather and soil conditions permit, turf or lawn should be part of each playing area. This area may be used for stunts, folk games, and rhythmical activities. Lawns at the front or sides of buildings should be used for these activities if a lawn area is not available at the rear. Weeds should be cut or eradicated with a weed destroyer before they reach tall growth or seed time.

Bench and Tables.   At least one bench and table should be available in a shady spot to provide for handcraft, table games, outdoor classes, and lunching. Patterns for game boards could be painted on the tops of the tables.

Open Air Grill.   Outdoor grills and fireplaces would make schools truly social centers for children and for the neighborhood. Here camp cooking could be studied and overnight camping experiences might be a reality even though no other opportunity for such experiences were available. The fireplaces could be used by the community for social events. Grills or fireplaces should be provided with protective screening.

Terraced Play Areas.   Grading should be done in areas where it is impossible to secure naturally level playground sites. At least one flat, smooth, fenced area is a necessity for a school with a small enrollment. For example, basketball at the elementary level requires a recommended space of 46 by 66 feet, which allows a court 40 by 60 feet with an outer safety lane of 3 feet. Other games can be played on this area. Several terraced areas should provide ample room for carrying on an excellent program in physical education. The expenditure of school funds for terracing as well as for fences is essential if children attending mountain and hillside schools are to have play opportunities equal to those offered children attending schools located in level sections of the state.

Erosion and Flooding.   School sites should be graded and maintained in such a condition that flooding and erosion cannot destroy the usefulness of the playgrounds. As an aid to early evaporation, water should be swept out of small depressions and from oiled, paved, and cement surfaces. Widths of old carpet or gunny sacks may be fastened to a pole and dragged over the ground to spread accumulated water. Drainpipes will be essential in some situations to guarantee early drainage. Drainpipes should also be used to remove water from jumping pits in order that pits may be used at any season of the year.

Recommended Outdoor Play Areas for an Elementary School

The following lists have been drawn up as guides for planning the outdoor play areas that should be provided for various age groups in the school, with provision also for community-use areas.

Kindergarten Outdoor Play Area or Preschool Play Lot

Apparatus area, surfaced with tanbark, shavings, or coarse sawdust and sand mixture
Sandbox, 8 by 20 feet, covered
Surfaced area for using wheeled toys
Live pet area
Area for using building boxes and planks
Digging area
Grass area
Surfaced area for games
Work area supplemental to classroom

Primary Outdoor Play Area

Apparatus area, surfaced with tanbark, shavings, or coarse sawdust and sand mixture
Sandbox
Surfaced area for using wheeled toys
Area for using building boxes and planks
Digging area
Work area supplemental to classroom
Open play areas
   1. Grass or stabilized soil·
   2. Multiple use paved area marked with circles and squares for small group games and hopscotch

Intermediate Outdoor Play Area

Apparatus area, surfaced with tanbark, shavings, or coarse sawdust and sand mixture
Multiple use area surfaced with resilient bituminous paving
   1. Space marked with permanent lines for small group games and hopscotch
   2. Courts for individual and team games
   3. Simple game areas
Field area, grass or stabilized soil
   1. Softball diamonds with backstops for practice and games. Diamond 35 to 45 feet between bases, batting radius allowance 175 feet
   2. Field space for soccer or football type games
Courts, paved area (combined with multiple use or separate)
   1. Volleyball type (high net, 25 by 50 foot court)
   2. Basketball with offset goals (8 or 9 feet high, court 40 by 60 feet)
   3. Handball (court 20 by 20 feet) with backboard
   4. Deck Tennis, paddle tennis type (low net, 18 by 40 feet or 20 by 44 feet)
   5. Tether ball (circle 12 feet in diameter with pole in center)
   6. Shuffleboard (6 by 52 feet)
   7. Bowling (3½ by 75 feet)
Other game areas
   1. Horseshoes (30 feet between stakes)
   2. Table Tennis (table 5 by 9 feet)
   3. Darts and table games
   4. Croquet (30 by 60 feet)

Upper Grade Outdoor Play Area

Apparatus area, surfaced with tanbark, shavings, or coarse sawdust and sand mixture
Field area, grass or stabilized soil
   1. Softball diamonds with backstops, including batting practice areas. Batting radius allowance 250 feet
   2. Fields with goals for games such as touch football, soccer, and speed ball (120 by 240 feet each)
Court areas, paved, turf, or packed soil
   1. Volleyball (25 by 50 feet)

  2. Badminton, paddle tennis, deck tennis (18 by 40 feet, for doubles)
  3. Basketball (50 by 84 feet)
  4. Tennis (36 by 78 feet)
  5. Handball (20 by 34 feet) with backboard
  6. Quoits and horseshoes (20 by 74 feet; quoit stakes 54 feet apart; horseshoes 30 or 40 feet apart)
  7. Shuffleboard (6 by 52 feet)
  8. Tether ball (circle 12 feet in diameter, with pole in center)

COMMUNITY RECREATION AREA

Water spray or wading pool
Swimming pool
Landscaped picnic area, approximately 8000 square feet for 10 acres
  1. Barbecue pits, benches, and drinking water
  2. Quiet area with fireplace, council ring, and small raised platform
Adult area, 4000 square feet for 10 acres
Multipurpose room

Playground Surfacing

Several types of surfacing are used for school playgrounds. A dirt surface requires special treatment to prevent dust. A sandy or rocky area, or one in which the soil is clay or adobe, needs treatment to make it safe for playground use. Turf, while expensive to plant and to maintain, makes a very satisfactory playground for some games. Various types of hard surfacing, including cement and bituminous mixtures, serve for the games requiring a smooth, hard surface. All playground areas should be levelled and graded enough to provide drainage. They should be free from loose stones, pebbles, or gravel, and from humps and depressions caused by uneven turf. Such accident hazards as exposed water faucets should, of course, be eliminated. No hard surfacing should be used under apparatus such as horizontal bars and horizontal ladders. Grass, tanbark, shavings, or a mixture of sand and sawdust should be used in such areas.

Dirt Surface. When the ground is very sandy or rocky, the only remedies are to haul in a covering of better soil and pack it down or to cover the area with some type of surfacing. Adobe and clay may be made less slippery and muddy by mixing it with sand or finely crushed rock and rolling it well. The chief drawback of a dirt playground is dust, which is a menace to health. Dust can be greatly reduced by treating it with a salt-water solution or with calcium chloride. The salt-water solution may be made by mixing crushed rock salt with water in the proportion of one-half to one pound of salt in a gallon of water. Sprinkling the ground with this solution once a week (preferably before the weekend) will keep the dust down.

Calcium chloride may be purchased either in the form of flakes or in solution. It is inexpensive, and about two pounds per square yard is enough to last an entire season. The flakes can be spread with a shovel, or if the area to be covered is large, a mechanical spreader may be used; the liquid may be spread over the surface with a street sprinkling cart. Calcium chloride should not be used on a surface which has been previously treated with oil, tar, or asphalt unless special preparations are made, but it can be used to advantage on any type of unpaved surface. Playing areas need not be closed during and following treatment. It is clean, odorless, harmless, and nonstaining. Once it becomes a part of the surface it will not track into buildings. It penetrates from three to five inches in depth and will remain effective for long periods. Besides preventing dust, this substance prevents surface cracking and slows the growth of weeds.

Turf.[1] Considerable attention has been given to the growing of grasses best suited to the semiarid conditions which are prevalent in California and to the hard use given turf fields by schools. Blue grass turf has been found to be impractical for this use, and Bermuda grass, which is sufficiently hardy and makes a thick turf, is apt to become lumpy and in some districts its use is considered a nuisance by the residents. The playing fields at the Agricultural Experiment Station of the University of California at Davis are among the best turf fields in the country. The seed prescription and the treatment for these fields was described by the Station as follows:

> The following grasses were included: perennial ryegrass (*Lolium perenne* Suttoni), crested dogstail (*Cynosure cristatus*), creeping fescue (*Festuca arenaria*), sheep's fescue (*Festuca elatior*), and creeping bent (*Agrostis* sp.).
>
> These seeds were mixed in the proportion of 50 per cent of perennial ryegrass and an equal amount of the others totaling 50 per cent. This mixture was sown on fall plowed land (well worked down and rolled) during February, at the rate of 250 pounds of seed per acre. It was sown by hand and covered by a light harrowing, and finished by rolling. The surface was then sprinkled and kept continually moist to prevent the formation of a crust until the stand was well established and the ground shaded. . . . The first named grass provides the upper story or framework and withstands hard wear at all seasons of the year. The other grasses form the lower story and creeping along the ground act as binders and give body to the turf. By using this mixture of several grasses a more complete binding together of the turf is effected than if a single grass was employed. The mixture also provides for vigorous growth and green appearance at all seasons. . . . I would recommend that the grasses be obtained separately and mixed before planting.[2]

Experience at San Luis Obispo with turf is told by Wilbur B. Howes, head of the Ornamental Horticulture Department of California State Polytechnic College. He advises concerning the selection of seeds, seed

[1] An excellent general reference regarding turf playground surfacing is an article by John Monteith, Jr., "Better Turf for Playgrounds and Playfields," *Recreation*, XXXV (May, 1941), 105-7, 128. The article discusses soil foundation, seeding, fertilizers, and height for mowing.

[2] Supplied by Professor George W. Hendry, Associate Agronomist at the University of California Agricultural Experiment Station. Quoted from *News Letter No. 9* of the California State Board of Education, Department of Physical Education. Sacramento: California State Board of Education, April 20, 1926.

planting procedures, the purchase of seed, and irrigation. The following is a résumé of Mr. Howes's recommendations:

The problem of a turf surface for playground use is one which has been with us for many years. Most school departments wish to turn off the water and dispense with the labor of maintenance of playgrounds the day that school is out and then begin maintenance and irrigation about the same time that school opens in the fall. I do not believe that there is any grass suitable for playground use that will stand this type of treatment.

Redtop (*Agrostis alba*) is one of the most satisfactory grasses to use in areas that have a very slight amount of alkali in the water or the soil. Another grass is Chewings Fescue. Any lawn or turf area will eventually become slightly acid in character, except in those areas where there is a hard clay subsoil and where the water table is liable to rise with continued watering. In those areas, the alkali content in the soil will rise to the surface and eventually kill out any of the grasses that prefer a slightly acid soil.

In alkali areas—and there are many in California, especially in the upper Sacramento and the lower San Joaquin valleys—I would suggest the use of *Lolium multiflorum*, Western grown ryegrass; also the use of Pacey's ryegrass. These two grasses must be planted thickly or they will become bunchy—300 pounds to an acre is recommended.

When planting seeds it is a good policy to see that the seeds mixed for planting are approximately the same weight and size. Otherwise, the heavier seeds will go toward the bottom of the mix and a patchy-looking lawn will result. It is advisable to plant each type of seed separately. This results in a more even lawn.

When planting lawns in April or early May, where warm spells of weather are liable to occur, plant one-half pound of white Dutch clover seed to every 200 square feet of surface. White Dutch clover will act as a nurse crop for the other finer grasses that are coming up underneath. The clover will germinate and be a fairly good-sized plant in less than ten days. It is seldom a clover lawn will last out one summer. Hot weather almost always kills it, but it has done its work by that time and the added cost of it is more than repaid by the protection it gives the other grasses.

The Texas carpet grass (*Axonopus compressus*), used successfully in southern Texas for polo fields and playgrounds, stands summer drouths. It grows from stolons and not from seeds. It may be the long-looked for grass for playfields and large turf areas, as it requires practically no care, little water, and is very resistant to alkali.

Kentucky blue grass is a good field grass for most localities. It should not be used in places where summer maintenance cannot be provided. It is probably the longest lived grass but it is so slow in getting established that a field seeded to it should not be used after seeding for at least ten months and preferably eighteen months. Most playgrounds cannot wait that long. That is one point in favor of Pacey's ryegrass. It is possible to use it for such games as football two months after it is planted. A satisfactory mixture for blue grass would be 200 pounds to the acre plus an overplanting of 50 pounds of white Dutch clover and, if the soil is sandy, an additional 50 pounds of Chewings Fescue.

Irrigation is one of the most important factors in keeping turf in good condition. Flooding with irrigation water is sometimes used. The surface must be level and a large head of water is necessary. The most serious drawback is the fact that the turfed area is out of commission for several days while the surface is drying off. Underground sprinkling systems are used in some areas; in others, overhead irrigation through the use of a type of traveling sprinkler. While more costly than flood irrigation, the use of the latter types for watering permit the turfed areas to be used the following morning, an important factor where many children are to be accommodated during school hours.[1]

Hard Surfacing. Some game courts such as tennis courts require a very hard, smooth surface. Cement is generally used for these. Such surfacing must be done by experts familiar with the specifications. Many school playgrounds are surfaced with some type of bituminous paving, commonly referred to as "blacktop." Specifications for playground surfacing have been drawn up by the Division of Architecture, California State Department of Public Works. The base is made of concrete aggregate, mixing type asphalt, Portland cement, and water. After the base has dried sufficiently, it is rolled and a carpet coat surfacing is laid.

Combining sawdust with an asphalt base has provided a useful playground surface at the schools in Santa Barbara. The process of applying this surface is described by Sterling S. Winans: [2]

> When a macadam base is completed a two-coat emulsion sawdust surface is applied as follows: First, spray or squeegee onto the surface of the macadam as much cold bitumul emulsion (L.X. quality) as will remain without running. Second, immediately after the bitumul emulsion is applied, cover the surface with an adequate amount of No. 6 sawdust or ground shavings—approximately one sack of sawdust per 200 square feet of surfacing. The surface is then rolled with a garden roller weighted with gravel or sand. Third, at the end of 24 hours, when the bitumul emulsion has had time to set and absorb or make adhesion with the sawdust, sweep off the loose sawdust with bassine brooms. Fourth, re-coat the first bitumul layer with a second coat of bitumul put on with squeegee or spray and immediately apply sawdust. Fifth, roll the surface and allow it to set for 24 hours, following which time the loose sawdust is removed.
>
> The double coating described has been very satisfactory over a term of five years and it appears to have a life usefulness in excess of twelve or fifteen years. The surface is nonabrasive in comparison with the old sand finished surfacing; it does not wear out shoes and clothing nearly as badly; and it is not so hard on the knees and elbows of children when falls occur.[3]

It should be possible to secure expert advice from city and county engineers or contractors concerning the best turf or hard surfacing that can be used locally on school grounds. No all-inclusive advice can be given, since factors affecting surfacing differ so materially in various sections of the state. The use of city and county road building equipment may be available to schools in some areas for this kind of construction work.

---

[1] Personal letter from W. B. Howes, California State Polytechnic College, San Luis Obispo, California, to Winifred Van Hagen, March 12, 1943.

[2] Sterling S. Winans was formerly Supervisor of Physical Education, Santa Barbara Public Schools. He is at present Director of the California State Recreation Commission.

[3] Personal communication from Sterling S. Winans to Miss Van Hagen, January 24, 1944.

PLAY EQUIPMENT FOR KINDERGARTEN AND PRIMARY GRADES

When necessary supplies and equipment are available and children are permitted to use the equipment of their choice, little or no asocial behavior will be seen in group play. Two to four different children will use such apparatus as hanging ropes, one after the other, during a play period. A variety of materials and pieces of equipment encourage group play on a level young children can themselves organize and carry out successfully. It is unnecessary for boys and girls to be separated while using playground equipment and apparatus.

Outdoor Apparatus

For young children, including preschool children who may come to the school playground, climbing apparatus is valuable. Low horizontal bars over which children can turn are also valuable. The heights of the bars that have proved most satisfactory for kindergarten are 36 inches from the ground and for grades 1, 2, and 3, 48 and 54 inches from the ground. A slide is useful, though not essential. For young children, the slide should be six feet high and have a safety platform. Swings, although commonly used on playgrounds, offer less physical exercise than many

Figure 22. Climbing apparatus develops all of the large muscles of the body and is challenging to children.

other kinds of apparatus. If they are used, the canvas swing seats should be not higher than 10 inches from the ground.

Much of the equipment for the playground can be made in the school shop or by local craftsmen. The following list gives some of the desirable items.

1. Climbing apparatus for hanging and climbing
2. Horizontal bars in units of two or three, graduated in height, for turning over and hanging (Figure 23)[1]
3. Horizontal ladder for hanging and hand traveling
4. Inverted V-shaped fence section (two walls), 5 to 6 feet high by 10 feet long. Each wall should have from 6 to 10 crosspieces nailed flat on the walls to afford footholds
5. Sandbox, 6 by 12 feet or 8 by 20 feet
6. Large wooden boxes, open on both ends, with hole handles
7. Barrels and kegs that can be rolled and pushed about
8. Ladder that can be placed on a slant or hung perpendicular to ground
9. Long 10- or 12-inch plank of 1¼-inch lumber that can be placed horizontally or be inclined for climbing up and running down
10. Sawhorses of different heights
11. Ridge pole 10 to 12 feet long and 3 inches wide, standing 8 inches from the floor [2]
12. Sturdy wheelbarrows large enough to carry small objects
13. Six-foot and eight-foot slides with safety platforms
14. Small tables and chairs
15. Work benches, tools, and scrap wood
16. Stairs for practice in stair climbing
17. Different-sized hollow building blocks finished for outdoor use

Sandbox and Sandbox Tools

Some of the simplest forms of play for younger children are sandbox activities. Valuable lessons are learned by the children as they fail or succeed in a given sandbox undertaking. They learn about mountains, tunnels, walls, and other phases of building. Such play is not inactive, since children must move about, get up and down, and control their actions to prevent accidents to their own and other players' constructions.

---

[1] Safety rules require that a soft area should be maintained around and under horizontal bars and ladder. The use of shavings (not redwood), rice husks, or sand spaded often enough to prevent packing and kept free from paper and sharp objects is recommended.

[2] This piece of equipment and the plank offer many opportunities for children to practice balancing in standing, walking, and running. Its use will benefit feet particularly if shoes and socks are removed. See *Home Play and Play Equipment for the Preschool Child.* Children's Bureau Publication No. 238. Washington, D. C.: U. S. Department of Labor, 1941.

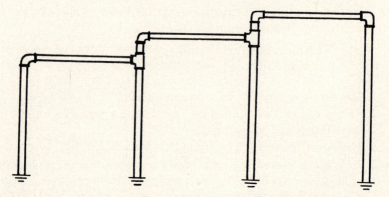

Figure 23. Horizontal bars in two or three sections must be of suitable height.

A sandbox may be built out of doors on the ground, with sides one foot high. A wide seat should be built around the upper edge of the sides. The size recommended is from 6 by 12 feet to 8 by 20 feet, depending on the number of children to be accommodated. The box should be large enough to permit at least six children to play together.

A sandbox for indoor use can be made from a wooden tub, oil drum, or galvanized tub with the sides cut down and smoothed off. A table may be used as the base of a sandbox. Sides should be added, the interior should be lined with zinc or galvanized iron, and the legs should be cut short so that the top edge is about level with the waists of the children. Since

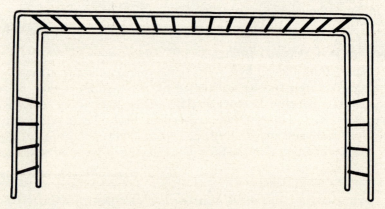

Figure 24. The horizontal ladder is another essential for the playground.

the weight of the sand makes the table difficult to move, it should not be too large. Casters should be put on the legs of the table.

Care of Sand.   Sand of a very fine grade should be used; white seashore sand is preferred. The sand should be put through a very fine sieve to remove foreign particles. Sand should be kept slightly damp by using a sprinkling can occasionally. It may be desirable to require hand washing before use of the sand is permitted. No child with sores on arms or hands should use the sand.

Sandbox Tools.   Numerous sandbox tools should be bought or constructed at home or at school. As a rule there should be small, medium, and large sizes of each of the following tools:

Cutters: Thin, sharp sections of wood, used to cut, scrape, and slice the moist sand

Tamping Blocks: Square or round and with or without handle; used to flatten and pack sand solidly

Sand Spade: Flat surface with handle formed at one end, similar to a butter paddle

Sand Plane: Flat block with handle fastened on upper surface for the entire length

Packing Boards: One for each hand, used to move quantities of sand and to mold areas with both hands simultaneously

Sand Knife: Pointed stick with one end flat, similar to an orangewood stick used for manicuring

Shaped Blocks: Ends cut in different shapes, for forming towers, steps, fences, and other objects

Sieves: Medium sized wire mesh

Molds: Various shapes and sizes

Play Equipment

Other equipment needed for kindergarten and primary grade children is mentioned in the list that follows: [1]

1. Tire casings to be rolled about
2. Tire casings hung from a height to form a swing
3. Ropes for hanging, climbing, and swinging
4. Shovels, pails, spoons, and pans
5. Sets of toy dishes
6. Doll buggies
7. Cloth bags or ball covers (six to eight inches in diameter) stuffed with rags and used for kicking and throwing to another person

---

[1] Scooters are not recommended because the continuous use of but one foot for pushing may cause a high hip to be developed.

8. Rubber balls of various sizes (5-inch, 6-inch, 8½-inch, 10-inch, 16-inch, and 24-inch)

9. Small mops, brooms, washtubs

10. Single jump ropes

11. "Flying Fleece" yarn balls

12. Tricycle with 16-inch and 20-inch ball-bearing wheels

13. Automobile equipped with pedals

14. Roller skates, several pairs. Use of but one skate should be forbidden, as a distorted pelvis may result.

15. Carts and metal wagons large enough to be loaded with blocks or used for carrying another child

APPARATUS AND PERMANENT PLAYGROUND FACILITIES

In order that all the children of a school may play simultaneously there should be ample land area to provide needed playing fields, diamonds, and game courts, and plenty of apparatus. Play among the different groups should go on in an organized and orderly fashion. Happy conditions of play depend in part upon the equipment available so that different interests can be satisfied.

Figure 25. A sandbox furnishes young children with opportunity for play in its simplest form.

Selection of Apparatus

The choice of apparatus is a matter of considerable importance. The expenditure of public funds for this important aspect of education should be made with the advice of experts.[1] Patrons of the schools who wish to give equipment for the playground, should be urged to use the recommendations of this guide or to consult a qualified adviser before purchases are made.

There are some types of equipment that provide good all-round physical activity for many children. No elementary school, grades one to eight, should be without climbing apparatus, sandbox, building blocks, horizontal bars, tether ball pole, basketball backstop and goals, volleyball net and posts, wooden handball backstop, and softball backstop and bases. If and when the finances are limited, playground apparatus other than these should not be bought until after adequate supplies of other physical education teaching tools, such as balls, bats, beanbags, line marking equipment, nets, and rackets, are purchased. It is recommended that no circle teeters, swings, ocean waves, merry-go-rounds, revolving platforms, whirl around swings, or merry whirls be installed until other equipment of greater physiological value to children is purchased.

Horizontal bars should be provided in several units, installed at the proper heights for the children who are to use them. Since they are often sold in heights for upper grade children, the installation should be made with regard to the needs of the younger children also. Use of high playground apparatus by younger children will be attempted only by the courageous and more experienced children who will not fear the comparatively long drop to the ground. Unless playground apparatus of lower heights is available the more timid children will be denied the early advantages resulting from swinging and manipulating their bodies through the air. The early and continuous use of such equipment as part of their play experiences even after the novelty of the equipment has worn off is necessary if children are to acquire normal strength, endurance, and balance, as well as nervous and emotional controls.

Slides have a universal appeal for young children. The necessary ladder climbing has value, while the slide builds up confidence in the child's ability to handle himself successfully. Everyone at some time has felt the desire to "slide down the cellar door" or some other inviting slope. Slides with safety platforms are recommended. Soft landing beds or mats are necessary.

---

[1] The Bureau of Health Education, Physical Education and Recreation of the California State Department of Education will provide counsel and help.

Figure 26.   Monkey rings are among the needed stationary playground equipment.

Swings also have appeal, but their acquisition is not recommended until other more essential pieces of playground apparatus and game supplies have been purchased. Little physical activity results from the use of swings unless users are allowed to stand up and pump and such activity should not be permitted. If swings are installed, a fence should surround the area given over to swings to protect other playing children from being struck by moving swings.

Teeters, low or high, are undesirable as playground equipment for schools. They offer little in the way of vigorous activity and they become an accident hazard if one of the two users decides suddenly to abandon his end of the teeter. Purchase of teeters is not recommended.

Recommended and Optional Apparatus.   The following list includes the major pieces of playground apparatus recommended for elementary schools, with the approximate area needed for installation.

RECOMMENDED AND OPTIONAL APPARATUS FOR SCHOOL PLAYGROUNDS

AGE GROUP	APPARATUS	MINIMUM AREA NEEDED
Kindergarten	*Recommended*	
	Climbing apparatus*—wood or pipe, 6'-7' high	12' x 12'
	Low horizontal bar—3' high	8' x 10'
	Slide, safety platform, 6'	10' x 15'
	Optional	
	Horizontal ladder, 4'9" or	10' x 12'
	Monkey rings,** 6'	10' x 12'
	Swings, canvas seats	8' x 8' for 2-swing unit
Primary	*Recommended*	
	Climbing apparatus, 7'-9' high	16' x 16'
	Horizontal bars, 48" to 54" high	8' x 10'
	Horizontal ladder, 5' high	8' x 24'
	Optional	
	Slide, safety platform, 8'	15' x 30'
	Swings, canvas seats	12' x 12' for 2-swing unit
	Circular traveling rings, low	25' x 25'
Intermediate	*Recommended*	
	Climbing ropes, hemp or manila, 1½" diameter	
	Horizontal bars, 60"-66"	10' x 12'
	Horizontal ladder, 6½' high	15' x 25'
	Optional	
	Monkey rings, 10' high	10' x 25'
	Parazontal bars	12' x 25'
	Giant stride, rope	35' x 35'
	Circular traveling rings, high	25' x 25'
Upper Grades	*Recommended*	
	Horizontal bar, 66"-72"	10' x 12'
	Climbing rope, hemp or manila, 1½" diameter	
	Optional	
	Horizontal circular ladder, 12' radius	25' x 25'

* Manufactured under various names, such as climbing trees, junglegyms, climbing towers, castle towers, and climbing maze.
** Some teachers prefer the mobility of the monkey ring in contrast to the rigid ladder.

Permanent Playground Facilities

Besides the playground apparatus, every school should have permanent game facilities and game areas. Courts and playing fields should be laid out to run north and south, so that players need not face the sun at any hour. Softball diamonds should be laid out so that the diagonal between home plate and second base runs in a north to south direction; the batter and the pitcher would thus not have to face the sun.

Court and Field Dimensions.[1] The dimensions of some standard field and court areas should be reduced for elementary school children. In Part II of this guide the court layouts for most of the games described are given in diagram form. Some of the standard game areas described and diagrammed in Part II are as follows:

Badminton Courts, p. 856

Basketball Court for Boys, p. 721

Basketball Court for Girls, p. 724

Croquet Court, p. 583

Deck Tennis Courts, p. 868

Handball Court, p. 550

Horseshoe Court, p. 765

Shuffleboard Court, p. 892

Soccer Field for Boys, p. 774

Soccer Field for Girls, p. 780

Softball Diamond, p. 567

Speed Ball Field, p. 904

Tennis Court, p. 912

Touch Football Field, p. 792

Volleyball Court, p. 800

Line Marking. Games with official rules, such as basketball, handball, paddle tennis, and volleyball, cannot be learned on courts without markings. In order to save time, lines for such games, as well as circles and parallel lines frequently used in relays and circle games, should be permanently marked on the playing areas. On hard surfaces, white traffic lacquer, colored oil paint, whitewash,[2] or cold water paint may be used to outline playing areas. Painting over the lines with shellac will prolong the period of their usefulness. Lines should be painted two inches in width. Dry lime also will remain on hard surfaces for several weeks.

On turf or dirt courts, dry slaked lime should be used. A line marking cart will make it possible to mark these courts with a minimum of time. One practical method of marking courts is to bury 2 by 4-inch redwood boards end to end so that the exposed 2-inch edge lies just below the ground surface. The exposed edges should be painted white. Redwood will not rot as readily as other wood.

Net Games. Net games provide a large part of physical education activity. There should be enough courts for such games so that boys and girls can have frequent opportunity to hit or catch the ball.

---

[1] See "Recommended Outdoor Play Areas," pages 81-82.

[2] Whitewash can be made by adding to each 8 quarts of unslaked lime, while it is slaking, 1 pound of tallow and 2 quarts of strong brine. This may be thinned as needed and applied with a brush or line marker. The mixture should be kept in a galvanized iron ash can, strong cask, or a large crock. A watering can with its nozzle pinched partly shut can be used for distributing the liquid.

Figure 27. Lines permanently marked on play areas facilitate class organization for different activities.

One of the best net games for elementary school use is paddle tennis. Beginning tennis skills can be learned by playing with a wooden paddle and an old tennis ball. Paddle tennis can be played on either a smooth, hard dirt surface or on an asphalt or concrete surface. If an official tennis court exists, four paddle tennis courts can be laid out on it crosswise and thus provide playing space for sixteen players instead of four. As a substitute for surfaced courts, a wooden platform can be constructed on which the ball bounces while the players stand on the ground.

For all net games it is preferable to have fixed posts with ratchets to keep the net taught. Posts 2½ inches in diameter and 5 feet long may be set in concrete or braced with blocks called "dead men" at the surface of the ground and at the bottom as shown in Figure 28. These braces give rigidity to the posts, which is essential if nets are to be stretched tightly enough. For paddle tennis the distance from the ground to ratchet or holes through which the cable of the net runs should be 2 feet 4 inches for elementary schools (2 feet 9 inches for adults).

If permanent posts cannot be installed, jumping standards or moveable standards may be substituted. They should be well weighted down

on the outside edge of the court with large bags of sand or fastened down
with guy ropes.

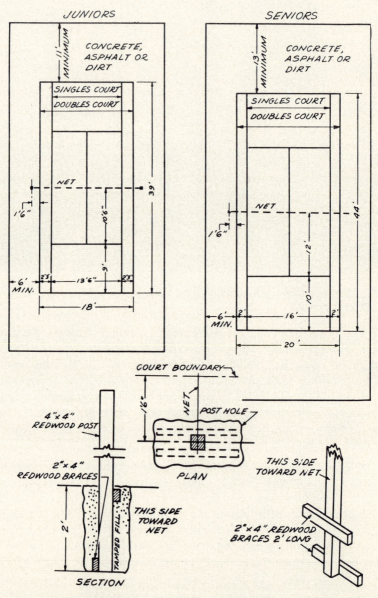

Figure 28. Diagram shows layout of paddle tennis courts with details
of installation of posts.

Nets treated for outdoor use should be provided. Wire fencing, grain sacks, or rope can be used as substitutes for nets if official nets cannot be purchased.

When possible, backstops for court or courts should be provided. Their presence adds tremendously to the pleasure of the game. The backstops should be not less than 8 feet high and 30 feet long, and they should be placed not less than 20 feet from the base lines of the court or courts. For the frame 1½ inch galvanized iron pipe should be used. Over the frame, ¼-inch galvanized wire mesh can be stretched.

Facilities for Jumping Events. When choosing space for the location of jumping events, consideration should be given to the preservation of areas for other play purposes. For instance, the broad jump runway and pit, requiring about 36 feet, could well be placed parallel to a fence or building. The approach for the high jump must be unobstructed and free for a distance of 20 to 30 feet on each side and 15 to 25 feet in front, and the pit itself requires a space 8 by 14 feet. Since the approach is on a diagonal toward the jumping pit, the high-jump pit might be located in a corner of a field. As with other facilities, the pits and approaches should be so located that the jumpers will not have to face the sun when competing.

1. *Broad Jump.* Elementary school and junior high school jumpers do not need an approach of more than 20 yards, although for adults the runway is 35 yards. The runway should be crowned for rapid drainage. A take-off board 8 inches wide, 2 inches thick, and 3 feet long[1] should be installed flush with the ground surface, from 3 to 12 feet from and paralleling the edge of the jumping pit. The top surface of the board should be painted white. Loosened dirt, moist sand, or moist clay should be spread over the ground for a space of at least six inches in front of the take-off board so that toe marks beyond the take-off board can be seen.

The National Collegiate Athletic Association rules for the broad jump specify a landing pit not less than 5 feet wide. For the elementary school this may be reduced to 4 feet. The length should be 16 feet, and the depth 8 inches. The walls of the pit should be shored with 2 by 4-inch redwood boards, with the inside edges beveled. Drainpipes should be installed to permit the use of pits throughout the year, and in particular during the early spring. The pit should be filled to ground level with sand, which should be moistened before use. From time to time it is necessary to loosen the sand in the pit to prevent hard packing. A pit leveler such as that shown in Figure 29 will be found useful.

---

[1] The rules of the National Collegiate Athletic Association require a take-off board at least 4 feet long.

2. *High Jump.* The high jump pit, as constructed today, is not a pit at all. The practice today is to lay a pile of wood shavings and to bound this pile on three sides with bags of shavings forming bolsters (Figure 29). The landing area should be 8 by 14 feet and the shavings should be 12 inches deep.[1]

Jumping standards should be six feet high, made of poles 4 by 4 inches, with a base for stability. These should be placed at least 12 feet apart on hard surfacing but near the pit edge.

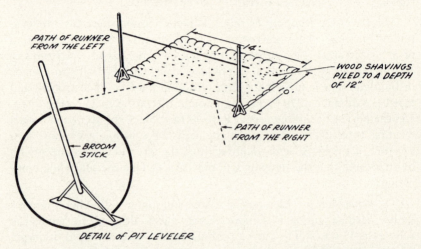

Figure 29. Diagram shows construction of high jump pit and detail of pit leveler.

The jump should be made over a bar of uniform thickness, either square with beveled edges or triangular. If square the bar should be 1⅛ inches thick; if triangular, each face should measure 1 3/16 inches. The support for the crossbar should be flat and rectangular, 1½ inches wide and 2⅜ inches deep. It should point toward the opposite upright, and the end of the crossbar should rest along the narrow dimension of the support. For elementary schools the type of jumping standards used for the pole vault are perfectly acceptable. In this type of standard, holes about 9/16 inch in diameter are drilled in the standard about 1 inch apart beginning at 2 feet from the bottom and extending to the top of the pole. Holes should permit pegs to extend parallel to the ground without any upward or downward tilt. Round pegs, to project no more than 3 inches beyond the uprights, are inserted in the holes on the pit side to support the crossbar. Instead of uprights with holes and pegs, standards equipped

---

[1] NCAA rules specify a minimum pit of 10 by 14 feet.

with sliding adjustable arms for holding the crossbar may be used. A bamboo bar may be used as the crossbar. If bamboo is used it should be taped at both ends and at each joint with friction tape.

Installation of Apparatus and Permanent Equipment

The proper installation of permanent equipment and the proper location of playground facilities are important. Horizontal bars, slides, traveling rings, climbing ropes and poles, and monkey rings should be installed adjacent to fences or buildings, with posts so placed that action of users of the equipment will parallel the line of the fence or building. It is important, however, to install the equipment far enough away from wall or fence so that the feet or bodies of those using the equipment will not come in contact with any obstruction. Permanent equipment should be installed away from open areas. Such areas should be kept free from obstruction for the safe and successful playing of running games and ball games.

The horizontal ladder, horizontal bars, and monkey rings should be installed far enough from any obstruction to permit the swing of performers while arms, body, and legs are fully extended. The crossbars of the horizontal bars should not be more than 1½ inches in diameter. The heights found most suitable for these are 48, 54, and 60 inches above the ground. Giant strides require an area large enough to permit the extended bodies of the users to swing out into space without touching any obstacle.

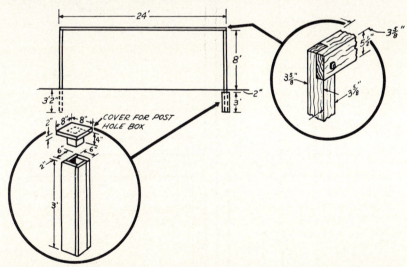

Figure 30. Diagram shows construction of soccer goal with detail of joint, post hole box, and cover.

Goal Posts or Net Posts. To support goal posts, redwood boxes, 3 feet deep with sides 1½ or 2 inches thick, should be set two inches below the turf. This two-inch drop will permit covers to rest flush with the turf when poles are removed. Covers should be 8 by 8 by 2 inches with a piece of 4 by 4 inch lumber as blocking to keep covers in position (Figure 30).

Tether Ball Pole. Tether ball is a game that interests boys and girls from the fourth grade through the eighth. It is an inexpensive means of

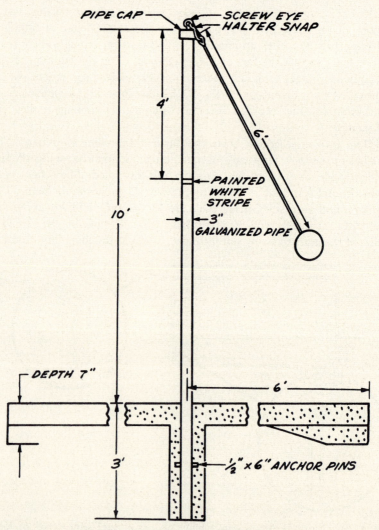

Figure 31.   Tether ball post construction is shown here.

teaching tennis-type skills. Either a small ball and paddle may be used, or a large commercially manufactured ball or converted volleyball may be batted with the hands. The installation of the pole is not difficult.

An iron pole 3 inches in diameter and 13 feet long, or a rounded, tapering, 13-foot pole of redwood of foundation or irrigation grade may be used. Either pole should be sunk three feet in the ground and should be braced by cement casing or stakes of foundation or irrigation redwood so that there will be no vibration. At the ground level a wooden pole should be 7½ inches in diameter, tapering toward the top. The pole should be painted, and 6 feet above the ground level a 2-inch band of a different color should be added. A screw eye should be placed at the top of the pole. Sash cord or light rope, 7 feet 6 inches long, should be attached to the screw eye (Figure 31). A circular cement base should be built, six feet in diameter. A foul line should be painted or grooved in the cement base running in a north to south direction, through the center of the pole.

Basketball Standards.   Basketball goals should be constructed so as to allow the support pole to be outside the court of play. This offset type of goal eliminates an accident hazard and provides opportunity for freer play. Standards can be made of wood, but 6-inch steel pipe and ½-inch steel plate makes a more satisfactory piece of equipment. The dimensions

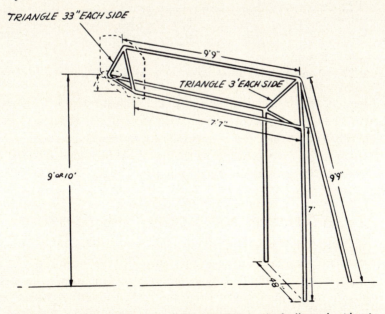

Figure 32.   Specifications for building offset basketball goal with triangular base are shown.

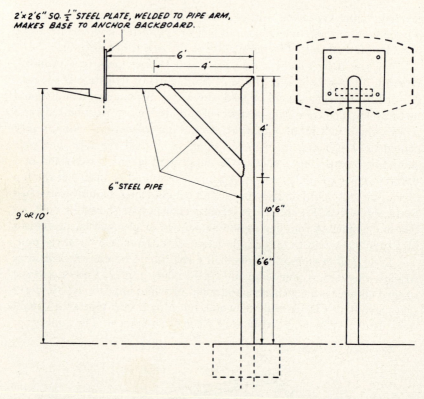

Figure 33.   Diagram shows offset basketball goal of single pole set in concrete.

and method of construction for a pipe and steel standard are shown in Figures 32 and 33. It should be noted that in Figure 33 the pipe is set in a concrete base. If the court is used only by the upper grades, nine feet is recommended for the height of the basket. When goals are used by the intermediate grades, the height should be eight feet. The official height is ten feet.

SAFETY MEASURES FOR FACILITIES AND EQUIPMENT [1]

Children should be permitted much leeway in the use of playground apparatus and facilities, but when first introduced to them they should be taught three things: (1) how to use each piece of apparatus safely, (2) how to follow directions when group participation is necessary; and (3) how to co-operate in protecting others. From the beginning there

[1] See "Safety in the Physical Education Program," Chapter I, page 16.

Figure 34. The correct and safe way to use play apparatus is shown in the drawings at the left; incorrect and dangerous ways of using apparatus appear at the right.

should be developed an individual consciousness of responsibility in aiding and protecting other persons from dangerous play or dangerous situations. Self-control must be developed, group control must be insisted upon, and general behavior conducive to a happy, wholesome playground must be the objective for both teacher and pupils. Children should take turns in acting as safety monitors. Teachers must be constantly on the alert to forestall accidents.

Regardless of how adequate or how meager the apparatus on the playground, there is always need to provide responsible leadership for teaching the proper use of the facilities, for establishing control methods, and for encouraging the frequent use of apparatus. Such supervision should maintain the area as a wholesome activity center and not a hazardous play area.

Adult Supervision of Grounds

Playground apparatus may be used frequently without serious accident hazards if members of boards of education, school trustees, and custodians share with teachers the responsibility of taking all reasonable precautions to prevent accidents. This will necessitate the early and prompt repair of equipment and its removal from use until the necessary repairs are made.

The governing board of a school district may be held liable for any judgment against the district on account of injury arising because of negligence of the district or its officers or employees.[1]

Accident Hazards. Teachers on the playground must train themselves to be aware at all times of all that is going on. They must be intensely alive to the need for seeing and forestalling situations that may cause accidents or endanger children, yet at the same time must not dampen the daring and ingenuity of children using playground facilities. The provisions for safety may be judged by considering such questions as the following:

1. Are facilities, ground surface, fence, water pipes and faucets, and other ground conditions free from hazards?
2. Are groups of children so placed that interference between them cannot occur?
3. Are children trained to be attentive to their own group activity and obedient to their leader?
4. Are leaders trained in safety precautions?
5. Do children show a sense of responsibility for the safety of others during activity periods?

---

[1] Education Code of California, Section 1007.

Figure 35. The correct and safe way to use play apparatus is shown at the left; incorrect and dangerous ways, at the right.

6. Do teacher and pupils use safety precautions during the practice of stunts, tumbling, and other situations where body contacts occur?

7. Do any accidents occur?

8. What type of accident has occurred?

9. What caused each accident?

10. Was a record kept of each accident?

11. Is defective apparatus removed from use until repaired?

Precautions to Be Observed

The everlasting vigilance of pupils, teachers, custodians, administrators, and trustees is essential for the prevention of injuries that may seem slight but that may have serious consequences. Each accident should be reported to the school administrator in writing. Some of the precautions to be observed are the following:

Protection of Younger Children. Adequate play space should be provided exclusively for younger children, with apparatus reduced in height to meet their age needs.

Proper Installation of Apparatus. Apparatus should be properly installed and kept in good working condition.

1. Broken chains, loosened sections, or broken parts should be removed from apparatus, repaired, and returned as promptly as possible.

Figure 36. Hazards of swings (shown at right) are minimized if safety seats are installed and children are instructed in proper use of swings as shown in drawing at left.

2. Upright posts should be buried deep enough for safety or embedded in concrete blocks. Iron posts are more desirable than wooden ones, which, unless made of redwood, will rot.

3. Horizontal bars should be so fastened that they do not turn in the hands and cannot work out of their frames.

4. The ground beneath apparatus should be free from stumps and rocks and hard surfacing; the landing area should be softened regularly by spading up the earth or sand, or shavings should be used.

Regular Inspection of Apparatus.   Once each month or more often, principal, custodian, or teacher should examine the entire playground area and permanent equipment for signs of accident hazards and evidence of wear which may lead to accidents.

Correct Use of Bat and Ball.   The correct manner of handling a bat and ball must be insisted upon. Since most boys and girls bat right handed, standing at left of home plate, thrown bats carry toward third base and on into foul territory to the left of the third base line. Therefore, all members of the batting team, substitutes, and spectators must be kept well out toward first base and well back of the first base foul line. This is an important safety procedure.

Elimination of Dust.[1]   To prevent the development of nasal, sinus, and eye infection or irritation, the dust problem should be studied and definite action taken. Dust conditions may be improved by several methods, as follows:

1. Surfacing portions of the school area with hard surfacing

2. Planting grass adapted to climatic conditions

3. Sprinkling or soaking down the grounds frequently during extended dry periods [2]

4. Using calcium chloride or a salt solution for the control of dust

Care of Perishable Play Equipment.   Children should be taught to care for balls, rackets, nets, and other play equipment.

Figure 37. Landing area under horizontal bars should be of shavings or loose dirt or sand.

---

[1] See pages 82-83.
[2] Arrangements may possibly be made with municipal or county street watering departments to perform this test.

1. They should help to mend broken equipment.
2. They should return equipment to closets or equipment boxes. Different children may be designated play equipment custodians, or squad leaders may be made responsible for returning equipment.
3. They should not sit on inflated balls.

Safety Suggestions

In the following list are important safety suggestions to guide the teacher in supervising play on apparatus.

1. Test the apparatus for rigidity, for loose nuts or bolts, or for broken parts.
2. Instruct children in safe ways to use apparatus.
3. Depending on the size of the apparatus, control the number of children that may use it simultaneously.
4. See that children use both hands when grasping bars on the climbing apparatus.
5. Warn children that to climb with wet hands is dangerous.
6. See that pits beneath horizontal bars and slides are large enough so that children will not fall on the edges.
7. Have children ask for assistance of a teacher when they want to undertake new or difficult stunts on apparatus.
8. Discourage the swinging of traveling rings over the crossbars.
9. Teach children to await their turn without pushing or going ahead of others in line.
10. Teach children the correct way to use the slide. Have them sit erect on the surface of the slide with feet together.
11. Do not permit primary school children on high slides; there should be low slides for their use.
12. See that there are no cracks in the slides that could hold stones or splinters.
13. Have children use steps to reach the top of the slide, see that no one is on the slide before descending, and leave the foot of the slide by walking forward out of the pit.
14. Do not permit children to kneel or stand on swing seats.
15. Allow only one child at a time to use a swing.
16. Do not allow children to swing when wearing skates.
17. Teach children to decrease speed when desirous of leaving the swing.
18. Chain swings to the posts or together before leaving the playground.
19. Do not permit empty swings to be pushed or twisted.

INDOOR PLAY SPACE

In areas of California where outdoor physical activity is impossible or inadvisable for several months out of the school year, indoor play space must be planned for elementary schools. The plans for such rooms could take into consideration the needs of the community for indoor play space as well as facilities needed for elementary school children. As a means of supplying such space, each school district should include in the plans for building a new plant or in additions to an old plant a multipurpose room. This room may be used as an auditorium, a gymnasium, a cafeteria or for other purposes. For a small school a room 40 by 60 feet, plus a 20-foot stage and a kitchen and storage space, is recommended. A 50 by 70-foot room is needed for a large school, plus the stage, kitchen, and storage space.

The room must be planned to allow maximum use as a playroom. The floor should be level, and should have a practical covering. Hardwood floors that are constantly used and are maintained in good condition are more costly in maintenance than is a concrete slab with a resilient covering. A floor surface that remains smooth and resilient through constant use and is easily cleaned is necessary.

The walls should be finished with a durable and easily cleaned material, and should be constructed to provide good acoustics. Built-in wall-hung tables are recommended because they do not interfere with a smooth wall surface, and because they can be lowered into place for the cafeteria in a minimum of time. The benches can be lowered separately for auditorium seating. The windows should be placed above the line of the door head to provide smooth wall surface and prevent window breakage.

The room should be heated as is any classroom, plus artificial ventilation to insure clearing the perspiration-filled air. If it is at all possible, showers for boys and showers for girls should adjoin this multipurpose room.

ESSENTIAL EQUIPMENT AND SUPPLIES

Tools are needed to teach children physical education. No reasonable person would expect to teach chemistry without laboratory equipment or to develop an orchestra without musical instruments. Modern teaching is depending more and more on perceptual learning; maps, globes, charts, moving pictures, and other audio-visual material are considered essential in the education of children. Likewise, it is true that the skills and co-ordinations so greatly needed in the development of the normal child require apparatus, game equipment, and a great variety of such supplies as balls, bats, and rackets.

All supplies needed for various game situations should be purchased in such quantities that players, when assigned to small squads, may practice simultaneously without long waiting intervals. For example, assigning only one volleyball, basketball, baseball and bat, or soccer ball to a class is an absurdity if early and rapid development of skill is desired for each child. A ball for every two pupils for pitching practice, bats for every three to five pupils for batting practice, or a dozen utility balls, volleyballs, soccer balls, or basketballs assigned to a room are none too many for effective squad instruction and continued practice. Children do not learn reading or arithmetic with but one book to a room, nor do they learn music and singing with one instrument and one songbook in a class. Similarly, learning in physical education requires an adequate supply of instructional materials.

Supplies for Primary Grades

Teaching tools and supplies for the primary grades have already been discussed (pages 86-90): Some of the supplies there listed may also be used by the intermediate group. Beanbags are used through all the grades, and it is recommended that every child have his own beanbag, although all should be made the same size and weight. Plastic cloth is found to be a suitable covering, and unpopped popcorn makes an excellent filler. Jump ropes should be used in all grades, and a short rope should be provided for each child. Several long ropes are needed for each class.

Balls for Various Games

Among the most used game materials are the various types of balls, which will be needed in quantities. Junior size basketballs should be used, since regulation size basketballs are too heavy and large to be handled successfully by most girls and by younger boys. Rubber balls for soccer, basketball, volleyball, and softball are useful during the rainy season and are particularly good if the surface of a playground is so rough as to cut or break leather casings. There are rubber softballs that are softer than the official softball; they are called soft softballs or soft playground balls. They are especially useful for teaching primary children the overhand throw and beginning catching, throwing, and batting games.

If the supply of balls is limited, extra balls may be made in the following way. A bunch of rubber bands is tied into a compact sphere; this is the core of the ball. Around this, string and yarn are wrapped until the desired size is reached. The wrapping must be tight and firm. The ball may then be covered with leather cut into two identical pieces of the shape

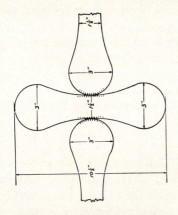

Figure 38. Diagram shows how to cut leather needed for covering a baseball.

shown in Figure 38. The ball may be made to fit into a standard size cover. The two pieces of leather are sewed together around the ball. Leather ball casings stuffed with rags or straw may be used in many game situations.

A ball must be properly cared for if it is to give maximum service. The following points should be remembered.

1. Each ball should be marked with the name of the school.

2. Bladders and leather casings should be stored in a dark, cool place.

3. The school should own a foot pump for inflating bladders. Bladders should always be inflated with a hand or foot pump, not with the lungs. During summer vacation, if not in use, they should be partially deflated. Bladders should not be stored flat but should be partly inflated. A ball should be inflated only to the pressure recommended by the manufacturer. In the absence of a gauge, the amount of inflation can be tested by pressing the heel of the hand into the ball. If the ball yields easily to pressure, it is sufficiently inflated.

4. Pupils should not be allowed to sit on an inflated ball.

5. Volleyballs and basketballs should not be kicked.

6. A bladder should be mended with tube patching or adhesive tape as soon as weak places become evident.

7. Leather casings should be treated with leather soap and leather oil several times during the school year and immediately preceeding the vacation if they are to be stored.

Gymnasium Mats

Gymnasium mats are a necessary part of school supplies if stunts are to be learned and practiced as extensively as is recommended. In stunts and tumbling it is necessary to have equipment that will break the force of the body impact with the floor or ground. Out of doors, turf may serve this purpose, but indoors or on a hard surfaced area mats are needed. Mats manufactured for this purpose should be purchased. In the elementary school these should be units small enough for the children to handle: 3 by 5 feet or 4 by 6 feet are recommended sizes. Mats made with plastic painted canvas are very satisfactory because plastic is dust resistant and pliable. Rubberized material is easily cleaned, but may be sticky in contact with rubber-soled shoes. Mats that do not have a special covering should be treated with waterproof paint to permit frequent cleaning with a disinfectant solution.

Shoes should be removed when pupils use mats.

When mats are not in use they should be hung on pegs. They should be lifted and not dragged on the ground.

Supply Box and Equipment Storage

A large, permanent supply box, well equipped with play materials, should be placed near outdoor play areas. These materials should be available during play periods and recess periods as well as during instructional periods. It is wise to store larger movable equipment in a building or room that can be locked and that will be accessible even when the school building is closed. Children should be taught to keep the equipment in order and to return each piece as soon as it is no longer needed.

Equipment for Outdoor Games of Skill

The following equipment will be useful not only in physical education classes but also in recreational programs of the school. They also may serve as the nucleus of a game lending library whose contents may be available to pupils for week-end or vacation periods.

Aerial darts (birds, wooden paddles, net)
Archery tackle (bows, arrows, quivers, guards, tabs, targets)
Badminton sets (birds, rackets, nets)
Croquet sets (mallets, balls, wickets, stakes)
Deck Tennis sets (ring, net)
Fly-casting equipment
Goal-Hi standards (see p. 649)
Horseshoes (shoes, stakes)
Lawn Bowling equipment (balls)
Paddle Tennis set (wooden paddles, ball, net)
Pateca (see p. 485)
Shuffleboard equipment (cues, disks)
Tennis equipment (rackets, balls, nets)
Tether Ball or Polo Ball set (pole, ball on cord)

Equipment for Indoor Games

Sitting games, table games, and other games suitable for classroom or playroom should be included in the experience of the elementary school child. Many of these are suitable for use by physically handicapped or temporarily disabled or incapacitated children. Afternoon or evening parties may call for special equipment of this kind. The list that follows may help administrators to build up a reserve of games valuable to the school's recreational and physical education program. The games may be included in a game lending library available to pupils.

Backgammon (board, backgammon pieces or checkers, dice)
Badminton (rackets, birds, net)
Beanbag games (beanbags, board)
Bowling (Indian clubs or milk cartons,[1] and softballs)
Carom (board and rings)
Checkers (board, checkers)
Chess (board, chessmen)
Darts (board and darts, either suction cup or pointed)
Pool (miniature table, balls, cues)
Putting Game (clubs, balls, putting holes)
Quoits (rings, posts)
Table Croquet (table, balls, wickets)
Table Tennis (table, ball, paddles, net)
Shuffleboard (court may be marked with chalk; cues, disks)

Directions for playing many of these games may be found in Part II of this guide. Other table games whose procedure and equipment are described in Part II are the following:

Box Hockey, p. 465
Maze, p. 479
Suction-Cup Dart Baseball, p. 674
Table Shuffleboard, p. 908.

Commercial Equipment for Quiet and Social Games

There are on the market great numbers of enjoyable games that can be used for quiet periods or social occasions. They may be purchased from local toy or sporting goods stores or ordered from the manufacturers. The following are games that have been found useful.[2]

Bat-O-Net: A feathered table tennis ball batted back and forth or caught in a bat pocket; no net, table, or court required (Ben Person, Inc., Pine Bluff, Ark., $3.95 a set)

Commando Game: Two tops projected from a camouflaged base to knock down tenpins ($6.62 a set)

Hockey Box ($12.35)

Horseshoe Pitching (indoor) (Bailey & Himes, Inc., Cambridge, Mass., $1.60 a set)

---

[1] See page 890.
[2] Supplied by Burford Bush, Recreation Specialist, California Recreation Commission.

Kikit: Ball propelled in box to opposing goals using movable paddles ($8.00 each)

Quoits: 5 peg cross board with 4 rope rings ($4.60 a set)

Shuffleboard (American Playground Device Co., Anderson, Ind., $9.75; Recreation Equipment Co., 724-26 W. 8th St., Anderson, Ind., plastic bakelite, $12.00, or wood, $8.00; Bailey & Himes, Inc., $16.90)

Skill Bowl: Bowling game (Allied Plastic, Inc., 1220 Huron Road, Cleveland 15, Ohio)

Tolo: Combination croquet and shuffleboard (George Burcham, Route 1, Box 817, Tracy, Calif., $5.95 to $8.85 a set)

Sky Pie: Plastic disc to be tossed back and forth and caught on "Pie Snager" (Hall Manufacturing Co., 622 Tularose Drive, Los Angeles 26, Calif., $1.00 a set)

Turf Bowling (Boccie) (Lignum-Vitae Products Corp., 89 Boyd Ave., Jersey City 4, N. J.)

XL Tops: Rotating and spinning a rubber top on a string between sticks held in the hands (Hammatt & Sons, 11356 Orangewood, Anaheim 5, Calif., $0.60 each)

Zelball: Portable Tether Ball (Zelball Company, Mt. Holly, N. J.)

Care and Replacement of Supplies

The budget for physical education equipment and supplies should include funds for replacement of worn-out equipment as well as a fund for the immediate repair of broken or unsafe sections of playground apparatus. Some supplies last a long time, but others must be replaced frequently.

How to Construct Some Useful Supplies

Many games require only simple equipment that can be made at school. Often the expense of the commercial product prevents the school from acquiring these worthwhile games. Suggestions for construction of some of these supplies are presented.

Shuttlecock. Children can make shuttlecocks by using corks 1 or 1½ inches in diameter. Ten to sixteen chicken or turkey feathers are needed for each cork. The feathers should be nearly the same size and length. The quills should be trimmed for 1 inch in order that they may be stuck firmly into the cork.

Around the outer edge of the cork, make openings into which the quills can be forced for half an inch. When the feathers are in place, an almost perfect circle about 2½ inches in diameter should be formed by their ends. To anchor the feathers at the base and above where the barbs start, weave light string or heavy thread in and out around the feathers.

When the starting point is reached, the weaving is reversed in order to form an anchoring loop around each feather. Remove as much slack in the string as possible.

Small rubber balls may be used instead of corks. These birdies will be livelier than the ones made from cork and feathers. Jackstone balls tied in 6-inch cloth squares may also be used.

Battledore. A battledore should be constructed from 3-ply wood, 5 by 12 inches. The exact measurements are given in Figure 39. A battledore could be used for table tennis as well as for games of the badminton type.

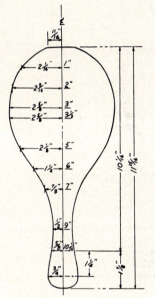

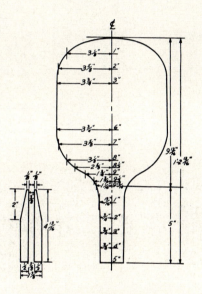

Figure 39. Dimensions for a battledore are shown here.

Figure 40. Specifications for making a paddle tennis paddle are shown here.

Paddle for Paddle Tennis. Paddles are constructed as follows. Use a piece of ½-inch plywood, 5 by 16 inches. The face or striking surface is an oval 5 by 6 inches and the handle is 10 inches long, 1½ inches wide at the grip end, tapering to 1 inch at the paddle end. The handles should be braced on each side as shown in Figure 40.

Pin-Spot Frame. A frame that can be used to mark quickly and accurately spots on which bowling pins are to be set can be constructed as shown in Figure 41. Official diameter of the bowling pin is 1⅛ inches, but the holes in the frame must be 1¼ inches to allow for the use of chalk inside the holes. The frame is placed on the floor and the spots marked through the holes with chalk.

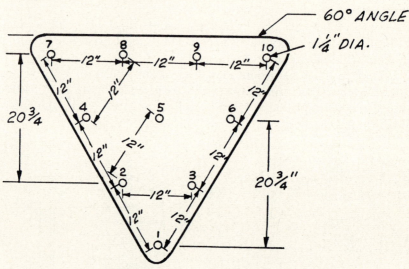

Figure 41.   Diagram shows how to make a pin-spot frame.

Tether Ball Substitutes. If no tether ball or volley tether ball is available, an acceptable substitute may be made out of a sponge rubber ball, baseball size. Using a thick packing needle and a double length of strong string, run the string through the center of the ball. The string should be about ten inches long. After the string is through the ball, pass it through the center of a 1¼-inch circle of strong leather and knot it. The leather prevents the knot from cutting into the rubber. Using a square knot, tie the free ends of the string to the free end of the pole cord.

A tennis or sponge rubber ball may be tied into a square of heavy cloth and the cloth may be attached to the pole cord.

A ball may be put into a tied or crocheted cover which is in turn attached to the pole cord. To tie a cover, securely fasten together in the middle eight lengths of strong string or heavy fishing line, each string being 14 inches long. Using square knots, fasten adjacent strings together (1 and 2; 3 and 4; 5 and 6; 7 and 8), the knots being ¾ of an inch from the center tie. Continue tying the next series of free strings (2 and 3; 4 and 5; 6 and 7; 8 and 1), at a distance of 1 inch from the first row of knots. The third row of knots should be 1¼ inches from the second row of knots. Inserting the ball, begin shortening the distance between the rows of knots. Bring all strings together and attach to the end of the pole cord.

Teaching Aids for Physical Education [1]

Books and visual aids of various types are available to the teacher who wishes to make use of them in the physical education program. New books dealing with different phases of physical education and recreation are essential for effective work. Teachers and pupils should have ready access to such materials. The county library or office of the superintendent of schools will secure needed reference books. Children should be encouraged to study games found therein and to present them to the group.

A good supply of phonograph records for rhythmical activities is a necessity. Each classroom should have available a phonograph with speed adjustment. Percussion instruments may be purchased or made at the school.

Numerous films have been made to demonstrate physical education skills and techniques. Teachers should have ready access to projection equipment and a supply of good films, filmstrips, and slides.

Posture charts are another teaching aid that the school should have. A list of charts and sources of supply is appended to Chapter VI.

The school should subscribe to one or more of the magazines dealing with physical education so that current articles and notes may be available to all teachers.

MINIMUM EQUIPMENT AND SUPPLIES

Every school will find it necessary to select from the many kinds of equipment and supplies that are available those it can afford. The minimum teaching tools believed to be essential to any school, with the quantities of each article recommended, are given in the following list. This list is designed to establish a standard from which to build. Once a school has acquired the basic supplies suggested, worn-out playground equipment can be replaced from year to year with a small annual budget. It is recommended that supplies and equipment in this minimum list be purchased before other stationary playground apparatus is bought. Administrators should purchase game supplies first and in sufficient quantities to allow each child full opportunity to handle the various kinds of materials, if a choice has to be made between the purchase of game supplies and stationary playground apparatus. This necessitates a planned program of purchasing supplies and equipment on a long-term basis.

---

[1] Reference materials for physical education, including books, magazines, phonograph records, films and filmstrips, and catalogues of teaching aids, are listed in the appendixes.

MINIMUM EQUIPMENT AND SUPPLIES FOR A PHYSICAL EDUCATION PROGRAM

Climbing apparatus
Graduated horizontal bars (1 or more sets for primary grades and 1 or more sets for upper grades)
Basketball backstop and goal
Handball backboard
Softball backstop, bases
Line marker cart
Amplifying phonograph with adjustable speed control, or piano
Phonograph records
Rhythm band instruments (made at school or purchased)
Scales, bathroom, for weighing children
Stop watch
Whistles, 6, for use by teachers and children [1]
Sandbox and sandbox tools
Large wooden boxes, open on both ends, with hole handles
Ladder
Ten- or twelve-inch plank of 1¼-inch lumber
Sturdy wheel toys
Gymnasium mats
Jump ropes, 1 short rope for each child, several long ropes for each class
Beanbags, 1 for each child in primary grades, several for each class in upper grades
Softball gloves
Catcher's mask and protector
Softball bats of different weights, 1 for each 4 children
Table for table tennis, 5 by 9 feet, 2½ feet high, with net, paddles, and balls
Tenikoit (ring for deck tennis)
Horseshoes and stakes (set)
Nets for volleyball, badminton, deck tennis, or paddle tennis (2)
Paddle tennis paddles (8) and balls (16); old tennis balls may be used
Indian clubs, 1½ pounds, or wood blocks (8), for relays, hit pin baseball, etc.
Shuttlecocks (3 dozen) or aerial darts; or Flying Fleece balls, 4½-inch diameter, washable
Rubber balls, 6- to 16-inch (one ball to two children in primary grades)
Soccer ball (rubber) or utility ball (1 for each 4 children)
Volleyball, lightweight (1 for each 4 children)
Basketball (3), junior size
Soft softball, 12-inch, smooth seam (1 for each 2 children)
Softball, rubberized (1 for each 2 children)
Tape for measuring distances
Tube patch set, for mending bladders; inflator (foot pump); wooden handled lacing needle; adhesive tape for mending equipment
Pinnies (aprons made of bright-colored cotton material used to distinguish teams), or colored scarves

SELECTED REFERENCES [2]

BOOKWALTER, KARL W. "Planning Health, Physical Education, and Recreation Facilities for Public Schools and Colleges." *The American School and University. A Yearbook.* 1946. Eighteenth Annual Edition. New York: American School Publishing Corporation, 1946.

---

[1] Whistles should be kept in a sterilizing solution when not in use.
[2] Appendix B also lists reference materials.

NATIONAL COUNCIL ON SCHOOLHOUSE CONSTRUCTION. *Guide for Planning School Plants.* Published by the Council with the Proceedings of the Annual Meeting, State Department of Education, Nashville, Tennessee, October 22-25, 1946. Revised 1949.

NATIONAL RECREATION ASSOCIATION. *Recreation Areas: Their Design and Equipment.* Prepared for the National Recreation Association by George D. Butler. New York: A. S. Barnes & Co., 1947.

A Guide for Planning Facilities for Athletics, Recreation, and Physical and Health Education. Chicago: Published for National Facilities Conference by The Athletic Institute, 1947.

WILLIAMS, JESSE FEIRING, AND BROWNELL, C. L. *The Administration of Health and Physical Education.* Philadelphia: W. B. Saunders Co., 1946, pp. 305-315.

Chapter VI
BODY MECHANICS: POSTURES IN PHYSICAL EDUCATION

The basis of all physical education may be summed up in the phrase "body mechanics," a term that describes the balance of body segments, both in motion and in repose, through muscular control. The values of good posture and of good form in all motor skills are as evident as are the dangers of faulty posture and the disadvantages of poor form in movements. It is the major responsibility of physical education to encourage good body mechanics and to correct, so far as possible, faulty body mechanics. While recognizing that posture is in a large part a matter of mechanics—balancing different weights in various positions through the pull of muscles—teachers of physical education realize also that the energy level of the individual and his emotional and psychological state are very important factors in posture. In encouraging good postures, therefore, as well as in correcting faulty postures, the teacher must understand not only the mechanics of posture but the role of energy and emotion in posture.

THE MECHANICS OF POSTURE

The human body has movable joints all the way from the neck to the ankle. Balancing the weights of the different body segments involves both gravity pull and muscular forces. If the system were in perfect balance mechanically, then the muscles would not be needed in maintaining the position, but since the individual is constantly engaged in achieving a balance and then through movement disturbing the balance, the muscles are also in constant use.

In the mechanics of posture, the individual's first problem is to learn how to balance the various body segments. If one achieves this balance, then the use of muscles to hold the individual erect is less and energy is saved. The head segment—which, in an elementary school child, weighs about 12 pounds—is supported by the cervical spine. In order to balance the head, the child should hold his head so that the opening of the ear is vertically above the mid-point of the shoulder and hip joint (Figure 42). When the head falls in front of a vertical line running through the shoulder point, the dead weight of the head mass must be carried by the ligaments and muscles at the back of the neck. In many movements and positions the head normally takes a forward position, as in writing at a desk, in stooping, and in playing some musical instruments.

Below the head is the trunk segment, which includes the spine and ribs. In general, all parts of this segment should remain balanced in a vertical line in standing and sitting positions. In all movements, however, the trunk may be involved in a continual series of changes, from front to back and from side to side. The lower end of the trunk rests on two points provided by the thigh bones. In standing, to avoid displacement of the body weight, one must keep the lower back almost straight. This position helps in maintaining flatness of the front abdominal wall. The weight of the body should be carried equally on both legs through the knee and ankle joints. The feet should be in a parallel position with the weight toward the outer side of the soles in standing and in sitting as well as in all patterns of movement.

It should be clear that the balance one may achieve at any one moment is lost whenever movement takes place, and then balance is recovered. Except in certain artificial postures, as in that of military attention, posture is never static.

Figure 42. In good sitting posture the opening of the ear should be vertically above the mid-point of the shoulder and hip joints.

The Role of Energy in Posture

In order to keep the individual in a constant state of balance, the muscles must work continually, contracting and relaxing, as they move the body segments and extremities. In this work, energy is expended. The ability, therefore, of the individual to regain balance and to move parts depends upon the possession of muscular energy. Some children have poor postural patterns because they lack the muscular power to bring the body segments into balance. Other children have faulty posture because of poor muscular co-ordination. These children need improved nutrition and rest, followed by developmental exercise. When energy is abundant and muscles are strong, these resources are reflected in the individual's movements and positions. Likewise fatigue expresses itself in a characteristic sag of the shoulders, a droop of the head, and an inelastic gait.

The Role of Emotion in Posture

The postures of a person reflect the drive of inner purpose and controlling idea. Examples of this psychological influence are portrayed in such phrases as "the stride of the general" and "the crouch of the slave." Heroes do not crouch and slaves do not stride, for they reflect in their movements the inner purposes and ideas that they possess. Children who are confident, self-respecting, and happy will have postures that reveal these states. Children with fears, timidities, and other feelings of insecurity often move and stand in harmony with these emotions. One significant approach, then, to the development of good postures is the cultivation of buoyant, self-respecting, happy personalities. Children who are treated as slaves will not be able to stand as heroes.

A feeling of self-confidence and adequacy comes with the assumption of good postures. We act as we feel, but we also feel as we act. Aside from the pleasurable sensation resulting from cleanliness and buoyant health, an individual derives pleasure and self-respect from the knowledge that he looks attractive. The utilitarian value of a fine physique and beautiful

Figure 43. Erect posture gives a feeling of well-being and inspires leadership. Slumped posture reveals a feeling of insecurity.

posture cannot be denied. Of necessity, employers and personnel directors base part of their judgment of candidates for positions on personal appearance and carriage. Poor body mechanics may cause such an unattractive impression that applicants are rejected.

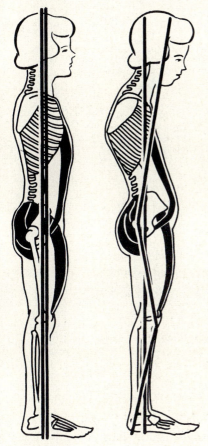

Figure 44. In good posture (left) all body segments are in good balance. The head is erect, chest up, abdomen in, hip and thigh muscles tight, and inner arch lifted. In slumped posture (right) the body segments are out of balance. The head is forward, shoulders round, chest flat, back hollow, hip and thigh muscles relaxed, and inner arches relaxed.

Good Forms in Posture

In following the basic principles of balanced motion children are not expected to show exact uniformity of postural patterns. It is important, however, that they exemplify certain principles in movement. Thus, all children will not run alike, but all children should learn to run with their toes pointing straight forward. Styles of walking will vary and yet all in walking should carry the weight on the outer borders of the feet. Individuals have different ways of throwing, yet all right-handed children should learn to throw with the left foot forward, left-handed children with the right foot forward. Good form in work skills should be learned.

Although there are innumerable good postures, all of them have certain elements in common. If they are good, there is an erectness of the trunk, a position of the head that favors speech and signifies alertness and readiness for action, and a poise of the entire weight on the feet in such fashion that movement can be made quickly in any direction. In contrast, if these essentials are lacking the individual stands with protruding head, depressed chest, humped back, and weight on the heels. At no moment is he ready for movement.

Figure 45

HOW TO LIFT

In order to avoid muscle strain, one should learn good form in such work skills as pushing, pulling, and lifting.

Incorrect and correct ways of lifting heavy objects are shown in the pictures on this page.

In the left-hand column, the man is lifting incorrectly. He stands too far away from the object and uses his back and abdominal muscles, with resultant strain and possible injury. In (1) he makes a bad start by leaning over and grasping the box. In (2, 3, and 4) his back muscles do the lifting with the resultant strain shown in (5).

Pictures on the right show the correct way to lift. In (1) the man decides the box is heavy and he stops to consider the best way to lift it. In (2) he stands close to the object and bends his knees as he grasps it. In (3) he stoops to lift, still keeping close to the box. In (4) his thigh muscles help in the lift, and in (5) he is ready to carry the box.

Courtesy National
Safety Council,
Chi

Faulty Body Mechanics

When studying postural defects in children, teachers must remember that many different factors are reflected in poor body posture. The inherited shape of the skeleton influences a child's postural pattern. For instance, a slender-boned child has a more difficult task in maintaining a balanced posture than does a broad-boned child. A child with a wide pelvis and endocrine deficiency often displays a characteristic knock-kneed position. Many postural patterns are the result of imitating an older person. Poor body mechanics in walking and standing can often be traced to the child's imitating the walk and standing position of mother or father.

Discouragement, consciousness of an unattractive appearance beyond the power of the individual to change, or a feeling of inferiority may be active factors in preventing children from maintaining good postures. Certain unfavorable factors that make it difficult, if not impossible, for children to maintain good posture are insufficient or troubled sleep; undernourishment with its train of physical evils; fatigue caused by overstimulation or long periods of inactivity; impaired hearing; eye strain; and other health hazards. Environmental conditions that may lead to postural defects are badly arranged, hot, or inadequately ventilated rooms, or unsuitable seating arrangements.

Poor posture may be due to serious structural changes occurring in the bones, muscles, and ligaments of the body. Thus, if one leg is shorter than the other, if muscles have been paralyzed by illness, if bones have been deformed by rickets, or if any one of several conditions exist, the posture faults may be extensive and severe. In such cases, admonitions to stand straight do no good because the individual is unable by voluntary act to follow the advice.

The problem of postures in children is not a simple one. It has many aspects. Some of the difficulties require the assistance of a physician, while others call for the expert services of a person trained in the field of corrective exercises. The chief function of the teacher in this respect is to help children form desirable postural patterns and acquire good habits in the many postures assumed. The teacher must also watch for the psychological and physiological factors that may affect the positions and movements of the individual, in order that remedies can be sought for harmful situations.

ENCOURAGING GOOD POSTURE

Although most elementary teachers are not now prepared to give particular exercises for correction of specific deviations from the normal, they can do much to improve the postures of boys and girls. Teachers should be posture conscious and should strive to have good postural habits themselves. They should be able (1) to recognize correct postures and deviations from normal postures,[1] (2) to teach basic skills for locomotion, work, and play, (3) to give posture instruction so effectively that correct body mechanics will be understood by children, and (4) to direct the interest of children so that they will try to maintain desirable body positions throughout all the activities of the school program. Children must learn to know what good posture feels like as well as what it looks like. This means the development in each child of a kinesthetic awareness of the correct distribution of body segments, acquired through many repeated experiences in adjusting the position of the different segments.

Once children understand and can assume correct posture, teachers must continually aid them in establishing good postural habits. It must be remembered, in the maintenance of desirable postures, that these positions are not static. Each time segments of the body are moved, postural readjustments must be made.

Teachers must include in their lesson plans specific instruction that will promote good body mechanics. Experience must be provided in climbing as well as in running, in jumping as well as in pushing, in stopping as well as in hanging. Games should be included that provide for development of all the muscles rather than of a few sets of muscles. A balance between rest and activity is necessary to prevent fatigue and tension. A class environment conducive to good body mechanics is one that not only provides proper seating and lighting but also offers interesting activities for every child.

Teachers and parents need to work together for the best growth and development of each child. The following items should be understood:

1. Need for extra rest for underweight and overweight children.
2. Need for outdoor play.
3. Need for uninterrupted sleep and rest with a minimum of movie and radio disturbance.
4. Need for good reading habits that include good sitting posture.
5. Need for proper fitting shoes, with an understanding that tennis shoes should not be worn constantly.
6. Need for hard, firm mattress.
7. Need to watch play habits of children.

---

[1] The technique of a posture examination is discussed in the following references:

Charles Leroy Lowman, Claire Colestock, and Hazel Cooper, *Corrective Physical Education for Groups*. New York: A. S. Barnes & Co., 1928, pp. 41-47.

Physical Education: A Wartime and Peacetime Program for Girls. A Report of the Women's Advisory Committee on Physical Education, appointed by the California Superintendent of Public Instruction. Published by the committee, 1943, pp. 20-22.

The last of these points is one that parents may overlook unless its importance is pointed out to them. Children, when playing on the floor with toys or with jackstones, are apt to sit with knees together and feet spread to the rear, or on one hip with both legs extended to the same side. These positions are harmful. It is recommended that parents and teachers tell children to sit with legs spread in a forward position or in tailor fashion; that is, with legs crossed in front, spine held erect, the forward motion of the body being made from the hips. In these positions weight and strain are removed from leg bones and from the bones, cartilage, and ligaments of the knees and feet. Another undesirable play habit is the continuous use of but one roller skate and the propulsion of a scooter or wagon through the use of a favored leg. A high hip may result, with distortion of the spinal column.

Activities to Aid Child's Desire for Good Postures

Teachers should strive to create within each child the desire for good postures. To help create this desire the following activities are recommended:

1. See that all children understand how to move correctly in all situations.
2. Explain that for some children growth proceeds faster than for others, and that tall children should never stoop to reach the level of shorter children.
3. Have available for the children pictures of famous men and women who stand or sit correctly. Make it easy for the children to see interesting books and magazine articles dealing with the subject of posture.[1] Such material should be changed frequently. Some magazines and Sunday papers often have useful pictures or articles on posture. These should be saved for future use after being displayed and discussed.
4. Have children write slogans about problems of posture.
5. Have children make posters that are related to their slogans; then hold an art exhibit inviting parents to view the posters.
6. Have children present talks on different phases of posture before school assemblies, the parent-teacher associations, or other community groups.
7. Encourage the writing and presenting of skits and plays in which children express their feelings toward desirable and undesirable

---

[1] Some suitable books on the subject are the following:
John Martin Hiss, *New Feet for Old.* New York: Doubleday, Doran & Co., 1937.
Dorothy Nye, *New Bodies for Old.* New York: Funk & Wagnalls Co., 1946 (revised).
Janet Lane, *Your Carriage, Madam!* New York: John Wiley & Sons, Inc., 1947.

postures. Sample plays may be found in the book, *Corrective Physical Education for Groups*.[1]

8. Have discussions on games and their contribution toward the improvement of posture.

9. Conduct posture week contests in which tags are given out the first day to teachers and pupils who maintain good postures, and taken away when anyone exhibits poor posture. The game is to see who can keep his tag until the end of the week. Frequent posture tag days will aid children to become posture conscious.

10. Place a narrow, full-length mirror in a conspicuous place, preferably the classroom or front hall, so that children, by glancing into the mirror as they pass by, may judge their posture. A white ribbon or strip of adhesive down the center of the mirror will help children to judge whether their bodies represent exclamation points or question marks.

11. Hold discussions on posture problems. Many themes can be employed for discussion groups, such as the mechanics of levers; weight distribution; the aesthetic and economic aspects of good posture; effect of poor posture on internal organs; the necessity of perseverance and the will to achieve; the probable long-time effect of continued poor posture (neuritis, backaches, eye strain, headaches, and general body aches).

12. Have children check each other's posture. These posture checks should be very simple for the children in the third grade. More complete posture checks can be made by the intermediate and upper grade children. Not only will they receive a deeper understanding of the difference between good and poor posture, but they will also help each other to correct and maintain good posture. In Chapter XIII of this guide is found an outline of a complete posture examination.

Posture Cues

There are some words that a teacher can use to remind pupils to readjust undesirable positions. Since bony structure and muscle pulls are different for each pupil, each becomes a separate problem for the teacher. The instructor should have a definite mental picture of what should happen when posture cues are given and how pupils may be helped to secure the desired position.

Stiff exaggerated positions are apt to result with younger children when reference is made to any area of the body other than the head or

---

[1] Charles Leroy Lowman and Others, *op. cit.*, pp. 482-88.

feet. Therefore, in the primary grades reference to spine, hips, abdomen, back or shoulders should be avoided.

The phrase, "Shoulders back—chests high," should not be given, as its use results, usually, in the assumption of exaggerated sitting or standing positions. In particular, pupils elevate the chest unnaturally, strain the lower back, and assume the undesirable hollow or sway-back position, with abdomen thrust forward.

The cues listed are recommended for younger children and for children in the intermediate and upper grades, according to their understanding of the terms used.

POSTURE CUES RECOMMENDED FOR CHILDREN IN KINDERGARTEN AND PRIMARY GRADES

Feet forward!	Feet pointing straight ahead!
Push up!	Grow tall!
Sit tall!	Heads high!
Stand tall!	Heads up!

POSTURE CUES RECOMMENDED FOR CHILDREN IN INTERMEDIATE AND UPPER GRADES

Stand tall!	Tuck buttocks under!
Push body up!	Abdomen up and in!
Stretch the neck!	Flatten lower back!
Chin easy!	Rotate arms out—return forearms
Lift chest!	and hands!
Sit tall!	Do not strain!
Shoulders easy!	Use opposing muscles!
Neck against collar!	Transfer weight over balls of feet!
Shoulder blades flat!	Test your balance!
Stretch tall!	Knees easy! [1]
Hips under!	Lift foot arches!
Feet parallel!	Weight off heels!
Feet forward!	Push with the toes!
Knee caps forward!	One line, not three!
Feet strong!	

POSTURE CUES RECOMMENDED FOR CORRECTION OF FATIGUE SLUMP OF OLDER CHILDREN

Chest high!	Abdomen up and in!
Feet forward!	Knees easy!
Hips under!	Tilt pelvic girdles!
Buttocks down!	Yawn hard and stretch all over!
Head high!	

CORRECTING FAULTY POSTURES

The most common postural faults among school children are the incorrect use of the feet and the ever-present "debutante slouch." Emphasis, therefore, on posture correction for children above the third grade

---

[1] Avoid using the direction "knees straight," since over-extension (backward thrust) of the knees is apt to occur, thereby causing an increased lordosis (sway-back) in the lumbar spine area.

should be placed on (1) the exercise to control the tilt of the pelvic bones; (2) games, exercises, and rhythmic patterns that strengthen side and front abdominal muscles; (3) games, exercises, and rhythmic patterns that strengthen upper back muscles; (4) apparatus exercises and games that strengthen the muscles of the shoulders and arms (shoulder girdle); and, (5) of special importance, exercises to strengthen the muscles of the feet.[1]

For younger children there should be frequent vigorous activity periods, systematic daily use of playground apparatus, the opportunity for frequent running, as well as daily exercise in handling and throwing large balls. Children should be taught how to move in correct form in all of the various activities. Rhythmical experiences are especially important for this age group. Locomotor skills can be taught easily through rhythms.

Correction of the fatigue slump, if accompanied by the sway-back position, requires first that the lower back position be improved through maintenance of the correct pelvic tilt. One or all of the following directions may be used: "Hips under; tighten lower abdomen; pull abdomen up and in; flatten lower part of back; push out the lower back by tilting pelvic girdle; lower the buttocks; shorten buttock muscles; tuck in your tail."

The Pelvic Bones and Postural Faults

Older children should be made to understand that the correction of poor postures comes about mainly through correcting the lower back position; that is, the elimination of any sway-back tendency that may be present. They must be taught how to avoid an exaggerated lumbar curve (hollow back) through mastery of the exercise in which simultaneously the fronts of the pelvic bones (pelvic girdle) are tilted up and the buttocks pulled down.

The Pelvic Tilt. The correct pelvic tilt straightens out any pronounced sway-back curve that may be present in the lumbar region of the back and at the same time removes from prominence the abdominal area in front and the buttocks in the rear.[2] With the correct tilt, body contours become streamlined. This tilt helps in securing correct alignment of the different body segments, one over the other, and assists in the removal of strain due to an unequal pull of antagonistic muscle groups over the different joints. It must be remembered, however, that a slight lumbar curve is natural.

---

[1] The major divergencies from correct posture and the corrective exercises to be used are discussed in the following references:
Physical Education: A Wartime and Peacetime Program for Girls. pp. 25-36.
Charles Leroy Lowman and Others, *op. cit.,* Chapters VI, VII, VIII.
[2] The importance of maintaining the correct pelvic tilt is emphasized in the following references:
Janet Lane, *op. cit.,* pp. 52-59.
Charles Leroy Lowman and Others, *op. cit.,* pp. 116, 206, 211.

Some children will learn immediately the muscle contractions that
result in the readjustment of the
pelvic position. Others will have to
work hard and over a period of time
before experiencing the readjustment that takes place when muscles
are contracted front and rear.

The teacher should work with
children individually. The child
should place his hands on the
teacher's waist, one hand in front
and the other in back, in order to
feel the muscular change that takes
place when the pelvic bones are
tipped up and down.

Valuable exercises for the pupil
in learning the process are these:

1. Lie on the back on the floor.
   Try to lessen the distance
   between lumbar spine and the
   floor or to flatten the back
   against the floor.

2. Stand with hips and shoulders
   touching a wall; heels do not
   touch. Try to lessen the distance between the small of the
   back and the wall. When the

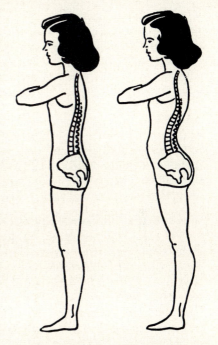

Figure 46. The correct pelvic tilt,
which lifts the front of the pelvis
and flattens the hollow of the back,
is illustrated at the left. Incorrect
pelvic tilt resulting in protruding abdomen and hollow back is shown
at right.

position is accomplished, walk around the room maintaining the new
position as long as possible. When the position is lost, try to get the
same results while standing still.

Teachers will find it difficult to give assistance in this very important corrective exercise if they cannot themselves perform the movement. When necessary they should seek instruction from supervisors
of physical education or teachers of corrective physical education in
their school districts, or from staff members of the physical education
departments of teacher-training institutions.

Shoulders and Their Control

When shoulders are mentioned the suggestion should be made to
relax tense muscles and allow the shoulders to take a natural position.
Never say, "shoulders back," or "throw your shoulders back." Use cue

words such as "shoulders easy," "shoulders natural," or "shoulders relaxed." A useful cue, if and when the lower back and hips are under control, is "shoulders down and shoulder blades in." Correct shoulder position can be attained by having children rotate or turn both hands and arms outward while they are hanging close to the body. By this exercise the chest is usually lifted automatically, thereby bringing the shoulder blades to the correct position for them, which is close to the ribs and adjacent to the spine. Since a continued outward turning of arms and hands is not a normal procedure, hands and forearms only are allowed to return to the position where fingers parallel the thighs. The points of the shoulders should not be allowed to rotate forward with the return of the forearms and hands to position. Arms should swing freely from shoulder sockets and shoulder and neck muscles should not be tensed.[1]

Feet and Their Influence on Posture [2]

The construction and function of the feet should be thoroughly understood, since care of the feet, together with early correction of abnormal functioning, is one of the problems that parents and educators must meet. Correct habits in use of the feet must be established if healthy feet are to be maintained. Older children should be taught a few basic foot exercises.[3] All children should be taught to stand and walk with feet practically parallel. The following suggestions for the care of the feet should prove beneficial.

1. Walk and stand with toes pointing forward and with weight borne on the outer areas of the feet (Figure 47).
2. Do not wear shoes and stockings too short. Corns, calluses, bunions, ingrown toenails, and other serious foot defects will result.
3. Do not wear rubber-soled shoes all day. They make the feet perspire excessively, and continuance of this condition causes the muscles of the feet to weaken, with resulting strain and fatigue.
4. Do not wear pointed shoes. They cramp the toes, causing corns, calluses, bunions, hammer toes, or overriding toes.
5. Bathe the feet frequently. Take care to dry the skin thoroughly between all the toes and in particular between the little toe and the neighboring toe.
6. Buy good shoes. They cost more but will last longer and will give better support to the feet.

Points in Fitting Shoes.[4]   When purchasing shoes for daily use the following points should be remembered:

---

[1] The development of the shoulder girdle is discussed by Janet Lane, *op. cit.*, pp. 66-73.

[2] The section, "Feet and Their Influence on Posture," was contributed by Pasadena Public Schools.

[3] Excellent foot exercises for group work are given by Charles Leroy Lowman and Others, *op. cit.*, pp. 407-10.

[4] The material "Points in Fitting Shoes" was contributed by the Department of Physical Education, Pasadena Public Schools.

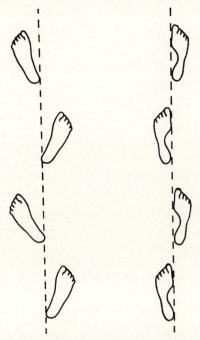

Figure 47. In walking, toes should be pointed straight ahead, with weight borne on outer areas of the feet as in the right column. Left column shows toes pointing out, which puts a strain on the arches of the foot.

1. Leather soles and heels, the latter broad and low with a rubber cap, are most desirable.
2. Broad toe areas permit freedom for and use of all the toes.
3. A straight last is desirable. The line on the inner border of the shoe, from the heel to the end of the big toe, should be a straight line. Pointed shoes inhibit the proper use of the big toes by pushing them inward and away from the best position for weight bearing and pushing.
4. Shoes should be sufficiently long. The length in any particular last changes approximately one-sixth of an inch from one size to the next half size. The position of the feet within the shoes when standing should be studied when shoes are fitted.
5. Accurate width for the anterior arch or ball of the foot is important. There should not be too much spread. The width in any particular last changes approximately one-sixteenth of an inch from one size to the next.
6. The central portion, or waist, of the shoe should fit the instep snugly.
7. The heel of the shoe should fit the heel of the foot snugly.
8. Proper support for the longitudinal arch is essential.
9. Shoes should permit weight bearing at four points: the heel; the base area of the big toe; the heads of the metatarsal bones (the ball of the foot); and the junction of the fifth metatarsal bone and the cuboid bone (outer border of the foot). The use of the big toe in weight bearing is important.
10. Oxford shoes which lace snugly over the instep are the most desirable for general use.

CORRECTIVE EXERCISES [1]

Most deviations from correct postural habits develop during the years of elementary schooling. Those are the years when teachers can stimulate children to desire and work for beautiful bodies. Corrective activities should be scheduled during these years, and teachers should have the aid of trained personnel from county and city school offices. For a large majority of pupils, junior and senior high school and college years will be too late for corrections. Hence it is important that teacher training institutions include basic body mechanics in the physical education courses for classroom teachers.

The distribution of the weight of the body has much to do in determining correct and incorrect posture. Starting with the feet, the base of support, the weight while in a standing position should be distributed upward through the main parts of the body as described in the following points:

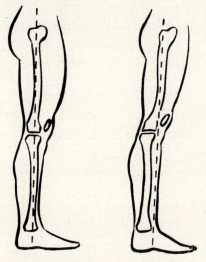

1. On the heels, outer borders of the feet, and toes, with all toes down
2. Legs and knees directly over the feet
3. Thighs over the knees
4. Pelvis over the thighs
5. Spine (which is the upright bony support for the trunk) over the pelvis
6. Head over the neck

The pull of gravity will help to maintain an upright position if bony structures are correctly centered one above the other, with each bearing the weight of the segments above. In an effort to stand straight some children push the knees backward into a hyperextended position.

Figure 48. Normal knee at left is in proper balance; illustration at right shows hyperextended knee.

This is undesirable because the weight of the body in this position is carried onto the heels and the pelvis tilts forward to cause a hollow back.

When muscle feel for good posture is learned and gravity is allowed to function, the maintenance of the upright position is freed from strain

[1] Much assistance in the preparation of this section was furnished by Lucile Grunewald, formerly Associate Professor, Division for Women, Department of Physical Education, University of California, Los Angeles.

and tenseness. Fatigue is minimized and improved circulation results. If segments of the body are unbalanced, faulty conditions such as pronated feet, sway-back, round upper back and shoulders, and sway-neck develop and muscle and nerve tensions result. Specialized exercises must be used to correct faulty weight carrying. Descriptions of exercises for specific parts of the body are given in the following sections.

Exercises to Improve the Feet

The feet should be at right angles to the legs, the toes should point straight ahead, and the weight should be carried equally on the heels, balls of the feet, and toes of both feet. A short heel cord may be congenital or it may be caused by the habitual wearing of high heels. A short heel cord, by lifting the back of the foot, thrusts the weight of the body forward onto the inner border of the foot (the spring arch), instead of on the outer border (the weight-bearing arch). The toes, to avoid the weight-thrust, toe out. The exercises indicated are for heel cord stretching and the adduction of the front part of the foot; that is, pulling the toes in so that they function in weight bearing.

1. *Heel Cord Stretching.* Stand facing table or wall for support. With feet parallel, weight on outer borders and toes, and while keeping heels on the floor, knees straight, and trunk erect, rock body forward and back, localizing all movement in the ankle joints. If there is difficulty in keeping heels down, place heels against a wall. The friction of the wall will keep heels on the floor.

This exercise may be done with feet on an angle board or with part of the foot on a pad or book. An angle board is a wedge-shaped platform 10 inches long, 15 inches wide, with upper edge 2½ inches from the floor. Stand on angle board, facing end of table or wall for support, with feet parallel, heels on floor, and toes curled over high edge of board. Sway back and forth, while keeping the heels on the floor. Action is in the ankles.

2. *Sand Scrape Exercise* (Figure 49). Place feet three inches apart and parallel, with heels, outer borders of the feet, and all toes on the floor. With the fore part of feet, pull in as if piling up sand with the inner borders of the feet. This exercise can be done either standing or sitting.

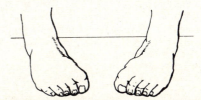

Figure 49. The sand scrape exercise strengthens the muscles of the arches.

Exercises to Improve Knee and Leg Position [1]

The weight or pull of gravity in the legs should go through the length of the thigh bones, middle of the knee joints, shins, and ankle joints. If the weight is carried on the inner side of the knee, there is a resulting knock knee or inward turning. Tight hamstrings (large tendons situated on each side of the space back of the knee) will cause faulty weight bearing in the leg and thigh. Exercises to correct these conditions follow.

1. *Thigh Muscle Contraction.* From prone (face) lying position, with toes together and heels out, pull heels together by contracting the outward rotators of the thighs and large buttock muscles, thus getting knees in better alignment.

2. *Hamstring Stretching* (Figure 50). From back lying position, right knee bent with foot on the floor, left leg straight, toes pointing toward the ceiling and fore part of the foot pulled in, raise left leg seven or eight times, each time raising leg a little higher. Relax leg between raisings. Repeat with right leg.

Figure 50. Steps in the exercise to stretch the hamstrings are (1) back lying position, right knee bent with foot on floor; (2) left leg straight, toes point toward ceiling; (3) raise left leg seven or eight times, each time raising leg a little higher as in (4) and (5). Relax leg between raisings. Repeat with right leg.

Exercises to Improve Lower Back Position

Many children need exercises to correct the abnormal forward curvature of the lower spine called hollow back, sway-back, or lordosis. Gravity constantly pulls the lumbar spine forward when a person sits or

---

[1] Good exercises for the feet and legs are described in the book, *Physical Education: A Wartime and Peacetime Program for Girls*, pp. 27-30.

Figure 51. The alternate knee-bending exercise helps decrease the pelvic tilt, flattens the lower back, and strengthens abdominal muscles.

stands in the hollow back position. The muscles of the lower back and the tissues which bind the muscles together, in resisting the gravity pull, become fixed and tense, thus restricting movement in the lumbar area of the spine. In the normal upright position the pelvis is the base of support for the trunk, and it is necessary, therefore, to control the pelvis. The lower back muscles and their tissues are primarily concerned in the maintenance of this adequate base. To correct a hollow back these muscles must be stretched enough to flatten the lower spine so as to permit gravity to pull through spine and pelvis.

The exercises that follow will prove useful in establishing greater mobility in the lumbar region, with a resulting improvement in sitting and standing positions.

1. *Knee-chest Exercise*. From hook lying position (on back with knees bent), grasp knees and pull them forcibly toward the chest, thereby stretching lower back muscles with resultant flattening of the lumbar spine. Hold position for an appreciable space of time. Then relax arms. Repeat exercise 12 to 14 times.

2. *Alternate Knee Bending Exercise* (Figure 51). Lie in hook lying position. Alternately bend knees to chest. By this exercise the pelvic tilt is decreased, and the lower back flattened, while the abdominal muscles are strengthened. Repeat 15 to 20 times.

3. *Pelvic Rotation*. From hook lying position place heels as close to buttocks as possible. Rest head on hands with elbows on floor. Contract

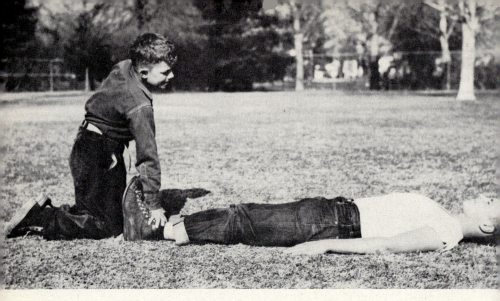

Figure 52. In step one for the sit-up exercise, the pupil lies on his back with legs extended, feet held by an assisting student.

buttock muscles, thereby pushing buttocks toward the heels while keeping back flat. Performer will get a feeling of tucking under as the pelvis is rotated under. Abdominal muscles must be relaxed. If it seems difficult to relax the abdominal muscles, perform the exercise from the prone lying position, which is lying face down, legs extended, arms at side and body relaxed. A pillow may be placed under the abdomen. Contract buttock muscles vigorously 25 to 50 times or until the pelvis is rotated without contraction of the abdominal muscles. Thereupon return to first position and repeat the exercise.

4. *Wall Standing Exercise.* Stand with back to wall, feet parallel, three inches apart, and with heels six inches from wall. Bend trunk forward and downward in a relaxed position. Start to bend knees slowly and at same time, while tucking under the pelvis, raise the trunk slowly upward so that entire spine, starting from the lowest part, touches the wall. Continue until body is erect with spine flattened, including the neck. Next, straighten knees slowly while spine remains in contact with the wall. When erect, give a slight push with hands and rock away from the wall. Maintaining improved position, walk about the room. Mastery of the tuck-under or pelvic tilt is of great importance for balanced, graceful walking and standing positions.

Exercises to Strengthen Lower Abdominal Muscles

It is important that the muscles of the lower abdomen be strong, since they have an important relationship to other muscle groups in the maintenance of correct posture.

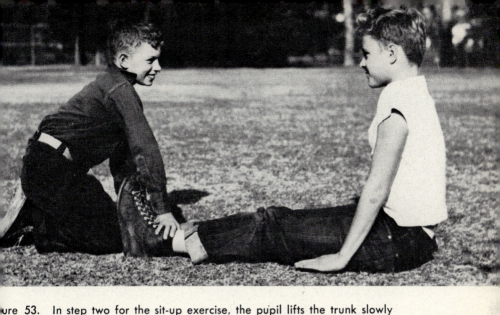

ure 53. In step two for the sit-up exercise, the pupil lifts the trunk slowly
d smoothly to an erect sitting position, without moving legs from the ground.
nk is returned to the ground slowly with back straight. Movement should occur
he hip joints, not in segments of the spine.

The following exercises will help in the development of the abdominal muscles.[1]

1. *Alternate Shoulder and Leg Lifting Exercise.* From hook lying
position simultaneously lift head and left shoulder and raise right leg
upward. Hold the position for several seconds while breathing naturally.
Relax. Repeat exercise, using opposite shoulder and leg. The passive
shoulder is kept on the floor. Arms are relaxed at all times. Repeat exercise
six times to each side.

2. *Alternate Knee Touching Exercise.* From hook lying position,
arms by side and relaxed, attempt to touch knee with opposite hand while
feet remain on the floor. Trunk and shoulder on side of reaching hand are
raised, but other shoulder remains on the floor. Repeat exercise 8 to 10
times to each side.

3. *Head Raising Exercise.* From hook lying position, arms by side
and relaxed, raise head as high as possible during three slow counts. Chin
should reach toward ceiling while head is being raised and held. This is a
strenuous abdominal exercise, since no flexors are involved. Repeat
exercise 8 to 10 times.

4. *Alternate Elbow and Knee Touching Exercise.* From hook lying
position, endeavor to touch with left elbow the bent knee as it is lifted,
and vice versa. Opposite shoulder remains on the floor. Repeat 10 times
to each side.

---

[1] Abdominal exercises particularly suitable for girls are described in the following references:
WAC Field Manual: Physical Training. FM 35-20. Washington, D. C.: War Department,
1943.
Physical Education: A Wartime and Peacetime Program for Girls, pp. 24-25.

5. *Sit-up*.   Lie on back with legs extended and with feet held in position on the floor by use of a strap, by slipping toes under a heavy bookcase, or by pressure applied to feet by an assisting pupil. Place hands on top of thighs to prevent the elbows from assisting during the perform- ance of the exercise. Lift trunk slowly and smoothly to an erect sitting position. Back is held in a straight line position throughout the exercise. The chest, held in an arched position, leads the way. Head is held in line with the shoulders. The return of the trunk to the floor is done slowly with the head leading, chest high, and back straight. Movement should occur in the hip joints, not in segments of the spine. Repeat exercise often but not for competition other than against one's own record.

The sit-up is an exercise that needs careful supervision and controlled performance.[1] It should not be attempted until the performer has well- developed abdominal muscles. This exercise is used to tone up abdominal muscles. A pupil with a hollow back should not use this exercise until he or she learns to correct and control the lumbar curve.

In order to eliminate the danger of hernia, the performer should learn not to set the abdominal muscles and the diaphragm. He should be taught to exhale during the act of sitting up and to inhale during the return of the trunk to the floor. Dr. Charles Leroy Lowman writes:

> The danger of hernia may be almost wholly eliminated if the throat is allowed to remain open when such exercises as sitting up from the Backward Lying Position or double leg raising are done. The locking of the diaphragm with increased abdominal pressure is prevented by exhaling with the sit-up and inhaling on the reverse movement. Thus the downward pressure with possible production of hernia is ruled out.[2]

Exercises to Improve Position of Upper Back and Shoulders

The following exercises will improve the round back condition of the upper back.

1. *Head-Shoulder Raising Exercise*.   From prone lying position, with a pillow under the abdomen, legs extended and together and arms extended along sides and relaxed, raise head and shoulders to maximum height, with movement taking place in the middle of the upper back between the shoulder blades. Chin should be kept in to flatten neck. Hold position but do not hold breath. Breathe easily. Relax. Repeat exercise 8 to 10 times.

---

[1] Warnings against incorrect use of the sit-up and similar exercises are given in the following references:

Physical Education: A Wartime and Peacetime Program for Girls, op. cit., p. 32.

"Physical Performance Levels for High School Girls," Summary Report of the Research Committee, National Section on Women's Athletics, *Journal of Health and Physical Education,* XVI (January, 1945), 308-11; 454-57.

Charles Leroy Lowman and Others, *op. cit.,* pp. 116-19.

[2] Charles Leroy Lowman and Others, *op. cit.,* pp. 118. By permission.

2. *Upper Spine Hyperextension.*   Stand facing a table, which should be at hip height. Keeping feet on floor, bend over and rest trunk on table. From this position, while hips remain on table, raise head and shoulders, flattening the upper back. Position is held while breathing is continued. Relax. Repeat exercise 8 to 10 times.

3. *Table Top Exercise* (so named because the back is transformed from a rounded position to a flat position).   From erect position, bend forward and downward in a relaxed position. Arms do no work. While in this position, raise head and shoulders, flattening the entire spine. Chin should be held in to flatten neck. Hold for an appreciable time but continue breathing. Relax. Repeat exercise 8 to 10 times, then go to erect position by raising trunk as one piece.

Figure 54.   The prone rocking exercise helps to strengthen the upper back and shoulder muscles.

4. *Prone Rocking* (Figure 54). Lie in prone position with arms extended over head. Keep hands together and keep feet together as they are lifted from the floor. Hold for several seconds, breathing naturally. Relax and repeat several times.

5. *Push-up from Prone Position.*   Squat and place hands on the floor in front of feet. Turn fingers slightly inward. In one movement move the feet backward with a jump to bring the body in a straight line, with the weight carried on the toes and hands. From this position bend the elbows and touch chest to floor. Push up to straight line position (Figure 55).

Push-ups from the prone position provide a vigorous exercise to strengthen shoulder and upper back muscles. In this exercise care must be taken to keep the back absolutely straight so that there is no strain on the lower back and abdominal muscles.

6. *Pull-up.*[1]   Grasp a horizontal bar with overhand grasp; that is, with palms turned out away from the face. Hands are placed far apart. The distance should be much wider than that indicated by the points of the shoulders. Feet should be touching each other and must completely clear the ground when the body is fully extended. Pull the body up until the chin is over the bar and return to original position. It is desirable to emphasize that the back muscles that control the position of the shoulder blades in relation to each other, the ribs underneath, and the spinal column are the ones exercised when the overhand grasp is used. Repeat the exercise often but not for competition other than against one's own record.

---

[1] Correct performance for the pull-up and other exercises are given by N. P. Neilson and Frederick W. Cozens in *Achievement Scales in Physical Education Activities for Boys and Girls in Elementary and Junior High Schools.* Sacramento: California State Department of Education, 1934.

The pull-up is an exercise that needs careful supervision and controlled performance. Teachers should see that children do not over-develop the pectoral muscles, located on the front of the chest wall with their ends attached to the upper arm. In many children these muscles over-balance the pull of the muscles of the shoulders and upper trunk. To counteract strong pectoral muscles, special developmental work should be provided for the muscles located on the upper back. The strengthening and resultant shortening of this group of muscles brings the shoulder blades nearer to the spinal column, with resultant expansion of the chest area. The pull-up or chinning exercise, provided it is done correctly, is a desirable exercise for strengthening the shoulder muscle groups.

Figure 55. In the push-up from prone position, steps are as follows: (1) from a position with toes and hands on floor and back straight, lower body to (2) and (3); then in (4) push body up to (5). In the lower row, the middle illustration shows the correct position; the ones at left and right are incorrect.

In order to eliminate the danger of hernia, the abdominal muscles and the diaphragm should not be locked during the upward pull. To avoid setting these muscles, individuals should be required to exhale during the upward pull, thereby keeping the throat open, and to inhale while returning to the starting position. The above breathing procedure lessens the possibility of hernia. Dr. Lowman recommends that performers count out loud while exhaling.[1]

---

[1] Charles Leroy Lowman and Others, *op. cit.*, pp. 117-19.

Pupils with a history or indication of heart difficulty should not work at pull-ups. Those having a history of pleurisy and with thin, flat chests should hang passively with arms far apart and later should progress to hand traveling events rather than to pull-ups.[1] Also, children who are very much overweight should work on hand traveling events rather than pull-ups.

In those schools that provide no horizontal bars, the development of strength and corrective action for the group of shoulder blade muscles can be achieved by having pupils take an extended overhead "Y" position of the arms, hands being some 30 to 40 inches apart. Pupils pull arms downward and at the same time resist the movement by contracting hand and arm muscles as hard as possible. Hands and elbows should be opposite ears all the time the downward pull is being executed. At the end of the pull, the elbows should be directly below the armpits and hugging the ribs, with fists opposite the points of the shoulders.

Exercises to Improve Head Position

The upper spine supports the head. When the head gets out of its normal position over the spine, gravity pulls it down and the muscles and ligaments of the neck, in resisting the pull of gravity, become fixed and tense. It is necessary, therefore, to stretch these tissues. The following exercises will prove beneficial.

1. *Head Raising from Hook Lying Position.*   With knees bent and feet flat on the floor, place elbows together and put hands over top of head. Grasp the head and raise it up from the floor. Then, with chin in against the chest, flatten the neck to the floor while arms give slight resistance. The exercise may be taken with face turned directly upward or to either side. Repeat exercise 5 to 10 times with face straight up. Repeat exercise 3 to 5 times with face turned to side.

2. *Head Raising from Erect Sitting Position.*   Sit tailor fashion with trunk erect. Drop head forward and place locked hands on rounded back portion of head. Force head up and back slowly against resistance supplied by hands. Muscles involved are those of the neck and thoracic (rib) region of the spine. No muscular action should take place in abdomen or lower back other than that needed to maintain good posture. As skill is gained, elbows should be held parallel to the shoulders and should at no time move to a point forward of the ears. Repeat exercise 10 to 20 times.

---

[1] Charles Leroy Lowman and Others, *op. cit.,* pp. 117-18.

THE EFFECT OF MENTAL, EMOTIONAL, AND PHYSICAL TENSIONS ON POSTURES

Sustained tension in voluntary muscles depletes energy and causes discomfort. The primary sign of fatigue is muscular tension, which at first may stimulate one to greater effort. This period of increased excitement is a warning, but it is seldom recognized. There are various signs of fatigue that teachers should recognize in themselves and in their pupils: the typical body slump of fatigue (the debutante slouch); tension in muscles of neck, shoulders, back, and feet; irritability, loss of power to concentrate, restlessness, a tired feeling, decreased output of work, over-excitement, or insomnia. An indication of the extent of tension and fatigue among people is the enormous sale of sedative and stimulating drugs, a sad commentary on the health habits of the American people.

Activity and Rest

Included in the school's program there should be instruction on how to rest and relax. To those trained to observe, the physical appearance and emotional reactions of many individuals are warning signs that indicate the immediate need for rest or change in the type of activity being experienced. Children as well as adults show the symptoms of tension. Not only should rest periods be a part of the kindergarten and primary program, but rest should be provided for any child that needs it. Types of activities should be varied so that vigorous play alternates with quiet play, sitting work alternates with work that involves movement, and the duration of work periods are in proportion to the interest span of the child.

Necessity of Learning Relaxation

Release of tension in voluntary muscles is necessary to relaxation of all parts of the body. This is a learned process, since the conscious effort to relax voluntary muscles requires training of muscle groups to give up their tensions. It is interesting to note that mental and emotional tensions tend to disappear as muscular tensions are decreased. Too often individuals are unaware of a tense forehead, neck, or shoulders, when sitting, studying, talking, or working. They must learn to recognize such conditions and to make a conscious effort to release such "tied-up" muscles.

Before trying to relax voluntary muscles it is necessary for pupils to recognize the sensation of tenseness in muscle groups. This can be accomplished by having them make a hard fist or tense the muscles of the neck or shoulder and hold them until an aching sensation is experienced. Following these tensing experiences, directed at different areas of the body, the contracting muscles are released; that is, pupils stop tensing and "let loose." Letting loose is the important item to master. Experiments in contraction are not designed to aid relaxation, but are used to demonstrate to pupils what groups of voluntary muscles should not be doing when not involved in the performance of a movement. This ability to release tensions in all parts of the body until the entire body, including throat and eye muscles, becomes limp is acquired only through practice. A varying period for learning will be necessary in most cases, since the rest-work rhythm of life is a learned process. Some learn it easily, others with greater difficulty. Success is dependent on a plan of living that assures the essentials of health by activity in the open, proper meals, regular exercise, regular hours for retiring and arising, and the prevention of chronic overfatigue.

Of the very greatest value in prevention of abnormal tension is the cultivation of a mood and a manner of living in which the dominant note is poise and calm rather than push and shove. Children are great imitators and adopt the emotional patterns of persons around them. If teachers are to help children avoid tensions, they must be excellent examples of poise. Moreover, it is essential that teachers avoid haste and hurry in their management of the classroom. Children should be taught to be alert, quick, and orderly in a calm and poised way. There is a fundamental difference between quickness and hurry; the one is orderly, expeditious, and without tension, the other is disorderly, wasteful of time, and productive of tension.

SELECTED REFERENCES [1]

Books

BANCROFT, JESSIE H. *The Posture of School Children.* New York: The Macmillan Co., 1919.

BAUMGARTNER, A. J. *Posture Training and Remedial Gymnastics.* Minneapolis, Minn.: Burgess Publishing Company, 1941.

BLANCHARD, VAUGHN S., AND COLLINS, LAURENTINE B. *A Modern Physical Education Program.* New York: A. S. Barnes & Co., 1940 "Examination of Posture," p. 242.

COLESTOCK, CLAIRE, AND LOWMAN, CHARLES LEROY. *Fundamental Exercises for Physical Fitness.* New York: A. S. Barnes & Co., 1943.

DUGGAN, ANNE SCHLEY; MONTAGUE, MARY ELLA; AND RUTLEDGE, ABBIE. *Conditioning Exercises for Girls and Women.* New York: A. S. Barnes & Co., 1945.

Health Education: A Guide for Teachers in Elementary and Secondary Schools and Institutions for Teacher Education. A Report of the Joint Committee on Health Problems in Education of National Education Association and American Medical Association with Co-operation of Advisory Committees. Washington: National Education Association, 1948.

Health in Schools. Twentieth Yearbook of the American Association of School Administrators. Washington: American Association of School Administrators. National Education Association, 1942. "Posture Education," pp. 125-126.

---

[1] Appendix B also lists reference materials.

HOWLAND, IVALCLARE SPROW. *The Teaching of Body Mechanics in Elementary and Secondary Schools*. New York: A. S. Barnes & Co., 1936.

KELLY, ELLEN DAVIS. *Teaching Posture and Body Mechanics*. New York: A. S. Barnes & Co., 1949.

LANE, JANET. *Your Carriage, Madam! A Guide to Good Posture.* New York: John Wiley and Sons, Inc., 1947 (second edition).

LOWMAN, CHARLES LEROY; COLESTOCK, CLAIRE; AND COOPER, HAZEL. *Corrective Physical Education for Groups: A Textbook of Organization, Theory, and Practice.* New York: A. S. Barnes & Co., 1928.

MORTON, DUDLEY JOY. *Oh Doctor! My Feet!* New York: D. Appleton-Century Co., 1939.

RATHBONE, JOSEPHINE LANGWORTHY. *Corrective Physical Education.* Philadelphia: W. B. Saunders Co., 1934.

Posture Charts, Models, and Posters

American Seating Company, 9th and Broadway, Grand Rapids, Michigan.
    Posters: "How to Sit Correctly" (set of seven posters illustrating effects of good and bad posture) (free)

Bristol-Myers Company, 45 Rockefeller Plaza, New York 20, N. Y.
    Chart: "Good Grooming for School" (free)

California Dairy Industry Advisory Board, 670 South Lafayette Park Place, Los Angeles 5, California.
    Posters: "Posture" (four colored posters, 11 by 17 inches, for girls, illustrating walking, sitting, standing posture and poor posture habits), (30 cents); "Physical Fitness" (six colored posters, 12 by 18 inches, cartoon style, showing importance of posture, play, physical examination, sleep, cleanliness, and nutrition) (free); "Physical Fitness" (second series; eight colored posters covering other health habits, including sitting straight) (free)

Juanita Riedinger, 10 Rich Avenue, Mt. Vernon, New York.
    Cardboard Model: "Posture Pete" (26-inch, heavy, durable, jointed cardboard model that can show all types of posture; $1.65)

Scholl Manufacturing Company, Chicago, Illinois.
    Local stores demonstrate measuring individual footprints; pictures of normal footprints and typical weaknesses (free)

Chapter VII

PLAY, GAMES, AND ATHLETIC ACTIVITIES

Active play makes up a large part of the physical education program. Play is one of the most important means of contributing to child growth and development. The large muscles are strengthened and actions co-ordinated by playing on the climbing apparatus, pedaling a tricycle, walking a balance board between building boxes, swinging across a horizontal ladder, chasing another child in a game of tag, throwing a ball, and playing a kicking game. Opportunity to contribute ideas to a group is provided in dramatic play, small group play, organized games, and athletic activities. Opportunity to create is offered to each child who engages in dramatic play centered around apparatus, sandboxes, digging areas, housekeeping activities, or community life. Each child should be given an opportunity for leadership in play through specific duties concerning organization of activity, use of equipment, or officiating.

DRAMATIC PLAY AND GUIDED PLAY

Long before children are ready to take part in organized games they play alone or in small groups, choosing activities and using the play mate-

Figure 56. Muscles are strengthened on the circular climbing tree.

Figure 57. Kick Ball is a simple game that teaches soccer skills.

rials that are at hand. As they express their ideas and relive experiences the activity becomes dramatic play. Through dramatic play the child's ideas and experiences are organized and clarified. The teacher works with each small group or individual child to see that the child's play experience is a happy one, and that the maximum benefit is derived from facilities provided. The provision of facilities for play and the arrangement of these facilities is of first importance. The ideal is to provide such a rich environment that boys and girls find a place to play, equipment suitable for play, and an atmosphere conducive to play. Both the indoor play space, including the classroom, and the outdoor play space should be arranged with centers of activity to provide for each child an opportunity for interesting play. Apparatus suited to the age of the child should be placed for most effective and safe use. The centers of interest may be varied daily by changing the type of equipment, adding to it, providing instruments for musical accompaniment, and allowing either more vigorous or more quiet activity according to the interest manifested by the children.

Guided play involves instruction, which may be given individually or in small groups. For example, guidance would be given to help a child in finding a firm grip on the climbing apparatus, using the sand toys properly, lifting the building blocks with the proper muscular co-ordination, and learning the appropriate patterns for simple rhythms and singing games.

Play activities should not be confined to the physical education instruction period. They should bear a significant relationship to the rest of the school experience. Dramatic play, guided play, and rhythmical activities in particular have many elements in common with social studies, music, and other parts of the school program and are most valuable when they are allowed to follow in natural sequence from the rest of the curriculum.

GAMES OF SIMPLE ORGANIZATION AND RELAYS

Organized games are a normal, natural outgrowth of guided play and dramatic play. In the simple games, as in dramatic play, small groups work together with very few, if any, rules other than one of sharing and getting along together. The games first played in the primary grades are those with little organization and simple rules, such as ball games, running games, and tag games. The object of the games is usually to chase someone who is "it" or to chase a group. Generally all the players are in one group, and children play as individuals with no team loyalty. These simply organized games may be adapted to suit the space or equipment available or to include groups of any size. Since they are easily understood and are enjoyed by all age groups, games with a low degree of organization are not confined to the early grades but continue in use through all grades and even in recreational programs for young people and adults. Many of the traditional party games such as Blind Man's Buff and Musical Chairs are of this type.

Intermediate age boys and girls are interested in being members of a group or a team. They enjoy games that have the team element if the techniques and rules are not too complex. It is necessary to provide for eight- and nine-year-old children the type of game that allows both individual and team play, such as Dodge Ball and Stealing Sticks. Besides involving the basic motor skills of running, dodging, stopping, and turning, the simple team games develop some of the skills of ball handling that are used in the more complicated team and dual sports. Because many of the elements of the highly organized games are learned in the simple team games, the latter are sometimes referred to as lead-up games. However, they are primarily valuable to the intermediate pupils because they offer an interesting and challenging activity suited to the physical and mental maturity of the players, not because they develop complex skills for use at some later time. Pupils in grades 4, 5, and 6 should play a greater percentage of simple team games than tag games. These games should involve a wide variety of skills.

Relays, in which pupils participate as members of teams, satisfy the early interest in being part of a team. Relay formations are often used to teach a particular type of throwing, catching, kicking, or handling various kinds of equipment. They also provide a game that is suited to a small area and still offers activity for many people at one time. Relay formations may be used for either vigorous or quiet activities.

INDIVIDUAL AND DUAL GAMES

Each boy and girl should have opportunity to engage in a variety of individual and dual games in addition to organized team games. These are games in which from one to four players participate, such as tennis and handball. Some of these are very simple, while others involve highly complex skills and techniques. Games of this type particularly suitable for physical education at the elementary level are deck tennis, handball, bowling, horseshoes, volleyball doubles, badminton, hand tennis, paddle tennis, quoits, tether ball, tennis, aerial dart tennis, shuffleboard, and croquet. Some children find greater satisfaction in playing these games than in participating in team games involving larger groups. Small schools that do not have enough pupils to play the organized team games will find the individual and dual games of especial usefulness.

Figure 58.   Table tennis can be played outdoors or indoors, in a hallway, an extra room, a playroom, or a classroom.

Individual and dual games have great recreational value; once they are mastered they offer to children and adults lifetime enjoyment. Most of them call for equipment which can be easily transported. Places to play many of them are found throughout the civilized world. The number of players required for a game is so small that the game may be played almost anywhere and at any time. Many of them have standard rules, officially adopted by athletic associations, and their techniques are uniform throughout the country or the world. Individual and dual games further the social development of the individual, as well as offering excellent opportunities for developing motor skills. The sense of social adequacy that comes from being able to play some of the common games well contributes much to an individual's emotional growth. All elementary schools should prepare pupils for successful participation in several of the standard individual and dual games.

An Old Game—Hopscotch

Many individual and dual games are very old. An excellent example of this type of game is hopscotch. It is enjoyable when played with a few companions or when played alone. It has no age limit. It is played in the country or on city sidewalks. It is traditionally a children's game, but adults often find it good activity on shipboard. It requires limited space and no equipment more complex than a pebble. A description of the game as played over a century ago has survived:

Among the school boys in my memory there was a pastime called Hop-Scotch, which was played in this manner: A parallelogram about four to five feet wide and ten to twelve feet in length, was made upon the ground and divided laterally into eighteen or twenty different compartments which

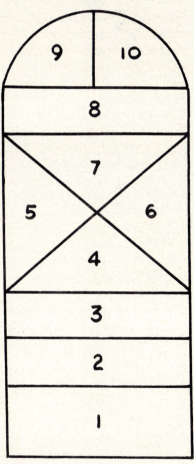

Figure 59. Diagram shows how to mark an area for hopscotch.

were called beds, some of them being larger than others. The players were each of them provided with a piece of tile, or any other flat material of the like kind, which they cast by the hand into the different beds in regular succession, and every time the tile was cast, the player's business was to hop upon one leg after it, and drive it out of the boundaries at the end where he stood to throw it; for, if it passed out at the sides or rested upon any one of the marks, it was necessary for the cast to be repeated. The boy who performed the whole of this operation by the fewest casts of the tile was the conqueror.[1]

INDIVIDUAL SPORTS

There are numerous active sports, such as swimming, riding horse-back, archery, or fishing, that an individual may engage in alone with no element of competition. Many of these sports are more enjoyable when several individuals participate, but even in groups competition is not an essential or important aspect of the activity. It is possible to stimulate interest in the mastery of techniques by measuring the player's skill against his own previous record or against another's record. These activities make a real contribution not only to the physical development of the individual but also to his emotional growth, since they give the participant a feeling of satisfaction in achievement. Some activities ordinarily thought of as games become individual sports when played alone; in this class are golf, shuffleboard, and bowling. Physical education can contribute to the ability of the individual to enjoy a healthy leisure time activity by teaching the skills of these individual sports. Many of them, of course, do not lend themselves readily to instruction during a class period, but others offer worthwhile material for physical education.

Swimming

Swimming is an individual sport that should be taught in the elementary school. The acquisition of swimming skills is vital, not only because the ability to swim often saves lives, but also because swimming is one of the best all-round physical development activities. It can be enjoyed as a recreational activity by persons of all ages and even by many physically handicapped individuals. Efforts should be made on the part of all school districts to include swimming in the physical education program. Unfortunately, too few elementary school plants have swimming facilities. If it is possible to do so, arrangements should be made to use pools in high schools or city or county parks. Even private pools may be utilized for instruction purposes. When new schools are in the planning stage, consideration should be given to the available facilities, or joint planning should provide for facilities in co-operation with other legally authorized

[1] Joseph Strutt, *Sports and Pastimes of the People of England.* London: 1810 (second edition), p. 339.

Figure 60. Boys and girls learn to swim easily at the elementary school age.

bodies, such as a city council, a recreation district, or a board of county supervisors.

The elementary school swimming program should aim to overcome in each pupil fear of the water, which in some may be acute. It should develop in each child the ability to float and to swim a short distance. The swimming classes can be coeducational and should be coeducational throughout the elementary grades if the facilities are adequate.

TEAM GAMES AND SPORTS

Highly organized team games, played with official rules, are generally not introduced until the seventh grade, although the skills and techniques involved in these games are taught earlier in the form of simple games and individual athletic events. Seventh- and eighth-grade boys and girls are interested in activities comparable to those engaged in by older adolescents and adults and at this age they enjoy team sports with official rules. The rules may need to be adapted to the maturity of the children, the

CLASSIFICATION OF GAMES BY TYPE IN RELATION TO THE MORE HIGHLY ORGANIZED GAMES TO WHICH THEY LEAD

GRADE	BASEBALL OR SOFTBALL	BASKETBALL	VOLLEYBALL	TENNIS OR BADMINTON	FOOTBALL OR SOCCER
3	Bases on Balls Bat Ball Boundary Ball Danish Rounders Kick Ball Kick the Wicket Sky High Ball Two Base Kick	Ball Passing Dodge Ball Keep Away			Bases on Balls Hand Polo Kick Ball Two Base Kick
4	Long Ball Throw Around	End Ball		Battledore and Shuttlecock	End Zone Soccer
5	Basket Softball Hit Pin Baseball Hit or Out SOFTBALL Work-Up	Captain Ball Circle Pole Ball Deck Floor Hockey End Goal Ball Free-Throw End Ball Pin Basketball	Net Ball	Badminton Games for the Schoolroom Paddle Badminton Paddle Ball	Circle Kick Ball Deck Floor Hockey Three-Section Soccer
6	Bowl Ball Circle Strike Glendale Ball Indian Ball Two Old Cat Whoopla Ball	Center Square Ball Goal-Hi Basketball Goal-Hi—Three Segments In-and-Out Basketball Net Basketball Nine-Court Basketball Three-Man Basketball	High Ball	Hand Tennis Nip Nop Paddle Tennis Swing Swat	Alley Soccer Kick Football Punt Back Soccer Kick Ball

7	Foot Baseball	BASKETBALL FOR BOYS BASKETBALL FOR GIRLS Frame Basketball Half-Court Basketball Knock-Out Freeze-Out Basketball Side-Line Basketball	Sponge Ball VOLLEYBALL Volleyball Doubles Volleyball for the Schoolroom Volleyball Modified	Sponge Ball Table Tennis	FLAG FOOTBALL Foot Baseball Football Lead-up Games Six-Man Soccer SOCCER FOR BOYS SOCCER FOR GIRLS TOUCH FOOTBALL
8	Sock-a-Ball	Basket Speed Ball	Volley Tennis	BADMINTON Backboard Tennis Deck Tennis Eight-Man Tennis Five-Man Badminton Mass Deck Tennis Six-Man Tennis TENNIS	Attack Base Soccer Bust the Leather Gymnasium Soccer Soccer Ball Tag

size of the group, or the available play areas and equipment. When such changes in official rules are made, the children should know what the changes are and why they are made. The rules, as modified, should be uniform throughout the school or school district. Softball may be introduced in the fifth or sixth grade, but the other sports, including basketball, soccer, speed ball, touch football, and volleyball, are more suitable for seventh- and eighth-grade pupils. At this period, too, the interests of boys and girls differ, and for that reason the sexes are separated for many of the games and athletics. Body contact team games should not be used in coeducational groups.

Team games and sports depend for their success on the united effort of several players to compete against a like group of opponents. Such games offer innumerable opportunities for the child to submerge his individual desires to the best interests of the group. When the child has reached the stage in his development when he is ready to play as a member of a team instead of as an individual, these team sports contribute to his social growth. Each child should have the experience of being a member of a team, and, as a team member, to work out the best method of playing the game.

Because most team games are very vigorous, they have profound influence on the functioning of the body. The use of the big skeletal muscles stimulates the body processes. It must be remembered, however, that the games chosen must be suited to the needs of the individual child. During the preadolescent and early adolescent years each pupil goes through a period of accelerated growth. Growth in different portions of the body does not go on at the same rate. Bones may grow out of proportion to muscular strength. The veins, arteries, and heart grow at a different rate. Because of these inharmonies in the growing process, long continued running, highly competitive games that are physically and emotionally exhausting, and feats of endurance requiring great muscular effort may cause great damage. Team games and sports are a vital part of the program, but great harm can be done when the needs of bodily growth and development are overshadowed by adult enthusiasm for personal prestige or for the achievement of so-called school glory.

Highly technical games are not desirable for intermediate grade children. One finds the tendency in too many school systems to push down into the lower levels of the school games that belong in the upper elementary grades or in high school. Younger boys and girls are thus forced to attempt games much too advanced for their physical abilities while they are denied opportunity to participate in games suitable to their age requirements. Less technical team games can develop the skills needed for mastering highly technical games so satisfying to older children and adults. These lead-up games involve skills of the standard games but are simple in organization and in procedure. The table on pages 154-55, classifying the simple games in relation to the more highly organized games to which they lead, indicates the grade level at which the activities ought to be introduced. Schools with but one teacher will undoubtedly be obliged to use pupils from other grades to make up teams, but the games should be modified accordingly. It should be kept in mind that these games must be satisfying in themselves. They should not be regarded as mere exercises to train pupils in skills of future value.

Classification of Children for Fairness in Competition

It is usually desirable for instructional purposes that children of similar stages of development and like abilities be grouped together for physical activities. Through the primary and intermediate grades the division into class units supplies for all practical purposes the only classification needed. In the upper grades children of the same grade and even the same age show greater differences in their physical maturity. At this time, when team games are being introduced, it is essential that children of similar development and abilities be grouped together for fairness in competition, as well as for instructional purposes. In order that team games may be played by participants of like physical maturity, pupils should be classified and playing schedules for team games and sports separately arranged for children in each class. In some schools the teacher may wish to set up a schedule in which all of the teams in a particular grade are of equal ability and strength. In this way each team has the same proportion of each class, instead of each team representing only one class.

A system of classification very widely used is the three-point classification worked out by the Oakland Public Schools.[1] This uses a combination of the three factors of age, height, and weight as the basis for classifying the children according to physical maturity. Numerical exponents are assigned to measures of height, age, and weight. The sum of the exponents for these three factors determines the class into which the particular pupil falls. There are eight classes, indicated by letters of the alphabet, ranging from A for the least mature, physically, to H for the most mature. In order to classify the pupils, the teacher must know each child's height in inches, his age in years and months, and his weight in

[1] A complete description of this method is given in the book by N. P. Neilson and Frederick W. Cozens, *Achievement Scales in Physical Education Activities for Boys and Girls in Elementary and Junior High Schools*. Sacramento: California State Department of Education, 1943, pp. 3-9.

CHART FOR CLASSIFYING BOYS AND GIRLS ACCORDING TO PHYSICAL MATURITY *

EXPONENT	HEIGHT IN INCHES	AGE IN YEARS AND MONTHS	WEIGHT IN POUNDS	SUM OF EXPONENTS	CLASS
1	50 to 51	10 to 10-5	60 to 65	9 and below	A
2	52 to 53	10-6 to 10-11	66 to 70	10 to 14	B
3		11 to 11-5	71 to 75	15 to 19	C
4	54 to 55	11-6 to 11-11	76 to 80	20 to 24	D
5		12 to 12-5	81 to 85	25 to 29	E
6	56 to 57	12-6 to 12-11	86 to 90	30 to 34	F
7		13 to 13-5	91 to 95	35 to 38	G
8	58 to 59	13-6 to 13-11	96 to 100	39 and above	H
9		14 to 14-5	101 to 105		
10	60 to 61	14-6 to 14-11	106 to 110		
11		15 to 15-5	111 to 115		
12	62 to 63	15-6 to 15-11	116 to 120		
13		16 to 16-5	121 to 125		
14	64 to 65	16-6 to 16-11	126 to 130		
15	66 to 67	17 to 17-5	131 to 133		
16	68	17-6 to 17-11	134 to 136		
17	69 and over	18 and over	137 and over		

* Neilson and Cozens, *op. cit.*, p. 6. Used by permission of Oakland Public Schools, developers of the chart.

pounds. For each factor a chart is consulted to find the exponent. The three exponents are added and the chart is consulted to find the child's classification letter.

The following example illustrates the procedure:

Child's height—57 inches .... exponent 6
Child's age—13 years and 2 months .... exponent 7
Child's weight—102 pounds .... exponent 9

Sum of exponents 22

Child is thus in Class D.

Scoring Team Games [1]

Boys and girls are interested in their achievement in games. Techniques for recording scores and determining averages for teams and individuals are important teaching aids. Official scoring techniques need not

---

[1] Material for this section was supplied by Harold Schoenfeld, Supervisor of Physical Education, Alameda County.

be used, but some simple means of showing improvement, a plateau, or even slumps in performance give children an opportunity to check strength and weakness of players as well as giving them a better understanding of the game.

Examples of a basketball scoring sheet and one for softball are shown here. The softball score sheet is devised for use by elementary schools and may be adapted for scoring any softball type game. A more complicated form of scoring may be used. Samples of such sheets and explanations are found in the official softball guides.[1]

BASKETBALL SCORING SHEET

NAME	FIELD GOAL	FREE THROW	FOULS	TOTAL POINTS
Jones, W	GG 0000	GO	P	5
Smith, B	00G		P₁ P₂	2
Petes, W				

G = Goal Made   O = Goal Missed P_1 = First Penalty P_2 = Second Penalty
Field Goal counts 2 points, Free Throw counts 1 point
NOTE: Jones made two field goals out of six tries and one free-throw out of two tries. He committed one foul. Smith made one goal out of three trials. He committed two fouls.

Batting Averages

Batting averages are computed by dividing the number of hits by the number of times at bat. A walk is not counted as a time at bat. If Jones came to bat six times and was given one walk and made three hits and two outs, we call him "at bat" five times and compute his batting average by the following formula:

$$\frac{3 \text{ (number of hits)}}{5 \text{ (number of times at bat)}} = .600$$

Pupils may be interested in referring to the sports section of the local newspaper for batting averages of players and team standings in the Pacific Coast League, National League, and American League.

INDIVIDUAL SKILL EVENTS

Team games involve skills that can be learned and practiced as worthwhile individual events. Basketball involves the activities of jumping for height, ball throwing for distance, and ball throwing for accuracy. Softball and baseball depend on the ability of players to throw a ball long

[1] *Official Softball-Track and Field Guide.* Washington, D. C.: American Association for Health, Physical Education and Recreation. *Official Softball Guide.* Leonia, N. J.: W. W. Wells Co.

SOFTBALL SCORING SHEET

Team _Greens_

Batting Order	Pos.	1	2	3	4	5	6	7	8	9	10
M. Jones	5	◆ —			② F9						
T. Hardy	4	① 5-3	◆ uu	③ K	⟩ ≡						
G. Smith	9	② F8		⟩ ≡ /w	⟩ /w						
H. Brown	7	⟩ ≡		⟩ w	③ 1-3 /						
D. Chase	3	③ K		① 5-3							
P. Black	7		◆ w	② F6							
N. Goodin	8		◆ ≡	③ K							
B. White	1		① 6-3		① K						
C. Miels	6		② F7		◆ E6						
Total		1	3	0	1						

① = first out
② = second out
③ = third out
— = one-base hit

= = two-base hit
≡ = three-base hit
"" = home run
F = fly caught

/ = player left on first
⟩ = player left on second
⟩ = player left on third
◆ = run

E = error
W = walk
K = strike out
▨ heavy diagonal mark indicates end of inning

NOTES. Players are numbered according to the following scheme: 1–Pitcher; 2–Catcher; 3–First Baseman; 4–Second Baseman; 5–Third Baseman; 6–Shortstop; 7–Left Fielder; 8–Center Fielder; 9–Right Fielder.

The scoresheet has been filled out for one team at bat for four innings. The position number of each player is recorded after his name.

The plays were as follows:

First inning. Jones hit a one-base hit. Hardy made the first out when the third baseman fielded the ball and threw it to the first baseman for an out. The second out was made by Smith when the center fielder caught his fly. Brown hit the ball for a two-base hit, bringing Jones home. The inning ended when Chase struck out. One run was made in the first inning.

Second inning. Black walked to first base. Goodin made a two-base hit, advancing Black to third base. The first out was made by White when the shortstop fielded the ball and threw it to the first baseman. The left fielder caught Mills's fly for the second out. Jones hit a home run to score Black and Goodin. The team was retired when Hardy struck out. The team scored three runs in the second inning.

Third inning. A two-base hit was made by Smith. Brown walked. Chase made the first out when the third baseman fielded the ball and threw it to first base. Smith advanced to third and Brown to second as the play was made. Second out was made by Black when the shortstop caught a fly. Goodin was struck out for the third out.

Fourth inning. A strike-out was made by White for the first out. Mills got to first base because of an error by the shortstop. Jones made the second out when the right fielder caught his fly. Hardy made a three-base hit, bringing Mills in for a run. Smith was walked. The side was retired as Brown made the third out when the pitcher fielded the ball and threw the runner out at first base.

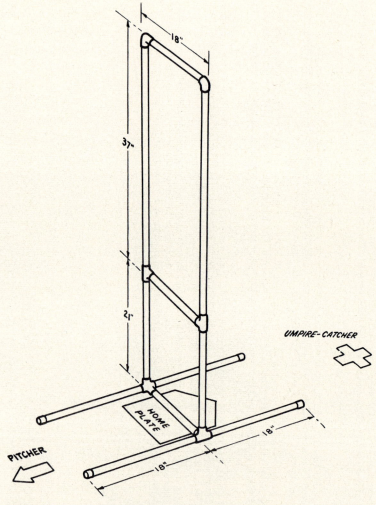

Figure 61. A pitching frame provides an accurate means for the player to check his pitching. It may be made of pipe.

distances and the ability to make short fast throws to bases or to home plate as well as ability in batting and running. Some of the elements in softball that require practice are pitching balls over a definite area (width of home plate and between knees and shoulder of the batter); batting; catching fly balls; jumping for balls; catching a rolling or bouncing ball; and running bases rapidly. Practice periods for the improvement of skills are needed for the different elements of the game.

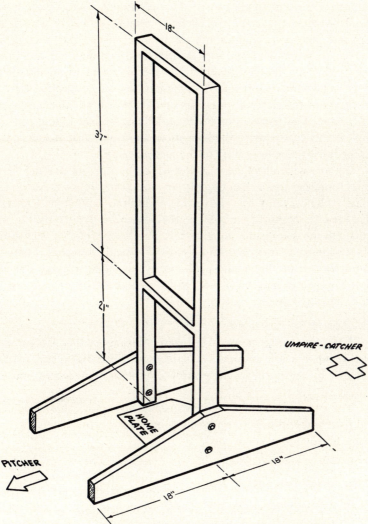

Figure 62.   A pitching frame may also be made of wood.

The performance of individuals in these skills can be measured. Measurements provide a basis for competition of an individual against his own achievement, competition between individuals, and competition between groups of individuals. Individual skill events may be used in an evaluation program, in a playday, or in a track and field meet.

An average of at least one instructional period per week for boys and girls in the upper grades should be devoted to individual athletic events or stunts, with opportunity provided for additional practice periods before school, at recess, the latter part of the noon hour, and after school. Good form and correct techniques, not the winning of contests, should be the concern of pupils and teachers during such instructional and practice periods. Usually individual athletic events are used as an instructional device to provide opportunity for children to perfect specific skills.

Study of the elements of games should precede the opening of a season for specified games. For instance, kicking and dribbling relays and simple games that provide the formations and teamwork of soccer should be scheduled at the beginning of the soccer season.

Schools with enrollments too small to permit the playing of team games requiring more than five players on a team should substitute individual athletic events for team games. Children who have a chance to learn these skills should enter high school with far greater ability to participate in the team games taught there than they would if they had had no opportunity to learn any of the skills of a regulation game. Many small schools overcome the handicap of size by providing playdays at which regulation games may be played with teams made up of children from more than one school.

Activities to Be Practiced

The activities that are listed here, if practiced consistently, will develop fundamental strength and special skills essential in successful performance on apparatus, in the playing of athletic team games, and in the mastery of stunts.

The events listed under "Fundamental Strengths" should seldom be used for competition between groups, but each performer may compete against his own previous record.

Fundamental Strengths [1]

Half Lever and Toes to Bar
Leg Lifts
Pull-up *
Push-up *
Sit-up

Softball

Softball Batting for Accuracy
Softball Fly Catching
Base Running *

Softball Throw for Accuracy *
Softball Throw and Catch
Jump and Reach *
Mass Running

Basketball

Basketball Free Throw
Basketball One Hand Shot
Basketball Pass for Accuracy
Basketball Throw for Distance *
Basketball Throw for Goal *
Run and Catch

---

[1] Starred items are described in N. P. Neilson and Frederick W. Cozens, *op. cit.*

Hand Traveling Events

Double Jumping on Both Rails
Double Jumping on Rungs
Hand over Hand on Both Rails
Hand over Hand on Rungs
Walking Sideward on Rail
Ring Travel
Rope Climb

Soccer and Speed Ball

Soccer Corner Kick for
  Accuracy
Soccer Dribble *
Soccer Dribble and Kick for
  Goal
Soccer Heading for Distance
Soccer Kick for Distance *
Soccer Kick for Goal

Soccer Punt for Distance
Soccer Throw-in for Distance *

Track and Field Events

Potato Race *
Runs *
Running High Jump *
Standing Broad Jump *
Standing High Jump

Elements of Other Games

Horseshoe Pitch
Tennis Serve for Accuracy
Volleyball Serve for Accuracy
Badminton Serve for Accuracy
Paddle Tennis Serve for
  Accuracy
Table Tennis Serve for
  Accuracy

Organization for Systematic Practice of Athletic Events

From eight to twelve individual athletic events can be practiced during the school year, out of which pupils may choose about half a dozen for determining their final rating. The events might be soccer dribble for speed, number of baskets thrown per minute, 50-yard dash, pull-up, push-up, jump and reach, base running, volleyball serve, softball throw for distance, standing broad jump. To show progress made, it is essential that pupils be tested twice on each event—once when the event is introduced and again at the conclusion of the season.

Squad Organization for Practice Periods. Children in the upper grades should be grouped in squads for practice of individual athletic events. Squad memberships should not exceed six pupils to a squad. The assignments should produce groups as homogeneous as possible in terms of age, height, and weight. Since some of the events are more challenging for and interesting to boys than girls, separate boy and girl squads may be organized, with the girls practicing a slightly different group of events than the boys.

After squads have been selected, the following procedure will provide smooth operation during the practice period:

1. Each squad should elect a leader.

2. Each squad leader should be responsible for (a) taking out the equipment or supplies needed for his squad to begin work, and (b) for returning to the storage room or classroom the supplies and equipment last used by his squad.

3. Each squad leader, on signal, should move his squad, under control and on the run, to the practice area.

4. Each squad leader should keep members of his squad actively occupied during practice periods.

Chart for Assignment of Squads. In order to distribute squad assignments with a minimum of confusion, the chart presented here will prove helpful.[1] It has been constructed with the following principles in mind:

1. In a 20- to 30-minute instructional period, there should be three 5- to 8-minute activity sessions, with each squad working on three different events during the period.

2. Squad activities should be so distributed that there will be no overlapping in the use of equipment and supplies.

3. The combination of events for squad assignments during an instruction or practice period should include some running, some throwing, and some jumping, provided available equipment and supplies permit such a distribution.

4. During a lesson period members of a squad should have events of different types so that individuals do not spend the entire period practicing events that exercise the same set of muscles.

5. In practicing athletic events there should be a regular progression from one event to another each day, and there should also be some repetition of events.

The events listed in the outer circle of the chart are for boys' squads; those in the center circle are for girls'. The number in parentheses following the name of the event refers to the number assigned to that event in *Achievement Scales in Physical Education Activities.*[2]

Superimposed on the center circle of the chart is a separate disk divided into sectors as is the larger chart, each sector being numbered for one of the squads. This disk is attached to the large chart at the center with a round-head fastener, so that it can be rotated. At the beginning of the practice or instruction period the teacher turns the disk so that the sector numbered 1 is opposite the sector listing the three events to be practiced by Squad 1. Squad 2 will then practice the events opposite the

---

[1] Chart developed by Arthur J. Schuettner, a member of the physical education staff of Los Angeles City College. Reproduced from *Physical Education in Small Rural Schools.* State of California Department of Education Bulletin No. 2 (April 15, 1938). Sacramento: California State Department of Education, 1938.

[2] N. P. Neilson and Frederick W. Cozens, *op. cit.*

number 2, and so on. On the next practice period the number 1 can be turned to the next sector, and so on for the number of days to be devoted to these events.

Each squad leader notes what activities his group is to undertake and decides what equipment and supplies will be needed for the first event. He secures the equipment while the members of his squad report immediately to the area where work is to begin. At the end of the first and second practice periods materials remain where they are and squad leaders and members move on. At the end of the third period the leader of the squad last using the materials returns them to classroom, equipment box, or equipment closet.

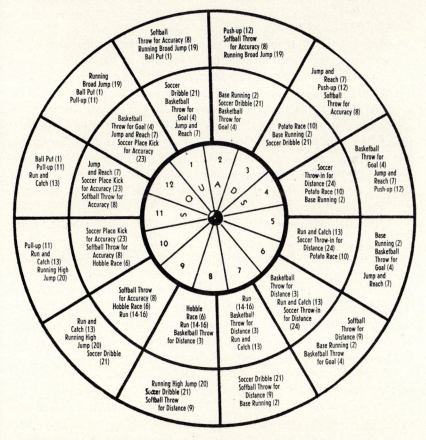

Figure 63. A chart with a movable center disk will aid in assigning squads to systematic practice of athletic events.

TRACK AND FIELD EVENTS

The track and field events usually taught in elementary schools are the standing and running broad jumps, the standing and running high jumps, and combination jumps such as the standing hop, step, and jump; sprints for very short distances; and relays. A quarter-mile track is desirable but not necessary for a good track and field program. Jumping pits should be provided, with approaches as needed.[1]

Certain track and field events have been eliminated from the physical education program of the elementary schools of California because their value has not been considered commensurate with the danger involved. Among events eliminated are the long distance runs and relays; the longer sprints; pole vaulting; the javelin throw; and weight events.

Broad Jump

Both the standing and the running broad jump are included in the elementary school physical education program. In the standing broad jump the take-off is from a standing position from behind the take-off board and the jumper attempts to jump as far forward as possible into the jumping pit. In the running broad jump the jumper approaches the take-off board at a run from some distance away, takes off from behind the scratch line, and jumps as far forward into the pit as he can. The scratch line is the edge of the take-off board nearest the pit. Each jumper is permitted four trial jumps, with the longest jump recorded as the record of the jumper. Running past the take-off or scratch line counts as a trial. Each foul counts as one trial jump.

The measurement is taken from the take-off line to the nearest point on the ground touched by the body or clothing of the jumper. Two officials are necessary for measuring jumps. One, with peg or pencil, marks the point at which the jumper's body or clothing touched the pit or the ground outside the pit. The zero end of the tape measure is slipped over the peg while the tape is stretched at a right angle to the front edge of the take-off board or extension of that line. The person holding that portion of the tape calls off the distance for the convenience of the recorder. The official nearest the take-off board also watches for fouls.

After each measurement the soil in the pit should be smoothed over with a pusher or other instrument. A rake is not recommended.

Technique for Standing Broad Jump. The performer stands almost toeing the scratch line with feet flat on the surface and fairly close together. To assist in lifting the body the arms are brought forward and

---

[1] For a description of the jumping pits, see pages 97-98.

then swung down and back. At the same time the jumper crouches with body bent forward but with hips directly over the feet. The jump is taken from both feet as the arms are swung forcibly forward and upward. To take off on only one foot is a foul.

The performer should strive for height. While the body is in the air, the knees are brought forward and upward toward the chin. Both the drive of the arms from high rear to the front-upward position and the spring from the take-off board should be performed with all the power and drive the jumper can command.

At no time before the jump is made may the toes overreach the front edge of the take-off board and make an imprint on the surface directly in front of the board. To do so counts as a trial jump.

The arms should be about shoulder height as the landing is made, the jumper trying to reach with them as far forward as possible. The landing should be made on both feet with the body still in a forward crouch position. Falling backward or sideward should be avoided. Performer should walk forward out of the pit.

Technique for Running Broad Jump. In the running broad jump, a preliminary run is taken to gain momentum for the jump. Practice will determine the distance to be run in each case, since runners' strides differ. Short runs are sufficient. A jumper should so plan his strides that the toes of the jumping foot, when touching the take-off board, will not make an imprint on the ground surface in front of the board. The take-off should not be far behind the scratch line, since the measurement is from the line. To prevent such errors each runner should learn to establish check marks to aid him during his performance. During the run the runner's jumping foot should touch the ground directly opposite these marks. Stones, lines, or handkerchiefs may be used to indicate spots. The run begins with short strides. The last strides are taken at top speed with the jumping foot touching the take-off board just behind the front edge. During practice, should the jumping foot overshoot the take-off board, the check marks are adjusted. Practice should be continued until correct positions are determined. The run should be practiced until it becomes automatic for the jumping foot to hit opposite each check mark.

A performer, without losing his running stride and without decreasing his speed, must take off with one foot. Body weight should be directly over the jumping foot. The take-off is from the entire foot, with knee bent to a maximum degree but without permitting loss of driving force by the entire leg. The toes impart the final push. The bend and spring of the leg is one continuous motion. The free leg is kicked forward and up at the same time the jump is taken. Simultaneously with the spring, the arms are thrown forcibly above the head. The head should be down and not back and the abdomen in and not out.

The performer must strive for height. Both knees are brought high in front of the body and, as the body approaches the ground, feet and arms are shot as far forward as possible without losing balance in landing. Some performers, to gain height, use a hitch kick near the mid-point of the jump; that is, the jumping leg is forced forward and the free leg is forced back, with both legs thrown out in front for the landing.

The landing is made in a forward direction, never sideward or backward. The performer, when leaving the pit, must walk forward. He should never turn around and walk out toward the take-off board, since the nearest mark to the scratch line is taken as the measurement of his jumping distance.

TEACHING SUGGESTIONS

1. Have participants run and use stretching exercises for a warm-up before attempting jumps.
2. At the beginning of the season, do not have pupils attempt full exertion for maximum results more often than once a week.
3. Have feet and inches marked on the side wall of pits as an aid in stimulating interest in jumping distances.
4. Standing opposite the take-off board, call "Up," as the performer takes off. This will help to get a performer higher into the air.
5. Place emphasis on the upward spring with the assistance of the arms.
6. Impress on jumpers that they should bend the knees and lower the head when landing.
7. See that the surface of pits is kept loose and the contents well distributed and that the sides of the pit are visible at all times. See that pit leveller is not allowed to remain in the pit after use.
8. During a meet, warn performers to examine the runway and set their own check marks before the event is called.
9. See that a performer keeps warm between jumps and loosens his leg muscles before each jump.
10. Have the performers spend much time in perfecting the approach for the running broad jump.

High Jump

Both the standing and the running high jump are included in the elementary school physical education program. In both types of jump the performer strives to jump as high as possible over a bar. The bar is moved up after each successful jump and the highest level at which the jumper is able to clear the bar is his record. A fair jump is one in which the jump is made from one foot. Three trial jumps are permitted at each height. During competition the jumping should not be started at too low a level. Jumpers should warm up well before competition begins.

Contestants jump in sequence as their names are called. After all have jumped those who failed (if any) take their second jump at the same height in the same order. Those who fail twice (if any) have their third trial in the same sequence. If anyone fails on the third trial he is eliminated from further competition. Displacing the bar, passing under it, crossing the line of the bar extended, or leaving the ground in an attempt count as trial jumps. The distance is measured from the top edge of the crossbar at its center to the hard ground surface directly below the crossbar (not within the pit).

Technique for Standing High Jump.   In a standing high jump, the jumper stands sideways to the crossbar and uses the foot farthest from the bar for the jump or take-off. The inside leg, next to the bar, is thrown forward, up, and over, with maximum effort, after the foot taking the jump has left the ground. The jumping foot trails the inside leg. Arms should assist during the jump. As the jumper improves in body control, he may, after the take-off, throw his head back to raise the buttocks in clearing the bar, and can either roll away from the bar or cut back to face the bar, depending on which form is easier. This basic jump is called the scissors jump and is the one most used by elementary school boys. The dive jump (head first) is not permitted.

Technique for Running High Jump.   The take-off for the running high jump is generally the same as for the standing high jump. Height is gained by using a running approach. Not more than 20 to 30 feet should be used for the approach, which may be from the right or left side according to the preference of the performer. Most performers prefer to make the jump from the outside leg (farthest from the bar), which should be the stronger leg.

TEACHING SUGGESTIONS

1. Have participants warm up well before attempting jumps.
2. During practice periods keep the bar below maximum heights that might be attained during competition, in order to stress form in jumping.
3. At the beginning of the season, do not have pupils attempt full exertion more often than once a week.
4. Use adhesive tape tabs, with feet and inches marked, at 2-inch intervals on a jumping standard, to help the jumper to see his mark.

5. See that the surface of the pit is kept loosened and that the shavings or other contents do not obscure the sides of the pit. Do not allow the pit leveler to be left in the pit.

6. Impress on high jumpers that they should straighten their knees as they reach the highest point of the jump.

7. See that a performer keeps warm between jumps and loosens his leg muscles before each jump.

Sprints

A sprint or dash is a run at top speed for a given distance. The sprints for older elementary school boys and girls should be not more than 75 yards in length and for younger children not more than 25, 35, and 50 yards, according to age and size. During sprints, runners tax themselves to the utmost for speed. A warm-up period should precede the practice of sprints, and maximum exertion should not occur too frequently.

Technique for Starting.   Much time should be spent on mastering the technique of the start or getaway, as this is one of the most important elements in sprinting.

Three directions are used in starting the races

1. "Get on Your Mark!"   Runners kneel on one knee behind the starting line, usually with the foot of the stronger leg to the rear. At the same time they place their hands on the ground behind the starting line. At no time may foot or hands touch or reach beyond the starting line until the signal to go is given. The distance of the front foot from the starting line varies with the size of participants but generally the distances used range from 4 to 7 inches. To determine the correct position for the rear foot, runners place the knee of the rear foot opposite the instep of the front foot. Older runners, once the position of this foot is determined, and in order to gain more pushing power, may dig holes for toes of both feet. To determine the best spots the ankles are flexed and where the toes touch depressions are made. The rear wall of the holes should form a right angle to the ground surface. These holes should be filled in after use if they are on the track.

2. "Get Set!"   Runners raise the knee of the rear leg and throw body weight forward over front leg, arms, and hands. The arms are straight, with wrists and elbows locked, thereby providing a stronger and steadier base. Hands are outside the knees, yet in line with the shoulders. The thumbs and first two fingers, or all the fingers, used in a tripod position, carry a large proportion of the body weight and assist in the maintenance of body balance. Backs are flattened, with head and hips on the same level. The chin is raised, with eyes focused on the ground some 20 yards distant.

3. "Go!"   On receiving this signal or at sound of a whistle or pistol shot, runners spring forward. The rear foot should give an extra strong push. Some performers during short sprints hold the breath throughout the sprint, since to relax the abdominal muscles interferes with the power of the leg action.

Finish Line.   Runners, as they approach the finish line, should put forth their greatest effort. They should not slow down but should run at top speed over the finish line. This means that they continue running at least 10 or 15 feet beyond the finish line before stopping. Runners place in the race in the order in which their bodies (not head, arms, hands, or feet) cross the finish line.

Technique for Running.   Runners, at the beginning of the sprint, should not straighten up immediately; to do so retards progress. The straightening process should occur gradually, with each runner reaching the erect position (or nearly so) some 12 or 15 yards distant from the starting point. The first strides should be short ones until the erect position is reached. Throughout the run, the body should be in a slightly forward position.

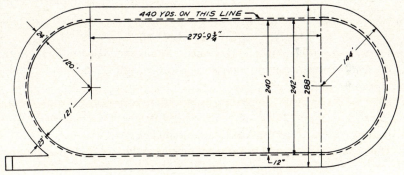

Figure 64.   A quarter mile track is shown in this diagram.

A natural stride should be used, with the balls of the feet taking the weight. Runners, as they advance, should not weave to the right and left. The legs must not be allowed to produce a criss-cross action to right and left in the rear of the body. The movement of legs and feet should be that of a hinge, directly forward and back. The arms co-ordinate with the opposite legs. Shoulders should be held in a normal position. An exaggerated twisting of shoulders to right and left should not be allowed to develop. Arms should be carried high and should swing forward and back without side swing across the body. Knees should be brought well up in front. Toes should point straight forward, or turn in slightly, with knees facing directly forward. Pupils who toe out badly or run "duck-footed" should practice toeing in slightly for correction. Runners who persist in running "duck-footed" will find the strain on the feet rather severe.

Fouls. Failure to observe certain rules results in a penalty being imposed on the offender.

1. Contestants may not start before the "Go" signal is given. To do so ("jumping the gun") is a false start. All contestants are directed to stand up and the offender is warned not to repeat the offense. If the same person offends a second time, he is disqualified and cannot run. If, however, the starter gives the signal and then recalls the runners because of an unfair start, no penalty is inflicted.

2. No part of a contestant's hand or foot may be touching the starting line or the ground in front of the starting line. *Penalty:* Same as for "jumping the gun."

3. When lanes are used, a contestant may not run outside his assigned lane. *Penalty:* (a) the runner committing the foul is disqualified; (b) if the foul occurs during a final heat, the referee has power to order a new race between all whom he considers entitled to such privilege.

TEACHING SUGGESTIONS

1. Have class run in couples or in squads. Pupils should run slowly, with the knees carried well up in front and the weight of the body carried on the balls of the feet.

2. See that pupils' arms swing naturally without cross movements.

3. See that each pupil walks and runs with feet pointed straight ahead. If he does not, exercises for correction should be given.

4. Have pupils, when practicing running, regardless of position among other runners, try to keep up with the speed of the group, and not drop out of race.

5. Do not have pupils run full distance at top speed more than once a week. They should work on form, frequently practicing fast starts with only a short run for each.

6. Teach pupils that thighs, legs, and ankles should work in harmony, with a hinge movement. To toe out or swing the feet across the body, rear or front, breaks the natural hinge joint action that should be present.

7. Teach runners to use toes and ankles, never their heels.

8. Warn runners not to throw up hands and arms as they cross the official finish line, since this action retards speed.

9. See that contestants, after a race, walk about slowly until normal breathing is re-established.

Relay Racing

Relay races are valuable in that numerous runners participate and the performance of each is vital to the success of his team. For ordinary purposes not more than six runners should be used on a team; to include more means too much standing around while awaiting a turn. It would be a better arrangement to form more relay teams. During track meets, however, there are usually four runners to a team.

Any number of teams may compete. Trial runs must be used when, because of a narrow track, all teams cannot compete simultaneously. Contestants in the final race must be members of a team that ran in one of the trial heats. No exchange of runners can be made.

The total distance to be run is divided into four or more equal segments, with an exchange mark to designate the end of each segment. The length of each segment should not exceed that recommended for sprints used in elementary schools. Members of each team are assigned to a position at or opposite an exchange mark where they await the arrival of a teammate.

The starting runner of each team holds a baton. Paper mailing tubes or 12-inch lengths cut from bamboo may be used. The baton must be passed to the next member of his team within a 20-yard exchange zone. This zone is formed by lines drawn 10 yards on each side of the exchange marks. The baton must be passed hand to hand between runners. It may not be thrown. If the baton is dropped while being passed, either runner may pick it up. If it is dropped from a runner's hand while he is outside the exchange zone, the runner must retrieve it.

TEACHING SUGGESTIONS

1. See that runner carries baton in left hand in order to give it into the right hand of the next runner. When received it should be changed to the new runner's left hand.
2. Spend considerable time in teaching pupils to exchange the baton quickly.

PLANNING AND CONDUCTING TRACK AND FIELD MEETS

Much planning must be done in order to have a successful track and field meet. Failure to plan carefully may result in a day full of disappointments.

General Announcement of Meet

A letter or bulletin containing the following information about the proposed track meet should be sent to the schools that are to participate:

1. Place, time, and type of meet to be held
2. Different classes of students who are to take part
3. Any special rules decided upon; for example, that spiked shoes are not to be worn
4. Eligibility requirements for participation
5. Method of scoring to be used, such as 5, 3, 2, 1, if four places are to be recorded, or 5, 3, 1, with but three places recorded
6. The date upon which entry blanks must be returned
7. List of events, with space underneath each event for writing (a) the number of entries in a given event and number of substitutes allowed; (b) the number and type of event each individual may enter; (c) the names of contestants
8. A statement to be signed by the person vouching for the entrants, giving the name of the school and his official position in the school.

Entry Blanks. With the announcement, entry blanks should be sent to schools. A suggested entry blank follows.

ENTRY BLANK

MAYDAY TRACK AND FIELD MEET
MIDDLETOWN UNION SCHOOL

Southfork School, May 1, 1951, 2:00 to 5:00 P.M.

Please enter the following pupils from _____ School

In events listed below:

40 Yard Dash (Class A)   High Jump (Class A)

1_____   1_____

2_____   2_____

Sub_____   Sub_____

Running Broad Jump (Class A)   Relay (4 boys, 40 yards each) (Class A)

1_____   1_____

2_____   2_____

3_____   3_____

4_____   4_____

Sub_____   Sub_____

[Continue list of events for each class]

I certify that these pupils are in good standing in my school and eligible to compete.

                                    Name

                                 (Position)

Rules. The rules and regulations under which the meet is to be conducted should accompany the entry blanks sent to schools. Following is a suggested list of rules.

1. Each school may enter two pupils and a substitute for each event.
2. No pupil may be entered for more than two events; the relay counts as one event.
3. The three-point classification is to be used (age, height, weight).
4. Pupils are to be classified 2 weeks before the meet.
5. Entry blanks must be returned a week previous to the meet.
6. Four places are to be scored; the points allocated for each are first place, 5 points; second place, 3 points; third place, 2 points; fourth place, 1 point.
7. No spiked shoes will be allowed.
8. Track suits are not essential.

Meet Officials

Much will depend on the officials. They should be selected and their duties made clear to them before the day of the meet. Either by personal conference or by written instructions the rules governing his special events should be explained to each official.

A games committee should (1) select the officials; (2) make the plans for the meet; and (3) pass on eligibility. Elementary school meets should be conducted under rules similar to those in official track and field handbooks. The rules may be simplified as needed. Committee members should not interfere with the work of the appointed officials, the action of the latter being determined by the rules of their activity.

Referee. The referee is the head official. He decides all questions in regard to the management of the meet that are not definitely assigned to other officials.

Inspectors. Two or more inspectors stand at places assigned them by the referee and assist him. They may not make independent decisions.

Clerk of the Course. The clerk of the course and his assistants notify contestants to appear at the starting line for races. They have charge of drawing for lanes, heats, and so on, for all runs and relays.

Starter. The starter has complete control of the contestants at the starting mark. He starts all races by the report of a pistol or by use of a whistle after the preparatory commands, "Get on your mark," and "Get set," are given.

Judges. For dashes and relays there should be a head judge and at least one more finish judge than there are places. The head judge assigns the judges to places. In case of disagreement among the judges, the vote of the majority rules. Each judge stands opposite the finish line and, paying no attention to other runners, selects his man and secures his number or his name and the school represented by him. The judges make out a list of all the winners of each heat and the schools they represent and give the list to the clerk of the course. They make out the records in the finals on official blanks and present them to the chief scorer.

Judges for events other than runs personally measure distances or heights and report these on official blanks to the chief scorer.

Scorer.   The chief scorer records, from information sent him from all judges and other officials, the order in which competitors finish, together with the record or score made. There may be several assistant scorers to aid the chief scorer.

Timekeepers.   There should be three timekeepers for each track event. If the three stop-watches disagree, the watch giving the middle time is official. If only two stop-watches are used, the slower time is official. Timers start their watches at the flash of the gun, not from the report.

Organizing the Meet

Committees must be appointed and the responsibilities of each committee must be made clear to the individual members. As much as is possible, committee chairmen should select helpers from among pupils of the host school.

Previous to the meet, the games committee must collect the names of the entrants sent in on the entry blanks and arrange them on new sheets under the heading of the different events. For example, if large numbers are entered for the runs, a series of heats must be arranged. The number of heats to be run is determined by the number of lanes available and the number of contestants. An attempt should be made to distribute equally among the several heats the contestants known to be fast so that the fastest runners will not be eliminated first. Winners of the heats run in the final race. The heats must be listed on the program or copies must be prepared for the clerk of the course, the starter, the judges, the scorer, and the referee.

Field events are run off continuously after the start of the meet, except when a performer is excused to take part in a running event.

The person in charge of the meet, with his committee members, should make a list of the needs of contestants and officials for every event. Later this list should be checked to see that no item has been overlooked. Some of the items to be included are in the following lists.

Preparation of Facilities for Contestants. The following should be arranged for before the meet:

1. Medical service. Arrangements should be made to have a physician or nurse present at the meet, if possible, or available on short notice. A first aid kit should be on the field.
2. Physical examination for all contestants previous to the day of the meet
3. A written statement from parents of contestants giving them permission to take part in the meet
4. A system of identifying contestants on the day of meet either by a large cloth number pinned on the clothing or by the classification index letter stamped on the arm with a rubber stamp
5. Adequate drinking water facilities
6. Dressing rooms and toilets plainly labeled
7. Sign boards or placards placed on high standards to show where events are to take place
8. An information center with a capable person in charge
9. A lost-and-found desk or room
10. A checking system for lunches, clothing, and valuables. Valuables should be placed in envelopes which the owner signs. The owner should then sign again before being given his property.

Preparation of the Grounds. In preparing the grounds for the meet the following should be completed:

1. Surface of the track prepared
2. Lanes for runs and relays, start and finish lines for each distance marked
3. Sand and shavings for jumping pits loosened
4. Additional jumping pits prepared if there are numerous entries for jumping events

Equipment. The following equipment should be made ready:

1. Standards and crossbars for high jump
2. Take-off board for broad jump
3. Leveling tools, shovels
4. Ropes and stakes to keep spectators from interfering with contestants
5. Chairs and table for scorers
6. At least three stop-watches
7. Gun and blank cartridges
8. Finish tape (cotton yarn is best)

9. Official badges
10. Scales for weighing contestants
11. Numbers for marking contestants, or rubber stamps and ink pad
12. Large scoreboard, score sheets, and pencils
13. Megaphones
14. Papers of safety pins

OFFICIALS FOR GAMES AND SPORTS [1]

Officials are necessary for most team and dual games and sports. Good officiating results in more harmonious and co-operative play. Principals and teachers should provide for proper officiating by serving as officials themselves or by preparing pupils to perform the functions. Daily officiating is desirable for playground activities during recess, noon, and after-school play periods. Although it takes time to train and assign pupils as officials, to organize schedules, and to aid officials in the performance of their duties, the resulting leadership experience is one of the outstanding contributions of physical education to the school curriculum. By using pupils as officials, the teacher is freed to give instruction to all groups and does not have to focus all his attention on one game.

Officials' Organizations

One of the many helpful devices that may be used to train pupil officials is the establishment of a club or committee for those pupils interested in officiating. Membership should be offered to those particularly interested in sports who are willing to give extra time in order to become proficient in the art of officiating. All boys and girls who are the least interested should be given opportunity to participate. Time must be provided for study of rules governing games and for practice in game situations. This period may be scheduled before school, at noon, after school, or during school time.

Officiating Techniques

Members of officials' clubs and committees should study game rules. They should have oral discussions and written tests. They should learn the rules and techniques of officiating both by practicing and by watching others perform in movies or demonstrations. When officiating, pupils should observe the following practices:

1. Be impartial in making decisions.
2. Call decisions promptly, decisively, clearly.
3. Be at the right place at the right time; that is, be "on top" of the game.

---

[1] Material for this section was supplied by Harold Schoenfeld, Supervisor of Physical Education, Alameda County.

4. Keep the object of the game, or the ball, in sight at all times.
5. Seek to anticipate trying situations.
6. Endeavor to keep activities moving at a rapid pace.
7. Keep out of the way of players so as not to interfere with activity of performers.
8. Be pleasant, polite, cheerful, but not personal, in the performance of the assignment.
9. Demonstrate good sportsmanship at all times.

Officials Needed for Various Games

Different games call for different numbers of officials.

Basketball. For boys' and girls' basketball a referee, who is the head official, and an umpire are needed. The referee should keep up with the ball and the umpire should stay behind it, both watching the full length of the court. The official nearest the ball should toss it up between opponents.

Each official should watch for held ball, out-of-bounds play, traveling while carrying the ball, illegal dribble, and so on. Each should be especially alert to call fouls for holding, pushing, blocking, charging, tripping, and unsportsmanlike conduct. Scorekeepers and timekeepers are also needed for basketball.

Soccer. For soccer, the official is called a referee in a boys' game and an umpire in a girls' game. There may be two officials, in which case they divide the field from the center, each taking a half of the field and counting all out-of-bounds plays in his half.

The referee is in charge of the game. He calls all fouls and violations and announces penalties for them. He determines when goals are made. He should follow the ball up and down the field. He should know the difficult rules, in particular those concerning different types of kicks, illegal play occurring within and outside penalty areas, use of hands and arms, and personal contact.

One linesman is on each side of the field. Each indicates the spot on his side where ball goes out of bounds. Each awards ball following out-of-bounds play. Scorekeepers and timekeepers are needed.

Speed Ball. Speed ball has one umpire and two linesmen or two umpires. The umpire must know the soccer rules which govern a ground ball, and basketball rules, which govern the ball when it is legally lifted into the air.

Linesmen, scorekeepers, and timekeepers operate as in soccer.

Softball, Kick Ball, Hit Pin Baseball. Two umpires are required. The head umpire is in charge of the game. He may remove a player or declare the game forfeited. He calls balls and strikes and determines plays made at home plate. The base umpire calls play on bases and field plays. He may remove players. The scorekeepers are very important in keeping the game moving smoothly.

Track Meets. Many trained officials are needed for track meets.[1] Study and practice in performing the different duties of track meet officials should be part of the study undertaken by those interested in officiating. Physically handicapped students, in particular, should be trained as referees and officials to serve during track meets.

Games Played Without Officials

Children should be given opportunities to carry on some game activities without the use of officials. An attitude of mind must be built up and group agreement must be reached on the acknowledgment of errors and acceptance of penalties. The following are essentials in the establishment of such situations:

1. All the players must know the rules.
2. All players must have the desire to play and be willing to abide by the rules.
3. There must be effective captains, who have been delegated authority by the group to make decisions. Such authority should be exercised infrequently.
4. Players must learn to call their own violations of rules and fouls committed. If they do not do this, the captains must take over and call errors made by players.
5. Teacher or group leader must become the final authority if captains cannot agree on a disputed point. A teacher or group leader who truly supervises knows the rules, yet discourages attempts by players or captains to have him make the decisions.
6. There should be immediate correction of rule interpretations by teacher or group leader when it is found the players are misinterpreting the intent of the rules.

TOURNAMENTS [2]

One of the most valuable devices to stimulate interest in games and athletics is the organization of a tournament or series of contests to determine the champion player or team. There are several kinds of tournaments suitable for use in elementary schools, some for scheduling games

---

[1] See pages 177-78.

[2] Further suggestions and examples for setting up all types of tournaments may be found in National Recreation Association, *Community Sports and Athletics*. New York: A. S. Barnes and Company, 1949, pp. 176-99.

over a long period of time and some for determining the championship fairly quickly. It is suggested that tournament games be scheduled for the after-school period, or in the recreation hour.

Round Robin Tournament

In a round robin tournament each player or team plays every other player or team. This type of tournament is particularly valuable for intramural contests since no players or teams are eliminated. It may, however, take a long time to schedule games between all teams if the number of teams is large.

In a schedule for round robin play there will be one less round than there are teams, and in each round games will be scheduled for all teams (half as many games as there are teams). A simple way to construct a round robin tournament chart is to write the numbers of the teams in sequence down the first column and up the second column in a counterclockwise direction. The teams standing opposite each other in the two columns compete for the first round. In the second round, the last team follows the first and then the numbers (skipping 1) follow in sequence down and up the columns. The same method may be used for any number of teams, as shown in the charts on page 184. If there is an uneven number of teams, a mythical team is added to make the number even. Wherever the mythical team appears on the schedule, the team opposite has a bye for that round—that is, it does not play.

Scheduling the Matches. The games should be scheduled to take full advantage of the time and facilities available. Care must be taken not to schedule two games for the same team in the same day if noon and after-school periods are utilized. The chart on page 185 is an example of the schedule that might be followed by seven teams, using two courts before lunch and during after-school periods for seven days (two school weeks). Three separate matches are played every day, two being played simultaneously either at noon or after school. At the end of the seven days of play every team has played every other team and percentage scores and team standings can be determined.

Percentage Scores. After the games have been played, percentage scores for each team can be determined and they can be ranked according to their standing. To determine the percentage score divide the number of games won by the number of games played and express the result in decimals to the third place. For example, Team 2 won 5 games out of 6 played. $5 \div 6 = .833$. On page 185 is an example of a method of recording percentage scores.

CHART FOR A ROUND ROBIN TOURNAMENT
SEVEN OR EIGHT TEAMS

FIRST ROUND	SECOND ROUND	THIRD ROUND	FOURTH ROUND	FIFTH ROUND	SIXTH ROUND	SEVENTH ROUND
1-8	1-7	1-6	1-5	1-4	1-3	1-2
2-7	8-6	7-5	6-4	5-3	4-2	3-8
3-6	2-5	8-4	7-3	6-2	5-8	4-7
4-5	3-4	2-3	8-2	7-8	6-7	5-6

Number 8 represents the mythical team if there are only seven teams to be scheduled. The team matched with the mythical team has a bye during that round and does not play.

CHART FOR A ROUND ROBIN TOURNAMENT
ELEVEN OR TWELVE TEAMS

FIRST ROUND	SECOND ROUND	THIRD ROUND	FOURTH ROUND	FIFTH ROUND	SIXTH ROUND	SEVENTH ROUND	EIGHTH ROUND	NINTH ROUND	TENTH ROUND	ELEVENTH ROUND
1-12	1-11	1-10	1-9	1-8	1-7	1- 6	1- 5	1- 4	1- 3	1- 2
2-11	12-10	11- 9	10-8	9-7	8-6	7- 5	6- 4	5- 3	4- 2	3-12
3-10	2- 9	12- 8	11-7	10-6	9-5	8- 4	7- 3	6- 2	5-12	4-11
4- 9	3- 8	2- 7	12-6	11-5	10-4	9- 3	8- 2	7-12	6-11	5-10
5- 8	4- 7	3- 6	2-5	12-4	11-3	10- 2	9-12	8-11	7-10	6- 9
6- 7	5- 6	4- 5	3-4	2-3	12-2	11-12	10-11	9-10	8- 9	7- 8

Number 12 represents the mythical team if there are only 11 teams to be scheduled.

Volleyball Tournament

Court	Time	Monday Teams	Winner	Tuesday Teams	Winner	Thursday Teams	Winner	Friday Teams	Winner	Monday Teams	Winner	Tuesday Teams	Winner	Thursday Teams	Winner
1	Noon	—	—	1-7	1	1-6	1	1-5	5	1-4	1	1-3	3	1-2	2
1	After School	2-7	2	—	—	7-5	7	6-4	6	5-3	3	4-2	2	—	—
2	Noon	3-6	3	2-5	2	—	—	7-3	7	6-2	2	—	—	4-7	7
2	After School	4-5	5	3-4	4	2-3	3	—	—	—	—	6-7	6	5-6	5

Percentage Scores

	Games Won	Games Lost	Percentage	Standing
Team 2	5	1	.833	1
Team 3	4	2	.666	2
Team 1	3	3	.500	3, 4, 5
Team 5	3	3	.500	3, 4, 5
Team 7	3	3	.500	3, 4, 5
Team 6	2	4	.333	6
Team 4	1	5	.166	7

Ladder or Perpetual Tournament

In a ladder tournament players are ranked according to their known or estimated ability in a certain game or sport, and each tries to maintain his position against challengers below him in rank. Nobody is eliminated, but players change positions as they win or lose. A chart for a ladder tournament is very simple. The names may be written on a chalkboard. One method is to attach metal card holders to a board, one above the other, numbering them consecutively from top to bottom. The names of the teams or players are written on cards, and these are inserted in the holders opposite the number assigned to or drawn by that team. When teams change places the cards can be slipped into the proper holders. Another method is to drive small nails into a board, one above the other, at regular intervals, numbering each according to its rank. Names are written on key tags and the tags slipped over the nails. The tags can be interchanged easily.

CHART FOR A LADDER TOURNAMENT

1	Mary Jones
2	Robert Stewart
3	John Adams
4	Anne Page
5	Robert Thompson
6	Jane Ross
7, etc.	

A person or team may challenge the first or second person or team immediately above him on the chart. Should the challenger win, the position of the names of contestants are changed on the chart. Should the challenger be defeated, the positions remain as they were. A person who fails to accept a challenge within the time limit agreed upon exchanges his name on the chart with that of the challenger. A loser may not challenge a winner a second time until the loser has played against a different contestant.

Tournament play should include not less than three challenges a week for each player or team, with more if facilities permit. Ladder tournaments are called perpetual tournaments because they may go on forever. If they appear to be continuing beyond the point where they stimulate interest, an end may be made by holding an elimination tournament between the four top players.

Progressive Tournament

A progressive tournament is used when it is desired to play a number of games simultaneously on a number of courts, with teams rotating at the end of each period of play to another court, where each meets a new team. Thus, at the end of each period of play winners move to the next lower numbered court, with the exception that the winner at Court 1 remains there, the loser in that court going to the highest numbered court. Members of losing teams remain where they are, except in the case of Court 1. This is an excellent type of tournament for playdays in which a number of teams participate in the same activity. Schools have been known to erect as many as 20 temporary courts for volleyball at a play-day when the progressive type of tournament was used. At one playday, with seven members to a team, a total of 260 persons played simultaneously. Net ball and basketball are other games that are often used in this kind of tournament.

The head official announces the number of minutes allowed for each round and the number of rounds to be played. Two or three minutes between each round are allowed for the recording of scores and the rotation of players. Play commences only on signal from the head official. In net games the losers exchange sides of the court before playing the next game.

Scoring.   The scores are recorded for each team at the end of the period. Winners may receive 5 points and losers 3 points, or the exact score may be recorded. At the end of the tournament a winning team may be determined by adding the total points won by each team.

Elimination Tournament

An elimination tournament is used to determine the best player or team by eliminating one team of a pair in each round. The winners of the first round are paired for the second round, and the winners of the next round play a match until in the final match a champion is determined. The chief disadvantage of this type of tournament is the elimination of each contestant from play as soon as he is defeated. When scheduled as the final activity of a series of games, however, this disadvantage is lessened. To provide the fullest activity for all players, an elimination tournament would not be used. To bring to an end a ladder tournament or series of league games, it would be appropriate.

The diagram on page 186 makes clear the method of bracketing teams for an elimination tournament with sixteen teams.

Byes.   An elimination tournament can be scheduled easily if the number of players is a power of 2—that is, 4, 8, 16, 32, or 64. When the

CHART FOR AN ELIMINATION TOURNAMENT
SIXTEEN TEAMS

First Round	Second Round	Semifinal Round	Final Round
A	(winner)		
B		(winner)	
C	(winner)		
D			(winner)
E	(winner)		
F		(winner)	
G	(winner)		
H			(champion)
I	(winner)		
J		(winner)	
K	(winner)		
L			(winner)
M	(winner)		
N		(winner)	
O	(winner)		
P			

number of players is not a power of 2, the problem is more complicated. A system of byes is used to schedule the first round so that the number of players in the second round will be a power of 2. By this system only a few of the contestants play the first round, the others—those who draw byes—advancing to the second round without playing. To determine the

CHART FOR AN ELIMINATION TOURNAMENT
NINE TEAMS

First Round	Second Round	Semifinal Round	Final Round
A (bye)	A	(winner)	
B (bye)	B		(winner)
C (bye)	C	(winner)	
D (bye)	D		(champion)
E (bye)	E	(winner)	
F (bye)	F		(winner)
G (bye)	G	(winner)	
H	(winner)		
I			

number of byes that will be drawn, the number of contestants is sub-
tracted from the next higher power of 2; the difference is the number of
players who draw byes. For example, if there are nine contestants, sub-
tract 9 from 16 (the next higher power of 2), and schedule 7 byes. The
chart on the preceding page illustrates the method of bracketing players
with byes.

Scheduling the Matches. Teams may draw for places in the first
round and then matches may be scheduled according to the time and
place available. If facilities permit, all matches for the first round may be
played off at the same time. It may be desirable to arrange the time and
place for each match ahead of time, or the teams themselves may arrange
each match as their names appear in the winning bracket. A sample schedule to be posted is shown here. The name of the winner should be written
on the chart as soon as the match has been played.

Paddle Tennis Tournament

	First Round			Semifinals			Finals		
Teams	Time	Place	Winner	Time	Place	Winner	Time	Place	Champion
Reds									
Whites									
Blues									
Greens									
Yellows									
Blacks									
Pinks									
Oranges									

Seeding Players. When a few of the teams or players are outstanding in ability, the matches are fairer and more enjoyable if the players of
superior ability are "seeded"; that is, placed on the schedule in such a way
that the superior players do not compete with each other in the early
rounds. Their names are placed either at the top and the bottom of the
chart or one in the first four, one in the second four, and so on. Thus,
in the chart on page 188 seeded players might be placed in positions A, E,
I, and M, and if each won his matches he would not meet another seeded
player until the semifinals. If there were only two players to be seeded,
they might be placed in positions A and I and, presuming each won his
matches, these two players would not meet until the final round. If they
were placed in the positions of A and B one of them would be eliminated
in the first round, which would be unfair both to the strong and the weak
players. When players are seeded they cannot draw for places on the
schedule, but the unseeded players should draw for the remaining places.

Consolation Tournament

In order to make an elimination tournament more interesting for the less skilled players, a consolation tournament may be arranged. The losers of the first round play a second round, and the winners of these matches play again, continuing until a consolation winner is determined.

SELECTED REFERENCES

BANCROFT, JESSIE H. *Games for the Playground, Home, School, and Gymnasium.* New York: Macmillan Co., 1937 (revised edition).

BLANCHARD, V. S., AND COLLINS, L. B. *A Modern Physical Education Program.* New York: A. S. Barnes & Co., 1940.

FRYMIR, ALICE W. *Basket Ball for Women: How to Coach and Play the Game.* New York: A. S. Barnes & Co., 1928.

GROMBACH, JOHN V. *Touch Football.* New York: A. S. Barnes & Co., 1942.

HUPPRICH, FLORENCE L. *Soccer and Speedball for Girls.* New York: A. S. Barnes & Co., 1942.

MASON, BERNARD S., AND MITCHELL, ELMER D. *Active Games and Contests.* New York: A. S. Barnes & Co., 1935.

MASON, JOHN LEONARD. *Sand Craft.* Boston: J. L. Hammett Co., 1937 (second edition).

MITCHELL, ELMER D. *Sports for Recreation and How to Play Them.* New York: A. S. Barnes & Co., 1936.

NATIONAL COLLEGIATE ATHLETIC BUREAU. *SO Soccer Guide.* New York: N. C. A. B. (P. O. Box 757, Grand Central Station, New York 17), 1950.

NATIONAL FEDERATION OF STATE HIGH SCHOOL ATHLETIC ASSOCIATIONS. Chicago: N. F. S. H. S. A. A. (7 S. Dearborn St., Chicago 3, Ill.), 1950.

IT	Track and Field Rules	SM	Six-Man Football Rules
IF	Football Rules	FC	Football Case Book
IB	Basketball Rules	BC	Basketball Case Book

NATIONAL SECTION ON WOMEN'S ATHLETICS. *Official Sports Library for Women.* Washington: American Association for Health, Physical Education and Recreation (1201 Sixteenth Street, N. W., Washington 6, D. C.)

Published annually or at approximately annual intervals.

The Official Basketball Guide

The Official Tennis–Badminton Guide

The Official Individual Sports Guide with Archery, Bowling, Fencing, Golf, and Riding

The Official Recreational Games–Volley Ball Guide

The Official Softball–Track and Field Guide

The Official Soccer–Speedball Guide

POWDERMAKER, THERESE. *Visual Aids for Teaching Sports.* New York: A. S. Barnes & Co., 1940.

UNITED STATES LAWN TENNIS ASSOCIATION. *The Official USLTA Tennis Guide and Year Book.* New York: U. S. L. T. A. (120 Broadway, New York 5), 1950.

UNITED STATES VOLLEY BALL ASSOCIATION. *The Official Volley Ball Guide.* Berne, Ind.: U. S. Volley Ball Association Printer (Box 109), published annually or at approximately annual intervals.

WELLS COMPANY. *Official Softball Guide.* Leonia, N. J.: W. W. Wells Co., published annually or at approximately annual intervals.

Chapter VIII

RHYTHMICAL ACTIVITIES

Rhythm is a basic aspect of nature. All peoples of the earth manifest rhythm; all animals show it; indeed all of nature portrays rhythm in the return of seasons, the growth of crops, and the change of ocean tides. The young child has an inner impulse for rhythm that manifests itself in movement, but because in immaturity the muscles are not fully developed and not under the full domination of the will, a child's movements lack the balanced, regular cadence of rhythm. As the muscles develop and control is established, the movements become more rhythmical. When greater co-ordination of the muscles is acquired, the whole body may be used in movement expressive of the child's emotions. Adults, too, often translate emotions into rhythmical movement. This natural rhythmic activity must be encouraged in the elementary school child because of the many benefits, emotionally and physically, derived from it.

Individuals with good motor ability have no difficulty in handling their bodies easily, rhythmically, and therefore effectively. Those with little motor ability are awkward, slow, and ineffective in their move-

ure 65. A rhythms program satisfactory for all children must give each d an opportunity to walk, skip, gallop, run, slide, hop, and jump.

ments, although they can develop motor skills and physical efficiency if given opportunity to practice the muscular co-ordinations demanded by rhythmical activity. A school rhythms program should be designed to help every boy and girl to develop through rhythmical movement a balanced and well co-ordinated body.

Balanced posture and physical efficiency are not the only desirable outcomes of a rhythms program. Rhythmical body movement also helps develop emotional freedom. Children use physical skills to identify themselves with their environment—with machines, animals, plants, people— and thus enrich their understanding of the community. As the child's physical efficiency develops, great satisfaction is derived from creating patterns of movement based on ideas and events in school and home experiences.

The development of many skills necessary for recreational enjoyment should result from a good program of rhythmical activities in the school. When boys and girls acquire skills necessary for leisure-time activity they are prepared for a happy and balanced social life. Practice of the rhythmic skills is thus a necessary part of the physical education program from kindergarten through the secondary school.

KINDS OF RHYTHMICAL ACTIVITIES

Rhythmical activities that provide worthwhile experiences for elementary school boys and girls fall into several classes.

1. Creative rhythms, which include (a) free rhythms, (b) identification rhythms, and (c) dramatizations
2. Singing games
3. Dances, which include (a) folk games and dances, (b) American Indian dances, (c) social dances, (d) modern, natural, or interpretive dances, (e) gymnastic, clog, and tap dances.

Introduction to creative rhythms and singing games is important at the earliest age at which learning takes place. Many of the games are enjoyed by all ages. Teachers in the primary grades are advised not to teach activities suitable only to the upper grades. In the upper grades, however, teachers may profitably use not only the rhythms recommended for those grades but also any the children may have missed while in the primary grades. When several grades are combined, as in a small rural school, the teacher must select activities that can be enjoyed by all, the younger children being introduced to more advanced rhythmical patterns through observation as well as by participation.

It is important that rhythms be introduced in an atmosphere of fun and enjoyment. The teacher should share in the rhythmical experience and participate in the fun. Rhythm and musical instruments should be used as accompaniment, and full use of a piano or phonograph should be made.[1] Finding a suitable place for conducting a rhythms program is often a problem. If a room with a smooth floor and no obstructions is not available, a program can be carried on out of doors—on a lawn, a tennis court, or other surfaced area.

Creative Rhythms

Creative rhythms include free rhythms, identifying rhythms, and dramatizations. Elementary school children should be encouraged to use movement to portray their ideas and emotional experiences. They may identify themselves with airplanes, trains, or wheels. They may dramatize events of their home life. Dance patterns created by the children themselves should be a part of the rhythmical activity.

Each child must be given an opportunity for walking, skipping, turning, running, sliding, hopping, and swinging. A free rhythms program allows the children to investigate the range of fundamental movements of the body. These fundamental movements include (1) axial movements—going up and down, sideward, forward, backward, and rotating, (2) locomotor movements—walking, running, skipping, leaping, hopping, jumping, sliding, galloping, and (3) nonlocomotor movements—pushing, pulling, striking, swinging, and lifting. Children should be provided with opportunities to use these axial, locomotor, and nonlocomotor movements with variations of time and intensity in different areas of space. Free choice of both type and tempo of movement is important, as is the free choice of rhythm accompaniment.

In practice, the development of creative rhythms depends in large part on the imagination and skill of the teacher in initiating simple patterns. For example, the teacher suggests that the children run as quickly as possible to the other side of the room. She then suggests that the children run around the room until they sense the rhythm of someone else. As the majority accepts a group tempo, the teacher beats that tempo on the drum. When the group gathers on the floor around the teacher, she starts a discussion on the different ways the children ran. The teacher asks if they would like to "run heavy" and "run light." Everyone is ready for this and one boy asks if he may beat the drum. The teacher lets him accompany the heavy and light runs.

The children now discuss the difference in the feeling in their bodies when they use a heavy and light run. "I feel strong when my feet pound

---

[1] An amplifying radio-phonograph can be used out of doors by means of a heavy extension cord, or a piano may be rolled to an open doorway to accompany a program out of doors. If a phonograph is used, it should have an adjustable speed control.

Figure 66. Children like to create their own accompaniment on drums.

the floor." "I liked the feeling of being high in the air on my toes." "Could we run to different records now?" a little girl asks. The rhythm period concludes with the children enjoying movements to various records.

This experience leads easily into familiarity with other ways of moving and with the difference of feeling when the tempo and intensity are changed. It becomes natural for children to identify themselves with persons, things, or animals in rhythms.

Because children learn from the experiences that are meaningful to them, they can learn about machines by actually having a feeling of being a train or a wheel, or about airplanes by having a feeling of being an airplane when it is taxiing, taking off, and flying. Children require, therefore, opportunity to identify themselves rhythmically with familiar things. The source of the experience may be a poem, song, field trip or incident.

The following scene is taken from a kindergarten room. The boys and girls sit on the rug as the teacher plays a train song. The children all recite a train poem with motions and appropriate train noises. They sing a song about the train. Next, the children are asked if they would like to be train engines and a chorus of "Oh, yes" is the result. What part would they like to be? Every child on this day wants to be the piston pushing the wheels. The children start moving upon the floor. As the motions of the different children become somewhat similar in quality and the boys and girls become pistons pushing those shining wheels, the teacher accompanies them on the piano.

What are they doing? Each child is pushing the big train up the track. That a sense of power, co-ordinated body movement, and the identification of pushing a train with each little arm, body, and foot is a satisfying experience for these children is shown by their eager participation.

Rhythmical dramatizations of ideas stemming from the daily experiences of the children are natural after the children have identified themselves with surrounding objects. The social studies provide a rich source for rhythmical dramatization of machinery and of occupations. If the children have acquired the skills of body movement and have had the opportunity to develop their own identification rhythms, then with the addition of a rich environment they will be in a position to create rhythmical patterns.

The teacher should try to arouse the interest of the children by providing pictures, posters, displays, and books along with the field trips or films. An active response on the part of the pupils can be stimulated by discussion when they want to try things, to be someone, or to be something. Group decision should be followed by a definite plan of action.

This plan of action should include the organization of the group and the participation of every individual as a musical and rhythmical pattern is developed by the children. The group should have opportunity to evaluate its activity in terms of the original plan and the effectiveness of participation. The culmination of the activity ought to provide each child with a sense of personal and group accomplishment. The children should increase their power of communication, appreciation of arts and crafts, and understanding of other peoples' cultures.

Two scenes from classrooms will illustrate rhythmical dramatization stemming from the social studies. The first scene is laid in the school rhythms room. The third grade is studying an American Indian community. After reading, collecting pieces for a museum, and seeing a film on Indian life, the children participate in that Indian life through rhythms. They decide to show how the Indians planted their corn. At first the motions are sheer pantomime from the film. The teacher asks, "What makes you feel you are planting seeds?" One boy answers, "Making big movements." With this suggestion, the children try making large body motions. Slowly the class accepts a pattern of movement that produces the desired feeling. The teacher beats the drum, and the children dance the accepted pattern. Then many of the children want to make a drum so that they can beat the rhythm as they dance.

The next scene takes place in a fourth-grade classroom where all the desks are pushed against the wall and every child has a rhythm instrument. Because the social studies unit deals with Mexico, the class is having a Mexican Christmas. For this festival the boys and girls learn the words and dance the steps of "La Cucaracha." They are accompanied by part of the rhythm band and the phonograph. This day half of the children work out rhythm patterns on their instruments while the other half create typical Mexican steps to the recording of "Chiapanecas." Before the end of the unit every child will have contributed to the class activity by creating a step, improving on a step, setting a rhythm pattern for an instrument, or by furnishing constructive criticism.

Singing Games

Singing games are a cultural heritage, their origins hidden in antiquity. Since the games are not complicated in their patterns they require

Figure 67. Singing games afford experience in rhythms and group co-operation.

little or no technical skill. At the same time they train a child in the use of his body in rhythmical experience. They give opportunity for dramatization, together with the satisfaction that is experienced from the use of oft repeated melodies. One of the important educational experiences for young children is the group co-operation necessary for the enjoyment of singing games.

Singing games have a definite place in the experience of kindergarten and primary children. The words and melodies necessary for playing the games may be taught during the music instruction period. Singing games should be used in play periods as well as in instructional periods.

DANCE IN PHYSICAL EDUCATION

A natural development from the free and creative rhythms and the traditional singing games are the various forms of the dance. Dancing may be an individual form of expression, as in the gymnastic, clog, and tap dances or the modern interpretive dance, enjoyed by dancer and spectator alike; or it may be a form of social recreation for young and old, as in the social dance or the group folk dances. The dance has many justifications. None appears more significant than the fact that man everywhere dances. Young children skip on the way to school, adolescents find the social dance romantic, adults participate in social or recreational dances, and both the learned and the unsophisticated discover, as spectators of the dance, their own latent impulses manifested and expressed. Havelock Ellis has written the following about the art of dancing:

> If we are indifferent to the art of dancing, we have failed to understand not merely the supreme manifestations of physical life, but also the supreme symbol of spiritual life. . . .
> Dancing is the primitive expression alike of religion and of love . . ., is intimately entwined with all human tradition of war, of labor, of pleasure, of education, . . . For the solemn occasions of life, for bridals and for funerals, for seed-time and harvest, for war and for peace, for all these things there were fitting dances.[1]

To omit from the physical education program the various forms of the dance would be a serious error. Rich cultural, social, and recreational experiences are to be gained, as well as valuable physical exercise, from the use of many of these forms.

Folk Dances

Folk dances have patterns similar to some games and for this reason are often spoken of as folk games. Both have patterns that are repeated over and over. They have, in addition, what football, baseball, and other games do not have— delightful music to accompany the action. These

---

[1] Havelock Ellis, *The Dance of Life.* Boston: Houghton Mifflin Co., 1923, pp. 34, 35, 37.

dances represent the national customs and folk interests, expressed in dance patterns. Each country has developed through the centuries its own characteristic dance steps and formations, ranging from the jolly peasant dance to the stately quadrille. We often think of America as lacking the traditions out of which such folk and national dances come, but many dances are truly part of America's folkways. The dances of the American Indian and the clog and tap dances of the American Negro are as indigenous to this land as the Chumak is to the Ukraine, the Flip to Holland, the morris and sword dances to England, the Czardas to Hungary, the Obertass to Poland, or the Seguidilla to Spain. The American pioneers, many of whom frowned upon social dancing, adapted the old country dances as forms of recreation. They developed the square and longways dances, the round dances, and the play party games into new and typically American dance forms that have survived in many parts of rural America. Today these dances are being revived all over the country as young people and adults find the "westerns" and squares a source of healthy fun and community recreation.

Figure 68.   Small boys in costume do the "Dance of the Little Old Men," a Mexican folk dance.

Folk dance instruction should begin usually in the third grade and continue throughout the elementary grades. There should be, on an average, the equivalent of one to two instruction periods weekly, depending on the facilities available. The teaching of folk dances should be correlated with social studies when possible, or with subject fields that deal with life problems of local and international groups.

Square and longways dances in their simplest form may be introduced in the intermediate grades. Because it involves the frequent change of partners, this type of folk dancing is popular with upper-grade boys and girls.

When school administrators recognize the values of folk dancing in a physical education program, they have at their disposal a tool for both socialization and recreation. Boys without sisters and girls without brothers, the shy, the awkward, the unsocial, and those with personality difficulties receive many benefits from dancing with members of the opposite sex. Under skilled adult leadership, ease of manner, kindliness, courteous behavior, and a feeling of responsibility for the success of social situations can be expected to be reasonable outcomes of folk dancing.

The study of folk dancing and folk games provides opportunity for improved boy-girl relationships and helps eliminate racial discriminations, "across-the-track" inequalities, and undesirable social cliques. To read about how to behave in social situations is not enough for the mastery of social techniques. Environments that provide opportunity for practice must be created by adults. Folk dancing offers a natural situation for such learning.

To provide a stimulating environment for folk dancing, men principals and men teachers as well as women should take an active part in the instruction. With a man and a woman teacher as partners, a normal atmosphere for folk dancing is set up. The goals of this program, as for all rhythms, are joy in participation and a feeling of personal and group achievement by every boy and girl in the elementary school. The cultural background of the dance should be used for setting the mood of the dance. A suggested plan for presenting a folk dance is to present the background and the rhythm and step pattern as a whole. Then the practice of the parts of the dance will come naturally as the learning progresses.

The American Indian Dance

Because they are rich in cultural meaning and afford opportunity for strong rhythmical movements and creative activity coupled with social learning, the dances of the American Indians should be introduced to children of the early grades.

The following discussion of the American Indian dance is condensed from an article by Lester Horton.[1]

Areas of Indian life can be divided into the Eastern Woodland tribes, tribes of the Plains, the Southwest, and Western Coastal tribes. In each area a cultural pattern arose due to the environment. The Eastern Woodland tribes were principally sedentary, living in large villages. The Indians of the Plains were nomadic, depending upon the migrations of the buffalo. The Indians of the Southwest were both sedentary and nomadic. The peoples of the Western Coast lived in villages, practiced slavery, and depended, to a great extent, upon fishing for a livelihood. The tepee, or conical tent, used in the west was made of buffalo hides. Transportation was by dog, the only beast of burden until the coming of the horse.

In the Plains area the dances developed around the hunt. They were used to instill courage and valor as exemplified in the Sun Dance and the Buffalo Dance.

Indian dances have a characteristic looseness in their knees when executing steps. Most of the steps have a caressing quality and touch the ground with a quick rebound. Exceptions to this are in the side glidings and rotations on the heel.

The steps listed may be used for classroom work in any grade level. Most of the steps fall into a 2/4 pattern. The steps may be combined in various patterns and combinations, regardless of the originating tribe or the type of step.

Characteristic Dance Steps of the Plains Indians

1. Toe Heel
   Step on ball of foot, lower heel as other foot comes forward. Executed with loose knees.

2. Toe Heel Fast
   Same as No. 1 but is executed much faster, which tends to keep the feet forward and from under the body.

3. Toe Heel Tap
   Tap toe forward, raise toe and pull foot back, lower heel as other foot comes forward. This gives a placement which may be counted toe, toe, heel, and the last toe heel is equivalent to one-eighth note. The body has an upright and forward spring on the first tap. This step is executed very rapidly and the feet seem to be always off the earth. There is a distinct rotary action back, up and over in the movement. The Comanche step of the Pueblo Indians is almost identical.

4. Toe Heel Across
   Step same as in No. 1, but the leading foot crosses over the back.

5. Toe Heel Spread
   It is customary among the Shoshoni men to execute the toe heel in a deep squat position. The feet are turned out and the body sways laterally away from the leading foot.

---

[1] Lester Horton, "American Indian Dance," *Educational Dance—The Journal of Dance in Education,* IV (October, 1941), 4-7. Used by permission of the author.

6. Kutenai Toe Heel
The feet are spread as in the Shoshoni step and turned outward. Before the toe is put down there is a high, springing movement of the knee. The heel hits lightly, the body pushes away from the leading leg. There is a continual vibration in the body.

7. Osage Toe Heel
The leading foot crosses extremely over the back foot and the toe is placed down, dragged back as the heel descends. This action cuts the back foot out, which is brought forward and repeated. The step does not allow for rapid progression. The effect is of a strut and is usually accompanied by a shaking of the complete musculature.

8. Blackfoot Point
Strike the point of the toe forward; as the foot recovers flat, the other toe strikes forward. Executed very rapidly and lightly.

9. Side Step
Step to side, foot forward, draw other foot to it. Repeat. Short and rapid with knees very loose.

10. Side Step Heel
Step sideways on heel. Twist on heel, letting the ball or toe point to drawing foot, which drags to a closed position. At the conclusion of one step the leading foot should be pigeon-toed in and the other straight forward. This is a characteristic women's step and is performed in a circle.

CHARACTERISTIC DANCE STEPS OF THE SOUTHWESTERN INDIANS

1. Women's Step from the Buffalo Dance
Stand with feet close together, knees flexed. Move toes to R, follow with heels. Repeat rapidly, keeping feet together. This step is performed in a straight line and usually retraces the line of direction. It may extend longer to one direction.

2. High Trot of the Buffalo Dance
The two buffalo execute a high trot step as a means of locomotion. The knees are brought high without destroying the verticality of the spine. The arms move downward in opposition to the legs. This is a characteristic step of the Pueblos.

3. High Trot Double
Performed on the balls of the feet. The knee is brought high and as the foot descends there is a double bounce, bringing the foot slightly forward. This is a "dust-making" step. A characteristic of all Pueblo dances is the held beat coming at different intervals either down or up (off the ground).

4. Eagle Dance Step
Tap the R toe obliquely forward or side drag the other foot. This step is executed very rapidly and at different time lengths. The body crouches low and the wing [on the side] of the tapping foot is held obliquely toward the foot. The other arm is raised without destroying the straight line of the wings.

5. Eagle Shuffle
Another characteristic step is the rapid shuffle. The knee is brought high and as the leg descends the foot scrapes forward similar to the action of running a thumb over a tambourine. The legs rotate back, down, and forward.

6. Eagle Pivot
The Eastern Pueblos use a pivot step in the Eagle Dance. The body weight leans away from the pulsing leg. Hop on one count and push the leg away from the supporting leg and tap the toe four times in a half circle. The supporting foot twists or hops to execute the circle. Full circles may be described or the step may be used as a means of locomotion by making half circles. Various counts are used and the circle always moves front.

7. "Kachna Step"

A characteristic step from the large group dances. Lift the R knee high and simultaneously drop or limp the left foot forward. Repeat. The rattle accompanies the right leg. The characteristic halt is used at different intervals, often with a double beat down with the leading leg. The halt may be a signal to change leading legs. This is a characteristic step of the Navajo "Mountain Chant." The supporting leg is loose and the step does not travel rapidly.

8. Jump Steps

A. Jump forward on L foot. Jump forward on R.

B. Jump forward on both feet. Jump forward on R and raise L sharply forward and up. Repeat or alternate.

C. Repeat B, pulling the free leg from the rear.

D. Jump forward on L foot. Hop on R foot and raise R to back. Hop back on R. Hop on R and raise leg back sharply. Repeat.

9. Hop Step with Heel Stroke

Hop on R foot. Strike L heel on ground rear and foot line forward. Hop on L foot and raise R leg back sharply. Repeat.

10. Hop Side

Hop gently to R on R foot and tap L heel at R heel and tap L heel away from R. Repeat.

The description of the gestures is not possible as they practically defy analysis. But many of the dances have a symbolic gesture understood collectively by the people. For example, in the Corn Dance a limp hand palm down denotes rain; and the palm up with two fingers extended symbolizes the sprouting corn. The line of the body, the action of the head, the manner in which the rattle is used, all have a meaning.

Social Dances

The skills of the social dance are necessary for the older pupils. If creative rhythms and folk dances have been an important part of a pupil's physical education program, then social dancing is a natural sequel to pro-

Figure 69. Folk dancing teaches the basic steps needed for social dancing.

vide rhythm skills necessary for preadolescents. Most of the dance steps will have been mastered through folk dancing, such as the polka, schottische, three-step, mazurka, minuet, and balance step. The two-step and waltz, the steps used most widely in social dances, should also have been learned in folk dances.

The courtesies connected with social events should be taught along with the rhythm and step pattern in couple dances. These include how the boy should hold the girl, where to place the arms, how the boy stands, how to ask a partner to dance, how to return the girl to her seat after the dance, how to introduce a partner, and how to converse. The mastering of these social graces will provide the dancers with sought-after poise. Self-confidence is also encouraged by the use of familiar, currently popular songs with a definite rhythm.

Modern, Natural, or Interpretive Dance

The modern dance derives its name from the effort to portray in movement significant ideas of current life. It finds its justification in the free representation of the idea or emotion rather than in some standard and traditional dance form. Much of its rhythm pattern stems from modern industrial life, although it is by no means restricted to that source.

This vital dance form represents a definite break with the past in much the same way that modern music, modern art, and modern architecture do. It is subject to the same excesses as are other forms of modern art.

While leaders of the modern dance movement do not agree on the term that should be used to describe this form of expression, the terms "natural" and "interpretive" are gradually being replaced by the term "modern." As an art form and as rhythmic expression this type of dancing has found a place in the lives of the people as well as on the stage.

Modern dance is an extremely vigorous form of rhythmic activity. It is built on techniques that develop maximum muscular strength, joint flexibility, and body co-ordination through such activities as twists, bends, jumps, turns, leaps, and falls. Localized controls developed by the dancer result in a harmonious use of the entire body. Elevation, timing, direction, and mood are important factors. Leaders proficient in teaching this type of dancing are careful to instruct children and youth in movements that conform to the anatomical structure and leverage actions of the body. Modern dance instruction includes techniques that strengthen foot, leg, thigh, back, chest, shoulder, and arm muscles. Improved postures and increased fitness often result. The skills that are learned emphasize not static postures but continuous, ever-changing movement. As skills improve, problems in movement and composition are presented to the class for individual or group solution. The outcomes are often delightful patterns or dramatic episodes from the life experience of an individual or a group.

This highly specialized phase of dancing is a fascinating area of learning for students in high school and college. It appeals to boys and girls equally when they realize the strength and endurance needed to achieve success in it and the pleasure resulting from increased body control. The teaching of modern dance in the elementary school is limited, usually, because of the lack of specialized teachers. It is, however, the culmination of a creative rhythm program begun in the kindergarten.

Gymnastic, Clog, and Tap Dances

Gymnastic, clog, and tap dances appeal to some because of the stunt elements that are often present and because a person can perform them effectively without a partner. These dances do not have as much to offer in the quality of the musical accompaniment or in creativity or the possibilities for social relationships as do other dance patterns. For demonstrations and exhibitions in the upper grades, gymnastic, clog, and tap dances are effective, especially in costume.

BASIC DANCE PATTERNS

In couple dances and the various folk dances suitable for elementary school pupils there are certain fundamental formations, positions, and steps with which the teacher should become thoroughly familiar.

Formations

Most of the group dances call for either (1) a circle formation, (2) a square, or (3) a longways set. Circles may be formed in several ways—a single circle, double circle, or triple circle. Boys may be in one circle, girls in another; they may face each other as partners or all face the center of the circle. Girls and boys may alternate in a single circle, partners facing or all facing in the same direction. Circles may move clockwise (in the direction taken by the clock hands), or counterclockwise (the reverse direction).

A square or quadrille is sometimes called a set. It consists of eight dancers, four couples (occasionally more or less), all facing toward the center of a square. The *head couple* (or Couple 1) are the partners with their backs to the music, the *end couple* (or Couple 3) stand opposite them, and the *side couples* (Couples 2 and 4) are on the right and left of the head couple. The girl is always to the right of the boy.

In a longways set, dancers (three or more couples) form two long columns, boys in one and girls in the other. Head or top couple are the partners at the end of the line nearer the music. An example of a longways dance is the Virginia Reel.

Occasionally other formations, such as line or file formation, are called for, and very often couples or single dancers take their positions anywhere on the dance floor.

The American square or longways dances are often "called"—that is, the steps or patterns to be performed are called out by a person who leads the group. Elementary school pupils can learn to call square dances and thus contribute to their own enjoyment as well as that of the group.

Positions

Pupils should learn the more common dance positions and courtesies.

Social Dance Position. Partners facing, boy's right arm around girl's waist, his left hand holding her right at shoulder level, her left hand resting on his shoulder. The open social dance position: partners face same direction, side by side, boy's right arm around girl's waist, girl's left hand on boy's shoulder; the outside hands may be on hips or joined in front of their bodies.

Skaters' Position. Partners stand side by side, boy's right hand holding girl's right hand, his left hand holding her left hand.

Varsovienne Position. Boy stands back of and to left of girl, both facing in same direction; girl raises both hands just above shoulder, palms forward, and boy places palms of his hands against girl's hands. On "point left," girl is on right side of partner; on "point right," boy moves to right side of girl.

Extended Arm Position. Facing each other, partners raise both arms to side; girl places her fingers, palm down, on upturned palms of boy.

Bow and Curtsy. Couples are often instructed to bow to each other. For the boy, a bow is a slight bend forward from the hips. The girl may execute a peasant curtsy as follows (count is "one, two, three, four"): 1. Step sideward with right foot. 2. Bring toes of left foot to heel of right foot; bend both knees. 3. Step sideways with left foot. 4. Bring toes of right foot to heel of left foot; bend both knees. She executes the formal or minuet curtsy as follows (sixteen counts). Step backward with right foot and transfer weight to right foot, left leg remaining straight; rotate left leg to the left so that heel is raised inward with little toe touching the floor. There should be full extension of the foot. Toes of right foot should be turned out (1, 2, 3, 4). With weight on right foot, bend right knee and lower body (5, 6, 7, 8). Rise to erect position by extending right knee (9, 10, 11, 12). Slowly transfer weight to left foot (13, 14, 15, 16). If balanced correctly, the performer should be able to lift the forward foot off the floor.

Steps

The basic step in square dances is a rhythmic fast walk or change-step, during which the feet are kept close to the floor. Skipping and hopping steps are taboo so far as quadrilles are concerned. Because the steps are danced from a caller's directions, courtesy must be observed in regard to noisy talk and movement.

Other common steps used in folk dances are described in the following list.

Allemande Left.   Gentleman takes L hand of the lady on his left in his L hand and turns her in place, walking completely around her.

Allemande Right.   Same as "Allemande Left" except that it is done with R hand in R hand of partner (lady on right).

Bleking Step.   2/4 time. Count is "one, and, two, and." Two measures or four counts are necessary to complete the step. Count 1: hop on R foot and at same time, with L leg in extended position, place L heel on floor, toes turned up. Simultaneously extend L arm forward at shoulder height. Bend R elbow while held at shoulder height. Give slight twist of body to L. Count "and": repeat, hopping onto L foot with R heel touching, toes turned up. R arm fully extended, L elbow bent. Slight twist of the body to R. Count 2: repeat above (double quick time) three times, R, L, R. Count "and": hold position. L heel on floor and L arm extended. (During alternate foot action, arms are alternately bent and extended.) Repeat all.

Buzz Step.   2/4 time. Count is "one, and, two, and." This is a pivot step used when swinging partner. Man holds partner in social dancing position but with lady so well out to the R that their shoulders are almost parallel. Count 1: each steps on R foot. Count "and": step forward on ball of L foot. Count 2: step with R foot on same spot as before. Count "and": step forward on L foot. Continue, turning, usually for eight measures. More weight is put on the R foot and a push or shoving movement is executed by the L foot as it is moved forward.

Cut Step.   2/4 or 4/4 time. Count is "one, and, two, and." To start movement stand with weight on R foot, L foot raised forward, knee extended. Count 1: drop L foot in front of R foot and transfer body weight to it. Count "and": as weight is transferred to L foot, swing R leg up backward, knee extended. Count 2: drop R foot and take weight on it. Count "and": swing L leg forward up, knee extended. Repeat with L leg remaining in front. Repeat with R leg remaining in front. Repeat with L and R legs alternating in front position. During this last movement two hops will have to be taken on each weight-bearing foot to allow time for rear leg to swing forward.

Draw Step. 3/4 time. Count is "one, two, three." Count 1: step to side with L foot, toes pointing forward. Count 2: start drawing R foot toward L foot, with heel leading, toes pointing directly to the side. Achieved by an outward rotation of the entire R leg from the thigh to the toes. Knee of R leg should be fully extended throughout the draw. Count 3: complete the draw, by bringing heel of R foot to instep of L foot. Weight remains on L foot until R heel reaches L foot, when a quick transfer of weight to the R leg occurs in order to free L leg for another step to the side. Continue movement to the L. Repeat, stepping R with R foot.

Gallop Step. The slide step done in a forward direction with L or R foot leading. See direction for Slide Step, page 207.

Grand Right and Left or Grand Chain. Grand right and left is used to secure a new partner or in a quadrille to meet one's own partner to escort her "home"; that is, back to position on the square previously occupied.

Dancers are in a single circle with partners facing. Giving R hand to each other, partners move forward and each offers his L hand to oncoming person. Passing that person each offers his R hand to third person coming toward him, then the L, and so around the circle weaving in and out. Boys always travel counterclockwise and girls clockwise.

Hopsa "Waltz." 2/4 time. Count is "one, and, two, and." Count 1: step with R foot to side. Count "and": hop on R foot; at same time swing L leg sideways, knee fully extended. Action takes place in hip, not the knee. Count 2: step left on L foot. Count "and": hop on L foot raising R leg sideways, knee fully extended. Usually done with a partner. Gentleman places his hands on waist of lady. Lady places her hands on shoulders of gentleman. It may be done with hands grasped and arms fully extended, shoulder high, or with all hands on shoulders. To begin the step with a partner, one steps with R foot, the other with L foot. Turns are made as desired.

Ladies Chain. 2/4, 4/4, 6/8 time. Count is "one, two, three, four," etc. Couples face each other with each man to the left of his partner. Ladies travel, exchanging positions, and return to own partner. Gentlemen remain where they are and turn first the visiting lady and then turn their own partners when they return to place. Count 1, 2, 3, 4: each lady extends R hand and takes opposite lady's R hand; each passes to the L and immediately offers her L hand to gentleman facing her (4 steps). Count 5, 6, 7, 8: each gentleman takes visiting lady's L hand in his L hand and places his R hand at her waist, or in her R hand, which she places palm up on her R hip. Each gentleman turns visiting lady around to his L in a small circle, while she walks forward (4 steps). Count 1, 2, 3, 4: each lady again takes R hand of approaching lady; they pass, and each offers L hand to own partner (4 steps). Count 5, 6, 7, 8: lady's own partner turns her around into original position (4 steps).

Mazurka Step.   3/4 Mazurka time. Count is "one, *two*, three." Accent is on second count. Count 1: slide R foot to side. Count 2: bring L foot to R foot and transfer weight to L foot (cut step); at same time extend R foot out to side and off the floor, knee in extended position. R leg is rotated to the right as "extend bend" is taken. Count 3: hop on L foot; at same time bend R knee sharply and bring R foot to instep of L foot. Repeat, continuing in the same direction. (To change direction stamp three times, R, L, R; during stamps turn body and face to the left.) Repeat, alternating direction following three mazurka steps.

Pivot.   Cross R foot over but close to L foot; rise on toes; turn completely around.

Polka Step.   2/4 time. Count is "and, one, and, two." The polka step is the two-step with the addition of a hop executed on the first "and." Count "and": hop on R foot. Count 1: step forward on L foot. Count "and": bring R foot to L foot and transfer weight to R foot. Count 2: step forward again on L foot.

Heel and Toe Polka.   2/4 or 6/8 time. Count is "one, and, two, and." Count "one and": touch R heel forward, toes up, and lean backward. Count "two and": touch R toes to rear and lean forward. One polka step and repeat above. The "heel and toe" step may be executed in front of toes of supporting foot, or at instep of supporting foot, instead of extending the leg forward and back as described above. Young children may use three running steps and a hold, instead of the true polka step.

Sequence of directions for Polka Step
1. Clap hands to music.
2. Hold one count and stamp three times with R foot. Then hold one count and stamp three times with L foot.
3. Hold a count and alternate foot stamping.
4. Gradually make sound less by rising on toes during stamping.

5. Advance by using three running steps and hold.
6. Advance by hopping once and running three steps.

Single Circle. Proceed R or L with gallop or slide steps—R or L foot leading for 16 measures. Return in opposite direction to original position L or R foot leading for 16 measures. Repeat for 8 measures. Repeat for 4 measures. Repeat for 2 measures. To change direction use a hop. Continue practicing until the hop and reversal are mastered. Practice in particular the two-slides routine.

Polka Series. May be done alone or with a partner.

1. Skip 8 steps in any direction and then polka 4 steps in any direction. Repeat, changing direction.
2. Take 2 polka steps, then 4 skip steps turning in place. Repeat.
3. Partners stand side by side with adjacent hands joined and extended backward. Each starting with outside foot, do one polka face-to-face. Swing arms forward and take one polka step back-to-back. Repeat around the room.

Schottische. 2/4 or 4/4 time. Count is "one, and, two, and" for 2/4 music, but "one, two, three, four" for 4/4 music.

Part I. Count 1: step R foot forward. Count 2: bring L foot to R foot and transfer weight to L foot. Count 3: step again with R foot. Count 4: hop on R foot and at same time swing L foot forward with knee bent. (L foot may be raised and extended to rear during hop.)

Part II. Count 1: step on R foot and hop on it; at the same time swing L foot forward with knee bent. Count 2: step on L foot and hop; at the same time swing R foot forward with knee bent. Count 3: step on R foot and hop; at the same time swing L foot forward with knee bent. Count 4: step on L foot and hop; at the same time swing R foot forward with knee bent.

Pupils may be taught Part I by having them run three steps, R, L, R, and hop on the R foot on count 4; repeat run and hop on L foot. Soon they can make the first running step a slide or glide step. There are many patterns that may be enjoyed while combining the runs and step hops (Part I and Part II).

Skip. 2/4 or 6/8 time. Count for either is "one, and, two, and." Count 1: step forward on L foot. Count "and": hop on L foot; at the same time bring R leg forward and up with knee bent. Count 2: step forward on R foot. Count "and": hop on R foot; at same time bring L leg forward and up with bent knee. Repeat all, starting with L foot.

Slide Step. 2/4 or 6/8 time. For slide in 2/4 time, count is "one, and, two, and." Count 1: slide R foot directly to side. Count "and": close L foot to R foot and transfer weight. Count 2: again, slide R foot to side. Count "and": close L foot to R. Repeat as desired. When done in forward direction, the same foot leads each time slide is taken. Add a hop when change of direction is desired.

Step Hop. 2/4 or 4/4 time. Count for step is "one, and, two, and" for 2/4 time. Count 1: step forward on L foot and raise R foot forward with knee bent or R foot raised backward with knee extended. Count "and": hop once on L foot with R foot and leg held in above position. Count 2: step forward on R foot, L foot raised front or back. Count "and": hop once on R foot with L foot raised front or back. Repeat all starting with L foot.

Step Swing. 4/4 or 3/4 time. Count is "one, two, three, four" or "one, two, three." Step in 4/4 time. Count 1: step forward on R foot. Count 2: swing L leg forward and at same time lift heel of weight-bearing foot off the floor. Count 3: step forward on L foot. Count 4: swing R leg forward and at same time raise heel of L foot. Repeat as

Figure 70.   The call "Swing your partner" is danced as a buzz step by many square dancers.

desired. In 3/4 time. Count 1: step forward on R foot. Count 2: swing L leg forward and across R leg. Count 3: raise R heel.

Swing. (Used in quadrille dances.) Boy takes girl as in waltz position, excepting that the ball of the R foot, both of the boy and girl, is placed on the outside and to the right of the other's R foot. Their R sides are next to each other with approximately six inches of space between them and in such alignment that if a line were drawn L shoulder to R shoulder of each person the two lines would be parallel. The boy should hold the girl firmly with his R hand in the small of her back. Both should stand straight and lean slightly backward, thus placing the center of balance over the pivot (R) foot of each person. Both the boy and girl pivot on the ball of the R foot. As the balance of weight is shifted the R foot should be allowed to rise and slide naturally in a close, tight circle on the pivot spot.

The L foot is used to propel the body around in a circle and should be kept slightly behind and to the L of the R foot. The propelling force is obtained by pushing downward and backward with the toe of the L foot as each shift of the R foot occurs.

Three-Step Turn. 4/4 time (count is "one, two, three, four") or 3/4 time (count of six). Three-four time music requires two measures of music to complete the step. Count 1: step R sideways. Count 2: cross L leg in front of R and execute a complete turn in place on balls of feet with weight transferred to L foot after the turn. Count 3: step R to side. Count 4: hold position. Repeat all starting to left with L foot.

Two-Step. 2/4 or 4/4 time. Count is "one, and, two, and." Count 1: step diagonally left with L foot. Count "and": close R foot to L and transfer weight. Count 2: step diagonally forward again with L foot. Count "and": hold. Repeat, beginning with R foot. As skill is gained, use gliding steps.

Tyroler Waltz. Partners stand side by side, inside hands joined. As hands swing forward and up, each partner executes one waltz balance (see page 210), turning away from partner. Joined hands then swing down and back, while partners face with a second waltz balance. ("Little Man in a Fix" uses a Tyroler Waltz as part of the pattern.)

Varsovienne Step. 3/4 time. Count is "one, two, three." Count 1: raise and bend L knee, thereby swinging L foot over instep of R foot. Count 2: step L. Count 3: step R. Count 2 may become a slide. Repeat and then after foot swing take three steps in place, making a half turn and point R foot. Repeat, beginning with R foot. For Varsovienne position see page 205.

Waltz Step.[1]   3/4 time. Count is *"one,* two, three." Accent is always on count one, and step is always taken on accented beat—be it forward or back. Never two-step to waltz music. Each count has the same value. Do not rush count three. Count 1: step forward on R foot. Count 2: step with L foot beyond R foot and transfer weight to L foot. Feet are never together on count two. Count 3: bring feet together (R foot up to L foot) and transfer weight to R foot. Count 1: step forward on L foot. Count 2: step beyond L foot with R foot. Count 3: bring feet together and transfer weight. Repeat as desired—forward, backward, turning R, turning L. The sliding foot always passes the weight-bearing foot on count two. When partners start to waltz, the gentleman always begins with a backward step on his L foot, and the lady begins with a forward step on her R foot. When starting to turn right, man begins with L foot; lady with her R foot. When starting a reverse turn (that is, to the left), man begins with R foot; lady with L foot.

Waltz Balance.   3/4 time. Count is *"one,* two, three." Count 1: step forward on L foot. Count 2: close R foot to L foot. Count 3: raise and lower heels. Knees and ankles should be easy, thereby getting an up-and-down motion.

SELECTED REFERENCES[2]

BALLWEBBER, EDITH. *Group Instruction in Social Dancing.* New York: A. S. Barnes & Co., 1938.

BURCHENAL, ELIZABETH. *Folk-Dances of Germany.* New York: G. Schirmer, Inc., 1938.

DUGGAN, ANNE SCHLEY; SCHLOTTMANN, JEANETTE; and RUTLEDGE, ABBIE. *The Folk Dance Library.* 5 vols. New York: A. S. Barnes & Co., 1948.

DUGGAN, ANNE SCHLEY. *Tap Dances for School and Recreation.* New York: A. S. Barnes & Co., 1935.

EVANS, BESSIE. *American Indian Dance Steps.* New York: A. S. Barnes & Co., 1931.

HOSTETLER, LAWRENCE. *The Art of Social Dancing.* New York: A. S. Barnes & Co., 1934.

KOZMAN, HILDA CLUTE. *Character Dances for School Programs.* New York: A. S. Barnes & Co., 1935.

MASON, BERNARD S. *Dances and Stories of the American Indian.* New York: A. S. Barnes & Co., 1944.

RADIR, RUTH. *Modern Dance for the Youth of America.* New York: A. S. Barnes & Co., 1944.

REYES, FRANCISCA S., and RAMOS, PETRONE. *Philippine Folk Dances and Games.* New York: Silver, Burdett and Co., 1927.

RYAN, GRACE L. *Dances of Our Pioneers.* New York: A. S. Barnes & Co., 1939.

[1] See directions for the waltz, pp. 840 ff.
[2] The appendixes also list phonograph records as well as books, magazines, films, and filmstrips.

Schwendener, Norma, and Tibbels, Averil. *Legends & Dances of Old Mexico*. New York: A. S. Barnes & Co., 1934.

Selden, Elizabeth. *Elements of the Free Dance*. New York: A. S. Barnes & Co., 1930.

Shaw, Lloyd. *Cowboy Dances: A Collection of Western Square Dances*. Caldwell, Idaho: The Caxton Printers, 1939.

—————. *The Round Dance Book*. Caldwell, Idaho: The Caxton Printers, 1948.

The Spanish-American Song and Game Book. Compiled by Workers of the Writers' Program, Music Program, and Art Program, of the Work Projects Administration in the State of New Mexico. New York: A. S. Barnes & Co., 1945.

Sutton, Rhoda Reynolds, and Brooks, Elizabeth. *Creative Rhythms*. New York: A. S. Barnes & Co., 1941.

Terry, Walter. *Invitation to Dance*. New York: A. S. Barnes & Co., 1942.

Waterman, Elizabeth. *The Rhythm Book*. New York: A. S. Barnes & Co., 1936.

Wissler, Clark. *Indians of the United States*. New York: Doubleday, Doran & Co., 1940.

Chapter IX
SELF-TESTING ACTIVITIES

A number of physical activities have a stunt quality; they appear to say, "Can you do this?" In this respect they challenge the individual to test himself and so have acquired the designation, self-testing. This type of activity offers individuals an increased opportunity to attain status within the group because of the possibility of excelling in certain skills. In addition, many activities of this type offer valuable opportunities to develop the muscular strength and co-ordination so essential to good body mechanics. Of greatest value in this respect are the total body activities, stunts, tumbling, rope jumping, apparatus games, and wrestling. Juggling, playing marbles, and spinning tops, although offering less physical exercise, have some value in the physical education program because of their age-old appeal to children.

STUNTS AND TUMBLING

Children are keenly interested in stunts. Very frequently they dare others to try an activity they are able to perform, and competition is keen. The universal appeal of stunts leads many pupils to practice them at home. This interest should be utilized to develop a program of stunts and tumbling that will stimulate the child's interest in building up body control and muscle strength. Such activities are an excellent form of exercise, causing a marked increase in nervous control and growth in the strength of arm, shoulder, back and leg muscles. These in turn result in increased bodily stamina, improved body control, and capacity to withstand heavier physical demands. Much practice is necessary before proficiency in execution is gained, but as skill is acquired the performer experiences a great emotional satisfaction.

Equipment and Its Care

Mats are needed for stunts and tumbling, although some of these activities can be conducted on grass plots or at the jumping pit. Mats can be used out of doors or, during inclement weather, within halls or classrooms. Homemade mats and discarded mattresses are not recommended. The selection, care, and purchase of mats are discussed in Chapter V. Mats should never be dragged over the floor or ground; they should be carried. They should be hung against a wall or should be placed on a mat rack when not in use.

Figure 71. To climb up a ladder and slide down a slide is a stunt for a primary-age child.

Shoes should be removed during instruction and practice periods. Girls should wear shorts, slacks, or jeans on days when stunts are scheduled.

Stunt Activities for Young Children (K, 1, 2, 3)

Children in the kindergarten and primary grades should be encouraged to become familiar with their physical surroundings and their own relationship to those surroundings through everyday experiences with such activities as running properly, hopping on one or both feet, skipping, twirling, galloping, turning somersaults, walking up a slanting ladder and sloping plank for short or longer distances, manipulating large wooden boxes and barrels, hanging by their hands or by their knees from different objects and climbing up and sliding down low slides. The above activities are typical of the type of stunt program they should have.

Early in the program for grade 3 the forward roll (somersault) and backward roll should be introduced and practiced until confidence, control, and perfection in execution is gained. Younger children can gain confidence through use of the forward roll. Skill in the forward and backward roll is necessary before the pupil may be introduced with safety to stunts calling for other inverted positions.

Activities Undesirable for Young Children. Because the following types of activities might injure children they should not be used: those that call for (1) extreme skill in balancing, (2) exceptional body control, (3) expenditure of great strength, or (4) prolonged periods of endurance. Neither should carrying of undue weight by any part of the body be required. Backward bending, splits, and activities that put an extra strain on joints should be avoided not only in these grades but in all grades. For example, the stump walk, knee dip, and fish-hook dive should not be taught, or their use permitted, since excessive strain is put on the ligaments surrounding the knee joint, and, once injured, the knee joint is the most difficult of all the joints to heal. Other stunts that should not be taught are table, bridge, or crab bend, since they overextend the back. Wooden Man puts a severe strain on the shoulders and may cause a shoulder dislocation if improperly done. Skin the Snake, when used as a speed event, is apt to cause too great a pull on the arms. When headstands or other inverted positions are used, extreme over-extension of the lower back region should be controlled by the raising or lowering of the head.

Stunt Activities for Pupils in Intermediate Grades (4, 5, 6)

In the intermediate grades, emphasis should be placed upon improvement of techniques, control in performance, and progression from simple

Figure 72. The forward roll allows the weight of the body to be taken on the hands and upper back with no pressure on the head.

to more difficult activities performed by the individual alone. No stunt should be used that requires the performer to carry a weight equal to or more than his own weight. The top performer in a dual, triple, or pyramid stunt should be considerably lighter in weight than is the base performer. This rule is extremely important, because until late adolescence certain cartilaginous attachments for muscle ends are not fully developed nor permanently attached to bone surfaces and may be severed from their attachment area if an excessive weight is placed on them.[1] For the same reason high pyramid stunts are not recommended for use in elementary and junior high school programs.

Children should not be encouraged to attempt new activities until old ones are fully mastered. A controlled performance with appreciable periods of rest during the stunt or at the finish should be required. Most stunts should start and end with the performer standing erect.

Stunt Activities for Pupils in Upper Grades (7 and 8)

Pupils in grades 7 and 8 show great interest in stunts. At this age boys and girls are capable of more sustained concentration and longer periods of vigorous participation in stunt activities. Group practice, under command, should result in increased control and improved performance. Individual, couple, and group combinations, and pyramid patterns in which height is not a factor should be practiced.

Introducing the Stunt and Tumbling Program

Schools that have not previously attempted the study of stunts and tumbling should start all pupils, regardless of grade level, with activities listed for primary grades and progress through materials suggested for intermediate and upper grades. Ernest Balch states that the ten basic elements to be mastered are the salute (used as a salutation before starting a stunt or when expressing thanks for applause), the rolls, headstand, cart wheels, handstands, hand walking, couple stunts, handsprings, pyramids, and diving. He, with others, states that mastery of the rolls (forward and backward) is one of the most important skills to be learned and that students should be introduced to them early in the program.[2]

[1] Charles Leroy Lowman, and Others, *Corrective Physical Education for Groups*. New York: A. S. Barnes & Co., 1928, p. 110.
[2] Ernest Balch, *Amateur Circus Life*. New York: The Macmillan Co., 1924, pp. 8-35.
B. and D. Cotteral, *The Teaching of Stunts and Tumbling*. New York: A. S. Barnes & Co., 1936, pp. 151-73.
L. I. McClow and D. N. Anderson, *Tumbling Illustrated*. New York: A. S. Barnes & Co., 1931, pp. 1-9.
W. R. La Porte and A. G. Renner, *The Tumbler's Manual*. New York: Prentice-Hall, Inc., 1938, pp. 9-21.

Rural Schools and the Stunt Program

Schools with such small enrollments as to prohibit pupil participation in team games should find the stunt program invaluable as a conditioning medium and as a means of having pupils take part in group experiences. Individual athletic events can be included for the older children as part of their stunt program.

Teachers should select stunts that will be suitable to children of different age groups. Children should be permitted to work on any activities they may wish, provided weight bearing is eliminated. There are numerous stunts done by couples that younger children will enjoy.

Suggestions for Teaching Stunts and Tumbling

Discussion of organization, classification, and evaluation techniques for stunts and tumbling is given here. In Part II of this guide selected stunt activities are described for each grade. Additional references for stunts and tumbling activities should be available to both teacher and pupil in school and county libraries. Pupils should be allowed to present stunts that they know and all should be encouraged to learn the new stunt. Teachers should not be surprised if girls show greater enthusiasm and proficiency than do boys. Being generally more supple than boys, girls gain proficiency more rapidly, with earlier emotional gratification, which causes them to persist more enthusiastically.

Organization Procedures. A stunt or tumbling lesson may call for the performance of an activity by one person alone, by two, three, or more in unison, or by the entire group. Several methods of class organization may be used, depending on age and ability of pupils and type of activity being presented.

1. Mass Grouping. When numbers to participate are not too large and the activity is not too difficult, mass grouping can be used. All can listen to the instruction, watch the demonstration, and work simultaneously but each at his own rate of speed. Later pupils work by count.

2. Squad Grouping. Large groups can be divided into squads, each with a squad leader who has had previous instruction in the activities to be introduced. This leaves the teacher free to give instruction or assistance where most needed.

3. Ability Grouping. Members of the group may be divided into squads according to known skills or for assignment to a special activity. The teacher may announce what activity is to be practiced and squad leaders then direct the activity. The teacher is then free to move

about and introduce new material as groups are ready to proceed to new experiences.

Skill in fundamental movements may be used as a gauge when it is desired to organize groups for stunt practice. Some of the fundamental activities involve the following skills:

1. Forward and backward rolls
2. The use of the inverted position—head-, forearm-, and handstands, cart wheels, handstand dip
3. Some form of jumping—leapfrog, jump the stick, the top, jumping jack
4. Careful balancing—forearm stand, hand knee shoulder stand
5. Springing—mule kick, heel knock, diving

Achievement Checking. Not more often than once a month pupils should be checked on improvement. The Stunt Achievement Chart (Figure 73) should prove useful in showing progress of individuals and of groups. The performance rating should be based on the form, control, and successful completion of each stunt.

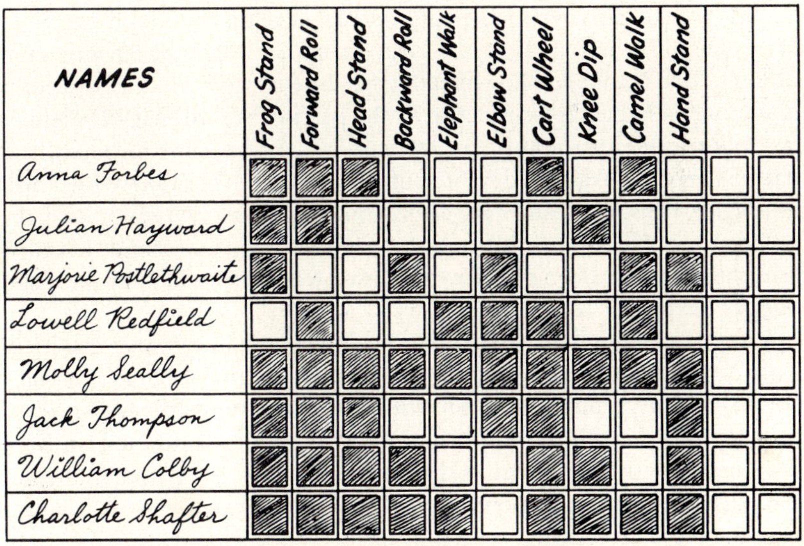

NAMES	Frog Stand	Forward Roll	Head Stand	Backward Roll	Elephant Walk	Elbow Stand	Cart Wheel	Knee Dip	Camel Walk	Hand Stand		
Anna Forbes	▨	▨	▨				▨		▨			
Julian Hayward	▨	▨						▨				
Marjorie Postlethwaite	▨			▨		▨			▨	▨		
Lowell Redfield		▨			▨	▨	▨					
Molly Scally	▨	▨		▨					▨	▨		
Jack Thompson	▨	▨							▨			
William Colby	▨	▨	▨	▨			▨	▨				
Charlotte Shafter	▨	▨	▨	▨	▨		▨	▨	▨			

Figure 73. Each child's achievement in stunts is checked on the stunt achievement chart by blacking out the square under the name of the stunt when that particular stunt is mastered.

Motivation. Several methods may be employed to stimulate the interest of participants:

1. Demonstration of class tumbling with all participating
2. Five-minute programs worked up by each squad

3. Competition to determine those showing the best form
4. Challenges; class divided into teams that challenge each other to do a particular stunt; points given for successful performance
5. Ladder tournaments using ten or more stunts and having a ladder for each one (see page 186).
6. Achievement charts posted to permit checking off activities as they are mastered

Safety Techniques in the Stunt Program

Teachers should not be apprehensive of teaching stunts. If the basic skills are thoroughly mastered by pupils, stunts need not be dangerous. Safety regulations for the performance of each stunt should be a part of the instruction.

Fear is an enemy of safe performance. A teacher of stunts and tumbling should never allow a pupil to perform any activity about which he has fear. Self-confidence must be built up gradually by acquiring skills that are fundamental to advanced stunts. Pupils should have complete confidence in the teacher.

Spotting. Teachers and pupils should develop the art of spotting; that is, guarding and assisting a performer until mastery of an activity is acquired. For example, when introducing the forward roll, the instructor should, while kneeling by the side of the performer, see that throughout the performance the head of the student is tucked against his chest, and that his back is maintained in a rounded or barrel position with knees tight against his chest and feet against his thighs. At the same time the teacher or spotter assists the pupil by pushing the shoulders down with his right hand and giving an upward push to the hips while his left hand is under the pupil's ankles.[1]

A spotter should be careful not to have his own head over the body of the performer, since flying feet may inflict a painful blow. The performer should complete his roll with a forward upward extension of his body together with a slight jump into the air so as to land on both feet simultaneously. Following the performance of each stunt the erect position should be held momentarily before performer moves *forward* from the place of action.

Safety Rules for the Teacher. The following points should be remembered by the teacher when a stunt period is in progress:

1. Have no practice periods without you (the teacher) or a trained spotter present and helping.

---

[1] W. R. La Porte and A. G. Renner, *op. cit.*, pp. 5-7.
See also Virginia Lee Horne, *Stunts and Tumbling for Girls.* New York: A. S. Barnes & Co., 1943.

2. Develop skill in spotting. It is more important for a teacher to develop this skill than to be an adept performer of the activity being presented.
3. Have a warm-up period before each lesson.
4. When pupils, regardless of grade placement, have had no previous instruction in stunts, begin with the activities for the primary grades and work forward from grade to grade.
5. Encourage pupils to protect others as well as themselves.
6. Remember that adolescent girls increase in weight around the hips and the center of gravity is lower in the trunk than previously; therefore, a re-emphasis on the mastery of basic skills is essential.

Safety Rules for Pupils. The pupils should be guided by the following safety rules while performing stunts:

1. Be sure area is clear of persons or objects before attempting a stunt.
2. Master the rolls thoroughly, since they are basic to all inverted stunts.
3. Always complete a stunt once it has been started.
4. Remember that a stunt worth doing is worth doing well.
5. Be sure others are ready when dual, triple, or group stunts are to be undertaken.
6. Avoid loud laughter or unnecessary noise. They may disturb or interfere with the success of a performer.

TEACHING SUGGESTIONS

1. Do not forget the warm-up period. It may consist of limbering-up exercises or a short run.
2. Teach performers to fall without twisting and especially to control body segments as the performance progresses.
3. Strive to develop group safety habits.
4. Have pockets emptied and glasses, pins, bracelets, and lockets removed.
5. If possible have stunts demonstrated before their study is undertaken.
6. Stand near or beside pupils when new activities are to be tried.
7. Teach pupils to be successful spotters.
8. Make waiting periods as short as possible.

ROPE JUMPING

Jumping rope is a very old pastime. In a volume published many years ago, *Sports and Pastimes of the People of England*, Joseph Strutt offers the following description of rope skipping:

This amusement is probably very ancient. It is performed by a rope held by both ends, that is, one end in each hand, and thrown forward or backward over the head and under the feet alternately. Boys often contend for superiority of skill in this game, and he who passes the rope about most times without interruption is the conqueror. In the hop season, a hop-stem stripped of its leaves is used instead of a rope, and in my opinion is preferable.[1]

Besides being a favorite game, rope jumping is an inexpensive activity and one that develops a sense of rhythm and total body control.

Equipment

Short and long ropes are needed for teaching purposes. Each child should be supplied with a short rope—one long enough to reach from the hips to the ground when doubled. A knot should be tied at each end to prevent raveling. Numerous long single ropes or long double ropes are needed for certain jumping patterns. Long ropes should be finger-thick and from 20 to 25 feet in length. Window sash rope is strong and durable. It can be cleaned in a washing machine.

Specific Values

Is jumping rope a sissy activity? One cannot say that it is, since the Army and Navy require its use as one means of developing endurance, and since boxers, football players, and track men use it in their training. Its physiological benefits are many. The leg muscles benefit directly because the stimulation given to the circulation results in a greatly increased return of venous blood from the legs to the heart. The exercise of jumping causes greater peristalsis of the intestines, resulting in better elimination. Flexibility of the chest wall is increased and thoracic breathing is stimulated, since respiration is quickened. The competition involved is individual and is not emotionally as irritating, disturbing, and exhausting as certain other forms of competition.

The organ called on to function most vigorously in rope jumping is the heart, but there is no possibility that the normal heart will be injured by this activity. Vigorous action results in a performer's getting his second wind; that is, after the first exhaustion caused by exertion the heart has increased the volume of blood pumped, causing a slowing of the pulse rate, easier breathing, and renewed energy. Since these adjustments take place only during continuous periods of sustained activity, they will be developed only in those who so exercise. Athletes, and boxers in particular, find rope jumping beneficial because of this fact as well as the benefit the leg muscles receive from the exercise.

---

[1] Joseph Strutt, *Sports and Pastimes of the People of England.* London, 1810 (second edition), p. 339.

Safety Measures

Children recovering from a prolonged sickness such as measles, whooping cough, scarlet fever, heavy cold, tonsilitis, influenza, diphtheria, or who are recovering from a recent operation should not be allowed to jump rope for several weeks.

Rest periods should be provided so that activity is not too long continued. When a long rope is used, a period of rest is assured for each child, since each must take a turn at swinging the rope or ropes. Performers strive for two goals. The first is to do tricks of varying types while hopping over one or two ropes. The second object is to jump a rope turned speedily. Failure in each gives a rest to the performer. The greater the number of tricks known, the greater the number of rest periods. Injury from speed jumping is prevented because errors are frequent when trying to clear the rope; also, those turning the rope cannot keep up the increased turning speed for any length of time.

Teaching Procedures

Boys and girls in the first grade often have difficulty in learning to jump rope. Young children, before using the rope, can learn to jump lightly with a steady, even timing by dramatizing a jack-in-a-box, grasshopper, or kangaroo.

ure 74. Rope jumping develops a sense of rhythm and total body control well as being a favorite activity.

Rope jumping to the first-grade child is a stunt of jumping over the rope at the right moment; to the third and fourth grader, it is an activity jumped to a rhyme in which one may show adeptness in performing unusual and difficult stunts; and to the intermediate child, or older boy and girl, it is an activity that can be made more challenging through tournament routines, or through rhythm routines to music.[1]

Rhythmical accompaniment makes jumping easier and more enjoyable. Victor record Number 20162, "Rhythms for Children," Parts 2 and 3, will be found helpful when developing jumping skill. Two other Victor records, Number 20164 and 22169, include several selections, of which the "Legend of the Bells" and "With Castanets" provide jumping rhythms.

Jumping Techniques

Teachers may find it necessary on the first day that long ropes are introduced to divide children into several groups. The groups will probably be those who can run in and jump, those who can stand still and jump as the rope is turned, and those who cannot jump. The last group will need most attention. One manner of developing skill is to swing the rope slowly back and forth like a pendulum without turning it but gradually raising it while the jumper jumps to the following rhyme:

Old Man Daisy
He went crazy,
Up the ladder
Down the ladder
Went Old Man Daisy.[2]

Front and Back Door Run In. An easy way of introducing rope jumping is to teach the old routine, "Chase the Fox!" The rope is turned and the jumper attempts to run through the "front door," that is, under the rope while it is being turned toward the jumper and is at its highest point. If successful, the jumper next attempts to run in, jump once, and run out. This is continued until six jumps are made successfully, whereupon the jumper relieves one of the rope turners. After this is learned the jumper is ready to try "back door" jumping; that is, he runs in when the rope is being turned away from him. One, both, or alternating feet may be used during the jumping. One of the hardest stunts is to run in, jump, and run out while two ropes are being turned simultaneously toward each other for front door or back door jumping.

---

[1] Helen Fahey, "Everyone Jumps Rope," *Journal of Health and Physical Education,* XI (September, 1940), 420.

[2] This rhyme and those that follow are used by permission of Helen Fahey, Special Assistant in Physical Education, Public Schools, Kansas City, Missouri.

Rhymes for Rope Jumping. There are many traditional rhymes that children chant as they jump rope. Three of these follow:

1

Chickety, chickety, chop
How many times before I stop?

2

Lady, lady, at the gate,
Eating cherries from a plate;
How many cherries did she partake?
One, two, three, four, five!

3

I asked my mother for fifteen cents
To see the elephant jump the fence,
He jumped so high, he reached the sky,
And never came back 'til the Fourth of July.

During the third rhyme the jumper does regular jumping to the first two lines. The rope is then gradually raised during the last two lines and the jumper has to jump higher and higher until he runs out on the word "July."

Rhymes for Speed Jumping. Some of the rhymes best liked for speed jumping are the following four:

1

H - O - T spells
Red hot pepper.

On the word "pepper" the performers jump as rapidly as possible until a miss occurs.

2

Mary, Mary, with a curl
Will you jump as my best girl?
Slow at first, now that's the way,
On we go to the break of day.

A boy and a girl jump together, using a short rope. The inside arm of each is around the waist of the partner. Outside hands hold the rope, which rests on the ground in the rear of the jumpers. As the rope comes forward they jump. The speed is increased on the last line and both continue to jump until a miss is made.

3

"Fire, fire," says Mrs. McGuire
"Where, where," says Mrs. O'Dare
"At the fair," says Mrs. Blair
"And it burns hotter and hotter."

Regular jumping occurs until the last word, "hotter."

4

Mother, mother, I am able
To stand on a chair and set the table;
Daughter, daughter, don't forget
Salt, vinegar, and red hot pepper.

Regular jumping occurs until the last word, "pepper."

Longer Rhymes for Older Children.   Pupils in the upper grades like to jump to longer rhymes and to those that signify actions to be performed. A few follow:

1

Down in the valley
  Where the green grass grows,
Sat little Mary as sweet as a rose.
  Along came Johnny
And kissed her on her nose
  How many kisses did she get?
1, 2, 3, 4, 5, 6, etc.

2

Mother, mother, I am ill,
Send for the doctor on the hill;
Doctor, doctor, shall I die?
Yes, my child, but do not cry.
How many flowers shall I have?
1, 2, 3, 4, 5, 6, etc.

Foot and Arm Patterns.   The material that follows describes various foot and arm patterns that can be used by a jumper, together with activities for ropes of different lengths.[1]

1. Short Rope
  Crossed Elbows.   Cross arms at elbows and turn rope with hands far out at sides.

---

[1] Adapted from article by Sue Hall, "That Spring Perennial—Rope Jumping," *Recreation,* XXXIV (March, 1941), 713-16. By permission of the author.

Rock. One foot in front of the other. Hop on front foot, then on back foot and continue rocking motion. Change feet and repeat.

Heel, Heel. Hop placing alternate heels forward on the ground.

Feet Together and Apart. Alternate jumping with feet together and feet spread apart.

Toe Tap. Hop with free leg and ankle extended forward, with little toe of forward foot tapping the ground.

Leg Swing. Hop on one foot, swing the other foot forward.

Jump Turn. Turn around while jumping in place.

Toe Tap in Back. Hop on one foot, tapping in back with the toe of the free foot.

Legs Crossed. Jump on both feet with one ankle crossed over the other.

Two Feet. Jump with both feet close together.

Single Hop. Hop on either right or left foot. Other foot is raised and held high with bent knee.

Skip. Skip in place and skip while traveling.

Dance Step. Hop while using a tap movement, such as brush and tap between hops.

2. One Long and One Short Rope. Long rope is turned by two players and third player runs in while jumping a short rope. He continues to jump both ropes together or two ropes in succession.

3. One Long or Medium Length Rope. Each turner makes a three quarter turn while swinging the rope and both jump the rope simultaneously.

4. Two Long Ropes. Players turn two long ropes. Each turner holds one hand slightly higher than the other. One rope is held still and to the side out of the way. Turners start turning one rope and then begin turning the second rope in the opposite direction. Third player runs in and jumps both ropes in turn as each strikes the ground. Jumping will be faster than for a single long rope but not as fast as "Salt, Pepper, Vinegar, HOT!"

5. Long Rope

Running Through School. (a) Run through a turning rope without jumping it. (b) Run in, jump one, and run out. Continue to add a jump for each grade. (c) For college years, go in the "back door" and jump, adding a jump for each year.

Baby's Cradle. Jump a rope swaying from side to side. Rope is held at same height throughout. Continue until a miss occurs.

Snake.   Wriggle, wave, or wag rope sideways on surface. Performer
jumps over wriggling rope and tries not to be bitten. For variety,
the rope may be raised while being wriggled.

Cut the Cheese.   Wriggle, wave, or wag the rope up and down.
Performer jumps over rope and tries not to let rope touch him.

Charlie Chaplin.   Jump a turning rope once for every other word.
Continue counting until a miss occurs.

> Charlie Chaplin sat on a pin
> How many inches did it go in?
> 1, 2, 3, 4, 5, 6, etc.

Going by Ages.   Jump a turning rope. Youngest player or players
turn the rope and second or third youngest player jumps first
and the oldest player jumps last. Jump once for every year of
the jumper's age. Jump until a miss occurs to determine how
many years the jumper will live.

Going A B C.   Jump until a miss occurs. The jumper who goes all
through the alphabet without a miss will be a bachelor maid,
or bachelor; first bride or first groom. Go through again and
learn first initial of girl's or boy's name.

> Raspberry, raspberry, raspberry jam,
> Tell me the initials of your (or my) old man.
> A, B, C, D, E, F, etc.

Cinderella.   Jump a turning rope once for every other syllable.

> Cinderella, dressed in white,
> Went upstairs to clean the flues.
> How many flues did she clean?
> 1, 2, 3, 4, 5, 6, etc.
>
> Cinderella, dressed in white,
> Went upstairs to turn on the lights.
> How many light bulbs did she use?
> 1, 2, 3, 4, 5, 6, etc.

One, Two Buckle (Button) My Shoe.   Jump a turning rope for
every other word. Work out pantomime while jumping. Run
out at end of verse.

> 1- 2 Buckle my shoe
> 3- 4 Shut the door
> 5- 6 Pick up sticks
> 7- 8 Lay them straight
> 9-10 Big fat hen
> 11-12 Ring the bell

    13-14 Maids a-courting
    15-16 Girls a-fixing
    17-18 Boys a-waiting
    19-20 That's a-plenty!

Teddy Bear. Jump a turning rope once for every other word. Work out pantomime. Run out at end of verse.

    Teddy Bear, Teddy Bear, turn around
    Teddy Bear, Teddy Bear, touch the ground
    Teddy Bear, Teddy Bear, buckle your shoe
    Teddy Bear, Teddy Bear, you'd better skiddoo
    Teddy Bear, Teddy Bear, go upstairs
    Teddy Bear, Teddy Bear, say your prayers
    Teddy Bear, Teddy Bear, switch off the light
    Teddy Bear, Teddy Bear, say good night!

JUGGLING

Juggling is an ancient activity. It requires perseverance, close concentration, and perfect timing.

Equipment

Tennis balls, jackstone balls, buckeye seeds, or walnuts are needed in a quantity depending on the number to be instructed.

Technique for Using Two Balls

1. In slow motion, player extends right or left arm forward and brings it upward in a circular motion toward the body.
2. Same exercise is continued with player practicing the throwing and catching of a single ball.
3. Next two balls are held in one hand, palm turned upward. Player throws ball No. 1 upward during circular motion and proceeds to release ball No. 2 before ball No. 1 is caught by the same hand. Movement is continuous, with player always throwing one ball and before catching it releasing the other ball.

    Height reached by balls will range from $1\frac{1}{2}$ to $2\frac{1}{2}$ feet. First attempts will not be too successful but by third practice period improvement will be noticed.

Technique for Using Three Balls

Balls No. 1 and 3 are held in the left hand and ball No. 2 in the right hand.

1. Ball No. 1 is thrown from left hand and is caught in the right hand after ball No. 2 is released.

2. Before ball No. 1 from left hand is caught by right hand, ball No. 2 in right hand is released, and

3. Before ball No. 2 from right hand is caught in left hand, ball No. 3 from left hand is released.

4. Continue throws, always remembering to release the second ball in a hand before catching the first ball with the other hand and while the third ball is in the air.

MARBLES AND TOPS

Yearly, school authorities face the question of whether to permit marbles and tops on the school grounds. The recommendation of physical education authorities has been not to encourage the use of marbles and tops during the school day, but to schedule instead games that necessitate the use of play equipment on the school grounds that offers more vigorous activity. There may be schools, however, where the use of marbles and tops during the school day should not be denied, especially where there is an inadequate supply of essential play equipment. The season for marbles and tops on school grounds should not exceed three weeks for each.

Marble Games

In Joseph Strutt's book *Sports and Pastimes of the People of England* is a quaint description of marble games used in the seventeenth century.

> Marbles seem to have been used by the boys as substitutes for bowls and with them they amuse themselves in many different manners.
> Taw, (a game) wherein a number of boys put each of them one or two marbles in a ring and shoot at them alternately with other marbles, and he who obtains the most of them by beating them out of the ring is the conqueror.
> Nine holes; which consists in bowling of marbles at a wooden bridge with nine arches. There is also another game of marbles where four, five or six holes, and sometimes more, are made in the ground at a distance from each other; and the business of everyone of the players is to bowl a marble by a regular succession into all the holes, which he who completes in the fewest bowls obtains the victory.
> Boss out, or boss and span, also called hit or span, wherein one bowls a marble to any distance that he pleases, which serves as a mark for his antagonist to bowl at, whose business it is to hit the marble first bowled, or lay his own near enough to it for him to span the space between them and touch both marbles; in either case he wins, if not his marble remains where it lay and becomes a mark for the first player, and so alternately until the game is won.[1]

Ringer (A Marble Game). The game Ringer is recommended as the wind-up for the marble season.

NUMBER OF PLAYERS: 2-6

SPACE: Playground—hard, smooth, level surface

PLAYING AREA: A ring with a diameter of 10 feet is drawn (Figure

---

[1] Joseph Strutt, *op. cit.*, p. 340.

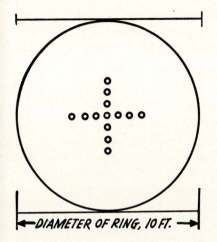

DIAMETER OF RING, 10 FT.

Figure 75. Layout shown is for Ringer, a marble game.

75). The outline of the ring should not be so deep or so wide as to check the roll of a marble. Two lines 9 inches long are drawn at right angles to each other in the form of a cross as a guide for placing the playing marbles. A lag line, a straight line tangent to the ring and touching it at one point, is drawn. The pitch line, a straight line tangent to the ring directly opposite the lag line and parallel to it, is drawn.

EQUIPMENT. Thirteen playing marbles. One marble is placed at the center and three each on the four branches of the cross, each marble being three inches from the next one.

Each player should have his own shooter marble. The playing marbles should be round and made of clay and should be not more than $\frac{5}{8}$ inch in diameter. During tournaments, all marbles in any one playing ring must be of uniform size.

The shooter of each player may be made of any substance except metal and should be not less than $\frac{1}{2}$ inch nor more than $\frac{5}{8}$ inch in diameter.

FORMATION. Two to six players may compete in a game. During tournaments not more than six persons may play in elimination games. Only two persons may play in a game during the finals of a tournament. Play takes place within the ring. All play is "for fair" and marbles must be returned to owners after each game.

THE LAG. The lag, in Ringer, is the first operation before actual play begins. It must precede each new game. Two lag players stand toeing the pitch line or they may knuckle down upon the pitch line. Each person tosses or shoots his shooter marble toward the lag line across the ring. The player whose shooter comes to rest nearest the lag line (on either side) wins the lag. The same shooter that is used in the lag must be used through the game which follows the lag.

The player winning the lag shoots first; others follow according to the distance between their shooters and the lag line, next nearest playing second.

KNUCKLING DOWN. During all shots, except the lag, a player's knuckle or knuckles must be in contact with the ground and the position must be maintained until the shooter leaves the hand.

PROCEDURE. To start the game each player in turn should knuckle down just outside the ring line, at any point desired, and should (1) shoot into the ring to knock one or more marbles out of the ring; or (2) shoot to hit or knock out of the ring the shooter of any opposing player if any such remain inside the ring.

If a player's shooter (1) knocks one or more marbles out of the ring, or (2) hits the shooter of an opponent, or (3) knocks an opponent's shooter out of the ring, the player continues to shoot, provided his own shooter remains inside the ring.

In the event a player's shooter passes outside the ring whether or not he has scored on the shot, he ceases to shoot but is credited with the marbles he scored.

If, after a miss, a player's shooter remains in the ring, the player must leave it there. His opponents are permitted to shoot at it.

If a player sends his shooter so that it rolls outside the ring, whether he hits a marble or misses, he picks the shooter up until his next turn, when he is permitted to take "roundsters" and may shoot from any point on the ring line.

PLAYING REGULATIONS. The following regulations control the method of play:

1. Whenever a shooter or marble comes to rest on the ring line, it is considered out of the ring if its center is exactly on the ring line or outside the ring. It is considered inside the ring if its center is inside the ring line.

2. Marbles knocked out of the ring are picked up by the player who knocks them out.

3. A player who hits an opponent's shooter inside the ring but does not knock it out of the ring picks up any marble he chooses and then continues to shoot, provided his own shooter remains inside the ring. He must not again hit the same opponent's shooter until (a) he hits another player's shooter, (b) he knocks a marble out of the ring, or (c) his next turn to shoot comes around.

4. A player knocking an opponent's shooter out of the ring is entitled to all the marbles won by that opponent, and the opponent whose shooter is knocked out of the ring is "killed," that is, he is out of the game. If the opponent who was knocked out of the ring has no

marbles, the player who knocked him out is not entitled to pick up a marble as a reward for the shot.

5. If a shooter in his play (a) knocks out two or more marbles, or (b) hits an opponent's shooter and a marble, or (c) hits two opponents' shooters, or (d) completes any other combination play, he is entitled to all the points scored on the shot.

6. If a shooter slips from a player's hand, and travels no more than 10 inches, the player calls "slips"; if the referee is convinced it is a slip, he may order, "No play," and permit the player to shoot again. The referee's decision is final.

7. The game ends when the last marble is shot out of the ring.

8. A match may be decided in one, three, or five games. The games won determine the winner of each match.

FOULS. Certain forms of play constitute fouls, for which penalties are imposed.

1. A player must not raise his hand until the shooter has left his hand. This violation is known as "histing."

2. A player must not move his hand forward until the shooter has left his hand. This violation is known as "hunching."

3. A player must not smooth or otherwise rearrange the ground. He may request the referee to clear obstructions.

Penalty for 1, 2, and 3: If, on the shot, any marbles are knocked out or dislocated, they must be restored to their position and the player loses his shot.

4. A player must not change shooters during the game; he may choose a new shooter on each lag provided he uses that shooter in the subsequent game. *Penalty:* The player is disqualified from the game.

5. A player must not receive coaching during the course of the game. *Penalty:* Forfeiture of all marbles he knocked out of the ring, these marbles to be returned to the game and placed on the cross.

6. An instructor must not give directions to either his own or any other player engaged in the contest. *Penalty:* Instructor is ordered from the playing field, if, after being warned once, he continues his violation.

7. A player must not walk through the ring. *Penalty:* The referee may require the forfeiture of one marble.

SCORING. The following rules govern scoring:

1. A player is credited with 1 point for each marble knocked out of the ring by that player.

2. A player is credited with all the points previously earned by an opponent whose shooter the player knocks out of the ring.

3. A player is credited with 1 point each time he hits the shooter of an opponent but does not cause the shooter to go out of the ring.

4. The player having credited to him the largest number of points at the completion of the game wins the game.

5. At the end of a tie game, where two or more than two players are contesting, those in the tie play a new game to break the tie.

6. A player refusing to continue a game once it is started is disqualified. If only two players are in the contest the game is forfeited 13-0 in favor of the one remaining in the game.

OFFICIALS. For tournament play there should be a referee and a scorer. If a scorer is not available the referee keeps the scores. The referee has complete charge of the play. He interprets the rules and has power to make decisions on any points not specifically covered by these rules. The referee has authority to disqualify players for unsportsmanlike conduct. The referee may order from the playing field and its vicinity the instructor or other interested representative of any player who conducts himself in an unsportsmanlike manner. The scorer keeps a record of the game, marking shot by shot the score of each player. The scorer may assist the referee in enforcing the rule against coaching and may call to the attention of the referee any infraction of the rules. The scorer at the end of each game notifies the referee what the score is and the referee announces the winner.

TERMINOLOGY. The following terms are used in marble games:

Marbles. The object marbles only—variously known as "commies," "ducks," "mibs," and "miggs"

Shooter. The attacking marble—variously known as the "taw," "moonie," and "glassie"

Knuckling. Resting a knuckle or knuckles on the ground when shooting

Shooting. Releasing the shooter marble by force from the thumb as it is held between the thumb and first finger

Hunching. Moving the hand forward across the ring line when shooting from the ring line, or moving it forward from the spot at which the shooter came to rest when shooting inside the ring

Histing. Raising the hand from the ground when shooting

Roundsters. The privilege of taking a different position on the ring line for shooting; permitted only at the start of the game or when taking one's turn at shooting after a shooter has passed out of the ring

Lofting.   Shooting in an arc through the air to hit a marble—the most
  skillful shot in the game of ringer
Bowling.   Rolling a shot on the ground to hit a marble
Fair play.   Playing for the fun of the game; the marbles are returned to
  their owners at the end of each game.

Top Spinning Meet

Spring is the time for a top spinning meet. Following its conclusion
no further activity with tops should be scheduled on the playground.
Before the meet is held the lead-up time for tops on the playground
should not exceed three weeks.

The events that follow are excellent in themselves but best when they
are used in a meet where one follows the other. Points are given to winners
in each event.

Scoring Values.   First place—3 points; second place—2 points; third
place—1 point.

Equipment.   (1) Fifty-foot measuring tape; (2) chalk, small block
of wood, or marble for each contestant; (3) stop watch or watch with
second hand; (4) top; and (5) string.

Top Spinning for Distance.   A base line is drawn. Contestant may
not step on or over this line. Each contestant in turn throws top in an
effort to have it spin as far as possible beyond the base line. The first point
of contact determines the measuring point. Each contestant has five trials
and is credited with his best distance.

Top Spinning Dash.   A start and finish line 100 feet apart should be
drawn. Each contestant has chalk, small block of wood, or a marble.
Standing behind the start line, each contestant holds his top ready
for the throw. On signal each throws the top as far as possible, runs
forward, places marker on spot of contact and watches until top stops
spinning. He then secures top, rewinds it, and placing foot beside marker
throws again. Action is repeated until top spins beyond the finish line
as the result of a successful throw. Spin is finished when side of top
touches the ground. If top fails to spin, contestant must retrieve it, return
to his marker and, with foot in position, throw again. Play continues
until first three places are determined. When there are numerous contestants this event should be run off in heats, with winners in each heat
taking part in the final test.

Top Spinning Against Time.   At the word "Go" each contestant
throws his top. Each contestant has five throws, and the spinning time
of the five throws is totalled. First, second, and third place winners are

determined by the total time earned during the five trials. If the top does not spin, no time is earned and the throw counts as one of the five trials.

Top Spinning for Accuracy. On the ground a bull's-eye target consisting of five concentric circles should be drawn. The inner circle has a radius of 1½ inches, and each succeeding circle is 1½ inches from the next smaller circle. The circles from the inside out are numbered 5, 4, 3, 2, 1. Each contestant has five throws at the bull's-eye from outside the outer circle. Each throw scores the number of points indicated for the circle within which the point of the top first strikes. A line takes the score of the lower numbered circle. If the top does not spin, no points are scored and the throw counts as a trial. The total number of points for the five throws determines the score of each contestant.

Top Spinning Upside Down. The top is wound and placed upside down on the ground. The left foot is placed on the end of the string and the top kicked with the right foot. If the kick is timed properly the top will turn over and spin. Five trials are permitted and each successful spin scores 1 point. Total number of points for the five trials determines the score of each contestant.

CLIMBING APPARATUS GAMES

One of the oldest forms of play is the use that children make of trees, fences, rocks, ditches, and other structures to test themselves in climbing, hanging, jumping, balancing, and vaulting. Even cracks in a sidewalk offer a challenge to children and the dare is accepted in terms of a rhyme that they chant as they seek to avoid stepping on a crack. Climbing apparatus affords opportunity to climb, to hang, to jump, and to vault. The mere act of climbing to a height is thrilling to young children and to perform the stunt, whatever it may be, is in itself satisfying.

But it is possible to secure all of these advantages and in addition to play games using the apparatus. In a game a premium is placed on being able to climb quickly, to run swiftly, and to make many of the usual movements better than another person. Hence, there is stimulus to effort and attention to practice.

Many apparatus games can be and have been invented by children. The following [1] are merely suggestive of what may be played.

1. Ordinary Tag.   Game of usual tag is played, the players clambering over climbing apparatus to escape being tagged.
2. Cross Tag.   A certain player is chosen to be caught. A player crossing between the tagger and the one chosen to be caught saves that

---

[1] Supplied through the courtesy of E. P. Finigan, 314 Twelfth Street, San Francisco, representing the Recreation Climbing Gym.

person. A new chase is started after the player who crossed between the tagger and the runner during the previous chase.

3. Elimination Tag. One player is "it." As each player is tagged he must climb down from the apparatus and get out of the game. The last player tagged is the tagger for the new game.

4. Safety Zone Tag. Ordinary tag with a zone or area of the climbing apparatus set aside as a safe retreat. Players in the safety zone cannot be tagged.

5. Relay Races. Following the usual procedures for a relay race, the routes and stunts are performed within the climbing apparatus.

6. Bird Catcher. Use the game Bird Catcher described on page 362, with action taking place on the climbing apparatus.

7. Body Guard. A small space is designated at one end of the climbing apparatus as a goal area. One player is chosen to be the Panjandrum, an important person requiring body guards. Two players are chosen to be his guards. The game starts with these three players in the goal area and the balance of players scattered over the apparatus. The three leave the goal area with the guards traveling in front of the Panjandrum. The object of the game is for the members-at-large to touch the Panjandrum without being tagged by his guards. The guards will shift around His Majesty to prevent the attack and the Panjandrum himself may avoid being tagged by moving around or between his guards. When a guard succeeds in tagging a player, the three return to the playing area, the person tagged exchanges places with the Panjandrum, two new guards are selected, and the game is continued.

8. Fortress. The group is divided into two armies. One army occupies the climbing apparatus and one army plans the attack. The object of the attacking army is to reach and secure a certain treasure placed under guard in the cupola of the apparatus. As soon as the treasure is captured the armies change positions.

9. Home Tag. Two or more safety or home areas are established at opposite ends of the climbing apparatus. One player is chaser and can tag anyone outside a safety area or home. If players rush to these homes too frequently to make a successful game, the chaser may call:

> Three times three are nine:
> Who does not run is mine.

Every player must then scramble from the home he may be occupying and the tagger gives chase.

WRESTLING

Wrestling is an excellent activity for boys. Its beginnings are seen in the tussling activities of small children. This kind of exercise develops strength and agility but it tends to end in quarrels because the combatants may be badly matched and rules of play unknown. In the free play of children after school this kind of activity is very popular. It is important to teach children the methods and rules of wrestling but such organized activity is not suitable for children in the lower grades.

In practicing wrestling, with its various holds and requirements for a fall, the contestants must be in appropriate clothing and mats must be available. The various holds, positions, and movements can be taught in class and later two contestants can be paired for application of the instruction. If mats and wrestling costumes are available, wrestling is an excellent activity for the upper grades. The different holds and falls should be taught by a teacher of physical education.

Indian Wrestling

This type of stunt wrestling should be performed on mats or on grass. The players lie down side by side on their backs, their heads in opposite directions. The elbow of one is hooked by the elbow of the other so that they are firmly anchored in place. At the count of one, the inner leg of each is raised to a vertical position and replaced; on the count of 2 it is again raised to a vertical position and then replaced; and on the count of 3, the legs again come up and, hooking the knee of the opponent, each tries to roll the other over backwards.

Hand Wrestling

In this form of wrestling the contestants stand facing each other. Right hands are grasped and the right feet are placed parallel and touching on their lateral borders. By pulling and pushing, each player attempts to cause the other to lose his position without himself moving either foot.

SELECTED REFERENCES [1]

BALCH, ERNEST. *Amateur Circus Life.* New York: The Macmillan Co., 1924.

BRADY, MARNA VENABLE. *Tumbling for Girls.* Philadelphia: Lea & Febiger, 1936.

COTTERAL, B. AND D. *The Teaching of Stunts and Tumbling.* New York: A. S. Barnes & Co., 1936.

————. *Tumbling, Pyramid Building, and Stunts for Girls and Women.* New York: A. S. Barnes & Co., 1926.

---

[1] Appendix B also lists reference materials.

HARBY, SAMUEL F. *Tumbling for Students and Teachers*. Philadelphia & London: W. B. Saunders & Co., 1932.

HORNE, VIRGINIA LEE. *Stunts and Tumbling for Girls*. New York: A. S. Barnes & Co., 1943.

LAPORTE, WILLIAM R., AND RENNER, A. G. *The Tumbler's Manual*. New York: Prentice-Hall, Inc., 1938.

MACHEREY, MATHIAS H., AND RICHARDS, JOHN N. *Pyramids Illustrated*. New York: A. S. Barnes & Co., 1932.

McCLOW, L. L., AND ANDERSON, D. N. *Tumbling Illustrated*. New York: A. S. Barnes & Co., 1931.

RODGERS, MARTIN. *A Handbook of Stunts*. New York: The Macmillan Co., 1928.

STALEY, SEWARD C. *Games, Contests, and Relays*. New York: A. S. Barnes & Co., 1924.

Chapter X
RECREATION AND PHYSICAL EDUCATION

Guidance in the constructive and worthy use of leisure has for many years been one of the principal objectives of education, and a major part of any physical education program is to prepare pupils in the fundamental skills of active recreational games and sports. This education should begin in the kindergarten or first grade and continue in progressive sequence through the secondary school if the maximum results in social, emotional, and recreational growth and development of the individual are to be obtained. In 1933 Nicholas Murray Butler, then President of Columbia University, stated that training for a vocation is relatively simple, but training for leisure is difficult and requires for its fullest success the co-operation of home and school; the school that overlooks sowing the seeds of a proper use of an obtainable leisure has done only part of its work.[1]

Education in recreational skills should not, however, be looked upon as merely the preparation for adult recreation. A leading authority on child development has expressed herself on this point in the following words:

> It is important in a discussion of skills and leisure to remember that the best preparation for the future is happy, satisfying, and worthwhile living in the present. The teaching of physical education skills, then, should not be based upon the remote objective of the preparation for adult leisure, but upon growth in skills which are both interesting and needed for children at their particular developmental level.[2]

It is a reasonable expectation that satisfying play experiences during school years will do a great deal towards insuring continued participation in active, wholesome recreation after school days are over.

It is now recognized that if the school is to accomplish to the greatest possible extent the objectives of education it must concern itself with the child's recreational life not only during the school day but during much of the leisure available for vigorous physical activity. The school should provide, if possible, for the recreation of pupils during free time and vacation periods. Finally, the school which takes its proper place in the community must be ready to supply much of the impetus, the leadership, and the facilities for adult community recreation.

---

[1] Nicholas Murray Butler, "Leisure: An Interpretation," *Recreation*, XXVII (December, 1933), p. 422. By permission.

[2] Dorothy La Salle, *Guidance of Children Through Physical Education*. New York: A. S. Barnes & Co., 1946, p. 9. By permission.

SCHEDULING THE RECREATION PROGRAM

The physical education instruction period is not nearly long enough to provide the amount of physical exercise needed daily by the elementary school child. Maximum growth and development of the bodies of children at this age depends on many hours daily of physical activity. It must be remembered that a child's needs for such activity are many times that of an adult. During the day, the recess periods, noon period, and the hours before and after school are normally utilized by the children in active play. Facilities, leadership, and supervision should be provided at the school during these periods.

Recess Periods

During recess very little time is provided for any play outside of individual play on apparatus or other small group activities. Many schools try to schedule the recess periods so that every child may use some equipment or apparatus for a brief period of activity, but there is limited time for organized games, and if any are played the opportunity for attending to personal needs without a feeling of haste is curtailed.

Noon Hour

The noon hour provides opportunity for recreation, but it must not interfere with the calm and quiet lunch period. If no other time in the school day can be used for recreation because of the length of time spent in transportation, an organized play period could be scheduled before lunch. When this makeshift program is a necessity, the mid morning lunch helps to carry the child over the long period between the breakfast hour and the lunch hour.

After a supervised, happy, restful lunch, children should be allowed to play quietly during the last half of the noon period. Equipment must be supplied for individual games, sitting games, tennis type activities, and other games played in small groups, so that an opportunity is given each child to enjoy an interesting activity. Many schools provide a room or a paved space outdoors for folk dancing which could be utilized during the noon hour.

It must be remembered that recess and the noon period provide opportunities for the child to attend to such personal needs as going to the toilet, washing the hands, or getting a drink. Organized activities should never interfere with the child's freedom to attend to these needs, and the person in charge of scheduled activities should allow plenty of time for them.

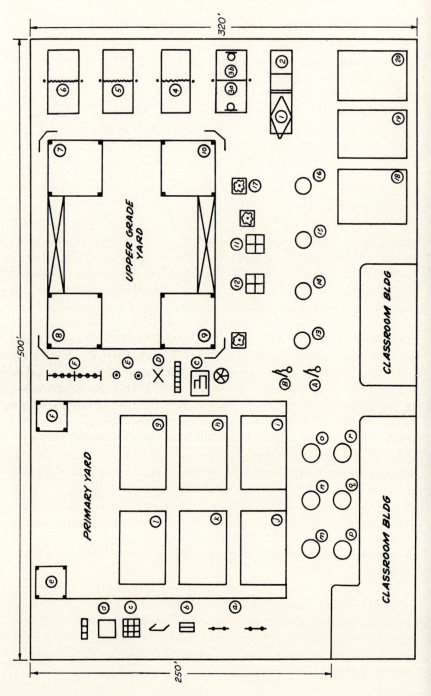

Extended School Day

A recreational program stemming from the instructional program that includes opportunity for physical activity can be scheduled as one of the activities of an extended school day. Arrangements may have to be made to reschedule buses so that all boys and girls may participate in the program. If school districts find it impossible to provide such an extensive program, physical recreation could be provided by lengthening the physical education period one day a week.

When a recreation period is participated in by different age groups the courts, fields, and playground apparatus must be scheduled on a rotating basis so that all boys and girls may have the opportunity for using facilities suited to their needs. A playground laid out to accommodate a large number of children of different ages is shown in Figure 76.

INTRAMURAL PROGRAMS

One means at the school's disposal for supplying time, equipment, and leadership for physical recreation is an intramural program of sports, games, and other activities. The intramural program should be based on activities taught in the physical education classes and should be so scheduled that every boy and girl has an opportunity to participate. Tournaments may be set up not only for team games but also for individual and dual games, both active and quiet. Pupils in small schools can take part in such a program if several grades are included as a unit. Larger schools can use classes or interest clubs as a basis for team organization.

Figure 76. The diagram on the adjoining page shows layout of school play areas suitable for 500 to 850 children. The whole school ground area is 320 x 500 feet, with classroom buildings in only a small part of the area. Key to the play area follows: Primary Yard: (a) swings; (b) slide; (c) low bar; climbing apparatus; (d) sandbox; horizontal ladder; (e) 25-foot diamond, fistball, etc.; (f) 25-foot diamond; (g through l) areas 40 x 60 feet for bat ball, end ball; (m through r) small circle game areas. Upper Grade Yard: (A and B) tether ball pole; (C) circular traveling rings; double horizontal bars; (D) horizontal ladder; climbing poles; (E) Giant Strides; (F) long traveling rings; (1) handball wall for hand baseball; (2) handball wall for handball; (3a and 3b) basketball; (4) volleyball, one bounce; (5) volleyball, one bounce; (6) volleyball, one bounce; (7, 8, 9, 10) baseball, kickball, fistball; (11, 12) four squares; (13, 14, 15, 16) circle games; (17) table games, carroms, etc.; (18, 19, 20) bat ball, captain ball, etc.

Organizing the Intramural Program

It is important that pupils take a large part in organizing the intramural program. Committees of pupils, elected by their fellows, should work with the teacher in selecting activities, drawing up schedules, and choosing teams. Making schedules and organizing tournaments of various kinds have been discussed in Chapter VII. Once the plans are put into effect, all pupils should accept responsibility for seeing that the details of the program are carried out efficiently and for making the program a success. Frequent change of committees, election of leaders, and rotation of responsibilities will make available to many boys and girls the opportunity to experience the responsibilities of leadership, followership, and participation in democratic situations. Pupils can act as officials for the games chosen. Managers, appointed or elected, should be responsible for keeping the roll of players, preparing record and score cards, choosing timekeepers and scorekeepers, assisting with the care of equipment, and notifying captains of changes in schedules. Handicapped pupils may take their part in such managerial duties.

Figure 77.   A school playground can provide a variety of activities for boys and girls after school.

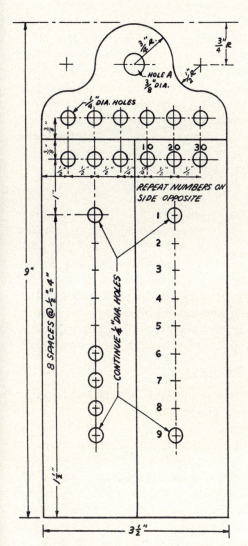

Figure 78. Diagram of a score-keeper's board.*

DIRECTIONS

1. Paint one - half of the board red, the other half white.
2. Bore hole "A" entirely through the board, all others to be only ½″ deep.
3. Numbers are stamped into the wood. The unnumbered holes at the top of the board hold the pegs not in use.
4. Provide three red and three white pegs 1¼″ long. Pegs may be cut from ¼″ dowel sticks and should fit snugly. If cut from slightly larger stock and slightly tapered, pegs will continue to fit as wear occurs. Pegs are used to keep score. As points are made, the peg in the lower numbered hole is advanced over the peg indicating the previous score. When points above nine are made the third peg is placed in the proper hole at the top of the board.

---

* Design of scorekeeper's board used through the courtesy of Mrs. Lillian Brown Schutte, Roosevelt Senior High School, Oakland, California.

Teams

A simple method of selecting teams is by lot. The names of boys and girls desiring to play a game are written on slips of paper and elected captains draw the slips until the teams are made up. This prevents the humiliation that many children experience daily when sides are chosen. For some games an effort should be made to equalize the playing skill of the groups. A satisfactory method of doing this is to use the three-point classification based on age, height, and weight which has been described previously.[1] Teams are then made up within the different grades or clubs so that each team has an equal number of pupils in the various classes, thus having about the same team strength. At the end of each season of play team memberships should be changed.

Types of Activities to Be Chosen

Individual and dual and team games can be used for intramural competition. Among those suitable are tether ball, paddle tennis, handball, badminton, net ball, soccer, long ball, end ball, field ball, volleyball, basketball, speed ball, and softball. Track and field events may be used. Less strenuous types of activities—such as horseshoes, outdoor checkers, croquet, table tennis, archery—may be chosen for pupils unable to take part in the vigorous team games. These games need not be reserved for physically handicapped children, however, for all children should be able to play quiet games. They are excellent for use during hot weather.

PLAYDAYS

The playday is uniquely American in its concept and organization. In a playday the pupils of a school or of adjacent schools or of a district meet together to take part in a number of sports, either for a day or part of a day. The purpose is not to determine interscholastic or individual championships but to give all children of the school or schools an opportunity to participate in a recreational program. The contests are arranged not between the best teams or players of individual schools but between well-matched teams made up of pupils from all participating schools. In a playday, therefore, the play is for enjoyment rather than for competition school against school. New friendships are made and frequently new games are learned.

Mrs. Herbert Hoover, in the foreword of an early pamphlet on the subject, wrote about playdays as follows:

> The aim, which is thoroughly American and democratic, is, in part, a development of our modern determination to give every girl—and every boy too—

---

[1] See page 153.

an equal opportunity for health. And I feel that an equal opportunity for joyous recreation is almost as important. Play, as all progressive educators realize, is an essential not only for physical fitness in children, but also for mental growth and poise and for social adjustment. Older girls and boys find in athletics of various types the best possible kind of play. The new plan for athletics to foster in our American youth the spirit of play, has been given the name of "Play Days." ... California was the first state to put on Play Days in widespread and wholly successful fashion. It showed that here was a method of athletic competition that gave scope to everybody. There was not just one star team in competition with another star team, either of which by its very nature could include only a few members. But there was "a team for everyone and everyone on a team." ... Thus in Play Days we have the democracy of athletics, of sports, which offers full and equal opportunity to all, from the most timid and uncertain of its novices to the most brilliant of its long-time devotees.[1]

Types of Playdays

Playdays are usually arranged so that schools within a convenient geographical district combine for mutual profit. Sometimes only one sport is planned—volleyball, paddle tennis, nine-court basketball, softball, hit pin baseball, or swimming. At other times the emphasis is on rhythmical activities. Festivals in which music, dancing, and other activities are added to team games to occupy a full day of fun offer every child a chance to take part in the activity he most enjoys. County-wide playdays, in which only the best players of each school meet for competition, are generally subject to unwise publicity and exploitation of the children. They do not add as much to the recreational program as the playday planned for all the children of a district. Publicized events which include only the star performers from a school are undesirable from an educational and civic viewpoint. More children have opportunity for participation and the most valuable outcomes result when not more than three or four schools combine leadership and resources for playdays.

A play hour is a form of get-together used by adjacent schools or by classes within a larger school when it is not feasible to devote a full day or half day to such events. Half of the hour may be devoted to relays, rhythms, running games, or stunts suited to all ages. The second half hour may be used for playing team and individual games.

Often team games cannot be played in rural schools because there are not enough children in the upper grades to form two teams for competition. Nevertheless, the children in these schools can study and master the individual athletic skills essential to team games, and opportunity to play in organized team games can then be given by planning and conducting interschool playdays or play hours. During these

---

[1] Ethel Perrin and Grace Turner, *Play Day, the Spirit of Sport*. New York: American Child Health Association, 1929, pp. 10-12. By permission.

Figure 79. Playdays are uniquely American in concept and organization. A variety of activities are shown in the upper picture. In the lower, games of volley-ball are being played on adjoining courts.

occasions children may join others for playing a game whose elements they have practiced at their own schools.

Play hours have been used quite extensively by teachers in one-room rural schools in an effort to give their children experiences in larger group undertakings. At intervals a get-together is arranged by such schools, the visiting teachers bringing all the children to the host school. An additional fifteen minutes permits group singing or the presentation of short dramatizations.

Organizing Playdays

Numerous methods may be used for organizing playdays. Usually three or four play periods are scheduled. Children are then arranged in three or four groups and they are rotated to the different types of activities—rhythms, running games, stunts and relays, or team games—each period of play. Play areas and floor areas are provided and equipment made ready for use. Play starts, stops, and rotations occur on a central signal that all observe. In some instances teachers remain in charge of a given activity for the four periods of play, receiving each group of new players and helping them to get under way. In other cases the teachers remain with the group originally assigned to them and travel with them from one activity to another. Still another method—perhaps the best in educational results—is to have the children manage both the games and the rotation of players to the next activity, the teachers serving only in an advisory capacity.

Activities Suggested for Playdays

Individual and team games, rhythms, stunts, relays, and running games may be used for playdays. The accompanying chart lists some of the most suitable activities in each group. Boys and girls can play together in all of the activities listed on the chart. Under Group A several individual and team games can be carried on simultaneously. In order to provide for such a wide variety of games, each school should be requested to bring specific equipment. The games, rhythms, and relays may have been learned before the playday, or some may be taught during the day to widen the experience of the children from the various schools.

When play periods must be limited, it is possible to play games such as volleyball, bat ball, field dodge ball, hit pin baseball in four periods of play, the total score for the quarters being credited to each team. Games that can be successfully played, in addition to those listed in the chart, are paddle tennis, deck tennis, softball, soccer, baseketball, bowling, horseshoes, shuffleboard, and croquet. In fact, any game that is taught in physical education can be adjusted to meet the playday situation.

Experience has shown that track and field and individual athletic events should not be included in the plans for a playday unless such events are used as a stunt between two contestants, a challenge being issued and a point earned for the team by the winner.

SUGGESTED ACTIVITIES FOR PLAYDAYS

GROUP A INDIVIDUAL AND TEAM GAMES	GROUP B RHYTHMS	GROUP C RUNNING GAMES	GROUP D RELAYS AND STUNTS
Bat Ball	Chimes of Dunkirk	Ball Stand	Shuttle
Long Ball	Captain Jinks	Oyster Shell	Stride Ball
Kick Ball	Virginia Reel	Squirrels in Trees	Over and Under
Hit Pin Baseball	Jump Jim Crow	Hound and Rabbit	Kangaroo
Tether Ball	Jolly is the Miller	Spider and Flies	Jack Rabbit
Progressive Dodge Ball	Broom Dance	Duck on the Rock	Pass and Squat
Handball	Nixie Polka	Forest Lookout	Square
Nine-Court Basketball	Gustaf's Skoal	Center Stride Ball	
Pin Basketball	Pop Goes the Weasel	Pig in the Hole	
End Ball	Sicilian Circle		
Captain Ball	Come, Let Us Be Joyful		
Boundary Ball			
Net Ball			
Volleyball			
Field Dodge Ball			

Scheduling the Activities

In making up the schedule for the playday, time should be allowed for registration and an opening program before the games. The order of rotation for the number of groups of children should be decided and scheduled. Time for lunch, a quiet period, and other events in a day-long program should be allotted. A suggested time table and schedule of the activities is shown in the accompanying chart.

If a pageant or program of short plays, singing, movies, or band or orchestra music is to be part of the playday, time for this must be scheduled. The period immediately following lunch is the preferred time for this activity.

SUGGESTED SCHEDULE FOR A PLAYDAY

9:00- 9:20	Registration
9:20- 9:30	Opening Program, Flag Raising, Directions
9:30-11:45	Games, with Groups Rotating

	A TEAM GAMES	B RHYTHMS	C RUNNING GAMES	D RELAYS AND STUNTS
9:30-10:00	Group I	Group II	Group III	Group IV
10:00-10:05		Rotation of Groups		
10:05-10:35	Group II	Group III	Group IV	Group I
10:35-10:40		Rotation of Groups		
10:40-11:10	Group III	Group IV	Group I	Group II
11:10-11:15		Rotation of Groups		
11:15-11:45	Group IV	Group I	Group II	Group III

12:00-1:30	Picnic Lunch
1:30-2:00	Auditorium Program
2:00-2:30	Moving Pictures
2:30-2:35	"Goodbye—Come Again!"

Classifying the Players

All schools participating in the playday should agree upon the method of classification to be used. Sometimes children are grouped by grades. The best method is to use the three-point classification method and to make up the teams within each group of members in the same class. This would mean that A's play against A's, B's against B's, and so on down the list. All teams could be made equal, however, by equally mixing the various classes on each team.

Preliminary Planning

Children should be encouraged to assume real leadership in the planning and carrying out of playday activities. Errors in judgment will occur, some committee members will not function entirely successfully, and some will fail as officials. An evaluation of the playday will bring out many needed improvements and it will be a stimulation to provide added opportunities for leadership and followership experience before the next playday occurs.

Invitations. Several weeks previous to a proposed playday the host school dispatches letters of invitation, stating the place and date and asking that an acknowledgment be made at an early date.

Committees. The host school appoints the following committees: (a) Program Committee, whose duties are to select the activities to be used, to make schedules, and to determine procedures for organizing teams; and (b) Committee on Facilities, whose duties are to prepare the playing fields and courts, to make equipment ready for use, and to number and mark the play areas so that visitors may find their positions rapidly. Other committees will be needed to act as receptionists, to register visitors, to care for transportation and parking, to prepare signs, to arrange for checking of lunches and valuables, to provide refreshments, to make arrangements for first aid, and to clean up.

Entry Blanks. Large playdays can be arranged more successfully if entry blanks are sent to invited schools three weeks in advance of the playday. The blanks should state the hour of arrival and departure, and should list the team games that are to be used at the playday as well as other activities such as challenges, stunts, and rhythms. They should be returned to the sender not later than one week before the playday. This permits the host school time in which to make necessary schedule arrangements and to organize the teams which will be composed of players from the different schools. Teachers should fill in the entry blanks, giving the names of the children who expect to go to the playday, their three-point classification letters, and, in the order of preference, the games they would like to play. Children should be told that it may not be possible for all to play every game they choose since facilities or time or team groupings may not allow this.

Conducting the Playday

When visitors arrive, hosts or hostesses should meet them and register them at an Information Center. Each child should be given an envelope containing his lunch or refreshment ticket. On the outside of the envelope should be written (1) his name, (2) the group to which assigned, and the name of host or hostess for that group, (3) the team games he is to play, (4) the number of the court or diamond, and (5) the time of play for each activity.

Players may be assigned to groups before arrival, or the assignment may be made on arrival. The host school should be prepared to use pupils from its own school to fill any vacancies on teams due to the absence of scheduled players.

Children in the primary grades should be assigned to different teacher leaders for stories, dramatizations, play on playground apparatus, singing games, tag games, story hour, and a rest period.

Prizes and Scorekeeping. Scores may be kept for each group if desired, but the practice of giving awards of any value should not be tolerated. Most organizers of playdays have done away with awards of any kind as well as scorekeeping, feeling that the joy in the game, the fun of playing, and the resulting sociability are reward enough without adding even paper ribbons for games won or lost.

Officials. During the playing of team games the children should act as officials. The host school usually provides the officials. There should be one general chairman whose business it will be to co-ordinate all the activities of other helpers. This chairman should be free to call on the services of any school officials throughout the day. The general chairman sees that each official is given a written statement of the duties he is to perform, together with the rules that govern the activity he may be assigned to supervise. This general chairman may be an exceptionally able pupil or an adult.

All teachers present at a playday should be assigned certain duties even if children of the host school are in charge of running the playday. The teachers should, throughout the day, be on the lookout to give assistance when needed to the pupil officials, watch for accident hazards, talk with and assist visiting parents and friends, encourage adults to participate, and enter into activities themselves as time permits.

Facilities for Participants and Spectators.   Parking space should be provided, with a committee of boys in charge to direct visitors. A greeting committee may welcome the occupants of each car and take them to their appointed places to receive information and check lunches and garments.

Dressing rooms, rest rooms, checking rooms, lost and found department, nurse's quarters or first aid station, lunch checking stations, refreshment stand, and information booth should be plainly marked. If they can be shown on a stencilled plan of the school grounds so much the better. If a large playday is undertaken there should be a nursery room, with a matron in charge, where parents may leave very young children.

If many spectators are to be present, they should be prevented from moving on to playing areas that are to be used. It may be necessary to rope off certain facilities. Chairs or benches should be provided. If possible, adults should be organized to play relays, rhythms, tag games, and team games.

Refreshments.   The selling of hot or cold drinks, ice cream, or sandwiches should be under the auspices of the school parent-teacher association and the funds revert to the school to meet expenses incurred for the playday. Luncheon areas should be provided and school children and adults should eat together—not as separate units representing each school present.

Supplies.   Visiting schools may be asked to bring their own balls, properly marked, to supplement the host school's supplies. There should be on hand a first aid kit, tape measures, marking materials, needles, thread, safety pins, extra whistles, paper and pencils, and a gong, trumpet, or large bell to notify participants when play is to begin or cease and when groups are to rotate.

Evaluation Period Following Playdays

Subsequent to the playdays, schools that participated should have an evaluation period for checking on the success or failure of the day. Recommendations for subsequent improvement should be listed and filed for future reference. Individual success in the execution of assigned duties should be noted and commendation expressed. This evaluation should be done in each school and may also be carried out with representatives of participating schools for the information of the next host school.

RELATIONSHIP OF SCHOOLS TO COMMUNITY RECREATION [1]

Legal authority for participation of California school districts in community recreation programs is contained in two State laws: The Civic Center Law [2] authorizes the governing boards to grant the use of school buildings and grounds for recreational purposes. The Community Recreation Enabling Law [3] authorizes cities, counties and public school districts "To organize, promote, and conduct such programs of community recreation as will contribute to the attainment of general educational and recreation objectives for children and adults of the State." It further provides that any two or more public agencies may co-operate with each other or with the Federal Government in developing such programs.

No single method of organizing, administering, or conducting a community recreation program is suggested; however, programs which have been conducted under the auspices of recreation commissions, on which local school districts are represented, usually have been successful in providing programs designed to serve the needs of all age groups.

A typical example of a pattern which has proven highly successful in California is the community in which the municipal authority and the·school district co-operate to establish and administer a system of public recreation. A director of recreation is employed jointly by the city and the school district to administer a co-ordinated program of school and community recreation, using both municipal and school facilities. A recreation commission, on which the city government and the school district are represented, serves as an advisory board. At least one member should be a woman. The superintendent of schools, the city manager, and the director of recreation should be ex-officio members of this commission. Valuable results are gained when a member of the commission also serves as a member of the city planning commission.

Planning School Facilities for Community Use

With the continued growth in California's population, school site acquisition and school building has increased. Far-sighted civic leaders have seen examples of poor economy and wasted resources resulting from unrelated planning, construction, and operation of facilities by public agencies and are attempting to bring about an awareness of the sound, broad concept of the school planned for use by the entire community.

---

[1] Contributed by Carson Conrad, California State Department of Education.
[2] Education Code, Sections 19431 to 19439. Sections 19401 to 19405 are also applicable.
[3] Education Code, Sections 24401 to 24411.

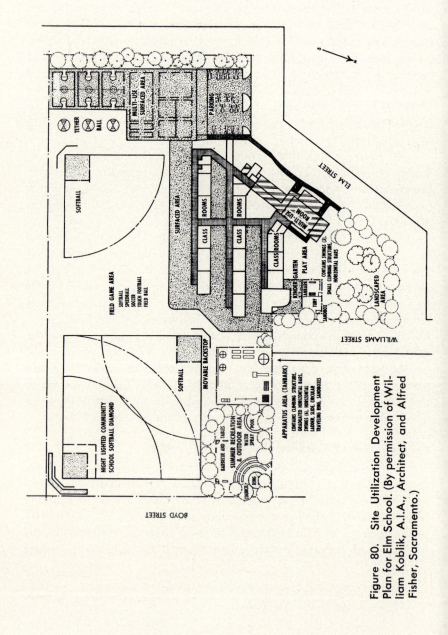

Figure 80. Site Utilization Development Plan for Elm School. (By permission of William Koblik, A.I.A., Architect, and Alfred Fisher, Sacramento.)

A splendid example of community planning for recreation recently took place in the California community of Vacaville, where a citizens' committee was set up to study local recreation needs. Representatives of the District's Board of Education and over thirty-five public and private agencies concerned with recreation or youth services in this northern California community were invited to participate. As a result, a Citizens' Planning Committee was formed.

After several months of committee consideration and follow-up meetings, many specific suggestions were submitted to the architect, who considered them in drawing up for the school district the Site Utilization Development Plan for Elm School, an elementary school then under construction. The importance of all-year playground activities was reflected in the plans for the summer recreation and outdoor education area. This section, landscaped to provide a park-like setting, includes the following areas: (1) picnic area, including barbecue pits and benches and tables, which can also be used for crafts; (2) a council ring, which can also be used as an outdoor classroom; (3) a water spray pool, which when empty of water can also be used for dancing and roller skating, since the concrete surface is made smooth by triple troweling; (4) a turfed open play area.

The apparatus area is laid out adjacent to both the summer recreation area and to the primary classrooms so that apparatus may be convenient for either use. Included in the plans for this hundred-foot-square area are the following pieces of equipment: climbing structure, graduated horizontal bars, horizontal ladder, circular traveling rings, swings with canvas safety seats, and safety-type slide. Benches are provided within the area, enclosed by a 3½-foot chain-link fence, and tanbark surfacing was recommended to insure maximum protection under apparatus.

The major portion of the playground is planned for field games, including softball, touch football, speed ball, soccer, and field ball. Approximately one-half of this field game area is turf, while the remainder is stabilized soil. A community-school softball diamond, lighted for night use, is included.

In addition to the surfacing surrounding the classrooms, a multiple-use surfaced area of approximately 25,000 square feet is planned. This all-weather area provides the following facilities: (1) three basketball courts, one with goals ten feet high, one with nine-foot goals, and the other with eight-foot goals; (2) space for court games, including volleyball, ring tennis, paddle tennis, and similar games; (3) space marked for hopscotch and circle games. Three tether ball standards are located adjacent to this area.

A parking area adjoins the multiple-use surfaced area, with a walk leading to a multi-use room. This room, approximately 40 by 80 feet, is planned for indoor recreation.

A preschool play lot of approximately 4,800 square feet, enclosed by a 3½-foot chain-link fence, is adjacent to the kindergarten classrooms. A portion of the lot is surfaced for all-weather use; however, tanbark is used under the climbing structure, horizontal bars, and swings. The remainder of the lot is turfed and benches for parents are provided. A sandbox 8 by 20 feet is planned for a corner of the turfed section.

Toilets are available on the site which may be open when classrooms and major school buildings are closed. Adequate drinking fountains have been properly located.

Joint planning insures more adequate facilities for both school children and other members of the community: the maximum use is generally made of buildings and facilities which have been planned by representatives of an entire community.

PROGRAMS FOR SPECIAL OCCASIONS

School administrators and teachers may contribute to the life of the community by planning and conducting recreational programs for many special occasions. Increasingly, citizens are turning to teachers to give them concrete leadership in such programs. Teachers do not need wide experience as recreation directors to undertake this leadership, for their experience in directing the play activities of children is an excellent preparation for leading adults in recreational activities.

The joy and relaxation that result from participation in a fun night are very real, provided the leadership is enthusiastic and all who attend are persuaded to join in. The activities need not be complicated. Group singing, simple dances, tag games, relays, and circle games may be used. Simple patterns, easily learned, that provide opportunity for laughter and sociability are preferred. To create a friendly atmosphere, activities should be provided that allow the frequent exchange of partners.

The recreation leader should provide more materials for use during an evening than will be needed, for often emergencies arise when certain activities on the prepared list must be omitted. The resourcefulness that comes from being familiar with a great variety of play activities and being able to adapt the program to meet an emergency is a prime requisite for success. Practice builds up this knowledge and ability. Teachers and children should make it a practice to jot down for easy reference descriptions of games and stunts enjoyed, songs and toasts heard, and amusing skits seen at different parties that they feel could be used profitably at some future social occasion for which they are responsible.

In initiating folk dances or rhythmical games, the music or rhythmic pattern should be presented to the group before the step pattern is introduced. It is usually advisable to break up the activity into the elements that make up the whole. The leader can make a game of each element as he presents it; the group should perform the movement until all are familiar with it. Each new part can be built onto the former one until finally a picture of the whole rhythm is gained. Then the group can swing into a spirited performance of the completed rhythm and repeat the dance a number of times. Enthusiasm, a sense of humor, knowledge of the activities, and laughing with and not at the crowd are attributes that go a long way toward making a successful leader.

It must be remembered that adults (and children) play for recreation rather than to perfect skills. Spontaneous fun and laughter are therefore the objectives to be sought for both children and adults. If the crowd is inattentive or noisy, standing still in silence will usually command attention. Until the group is controlled and ready to give attention, it is useless to try to give directions.

Mistakes should be overlooked and leniency toward blunders should be the policy. Emphasis should be put on the joy of playing rather than boosting competitive rivalries. Rhythms with simple patterns are much more desirable and are more quickly learned than are those with complicated step patterns.

Even in a small community many of the people who attend a fun night may be strangers to each other. A typical fun-night program, therefore, should begin with a "mixer"— an activity in which the participants are introduced to each other, or in which couples and groups are mixed up and new combinations formed. Stiffness and formality must be avoided, for the keynote of the whole program is one of fun and informality. After all the guests have arrived and the ice is thoroughly broken by some enjoyable mixers, the program may continue with rhythmical activities—folk dances or folk games—singing, relay races, and active or quiet games. Any or all of these types of activities may be planned. The whole group may participate in one activity or the guests may be divided into smaller groups to play several games simultaneously. If desired, a progressive party may be planned, in which the guests move from one activity to another in groups. It is well to close the evening by having all the guests join in a dance or group game that brings them all together again.

Typical Fun Night Programs

The following five programs are merely suggestions for making up the list of activities to be used for a fun night. Many of the rhythmical activities and games are described in detail in Part II of this guide. Descriptions and directions for others will be found in the following pages. There are many books of games that will assist the recreation leader in making up programs similar to this.

PROGRAM I [1]

Rhythmical Activities

Bean Porridge Hot	Did You Ever See a Lassie?
How D'Ye Do, My Partner	Broom Dance
Come Along	Skating Away
Danish Dance of Greeting	A-Hunting We Will Go
Lott Ist Todt	

Singing

1. Rounds, cheers, toasts, and songs, such as the following:

Black Eyed Susan	Mary's Bees
Rheumatism	Mummy Song
Perfect Posture	Little Tommy Tinker
Cheer Up Teachers	Pussy Willow Round
Throw It Out the Window	Ham and Eggs
States Song	

2. Vocal combats, in which two groups sing different songs simultaneously, such as

"The Long Long Trail" with "Keep the Home Fires Burning"
"Spanish Cavalier" with "Solomon Levi"

Games

Right and Left	Back to Back
Spelling Bee	Hound and Rabbit
Grand Opera Tag	Beetle Goes Round

Relays

Eggshell Relay	Balloon Relay
Nose Powder Relay	Hand Squeeze Relay

Rhythms for Closing the Program

Rye Waltz	Good Night, Ladies

[1] Programs I, II, and III are typical of programs for elementary, high school, and adult groups conducted by Winifred Van Hagen.

PROGRAM II

Rhythms

    Grand March   Jolly is the Miller

    Rig-a-jig-jig   Nixie Polka

    Jump Jim Crow   Gustaf's Skoal

    Bear Went Over the Mountain   Virginia Reel

Singing

    For suggestions see Program I

Games

    Coin Hand Shake   Double Circle

    Hook On   The Ocean is Stormy

    Simon Says

    For other suggestions see games in Program I or III.

Rhythms for Closing the Program

    Little Man in a Fix   Good Night, Ladies

    Old Dan Tucker

PROGRAM III

Open the program with a short talk and group singing.

Mixer

    Name Knowing Contest

Rhythms

    Rolling Stones   Cats and Rats (musical)

    Chimes of Dunkirk   Portland Fancy

    Carrousel   Captain Jinks

    B'eking   Sicilian Circle

Games

    Hook On   Dumb Spelling Bee

    Three Around   Jack Rabbit Relay

    Forest Lookout   Double Handcuff

    Hindoo Tag   Center Catch Touch Ball

                                   (using handkerchiefs)

Rhythms for Closing the Program

    Rovenacka   Badger Gavotte

    Cshebogar   Good Night, Ladies

PROGRAM IV [1]

Games

Double Handcuff	Hide in Sight
How Do You Like Your	Calabashes
Neighbors	Queen's Headache
Up-Down	Jockey Race

Folk Games (found in *Handy II*,[2] Section P, "Singing Games, Set Running and Circle Dances").

Shoo Fly (page 7)	Jingle at the Window (page 20)
O, Susanna (page 29)	Turn the Glasses Over (page 12)

PROGRAM V

Mixers

Alphabet Mixer	Riot Mixer
Paul Jones Figures	Mixing Circles

Folk Games and Dances

Knights and Ladies	Bean Porridge Hot
Jolly is the Miller	Jump Jim Crow
Carrousel	

Game

The Ocean is Stormy

Relays

Object on Head Relay	Tin Can Relay
Ring Relay	

Mixers or Introductions

Alphabet Mixer.   A letter placed on a card 4 inches by 6 inches is pinned on the clothing of each person playing. It is best to use all the letters of the alphabet, with an additional set of vowels. Players are asked to join hands with other players so that when joined they spell a word. For example, the players having the letters *c*, *r*, *a*, and *d* join together and spell *card*. The word would then be written on their slips by the schoolmasters appointed to do so, whereupon players are free to try to form another word. A prize may be given to the player having the most words on his slip at the end of the playing time.

---

[1] Programs IV and V were prepared by Harold Baldwin, formerly Director of Physical Education for Boys, Claremont Junior High School, Oakland.
[2] *Handy II*, edited by Lynn Rohrbough. Delaware, Ohio: Co operative Recreation Service.

Coin Hand Shake. Before the party begins, the leader explains the game to two or more persons, and gives each one some pennies. When the guests arrive the leader announces that certain people in the group have had their hands crossed with gold and that the tenth person to shake hands with each of these individuals will be given the gold. The tenth person to shake hands with the key people will be given a penny. When shaking hands all of the guests are instructed to ask questions of each other such as "Where were you born?" "What did your father do?" "What is your birthday?" "Do you have a pet?"

Continuous Receiving Line. The second person to arrive (No. 2) introduces himself to No. 1, and then No. 2 stands beside No. 1. No. 3 introduces himself to No. 1. No. 1 introduces 3 to 2 and then 3 stands beside 2. They continue the introductions until all guests have gone down the introduction line.

Grand March Figures With Calls. When taking part in a quadrille or square dance figures, when marching, or when dancing with a lady, the gentlemen should be on the left side, next to the heart of his lady.

From the beginning impress on marchers that throughout grand march figures, there should be full arm distance between couples.

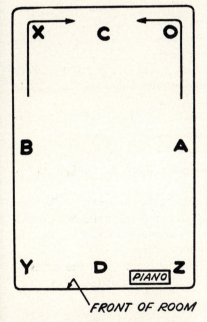

Figure 81. Diagram shows area marked for Grand March figures.

FIGURE I

"LADIES ON THE LEFT, GENTLEMEN ON THE RIGHT." As leader faces rear of room ladies stand in line between points X and Y (Figure 81). Gentlemen stand in a line between points O and Z.

1. Ladies face toward X and gentlemen toward O and all march toward each other. On meeting at C, they march single file down the center of the room, toward the music, each lady stepping in front of the oncoming gentlemen.

2. At D ladies march to their right, gentlemen to their left, meet at C and down the center toward D by twos.

3. Separate at D by twos, first couple to left, second couple to

right, partners together; return to C and come down the center by fours.

4. Separate by fours, alternating left and right, and come down the center by eights.

5. Separate by eights and come down the center by sixteens or by eights. Members of the first line of Group A (on right of leader as he faces the marchers) will be the leaders; second line of Group A will be third; third line of Group A will be the fifth, etc.

6. Separate by fours and come down the center by fours. Note: A good time to halt the group when Area D is reached and express appreciation for musician's services by word and by hand clapping.

7. Separate by twos, right and left. Groups march around the room with the two groups passing each other until leaders stop and face each other fairly near point D.

FIGURE II

"FOUR ABREAST—GENTLEMEN ON THE OUTSIDE." Groups A and B advance simultaneously with partners stepping apart from each other far enough to permit another person to march between them. Four lines march forward and around the outer edges of the room, ladies passing through the center of the four lines.

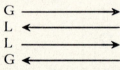

At the opposite end of the room (between X and O), reverse the order, the gentlemen passing through the center, the ladies on the outside.

L ——————→
G ←——————
G ——————→
L ←——————

Leaders stop at Y and Z to wait until the figure is finished and to receive directions for the next figure.

"GENTLEMEN ON THE OUTSIDE—LADIES UNDER THE ARCH." The same figure as above but Group A makes an arch and the ladies of Group B march under it. At the end of the room, Group A continues to make the arch and the gentlemen of Group B march under it.

Repeat the figure with Group B forming the arch, the ladies of Group A marching under it and then the gentlemen of Group A.

FIGURE III

"CONTINUOUS ARCH." All couples of Group A, as they march forward, join inside hands and form an arch. At the same time all couples of Group B march forward and pass under the arch. At C, the members of Group B who passed under the arch form the arch for Group A to pass under. Leaders stop at Y and Z.

Figure IV

"Over and under." Couples join inside hands and keep them clasped. Couples stand still until the advancing couple reaches them, when they, too, begin to advance. Crowding forward should not occur.

While marching forward, partners of Couple 1 of Group A separate from each other at D, and allow Couple 1 of Group B to pass under the arch made by their hands. Continuing to advance, Couple 1A pass under the arch made by hands of 2B; separate and pass outside 3B; under 4B; outside 5B, etc.

At the same time Couple 1 of Group B, having passed under hands of 1A, form an arch and pass outside of Couple 2A; under arch made by 3A; outside 4A; under 5A, etc.

Finally, every couple is weaving over and under or under and over as the case may be, the leaders continuing the figure until they return to Y and Z (Figure 82) where they stand and talk until all have finished the figure.

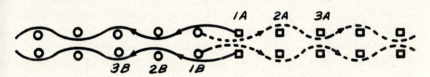

Figure 82. Diagram shows how couples weave over and under in Grand March figure.

Figure V

"Left and right." Couples take skating position—left hand in left hand and right hand in right hand. Couples stand still until the advancing couple reaches them, when they, too, begin to advance. Crowding forward should not occur.

Couple 1A walk to left of and pass Couple 1B; in front of and to the right of Couple 2B; in front of and to the left of 3B, etc.

Couple 1B walk to left of and pass Couple 1A; in front of and to the right of Couple 2A; in front of and to the left of 3A, etc. Finally all couples are marching to the left or right of each advancing couple until the leaders reach Y and Z where they rest until the figure is finished. Advancing couples should greet each other in a friendly way.

FIGURE VI

"ADVANCE BY SMALL CIRCLES." Couples stand still until the advancing couple reaches them, when they, too, begin to advance. Crowding forward should not occur.

The first couple of groups A and B march toward each other. They join hands and the four march in a circle to their *left, once,* until they are facing their original positions, whereupon Couple 1A drop the hands of Couple 1B and, passing them to the *left,* advance and join hands with Couple 2B and the four move to their *right* in a small circle (Figure 83).

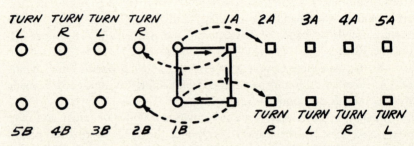

Figure 83.   Diagram shows how to advance by small circles in the Grand March.

After passing to the left of Couple 1A, Couple 1B join hands with Couple 2A and they circle to their *right once;* Couple 1A join hands with Couple 3B and they circle to their *left.* At the same time Couple 1B join hands with Couple 3A and they circle to their *left once.* Couples continue circling with oncoming couples after Couples 1A and/or Couple 1B meet with and turn them. Each time a circle is completed each couple, with inside hands joined, passes by the other couple on the same side as the direction of the circle. If they circle *right,* they pass to the *right* and turn the next two persons to the *left;* pass them on the *left* side and turn next two to the *right;* pass them on the *right* side and turn next two persons *left,* etc. This procedure is essential as players may become very dizzy if the movement is always to the left or to the right. Emphasize the fact that couples make but one complete turn each time they meet a new couple. If this procedure is followed no couple will have to stand and wait for an oncoming couple.

FIGURE VII

"BRIDGE OF SMILES." Two lines at Y and Z march forward and at D turn and march down the middle of the room by fours. At C all lead off to the left by twos, Couple 1A leading, Couple 1B next, Couple 2A third, Couple 2B fourth, etc.

Couple 1A leads the group to D. At this point partners of Couple 1A face each other, join hands, and slide forward three or four steps toward C. They then stand still and with four hands joined form an arch. Couple 1B then slide under the arch, stand *close* to Couple 1A and form an arch; Couple 2A pass under the arch made by Couple 1A and 1B and stand *close* to 1B; Couple 2B pass under the arch made by the three couples and stand *close* to 2A. This procedure is continued by the remaining couples. Due allowance must be made by the participants for circling to the left or right when approaching area C.

When Couple 1A become the last or end couple of the arch, they drop hands and pass forward under the hands of the other couples. The rest follow them. When Couple 1A reach the head of the arch they march forward around the room, the others following them as they emerge from under the arch.

Figure VIII

"All slide or chasse." Similar to Figure VII. When Couple 1A reach the center of the room at C or D, partners face each other, join hands, and start toward the opposite end of the room with three or four chassé or slide steps. They then drop hands and step back from each other three or four paces and stand still. Couple 1B follow them with the same sliding step and when just beyond Couple 1A they separate and stand shoulder to shoulder with Couple 1A. Couple 2A advance next and then Couple 2B. Figure is continued until all have advanced. When Couple 1A become the last or end couple, they join hands and slide forward between the lines with the others following until .they reach the head of the line, whereupon they may march off slowly around the room to form a large double circle, the others following, for the playing of a rhythmical game or for a "Paul Jones," or they may come down the center of the room by twos and continue all or some of the following figures.

Figure IX

"Grand right and left (or grand chain) around the hall." [1] Couple 1A lead the group down the center of the room to C or D with all other couples following. Partners then separate, the lady of Couple 1A leading all the ladies in single file around the outside of the room while the gentleman of Couple 1A leads the men around the opposite side of the room. When Couple 1A meet they start a Grand Right and Left around the room, performing the action with each person as they advance.

[1] For description of "Grand Chain" or "Grand Right and Left," see page 207.

Those waiting to begin the weaving must not advance to meet the oncoming leaders. Arm distance between marchers must be maintained. During the figure, right shoulders should pass right shoulders and left shoulders pass left shoulders. The position of the leader will determine which hand of the waiting person should be first extended.

Figure X

"Complete wheel and grand right and left." When, from opposite directions, the lady and gentleman of Couple 1A meet, they hook their right elbows and completely turn each other before advancing and hooking left elbows with the second person in order to turn that person. Action is continued until all have performed the figure.

Figure XI

"Grand right and left by couples." Manipulate marchers so Couples 1A and 1B will be facing each other with the members of their group behind them. All couples join their inside elbows and so remain. All are asked to note in particular the direction in which they are to march. The figure of the Grand Chain is used with advancing couples turning each other completely around before moving forward to meet waiting couples. Only the outside elbows of the couples can be used for contacting and swinging new couples. Elbow hooks should not be broken until the finish of the swing.

Figure XII

"Down the center by fours." Two leading couples meet at C and, joining elbows, come down the center by fours. Always arm distance should be maintained between the different lines of marchers.

Figure XIII

"Down the center by eights." Lines of four separate, meet, and march down the center by eights. An excellent point at which to halt the group and again thank the musician or musicians.

Figure XIV

"Follow the leader." Marchers should be in lines of eight with lines arm distance apart. Marchers in each line join hands and keep them joined. Leader, with his left hand, grasps the right hand of end player on the right end of the first line, and leads members of first line in front of and across their own line; behind their own line and in front of the second line; in front of the third line; in front of the fourth line, thus performing a spiral movement. The figure is continued until the leader has been through all the aisles.

As leader passes the end person on the right end of each line, he instructs that person to join hands with the last person of the lengthening line when the last person reaches the spot.

FIGURE XV

"WIND THE WHIP." When Figure XIV is finished leader marches in a circle with others following. Circle is made to grow smaller and smaller until center is reached.

FIGURE XVI

"CRACK THE WHIP." When center of the whip is reached, leader reverses direction and leads group out again and into a large circle in preparation for a game such as "Bean Porridge Hot," performed in a single circle, or the "Danish Dance of Greeting."

TEACHING SUGGESTIONS

1. The first two couples, who will be leaders, should be carefully chosen. They should try to keep in line with each other when on opposite sides of the room, and their pace should not be too rapid or steps too long. They should be cautioned to watch the leader for signals and directions.

2. All marchers should be told not to crowd up on the persons immediately in front of them. If the room will permit, a full arm's reach between marchers should be maintained at all times.

3. During certain figures marchers must stand still and not crowd forward. They remain inactive until the advancing leaders reach them, whereupon they become active.

4. Once or twice it is well to halt the group near the musician and express to that person, by vigorous hand clapping and by word of mouth, *never by whistling*, the appreciation of the group for service being rendered.

5. Phonograph records can be used. It will be advisable to have some one reliable person take charge of the machine since the needle will have to be raised frequently in order that the group may receive instruction.

6. If a musician or phonograph is not available, the beat of a drum, tambourine, or tin basin will give the cadence needed. Popular songs may be sung when the group understands how to execute the figures.

7. All teachers present should take part in the Grand March.

8. If the group is familiar with the various steps in Figure 1, omit numbers 3, 4, 5, and 6.

9. Boys should be shown early in the instructional period how to offer the right arm to their partner. The elbow should be bent at more than a right angle in order that the fingers of the girl's hand may rest easily on the forearm without the constant need to pull up the hand position because of the downward slant of her partner's arm.

"I'm Glad to Meet You."   A double circle is formed. Members of the two circles march in opposite directions. When a whistle is blown, all stop and introduce themselves to the nearest person in the opposite circle. This is continued for several rounds.

Inquisition.   Partners march in a double circle. On a signal, ladies face about and all do the Grand Chain. On a second signal, all stop and chat with the one opposite. The leader asks each to find out his opposite's favorite actor, his birth state, whether he can swim, what his favorite dessert is, or his middle name. The director may ask for reports.

Mixing Circles.   Four concentric circles are formed, ladies on the right side of their partner. Each alternate line of fours is named A and B or 1 and 2. March music is played. The persons on the inside circles will have to shorten their steps somewhat so that those on the outside can keep up with them. The groups continue marching until a call is given, whereupon they immediately execute the call. As soon as the figure is finished the group starts marching forward again. Various calls are given such as:

"LADIES FOUR STEPS FORWARD."   Gentlemen mark time in place or shorten their steps and the ladies march forward to the side of the fourth gentleman ahead.

"GENTLEMEN TWO STEPS FORWARD."   Ladies mark time while gentlemen move to the side of the second lady ahead.

"LADIES CHAIN."   The ladies with their partners in lines A or 1 face about. Ladies do the chain, the gentlemen turning the two ladies as they advance to the gentlemen. All face forward and march forward.

"GRAND RIGHT AND LEFT."   All the ladies face about and begin the figure with the gentlemen facing them. When the partner is reached, ladies face forward and all march forward.

"SWING YOUR PARTNER."   Each gentleman swings his own partner twice in place and then all march forward.

Name Knowing Contest.   A circle is formed. Each guest learns the names of his neighbors to the right and to the left. When challenged by the leader, the player must give his neighbors' names before the leader can count to ten. If he misses, he takes the leader's place.

re 84. Elementary school boys and girls as well as their parents like to
ce a "Paul Jones."

"*Paul Jones*" *Figures With Calls.*[1]   The calls and. steps for "Paul
Jones" are described.

1.   (a) "Everybody up for the 'paul jones,'" or (b) "Get partners
and start dancing."   All dancers in the room (a) form a large circle, or
(b) secure a partner and dance until the next call is given. As far as possible, when forming a circle, each gentleman present should stand between
two ladies. If ladies are standing side by side in the circle, gentlemen
should never stand side by side but should place themselves immediately
between two ladies. The following calls and explanation will enable a
leader to direct a successful "Paul Jones."

2.   "Ladies in the center, gents take a walk," or "Gents in the
center, ladies take a walk."   While the women (or men) move in
toward the center and stand about informally, or form a circle and stand
still, the men (or women) join hands and march in a circle to the left
or the right. Leader then calls: "All dance." Each gentleman takes the

[1] The description of the figures for this traditional dance were contributed by Harold Baldwin,
Oakland Public Shcools.

lady nearest him from the center group, or from the circle, and dances with her until the next figure is called.

3. "CIRCLE FOUR." Each two couples nearest to each other on the floor join hands and, making a small circle of four, move in a circle to their own left or right. Leader then calls: "EXCHANGE PARTNERS AND DANCE." Each gentleman in a circle takes the other gentleman's partner in his circle and dances with her.

4. "SIX HANDS ROUND." The nearest three couples to each other on the floor join hands and, making a small circle of six, move in a circle to their own left or right. Leader then calls: "EXCHANGE PARTNERS AND DANCE." Each gentleman takes a lady in his circle, not his partner, and dances with her.

5. "GENTS INSIDE THE CIRCLE, LADIES OUTSIDE THE CIRCLE," (or vice versa). Men (or women) step toward the center and form a circle, while the women (or men) form a circle outside the others. When the groups are ready, the leader calls: "LADIES MARCH TO THE RIGHT, GENTS TO THE LEFT," (or vice versa). Leader then calls: "ALL SWING." Each gentleman takes a partner, swings her around in place twice and then dances with her. The leader may use the call: "EVERYBODY DANCE." Each gentleman secures a lady and dances with her.

6. "EXCHANGE PARTNERS." This call is given while partners are dancing. The gentlemen release their partners, take new ones, and continue dancing until a new figure is called.

7. "ONE LARGE CIRCLE." When a large circle is formed the leader calls: "GRAND RIGHT AND LEFT." Always the gentlemen make a quarter turn so that their left hands are on the inside of the circle, as they face forward, in order to begin marching forward in a circle. The ladies face in the opposite direction to that taken by the gentlemen. The ladies' left hands will then be on the outside of the circle. Each giving his right hand to the one facing him, ladies and gentlemen march forward passing each other on the side of the free hand (left), right shoulders adjacent when passing. They then give their left hand to the next advancing person and pass on the side of the free hand (right), left shoulders adjacent when passing. Continue marching, offering right and left hands alternately, passing in and out, or out and in, as the case may be, until the gentlemen reach the ladies with whom they began the figure of the Grand Right and Left; or until the leader calls: "ALL PROMENADE." Each gentleman takes the lady advancing toward him and together they walk around the circle until the leader calls: "EVERBODY DANCE."

8. The last call is "PROMENADE THE HALL." Each gentleman returns his lady to her seat.

TEACHING SUGGESTIONS

1. If, during the execution of a figure, gentlemen fail to secure partners, they should be very alert to see if any ladies are without partners and, on seeing any, quickly secure one for a partner.

2. The leader should speak with a voice that carries, to keep the activities moving at a lively tempo.

Right and Left. A single circle is formed. Players stand shoulder to shoulder. The director stands in front of a guest and introduces himself and they chat for a moment or two. The director then moves to his right and the person to whom he introduced himself steps into the circle and moves to his right and each introduces himself again. When a player moves out of the circle into the center, the space vacated must not be eliminated by circle players edging toward each other. After several players have left the circle, a whistle is blown and each person within the circle tries to secure a vacant place. The player who cannot find a place is the odd player and he begins the game again.

Riot Mixer. Players are told that various directions are to be given, and that they are to carry out the directions by assuming indicated positions with a neighbor when the calls are given. Examples of calls are "skating position," "same last initials together," "back to back," "right elbows linked," "little fingers linked," "fingers laced," "circles of two," three, four, five or six. A finish direction could be "each man kneel on one knee with a lady sitting on the other knee." If forfeits are being given, the last ones to finish a given call are penalized.

Rolling Stones. Music is played for skipping. A single circle is formed, with the director in the center. When the music begins, the director skips around inside the circle. The instant the music stops (or on a signal, with music continuing), the director dashes for a partner and both begin skipping immediately. When the music stops again or signal is given, both dash for new partners. Next time the music stops, all four dash to get partners. This is continued until all have partners.

Rhythmical Activities

Come Along. Any skipping music is played. Players stand shoulder to shoulder in circle formation. Impress upon the players that as circle players leave their places to follow the leader the vacancy is to be maintained. They must not close in and obliterate the open space because when the music stops all try to find a place in the circle. The leader tags persons, who follow him until the music stops, and the player who fails· to find a place in the circle starts the game again.

Good Night, Ladies (see page 608). A double circle is formed, partners facing, girls on the inside and boys on the outside. During the singing of the verse the girls stand still and the boys move to the left.

"Good night, ladies"— each shakes hands with partner.

"Good night, ladies"— each shakes hands with the second lady.

"We're going to leave you now"— gentleman takes skating position with the third lady and faces in the line of direction.

Chorus—partners skip, slowing down and facing each other while singing "O'er the deep blue sea."

Game is repeated, with gentleman shaking hands with the lady he has just skipped around with.

Other verses are: Good night, ladies. Come again, ladies. Sweet dreams, ladies. One kiss, ladies.

As this is generally the last activity of the evening, everyone should be urged to join in.

John Brown. Any good quadrille music may be used for this dance. Eight players stand in quadrille formation. An extra player stands inside each set. On the first four measures the ladies step forward and greet John Brown (the center player); on the next four measures the gentlemen step forward and greet John Brown. On the next eight measures the couples face each other and perform the Grand Chain or Grand Right and Left, in which John Brown joins. The players then take partners and promenade around the circle for the last eight measures. The person who fails to get a partner becomes the next John Brown.

Jolly is the Miller. (Victor Album E-87 and Victor Record 20214.) See page 443. Instead of stepping forward and back, the inside circle reverses direction and both lines skip until the music is stopped or a whistle is blown, when a new partner is chosen.

Knights and Ladies. The dance is done to march music. A double circle is formed, ladies inside and gentlemen outside, partners facing. They turn so that circles move in opposite directions. When a whistle is blown or the music stops, each gentleman kneels and his partner runs and sits upon his knee. The last three or four couples to reach each other are the hoboes.

Yankee Doodle (see page 455; use Victor Record 20166 or Decca Record 25050, Album A525). A double circle is formed. During the verses, partners march around the circle, gentlemen on the inside. During the chorus, partners face, join hands, and slide four times in the line of direction to word "up," then slide four times back to the word "dandy." On the word "mind" gentlemen turn partners with six walking steps, then partners separate, each advancing to his own left to meet a new partner. The game is repeated with the singing of the second verse, and is continued as long as desired.

Other Suitable Folk Dances. The following dances, which are described in Part II of this guide, have been used successfully for social occasions.

Across the Hall	Nigarepolska
Badger Gavotte	Noriu Miego
Broom Dance	Oh! Susanna
California Schottische	Old Dan Tucker
Captain Jinks	Paw Paw Patch
Carrousel	Pop Goes the Weasel
Cats and Rats	Rovenacka
Chimes of Dunkirk	Rustic Reel
Crested Hen	Sicilian Circle
Cshebogar	Skip to My Lou
Dance of Greeting	Soldier's Joy
Did You Ever See a Lassie?	Tantoli
Gustaf's Skoal	Turn Around Me
Heel and Toe Polka	Valeta Waltz
How D'ye Do, My Partner	Varsovienne
Jump Jim Crow	Virginia Reel

Singing

Rounds (all sung to the tune "Brother John")

Black-eyed Susan,	Perfect posture.
Black-eyed Susan,	Perfect posture.
How are you?	Do not slump.
How are you?	Do not slump.
Very well I thank you.	You must grow up handsome.
Very well I thank you.	You must grow up handsome.
How are you?	Hide that hump.
How are you?	Hide that hump.
Cheer up, teachers.	Rheumatism.
Cheer up, teachers.	Rheumatism.
Smile a while.	How it pains.
Smile a while.	How it pains.
It isn't going to hurt you.	Up and down the system.
It isn't going to hurt you.	Up and down the system.
Ha, ha, ha.	When it rains.
Ha, ha, ha.	When it rains.

Nursery Rhymes (music, "Throw it Out the Window")[1]

Mother Hubbard	Jack Horner
Old King Cole	Jack and Jill
Mary Had a Little Lamb	Jack Sprat
Little Miss Muffet	Queen of Hearts
Simple Simon	Peter, Peter, Pumpkin Eater

Vocal Combats (One group sings one song, while another group sings a second song that will blend with the first but has a different tune and words.)

"Long Long Trail" with "Keep the Home Fires Burning"

"Home Sweet Home" with "Old Gray Mare"

"Solomon Levi" with "Spanish Cavalier"

"Humoresque" with "Way Down Upon the Swanee River"

Relays

Relays may be used with a selected group while the majority rest, or may be participated in by the entire group, divided into teams. The object of a relay is for the players in turn to perform a specified stunt or activity, one team being matched against another to see which team can finish first.

Balloon Race. Teams are formed of couples. Head couple of each team link inside arms and may not break apart. On a signal they bat a balloon forward around a chair or a person and then bat it back to the second couple on their team.

Nose Powder. Each player pushes a penny with his nose across a strip of shelf paper about four feet long placed on the floor. The second player pushes it back, the third player pushes it across again, and so on until one team wins.

Object on Head. A potato, an apple, or a saucer is balanced on the head while the player walks across the room and back.

Ring Relay. A large ring is passed down the line. The first player takes the ring from his right to his left forefinger and then slips it, using the forefinger only, to the right forefinger of the person next to him. This is continued until the end player has the ring on his left finger.

Stepping Stones. Each team has two newspapers folded in half or two pieces of cardboard of about the same size as the newspaper. Teams are formed of couples. On the signal, the man of each head couple places one of his papers on the floor in front of his partner and she steps on it. He places the second newspaper down and removes the first as

---

[1] *Handy I, Handy II,* edited by Lynn Rohrbough. Delaware, Ohio: Co-operative Recreation Service. Section S, Musical Recreation.

his partner steps onto the second. They cross the room in this manner, and then run back, arm in arm, to give the papers to the second couple.

Tin Can. Tin cans are used as stilts. Strings are attached to each can so that the cans may be held in place while the person is walking.

Games

Calabashes. Two lines are formed about 8 feet apart, the ladies sitting on one side and the gentlemen on the other. Each person secretly chooses one of the opposite sex for a fairy godmother or fairy godfather. To begin the game two men cross to the ladies' side, and each one asks any lady he cares to if she would like to be his fairy godmother. If he is the one the lady had secretly chosen she returns and sits with him on his side of the room. If not the one she has decided on, she replies "Calabashes." At all times there should be two men up. Each person has three trials. When the men's line is completed, the ladies have their turn. If a person sees that the one he had mentally selected has been secured, he may choose another.

Double Handcuff. The group is paired off by twos, and a string approximately 40 inches long is given each person. The gentleman ties separately the two ends of his string around the two wrists of his partner. The partner then ties one end of her string around one of the wrists of the gentleman, passes the loose end inside of his string (attached to her wrists) and then attaches that free end to the gentleman's other wrist. The game is to release one from the other without breaking the string. To do this, slip a loop made from the string of the gentleman under the string tied around a wrist of the lady and then pull the same loop over her hand. Ask those who know the trick not to show immediately how it is done.

Dumb Spelling Bee. A spelling bee is held in which signs are substituted for vowels as follows: A—right hand raised; E—left hand raised; I—point to eye; O—point to mouth; U—point to another person. Players are divided into groups, with a captain for each. Captains ask any player of their group to spell a word, substituting the signs for the vowels. If the speller sounds a vowel he has to exchange places with his captain.

Fist Challenge. Two lines of players, A and B, face each other, four or more players in a line. Line A passes a coin up and down the row while trying to prevent the members of line B from knowing where the coin is. B players point out the hand of any A player which, in their opinion, does not hold the coin. If the guess is correct, that hand is put behind the player and not used during the game. If the hand holding the coin is challenged by mistake, the number of hands still in the game are counted against Group B. Team B then takes the coin and play is resumed. The lowest score wins.

Grand Opera Tag. A game of tag is played. To escape being tagged a player must spread his feet apart, fold his arms, and sing loudly.

Handkerchief Passing. A group of about eight persons forms a team. Each group has a handkerchief. A circle is formed and at the word "play" the handkerchief is passed around the circle, each player handling it. When a whistle is blown the person having the handkerchief must stand on one foot. If a player is caught a second time the player must stand on one foot and hold a hand high in the air. A player must drop out if he puts his foot down or if caught a third time. Play until all players are eliminated.

Hide in Sight. The leader has piece of string about four inches long. While players close their eyes the leader hides the string in plain sight within the room. Players are then asked to hunt for the string and when they see it to sit down without saying anything. When all are seated, the first one who discovered the string becomes the hider.

Hindoo Tag. A game of tag is played. To escape being tagged, players must stop and place foreheads on the floor. As soon as the tagger goes away from the player's vicinity he must stand up again and join the game.

How Do You Like Your Neighbors. Group is seated in a circle with the exception of the leader, who has no chair and stands inside the ring. The leader addresses any individual and says, "How do you like your neighbors?" That person may answer in one of two ways: (1) "I like them very much," or (2) "I don't like them at all." If the person says, "I like them very much," everyone must rise and try to secure a new seat, at which time the leader also tries to capture a chair. The one left without a chair becomes the person to ask "How do you like your neighbors?" If the person addressed says, "I don't like them at all," the leader then asks, "Whom would you like?" The player addressed then calls the names of two people, whereupon the two seated next to him and the two whose names are called exchange places, the leader trying to get one of the seats.

Jockey Race. This is the familiar game played on shipboard, using players as jockeys. Six parallel lanes 24 feet long are marked on the floor and divided by cross lines every two feet, making 12 squares in each lane. The crowd is asked to collect into groups according to the lanes. Each lane and group is named or numbered. Each group selects a jockey, who stands at the end of the lane for his group. Two dice are rolled by the leader. If a jockey's number is shown on one of the two dice, he advances one square. There are several ways of competing, as follows:

1. Straight Ahead—advance the number of squares for each number on the dice turned up
2. Obstacle Start—a doubles is necessary to begin
3. Obstacle Finish—a doubles is necessary to finish
4. Obstacle in Center—a doubles is necessary to leave square number 6
5. Mule Race—last player left receives acclaim or prize

Popularity Circles. Two circles are formed, ladies in one, gentlemen in the other. The circle with the larger number of players marches on the inside. On a signal, circles march in opposite directions. When a whistle is blown or chords of music are sounded, players try to secure partners from the opposite circle. Those unsuccessful retire to the center. Others march as partners in the direction the boys were marching. Whistle or piano chords are sounded and partners separate, the girls reversing their direction. A signal is given and a new partner is secured, the center players having another opportunity to get a partner. Continue as long as desired.

Queen's Headache. A queen is seated on a throne. The leader announces that the queen has a terrible headache; in fact, it is so bad that she must be blindfolded. After the leader gives each a number, he signals them one at a time to cross over to the other side of the room. If the queen hears one she groans, whereupon that individual must sit down on the floor at the spot where he is when the queen groaned. The fun is to see how many can escape having to sit on the floor.

Ten Times Around. Circles of about eight players are formed and a captain is chosen for each group. A handkerchief is passed ten times around each group, each person handling the handkerchief. When the handkerchief passes the captain, he calls the number in a loud voice. The object is to see which group finishes first.

Up-Down. All the players, with the exception of the leader and one additional player, are seated, there being an intervening space between each chair. On signal, the players march in and out around the chairs and the leader calls either "Up" or "Down." If he says "Up" each person stands behind a chair. If "Down" is called each sits on a chair. The leader removes one or more chairs each time a call is given.

Progressive Games [1]

Sometimes a leader desires to vary the usual program of a fun night so that team games become the motif. This may be done by using a num-

---

[1] Directions for progressive games can be secured at small cost from the National Recreation Association, 315 Fourth Avenue, New York 10, New York.

ber of activities in which the players in designated numbers rotate from game to game as signals are given. Teachers should make a practice of building up their collection of game materials and statements of the rules of play needed for each of the games that will be used during such an evening's program.

Each person present is given a score card and each keeps his own record. At the end of the final period of play, all score cards are collected by the captains and are given to the persons assigned to determine the persons having the highest and the lowest score.

The persons present should be divided into groups with not more than six persons to a group. All the groups and all the games should be numbered. When beginning the play, members of each group report to the game having the same number as their set. Play begins and stops on a signal given by the leader. On the first rotation, the group having the highest group number reports to game Number 1, the other groups moving to the next highest game number.

Five, eight, or ten minutes is the usual time allowed for the playing of a game. Two or three minutes should be allowed for the players to record on their score card their score for the game and for the groups to rotate to the new game and receive instructions on how to play the game.

Each group may elect a captain or the leader may select captains before the party and instruct them in their duties. If this latter method is used, the captains remain at the assignment given them throughout the evening, directing each new group how to play his or her particular activity. If the first method is used, each captain remains with his group and travels with them from game to game.

Games should be arranged next to the walls of the gymnasium or auditorium with enough space between each game so that no interference will occur. Tables must be supplied for some games and chairs should be available for those desiring to sit until their turn arrives.

The descriptions of a few games are presented to aid leaders in a better understanding as to what is needed for rotative game parties for boys and girls, men and women. The ingenuity of students and teachers will result in the invention and construction of many others. The expense involved should be small, as much of the needed equipment can be made from discards or by using articles found in the home, such as stove lids, pie pans, broom handles, coffee cans, boxes, fruit jar covers, and hose washers.

Tiddlywinks. Tiddlywinks is played from a piece of felt or blotter. The small disks are flipped into a circle and score is indicated by the number in the area where disk lands. If disk falls on a line, no score is allowed. The playing diagram may be drawn on the floor or it may be used on a table. (Figure 85.)

Chair Quoits. Quoits may be rope rings or may be constructed from garden hose. The chair is turned upside down and the quoits are tossed toward the legs of the chair. Twenty-five points are scored for each ringer.

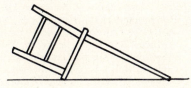

Figure 85.   Diagram shows how to mark out an area for tiddlywinks.

Figure 86.   The legs of an upturned chair may be used for chair quoits.

Shuffleboard.   Four stove lids, cake tins, or pie pans and one broom handle provide the necessary equipment. The plates are pushed one at a time toward the diagram marked on floor. (Figure 87.)

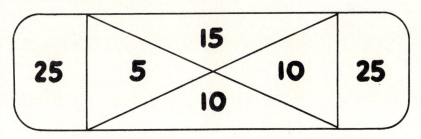

Figure 87.   Diagram shows how to mark an area for shuffleboard.

Swing Bowling.   Ten Indian clubs are set up in triangular formation about eight or ten inches apart. A baseball is tied into a towel and is attached to the end of a rope suspended above the Indian clubs but hanging low enough to touch the clubs. The player draws the baseball to any angle he chooses and lets it swing, thereby hoping to knock down as many clubs as is possible with the forward swing of the weighted rope. Clubs knocked down on the return swing of the ball may not be counted.

SELECTED REFERENCES [1]

BURCHENAL, ELIZABETH. *Folk Dances from Old Homelands.* New York: G. Schirmer, Inc., 1922.

—————. *American Country-Dances.* New York: G. Schirmer Co., 1918.

CRAMPTON, C. WARD, AND WOLLASTON, MARY A. *The Song Play Book.* New York: A. S. Barnes & Co., 1917.

DICK, WILLIAM BRISBANE. *Dick's Quadrille Call-Book.* New York: Fitzgerald Publishing Corp.

ELSOM, J. C., AND TRILLING, BLANCHE M. *Social Games and Group Dances.* Philadelphia: J. B. Lippincott Co., 1927.

"Good Morning." Music, Calls, and Directions for Old-Time Dancing as Revived by Mr. and Mrs. Henry Ford. Dearborn, Mich.: 1943 (fourth edition).

Handy I and *Handy II.* Edited by Lynn Rohrbough. Delaware, Ohio: Co-operative Recreation Service. The "Handies" are made up of kits which can be purchased separately. Especially good for fun nights are the following kits:

Musical Recreation, Section S, "Social Songs, Rounds"
Section G, "Mixing Games"
Handy II. Kit T, "Old Fashioned Quadrilles"
Handy II. Kit R, "Singing Games from the South"
Handy II. Section P, "Singing Games, Set Running, and Circle Dances"
The Recreation Kit, "American Folk Dances"

LA SALLE, DOROTHY. *Rhythms and Dances for Elementary Schools.* New York: A. S. Barnes & Co., 1926.

SHAW, LLOYD. *Cowboy Dances.* Caldwell, Idaho: The Caxton Printers, 1939.

Special Activities in Physical Education for High School and Adult Groups. State of California, Department of Education Bulletin No. 14 (July 15, 1934). Sacramento: California State Department of Education, 1934.

---

[1] The appendixes also list reference materials.

Chapter XI
CAMPING AS AN INTEGRAL PART OF THE
SCHOOL CURRICULUM [1]

Primitive man, squatting outside his cave along the bank of a stream, set a pattern of living that of necessity continued for many generations, and his descendant, modern civilized man, voluntarily repeats the pattern again and again through camping experiences, quite unaware why they are so satisfying. Hunting and fishing, necessities·for primitive man and two of the most popular avocations of men today, are intimately related to camping. The fireplace in a modern home is treasured not so much because of the heat it affords but because of the joy it brings to those who can sit beside it and watch the flame and smoke and embers reminiscent of campfires.

Educators have done much in recent years to bring reality into the learning experiences of children in school. The stiff formality of classrooms has been relaxed in favor of informality and interested pupilteacher co-operation in learning. Increasing numbers of schools are leading pupils into participation in community life and into living in wilderness areas to study at first hand the realities of life outside the classroom.

ORGANIZED CAMPING IN THE SCHOOL PROGRAM

Organized camping has come into the school program because camping affords a kind of education that is not possible in the schoolhouse or on the playground. The experiences that come from close contact with nature require the woods and fields; they can never be approximated by reading about them. These experiences include meeting adverse weather conditions, providing for one's own comfort, preparing one's own food, working with others of different races and religions in a camp environment. Among the values derived from these experiences are work experiences, an understanding of the plant and wildlife of the woods and the fields, training in self-reliance, development of physical sturdiness, and the ability to live and work co-operatively with others.

At present only about five per cent of American children have an opportunity to enjoy organized camping experiences. A large percentage

[1] Material for this chapter was prepared by the 1947-48 School Camp Steering Committee of the City-County Camp Commission, San Diego, California. Jay Davis Conner, Chairman, Robert W. Bergstrom, Denver C. Fox, Vesta Petersen, Edwin J. Pumala, Joseph C. Robinson, Peter H. Snyder, Burton C. Tiffany, and James C. Clark, Editor-Co-ordinator.

[283]

Figure 88. Children learn to live and work together at the school camp.

of this group are the children of well-to-do families and of families with very low incomes. Most children have no opportunity to attend camps. Recognition of that fact and appreciation of the educational values of camping for children have led to the conclusion that camping and outdoor education should be instituted by the public schools as a part of the general education program.

Such a program, when organized properly under qualified leadership, should enrich and make more popular the camping programs now operated by private and voluntary youth-serving agencies. In this way a much larger percentage of children of school age may be afforded at least an introductory experience in organized camping.

The public appears to be ready for school camps. Public support for conservation of natural resources recognizes the part that citizens play in protection of the woods and of animal life. Moreover, parents and educators have shown a readiness to include camping in the school curriculum and, when attempted, the experience has generally been a rich and rewarding one for children.

CAMPING AND OUTDOOR EDUCATION IN CALIFORNIA

California is unusually fortunate in the natural facilities for camping available in every section of the state. Like all modern states California is building cities, and the children of these centers of population may grow into adulthood without knowing the woods, fields, streams, and mountains if the school does not act to bring them in contact with nature in her many forms. But California, along with other states, is beginning to attack the problem.

School camping has passed beyond the theoretical stage in California. While a number of school districts have conducted week-end and vacation camps for several years, the San Diego city schools and the schools of San Diego County and the Long Beach public schools have led the way in California in demonstrating how camping experiences may be used to enrich the program of public education during the regular school year. The San Diego project is referred to more specifically here because this pioneer venture has been operated continuously since March of 1946, while the Long Beach project started in May, 1948. Throughout the nation this kind of education is beginning to grow in popularity and frequency.

THE SAN DIEGO CITY-COUNTY CAMPING EDUCATION PROGRAM

The idea of a public year-round camp for the school children of San Diego was conceived by a number of nature-loving citizens and championed by parent-teacher groups, a member of the county board of supervisors, a member of the city council, and various individuals. A committee was formed, the outgrowth of which is the present San Diego City-County Camp Commission. This was organized in 1943 by joint ordinance of the City Council and the County Board of Supervisors. A five-member board representing city and county governments, public schools in both city and county, and parent-teacher organizations, the Commission has over-all responsibility for conducting the business of the camp and setting policies. The camp program is under continuous study by a Steering Committee, which also recommends policies and co-ordinates the activities of the camp and the school systems of the city and county. This committee is composed of elementary school principals and administrators of the schools in the city and the county.

In 1944 the Commission acquired Camp Cuyamaca by lease without charge from the State Park Commission. The camp itself consists of ten acres in a small valley in Cuyamaca State Park. The elevation is about 4,000 feet, and accessible peaks rise to about 5,500 feet. There are scattered stands of oak and pine—some of fair size—interspersed with open meadows and chaparral. Bird and animal life is plentiful and varied. A small stream cuts through the camp area. One main advantage of the site is that a fair amount of snow falls there, but never enough to cut the camp off from food and fuel supplies. The main buildings, including four dormitories, two meeting halls, a dining hall and kitchen, the staff quarters, and the shops are weatherproofed and can be made comfortable in winter. They are plain, substantial structures originally built for the Civilian Conservation Corps.

Limitation of funds and facilities made it necessary to limit participation to pupils of a particular grade for this pioneer venture at Camp Cuyamaca. The sixth grade was chosen for several practical reasons. Children of this level of maturity are capable of carrying on organized activities and are able to assume considerable responsibility for themselves. Sixth graders are under the direction of a single teacher for most of their work, and it was felt that groups who were accustomed to working together could adjust to living together more easily than junior high school children—an important factor because, for reasons of expediency, the encampment is limited to one school week. Moreover, the site is suited to many activities for children in the ten to thirteen year age group.

In the first year and a half of its life the camp and its program evolved through trial and error. Of the many lessons learned during this period, three are especially pertinent here:

1. Counselor-teachers must be well-balanced persons of considerable intelligence and they should have training that is exceptionally broad. Teaching experience is highly desirable.
2. The number of children to a counselor should not be more than 8 to 10. This is the standard that prevails in private camps, though it may well be that well-prepared counselors could be responsible for 16 to 18 children.
3. The staff members should have two days each of relief per week and opportunity to leave camp during these periods. Overloading and overworking counselor-teachers ultimately puts the well-being of the children in jeopardy.

With the beginning of the 1947-48 school year the camp entered a new phase. The San Diego City Board of Education provided five certificated teachers to serve as camp counselors and an experienced elementary school principal to serve as camp director. The Rosenberg Foundation of San Francisco provided funds for a documentary study of the camp and its relationship to the schools. Much effort was spent in refining the camp curriculum and in making camping experience an integral part of the education of the San Diego public school child.

The fundamental factor that is considered in planning all operations at Camp Cuyamaca is the level of maturity of the children. For instance, in hiking trips it is necessary to begin with short walks, proceed to hikes of a few miles, and then undertake an all-day hike. It takes longer than a week for all children to reach the same degree of hiking endurance. It is necessary, consequently, to offer hikes of three different lengths: a two and one-half mile hike which gives the strongest a real test, a shorter hike over less formidable terrain for the average hiker, and a leisurely walk for the few children incapable of hiking.

To arrange these hikes requires careful planning and careful management. Routes must be mapped out which are not only appropriate to the varying abilities of the children, but are also of equal interest. For it would jeopardize the success of the camping trip if any child felt that he had missed an exciting, enviable experience without having a compensating adventure. Moreover, the Cuyamaca policy is to let children choose which activity they will pursue. This creates a feeling of freedom, promotes democratic participation in the life of the camp, and provides ultimate satisfaction with the outcome of the experience. Children almost always choose activities suited to their capacities if all the offerings have

re 89. Hiking in new surroundings is an exciting adventure to child campers.

equivalent interest and if they are presented in such a way that all appear equally desirable. The camp staff is aided in evaluating the wisdom of the children's choices of activity through study of the complete health data kept by schools and supplied to the camp. In special cases, parents and attending physicians also supply information that enables the staff to provide adequate protection and care. Effort spent in making the camp experience safe for physically handicapped children is rewarding because it enables them to share selected activities with their companions and gives them a psychological lift.

In addition to the organized hikes, considerable hiking necessarily occurs in connection with other camp experiences. Thus, children in a nature study project or in a quest for proper wood with which to make bows and arrows or in the effort to follow the tracks of some animal will naturally hike through the woods and along the streams. The teacher may have a real share in the group decision without making her judgment arbitrary if she helps to arrange the activities in groups from which choices are to be made and helps to set up minimum standards of attainment in several areas from which the children choose.

Physical Education at Camp

It has been said that the first physical educator was the parent who taught his son how to throw, to jump, and to climb. This sort of physical education grew out of the needs of the simple society of the tribe and served its purpose as it contributed to the welfare and stability of the group. The activities that make up the physical education program at a camp are taken from these simple group patterns. Instead of being confined to the organized games and dances that are so characteristic a part of the physical education program of the school, physical education at camp is a continuous part of the natural activity of camp life.

All of the physical activities at Camp Cuyamaca are purposeful. In addition to going on all-day hikes, the children make shorter expeditions daily when weather permits. These are trips of exploration and discovery in the course of which they gather specimens for their own collections and the camp museum and obtain materials for use in arts and craft shops. Clay modeling, carving in soft stone, and woodworking with local materials provide the type of steady, mild, and satisfying physical activity appropriate to sixth-grade children. These activities are often scheduled for the afternoon hours, the more vigorous activities taking place in the morning.

Most of the physical activity at Cuyamaca is closely connected with work-experience ranging from sweeping to tree planting—or with studies of nature in the investigation of Indian remains and similar interests. This policy enables the camp to fulfill its educational purposes and to give the children an interesting and diversified experience. Learning under these circumstances is a pleasure to youngsters of sixth-grade age. Moreover, the child who is truly interested in a constructive activity is seldom a behavior problem.

An organized program of competitive sports has no place in the Cuyamaca program. The children are so occupied in exploring and living in their new environment that they have little desire for this type of play. It is the intention of the camp to provide an experience in enjoyable, constructive group living. This would be more difficult to achieve if competition were introduced into the short, intense camp period.

Purely recreational activities are introduced into the flexible schedule as circumstances dictate. Playing on the "monkey bridge" is a favorite pastime. This bridge consists of a rope stretched across a stream supported on either bank by perpendicular cross or "x" frames. Rope hand rails are attached to the foot rope by crisscrossing shorter ropes. Whoever crosses the bridge must walk Indian-fashion, one foot in front of the other, using the hand rails for support. On clear nights, children enjoy stories and songs around a campfire. On rainy days the counselors provide sessions of stunts, tumbling, and folk dancing. Following an occasional snowfall, play is chiefly of the snow-balling and snowman-making variety. The camp has toboggans, but winter sports requiring highly developed skills appear to be impractical at Camp Cuyamaca.

Room is left in the camp schedule for the unplanned, impulsive activities of leisure. The children have opportunities to do what they please—to wander down to the paddock and talk to the donkey, to stand at the camp's edge and watch feeding deer. Since rest is as important as activity, an hour after lunch and approximately half an hour after dinner are set aside for quiet games, quiet talk, reading, writing home, and sleep.

The physical education features of the program at Camp Cuyamaca are significant although they are not conspicuous. In the gymnasium and on the playground, ladders are installed for climbing because development of climbing skills is one essential for the proper development of young children. At Camp Cuyamaca there are trees to climb, there are logs that serve as balance beams, there are brooks and gullies to be jumped, hills and mountains to be climbed, and distant goals to be reached. These facilities provide opportunity for development of fundamental skills in a natural setting. But in addition the camp program adds greatly to the child's interest in and knowledge of many phases of outdoor living that

Figure 90. On clear nights, the blaze of the campfire fascinates the young camper.

also are part of his education. Indeed, interest in and appreciation of the outdoors is quite as important as the particular skills that might be developed.

The more the children help to take care of themselves the less outside dictation and discipline are required. Working with others in camp life serves to lessen tensions, enables the children to participate democratically in the life of the group, and results in wholesome attitudes and behavior which may last beyond the camp experience if parents and teachers incorporate these patterns into the child's everyday life when he returns. Also, this kind of work-play experience helps to dissolve the artificial barriers separating work and play, mental and physical activity, and recreation and learning. It has been found most practical to help the children to apply what they know to the real situation at hand, rather than to attempt to add a great deal of new knowledge during the brief camp experience. Necessity—the necessity to take care of one's self and to lead a satisfying group life—is in this case the mother of learning. Instruction by relating knowledge to necessity makes the children respond with interest and genuine effort.

Inevitably—since the camp philosophy recognizes the oneness of mind and body—such psychosomatic problems as a slight rise in temperature due to homesickness must be frequently solved. Balance and good judgment on the part of the staff, particularly the nurse, are required. The position of the nurse in camp is, in fact, critical. She must, to do her job properly, have a deep interest in children and teaching skill as well as technical competence. The counselors and director should have a good basic understanding of the principles of health, and a special understanding of the relation of health to the types of physical activity involved in camping. It is inevitable that no matter how well prepared the counselors are when they join the staff, a certain amount of in-service training will be required to prepare them to meet and deal with the special circumstances of this particular camp, such as degree of altitude, living arrangements and hazards ranging from snake bite to a slippery shower room floor. Continuous study must also be made of the related health and physical activity programs in order to maintain high standards and realize the full educational potential.

THE COMMON HERITAGE

It is inevitable that the confusions of a world-wide social, economic, and political revolution should lead man to forget the simple priorities of life that remain for all men everywhere. The atomic age with its tremendous achievements in science speaks so loudly that many persons never hear the call of simple things. And yet it is the simple things that gladden the heart of man—feeling warmth when cold, sleeping when tired, the splash of cold water on a warm face, the smell of new-mown hay, the song of birds at daybreak. Camping gives to children a natural contact with this common heritage from the past and also makes them happy. For the land is still man's habitation. Although he has mastered the air and sails upon the sea and goes under it with his war craft, he returns to the land which nourishes him and revives his energies.

The men and women of each generation build their lives out of the experiences that they have. Camping as an integral part of the public school program can make certain that one great area of experience is not lost and one heritage not forgotten.

SELECTED REFERENCES [1]

Books

AMERICAN CAMPING ASSOCIATION. *Marks of Good Camping.* New York: Association Press, 1941.

BROWN, CORA L., AND OTHERS. *Outdoor Cooking.* New York: The Greystone Press, 1940.

Camping and Outdoor Experiences in the School Program. Washington 25, D. C.: U. S. Office of Education, Federal Security Agency, 1947.

---

[1] Appendix B also lists reference materials.

CLARKE, JAMES MITCHELL. *The Cuyamaca Story: A Record in Pictures of San Diego's City-County School Camp.* Prepared for the San Diego City-County Camp Commission under direction of the School Camp Steering Committee, 1948, through the generosity of the Rosenberg Foundation of San Francisco. San Diego, California: San Diego City-County Camp Commission, 1948.

DROUGHT, R. ALICE. *A Camping Manual.* New York: A. S. Barnes & Co., 1943.

Extending Education through Camping. New York City Board of Education Report of School Camp Experiment. New York: Life Camps, Inc., 1948.

GROVER, EDWIN D. *The Nature Lover's Knapsack. An Anthology of Poems.* New York: Thos. F. Crowell Co., 1947 (enlarged edition).

LINDERMAN, WANDA T. *The Outdoor Book.* New York: Camp Fire Girls, Inc., 1947.

NATIONAL RECREATION ASSOCIATION. *Nature in Recreation.* New York: National Recreation Association, 1938.

Film

Camping Education—California's Pilot Project. Color, sound. May be rented from San Diego County Schools Camping Trust Fund, c/o Camp Commission, 405 Civic Center, San Diego 1, California, at $5.00, plus shipping charges.

Chapter XII
EVALUATION IN THE PHYSICAL EDUCATION PROGRAM

No physical education program can be complete without evaluation. The teacher and the administrator must know what the program is accomplishing. Is it developing the pupils' physical fitness and contributing to their emotional and social growth? Is it meeting the particular needs of the individual pupil? If so, how much is it contributing to his growth? Could the program be modified to increase its effectiveness? Is there too much emphasis on games and sports, too little attention given to rhythmical activities? Are a few individuals getting all the teacher's attention, to the detriment of those who are handicapped or immature socially or physically? Are the facilities adequate to carry out the program? Answers to these and similar questions will give the teacher and the administrator an indication of the relative success or failure of the program.

Reliable answers to these questions can only be made if evaluation procedures are a part of the physical education program. Tests devised to measure various kinds of ability must be given to all who take part in the program. Some kinds of ability can be easily measured in feet, seconds or exact number of performances. For other kinds of learnings no objective tests of achievement have been devised. Courtesy, courage, and sportsmanship cannot be timed and measured as can running, jumping, or ball throwing. Changes in behavior, improvements in posture, and performance in game situations can, however, be appraised by an observant and understanding teacher. Subjective appraisals of growth have a definite place in the process of evaluating a pupil's needs and abilities.

In forming judgments the appraiser must measure achievement against standards. If the children have made satisfactory and apparent progress toward achieving the specific skills appropriate to their age, the program can be adjudged a success. If there are failures, the causes of failure must be assessed and remedies found.

A wholly objective method of rating a total physical education program has not been devised. It is true that one may count the basketballs and measure the playing fields and compute the percentage of time given to various types of activities in the program. But since no fixed standards for the relationship of facilities to pupils or for the amount of time a class must spend mastering basketball skills can be set up, such measurements must be partially subjective. Here again the teacher and administrator must rely on judgment to determine how well the planning and teaching procedures have succeeded in carrying out the basic objectives of physical education. Competent judgment of the adequacy of a program must be made through a study of the results as compared with the results in the same or other schools with other methods. In the final analysis, the evaluation of the total program can only be in terms of what it accomplishes for the individual.

OBJECTIVES OF EVALUATION

The first essential in evaluating a program is a clear understanding of the aims and objectives of physical education. They have been stated in terms of physical status, motor skills, mental learnings, personality integration, and social adjustment. The conscientious teacher who is concerned with the outcomes of the program should attempt to determine what progress has been made in each of these areas. Such measurement of progress will serve as a basis for judging the effectiveness of teaching procedures and diagnosing the weaknesses of those procedures, and will focus attention upon the specific needs of individuals in each group.

The administrator needs to survey facilities, personnel, and curriculum to discover weaknesses and needs. Although weaknesses of some kinds may be apparent without elaborate tests, a thorough survey based on appraisal of many different factors is more effective than a mere statement of need or an unsubstantiated opinion.

The pupil, too, should benefit from the evaluation program. He should be informed of the results of tests so that he can see his own achievement as measured against his own previous records and against records of his classmates. The evaluative process will give the pupil a better understanding of the objectives and content of the program and will be a valuable motivation if it shows him personal accomplishment and increase of status.

OBJECTIVE AND SUBJECTIVE METHODS OF EVALUATION

Evaluative procedures should not be restricted to the measurable abilities and skills. It is important to know the exact performance of children in numerous motor activities, but it is equally important to know what interests they manifest, what habits they have, and what attitudes they show. Evaluation, therefore, entails a judgment of what has taken place in each child as evidenced by changed behavior, as well as measurement of the skills, attitudes, and knowledge he has acquired. Both objective and subjective methods of evaluation must be used to establish a true and complete picture of achievement and growth.

Objective or quantitative measurement is a concrete measuring or testing procedure which provides a score, usually numerical, that does not depend upon the personal judgment or bias of the test administrator. Objective measurement can be used to determine physical status, specific elements and combinations of motor skills, and information about the rules, form, and strategy of games. Results of tests are in units of time, distance, height, or number of times the skill is performed. All tests should be so constructed and so administered that they will yield valid and reliable information. A test is valid if it measures what it is intended to measure. A test in throwing a softball accurately will measure a throwing skill but it will not measure all the aspects of throwing nor does it measure ability in an actual game situation. Tests of a pupil's ability in performing pull-ups can be used to measure the physical strength of certain muscles but not to indicate total physical strength. A test is reliable if the same individual can repeat it a number of times with consistent results. Isolating the elements of a skill to be tested and devising a valid and reliable test is not an easy matter; it involves a great deal of research and experience.

Many traits, learnings, and skills do not lend themselves readily to objective measurement but must be evaluated subjectively through careful observation of evidence and exercise of judgment. It is more difficult to make valid and reliable subjective evaluations than it is to administer an objective test, but unless subjective judgments are used in addition to objective tests, progress toward many of the more important aims of the physical education program cannot be measured. The form used in the performance of motor skills and the effectiveness of those skills in a game or team situation cannot be evaluated except by observation. Knowledge of facts may be tested objectively, but the understanding and application of those facts must be observed and interpreted. As yet no adequate measures of the complex of factors which determine personality integration and social adjustment have been devised, but the manifestations of such integration and adjustment should be observed by the teacher and her teaching procedures adapted to the needs of each individual in these respects.

Devices for making subjective evaluations must be as carefully prepared and used as are the objective tests. Mere guesses or opinions are of little value in analyzing the worth of a program. The teacher must know exactly what achievement ought to be expected and how to judge whether or not the pupil is making progress toward the objective. In posture, for instance, a fairly reliable judgment may be made only if the teacher knows what good posture is and observes the child's standing and sitting posture at various times, checking on each particular item.[1] In game skills such as batting, elements of good performance must be known and checked point by point while the pupil is actually batting a ball. Behavior inventory sheets may be drawn up for checking indications of improved behavior in terms of responsibility, leadership, courtesy, or other desirable traits that may be expected to improve through experiences offered by physical education.

EVALUATING THE PROGRESS OF THE INDIVIDUAL

One of the principal objectives of physical education is to teach students the skills of many games, sports, and rhythmic activities. Accomplishment in these areas is one of the most concrete and readily demonstrable results of a well-planned and well-taught program of physical education. This achievement can be measured. The problem, however, is not a simple one, for the ultimate results of such learning are demonstrated in the ability of the individual to use those skills effectively in a game situation. Isolated elements of those skills may be measured with a reasonable degree of accuracy, but the final evaluation of the use of those skills must usually be made subjectively by an experienced observer.

For example, in tennis it is simple to mark off the areas in which a well-placed serve should land, and then to count the number of times the server is able to place the ball in those areas in a given number of trials. A person may successfully place the ball in those areas ten times out of ten trials, but may do it by using less speed, force, and deceptiveness than would be effective in a game. These factors are important in determining the ability to use the total skill in a game situation, but they are difficult to measure with simple tests. It becomes evident, then, that these factors must be evaluated by the teacher through observation.

Subjective Ratings

Subjective rating of form, force, speed, and effectiveness in the performance of a total skill in its natural setting is one of the most important aspects of evaluation, though many teachers do not consciously consider it a part of the testing program. In a rating chart for softball batting, for example, the elements of softball batting are listed and checked against actual performance. The accompanying list, taken from a softball batting chart,[2] is comprehensive and yet is in simple terms so that either a pupil

---

[1] See Chapter XIII, "An Analysis of Skills Developed Through Elementary School Physical Education," which includes the characteristics of good posture as well as analysis of skills developed through activities in all grades.

[2] By permission of Esther French, Department of Health and Physical Education for Women, Illinois State Normal University.

or the teacher may check performance. Similar forms may be devised for other skills. It is only necessary to analyze with care all the elements of a skill which may be rated by careful observation.

RATING OF PERFORMANCE IN SOFTBALL BATTING

Performer's Name .... Date ....

Rater's Initials ....

	RATING	ERRORS
1. *Grip*	........Good ....Fair ....Poor	........Hands too far apart ....Wrong hand on top ....Hands too far from end of bat
2. *Preliminary Stance*	........Good ....Fair ....Poor	........Too near the plate ....Too far from plate ....Too far forward toward pitcher ....Too far backward toward catcher ....Rear foot closer to plate than forward foot ....Bat resting on shoulders ....Shoulders not horizontal
3. *Stride or Footwork*	........Good ....Fair ....Poor	........Fails to step forward ....Fails to transfer weight ....Lifts back foot from ground ....(Other)
4. *Pivot or Body Twist*	........Good ....Fair ....Poor	........Fails to twist body ....Fails to "wind up" ....Has less than 90° pivot ....(Other)
5. *Arm Movement or Swing*	........Good ....Fair ....Poor	........Arms held too close to body ....Rear elbow held too far up ....Bat not held approximately parallel to ground ....Batter does not use enough wrist motion ....Wrists not uncocked forcefully enough
6. *General* (Eyes on ball, judgment of pitches, etc.)	........Good ....Fair ....Poor	........Movements jerky ....Tries too hard; "presses" ....Fails to look at exact center of ball ....Poor judgment of pitches ....Appears to lack confidence ....Poor selection of bat

Additional Comments: ....

....

....

Objective Measures of Game Skills

Objective measures of game skills can be made by testing performance in isolated elements. Batteries of tests for specific sport and game skills have been devised and presented by various research workers. Many of these batteries are still in experimental form, being too long, too complicated, or not sufficiently reliable or valid for general use. A few, however, have been simplified and validated and are useful in testing skills involved in the games of softball, soccer, tennis, volleyball, and basketball. The scores made on these items will provide objective evidence of the ability of each individual to apply the skill acquired in a situation which, while it may be artificial, still retains many of the elements of the game situation.

Many tests for specific sports may be found in the guides in the Official Sports Library for Women, prepared by committees of the National Section on Women's Athletics of the American Association for Health, Physical Education and Recreation, and published by the Association.[1] These guides, which contain the official rules for each sport, should be in every elementary school library. It is strongly urged that the teacher read the sections on testing in each current edition to inform himself of new batteries of tests and of revisions and improvements in the previously presented batteries.

Thirty-three tests for boys and twenty for girls in the events commonly used in grades 5 to 12 are described in *Achievement Scales in Physical Education Activities*.[2] The method of giving the tests and scoring the pupils is described in detail. Pupils in the upper grades may learn to use the scoring procedures and score their own performances. In the list of skill tests that follows, details of the test are omitted from items which can be found in the above-mentioned book, a page reference being substituted.

1. *Softball* (and other games using a softball)
   a. Throwing for accuracy (*Achievement Scales*, p. 22)
   b. Base running (*Achievement Scales*, p. 17)

2. *Soccer, speed ball, and field ball*
   a. Dribble (*Achievement Scales*, p. 30)
   b. Kick for distance (*Achievement Scales*, p. 31)
   c. Kick for accuracy (*Achievement Scales*, p. 32)

---

[1] Listed in Appendix B.

[2] N. P. Neilson and F. W. Cozens, *Achievement Scales in Physical Education Activities for Boys and Girls in Elementary and Junior High Schools*. Sacramento: California State Department of Education, 1934. This book is furnished to elementary schools and to junior high schools by the State Department of Education. Teachers of physical education in the intermediate and upper grades should have desk copies of this book.

d. Throw for accuracy (for games such as kick ball or hit-pin base-ball). The performer stands with one foot on base and throws five soccer balls, using a sidearm throw, to a player standing on a base 45 feet away. The throw is scored 1 point if it can be easily reached and caught on the fly by the player on base.

3. *Basketball*

a. Throw for distance (*Achievement Scales*, p. 19)
b. Throw for goal (*Achievement Scales*, p. 19)
c. Ball handling (see Figure 91). Player takes ball in Area A, makes an angle pass at the wall and recovers in Area B. Player immediately passes to wall again and recovers in A (continuing for 15 seconds). If ball is caught in the wrong area player must retrieve it and must bounce to the correct square before continuing. *Score:* Number of passes completed in 15 seconds. Three trials are given and the best score counted.

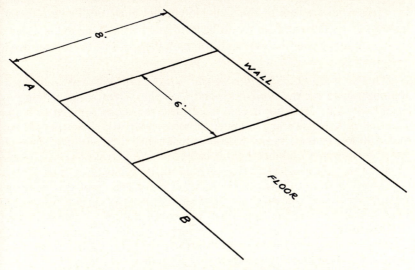

Figure 91. Diagram shows area for ball handling test.

d. Dribble and shoot.[1] Player stands behind center of free-throw line, then dribbles ball to left and retrieves it outside the free-throw circle and immediately shoots for the basket. This is repeated to the right, alternating for the total of ten shots. *Score:* Score 2 points for each basket made and 1 for each time ball hits rim but fails to go in. Basket or rim

[1] Adapted from Joanna T. Dyer, Jennie C. Schurig, and Sara L. Apgar, "A Basketball Motor Ability Test for College Women and Secondary School Girls," *Research Quarterly*, X (October, 1939), 128. By permission.

hit is not counted if dribble is illegal or either foot is inside circle at time of shooting. The final score is the sum of scores for 10 shots.

e. Repeated passes.[1]   A restraining line is drawn 9 feet from the wall and parallel to it. Player stands behind the line. Player throws the ball against the wall, catches it as it rebounds, and throws again as quickly as possible. This is continued for 15 seconds. Player may cross the line to retrieve the ball but must be behind the line for each throw. *Score:* Number of passes completed in 15 seconds.

4. *Tennis*

a. Backboard test of tennis ability.[2]   A backboard or wall should be provided, allowing 15 to 20 feet in width for each person taking the test at one time. The wall should be approximately 10 feet high. A line should be drawn on the wall to represent a tennis net. It should be three inches wide, with the top of the line three feet from the floor. Five feet from the base of the wall and parallel to the wall a restraining line should be drawn. Two tennis balls, in good condition, and a racket, tightly strung, should be provided for each player. The tester will need a stop watch.

On the word "Go!" of the signal, "Ready, go!" the ball is dropped and allowed to hit the floor once and then the player starts rallying it against the wall. Rallying is continued until the signal is given to stop. The ball may bounce any number of times or it may be volleyed. At the beginning of the test and whenever a new ball is put in play, the ball must be allowed to bounce before being hit. Any stroke may be used, but all strokes must be played from behind the restraining line. The player may cross the line to retrieve the ball but hits made from this position are not scored. If the ball gets out of control the player may take another ball. *Score:* Each time a ball strikes the wall on or above the net line, having been hit from behind the restraining line, 1 point is scored. Three trials are given, and the score is the sum of the points made. The length of each trial is 30 seconds.

5. *Volleyball* [3]

a. Repeated volleys test.   A backboard or wall should be marked with a line 10 feet long at the net height, 7½ feet from the floor or ground. Three feet from the base of the wall and parallel to it, a restrain-

[1] Adapted from M. Gladys Scott and Esther French, *Better Teaching Through Testing.* New York: A. S. Barnes & Co., 1945, p. 140. By permission.
[2] Adapted from Joanna Dyer, "Revision of Backboard Test of Tennis Ability," *Research Quarterly,* IX (March, 1938), 25. By permission.
[3] Adapted from Naomi Russell and Elizabeth Lange, "Achievement Tests in Volleyball for High School Girls," *Research Quarterly,* XI (December, 1940), 33-41.

ing line 10 feet long is drawn. Volleyballs will be needed, and the tester should have a stop watch.

The player being tested stands behind the 3-foot line, and with an underhand movement tosses the ball against the wall. When it returns, the player volleys it repeatedly against the wall above the net line for 30 seconds. The ball may be set up as many times as desired; it may be caught and restarted with a toss as at the beginning. If the ball gets out of control, it must be recovered by the player and brought back to the restraining line to be started over again as at the beginning.

Each pupil is given three trials. A rest period should be given between trials. *Score:* The score is the number of times the ball is clearly batted (not tossed) from the restraining line to the wall above or on the net line. The best score of the three trials is the test score.

b. Serving test. A regulation volleyball court, 30 by 60 feet, is divided into a service end and a target end. The target end is divided into scoring areas by chalk lines as follows: (1) 12½ feet from the net and parallel to it; (2) 5 feet inside the end line and parallel to it; and (3) 5 feet inside each side line and parallel to it, running from the net to line 2. Each area so outlined is given a score value (Figure 92).

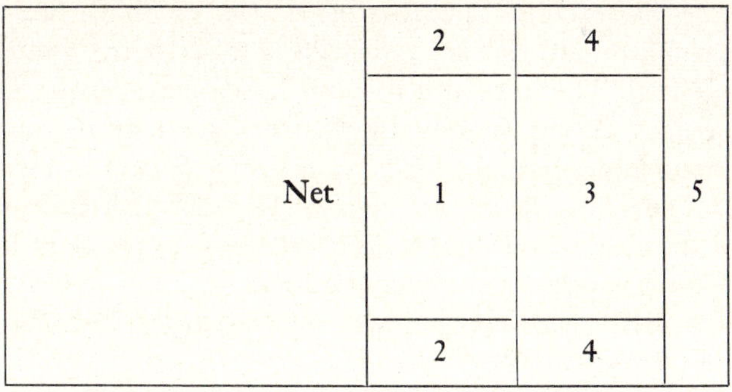

		2	4	
Net	1	3		5
		2	4	

Figure 92. The scoring value for each division of the volleyball court used in the serving test is shown in this diagram.

The player being tested stands behind the end line in the service end of the court and is given ten serves into the target side of the court. Any of the three types of legal serve is permitted. A let ball is served over. *Score:* Score the point value of the area on which the ball lands. A ball landing on a line separating two areas is scored at the higher value. A ball landing on side or end lines scores value of the area adjacent. If the server commits a foot fault while serving, no score is recorded. The sum of the area scores for the ten serves is the total score. Each pupil should be given two trials of ten serves and the better of the two trial scores should be counted.

Measurement of Fundamental Skills

One of the primary objectives of physical education is the development of physical strength and endurance, and these characteristics can generally be measured objectively through tests of individual athletic skills such as running, jumping, the pull-up, the push-up, and the sit-up, with scores in units of time, distance, or number of times the skill is performed. Neilson and Cozens list numerous tests of these skills.

1. *Run* (40 yards) (*Achievement Scales*, page 27)
2. *Running broad hop* (*Achievement Scales*, page 28)
3. *Running broad jump* (*Achievement Scales*, page 29)
4. *Running high jump* (*Achievement Scales*, page 29)
5. *Standing broad jump* (*Achievement Scales*, page 34)
6. *Sit-up.* The performer lies on his back with legs separated and feet about 25 inches apart. He places his hands on the back of his neck with fingertips touching and rests the elbows on the floor. A partner places his hands on the performer's ankles and holds his heels in contact with the floor during the exercise. The performer sits up to vertical position, turns the trunk to left, touches right elbow to left knee, and returns to starting position. The fingertips of both hands must remain in contact behind the neck during the exercise, but the back may be rounded and the head and elbows brought forward in sitting up and in touching the knee. Both knees must be on the floor. Performer then repeats the sit-up portion of the exercise but touches the left elbow to the right knee. The test is continued, performer touching alternate knees. *Score:* Number of times the performer raises himself from a lying to a sitting position.
7. *Push-up* (*Achievement Scales*, p. 25)
8. *Pull-up* (*Achievement Scales*, p. 24)

Recording Test Results

Record cards and sheets on which pupils' achievement can be recorded over a period of time can be devised by each school. These should be based on the tests to be given, which should, in turn, be based on the physical education program in use. Examples are shown of three different types of records:

a. An individual record card, on which the best score made in three trials for each of eight events may be recorded. Space is also left for recording the scale score in each event.

b. A class record sheet, on which the scores for a specific skill test given to all members of a class on five different dates may be recorded.

c. A check sheet listing specific skills on which each member of a class has been tested. This sheet is drawn up for primary grades, and the score or mark should be some simple rating of performance.

SAMPLE INDIVIDUAL RECORD CARD

Pupil_____				Height Exponent _____		
				Age ʹʹ _____		
				Weight ʹʹ _____		
Grade_____				Sum of Exponents _____		
				Class _____		

Event	Date of Test	Trial Scores			Best Score	Scale Score
		1	2	3		

Utilization of Test Results

The evaluation process is not completed when the various tests for skills and strengths have been administered. The results of the tests should be used for comparison either with scores made by others or with previous scores made by the same individual or group. The abilities of one individual may be measured against those of another individual. Pupils with outstanding ability may be encouraged to develop their skills further. Pupils who fall below the average may be stimulated to improve their weak points. If a comparison is made with previous records, the scores will show the progress of the individual or group. They may point out the efficiency of one teaching method over another.

SAMPLE CLASS RECORD SHEET

Event _____

Instructor _____

Dates of Tests: 1 · | 2 | 3 | 4 | 5

Name of Pupil	Grade	Test 1 Trials	Test 2 Trials	Test 3 Trials	Test 4 Trials	Test 5 Trials	Best Score

SAMPLE CLASS CHECK SHEET FOR SPECIFIC SKILLS

Pupil's Name	Walk: march time to music	Walk: march time without music	Walk: march time accent first beat with foot	Walk: march time accent third beat by hand-clapping	Walk: combined hand clapping and foot accent on 1 and 3 beat	Walk: clapping and accenting on 2 and 4 beat	Walk: ¾ time	Walk: changing tempo ¾ time	Walk: changing tempo 4/4 time	Walk: 2 beats to one step
1.										
2.										

Scores made in tests may be used to group pupils according to ability for competition.

The usefulness of test results depends on the relationship of these results to a standard of some kind. If the standard is in terms of physical maturity its usefulness, particularly in the elementary school, is greatly enhanced. Standards based on the three-point classification index of physical maturity were worked out by Neilson and Cozens for all the events included in their *Achievement Scales*. By finding the scale score for each pupil's test score, in terms of his physical maturity and sex, the teacher may make a meaningful comparison of pupil against pupil, or grade against grade.

Knowledge Tests

Written tests should be an integral part of any well-planned program of physical education. Such tests should cover knowledge of rules, techniques, principles of play, strategy, and elements of form in the various activities taught. These tests should be short, simple, objective, and should consume only a very small portion of the class time for physical education. They should be of such a nature that they can either be corrected in class or checked quickly and returned to the class on the following day for discussion. For the teacher who wishes to supplement her information about objective written tests, Bovard and Cozens[1] and McCloy[2] presents excellent discussions based on the materials of physical education. Good sample tests for most of the activities covered in physical education will be found in the book by Blanchard and Collins.[3]

Class Organization for Group Testing

It is essential that a minimum amount of time be spent on the actual administering of a test. Organization of the group for testing, equipment to be used, score sheets, and testing procedure should be planned in advance.

In order to facilitate the administering of a series of tests in a class period, squad organization with student leaders may be used. This arrangement frees the instructor from the responsibility of personally administering each test and gives her an opportunity to supervise the entire testing program, thereby insuring that it will move along smoothly and efficiently.

[1] J. F. Bovard, F. W. Cozens, and E. P. Hagman, *Tests and Measurements in Physical Education*. Philadelphia: W. B. Saunders Co., 1949 (third edition).

[2] C. H. McCloy, *Tests and Measurements in Health and Physical Education*. New York: F. S. Crofts & Co., 1942 (second edition).

[3] V. S. Blanchard and Laurentine Collins, *A Modern Physical Education Program for Boys and Girls*. New York: A. S. Barnes & Co., 1940.

The following suggestions may be useful in organizing the class for testing:

1. Squad leaders should be instructed in, and given an opportunity to practice with, the various measuring devices (stop watches, tapes, yardsticks, etc.) in advance of the actual testing.
2. The area for each test should be clearly marked.
3. All equipment and markings should be in readiness in advance of the testing.
4. A recorder should be appointed to work with each squad leader.
5. Each squad leader should be given written directions indicating the order in which the individual tests will be given and directions for administering and scoring each test.
6. Each recorder should be supplied with a score card and pencils.
7. All squads should be instructed to advance from one test to the next only on a predetermined signal.
8. Squad size should not exceed ten pupils.
9. If possible, arrangements should be made for the squad leader to test more than one individual at a time.

The tests should be explained and demonstrated, the correct mechanical use of the body emphasized, and pupils allowed to practice for a day or two before tests are given in order to eliminate errors due to misinterpretation of the directions.

All score charts, field or wall markings, measuring tapes, watches, and the like should be put in readiness ahead of time. The surface used for running events should be turf or smooth dirt. A pit with sawdust or sand that is kept freshly loosened, or a turf surface, should be used for jumping events. Stop watches, if available, should be used for all timed events. In the absence of a stop watch, a watch with a second hand, preferably one with a sweep second hand, may be used.

EVALUATING THE TOTAL PROGRAM

Evaluation of the program as a whole depends to a great extent upon the evaluation of each pupil's progress. It is a mistake to adjudge a class program successful simply because it produces a good basketball team or an outstanding dance group. Every member of the class may not be represented on that team or in the dance. There may be some whose needs were greater than others but who were neglected in the effort to develop a championship team. If so, the physical education program has failed. If, on the other hand, each member of the class has made progress toward overcoming his weaknesses, physical, social, or emotional, the program has in a measure succeeded. There is, however, a need for evaluating the total program in terms of group achievement as measured against the objectives for that group.

Standards for Evaluation

The physical education program as a whole should be evaluated by reference to standards that relate to the aims of the program. The following four standards are proposed:

1. The program should use activities that arise out of the basic urges and drives of each age group.
2. The program should provide vigorous activity of the organic systems, suited to the condition and stage of development of the individual.
3. The program should be conducted with reference to the social learnings that are inherent in group relationships.
4. The program should provide the opportunity to acquire the motor skills necessary in the play life of the child and his use of leisure.

The worth of the program can be estimated by asking and answering specific questions that relate to each of these standards.

1. *Activities That Arise Out of the Basic Urges and Drives.* In their early years children have urges and drives that lead them to chase others, to climb, to throw at marks, to run and skip, and to make many other movements that are natural to them. As they grow older, their impulses lead them to desire different activities. The program should be judged with reference to the extent to which such natural activities are employed. The extent may be judged by the answers given to such questions as the following:

   a. Are the needs of the age group considered?
   b. Is the skill of the age group considered?
   c. Is the interest of the age group considered?

2. *Vigorous Activity in Proportion to Individual Need.* The activities in general should be vigorous. There are conditions that require moderate or mild activity, but the normal expectation should be that children will secure strong stimulation of the organic systems. It is the exercise of the vital organs that builds vitality. When lack of proper space or equipment prevents the teacher from conducting activities that result in stimulation of the heart and lungs, then the program is defective. The vigorousness of the program may be tested by questions of the following type:

   a. Was adequate and stimulating leadership given to pupils permanently or temporarily assigned to a modified physical education program?

b. Were efforts made for children to appreciate their own limitations?

c. Did every child have opportunity for suitable vigorous activity?

3. *Social Learnings.* The experiences that individuals have determine what sort of attitudes and ideals they adopt and how they conduct themselves. It is certain, then, that the experiences of the school are factors in the social learnings of children. Of the school experiences, some of the most important occur in physical education activities. Children care and care greatly about what happens in their games and play, and the crux of such experiences is the relationship of the individual to others. Concepts of fairness, kindliness, honesty, courtesy, loyalty, generosity, courage, doing one's best, and many others are firmly bound to the motor experiences of physical education. The particular slant that children acquire on these and other matters comes from the leadership of the program. Many unfavorable attitudes arise out of physical education experiences because of irritations over the poor organization of plans and materials. The effectiveness of the program in affording leadership and avoiding tensions may be tested by the following questions:

a. Was each child given an opportunity to contribute to the group planning and participation?

b. Were opportunities grasped for teaching social conduct, honesty, and fairness?

c. Were opportunities used for furthering leadership abilities of students during class and other periods of the day?

d. Were teaching materials available in sufficient quantity for early and effective learning and mastery?

e. Were courts adequately outlined and were rules effectively enforced?

f. Were lessons planned ahead of the class period, supplies secured before lessons began, and minimum time used for organization purposes?

4. *Skills for Play Life and Leisure.* A choice must be made among the enormous number of motor activities available for instruction. Some are better or more useful than others. If children learn while in school the dances and games that they enjoy using in their free play time, such activities are relatively more worthwhile than activities that they never practice. This criterion of value can be applied again and again throughout the elementary school, and over the years it should lead to the choice of activities that will contribute to a wholesome use of leisure.

It is a mistake, however, to select only activities that carry over into play at a later period of the child's life. The enjoyment of motor activity in its many forms is the important thing for the elementary school child.

One indication, then, of the functional service of an activity is the interest of the children in the experience. The teacher or administrator may check this interest by answers to such questions as the following:

a. Was interest successfully indicated in activities new to the group?
b. What activities resulted in tangible enthusiasm? Why?
c. Were seasonal activities carried on too long?
d. Were too few activities taught? Why?
e. Was the program too limited in content?
f. Were opportunities arranged for pupils to participate voluntarily, through intramural programs, in activities taught during class periods?

Devices for Evaluating the Program

Questionnaires and check lists covering the specific parts of a program are sometimes used by groups of teachers for self evaluation. Such questionnaires should be constructed in terms of the standards for a well-balanced physical education program.

A score card based on a national study is now available for evaluating the physical education program of the elementary school. This score card is published in *The Physical Education Curriculum*, a publication of the Committee on Curriculum Research of the College Physical Education Association.[1] After nineteen years of research and study this committee reported its findings in a discussion of a balanced physical education program for the elementary school and for the junior and senior high school. The score card covers the following points: (1) program of activities, (2) outdoor areas, (3) indoor areas, (4) organization and administration of class programs, (5) medical examinations and health services. The programs for seventh and eighth grades are included in the junior high school score card. The publication and the score card are a helpful device in evaluating a local physical education program.

SELECTED REFERENCES[2]

BACON, FRANCIS L. *Outwitting the Hazards*. New York: Silver Burdett Co., 1941, pp. 57-101.

BLANCHARD, VAUGHN S., AND COLLINS, LAURENTINE B. *A Modern Physical Education Program for Boys and Girls*. New York: A. S. Barnes & Co., 1940.

[1] *The Physical Education Curriculum*, compiled by William Ralph La Porte. Los Angeles: University of Southern California Press, 1949 (fourth edition).
[2] The appendixes also list reference material.

BOVARD, J. F., COZENS, F. W., AND HAGMAN, E. P. *Tests and Measurements in Physical Education.* Philadelphia: W. B. Saunders Co., 1949 (third edition).

CRAINE, HENRY C. *Teaching Athletic Skills in Physical Education.* New York: Inor Publishing Co., Inc., 1942.

LA PORTE, WILLIAM RALPH. *The Physical Education Curriculum.* Los Angeles: The University of Southern California Press, 1949 (fourth edition).

WILLIAMS, JESSE FEIRING. *Principles of Physical Education.* Philadelphia: W. B. Saunders Co., 1948 (fifth edition).

PART TWO

ACTIVITIES FOR PHYSICAL EDUCATION IN GRADES ONE THROUGH EIGHT

Chapter XIII

AN ANALYSIS OF SKILLS DEVELOPED THROUGH ELEMENTARY SCHOOL PHYSICAL EDUCATION

Part I of this book concerns the characteristics of a good physical education program in the elementary school. It discusses not only the selection, planning, and scheduling of activities and the standards for facilities and equipment, but also methods, procedures, and examples for the various phases of the program. In Part II, physical education activities appropriate for each grade level from the first to the eighth are described, each grade providing more advanced skills and game situations. Some of these activities are carried on through all the years of school and to miss an early introduction to them is a loss to the individual that can never be fully compensated for later. On the other hand, to introduce an activity too soon disregards the principle of readiness and the facts of physical development. Obviously, however, teachers of one- and two-room schools must make selections from and modifications in the activities offered to meet the local conditions and needs of their particular schools.

Teachers of younger children should not select activities from upper grade levels, but teachers of older children may desire frequently to return to lower grade content for review material and to play games that were not learned previously. Other manuals and books should be used as sources for teaching material. Hundreds of fascinating books are available at city and county libraries, and professional libraries in large school systems are usually rich in reference materials.[1]

In choosing and adapting these activities to the teacher's own situation, the objectives discussed through the first chapters of this book should be kept in mind. In addition, the elements of the characteristic skills to be developed through the use of the games and relays, the rhythmical activities and the stunts should be thoroughly understood. Only by analyzing these elements fully can the teacher recognize good and bad performance, organize the steps for instruction, and use the activities effectively.

Included in the basic physical education skills are skills relating to locomotion, skills relating to safety in work, and skills relating to games. Skills of locomotion are fundamental to physical activity and children should be taught to use these skills efficiently from the very beginning of

---

[1] The appendixes contain lists of such reference materials, including books, magazines, phonograph records, films, and filmstrips.

their school experience. To avoid muscular strains and joint sprains, boys and girls must be taught throughout all grades the skills that provide safety in work and play. The particular game skills, such as batting and throwing, catching and kicking, must be learned before organized games are presented, and as the more highly organized games of the upper grades are introduced the techniques of each skill should be taught so that the full benefit will be derived from the activity.

An analysis of the characteristic skills developed through activities for the various grades is presented in three groupings: primary, intermediate, and upper grades. The elements of correct performance of each skill are listed in outline form, in order that the teacher may have a quick review of the points to be kept in mind as the activities are presented. Because the skills underlying good posture are an essential part of physical activity in all grades, an outline of good posture characteristics precedes the analysis of fundamental skills. The characteristics of good posture should be used as a teaching guide in all grades, since if good posture and balance are definitely taught in the elementary school, beginning with the primary and continuing through the intermediate and upper grades, poor posture habits will have little opportunity to develop.

I. Characteristics of Good Posture

   A. Standing Posture

      1. Viewed by the observer from the side of the child

         a. Feet

            (1) Ankle bone directly under knee joint

            (2) Toes pointing straight ahead

            (3) Weight evenly divided on feet, not on heels or toes alone

         b. Knees

            (1) Relaxed with no bulge in calf muscles

            (2) Middle of joint directly over ankle bone

            (3) Not in back-kneed position (knee joint should be capable of being pushed back farther)

         c. Lower back and abdomen

            (1) Slight curve forward in lower back

            (2) Middle of pelvis over knee joint

            (3) Abdominal muscles flat but relaxed

         d. Upper back and chest

            (1) Shoulder blades flat

            (2) Slight curve backward in upper back

            (3) Chest raised over abdomen

            (4) Shoulder joint directly over hip joint with arms hanging at side of body

e. Head
  (1) Ear in line with shoulder, hips, knee, and ankle joint
  (2) Back of head up and chin in

2. Viewed by the observer from the back of the child
  a. Head, shoulders, and arms
    (1) Head evenly balanced between shoulders
    (2) Shoulders and shoulder blades even
    (3) Arms hanging same length at side of body
  b. Hips and spine
    (1) Hips even (check with hands on hips)
    (2) Air space between arms and body equal as the arms
        hang at the side
    (3) Spine a straight line from middle of head to middle of
        pelvis
  c. Knees (check also from front view)
    (1) Pointing straight ahead and not turning in toward each
        other
    (2) Knee caps not turning toward the inside of knee
  d. Ankles and arches
    (1) Long arches in a straight line from heel to large toe
    (2) Ankle bones not prominent but in line with foot
    (3) Front or metatarsal arch with a small wrinkle or depres-
        sion and free from bulge or callus

3. Directions for correcting poor standing posture
  a. Put weight equally on both feet, and equally on both the
     heel and the toes.
  b. Point toes straight ahead.
  c. Roll knees outward to make them point straight ahead, using
     outer thigh muscles.
  d. Tuck pelvis under as buttock muscles are tightened.
  e. Lift chest over pelvis.
  f. Balance head with back of head up and chin in.
  g. Breathe normally; do not hold the breath.

B. Walking Posture
  1. Body in alignment or balance as in standing posture
  2. Legs swinging freely from hips
  3. Knees bent so that the feet clear the floor and toes point
     straight ahead
  4. Heels touching first, followed instantly by the ball of the foot
     and the toes
  5. Toes giving the push to the walk
  6. Arms swinging freely from the shoulders

C. Sitting Posture
  1. Relaxed or resting
     a. Head and body in good balance as in standing position
     b. Hips supported against the chair back
     c. Knees bent at right angles and feet flat on the floor
  2. Working at a desk
     a. Body moving forward from a resting position to a working
        position using the hip joints (bend does not come in the
        spine)
     b. Head, upper body, and pelvis remaining in normal positions

II. Skills Developed Through Primary Grade Activities

  A. Skills of Locomotion
    1. Walking
       a. Balance body directly over feet.
       b. Keep spine straight but not rigid.
       c. Swing legs from hips.
       d. Bend knees enough for feet to clear floor.
       e. Push off from toes of rear foot.
       f. Touch heel of foot first, next ball of foot, and then toes to
          take a step.
       g. Walk with feet parallel and point toes straight ahead.
       h. Swing arms freely from shoulder, not from elbow.

    2. Running (medium speed)
       a. Speed up the walk tempo to run.
       b. Touch ground with balls of feet first, not with heels.
       c. Lean body forward at a slight angle from the vertical.
       d. Bend knees moderately.
       e. Use arms to help carry body weight forward.

    3. Jumping
       a. Send body high or far into air.
       b. Land with weight of body taken on both feet with knees
          bent.
       c. Carry body weight forward toward hands in jumping far.
       d. Use arms as balance while body is in air.
       e. Use all of body muscles to get power for the jump.

    4. Hopping
       a. Send body up and down supported by one foot.
       b. Balance body with arms out from sides.
       c. Balance also with nonsupporting leg.
       d. Keep supporting foot in perfect balance and pointing
          straight ahead.

    e. Use toe grip for better support on hopping foot.

5. Leaping
    a. Change weight of body from one foot to the other while body is in the air.
    b. Push off on supporting foot.
    c. Send body high and far into air.
    d. Land on alternating feet, first on ball of foot.
    e. Bend ankles and knees for an easy landing.
    f. Take off on one foot and land on the other with continued motion.

6. Skipping
    a. Step and hop in an uneven rhythm.
    b. Get body off the floor on the hop.
    c. Get balance and height by using the arms.
    d. Alternate feet to take body weight.
    e. Relax ankles and knees as body touches floor.

7. Sliding
    a. Step and hop in an uneven rhythm to the side.
    b. Move always to the side.
    c. Step to the side and draw other foot to side of supporting foot and put weight on it.

8. Galloping
    a. Use slide pattern moving forward.
    b. Lead always with same foot.
    c. Step ahead and bring back foot up to supporting foot and put weight on it.

B. Skills Relating to Safety in Work
1. Hanging
    a. Support body by both arms.
    b. Grip with back of hands toward body.
    c. Hang securely enough to be able to mount an obstacle.

2. Climbing
    a. Pull body up a ladder or rope, or over an obstacle.
    b. Use hand, upper arm, and shoulder girdle muscles with upper body to lift body weights easily.
    c. Co-ordinate legs and trunk muscles with upper body to lift body upward.

3. Lifting
    a. Stand close to object.
    b. Bend knees before grasping article.
    c. Lift by throwing effort on large muscles of legs.

  d. Keep back erect.

  e. Open a low window by standing with back toward window and use leg muscle to lift as hands pull open window.

  f. Pick up a small object from floor by bending knees, not stooping over from waist.

4. Carrying

  a. Keep extra weight as near body as possible without disturbing body balance.

  b. Distribute weight equally on both sides of body if possible.

  c. Maintain as erect a posture as possible.

5. Pushing or Pulling

  a. Get body in line with object.

  b. Get center of gravity low.

  c. Keep body in line with applied force.

  d. Point toes straight ahead with one foot ahead of the other.

  e. Set up a natural rhythm for entire body.

C. Skills Relating to Games

  NOTE: Written for right-handed and right-footed children; in general, the reverse direction applies for left-handed children.

1. Stopping

  a. Bend knees and drop center of gravity *low to ground*.

  b. Use toes to grip ground.

  c. Do not slap the feet.

  d. Keep body over feet; do not allow body to go ahead of a direct line over feet.

2. Dodging

  a. Move body weight to side with knees bent.

  b. Drop weight low before shifting in direction of dodge.

  c. Use toes for gripping to maintain balance.

  d. Use arms for balance.

3. Tossing

  a. Grip with one or both hands according to size of object.

  b. Swing object forward and back to the right and bring body weight backward

  c. Bring object forward with weight on left foot as it is released toward target.

  d. Bend knees as object is released.

  NOTE: Children should have had experience in bouncing and catching a ball.

4. Overhand Throwing

  a. Hold ball in throwing hand so that it is comfortably gripped.

b. Keep eyes on target.

c. Swing arm down, back, and up as weight and body goes backward.

d. Bring ball over shoulder about ear height or near top of head.

e. Keep the elbow high and bent.

f. Straighten arm as fingers release ball toward target and transfer body weight to forward foot.

g. Follow through by pointing hand toward target, and possibly by stepping forward.

5. Catching

   a. Keep in line with ball.

   b. Move toward ball, never back away.

   c. Give or draw back with the hands as object is caught and bring it in toward body.

   d. If ball is above waist, catch with thumbs together and palms forward.

   e. If ball is below waist, catch with little fingers together.

   f. Keep fingers relaxed.

6. Kicking

   a. Stand with left foot slightly in back of and to left of ball.

   b. Swing right foot backward directly behind ball with knee bent and arms raised for balance.

   c. Swing right leg forward with a sharp straightening of the knee as the *instep*, not *toe*, comes in contact with ball.

   d. Continue follow-through as right leg swings forward and the body weight comes onto the toes of the supporting foot.

      NOTE: This same procedure is used in a punt or drop kick with the exception that the ball is held in the hands and dropped as the player steps forward with the left foot to kick with the right.

III. Skills Developed Through Intermediate Grade Activities [1]

   NOTE: Review all skills for primary grades.

   A. Throwing

      1. Underhand Pitch (softball)

         a. Place both feet together on pitcher's plate, facing target.

         b. Hold ball in right hand resting it in left hand in front of body.

         c. Swing right arm back parallel to body with weight on right foot, but do not move the feet.

         d. Twist to right as left shoulder faces target.

[1] See Characteristics and Needs of Pupils in Grades 4, 5, 6, Chapter IV, pp. 49-51.

    e. When the arm swings forward parallel to body, shift the weight as *one* step is taken on left foot.

    f. Follow through with hand pointing toward target and a possible forward step.

2. Two or One Hand Underarm Pass (basketball, speed ball)
   a. Use two hands always at beginning.
   b. Combine with catching rhythm in slight forward stride position.
   c. Swing ball backward as body weight goes backward.
   d. Swing ball forward close to body and carry weight to left foot with a forward step.
   e. Get a rhythmic swing with step into stride position.

3. Chest Pass (basketball)
   a. Stand in a forward stride position.
   b. Hold ball with both hands, fingers gripping ball, and elbows bent.
   c. Bring ball downward and inward as body weight goes to backward foot. (Keep elbows close to body.)
   d. Straighten elbows as ball is released and weight is transferred to forward foot.
   e. Point both hands toward target during the follow-through.

B. Batting
   1. Hold bat with trade-mark up.
   2. Place feet parallel, pointing in direction of home plate.
   3. Keep body relaxed.
   4. Keep elbows away from body.
   5. Keep left arm parallel to ground.
   6. Grip bat with left hand just above end of bat and right hand comfortably above it. Do not rest bat on shoulder.
   7. Turn face to pitcher; keep eyes on ball.
   8. Swing bat backward parallel to ground as weight goes back.
   9. Swing bat forward parallel to ground as weight comes forward onto a left step.
   10. Follow through with bat to left hand which *drops bat on ground* as the runner starts for first.

C. Hitting with Paddle or Racket
   1. Forehand
      a. Grip comfortably with fingers spread in a handshake position with the paddle or racket head slightly higher than the handle. Thumb and first finger should form a slight "V" on the side of the handle continuous with the thin edge of the paddle's striking surface.

b. Wait for the ball with paddle in front of body, facing the net; feet slightly apart and knees bent.

c. Swing the paddle slightly up and back as the body turns sideways and left foot steps across so that the left shoulder is toward the net, and the weight of the body is on the right foot.

d. Swing the paddle parallel to the ground as the weight of the body is transferred forward and thus into the stroke.

e. Hit the ball squarely when it is about at waist height and out in front of left leg. (Ball must be hit before it passes the body.)

f. Continue the stroke as far as the player can reach as the weight is transferred forward, and finish facing the net ready for the next stroke.

2. Backhand

a. Grip in forehand position and move the thumb around the handle a little to the left.

b. Wait for ball in forehand position, shifting the grip just before the backward swing of the paddle.

c. Swing the paddle slightly up and back as the right foot steps across so that the right shoulder is toward the net and the weight of the body is transferred backward onto the left foot.

d. Swing the paddle forward parallel to the ground as the weight of the body is transferred forward onto the right foot.

e. Hit the ball squarely when it is about at waist height and in front of the right leg. (Get behind the ball.)

f. Continue the stroke to follow through as in forehand and finish facing the net ready for the next stroke.

D. Pivoting (basketball) [1]

1. Place feet apart, knees slightly bent from either a jump or a running step.

2. Turn either to the right or to the left.

3. For a rear pivot or reverse turn, step back with one foot to turn the body from a quarter to a half turn. Keep the pivot foot in contact with the floor.

4. For a front pivot, step forward with one foot, and turn the body, keeping the pivot foot in contact with the floor.

---

[1] See Basketball Techniques, page 727.

E. Guarding (basketball)

1. Always keep body between opponent and goal.
2. Be ready to intercept passes.
3. Move with opponent by using quick, short, slide steps.
4. As long as the opponent has the ball, never jump from the floor.
5. Do not come in contact with opponent's body at any time.

F. Soccer Skills [1]

1. Dribble
   a. Put ball between the feet.
   b. Tap ball every few steps, using the inside of first one foot and then the other.
   c. Keep arms free at side for balance.
   d. Dribble as fast as possible while running.

2. Punt
   a. Hold the ball in front of the body about at waist height and at arm's distance.
   b. Step forward onto the left foot.
   c. Bend the knee of the right leg slightly.
   d. Release the ball just as the right leg is swung forward and upward and the instep of the foot contacts the ball.
   e. Carry the weight of the body on the left foot and follow through by pointing the toes of the right foot forward.

3. Stopping a Kicked Ball
   a. Keep feet in slight stride position with knees easy.
   b. Take one step toward ball.
   c. Bend knee of nonsupporting foot to trap ball between knee and ground; or stop ball with sole of nonsupporting foot.

G. Volleyball serve [2] (underarm)

1. Stand in a forward stride position with left foot forward.
2. Face net.
3. Hold ball in left hand.
4. Swing right arm backward as weight is shifted to back foot.
5. Swing right arm forward to shift weight toward left foot.
6. Hit ball out of left hand with heel of right hand as the right hand is swung forward and the body weight is transferred to the left foot.
7. Point hand at end of swing directly toward path of ball.

---

[1] See Soccer Techniques, page 784.
[2] See Volleyball, page 801.

IV. Skills Developed Through Upper Grade Activities [1]
NOTE: Review skills for primary and intermediate grades.

A. Basketball Shooting [2]

1. Two-hand chest shot for goal
   a. Face direction of throw, feet in forward or side stride position.
   b. Relax body with ankles and knees slightly bent.
   c. Keep eyes on backboard for banked shot, and on near point of rim of basket for open shot. (Banked shot hits the backboard before going through basket.)
   d. Grip ball at sides, with fingers spread, elbows down.
   e. Bring ball slightly down as the body is bent forward and then upward close to chest before the ball is pushed forward toward the basket.
   f. Straighten ankles, knees, hips, and elbows as the ball is released.
   g. Rotate hands inward as the ball is released.
   h. Follow through with hands pointing toward basket and weight carried forward.

2. One-hand shot for goal [3]
   a. Stand with right foot forward, close to basket, with left foot maintaining body balance.
   b. Take the ball in the right hand and turn the wrist clear to the left and "cock" it back.
   c. Support the ball with the left hand beneath it and with the right hand directly behind the ball. Rest the ball on the fingers, not the palms of the hands.
   d. Do a knee-bend with most of the weight on the balls of the feet.
   e. Shoot the right arm in an upward motion toward the top of the arc in which the ball will travel.
   f. Flip the ball with a slight wrist and finger motion as the arm and leg straighten.
   g. Concentrate eyes and thought on the basket as the ball leaves the hand.
   h. Follow through naturally; do not jerk the arm back.
   i. Jump straight in the direction of the basket.

B. Football Forward Pass [4]

1. Stand in a forward stride position with the left foot forward.

2. Grip the ball close to the end with the palm of the hand in contact with the ball and fingers spread.
3. Transfer weight backward on right foot as ball is brought back with elbow up and away from the body.
4. As the ball is brought forward past the ear, transfer the weight of the body onto the left foot. With a wrist snap roll the ball off the fingers as the nose of the ball is pointed toward the target.
5. For long passes, start the pass farther back than the ear and gain more muscle power by using the back and leg muscles.

C. Baseball Pitch (hardball) (right-handed)
1. Grip the ball between the thumb and first two fingers.
2. Stand facing the batter with the right foot on the plate.
3. Get signal from catcher.
4. Wind up by swinging arm completely around a couple of times. (No one is on base.)
5. Bring ball up above forehead to gloved hand.
6. Raise left leg forward as the right arm comes down and back, and the body twists to the right.
7. Raise arm to bring ball back of head with elbow bent.
8. Throw ball from overhead or past ear with a fast wrist snap as right shoulder and body twists to the left and the left foot steps forward.
9. Follow through with arm to left of body and by stepping onto right foot.
10. Regain balance on both feet in order to move quickly in any direction.

D. Tennis Serve
1. Grip the racket in a handshake position with the fingers spread. Some players like to move the hand very slightly to the left so that the grip is not identical to forehand.
   NOTE: A handshake position means that the racket is held with the edge of the racket up as the grip is taken.
2. Stand as close to the center marker as is legal with the left foot at a 45° angle with the base line and the right foot parallel to base line.
3. Swing the racket past the legs and up behind the head as the weight is transferred to the back foot.
4. Drop the head of the racket at the height of the swing.
5. By bringing the elbow close to the head, swing the racket up to the right over the server's head as high as the straightened elbow and wrist will take it.
6. Carry the racket through to the left side of the body.

7. Toss ball upward with an upward swing of the left arm as the right arm starts the racket on its backward swing.

8. Toss ball high enough so that it will start down at the height of the racket swing.

NOTE: The toss and racket swing will have to be practiced separately at first, but when developed the toss and racket swing are simultaneous.

E. Volleyball Volley

1. Lift ball by open hands into air.
2. Relax and open fingers.
3. If ball is below waist, face palms forward with fingers down.
4. If ball is above head, face palms upward.
5. Get body directly in line with ball.
6. Stand in stride position with knees bent as action occurs.

Chapter XIV

ACTIVITIES FOR FIRST GRADE

Activities are alphabetically arranged by title within the following three classes:

The games fall into several classes. They are indexed here by type for the convenience of the teacher.

Games

BEANBAG THROWING FOR DISTANCE

NUMBER OF PLAYERS: 5-12

SPACE: Playground, gymnasium, auditorium

PLAYING AREA: A throwing line long enough to accommodate all players

EQUIPMENT: A beanbag or ball for each child

FORMATION: Children line up behind the throwing line, keeping both feet behind it while in the act of throwing.

PROCEDURE: After the signal, when ready, each child throws his beanbag overhand as far forward as he can. When all the children have thrown they advance on the run and each secures his own beanbag. Throwing is repeated on signal after all children have returned to position behind the line.

TEACHING SUGGESTIONS

1. Determine which children throw the greater distances. Form them into a group by themselves. Place other children into groupings according to throwing ability and have them progress from group to group as skill is acquired.
2. Have frequent practice periods over the weeks and months.
3. Have the children throw with the hand that is normal for them, either right or left. Teach the proper use of the foot in connection with the throw. If the right hand is used, then the left foot should be forward.
4. Play this game with a toss instead of an overhand throw if all the children have not learned to throw overhand.

BUTTERFLIES AND FLOWERS

NUMBER OF PLAYERS: 5-12

SPACE: Playground, playroom, gymnasium, hallway, classroom

EQUIPMENT: Piano or phonograph

FORMATION: Players are divided into two groups, one group to be flowers and the other to be butterflies. Each flower takes a squatting position three or four feet distant from other flowers.

PROCEDURE: While soft music is played the butterflies spread their wings and run softly among the flowers. When the music stops the butterflies must stop immediately. From their squatting positions the flowers reach out and try to tag the butterflies. If tagged the butterflies squat with the flowers. This continues until all the butterflies are caught, whereupon the butterflies become flowers and vice versa.

A butterfly who fails to stop or who seeks safety after the signal is given stands by the teacher for a period to watch how successful butterflies work.

TEACHING SUGGESTIONS

1. Limit the size of space in which the flowers and butterflies may play. If this is not done, the butterflies will remain too far away for successful tagging.
2. Use a whistle, drum, or other signal-giving instrument to indicate the stopping times if music is not available.

CAGED TIGER

NUMBER OF PLAYERS: 5-12

SPACE: Playground, gymnasium, auditorium, playroom, stage of auditorium

PLAYING AREA: Large circle marked on floor to form the cage boundaries

FORMATION: One player, the tiger, is placed within the cage. The other players scatter outside the cage boundaries.

PROCEDURE: The tiger wishes to get out of the cage. The other players wish to keep the tiger in the cage, and, at the same time, wish to enter and leave the cage without being caught or tagged by the tiger. Players enter and tease the tiger but are privileged to leave the cage if it appears they may be tagged by the tiger. Players may run through the cage and out the opposite side. The tiger may tag any one who has a foot contacting the cage circumference or is completely within the cage, but he himself must stay inside the cage until he tags someone. The tagged person becomes the new tiger and the game continues.

TEACHING SUGGESTIONS

1. Encourage all children to be venturesome.
2. Discourage those who wish always to be tagged.
3. Experiment with the size of the circle used until a lively game results.

CAT AND MICE

NUMBER OF PLAYERS: 4-12

SPACE: Classroom

FORMATION: A player is selected to be the cat and a number of children from different parts of the room are chosen to be mice. The cat hides behind or under the teacher's desk.

PROCEDURE: The mice creep up to the desk and when all have arrived one scratches the wood of the desk, whereupon the cat gives chase and tags as many mice as possible before the mice reach their own holes (their desks). The first mouse caught becomes the cat for the next game, and new mice are chosen.

TEACHING SUGGESTIONS

1. Discourage the desire of some children to be caught immediately. They may be removed from the game to watch for a while.
2. Emphasize that it is more fun to be mice than to be the cat, and to escape successfully.
3. Teach children that the real skill of the game is to elude the cat as every real mouse would wish to do.
4. Teach personal control for the cat in waiting for the signal and alertness on the part of the mice.

CHASE THE ANIMALS AROUND THE CORRAL

NUMBER OF PLAYERS: 4-12

SPACE: Playground, playroom, gymnasium, hallway, auditorium

EQUIPMENT: Balls of various sizes; beanbags; different sized blocks of wood. Children give each object a name, such as bear, wolf, coyote, elephant, or tiger.

FORMATION: Children form a single circle, facing inward (teacher with the children).

PROCEDURE: The teacher starts around the circle an animal (a named object) that each child must handle. When it reaches the teacher it must be sent around again and a second object sent after it. After two objects have been around the circle, the teacher starts the third, and so on. If an object is dropped, the child who dropped it must pick it up and pass it on before receiving the next object. If a second animal overtakes the first, the former is captured and is out of the game.

TEACHING SUGGESTIONS

1. Make the game progressively difficult by increasing the number of objects to be sent around simultaneously, by varying in size, shape, or weight the objects used, or by increasing the distance between circle players.
2. At times reverse the direction taken by the objects.
3. Develop the children's ability to handle objects of different size, shape, and weight.

FAIRIES AND BROWNIES

NUMBER OF PLAYERS: 4-12

SPACE: Playground, gymnasium, hallway, auditorium

PLAYING AREA: Two lines drawn 40 or 50 feet apart and parallel, 6 to 25 feet long, depending upon the number of players

FORMATION: Players are divided into two equal groups, the fairies and the brownies. Each group stands behind one of the lines. The fairies turn their backs toward the brownies. A leader or lookout watches the game and gives the necessary signals.

PROCEDURE: Brownies creep forward quietly. The lookout, when he sees that the brownies are near enough to make it possible to tag players, calls out "Look out for the fairies!" The fairies then turn and chase the brownies, each fairy tagging as many brownies as possible before the latter cross their safety line. All the brownies tagged become fairies and join that group.

The game is repeated, the brownies turning their backs. Players are not permitted to look over their shoulders while awaiting the approach of the oncoming players.

The winning side is the one having the greater number of players at the end of six chasings or at the end of the available time period.

TEACHING SUGGESTIONS

1. Before giving the signal, encourage all children to approach close to the chasing group.
2. Discourage those who deliberately try to be tagged.
3. Teach personal control in not looking, and ability to respond immediately when the signal is given.

GALLOPING AND SKIPPING

NUMBER OF PLAYERS: 5-40

SPACE: Playground, gymnasium, classroom, auditorium

EQUIPMENT: Piano or phonograph

FORMATION: Children form a circle or stand in line or file formation.

PROCEDURE: All children gallop to music. To gallop the child advances forward, either right or left foot leading, the rear foot coming to but not passing beyond the leading foot.

All children skip. For children who do not know how to skip, the teacher first has them hop on one foot twice, then bring the elevated foot to the floor so that they are standing on both feet. This drill is repeated, the children alternating the hopping foot. Next each takes one step forward and hops once on the same foot, steps with the other foot and hops on it once, and continues until he can skip.

TEACHING SUGGESTIONS

1. Allow some children to skip with one foot leading all the time. This will be overcome later.
2. Do not expect too much skill in the beginning. Numerous practice periods will be necessary.
3. Have children who skip easily demonstrate for the others.

GALLOPING LIZZIE [1]

NUMBER OF PLAYERS: 6-12

SPACE: Playground, playroom, gymnasium, hallway

EQUIPMENT: Large balls, beanbags, knotted towels, or stuffed leather ball casings

FORMATION: Children stand in a circle fairly close together and facing in. One player stands outside the circle. The ball is given to a circle player.

PROCEDURE: The ball is passed from player to player or is thrown across to an opposite player. The outside player tries to tag a circle player while he has the ball in his hands. When the outside player is successful in tagging a player he changes places with him. If a circle player drops the ball he becomes the tagger, the former tagger taking his place.

TEACHING SUGGESTIONS

1. When the number to play is above 12, form two circles and provide each circle with a ball.
2. Vary the direction in which the ball may travel.

GOOD MORNING [1]

NUMBER OF PLAYERS: 5-40

SPACE: Classroom

FORMATION: Children are seated at their desks. One child stands in the front of the room with his back toward the group. The teacher silently indicates the child who is to advance.

PROCEDURE: A member of the group (Martha) approaches the standing child and says, "Good morning, John," and John, without turning his

[1] Developed by Margaret Van Voorhees.

head, guesses the name of the speaker. If unsuccessful, Martha repeats her salutation. If still unsuccessful John returns to his seat and Martha becomes the guesser.

If successful John remains the guesser and a new player approaches and greets him. So the game continues.

TEACHING SUGGESTIONS

1. Encourage children to speak distinctly and with enough volume for all in the room to hear the name given.
2. Have the children move rapidly from their seats to the front of the room and back again.

THE HUNTSMAN

NUMBER OF PLAYERS: 4-12

SPACE: Classroom, playground

FORMATION: Children are seated at their desks. A leader is chosen.

PROCEDURE: The leader wanders up and down the aisles and asks, "Who would like to go with me to hunt ducks?" (or bears, rabbits, foxes, or lions). As the leader approaches, the children who wish to do so fall in behind the leader and follow him. When the leader sees that the children are in file formation and as far as possible from their seats, he jumps up and down and calls loudly "Bang!" whereupon all the children scamper for their seats. The first one to reach his seat becomes the leader for a repetition of the game.

TEACHING SUGGESTIONS

1. Act as leader until the children master the fact that the leader tries to get all the children away from their own desks.
2. Give the names of different animals to different groups of children if desired. These named groups should not be bunched but should be seated individually in different areas of the room.
3. When played out of doors, have the children stand within a given area until called and have them try to return to this area at the word "Bang!" The first one entering it will be the new leader.

JACK BE NIMBLE

NUMBER OF PLAYERS: 3-12

SPACE: Playground, playroom, classroom, gymnasium, hallway

EQUIPMENT: Paper cones 6 to 8 inches high with a base not more than 6 to 8 inches across, representing candles, one for each group of players

FORMATION: Children are divided into groups of three to six players. Each group stands in file formation before its own candle.

PROCEDURE: On a signal, the first child in each file steps to his candle and jumps over it, jumping with both feet together. Following the jump, on a second signal, the child goes to the rear of his file. Another signal is given for the second player to jump, and so on until each child has jumped over the candle.

TEACHING SUGGESTIONS

1. See that the children wait for commands and do not give the jumping signal until the previous jumper has reached the rear of his file.
2. Teach the children to use their arms for balance, and to land on both feet with the ankles, knees, and hips bent.

LEADER AND CLASS

NUMBER OF PLAYERS: 4-40

SPACE: Playground, playroom, gymnasium, hallway, auditorium

EQUIPMENT: Utility balls, volleyballs, or beanbags, one for each group

FORMATION: Children are divided into groups of four to six players. Members of each group stand side by side in a line. The one at the head of the line becomes the leader, and he faces his group, standing eight to ten feet away.

PROCEDURE: The leader tosses a ball to all the players of his group in turn, who throw the ball back to him. Any player missing the ball goes to the foot of his line. If the leader misses a ball, he goes to the foot of his line and the next player at the head becomes the leader.

If the ball goes around the group twice and the leader has not missed, he takes his place in the line just above the last player who missed.

TEACHING SUGGESTIONS

1. As skill is gained, increase the distance between the leaders and their group.
2. Teach players to make accurate throws.
3. Give leaders two or three objects to throw, of different sizes and weights.
4. Teach accuracy in catching a moving object.
5. If there are more than six players, divide them into small groups so that there will be no long waiting period between throws.

LINE WALKING

NUMBER OF PLAYERS: 5-40

SPACE: Playground, gymnasium, classroom, auditorium

PLAYING AREA: Several parallel lines three or more feet apart; horizontal walking rails; or balance beams

FORMATION: Children are divided into groups and line up at one end of selected line areas.

PROCEDURE: Walking slowly, children try to have the inner border of each foot touch the line. If balance beams are used a definite error can be recorded, since each foot must contact the inner rail in order to stay on the board.

TEACHING SUGGESTIONS

1. Dramatize the activity by having the line represent a tightrope over Niagara Falls or some stream or river known to the children.
2. Have the children do certain stunts as they walk—extend the arms sideways, forward, or over the head; lift the knees to a right angle before the next step is taken; kneel with weight on one leg so that the other knee touches the floor or board.
3. Do not make this a contest between children, but emphasize individual control, skill, and posture.

MAGIC CARPETS

NUMBER OF PLAYERS: 4-12

SPACE: Playground, playroom, gymnasium, auditorium, hallway

PLAYING AREA: Circles or squares are drawn on the floor fairly close together, the diameters being not less than three feet. Cardboard and linoleum squares or newspapers may be used, scattered about in fairly close proximity to each other. They are known as magic carpets.

FORMATION: A leader is chosen. The remaining players form a long line behind the leader, all joining hands with the persons in front and back of them.

PROCEDURE: Skipping or running, the leader guides the line back and forth and around about so that the players cannot escape stepping on the magic carpets. A signal is given and the players stop wherever they may be. Those caught on magic carpets are eliminated. Continue until the winner or winners are determined.

TEACHING SUGGESTIONS

1. Have children run or skip to music.

2. Make the signal to stop the sudden cessation of the music, the clapping of hands, or the blowing of a whistle.
3. Discourage children from trying to avoid passing through the carpets.
4. If the group is a large one, designate the last five players who remain uncaught the winners.

OBJECT TOUCHING

NUMBER OF PLAYERS: 5-12

SPACE: Classroom

FORMATION: Children are seated. One player is selected to start the game. The others follow in the same sequence as seated.

PROCEDURE: The leader touches some object in the room and returns to his seat. Number 2 touches that object and then a second object. Number 3 touches object one, two, and then touches a third object. The game continues, with each child trying to touch objects in the proper sequence and ending by touching a new object. When an error occurs, the game is replayed with a new leader from a different area of the room, or the original game continues with each child having an opportunity to touch the objects in sequence regardless of the error made by a previous child.

TEACHING SUGGESTIONS

1. Jot down in the proper sequence the names of the objects touched.
2. Credit to the score of each child or toward a team score the number of successful touches before the error occurs.
3. Use as a hot weather game.
4. Develop the ability to remember in sequence the objects touched.

ONE, TWO, BUTTON MY SHOE

NUMBER OF PLAYERS: 5-12

SPACE: Playground, playroom gymnasium, auditorium, hallway

PLAYING AREA: Two parallel lines 30 feet apart

FORMATION: One child, the leader, stands ahead of but to one side of the players who stand scattered out behind one of the lines.

PROCEDURE: When the leader sees that all are toeing the line he says, "Ready," then in unison the following dialogue is carried on:

Children: "One, two ___"
Leader: "Button my shoe ___"
Children: "Three, four ___"

Leader: "Knock on the door ___"
Children: "Five, six ___"
Leader: "Pick up sticks ___"
Children: "Seven, eight ___"
Leader: "Run, or you'll be_____late."

At the word "late," and not before, all the children run forward, cross over the second line with both feet, turn and race back, the first one to cross the home line being the next leader. The previous leader joins the group for a repetition of the game.

TEACHING SUGGESTIONS

1. Have the leader vary the rhythm of the line "Run, or you'll be late" thereby keeping the others on the alert until they hear the word, "late." Emphasize suspense, as it adds fun and zest to the game.
2. Require those who break over the starting line before the word "late" is used to stand three or four feet behind the starting line.

PUSSY WANTS A CORNER

NUMBER OF PLAYERS: 5-12

SPACE: Playground, gymnasium, auditorium, playroom

PLAYING AREA: Bases scattered about, each base not less than ten feet from any other base; one base for each player except the pussy. Chalk marks, stones, beanbags, circles, linoleum squares, or cardboard may be used for the bases.

FORMATION: Each player stands on his base. The player chosen to be pussy has no base.

PROCEDURE: The pussy moves about saying "Pussy wants a corner!" Players on bases try to exchange places with each other without being seen by the pussy. If pussy manages to reach a base while it is vacant she exchanges places with the player who has just left that base, who then becomes the pussy. Sometimes the teacher or the pussy may call "All change bases," whereupon every player must leave his own base and try to secure another. Pussy seeks a base too. The one left without a base becomes the pussy.

TEACHING SUGGESTIONS

1. Do not spoil the activity by having bases too close together.
2. Allow players to try to confuse Pussy by calls, by signals, by sudden dashes.
3. Keep the game moving rapidly. Long waits and timidity in exchanging bases slow up the fun of the game.

RAILROAD TRAIN

NUMBER OF PLAYERS: 4-15

SPACE: Playground, classroom, playroom, gymnasium, auditorium

FORMATION: One player is selected to be the trainmaster, another to be the starter. The remaining children are given the names of parts of a train or of objects carried on a train.

PROCEDURE: The trainmaster tells a story, using the names of the various parts of the train or of the objects carried in the train. As a child's train name is mentioned, he runs to the starter and lines up behind him, putting his hands on the shoulders or hips of the person in front of him.

When all have joined the train, or whenever the starter wishes, he gives the starting whistle and the train moves off around the room, gaining momentum as it advances. The starter leads the train in any direction he may desire.

TEACHING SUGGESTIONS

1. For large groups, give the same object name to several children and make up several trains by appointing several starters.
2. Suggest to the children that they all try to use the same foot at the same time while the train is in motion. This will give a rhythmic motion to the trains.
3. Develop concentration and identification with a given object.
4. If the train breaks apart, have all return to the roundhouse to await assembling of a new train.

RUN, RABBITS, RUN

NUMBER OF PLAYERS: 4-12

SPACE: Playground, playroom, gymnasium, hallway, auditorium

PLAYING AREA: A nest or home base large enough for all the rabbits to stand within it

FORMATION: Half the group are rabbits, half are foxes. Each group selects a leader. The rabbits stand in the nest while the foxes are free to move about in the woods, at the same time staying near their leader.

PROCEDURE: The mother rabbit takes her children out to play in the sunshine and to look for food. They go softly for fear the old fox and his children may see them.

The fox moves about, with his children following him, and when he thinks it advantageous he cries loudly, "Run, rabbits, run!" Up to this time no fox may chase a rabbit. On hearing the cry the rabbits try to reach their nest before the foxes can catch them. Those caught become foxes and on later occasions try to catch the remaining rabbits when next they venture out. The game is repeated until all the rabbits are caught, whereupon they become the foxes and the foxes the rabbits. The last rabbit to be caught becomes the new mother rabbit when next the group become rabbits. The old fox selects a new fox to take his place.

TEACHING SUGGESTIONS

1. Encourage the foxes not to keep too close to the rabbits' nest.
2. Encourge the rabbits to be brave and venturesome.
3. Discourage those children who seek to be caught by having them for several minutes stand beside the teacher and watch how successful players maneuver their positions and the speed with which they run.

SKIP `TAG

NUMBER OF PLAYERS: 1-12

SPACE: Playground, playroom, gymnasium

FORMATION: Players form a single circle, all facing inward. A tagger is chosen, who stands outside the circle.

PROCEDURE: The tagger, while skipping around the outside of the circle, tags a circle player. The circle player skips after the tagger and tries to catch him. If the tagger reaches the vacant space left by the circle player, the circle player becomes the tagger and the game continues. If the tagger is caught by the circle player, he remains the tagger.

TEACHING SUGGESTIONS

1. Do not permit the tagger to skip for a long distance before tagging a circle player.
2. Do not permit running, or skipping with only one foot.
3. Do not permit favoritism in the form of choosing a certain player several times in succession.
4. Do not permit boys continually to choose boys or girls to choose girls.
5. Encourage real effort by the tagger to reach the vacant place in the circle.
6. Develop skipping skill as a game objective.

SQUIRRELS AND NUTS

NUMBER OF PLAYERS: 4-12

SPACE: Classroom

EQUIPMENT: Two small objects to represent nuts.

FORMATION: Two squirrels are chosen and each is given a nut. The remaining children put their arms on their desks with one hand extended palm up and open. Their heads are placed on their arms with their eyes shut.

PROCEDURE: Each squirrel runs on tiptoe up and down the aisles and drops his nut into an open hand. The player who receives a nut starts chasing the squirrel that gave him the nut and tries to catch the squirrel before the latter can reach his nest (his own seat).

If a squirrel is caught before reaching his nest, the person who tags him becomes the new squirrel. If the squirrels are successful in reaching their nests, the first squirrels again drop the nuts into new hands.

TEACHING SUGGESTIONS

1. See that seated children *at all times* keep their feet under their desks and out of the aisles.
2. Use only one squirrel until the game is learned.
3. Encourage the squirrels to drop the nuts into a hand while they are well away from their own nest. This will increase the fun of the game.
4. Discourage long runs before the nut is given to a seated player.

SQUIRRELS IN TREES

NUMBER OF PLAYERS: 7-13

SPACE: Playground, playroom, gymnasium, auditorium, hallway

FORMATION: Two-thirds of the players form by couples with their hands on the shoulders of their partners. In this manner they form hollow trees. The trees should be scattered about in no set formation with considerable space between them. The remaining one-third of the children enter trees as squirrels and stand there. There should be one or more players without a tree home.

PROCEDURE: The teacher, or a leader, claps his hands or blows a whistle, whereupon all the squirrels, including the homeless ones, run to secure a new home. Squirrels who leave a tree may not return immediately to the same tree. Those unsuccessful in securing a tree become homeless squirrels. The game is continued as long as desired. Three changes should be made in the positions of players so that all children have the chance during some part of the game to be squirrels.

TEACHING SUGGESTIONS

1. When the game is new, use only one homeless squirrel.
2. Do not permit two squirrels to occupy one tree.
3. Give the signals in rapid succession.
4. Have the trees scattered over an area large enough to encourage a vigorous run when changes are made.

STOP AND START

NUMBER OF PLAYERS: 4-12

SPACE: Playground, playroom, gymnasium, auditorium

EQUIPMENT: Whistle

FORMATION: Children stand about the room watching the leader.

PROCEDURE: The leader points in any direction desired and the children move in that direction. The whistle is blown and children stop and turn in order to watch the leader for the next direction. Children who fail to stop immediately or who fail to follow directions form a second group of players on the opposite side of the leader. The object of the game is to see who will be the last player in the original group.

TEACHING SUGGESTIONS

1. Give directions in rapid succession.
2. Vary the game by telling the children to fly, hop, skip, run, crawl, or jump as they move.
3. If the group is a large one, stop the game when there are three, four, or five left in the original group and declare these the winners.
4. Teach children to stop by showing them how to "tuck under" as they bend their ankles, knees, and hips for an easy stop.
5. Improve the turn by showing how important the feet are in keeping balance and how much easier it is to turn in the direction in which the feet are pointing, so that the feet will not need to be crossed.

SWAT 'EM

NUMBER OF PLAYERS: 5-12

SPACE: Playground, auditorium, playroom, gymnasium

FORMATION: Players make a circle by joining hands. One player stands outside the circle.

PROCEDURE: The outside player runs around the circle and while running tags a circle player. That player must run in the opposite direction. Each runner tries to be the first to reach the vacant place in the circle. The unsuccessful player continues to run and tag.

TEACHING SUGGESTIONS

1. If there are but a few players, draw a circle on the floor or ground and insist that runners remain outside the circle area while trying to reach the position of the person tagged.
2. Train children to pass to the right when passing each other.

3. Watch for evidence of fatigue and change the tagger if it seems advisable.
4. Do not permit the taggers to choose certain players over and over. All should have a chance to run.
5. Do not permit long runs before a person is selected to be tagged.
6. Add fun to the game by having the runners stop and bow when they meet, shake hands, run around each other, or jump up and down a given number of times before continuing their runs.
7. Try having girls tag boys and boys tag girls.

WHAT TO PLAY

NUMBER OF PLAYERS: 4-40

SPACE: Playground, playroom, gymnasium, hallway, auditorium, classroom

FORMATION: Children form a large single circle, all facing inward. One child is chosen to start the game.

PROCEDURE: As the chosen child moves toward the center of the circle, the circle children join hands and move to the left. While moving they sing, using the tune, "Mulberry Bush" (page 352).

> Mary, show us what to play,
> What to play, what to play,
> Mary, show us what to play,
> Show us what to play.

When the circle singers finish, the child in the center says, "Play this," showing the group some action such as hopping, jumping, shaking hands, bending forward or sideward, skipping around the circle, or moving parts of the body such as a leg or arm. The class imitates the action until the leader or teacher says, "Stop." The center child retires to the circle group and selects a new center player. A boy selects a girl and a girl chooses a boy. The song is resung and the game is repeated.

TEACHING SUGGESTIONS

1. See that each child chosen thinks up his own action and does not repeat what the previous child did.
2. Encourage vigorous action rather than passive movements.
3. Substitute the name of any child present for the name, "Mary."
4. When played in the classroom, have the children stand beside their desks and perform the designated activity.
5. Do not permit the same children to be chosen as leaders over and over again. All should have an opportunity to lead.

Rhythmical Activities

CATS AND RATS [1]

FORMATION: Players form two lines facing in opposite directions. Pupils opposite each other are partners. Partners should know each other so as to be able to pick each other out when the run occurs. One line is named the cats, the other line the rats. Each cat will chase his own rat.

DESCRIPTION: This is a marching and chasing game. All sing the verse, while the leaders of the two lines march their players away from the other line. When they reach the word "away," and not before, lines break, with each cat chasing his own rat. When caught, players return to original places and rats become the cats for a repetition of the game.

Out of doors it may be necessary to limit the area where the run is to occur, such as within the shade of a building or within a fenced-in section. Local conditions or restrictions will determine the best situation for a successful game. This is a useful activity when relief from passive work is desired.

Cats and Rats

Arranged by Grace Van Ness

Now here comes sly old pus - sy cat
You'd best be - ware, you lit - tle rat!

Pus-sy wants with you to play, So you'd bet-ter run a-way!

CHARLIE OVER THE WATER [2]

FORMATION: Single circle, one or more players in the center

DESCRIPTION: Joining hands, circle players walk, skip, or gallop around the center players. On the word "me" all stoop and the center player(s)

---

[1] M. R. Wild and D. E. White, *Physical Education for Elementary Schools.* Cedar Falls, Iowa: Iowa State Teachers College, 1924. By permission.
[2] William Wells Newell, *Games and Songs of American Children.* New York: Harper & Bros., 1911. By permission.

tries to tag a circle player before he can stoop. If tagged, the person tagged exchanges places with the center player.

Almost any summer evening, in certain streets of New York, children may be seen playing this round, which they sing on one note, with a shriek to conclude it.

Charlie Over the Water

Char-lie o-ver the wa-ter, Char-lie o-ver the sea,

Char-lie catch a black-bird, Can't catch me.

DID YOU EVER SEE A LASSIE? [1]

Victor Record No. 21618; and No. 45-5066 (Album E 87)

1. Did you ever see a lassie (or laddie), a lassie, a lassie
2. Did you ever see a lassie (or laddie) do this way and that?
3. Do this way and that way, and this way and that way,
4. Did you ever see a lassie (or laddie) do this way and that?

FORMATION: Children form a single circle with hands joined, boys and girls alternating. A leader is selected to stand in the center.

DESCRIPTION: Moving to right or left, all sing. During the singing of lines 1 and 2 the center player decides what action to show the others.

During lines 3 and 4, the circle players stop walking and skipping and imitate the action of the leader. Movements should be rhythmical. The use of large, vigorous movements such as bending body forward and touching floor with hands, jumping high into the air, clapping hands under a raised leg, or running in place should be encouraged.

At the end of the verse the center player selects a new leader. The selection of boys by girls and of girls by boys should be encouraged.

---

[1] Music from *Our First Music*. Sacramento: California State Department of Education, 1942. By permission of C. C. Birchard & Co.

Did You Ever See a Lassie?

Old Game Song

Did you ev - er see a las-sie, a las-sie, a las- sie. Did you ev - er see a
(or lad-die)

las - sie do this way and that? Do this way and that way, And

this way and that way. Did you ev - er see a las-sie do this way and that?

THE FARMER IN THE DELL [1]

Victor Record No. 21618; and No. 45-5066 (Album E 87)

FORMATION: Children form a single circle, players facing the center. One child is appointed to be the farmer. He enters and remains inside the circle during the singing of the verses.

DESCRIPTION

Verse 1. Circle players, with hands joined, move to the right or left as desired during the singing. The farmer looks about and decides on the person to be chosen.

Verse 2. The farmer chooses a wife by taking another player into the center of the circle with him.

Verse 3. The wife chooses a child.

The choosing continues until the end of the verses. The cheese may be "clapped out," that is, the circle players move in and clap their hands over the head of the cheese. The last player chosen becomes the new farmer for a repetition of the game.

[1] William Wells Newell, *op. cit.* By permission of Harper & Bros., publishers.

Variation 1.   The eighth verse may be sung, "The cat chases the rat," and during the singing the cat chases his rat. The rat moves in and out of the circle, while the circle players help him and obstruct the movement of the cat.

Variation 2.   The eighth verse may read, "We'll all chase the rat," and at the end of the verse the circle players chase the rat, who has been permitted to escape from the circle during the verse.

Variation 3.   Several farmers may be chosen, and each one chooses a wife. Each wife then chooses a child, and so on.

The Farmer in the Dell

2. The farmer takes a wife, etc.
3. The wife takes a child, etc.
4. The child takes a nurse, etc.
5. The nurse takes a dog, etc.
6. The dog takes a cat, etc.
7. The cat takes a rat, etc.
8. The rat takes the cheese, etc.
9. The cheese stands alone, etc.

GO 'ROUND AND 'ROUND THE VILLAGE [1]

FORMATION: Children form a single circle with hands joined, boys and girls alternating. Several independent players stand outside and on opposite sides of the circle. They should not crowd up on each other.

DESCRIPTION: All sing the verses.

Verse 1.   Circle players move to right or left and those on the outside move in the opposite direction.

[1] From Cecille Jean Barnett, *Games, Rhythms, Dances.* Oshkosh, Wis.: J. O. Frank and Sons, 1941. By permission.

Go 'Round and 'Round the Village

Arranged by C. J. Barnett

Go 'round and 'round the vil-lage. Go 'round and 'round the vil-lage. Go
'round and 'round the vil-lage, As we have done be-fore.

Verse 2. Go in and out the window,
          Go in and out the window,
          Go in and out the window,
          As we have done before.

   3. Now stand and face your partner, etc.

   4. Now kneel to show you love her (him), etc.

   5. Now measure how much you love her (him), etc.

   6. Now follow me to London, etc.

Verse 2. Circle players stand still and, lifting their arms, form arches. Outside players, all moving in the same direction, weave in and out under the raised arms and finish inside the circle.

Verse 3. Outside players select partners. Boys select girls, girls select boys.

Verse 4. Outside players drop onto one knee in front of their partners.

Verse 5. Outside players extend their arms sideways as far as desired.

Verse 6. Outside players and their partners step out of the circle and, taking hands, skip around the outside.

At the end those first chosen: (1) return to the circle and their partners start the new game; or (2) all chosen players repeat the game with each choosing a partner until no circle players remain. This second form is often more desirable than the first form, particularly if there is a large number of pupils to participate. The more activity for the group the better.

HOW D'YE DO, MY PARTNER[1]

(Swedish)

Victor Record No. 21685

FORMATION: Double circle with boys on the outside. Partners face each other.

DESCRIPTION

Line 1. Boys bow.

Line 2. Girls curtsy.

Line 3. Partners take each other's right hand and shake it.

Line 4. Partners, still holding right hands, grasp left hands and at the same time turn so that they stand side by side and shoulder to shoulder, in skater's position.

Chorus: Couples skip while singing the chorus. They must *slow down* during Measure 7 and bow to each other during Measure 8. Members of both circles then move one step to their own right or left and secure a new partner.

The entire pattern is repeated as many times as desired.

Variation 1. During the first two lines boys and girls bow twice simultaneously.

Variation 2. For classroom use, the game is played in a single circle with partners facing. During the chorus all face inward, join hands and, holding them high, skip or slide in the desired line of direction.

How D'Ye Do, My Partner

How d'ye do my part-ner How d'ye do to-day

Will you dance in the cir-cle? I will show you the way.

[1] From C. Ward Crampton and M. A. Wollaston, *The Song Play Book.* New York: A. S. Barnes & Co., 1917. By permission.

KITTY WHITE [1]

FORMATION: Single circle, boys and girls alternating. A mouse and a kitty are chosen. The mouse is inside the circle, the kitty outside.

DESCRIPTION: The circle players join hands and move to left or right while singing the first four lines. Meanwhile Kitty White creeps around outside the circle and peeks in at little Mousie Gray. When the last word of the fourth line is reached, "And quickly runs *away*," the circle players stop moving and drop their hands. The mouse runs out and in through the circle, chased by Kitty White. The kitty may be required to follow the trail taken by Mousie Gray. During the singing of the last four lines the circle players clap their hands. When the mouse is caught, both players, after selecting a new mouse and kitty, return to circle positions. It is suggested that two mice and two kittens be used.

Kitty White

Kit-ty White so sly-ly comes To catch the Mous-ie Gray; But mous-ie hears her soft-ly creep And quick-ly runs a-way. Run, run, run, lit-tle mouse, Run all a-round the house; For Kit-ty White is com-ing near, And she will catch the mouse, I fear.

[1] Jessie H. Bancroft, *Games*. New York: The Macmillan Co., 1937. By permission.

LITTLE POLLY FLINDERS [1]

Arranged by C. J. Barnett

Lit-tle Pol-ly Flin-ders sat a-mong the cin-ders warm-ing her

pret-ty lit-tle toes. Her mo-ther came and caught her and spanked her

lit-tle daugh-ter for burn-ing up her nice new clothes.

Line 1. Little Polly Flinders
2. Sat among the cinders
3. Warming her pretty little toes.
4. Her mother came and caught her
5. And spanked her little daughter
6. For burning up her nice new clothes.

FORMATION: Children form a single circle, facing in, or two straight lines with pupils shoulder to shoulder, lines facing each other.

DESCRIPTION: All sing words while performing the following actions:

Line 1. Turn to right and walk, walk, walk, walk.

Line 2. Turn about and walk, walk, walk, walk.

Line 3. With lines facing each other (or facing center of circle if in circle formation), raise right foot in the air; raise left foot in the air.

Line 4. Run backward with small running steps.

Line 5. Pretend to rub eyes and at the same time shake the head.

Line 6. Face right and with arms outstretched at the side, walk forward slowly. On word "clothes," place the heel well forward on the floor.

---

[1] From Cecille Jean Barnett, *op. cit.* Music and verse by permission of J. O. Frank & Sons, publishers.

LOOBY LOO [1]

Old Singing Game

Here we go Loo - by   Loo,___   Here we go Loo - by   light.___

Here we go Loo - by   Loo,___   All on a Sat - ur - day   night.___

I   put my right hand in,___   I   put my right hand out;___   I

give my right hand a   shake shake shake and turn my - self a - bout, Oh,

Verse 2.   I put my left hand in,
            I put my left hand out;
            I give my left hand a shake, shake, shake
            And turn myself about,

        3.   I put my two hands in, etc.
        4.   I put my right foot in, etc.
        5.   I put my left foot in, etc.
        6.   I put my head 'way in, etc.
        7.   I put my whole self in, etc.

Victor Record No. 20214

FORMATION: Children form a single circle, facing in.

---

[1] *Our First Music.* Sacramento: California State Department of Education, 1942. By permission of C. C. Birchard & Co.

DESCRIPTION: Music consists of chorus (A), eight measures, followed by verse (B), eight measures. During the chorus the pupils join hands and slide, skip, run, or walk to the left or right. During the singing of the verses (B), pupils stand still and dramatize the verse. The chorus is repeated after each verse.

The game represents the experiences of a little boy who is loath to take a bath. Large and vigorous movement should be encouraged. Suggested actions are as follows:

Verse 1. Stretch right arm toward the center of the circle. Turn about and stretch the arm away from the circle. Turn back to the center and shake the right hand vigorously. Turn body around in place.

Verse 2. Stretch left arm toward center of circle. Turn about and stretch left arm away from the circle. Turn back to center and shake left hand vigorously. Turn body around in place.

Verse 3. Stretch both arms toward the center of the circle, etc.

Verse 4. Stand on left foot and lift right foot from the ground, etc.

Verse 5. Stand on right foot and lift left foot from the ground, etc.

Verse 6. Bend head forward, etc.

Verse 7. Jump forward, jump backward, shake self vigorously, and turn about.

MULBERRY BUSH [1]

Victor Record No. 20806; and No. 45-5065 (Album E 87)

FORMATION: Players stand in a circle and each clasps the hands of his neighbors.

DESCRIPTION: When singing the chorus, players circle by skipping. During the verses they stand still and dramatize the action mentioned in the verses.

The actions should be performed with big movements and vigorously. When the refrain "So early in the morning" is sung, each player stands and spins around rapidly in place. The chorus is repeated after each verse.

> Verse 1. This is the way we wash our clothes,
> We wash our clothes, we wash our clothes;
> This is the way we wash our clothes
> So early Monday morning.

---

[1] Music and words from Jessie H. Bancroft, *op. cit.* By permission of The Macmillan Co., publishers.

Mulberry Bush

Here we go round the mul - ber - ry bush, The mul - ber - ry bush, the mul - ber - ry bush, Here we go round the mul - ber - ry bush, So ear - ly in the morn - ing.

Chorus: Here we go round the mulberry bush,
The mulberry bush, the mulberry bush,
Here we go round the mulberry bush,
So early in the morning!

2.   This is the way we iron our clothes, etc.
So early Tuesday morning.

3.   This is the way we scrub the floor, etc.,
So early Wednesday morning.

4.   This is the way we mend our clothes, etc.,
So early Thursday morning.

5.   This is the way we sweep the house, etc.,
So early Friday morning!

6.   Thus we play when our work is done, etc.,
So early Saturday morning!

OATS, PEAS, BEANS [1]

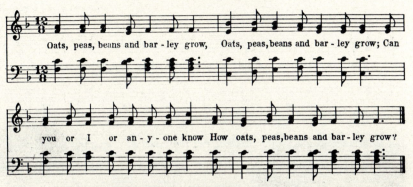

Oats, peas, beans and bar - ley grow,   Oats, peas, beans and bar - ley grow; Can

you or I   or an - y - one know How oats, peas, beans and bar - ley grow?

Verse 2.   Thus the farmer sows his seed,
Thus he stands and takes his ease;
He stamps his foot and claps his hands,
And turns around to view the land.

3.   Waiting for a partner,
Waiting for a partner,
Open the ring and choose one in,
While we all gaily dance and sing.

4.   Now you're married, you must obey,
You must be true to all you say,
You must be kind, you must be good,
And keep your wife in kindling wood.

Victor Record No. 20214; and No. 45-5067 (Album E 87)

FORMATION: All form a single circle, with one or more players in the center.

DESCRIPTION: All sing the words while performing the actions.

Verse 1.   All move to left or right. Farmer stands in the center. Farmer sows his seed; folds his arms; stamps his foot; claps his hands; and placing a hand over his eyes revolves, viewing his lands as he does so.

Verse 2.   Circle players stand still and follow the actions of the farmer.

Verse 3.   Circle players move again while farmer chooses a partner. Selection should be finished by end of the verse.

Verse 4.   Everyone skips, the farmer and his wife going in the opposite direction to that taken by the circle players.

[1] *Our First Music.* Sacramento: California State Department of Education, 1942. By permission of C. C. Birchard & Co.

OUR EXERCISES [1]

Arranged by C. J. Barnett

We touch our toes and then our heads, touch our toes, then our heads, we

touch our toes and then our heads, let feet go stamp, stamp, stamp.

Verse 2.   We touch our knees and stretch up tall
Touch our knees, stretch up tall.
We touch our knees and stretch up tall.
Let hands go: clap, clap, clap.

FORMATION: Children form a single circle, with boys and girls alternating.

DESCRIPTION: Children sing and follow the action of the words. Various movements are added as suggested by the class.

PUSSY CAT [1]

FORMATION: Children form a single circle, boys and girls alternating, one or more players in the center as pussy cats.

DESCRIPTION: Circle players sing lines 1 and 3; center players sing lines 2 and 4.

Line 1.   Circle players join hands and walk around the circle.

Line 2.   They reverse direction.

Line 3.   They unclasp hands and walk toward the center, shaking a finger at the pussy cat.

Line 4.   On the last word, "chair," the center player jumps high into the air and the others run back to place in circle formation.

A new pussy is chosen and the game is repeated.

---

[1] From Cecille Jean Barnett, *op. cit.* By permission of J. O. Frank & Sons, publishers.

Pussy Cat

Arranged by C. J. Barnett

Pus-sy cat, pus-sy cat where have you been? I've been to
Lon-don to vis-it the queen. Pus-sy cat, pus-sy cat what did you
there? I fright-ened a lit-tle mouse un-der the chair.

Line 1. Pussy cat, pussy cat, where have you been?
2. I've been to London to visit the queen.
3. Pussy cat, pussy cat, what did you there?
4. I frightened a little mouse under the chair.

THE SLEEPING PRINCESS

Music: "The Sleeping Beauty" [1]

FORMATION: Children form a large circle, hands joined; one player is selected to be the princess inside the circle. Eight or ten boys and girls chosen as ladies-in-waiting and courtiers form a smaller circle around the princess. Outside of the circle stand two players chosen to be prince and wicked fairy.

DESCRIPTION: The teacher introduces the story: "Once upon a time in a large castle there lived a princess with the members of the court who admired her, waited on her, and did her bidding. She had one enemy, a fairy who had been angered because she had not been invited to the christening party of the princess. She harbored her hatred and when the princess was grown she appeared one day and pronounced a curse."

Verse 1. The two groups move in opposite directions while singing:

---

[1] Music from Caroline Crawford, *Dramatic Games and Dances.* New York: A. S. Barnes & Co., 1914. By permission.

"The princess is so beautiful, beautiful, beautiful,
The princess is so beautiful, beautiful!"

Verse 2. Children stand still and wag their fingers or clap their hands warningly at the princess while they sing:

"Oh, little princess, do take care, do take care, do take care,
Oh, little princess, do take care—there's a wicked fay."

Verse 3. The wicked fay breaks through the joined hands of the circle and seeks out the princess while all sing:

"There came a wicked fay right there, fay right there, fay right there.
There came a wicked fay right there, and she sang:"

Verse 4. The fairy, extending her arms and turning around slowly so as to include the princess and the members of her court, sings alone or others may join in the singing. As the curse is pronounced, one by one the center players drop to a knee and close their eyes:

"Princess, sleep for a hundred years, a hundred years, a hundred years,
Princess sleep for a hundred years, and each of you."

The Sleeping Beauty

Arranged by Elizabeth Rose Fogg

Verse 5. Teacher: "For many years no one disturbed the princess and her followers and tall trees grew up around the castle." Outer circle players move in slowly and with hands joined raise their arms to form the trees of the forest. They sing:

"A giant hedge had grown up high, grown up high, grown up high,
A giant hedge had grown up high, and hid them all."

Verse 6. Teacher: "A prince, exploring, finds the hedge and grows curious. He seeks for an opening and finally breaks through the barrier after a struggle with the tough branches and finds the princess." All sing:

"There came a prince then through the hedge, through the hedge,
  through the hedge,
There came a prince then through the hedge and he sang:"

Verse 7.   Approaching the princess, the prince sings alone:

"Oh little princess, do awake, do awake, do awake,
Oh little princess, do awake, and be my bride!"

Verse 8.   Those in the outer circle drop their hands and move backward.
The courtiers and ladies-in-waiting awake as the prince takes the hand of
the princess. While he is helping her to her feet all sing:

"The little princess then awoke, then awoke, then awoke,
The little princess then awoke, to be his bride."

Verse 9.   The outside circle stands still. Together, the prince and princess, arm in arm, walk about in the center with the others following them
two by two and arm in arm. All sing:

"They had a wondrous wedding feast, wedding feast, wedding feast,
They had a wondrous wedding feast, wedding feast."

Verse 10.   The couples in the center join hands with each other and skip
around in their own small circles while the outside circle players gallop to
the right or left while all sing:

"The people all were merry then, merry then, merry then,
The people all were merry then, throughout that land."

During the singing of "throughout that land," which should be
greatly retarded, those in the center bow to each other. Those in the big
circle bow toward the prince and princess.

The center players select persons to take their parts and repeat the
game.

WHEN I WAS A SHOEMAKER [1]

FORMATION: A single circle is formed.

DESCRIPTION: Children sing and perform actions appropriate to the words.
In the first verse they tap with imaginary hammers. The gentleman places
his hands in his coat pockets and promenades up and down. The lady
gathers her skirts haughtily together. Additional verses may be made up
by the children.

---

[1] William Wells Newell, *op. cit.* By permission of Harper & Bros., publishers.

When I Was a Shoemaker

When I was a shoe-ma-ker, and a shoe-ma-ker was I, And this a way, and a this a way, And a this a way went I.

Verse 2.   When I was a gentleman,
           And a gentleman was I,
           A this a way, and a this a way,
           And a this a way went I.

3.   When I was a lady,
     And a lady was I,
     A this a way, and a this a way,
     And a this a way went I.

ADDITIONAL RHYTHMICAL ACTIVITIES IN CALIFORNIA STATE SERIES MUSIC TEXTBOOKS

New Music Horizons. First Book. Edited by Osbourne McConathy and Others. (Copyrighted, 1944, by Silver Burdett Co.) Sacramento: California State Department of Education (1950).

For teaching suggestions, refer to *Teacher's Manual for Primary Grades.* Page references below are to student's book.

Our First Music. A Complete Book for Teachers. Edited by Theresa Armitage and Others. A Singing School series (copyrighted, 1941, by C. C. Birchard & Co.). Sacramento: State Department of Education, 1942.

SELECTED REFERENCES ON RHYTHMS [1]

Bentley, Berenice Benson, and Mathewson, Sophie B. *Music in Playtime.* Chicago: Clayton F. Summy Co., 1948.

A collection of easy melodies for rhythms, singing games, and play activities, with helpful suggestions for nursery school and kindergarten activities.

James, Phoebe. *Accompaniments for Rhythmic Expressions.* Pacific Palisades, California: Phoebe James, 1946.

A book of simple piano arrangements. Contains free rhythms, interpretative rhythms, and creative rhythm sequences.

————. *Songs for Rhythmic Expressions. Primary Grades.* Pacific Palisades, California: Phoebe James, 1944.

Songs descriptive of the rhythms expressed. There are free rhythms, animal rhythms, rhythmic note patterns and percussion ideas. In back of the book songs are arranged for piano.

————. *Harbor Rhythms.* Pacific Palisades, California: Phoebe James, 1948.

A rhythm book concerned with boats, harbor activities, and cargoes.

Oltz, Carle. *Rhythm Time.* Chicago: Clayton F. Summy Co., 1946.

Simple piano arrangements for basic free rhythms and identification rhythms for kindergarten and primary grades.

Rossman, Floy Adele, Editor. *Singing All the Way.* New York: Paull-Pioneer Music Co., 1931.

An inexpensive collection of lullabies, nursery songs, singing games, and folk songs with the words and music that can be used in kindergarten and primary grades.

Salt, Ellis Benton; and Others. *Teaching Physical Education in the Elementary School.* New York: A. S. Barnes & Co., 1942.

---

[1] Consult the bibliography and listing of phonograph records in the appendixes.

Of particular interest to those who wish to introduce creative activities is Chapter 9, pages 188-231. Music is included.

Sehon, Elizabeth; and Others. *Physical Education Methods for Elementary Schools.* Philadelphia: W. B. Saunders Co., 1948.

Chapter 8, "Creative Rhythms" is devoted to problems that puzzle many teachers when the term "creative" is used. Chapter 9, "Folk Singing Games and Folk Dances," discusses procedures in presenting activities, different group formations that are often used, gives definitions of numerous steps used in rhythm patterns and the names of singing games and folk dances, their national background, books where they may be found, and the phonograph record numbers.

Sheehy, Emma Dickson. *There's Music in Children.* New York: Henry Holt & Co., 1946.

Tells parents and teachers how they may bring out the natural love for music inherent in every child. Chapter IV discusses singing games; Chapter V is devoted to the dance and how teachers may help children; Chapter VII deals with the radio and phonograph.

Sutton, Rhoda Reynolds; and Brooks, Elizabeth. *Creative Rhythms.* New York: A. S. Barnes & Co., 1941.

With ever increasing emphasis on creative activity and the deepening realization that children can compose in dance form, hundreds of teachers ask each year, "What and how shall we teach children?" This book will be extremely helpful in supplying suggestions, in lesson development, and in the use of percussion instruments.

Stunts

Stunts for children in the first grade are the performance of simple basic skills. These skills are challenging to a child of this age, however, and should be incorporated in the instructional program.

The following stunts, to be performed by children individually, can be done in the playroom or gymnasium, on the playground, or on a lawn out of doors. Some require playground apparatus.

STUNTS REQUIRING NO APPARATUS

1. Skip for a distance of 20 feet (one foot leading is permissible).
2. Walk a line for 10 feet with one foot touching the line every other step.
3. Hop forward on each foot for 10 feet.
4. Turn somersaults on lawn, mat, strip of carpet, canvas, or linoleum rug.
5. Walk on all fours with knees bent.
6. Swing into space from a low elevation.
7. Sit on heels with hands resting on knees. Waddle forward as ducks do.
8. Move quietly on all fours and stretch forward and back as dogs and cats do.

9. With hands on floor and close to feet, knees straight, walk forward, while using foot and hand on same side of body.

10. Move head directly forward and back as blackbirds do, while walking forward. At the same time lift feet well off the floor.

11. Twirl to the right, then to the left.

STUNTS REQUIRING APPARATUS

1. While grasping low level fence-bar or horizontal bar, turn body over the bar.

2. Climb over and through the climbing apparatus.

3. Swing on a suspended rope.

4. Walk up a slanting plank, while holding onto its sides. Walk down while facing the same way.

5. Climb a low perpendicular or slanting ladder and return to the ground.

6. Use any activity performed on the playground which would be a challenging stunt to other children.

Chapter XV

ACTIVITIES FOR SECOND GRADE

Activities are alphabetically arranged by title within the following three classes:

The games fall into several classes. They are indexed here by type for the convenience of the teacher.

Games

BACK TO BACK

NUMBER OF PLAYERS: 9-21

SPACE: Playground, playroom, gymnasium, auditorium

FORMATION: Players are arranged in couples about the room. They stand back to back with the four elbows hooked. The odd player stands in the center of the playing space. In other words, he is in "the mush pot."

PROCEDURE: At the signal, "Everybody change," partners leave each other and try to hook up with a player across the room. At the same time the odd player tries to get a partner. Players are not safe unless all four elbows are hooked. The game continues with each odd player trying to get a partner.

TEACHING SUGGESTIONS

1. Play five or six times.
2. Give commands sharply and distinctly. A whistle may be used.
3. Have players choose different partners immediately following a hook-up.
4. When boys and girls are playing together, have boys seek girls and girls seek boys unless the numbers are uneven.
5. Use this game for fun night parties.

BIG BLACK BEAR [1]

NUMBER OF PLAYERS: 5-15

SPACE: Playground

PLAYING AREA: A home base or den large enough to hold all the players

FORMATION: One player (the bear) hides, the rest being the seekers.

PROCEDURE: Time is given for the bear to hide, whereupon the seekers, keeping somewhat together, hunt for the bear. As they seek they chant together, "Oh where, oh where is the big black bear?" The bear remains hidden until the seekers are close to him, whereupon he dashes out and tries to tag as many runners as possible before they reach home base. The next bear is chosen by the teacher or the players, or the last person tagged becomes the bear. The game is repeated.

TEACHING SUGGESTIONS

1. Keep children together while hunting the bear.
2. Give praise to the bear who catches the most seekers.

[1] Developed by Margaret Van Voorhees.

BIRD CATCHER

NUMBER OF PLAYERS: 7-16

SPACE: Classroom

PLAYING AREA: A nest and a bird cage are marked at the front corners of the room. Each should be large enough to hold all the players while they stand close together.

FORMATION: A mother bird and a bird catcher are chosen. Each stands near his special area. The remaining players are seated. The names of birds are given to the players, including the mother bird and the bird catcher. There should be several of the same species of bird seated in different parts of the room.

PROCEDURE: The mother bird summons birds of a given species by calling the name so that all can hear. All the birds of that name run to the rear of the room and from there try to reach the nest. The bird catcher may not start chasing until all the birds have reached the rear of the room. Thereafter he may tag as many birds as possible before they reach the nest. Birds so caught go to the cage of the bird catcher. The last two players caught become the new mother bird and bird catcher. If more than one group is playing, that group wins that has the largest number safe in the nest after all runs have been made.

TEACHING SUGGESTIONS

1. Give rows of players the same name, after which all the players in the room change their seats. This will prevent, for example, having all the orioles fly from one general location.
2. As children become expert in dodging, add a second bird catcher.
3. When played out of doors, draw a line opposite the nest and bird cage behind which the birds must stand until summoned by the mother bird.

BOILER, BOILER, BOILER, BLUE

NUMBER OF PLAYERS: 5-12

SPACE: Playground, playroom, gymnasium, auditorium

FORMATION: One player is chosen to be the tagger. The others are scattered about the playing area.

PROCEDURE: The tagger, clasping his hands in front of him, calls out,

> Boiler, boiler, boiler, blue
> If you're careless I'll catch you!

and thereafter tries to tag a player with his clasped hands. If successful, he joins one hand with the tagged player and the two repeat the rhyme and try to tag a third player with their clasped hands. When caught, the third player clasps his own hands, repeats the rhyme, and starts chasing other players. This is continued until all have partners or there is just one player left. The last player to be caught wins the game.

TEACHING SUGGESTIONS

1. Do not permit the players to scatter in too many directions nor too far apart. The area of a basketball court or volleyball court is sufficiently large.
2. Watch for evidence of fatigue and change the taggers if necessary.
3. Do not call a person caught if tagged by a player's free hand.

BOUNDARY TAG

NUMBER OF PLAYERS: 10-20

SPACE: Playground, playroom, gymnasium, auditorium

PLAYING AREA: A square, the length being 20 feet for each side; or a circle with a radius of 15 feet

FORMATION: Players are divided into two or more teams. Each team, standing outside the square, occupies a side of the playing area. Teams face in the same line of direction around the playing area. Players line up behind their captains, each with his arms locked around the waist of the player in front of him.

PROCEDURE: At a signal, teams run forward, following the lines of the playing area. Each captain attempts to tag the end player of the line ahead of him. The tag does not count if the chain of the team is broken. When a captain succeeds in touching the last man of the team ahead of him without having his team break apart, teams reverse directions and begin a new game.

TEACHING SUGGESTIONS

1. Place children at the corners to represent posts, or use Indian clubs, chairs, or jumping standards to mark the playing area. Neither the children representing posts nor other boundary markers may be touched while being passed.
2. When three or four teams compete at the same time, eliminate the team whose end player is tagged. Play until only one team remains.

CAT AND RAT

NUMBER OF PLAYERS: 10-16

SPACE: Playground, gymnasium, hallway, auditorium

FORMATION: A cat and a rat are chosen. The remaining players form a ring by joining hands. The cat is on the outside and the rat on the inside of the ring.

PROCEDURE: The cat tries to catch the rat. The ring players favor the rat, allowing him to run in and out of the circle under their clasped hands. They try to prevent the cat from following the rat by lowering and raising their arms. When caught the rat joins the ring players; the cat becomes the rat and chooses a new cat.

TEACHING SUGGESTIONS

1. Do not permit the cat and rat to run away from the other players.
2. Change the cat and rat if the run is too prolonged, and one or both give evidence of fatigue.
3. When there is a large number of players, form more than one ring or use two or more cats and rats, having the cats designated by a handkerchief tied on the arm or a colored loop extending over one shoulder and under the opposite arm.

CENTER BASE

NUMBER OF PLAYERS: 7-16

SPACE: Playground, playroom, gymnasium, hallway, auditorium

EQUIPMENT: Ball, beanbag, knotted towel, or a leather ball casing stuffed with straw, paper, or other material

FORMATION: Children stand in a single circle all facing the center. Have a distance of at least four feet between the players. One player stands in the center holding the ball.

PROCEDURE: The center player throws the ball to a circle player and leaves the circle immediately. The one to whom the ball was thrown must catch it, take it to the center, place the ball on the ground, and then begin to chase the first player. The former tries to return to the ball and touch it without being tagged. The first player, if tagged, joins the circle players and the second player becomes the thrower. If the first player succeeds in reaching the ball he remains, throws the ball again, and runs.

TEACHING SUGGESTIONS

1. Do not permit the runners to go too far afield. To do so slows up the game.
2. Do not allow a player to run to the point of marked fatigue.
3. If there is a large number of players, have several circles playing the game simultaneously rather than increasing the number in one circle over 16.

CHANGING SEATS

NUMBER OF PLAYERS: 10-40

SPACE: Classroom

FORMATION: Children are seated. Place a book on vacant desks signifying that those seats are not to be used.

PROCEDURE: The leader gives commands such as "Change right!" "Change rear!" "Change front!" "Change left!" "Change two seats forward!" Players stand and move in the direction of the command, then sit down. The players who are forced into the aisle next to a side wall, to the rear, or to the front where there are no seats, run immediately to the vacant seats at the opposite side, front, or rear of the room.

TEACHING SUGGESTIONS

1. Impress upon the children that when they are seated all feet must be kept under the desks.
2. Substitute skipping or hopping.
3. Make commands rapidly and continue until all have had a chance to run.
4. Use this activity to relieve tension after a long period of desk work, or when inclement weather prevents outdoor games.

CROW RACE [1]

NUMBER OF PLAYERS: 5-40

SPACE: Playground, playroom, gymnasium, hallway, auditorium

PLAYING AREA: Two parallel lines 20 feet long and 15 feet apart

FORMATION: Children line up on one line and, with arms outside their knees, grasp their ankles.

PROCEDURE: On a signal, each player hops or walks rapidly toward the opposite line. The one to cross the line first with both feet and with hands still grasping his ankles wins the race.

TEACHING SUGGESTIONS

1. Disqualify children in the race who remove their hands from their ankles.
2. Insist on the strict observance of rules governing relay or other types of races to increase the enjoyment of the game.
3. Teach children to balance while grasping ankles in this position.

---

[1] Developed by Margaret Van Voorhees.

DOUBLE CIRCLE

NUMBER OF PLAYERS: 15-40

SPACE: Playground, hallway, auditorium, gymnasium

FORMATION: Players are arranged in a double circle. Members of one circle face clockwise; members of the second circle face counterclockwise. Thus the two circles will move in opposite directions. One circle has an additional player.

PROCEDURE: On a signal the players skip around in their own circle until a whistle is blown or music is stopped, whereupon each player endeavors to secure a partner from the other circle. The player who fails to secure a partner is said to be in "the mush pot." Play is continued.

A similar game is Last Couple Down; it is often used as an active mixer for older groups. The couples not only must be together, but must squat on the floor when the music stops.

TEACHING SUGGESTIONS

1. When boys and girls play together, do not permit boys to seek boys and girls girls unless the numbers are uneven.
2. Vary the game by having the players run, hop, gallop, or run on tiptoes.
3. Use for party or fun night occasions.

FLOWERS AND THE WIND

NUMBER OF PLAYERS: 10-20

SPACE: Playground, playroom, gymnasium, hallway, auditorium

PLAYING AREA: Two parallel base lines 30 feet long and 50 feet apart

FORMATION: Players are divided into two groups. The groups stand behind the base lines facing each other. One group represents flowers. This group selects a flower name without letting the other side know what the name is. The second group represents the wind.

PROCEDURE: The flowers advance with a skip or run to within a short distance of the base line of the wind. On their arrival the wind players try to guess correctly the name of the flower chosen. When the name is called the flowers turn and run to pass over their base line without being tagged. Each wind player tags as many flower players as possible before the flowers cross their base line to safety. Those tagged join the wind players. The remaining flowers choose a new name and the game is continued until all are caught, whereupon the flowers become the wind and the wind the flowers.

TEACHING SUGGESTIONS

1. Reverse positions of the wind or the flowers following each successful guess.
2. Encourage the timid players to advance close to the opposite base line. If necessary parallel lines may be drawn two or three feet in from the base lines, the flower players being required each time to toe the line.
3. Do not allow wind players to stand on or over their base line while trying to guess a flower name.

HOUND AND RABBIT

NUMBER OF PLAYERS: 10-16

SPACE: Playground, playroom, gymnasium, auditorium, hallway

FORMATION: Players stand in sets of three, scattered about the playing area with a distance of from 8 to 12 feet between sets. Two players of each set stand with their hands joined and facing each other. The third player stands inside the small circle made by the joined hands. The former represent hollow trees, the latter rabbits inside the trees. Two players of the group are unassigned, one being a homeless rabbit, the other a hound.

PROCEDURE: The hound chases the rabbit. The latter may take refuge in any tree by dodging under the arms of two players. As soon as the hunted rabbit enters a tree the rabbit already there must try to reach another tree, as no tree may shelter two rabbits at a time. The hound then chases the second rabbit. If the hound catches a rabbit by tagging him, the positions are reversed and the chase continues.

TEACHING SUGGESTIONS

1. Give all children the opportunity to be runners; therefore, make three changes in playing positions before finishing the game.
2. Do not permit certain trees to be used over and over but see that the trees are so located that all will be available.
3. Watch for signs of fatigue and change the runners as it seems necessary.
4. Do not permit long runs but insist that nearby trees be entered.

HUMPTY DUMPTY, STRAWBERRY PIE

NUMBER OF PLAYERS: 5-40

SPACE: Classroom

EQUIPMENT: Cork, spool of thread, nail, or ink eraser

FORMATION: All but one player leave the room or while seated cover their ears and with foreheads resting on the desks close their eyes.

PROCEDURE: The odd player hides the selected object some place within the room, accessible to all but not too much in evidence. The children are told to return to the room or to open their eyes and hunt for the object.

As the children discover the hiding place, they go to their seats as quietly and inconspicuously as possible; when seated, and not before, each announces, "Humpty Dumpty, Strawberry Pie!" Play continues until all have spotted the object or until the teacher calls off the hunt. The child who first discovers the object becomes the player to rehide it.

TEACHING SUGGESTIONS

1. Teach children to keep a secret and control the announcement of discovery as a game objective.
2. Impress on the children that they should in no way indicate to others where the object is located.

LOOK OUT FOR THE BEARS [1]

NUMBER OF PLAYERS: 5-16

SPACE: Playground

FORMATION: One child is chosen to be the bear. The rest of the players occupy a den.

PROCEDURE: The group members turn their backs on the bear and count to two hundred. The bear hides during the counting. When the counting is finished children scatter to find the bear. The first child to find the bear calls loudly, "Look out for the bear!" whereupon all the players race for the den. Those tagged by the bear before reaching safety join him, counting is repeated, and the bears hide together. The game continues until all are caught. The last one tagged becomes the new bear.

TEACHING SUGGESTIONS

1. Discourage peeking by members of the group.
2. Encourage the bear to tag as many runners as possible during each running period.

LOST CHILD [1]

NUMBER OF PLAYERS: 5-20

SPACE: Classroom, playground

FORMATION: One child is called to the front of the room and stands with his back toward the children. He is the guesser.

---

[1] Developed by Margaret Van Voorhees.

PROCEDURE: The teacher signals for some child to leave the room or to hide in some convenient place. Thereupon the remaining children exchange seats. The guesser turns about and tries to guess which child left the room. If he finds it difficult, some assistance may be offered but it must not be too obvious. If successful in naming the absent player, the guesser has another turn. If unsuccessful, the player is retired. A new guesser is chosen and a new player leaves the room.

MIDNIGHT

NUMBER OF PLAYERS: 6-20

SPACE: Playground, playroom, gymnasium, auditorium

PLAYING AREA: A fox's den and a sheepfold some distance away from the den

FORMATION: One player, the fox, is in his den; the others, the sheep, are in the sheepfold.

PROCEDURE: The fox leaves his den and wanders around the meadow, whereupon the sheep sally forth and, approaching the fox, ask him, "What time is it, Mr. Fox?" Should the fox say, "Three o'clock," or "Five o'clock," or "Ten o'clock," the sheep are safe but when the fox says, "Midnight!" the sheep must run for the sheepfold, as the fox may then begin to chase them. The fox tags as many sheep as he can before they find shelter in the fold. The caught sheep go to the fox's den and thereafter assist the first fox in capturing sheep. The original fox is always the first one to leave the den. The last sheep caught becomes the fox for the new game.

TEACHING SUGGESTIONS

1. When there are two or more foxes chasing, have all of them, while running, hold the right or left arm high in the air, letting the sheep know which players are the foxes.
2. Do not permit the players to scatter over too large an area. Often the shadow cast by the building can be used as the playing area.

MOVING DAY

NUMBER OF PLAYERS: 12-40

SPACE: Classroom

PLAYING AREA: Children sitting in adjacent rows play the game together. Vacant seats in each row and one additional one for the two rows must be marked by having a book placed on each one. The seats of these desks may not be used.

FORMATION: For each two rows a renter is chosen who walks up and down the street between the houses.

PROCEDURE: As the renter moves along the street the house owners in front and behind him exchange homes. The renter tries to get one of the vacant houses. If successful the new renter begins his house hunting.

TEACHING SUGGESTIONS

1. If the game is dragging, have the leader call, "It's May Day!" whereupon everyone in the room seeks a new residence in a new part of town, but he may not occupy any house on the street where he formerly resided.
2. Insist that feet must be kept out of the aisles.

NUMBERS EXCHANGE

NUMBER OF PLAYERS: 9-15

SPACE: Classroom

FORMATION: All players are numbered. One is chosen to be the tagger. He stands with his back against the front wall of the room. The remaining players sit at their desks. Books are placed on the desks of the seats that are not to be used.

PROCEDURE: The leader calls out two numbers. The players with those numbers try to exchange seats without being caught by the tagger. The tagger may not take a vacant seat but must try to tag a runner. A runner may not return to his own seat once he has left it. If a runner is tagged he becomes the tagger. The former tagger returns to his own seat. The game continues.

TEACHING SUGGESTIONS

1. Impress on the children that feet must be kept under the desks and out of the aisles.
2. Do not permit the tagger to leave the wall until the numbers have been announced.
3. As skill is gained, use two taggers.

RING CALL BALL

NUMBER OF PLAYERS: 6-16

SPACE: Playground, playroom, gymnasium, auditorium, hallway

EQUIPMENT: Ball, beanbag, knotted towel, or stuffed leather ball casing, one for each group of players.

FORMATION: Players are divided into groups of not more than eight players. Each group forms its own circle, and elects a center player, who is given the ball.

PROCEDURE: The center player of each circle calls the name of a player of his group and then throws the ball high into the air. The one called runs forward and tries to catch the ball on the fly or following the first bounce. If the player catches the ball he becomes the thrower. If he does not catch the ball he returns to his place in the circle and the former thrower rethrows the ball.

TEACHING SUGGESTIONS

1. When the names of children are not known, give the members of each group a number, beginning with number one.
2. Insist that the name or number be announced before the ball leaves the hands of the center thrower.

SPIDER AND FLIES

NUMBER OF PLAYERS: 6-16

SPACE: Playground, playroom, gymnasium, auditorium

PLAYING AREA: Two goal areas marked off some 40 feet apart. Halfway between them a circle is drawn on the ground, the size depending on the number of persons to play.

FORMATION: One player is chosen to be the spider and crouches in the center of the circle. The remaining players, the flies, occupy the two goals.

PROCEDURE: The flies advance and, walking, skipping, or running, move around close to the circumference of the circle. All travel in the same direction. At any time the spider may give chase to the flies, tagging as many as possible before the flies reach a goal. If tagged, a fly becomes a spider and joins the first spider in his circle. The original spider always gives the chasing signal; hence other spiders may not leave the circle until the signal is given. The last fly caught becomes the first spider for a new game.

TEACHING SUGGESTIONS

1. Encourage timid flies to approach and keep close to the circle while moving around it.
2. Have the circle large enough to hold all the players when standing close together.

Rhythmical Activities

A-HUNTING WE WILL GO

Music: "Hunting" [1]

Victor Record No. 22759

Line 1. Oh, a-hunting we will go,
    2. A-hunting we will go,
    3. We'll catch a fox and put him in a box,
    4. And then we'll let him go.

FORMATION: Sets of two parallel lines, not more than six players. Partners face each other, boys on one side, girls on the other side.

DESCRIPTION

Lines 1-2. The first (head) couple join hands and skip down between the lines. The other players stand in place and clap their hands in rhythm.

Lines 3-4. The head couple face about (turning inward without losing the grasp) and return to the head of their set.

Chorus. Partners in each set join hands and skip to the left in a circle, following the head couple. When the head couple reach the place previously occupied by the last or end couple, they form an arch under which all the others skip.

The second couple now becomes the head couple. The game is repeated until all have regained their original positions.

Hunting

Old Game

[1] Music from *Our First Music*. Sacramento: California State Board of Education, 1942. By permission of C. C. Birchard & Co.

CHIMES OF DUNKIRK [1]

Victor Record No. 21618.

First Pattern

Formation: A single circle, boys and girls alternating, is formed. Partners face each other with hands on own hips.

Description

Measures 1-2.   All stamp (not too heavily) left, right, left.

Measures 3-4.   All raise arms over head (so that faces can be seen between the arms). All bend bodies sharply to the left and clap hands over head; bend to the right and clap, bend to the left and clap. This represents the ringing of the town's bells.

Measures 5-7.   Partners take each other's hands with arms extended sideways. Starting with the left foot, they run in a small circle while turning their partners once around.

Measure 8.   Players run forward on the last measure and secure a new partner.

The dance is continued until the music ends.

[1] C. Ward Crampton, *The Folk Dance Book.* New York: A. S. Barnes & Co., 1909. By permission.

SECOND PATTERN [1]

FORMATION: A double circle is formed, partners facing, boys on the outside

DESCRIPTION

Measures 1-2. All stamp left, right, left.

Measures 3-4. All raise arms and clap as described in First Pattern.

Measures 5-8. Starting with the left foot, all turn partners once with seven running steps. On Measures 7 and 8, each player moves to his or her left and secures a new partner.

The dance is continued until the music ends.

COME, SKIP WITH ME [2]

1. Come, skip with me,
   Partners we'll be,
   Round in the ring we're dancing.
2. See, here we stand;
3. Now, shake my hand;
4. Then off we are prancing.

FORMATION: A single circle, boys and girls alternating, is formed. Several boys or girls are selected to go inside the circle.

DESCRIPTION: Children inside the circle perform the actions.

1. Boys choose partners and dance around with them in own small circles or around the inside of the big circle.
2. Partners face and drop hands.
3. Partners shake each other's right hands.
4. With right hands still joined and left hands on hips, they skip around in small circles.

The dance is repeated, all shaking left hands instead of right.

The game is repeated, with boys returning to circle positions and girls inside the circle choosing new partners. A child should not be allowed to choose a player for a second time if other children have not been chosen. The game can be played with both boys and girls in the center, each choosing a partner of the opposite sex.

---

[1] A very useful pattern for fun night parties.
[2] Valborg Kastman and Greta Köhler, *Swedish Song Games.* Boston: Ginn & Co., 1913. By permission.

Come, Skip with Me

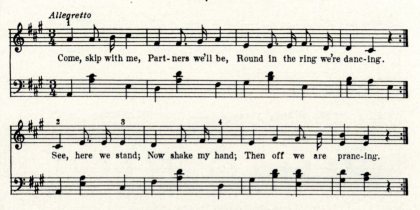

Come, skip with me, Part-ners we'll be, Round in the ring we're danc-ing.

See, here we stand; Now shake my hand; Then off we are pranc-ing.

DANCE OF GREETING [1]
(Danish)

Victor Record No. 20432

FORMATION: Children form a single circle. All, with hands on hips, face the center. Each boy stands on the left side of his partner.

DESCRIPTION

Measure 1. All clap, clap, turn toward partners; boy bows and girl curtsies.

Measure 2. All repeat but turn their backs on partners during the clapping and bow to their neighbors.

Measure 3. All stamp with the right foot, stamp with the left foot.

Measure 4. Each person turns around to his or her place with four running steps. Partners may turn left or turn right as each desires or the entire group may turn to the left or to the right.

Measures 1-4 repeated. Steps are repeated from the beginning.

Measures 5-8 (Chorus). All join hands and run to the right or left for four measures—16 steps. They take four running steps to a measure. This will need practice.

Measures 5-8 repeated. Running steps are repeated in the opposite direction.

[1] M. R. Wild and D. E. White, *Physical Education for Elementary Schools.* Cedar Falls, Iowa: Iowa State Teacher's College, 1924. By permission.

Dance of Greeting

Arranged by Grace Van Ness

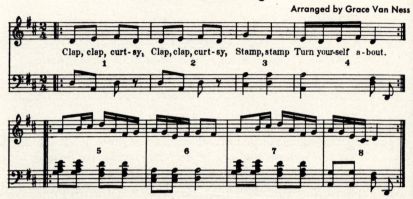

Clap, clap, curt-sy, Clap, clap, curt-sy, Stamp, stamp Turn your-self a-bout.

NOTES. This game can be played in the aisles of the schoolroom. Two rows of children face and form an elongated circle around a row of desks and play in that formation. If music is not available the words can be sung.

Instead of running around the desks, children may join hands and, holding them high, take a brisk run in place. This latter variation is an excellent one to use with adults who have been sitting in auditorium seats for a long period of time.

I SEE YOU [1]

Victor Record No. 20432

FORMATION: This is a longways dance, with four lines of dancers, arranged as in the following diagram:

(a)	x	x	x	x	x	x	(boys)
(b)	o	o	o	o	o	o	(girls)
(c)	x	x	x	x	x	x	(boys)
(d)	o	o	o	o	o	o	(girls)

Lines *a* and *b* face lines *c* and *d*, and between *b* and *c* there should be enough space to permit players to skip in small circles.

DESCRIPTION: Players in lines *a* and *d* play peekaboo with each other by bending alternately to the left and the right of the partner in front, with hands on the partner's shoulder. At 1, they look over the left shoulder; at 2, over the right shoulder. At "Ti-ra-la's" the tempo of the peekaboo is doubled. At 12 (Measure 9) the rear players clap their hands once, and start skipping forward; passing to the left of partners, they meet in the center. There they take hands and continue skipping to the left in small

---

[1] Valborg Kastman and Greta Köhler, *op. cit.* By permission of Ginn & Co., publishers. Words by courtesy of Jacob Bolin.

circles. At 13 (Measure 13) they clap once again, separate, and return to their own partners, take hands, and skip once around to the left with them. At the end, the former rear players (lines *a* and *d*) stop in front of their partners and lines *b* and *c* become the rear players and repeat the game. All players sing the words.

I See You

LAZY MARY [1]

FORMATION: A mother and daughter are in the center of a ring of players, the daughter kneeling with closed eyes.

DESCRIPTION: Mother advances and sings:

> Lazy Mary, will you get up,
> Will you get up, will you get up,
> Lazy Mary, will you get up,
> Will you get up to-day?

[1] From William Wells Newell, *Games and Songs of American Children.* New York: Harper & Bros., 1911. By permission.

Lazy Mary

La - zy Ma - ry, will you get up, will you get up, will you get up?

La - zy Ma - ry, will you get up, Will you get up to - day?___

Mary sings:

> What will you give me for my breakfast,
> If I get up, if I get up,
> What will you give me for my breakfast,
>   If I get up to-day?

The reply is, "A slice of bread and a cup of tea," whereupon Mary answers, "No, mother, I won't get up," and responds similarly to the call to dinner; but for supper the mother offers, "A nice young man with rosy cheeks," which is accepted with the words, "Yes, mother, I will get up," whereupon the ring members clap their hands.

> Others are chosen and the game continues.
> The round is familiar in New York streets.

LONDON BRIDGE [1]

Lon - don Bridge is fall - ing down, fall - ing down, fall - ing down,

Lon - don Bridge is fall - ing down, my fair la - dy.

---

[1] William Wells Newell. *op. cit.* By permission of Harper & Bros., publishers.

Verse 2. What did the robber do to you? do to you, do to you?
What did the robber do to you, my fair lady?

3. He broke my watch and stole my keys, stole my keys,
He broke my watch and stole my keys, my fair lady.

4. Then off to prison she must go, she must go,
Then off to prison she must go, my fair lady.

Victor Record No. 20806

FORMATION: Two players with uplifted hands form an arch, representing the bridge under which the train of children passes as they sing, each clinging to the garments of his predecessor and hurrying to get safely by.

DESCRIPTION: As the words "off to prison she must go" are sung, the person passing under the arch of the bridge is caught by the lowered arms of the guardians of the bridge. They take him off to the side and ask, "Will you have a diamond necklace or a gold pin?" "a rose or a cabbage?" or some equivalent question. The keepers have already privately agreed which of the two of these objects he shall represent, and, according to the prisoner's choice, he is placed behind one of the two keepers. When all are caught, the game ends with a tug of war, the two sides pulling against each other; the line which does not break is declared the winner.

MARUSAKI [1]

FORMATION: All players stand in the aisles of the schoolroom or auditorium, or they may form a circle.

Verse 1. Marusaki (1) lives in far Japan,
She wears a long dress and waves a fan.
When (2) she makes a bow, she bends so low,
She (3) sits on a mat on her heels just so.

2. She (4) learns to do writing with a brush
Always very careful, never in a rush,
She (5) makes a low bow and bids us come (6)
To see the fete of chrysanthemum.

3. Then (7) away we'll haste to fair Japan,
Each one with a sunshade and a fan;
When the visit's over, home we'll come,
Each one bringing home a chrysanthemum.

DESCRIPTION: Each person sings and performs the following pantomime as the appropriate point is reached in the song.

---

[1] State of New York, *General Plan and Syllabus for Physical Training*. University of the State of New York, 1925. By permission.

Marusaki

Mar - u - sa - ki lives in far Ja - pan,

She wears a long dress and waves a fan:

When she makes a bow, she bends so - o low,

she sits on a mat on her heels just so.

Verse 1 . (1) Points to far-away place. Makes gesture to long dress and waves a fan. (2) Begins Japanese bow by placing one hand on one knee and dropping to the floor on that knee; then the other hand and knee; at "low" drops head toward the floor. (3) Sits back on heels and remains until (5).

Verse 2. (4) Through eight measures holds one hand as if holding a paper, and makes printing motions with the other hand. (5) Rises to knees and bows head. (6) Stands, using hands as in (1).

Verse 3. (7) Moves forward for the first line of the verse, backward for the second line, etc., with short steps on toes, two steps to a measure.

NUTS IN MAY [1]

Music: "Mulberry Bush," page 352.

1. Here we come gathering nuts in May,
   Nuts in May, nuts in May.
   Here we come gathering nuts in May,
   On a cold and frosty morning.

2. Whom will you have for nuts in May,
   Nuts in May, nuts in May?
   Whom will you have for nuts in May
   On a cold and frosty morning?

3. We'll have (Mary) for nuts in May,
   Nuts in May, nuts in May,
   We'll have (Mary) for nuts in May,
   On a cold and frosty morning.

[1] Jessie H. Bancroft, *Games.* New York: The Macmillan Co., 1937. By permission.

4. Whom will you send to fetch her away,
    To fetch her away, to fetch her away?
   Whom will you send to fetch her away,
    On a cold and frosty morning?

5. We'll send (Alice) to fetch her away,
    To fetch her away, to fetch her away,
   We'll send (Alice) to fetch her away,
    On a cold and frosty morning.

FORMATION: The players stand in two facing lines, with a wide space between them which will permit the lines to advance toward each other and retreat. Each player clasps the hands of his neighbors to the right and the left.

DESCRIPTION: The first line sings the first verse, advancing toward its opponents and retreating. The second line then advances and retreats and sings the second verse. The first line again advances and retreats, singing the third verse, naming some player who stands in the opposing line. The second line, unwilling to yield a player so easily, then advances and retires, singing the fourth verse, in which it suggests that some one be sent to take the one who has been selected for "nuts," and the first line then advances and retires, singing the last verse, in which it names some player from its own side whom it considers a good match for the player called from the opposite side. The lines then stand still while these two players advance to the center, draw a mark on the ground, or throw a handkerchief down to serve the purpose, take hold of right hands across the line, and have a tug of war. The player who is pulled across the line becomes the captured "nut" and joins the side of his captors. The game is then repeated, with the change that the lines of players sing the verses that were sung by their opponents the previous time, the second line of players starting with the first verse. This should be continued until all of the players have taken part in the tug of war. The line wins which gets the more "nuts."

Variations: For a large number of players, instead of a tug of war between two players only, the two lines may advance, each player joining hands with the one opposite, and all taking part in the tug of war. Still another method is to have the two players who are named join hands, with the players of their respective sides all lined up behind them for a tug of war, as in London Bridge.

PUSSY CAT, PUSSY CAT

Music: See page 354.

1. Pussy cat, pussy cat,
2. Where have you been?
3. I've been to London to visit the queen.
4. Pussy cat, pussy cat,
5. What did you there?
6. I frightened a little mouse under the chair.

FORMATION: All form a double circle, partners facing, those on the outside numbered 1's, those on the inside 2's.

DESCRIPTION: Number 1's ask the questions.

1. Number 1's shake right forefinger at partner. Number 2's stand still and look somewhat surprised.
2. Number 1's clap hands four times. Number 2's still look surprised and back away slightly.
3. Number 2's make a curtsy if girls, or a bow if boys, while Number 1's stand still.
4. Number 1's shake fingers again.
5. Number 1's clap hands four times in rhythm.
6. Partners join hands and twirl around in their own small circle.

SEVEN STEPS [1]
(Austrian Version)

Methodist Record No. 101

FORMATION: All form in couples, with partners side by side, the girl on the right of the man, with inside hands joined. The couples arrange themselves one behind the other in circle formation. (The dance may be done in column formation with no change of partners.)

DESCRIPTION: The basic step is a walk.

Measures 1-4. Seven steps forward. Beginning with the outside foot, the boy with the left foot and the girl with the right, all run seven steps forward and pause on the eighth count.

Measures 5-8. Seven steps backward. Beginning with the inside foot, all run backward seven steps and pause as before.

Measures 9-10. Three steps apart. Partners release hands and, beginning with the outside foot, run three steps away from each other and pause on the 4th count of measure.

---

[1] The World of Fun Series. Produced by the Audio-Visual Department of the Methodist Church, Nashville, Tennessee, 1947. By permission. May be purchased with records from the Methodist Publishing House, 85 McAllister Street, San Francisco 2, and 125 East Sunset Boulevard, Los Angeles 12.

Measures 11-12. Three steps back together. Beginning with the inside foot, partners run three steps toward each other and pause.

Measures 13-16. Swing. Partners swing once around in place with eight running steps, holding hands as they run.

Measures 17-18. Three steps apart. Releasing their grasp, partners run three steps away from each other and pause.

Measures 19-20. Three steps back together. Partners take three steps toward a new partner and pause, the boy moving forward to the next girl to his left.

Measures 21-24. Swing. New partners swing as before, and finish in position, with inside hands joined, ready to begin again.

SEVEN STEPS [1]
(Variation)

Methodist Record No. 101

FORMATION: Couples form a circle, facing clockwise, boys on the inside. Partners join inside hands.

DESCRIPTION

Measures 1-4. Beginning with the outside foot (boy's right, girl's left), partners take seven running steps forward, two to each measure. They stamp on seven and pause.

Measures 5-8. Beginning with the outside foot again, they take seven running steps backward, stamp on seven and pause.

Measures 9-10. Moving sidewise, away from each other, beginning with outside foot, partners take three running steps, and hop on the outside foot.

Measures 11-12. Moving toward each other, both take three running steps, hop on inside foot, face partner and take shoulder-waist position.

Measures 13-16. Partners step hop together around in place.

Measures 17-18. Repeat measures 9-10.

Measures 19-20. They repeat measures 11-12. (All move to a new partner.)

Measures 21-24. They repeat measures 13-16.

---

[1] *We Sing.* Boston: C. C. Birchard & Co., 1940. By permission.

Seven Steps

Adapted by David Stevens

Finnish, Norwegian, or
German Song Dance
Piano by Gladys Pitcher

THE SLEEPING MAN [1]

Music: See "Mulberry Bush," page 352.

> Here we go 'round the sleeping man,
> The sleeping man,
> Sleeping man,
> Here we go 'round the sleeping man,
> So early in the morning!
>
> He will wake up and try to catch us,
> Try to catch us,
> Try to catch us,
> He will wake up and try to catch us,
> This bright and happy morning.

FORMATION: Dancers form a single circle, with boys and girls alternating. All join hands. One or more sleepers are in the center, depending on the size of the group.

DESCRIPTION: Circle players walk or skip around the center players. At the conclusion of the song those in the circle drop hands and run for a goal or goals that have been selected, while the sleeping man (men) tries to catch as many as he can. All caught go to the center and become helpers of the sleeping man.

THE SNAIL [2]

FORMATION: A single circle is formed, all facing left. Each one reaches backward with his left hand and takes the right hand of the person behind him. One person is the leader.

DESCRIPTION: The group may walk, run, or skip.

1. The leader walks around and around in an ever-decreasing circle, so that at the end of the verse he is at the center of a spiral of players.

2. The leader countermarches so as to unwind the spiral.

> 1. Hand in hand you see us well,
>   Creep like a snail into his shell.
>   Ever nearer, ever nearer,
>   Ever closer, ever closer,
>   Very snug, indeed, you dwell,
>   Snail within your tiny shell.

[1] Used by permission of Pasadena Public Schools.
[2] From C. Ward Crampton and M. A. Wollaston, *The Song Play Book.* New York: A. S. Barnes & Co., 1917. By permission.

The Snail

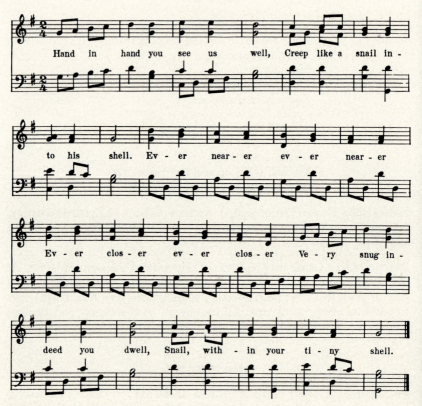

Hand in hand you see us well, Creep like a snail into his shell. Ev - er near - er ev - er near - er
Ev - er clos - er ev - er clos - er Ve - ry snug indeed you dwell, Snail, with - in your ti - ny shell.

2. Hand in hand you see us well,
Creep like a snail out of his shell.
Ever farther, ever farther,
Ever wider, ever wider,
Who'd have thought this little shell
Could have held us all so well.

THE SWING [1]

FORMATION: Groups of three form circles. Two players join inside hands to form the seat of the swing. The third child stands behind them. Grasping their arms, the third child "pushes the swing" in rhythm.

---

[1] State of Missouri *Course of Study, Physical Education for Elementary Schools.* By permission. See also *Our First Music.* Sacramento: California State Department of Education, 1942. "Swinging," p. 6.

DESCRIPTION

Measures 1-3.   Members on the left place the left foot forward; players on the right place the right foot forward. All sway forward and lift the heel of the supporting foot. The rear foot is lifted from the ground. At the same time the arms of all three are raised forward and up. All sway back onto the rear foot, lifting the front foot, and at the same time swing the arms down and back. This movement is continued for 7 measures.

Measure 4.   The children forming the swing raise their joined hands. The person swinging runs under their arms and on to the next group.

Measure 5.   The pattern is repeated as often as desired.
    The positions of players are changed so that all experience the fun of pushing the swing.

The Swing

TURN ME 'ROUND [1]

Words and Music by C. J. Barnett

Turn me 'round, turn me 'round, turn me 'round, clap, clap, clap.

Turn me 'round, turn me 'round, turn me 'round, clap, clap, clap.

Slide to the side, slide to the side, slide to the side,—stamp, stamp, stamp.

Slide to the side, slide to the side, slide to the side,—Clap - Bow.

FORMATION: A double circle is formed, partners facing, boys on the inside.

DESCRIPTION: Children may sing words as they perform the dance.

Measures 1-3.   Partners link right arms; they take small running steps, turning partner in place and back to original position (12 steps).

Measure 4.   Each releases partner's arm and claps own hands three times and holds (or claps partner's hands).

Measures 5-7.   Linking partner's left arm, each takes small running steps, turning partner (12 steps).

Measure 8.   Each releases partner's arm and claps own hands three times and holds.

Measures 1-8 repeated.

---

[1] Words and music from Cecille Jean Barnett, *Games, Rhythms, Dances.* Oshkosh, Wis.: J. O. Frank & Sons, 1941. By permission.

Measures 9-11. Each faces partner, hands on hips (or takes partner's hands, arms extended), and slides. Outside circle players take six slide steps to the right, while inside circle players take six slides to the left.

Measure 12. All stamp feet three times and hold.

Measures 13-15. Facing partner, hands on hips, outside circle players take six slide steps to the left, inside players to the right.

Measure 16. All clap own hands once and bow to partner. Girls make peasant curtsy and boys bow from the hips. (Note: If necessary, review peasant curtsy, page 205.)

Measures 9-16 repeated.

The entire dance is repeated.

ADDITIONAL RHYTHMICAL ACTIVITIES IN CALIFORNIA STATE SERIES MUSIC TEXTBOOKS

New Music Horizons. Second Book. Edited by Osbourne McConathy and Others. (Copyrighted, 1944, 1948, by Silver Burdett Co.) Sacramento: California State Department of Education (edition in preparation).

Students' book and book of accompaniments and interpretation for the teacher. Page references are to the latter book.

Our Songs. Edited by Theresa Armitage, Peter W. Dykema, and Gladys Pitcher. A Singing School series (copyrighted, 1939, 1940, by C. C.

Birchard & Co.). Sacramento: California State Department of Education, 1942.[1]

Students' book, teacher's manual, and book of accompaniments. Page references are to the last named book.

Copying Mother	6	Big Brown Bear	54
My Funny Jumping Jack	7	Minuet from Don Juan	94
Hobby Horse	15	The Waves and I	105
Trot, Trot, Trot	16	My Fiddle	118
Nelly Bly	18		

SELECTED REFERENCES ON RHYTHMS [2]

Annis, Elsie K., and Mathews, Janet. *Rhythmic Activities* (The World of Music). New York: Ginn & Co., 1944.

Schmidt, Anna, and Ashton, Dudley. *Characteristic Rhythms for Children.* New York: A. S. Barnes & Co., 1931.

Twenty-seven musical selections are given, with suggestions for their use.

Shafer, Mary S., and Mosher, Mary Morgan. *Rhythms for Children.* New York: A. S. Barnes & Co., 1938.

Music and action possibilities are given for 44 activities.

Stunts

The simple skills of Grade I should be used as a basis for the teaching of new stunts and more complicated skills in Grade II.

A warm-up period should precede any practice of stunts.

Many of the stunts taught in this grade require no apparatus and can be performed indoors or outdoors. A few others are designed for use with playground equipment.

STUNTS REQUIRING NO APPARATUS

Hop.   Hop forward on one foot for 10 feet. Turn and hop back on the other foot. The elevated foot should not touch the ground during the hopping.

Walk.   Walk a line for 20 feet with the inner border of the right foot touching the line every other step. Repeat, with the left foot touching the line.

Skip.   Skip for 40 or 50 feet, using right and left foot alternately.

Line Walking.   With body erect, arms extended sidewards, walk a line for 10 feet with one foot in front of the other and on the line each step.

---

[1] Former series (adoption period July 1, 1942, to July 1, 1950).
[2] Consult the bibliography and listing of phonograph records in the appendixes.

Jump.   Jump forward for 20 feet using both feet simultaneously.

Somersaults.   Turn somersaults on a mat or on the lawn in order to get the feeling of "heels over head."

Stiff Knee Walk.   Walk on all fours with knees stiff.

Rabbit Hop.   Imitate a rabbit. Squat and place the hands on the floor. With a jump bring the feet even with the hands. Advance hands again. The knees are kept together and are brought up to a position inside the hands.

Airplane Zooming.   Jump into the air and make a quarter turn to the right. Repeat three times more to make a complete turn. Repeat, turning to the left.

STUNTS REQUIRING APPARATUS OR EQUIPMENT

Climb Through the Stick.   Grasping the ends of a stick (a broom handle will serve) in front of the body, climb through the stick by bringing first one leg and then the other between the stick and the arms, and by moving the stick up over the back and head and down in front of the body. Move the stick backwards to the starting position without letting go.

Ladder Walking.   Walk up a slanting ladder holding on to the sides. Back down without changing position.

Fence Climbing.   Climb up, over, and down a practice fence.

Monkey Swing.   Hang by the arms and swing the body back and forth. Keep the knees and ankles together throughout the swings.

Hang and Drop.   Hang from playground apparatus and drop to the ground. As feet contact the ground, bend the knees and ankles, thus preventing a severe jar.

Horizontal Ladder Travel.   Travel forward across the ladder by grasping each rung of the ladder.

Chapter XVI
ACTIVITIES FOR THIRD GRADE

The activities are alphabetically arranged by title within the following four classes:

The games fall into several classes. They are indexed here by type for the convenience of the teacher.

Games

BALL PASS

NUMBER OF PLAYERS: 5-15

SPACE: Playground, playroom, gymnasium

EQUIPMENT: (1) Soft rubber ball, 15-inch playground baseball, knotted towel, beanbag, or slightly deflated basketball, volleyball, or soccer ball; (2) a base for each child with the exception of one player. The bases should be scattered about the playing area but should not be too far removed from each other. The bases may be made from the ends of boxes, sandbags, beanbags made of canvas, pieces of wood, squares of heavy wrapping paper, corrugated paper, cardboard, linoleum, or small circles chalked on hard surface.

FORMATION: One player is appointed to be the rover. He has no base and is given the ball. Other players stand with one foot in contact with their individual bases.

PROCEDURE: Players on the bases beckon to one another to exchange bases. As they seek to reach each other's bases, the rover, while standing still, tries to hit one of the runners with the ball. If he succeeds, he takes the base of the player struck with the ball, and the play continues with a new rover. The rover may steal a base whenever he can reach a vacant one, in which case the player who left the base becomes the rover.

TEACHING SUGGESTIONS

1. Have the rover retrieve the ball after throwing it and missing a player, unless it goes outside the area occupied by the bases. In that case, have the nearest player bring it into the area and pass it to the rover. The player's base cannot be stolen, nor may he be struck with the ball while he is off base for the purpose of securing the ball.
2. If the number to play is large, form several groups, each with its own bases and ball.
3. Have each group appoint its own captain whose duty it will be to keep the game going at a lively pace once the rules are mastered.
4. Advise children to throw the ball ahead of a running player.

BALL PASSING

NUMBER OF PLAYERS: 6-40

SPACE: Playground, playroom, gymnasium

EQUIPMENT: Five or six objects of various sizes and weights: basketball, tennis ball, rubber ball, soccer ball, volleyball or baseball, knotted towels, beanbags, or sticks of wood

FORMATION: Divide the players into two or more teams depending on the number to play. Each team is given a name or number. Players of both teams form a single circle, facing inward.

PROCEDURE: The game is played for a given number of minutes with as many repetitions as desired.

The teacher starts an object around the circle, then additional objects or balls are introduced until five or six are being passed. Those children who miss an object or ball must secure it and put it into play as soon as possible. Circle players should not try to give a new ball or object to a player having difficulty with an object or ball.

SCORING: Each time players drop or miss an object it scores against their team. The player must call loudly the name or number of his team on missing the object. He remains in the game. The team with the lower score at the end of the playing time wins.

TEACHING SUGGESTIONS

1. Keep the score or appoint a scorekeeper and assist him in his duties.
2. As the children gain proficiency, increase the distance between them.
3. Stop play if necessary to impress on the children that when they miss they must call loudly the name or number of their team.

BASES ON BALLS [1]

NUMBER OF PLAYERS: 8-20

SPACE: Playground, gymnasium

PLAYING AREA: Baseball diamond with bases 35 feet apart

EQUIPMENT: (1) Soccer ball, 10-inch rubber ball, beanbag, or knotted towel [2]; (2) whistle

FORMATION: Players are divided into two teams, and players of each team are numbered to establish rotation order. When all members of a team have kicked, a half inning is finished and the other team has its turn. Team A sends player Number 1 to field balls within the diamond. Remaining players stand behind the line connecting third and home bases. Number 1 of Team B stands behind home plate, and remaining members of his team line up behind the line connecting first and home bases.

PROCEDURE: The player at home base places the ball on the surface of home plate. Taking one step, he kicks the ball and immediately starts around the bases, touching each in turn. The runner tries to reach home

---

[1] Used through courtesy of Los Angeles Public Schools.
[2] A knotted towel or beanbag is thrown, not kicked.

base before the fielder secures the ball and returns with it to home plate. As soon as the fielder touches home plate with a foot or the ball while the ball is in his hand, the runner must stop where he is. The bases he has touched are recorded. His run is finished and he retires to end position on his team. Number 2 on the kicking team then steps to home plate and Number 2 of the fielding team enters the diamond. Play continues.

Fly Ball: If a fielder catches a fly ball (a kicked or thrown ball before it touches the ground), no score is made by kicker and a new player from each team takes his position.

Fair Ball: A ball that travels within the area outlined by home plate and first and third bases is a fair ball.

Line Ball: A line ball (one that lands on a boundary line) is a good ball and continues in play.

Second Trial: A player is allowed a second kick if on the first try he fails to send the ball within the official court boundaries. On a second failure, his play is finished and he retires to end position of his team.

SCORING: The kicking team scores for each base reached before the fielder contacts home plate, as follows: 1 point when first base is reached; 2 points when second base is reached; 3 points for third base; 4 points for home base. The team wins whose members score the higher number of points at the end of an agreed upon number of innings or at the end of the playing period.

TEACHING SUGGESTIONS

1. Simplify the game by having the person at batting position throw the object instead of kicking.
2. Have those kicking keep their eyes on the ball until the kick is made.
3. Change position of the teams when five players on both teams have run or fielded. On the return of teams to their former position those who have not performed will begin the play.
4. Have children manage their own game by having a child with a whistle stationed behind home plate to signal whenever a fielder touches home base. The runner stops at the whistle and the number of bases he has touched is recorded.

BAT BALL

NUMBER OF PLAYERS: 8-14

SPACE: Playground, gymnasium

PLAYING AREA: Court 36 by 72 feet (Figure 93)

EQUIPMENT: (1) Volleyball or utility ball; (2) base post—a jumping standard, chair, or sandbag

Procedure

The object of the game is for each batter in turn to try to bat a ball from the serving line into Area A and then run down the field, around the base post, and return across the scratch line without having been struck by the ball. The opposing team, meanwhile, tries to obtain the ball and put the base runner out by throwing the ball and hitting the runner between the knees and the shoulders.

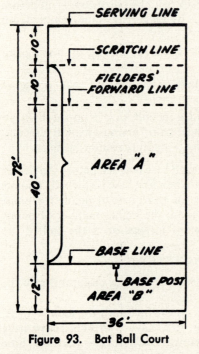

Figure 93.   Bat Ball Court

FORMATION: Players are divided into two equal teams of four to seven. Players of each team are numbered and they rotate in sequence when their team is at bat. The team at bat lines up behind the serving line; the other team takes its position in Area A, behind the fielders' forward line, and in Area B, where no more than two fielders may stand at one time.

PLAYING PERIOD: The game is played in seven innings. An inning is finished when both teams have had a period at bat. Teams change places after three outs.

BATTING: The batter must stand with both feet behind the serving line until after the ball has been hit. The ball is thrown into the air by the batter and then struck by the open hand, fingers extended. The ball must cross the scratch line on the fly and enter Area A. A line ball (one which hits a boundary line) is fair.

Two batting trials are allowed each batter, but if on the first trial the ball goes over the scratch line and lands outside of Area A, the batter is out. If on the second trial the ball fails to cross the scratch line and enter Area A, the batter is out. If on a fair ball the batter fails to run within five seconds, he is out.

RUNNING: Following a successful ball, the batter must immediately run down the field, around the base post, and back across the scratch line. He must keep moving. If during his run he is struck by the ball between the shoulders and the knees he is out. If he completes the run without going out of bounds and without being struck by the ball he wins two points for his team. As soon as he completes the run or is struck out, the next batter on his team is up (unless there are three outs, in which case the other team is at bat).

FIELDING: As soon as a fair ball crosses the scratch line, fielders try to retrieve the ball and throw it so as to strike the runner between the knees and shoulders. The following rules govern the fielders:

1. Fielders may not cross the forward line until the ball crosses the scratch line.
2. Fielders may not run with the ball while within the playing area. If, while running, a fielder throws the ball at the runner and misses him, it counts as a foul and the runner continues his run. If, while running, a fielder throws the ball at the runner and hits him, it counts as a foul and also as a completed run for the batting team; the runner need not continue the run.
3. Fielders may pass the ball to a teammate closer to the runner, but two fielders cannot so pass to each other twice in succession without throwing to a third player.
4. If the ball goes out of the playing area, a fielder may get it and throw it from the boundary line to a teammate but not at the runner.
5. Not more than two fielders may be in Area B, behind the base line, at any given time.

OUTS: The batter is out under the following conditions:

1. When he is fairly hit by a ball
2. When a fielder catches a fly ball
3. When he commits one of the following errors:
   a. Failure to serve with open hand, fingers extended
   b. Failure to serve a fair ball in two trials, or on first trial to send the ball across the scratch line but within Area A
   c. Failure to remain behind the serving line until the ball is struck
   d. Failure to cross the scratch line within five seconds after batting a fair ball
   e. Failure to remain within the boundary lines while running
   f. Failure to leave Area B before 20 seconds are counted. The runner may return to Area B in a further attempt to encircle the base post before completing his run.
   g. Failure to keep moving. The first offense gives one point to the fielding team, the second offense puts the batter out.
   h. Failure to encircle the base post in his run.

FOULS: The batter fouls when he stops moving during his run (see Outs, 3, g). The following are fouls when committed by the fielding team, and each counts 1 point for the batting team:

1. Running while holding the ball
2. Bouncing the ball

3. Holding the ball more than five seconds
4. Passing the ball to the same player twice in succession without an intervening play to another fielder
5. Throwing the ball while running, whether or not the runner is hit
6. Hitting the batter with the ball before the batter crosses the scratch line on his way to the base post.

If the fielding team has more than two players at a time in Area B, the penalty is 1 point for each fielder over two present.

SCORING: Each successful field run scores 2 points for the batting team. If a runner is hit by the ball thrown by a *running* fielder, this counts as a field run, and also counts an additional point as a penalty for the fielder's foul. Each foul made by the batting side scores 1 point for the fielding team, and each foul made by the fielding team scores 1 point for the batting team. The team wins that has the higher score at the end of seven innings.

OFFICIALS: For match play there should be two officials: (1) a starter who serves also as a scorekeeper; (2) a base referee who sees that the base post is included in player's run. Both officials watch for fouls, outs, and legal runs.

TEACHING SUGGESTIONS

1. For older players, place the scratch line 15 feet from the serving line.
2. If teams are smaller than seven players, narrow the court; if larger, widen the court, but the length should remain the same.
3. Substitute a beanbag for the ball, in which case the bag is thrown rather than batted.
4. When playing time is limited, organize the game for two or four periods of play instead of innings.

BEANBAG BOXES

NUMBER OF PLAYERS: 2-6

SPACE: Playground, playroom, classroom, hallway

EQUIPMENT: (1) Five beanbags, small balls, oaktree blister balls, buckeye tree balls, small blocks of wood, or blackboard erasers; (2) three cardboard or wooden boxes of different sizes fastened one inside the other with a space of approximately six inches between the walls of the boxes. The diameter of the center box should be approximately six inches. The boxes may remain flat on the floor or they may be tilted.

FORMATION: A throwing line is drawn not less than eight feet from the front edge of the largest box. Players must stand with both feet back of the throwing line when playing.

PROCEDURE: The first player, supplied with beanbags (or substitute), steps to the throwing line and throws his five beanbags, one at a time, attempting to have them fall completely within a box area. Beanbags which remain lodged on the edge of a wall partition do not score. When the player has thrown, the bags are collected and the second player tries.

SCORING: A beanbag falling in the center of the smallest box scores 15 points; a beanbag falling into the middle space scores 10 points; one falling into the outside space between the third and second box scores 5 points.

At the beginning of the game the players decide how many points they will play for: 25, 50, 75, or a smaller number, depending on the arithmetical skill of the players. The player who first earns the total number of points agreed upon is the winner.

TEACHING SUGGESTIONS

1. If a large number of children are to play, have several sets of beanbags and nests of boxes.
2. Do not permit the thrower to step over the throwing line.

BEANBAG PASSING

NUMBER OF PLAYERS: 4-20

SPACE: Playground, playroom, gymnasium, auditorium

EQUIPMENT: Beanbag for every other player, or half the group. One beanbag should be of a distinctive color.

FORMATION: Players form a single circle, all facing inward. There should be a space between the players, the amount depending on the skill of the group in tossing and catching. Every second child is given a beanbag, the leader having the colored one.

PROCEDURE: At a signal the players holding beanbags turn to the right and toss their bags to their right-hand neighbor. Immediately those same players turn to the left to receive the beanbag which will be coming to them. The game ends when the leader receives the distinctive colored beanbag with which he started play.

The game may be repeated as often as desired. As players become proficient, additional beanbags are introduced and the distance between players is increased.

TEACHING SUGGESTIONS

1. For a large number of players, form two circles and appoint a captain for each group.
2. Change the throwing directions frequently.
3. Speed up the game as skill is acquired.

BEANBAG RING THROW

NUMBER OF PLAYERS: 4-40

SPACE: Playground, playroom, classroom, gymnasium

PLAYING AREA: For each team an 18-inch circle drawn on the ground; a restraining line opposite each circle and 10 feet distant from it

EQUIPMENT: For each team five beanbags, rubber heels, blackboard erasers, or other objects for throwing

FORMATION: Members of each team are lined up in file formation behind that team's restraining line.

PROCEDURE: At a signal the captain of each team, while standing behind the restraining line, throws each beanbag in succession towards his circle. Any bag which touches the circumference of the circle cannot be counted in computing the score. After the score is recorded the player runs forward, picks up the beanbags, and carries them to the next player of his team, thereafter going to the end of his file. Play continues until all have thrown. The time element is not so important as accuracy in throwing.

SCORING: One point is earned for each bag completely within the circle. The team wins that has the highest score after all players have thrown.

TEACHING SUGGESTIONS

1. See that each child in a class has his own beanbag. The bag should have some distinguishing mark or emblem. It should correspond in size and in weight to the other bags.
2. As skill is gained, increase the distance between the circles and the restraining lines.
3. If played in the classroom, draw the circles directly opposite the aisles formed by rows of desks.
4. See that feet are behind the restraining lines while throws are made.

BOUNDARY BALL

NUMBER OF PLAYERS: 8-16

SPACE: Playground, gymnasium

PLAYING AREA: Two parallel goal lines, 60 feet long and 60 feet apart, with a center line halfway between and parallel to the goal lines

EQUIPMENT: For each team a utility ball, volleyball, soccer ball, basketball, or beanbag; each team should have a different type of ball or color of beanbag so that they can be distinguished.

FORMATION: Players are divided into two teams. Players of each team occupy the area between their own goal line and the center line.

PROCEDURE: At a signal, members of each team attempt to throw the ball so that it will bounce or roll across the opponents' goal line. Balls going across a goal line on the fly, or passing beyond the ends of the goal lines, do not score.

Players try to prevent balls from crossing their own goal lines. Players move about freely within their own side of the playing area but may not enter the opponents' territory.

Following the first throw, balls are thrown back and forth at will. Players may run with the ball to the center line before throwing. Each player securing the ball must throw it himself and not pass to a teammate.

The game is played either (1) by time periods, or (2) by innings, in which case each time a legal ball crosses the goal line a half inning is played. After each goal, the ball is returned to the captain of the team that threw it and is put into play again.

SCORING: Each ball which rolls or bounces over a goal line scores 1 point. The team wins which has the higher number of points at the end of an agreed upon number of innings or at the end of the time period allowed.

If a player steps on or across the center line, 1 point is given to the opponents.

When beanbags are used a fly ball passing over a goal line scores 1 point as well as a beanbag which slides on the ground across a goal line.

TEACHING SUGGESTIONS

1. If but a few children are to play, make the length of the goal lines shorter but keep the same distance between them.
2. When the ball passes beyond the field of play, have the nearest child to it secure the ball, run with it to his goal line, and immediately throw the ball to a team member, thereafter entering his own playing area.

CENTER BALL [1]

NUMBER OF PLAYERS: 5-10

SPACE: Playground, playroom, gymnasium

EQUIPMENT: Volleyball, soccer ball, playground baseball, beanbag, or stuffed leather ball casing

FORMATION: Players form a circle, with one player in the center who holds the ball.

---

[1] Developed by Margaret Van Voorhees.

PROCEDURE: The center player throws the ball to a circle player and immediately runs around the outside of the circle, returns to the opening where he left the circle, enters the circle, and tries to touch or pick up the ball. In the meantime, the player to whom he threw the ball runs to the center of the circle, places the ball on the ground, and then chases the running player, trying to tag him.

Should the runner be tagged, he must retire to a circle position; should he reach the ball and touch it ahead of the person chasing him, he remains the thrower and the game is repeated.

TEACHING SUGGESTIONS

1. If the group is large, provide extra balls and form smaller groups, each with a captain.
2. See that the runner enters the ring where he left it.

CHASE BALL [1]

NUMBER OF PLAYERS: 20-40

SPACE: Playground, playroom, gymnasium

EQUIPMENT: For each team two balls of different sizes and weights, such as a volleyball and baseball; basketball and tennis ball; or beanbag and stuffed leather ball casing

FORMATION: Players of each team are divided into two lines facing each other some eight feet apart and with about six feet between each player. Two balls are placed on the ground in front of each captain.

PROCEDURE: On a signal each captain tosses a ball to the first player in his line so that it will start a trail down one line and back the other to the end player of his team who is facing the captain. When the third player of his team has the first ball, the second ball is started in pursuit, the object being for it to overtake the first ball. All balls must be passed immediately or a foul with a minus count will be called against the team. Balls are kept at the end of the line until the winner of the teams is determined, whereupon the game is replayed, the balls starting from the end and working back to the captain. If a child drops a ball, have him run immediately, pick it up, return to his position in the line, and then throw it across.

SCORING: A team may win by a combination of credits. (1) If a second ball overtakes a first ball 1 point is credited to that team. (2) The team whose second ball is first held high in the air by the last player scores 1 point. The team that makes more points during the playing of the game (three out of five races) wins the game.

---

[1] Developed by Margaret Van Voorhees.

1. When teams are small, increase the distance between players.
2. Try to eliminate wild throws and too great haste.

CHINESE WALL

NUMBER OF PLAYERS: 5-20

SPACE: Playground, gymnasium, playroom, auditorium

PLAYING AREA: Two parallel lines 40 to 50 feet long drawn from 10 to 12 feet apart. The space between the lines represents a Chinese wall. Some 30 feet from the wall, on each side, draw parallel restraining lines.

FORMATION: One player, the coolie or guard, stands within the wall boundaries and may not leave the area. Remaining players stand behind one of the restraining lines.

PROCEDURE: The coolie calls loudly, "Scale the Wall!" whereupon all players run forward, cross the wall, and go beyond the opposite restraining line. As they pass over the wall the coolie tags as many runners as he can. The runners who are tagged drop out of the game. The game continues until the coolie has tagged all players. The last person tagged becomes the coolie for a new game. If the coolie leaves his area a person tagged by him is safe.

TEACHING SUGGESTIONS

1. Have players line up behind the restraining line each time before the call is given by the coolie.
2. If but a few are to play, shorten the length of the restraining line.

CRACKABOUT [1]

NUMBER OF PLAYERS: 6-20

SPACE: Playground, playroom, gymnasium

EQUIPMENT: Lightweight volleyball, utility ball, large beanbag, or knotted towel

FORMATION: One player is given the ball. The remaining players scatter about.

PROCEDURE: The player holding the ball tries to hit another player by throwing the ball. He may run with the ball while trying to make the contact. If successful in his throw he shouts, "Crackabout!" whereupon all the players rush to get the ball. As soon as it is secured by a player he calls "Crackabout," the others scatter again, and play is continued.

---

[1] Developed by Margaret Van Voorhees.

TEACHING SUGGESTIONS

1. Use in cold weather, as action is strenuous and continuous.
2. Teach the skill of stopping, in order to avoid accidents, when the children rush to get the ball.

DANISH ROUNDERS

NUMBER OF PLAYERS: 10-20

SPACE: Playground, gymnasium

PLAYING AREA: Softball diamond with bases 35 feet apart or half a tennis court with bases at four corners. Ten feet from home plate a pitcher's circle is drawn, with a radius of three feet (Figure 94).

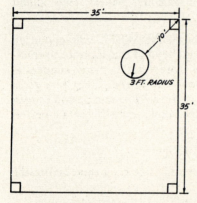

Figure 94. Diamond for Danish Rounders

EQUIPMENT: Tennis ball

FORMATION: Players are divided into two teams, with one team at bat and the other team fielding. The fielding team has a pitcher and a catcher. An inning is finished when all members of both teams have batted. An agreed upon number of innings may be used, or two playing periods of equal duration. In the latter case, players of the batting team continue to return to bat until the time period is finished, even if some had previously been put out.

PROCEDURE: The pitcher throws the ball slightly above the head of the batter. The latter tries to hit the ball with his hand and, successful or not, runs for first base and farther if possible. The catcher and the fielders try to return the ball to the pitcher, who touches the ground within the pitcher's circle with the ball and calls loudly, "Down!" If the ball is downed before the runner reaches the base, he is out; if after, he is safe.

Any number of players may be at a base at the same time and on a strike may remain at the base or run, as desired. If but one batter remains to bat, bases being full, the batter has three trials but must run to first base each trial. He may be put out by the pitcher downing the ball. During these trials, basemen may try to get home.

OUTS: When "down" is called any base runners who are off bases are out. A fly ball caught puts out not only the batter but also any players running between bases. Three outs do not change the side; play is continued until all members have batted.

SCORING: A successful return to home plate, each base having been touched, scores 1 point. The team wins which has the larger number of points at the end of the agreed upon number of innings or time periods.

DODGE BALL

NUMBER OF PLAYERS: 8-20

SPACE: Playground, gymnasium, playroom

PLAYING AREA: Children join hands, form a circle, and then, dropping hands, step backward one step. With chalk or a pointed stick, a circle is drawn in front of the feet of the players.

EQUIPMENT: Utility ball, volley ball, soccer ball, or knotted towel

FORMATION: Players are divided into two teams. One team remains outside the circle while the other team steps into the circle.

PROCEDURE: Players outside the circle try to hit the circle players with the ball by throwing it rapidly. The circle players, to avoid being hit by a fly ball, may move about, jump, or stoop, but they may not leave the circle. Circle players do not touch the ball at any time.

Outside players may enter the circle to secure the ball but they *must throw* the ball to another team member. They may not carry the ball outside the circle themselves nor may they throw at a circle player while within the circle.

SCORING: Several methods of scoring may be used. (1) Circle players, hit by a fly ball on any part of the person other than the head, at once join the outside players and try to hit remaining circle players. The last player to remain in the circle is the winner. (2) Two time periods of equal length may be used, with each team having a turn in the center. Players who are legally hit raise an arm to signal the scorer to tally a hit against their team. They remain in the circle and continue to play. The team with the smaller number of hits at the end of the playing period wins the game. (3) Play may be against time, the team winning which eliminates all the circle players in the shorter time. In this form of play, those hit retire from the game and do not assist outside players.

TEACHING SUGGESTIONS

1. If outside players, while throwing, step on the circumference line and, at the same time, succeed in hitting a player legally, do not score the throw.
2. Do not score a bouncing or rolling ball which contacts a circle player.
3. Declare a thrown ball which bounces off a circle player a dead ball and no longer in play until secured by an out-of-the-circle player.

DOUBLE TAG

NUMBER OF PLAYERS: 6-20

SPACE: Playground, auditorium

FORMATION: Couples stand with adjacent elbows hooked. One player is chosen a tagger and the other a runner.

PROCEDURE: The runner must try to join a couple and hook elbows with one of them. Couples move about trying to prevent the runner from doing this. If the runner is successful, the one whose partner's elbow was hooked immediately becomes the runner and tries to escape the tagger by joining another couple. If the tagger catches the runner, that runner becomes the tagger and the former tagger the runner. The new runner should seek safety immediately.

ELEPHANTS FLY

NUMBER OF PLAYERS: 5-20

SPACE: Playground, playroom, gymnasium, auditorium, hallway, classroom

FORMATION: Players stand in circle formation, or in line formation with the leader standing in front of the middle of the line. One person is chosen to be leader.

PROCEDURE: The leader calls, "Butterflies fly!" and all children wave their arms. He may then say, "Crows fly," and the action is repeated. If he should say, "Elephants fly!" and any child waves his arms, that child exchanges places with the leader, since elephants do not fly, even if the leader so stated.

TEACHING SUGGESTIONS

1. Encourage leaders to make their statements in rapid succession and in an emphatic way.
2. Call the names of familiar animals in order to speed up the game.

EXCHANGE TAG

NUMBER OF PLAYERS: 6-20

SPACE: Classroom

FORMATION: Children are seated at their desks or, if the room permits, they stand in a circle. A child is selected to be the tagger. If the names of the players are not known to each other, give each child a number to be remembered.

PROCEDURE: The leader calls the names or numbers of two children. Those two try to exchange seats or places in the circle before the tagger can tag them. If players are not tagged before reaching the desired places, new numbers are called. Any player tagged becomes the tagger and the old tagger retires.

TEACHING SUGGESTIONS

1. See that all the children's names are called and not just those of a small clique.
2. When the game is mastered, call the names of three or four players who will try to exchange places simultaneously.

FIRE ENGINE

NUMBER OF PLAYERS: 6-40

SPACE: Playground, gymnasium

PLAYING AREA: A starting line and a parallel line some 40 feet distant are drawn. The length of the lines will depend upon the number of children playing.

FORMATION: The players are divided into small groups and each group is given a number. All the players, regardless of their group affiliation, stand behind but near the starting line. A child is selected to be the Fire Chief.

PROCEDURE: The chief, at the side and halfway between the lines, gives a fire alarm signal. There may be as many signals as there are numbered groups. To give the signal the fire chief may clap his hands, count aloud the desired signal, or jump into the air the desired number of times. At the end he shouts loudly, "Fire!" The members of the group whose number has been given start running when they hear the word "Fire." They must run across the far line and then return and cross the starting line. If the chief calls, "General Alarm! Fire!" all the players run. This signal should not be given too frequently. The player who returns first across the starting line becomes the new fire chief.

TEACHING SUGGESTIONS

1. Have the fire chief move quickly into his position.
2. Have the children completely cross the second line with both feet before turning. To toe the line with one foot is not enough.
3. Teach the children how to turn or pivot without crossing their feet.

FLOOR TAG

NUMBER OF PLAYERS: 8-40

SPACE: Playground, playroom, auditorium

FORMATION: The children are divided into small groups of eight or less, with one child in the center of each group. The center player is the tagger; the others squat and place one hand on the floor.

PROCEDURE: Group players may rise as they wish and move about. The tagger attempts to tag a member of the group before that member can squat and touch the floor. If successful, the center player exchanges places with the person tagged.

TEACHING SUGGESTIONS

1. Limit the playing area, and experiment to determine the size that will result in a lively game.
2. See that children move to a new location upon arising from a squatting position.

FLYING DUTCHMEN

NUMBER OF PLAYERS: 10-20

SPACE: Playground, gymnasium, hallway, auditorium

FORMATION: Players join hands and form a circle. Two players are selected to run together. They join inside hands and keep them joined.

PROCEDURE: The running couple start around the outside of the circle. While running, the inside player quickly tags the clasped hands of two players in the circle. The tagged couple, with hands clasped, start running in the opposite direction from the ones who tagged them and try to reach their former position before the players who tagged them can reach it. If successful they remain in the circle. If unsuccessful they become the new taggers.

TEACHING SUGGESTIONS

1. When the group to play is large, form two circles.
2. Do not permit favoritism in the continued reselection of certain players.
3. Have running couples tag early in their run. Not to do so makes the game drag.
4. Have couples keep to the right as they pass each other.
5. Declare players in the circle who drop each other's hands automatically out of the game.
6. Have those who have been tagged sit down, to indicate that they have had their turn, and thus give others a chance to play.

FOLLOW THE LEADER

NUMBER OF PLAYERS: 5-40

SPACE: Playground, playroom, gymnasium, hallway, auditorium

FORMATION: A leader is selected. The remaining children line up behind the leader in file formation.

PROCEDURE: The leader sets patterns for the children to perform. He may jump forward, climb apparatus, crawl under a bench, run, skip, walk with long strides, perform stunts, or, twisting and turning, lead the group where he desires. The others follow and try to perform accurately the patterns set by the leader. Children who fail to perform the stipulated activity go to the rear of the file.

TEACHING SUGGESTIONS

1. Once the game is mastered, appoint new leaders frequently.
2. Use this game to aid children in the development of originality together with vigorous and energetic following of patterns set.

FOREST LOOKOUT

NUMBER OF PLAYERS: 15-41

SPACE: Playground, playroom, gymnasium, auditorium

FORMATION: Two circles are formed, the members of the outside circle standing behind inner circle players. The outside players represent fire fighters, the inside members trees. One player is chosen to be the lookout. He stands in the center.

PROCEDURE: The lookout calls loudly, "Fire in the mountain, run, run—

RUN!" and at the same time claps his hands. On hearing the last "Run" the outside players start rapidly around the circle to right or left as may be desired, all moving in the same direction. While the fire fighters are running, the lookout quietly steps in front of some inner circle player. The runners who see the lookout do this do likewise. The player who can find no tree becomes the lookout, and the former trees and fire fighters exchange places.

TEACHING SUGGESTIONS

1. Frequently require players to step several steps backward since the diameter continually grows smaller.
2. Have the lookout endeavor to deceive the fire fighters as to the last command.

GALLOPING BRONCOS

NUMBER OF PLAYERS: 10-20

SPACE: Playground, gymnasium

PLAYING AREA: A basketball court or area similar in size, with lines marked

EQUIPMENT: Volleyball, soccer ball, speed ball, or beanbag

FORMATION: Players are divided into two teams, A and B. Half the members of Team A stand outside and scattered along one side of the court. The remaining players of Team A stand facing them on the opposite side of the court. A member of the team holds a ball. Team B players are lined up beyond, and outside, one of the end lines of the court.

PROCEDURE: The game may be played in 3, 5, or 7 innings, or it may be played with the teams having an equal time period for scoring purposes. An inning is finished when all members of a team have run down the court and back.

At a signal, members of Team B, while remaining within the side lines of the court, try to run toward and cross over the opposite end line without being hit by the ball. The signal is repeated and they return to the starting area. A record is kept of the number of players not hit.

Team A members, while outside the court, are privileged to hit as many Team B players as possible during the run. Team A members may not enter the playing area except to secure the ball. The ball must then be thrown to a teammate out of bounds. As players are hit they are not eliminated from the return run.

Outs: Runners who pass outside the side boundary lines of the court put themselves out of the inning that is being played. Otherwise there are no outs.

Runs: (1) A run is made each time a runner is successful in crossing the end of the court without being hit by the ball. Tally of runs is kept following the completion of each inning. (2) A run is credited to the running team if a member of the throwing team while standing or running *inside* the playing area throws the ball at a member of the running team regardless of whether a runner is hit.

SCORING: One point is given for each run made or credited. The team wins that has the higher total of runs during the playing period.

TEACHING SUGGESTIONS

1. Since the success of the game depends on the size of the area, determine its size by the number of players.
2. Have the throwers practice running in, securing the ball, and throwing it immediately to a teammate out of court, while other players run up and down the court.

HAND POLO

NUMBER OF PLAYERS: 8-20

SPACE: Playground, gymnasium, auditorium

PLAYING AREA: A court with maximum dimensions of 40 by 60 feet. At each end a line is drawn to enclose an area three feet deep, called the goal area. The width of the goal area remains constant regardless of length or width of the field.

EQUIPMENT: Soccer ball, basketball, volleyball, or large utility ball

FORMATION: Players are divided into two teams of from four to six members: each team has one center fielder, two to six fielders, one to three goal guards. Players are numbered, starting with center fielder. See diagram for position of players at start of game (Figure 95).

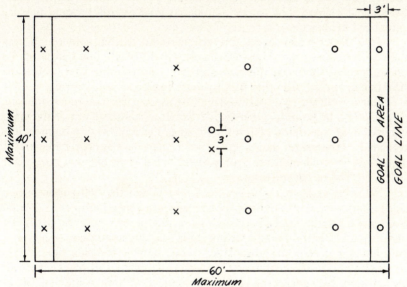

Figure 95.   Court and Position of Players for Hand Polo

PROCEDURE: The game should be kept as simple as possible. The object is to push or roll the ball along the ground and across the opposing team's rear goal line. To start the play team members are assigned to the following duties:

Center Fielders: They stand facing the side lines with their left shoulders nearest their own goal at the center of the field with the ball on the ground between them. Each places a hand on the ball. The center fielder's duty is to (1) roll the ball to a teammate; (2) advance the ball with one hand toward the opponent's goal, while the ball is on the ground;

or (3) when there is no other choice, lift the ball with one hand and throw it to a teammate. That player must bring the ball to the ground before advancing it. Members of both teams must be in their half of the field and must remain so until the ball is put in play by the referee's whistle or command.

Fielders: They may advance to a goal line in an attempt to push or roll the ball over a goal line. The ball may not be thrown or be permitted to bounce over the goal line. A bouncing or fly ball must be brought to the ground by a player, with one hand, before it can be pushed or rolled in any direction.

Goalkeepers: These players may not have both feet outside their goal area at the same time. They may use one or both hands to stop the ball, bat the ball, or pick up the ball to throw it away from their own goal area.

Rotation of Players: Following each scoring play a rotation occurs. Center fielders become goal guards, taking position of the highest numbered goal guards. The lowest numbered goal guards become fielders. Number 2 fielders become center fielders, etc.

Held Ball: When several players surround the ball and rough play may be imminent, the referee declares a "held ball." The ball is placed on the ground between the two opponents nearest the spot where the held ball occurred. All other players must be six feet way. On signal, play is resumed with the two players trying to advance the ball to a teammate.

Ball Out of Bounds—Over Goal Line: If a ball passes out of the playing area over a goal line (1) on the fly or (2) as a result of a bounce, it is returned to the center and is again put in play by the center fielders. If a goalkeeper accidentally rolls or pushes the ball over his own goal line it scores for the opponent team.

Ball Out of Bounds—Over Side Line: When the ball passes over a side boundary line, it is put in play by the nearest member of the opposite team while standing outside of the field at the point where the ball went out of bounds. If this point is within three feet of the junction of an inner goal line and a side line, the player, while outside the side line, moves 10 strides nearer the center of the field. In front of this player and not less than six feet apart, the remaining fielders of both teams line up in two straight lines facing each other. Members of each team may be in either line. These players may not advance toward each other or toward the ball until the ball is in motion. On signal, the out-of-bounds player rolls the ball forward toward the center of the field but between the two lines.

FOULS: Fouls are of two types, personal and technical.

Personal Foul: Charging, hitting, kicking, or tripping another player is a personal foul. *Penalty:* The player leaves the game and may not return. If no substitute is available, the team continues to play with reduced membership.

Technical Fouls: The following are technical fouls: (1) A fielder using both hands simultaneously on the ball; (2) any player kneeling on one or both knees; (3) stepping within a goal area with either foot (a line step is not penalized); (4) the goal guard stepping out of the goal area with both feet. *Penalty:* If a fielder fouls, the ball is given to the nearest goal guard. The goal guard may throw the ball. If the goal guard fouls, the ball is placed on the ground 10 feet in front of the goal guard who fouled. The nearest fielder to the ball takes the play. All other players must be at least six feet away. On signal, play is resumed with the fielder permitted an unguarded stroke.

PLAYING TIME: Game may be played in (a) 3-minute quarters, or (b) 5-minute halves. A rest period should be scheduled between each quarter or between halves.

SCORING: One point is scored each time the ball rolls across the opponents' goal line. Tie score stands.

TEACHING SUGGESTIONS

1. Teach fielders not to bunch, but to keep in their part of the field.
2. Teach fielders to grasp, with hand not in use, the belt or dress at the back. Hands may be changed as desired.
3. In rural schools with small enrollments, reduce size of field both as to width and length.
4. Have players practice bringing fly and bouncing balls to the ground.
5. Encourage short accurate rolls to other players. Batted balls are permissible.

KEEP AWAY

NUMBER OF PLAYERS: 8-16

SPACE: Playground, gymnasium

PLAYING AREA: Court 40 by 60 feet

EQUIPMENT: (1) Volleyball, 10-inch rubber ball, beanbag, or knotted towel; (2) two sets of different colored pinnies [1] to distinguish teams

FORMATION: Players are divided into two teams of equal size, members of both teams being scattered over the playing area. The ball is handed to one player.

PROCEDURE: On a signal, the ball is passed from player to player, each

---

[1] Pinnies are made from lightweight colored cotton material and are made to slip over a player's head easily so that the color shows both on the chest and back. They may be ordered through physical education uniform manufacturers or made in the school. Sashes or arm bands of material may be used instead of the more complicated pinnies.

team trying to keep the ball away from the opponents while passing to teammates.

Fouls: Tripping, pushing, holding, kicking, or any other outstanding roughness is a foul, and the ball is given to the opposite team. A player is eliminated if his play continues to be rough.

There is no scoring. The object is to see which team can keep the ball in play for the longer period.

TEACHING SUGGESTIONS

1. Do not allow a player to hold the ball. It must be kept in play.
2. Do not allow rough play.
3. If a ball goes out of bounds, have a player of the team which did not send it out retrieve it for his team.
4. Encourage players to watch each other and signal for passes without shouting.
5. Use stop watch when available to determine longest period of continuous play by members of a team.

KICK BALL

NUMBER OF PLAYERS: 8-20

SPACE: Playground, gymnasium

PLAYING AREA: Softball diamond with bases 30 feet apart; pitcher's line 15 to 20 feet from home plate

EQUIPMENT: (1) Four bases made of wood, linoleum, or sacks filled with sand or sawdust; (2) utility ball or soccer ball. Never use a volleyball, as it is not built for kicking.

FORMATION: Players are divided into two teams. One team stands behind home plate and each member takes his turn as the kicker. The other team goes to the field, with a pitcher and catcher elected by the members. After three members of the kicking team have been put out, the kicking team goes to the field and the fielding team become the kickers. Players rotate positions on the field so that all eventually have a chance to be pitchers and catchers.

PROCEDURE: The game is played according to softball rules, with the following exceptions: (1) The pitcher *rolls* the ball to the waiting kicker, who attempts to kick the ball into the field and then to run to first, second, third, and home bases before being tagged or thrown out by the other team. He may not steal or play off bases while the ball is in the pitcher's hands preparatory to a roll. (2) A base runner is out if "tagged out" or "thrown out" before reaching *first, second, third,* or *home* plate. He is tagged out if the ball is in the hands of the baseman or fielder when he tags the base runner. Runner is thrown out if the base is touched, before the runner reaches it, either (a) by the ball while in the hands of the baseman or fielder, or (b) by some part of the body of the baseman or fielder while holding the ball.

SCORING: Each successful run to home plate scores 1 point. The team wins that has more points at the end of seven innings (that is, when each team has had seven turns at bat).

TEACHING SUGGESTIONS

1. Keep the rules simple but insist that they be strictly observed.
2. Teach children to judge whether the ball or runner gets to a base first—there is no tie between ball and runner.

KICK THE WICKET

NUMBER OF PLAYERS: 10-22

SPACE: Playground, gymnasium

PLAYING AREA: Softball diamond with bases 30 feet apart

EQUIPMENT: (1) Four bases; (2) portion of a bicycle tire or garden hose about 18 inches long, known as the wicket; (3) two bricks placed on end opposite each other two feet inside of home base and 18 inches apart. The wicket is so placed that the ends rest on the bricks.

FORMATION: Players are divided into two teams, 11 men on a team: one home base guard who stands to the left and slightly back of home base; three players stationed within the diamond; a player at each of first, second, and third bases; and four players in the outfield.

PROCEDURE: Each member of a team in turn kicks the wicket, which must land inside the diamond. A wicket that contacts a base line is a fair wicket. Foul kicks are called when the wicket lands outside the diamond.

After each legal kick a runner tries to make as many bases as possible. Circling the bases and touching home base without being put out constitutes a run. The run does not have to be continuous.

Return of Wicket: Fielders try to return the wicket to the home base guard, who in turn taps one of the bricks with the wicket.

Men on Bases: Not more than one player may be on a base. Base runners must have a foot in contact with the base until the wicket is legally kicked.

Innings: An inning is finished when three outs have been made by both teams. A game consists of any agreed-upon number of innings between five and nine, depending upon the time available.

Outs: (1) A wicket caught before it touches the ground puts a runner out; (2) a runner is out if he is off his base when a brick is tapped with the wicket; (3) four foul kicks retire the kicker; (4) after three outs the inning changes.

Rotation of Players: With each change of inning, the positions of fielders are rotated, home base guard going to the outfield and all others being advanced one position. Team members who are kicking are numbered and follow each other in that sequence.

SCORING: The team wins which has the higher number of runs at the end of the agreed upon innings. Runners must touch home base with a foot in order to make the run legal.

TEACHING SUGGESTIONS

1. Lessen the distance between bases if experience makes it advisable.
2. Teach the children to kick by using the instep—not the toes.
3. Demonstrate how the toes must be pointed forward at the end of the kick to make the wicket go ahead and not just up into the air.

LAME FOX AND CHICKENS

NUMBER OF PLAYERS: 5-20

SPACE: Playground, playroom, gymnasium, auditorium

PLAYING AREA: A fox's den and a chicken yard established some 50 feet distant from the den. The sizes will depend upon the number playing.

FORMATION: A fox stands in his den. The chickens stand in their yard.

PROCEDURE: Leaving the chicken yard, the chickens advance as near as they dare to the den and tease the fox by chanting, "Lame fox! Lame fox! Can't catch me!" while the fox moves in any direction that he desires within his own den. When the fox feels the right moment has arrived he dashes out to try and catch as many chickens as he can before they can enter the chicken yard.

The fox, on leaving his den, may take but three running leaps and thereafter must hop on one foot. He may change his hopping from foot to foot as he tires. As the chickens are tagged they become foxes and must go immediately to the fox's den and wait for him. When all the chickens have entered the chicken yard, the fox returns to his den. As the action of taunting the fox is repeated and he leaves his den, the new foxes go out with him and try to tag as many chickens as they can. The new foxes must observe the rule of only three steps beyond the den and hops thereafter. The chicken last caught wins the game and becomes the first lame fox in the new game.

The first fox always decides when he and the other foxes will leave the den. He should not slow up the game by prolonging his stay in his den.

THE OCEAN IS STORMY

NUMBER OF PLAYERS: 10-40

SPACE: Playground, playroom, gymnasium, auditorium

PLAYING AREA: Small circles marked on the playing area. They should not be too close together. One circle for each two players, with the exception of the two chosen to be the "whales." Circles may be marked by chalk, or by using newspapers, linoleum squares, corrugated cardboard, or tire casings.

FORMATION: Players divide off in pairs and each pair occupies a circle. Two players become the whales. The couples, including the whales, decide in secret which fish the two of them will represent, such as codfish, mackerel, or rainbow trout. Couples keep their original name throughout the playing of the game.

PROCEDURE: The whales hook elbows and, having no home, move about calling the names of fish as they move. Couples whose fish name is called leave their circle, hook elbows, and drop behind the whales, following them thereafter until the whales call, "The Ocean is Stormy!" whereupon they, together with all who are following them, dash arm in arm to secure a vacant circle. Those unsuccessful are the new whales.

The leader, when he feels it will liven the game, may call loudly, "Typhoon! Typhoon!" whereupon everyone, including those standing in circles, must try to secure a new living place.

TEACHING SUGGESTIONS

1. Have circles with a diameter of not more than 1½ feet.
2. Use names other than those of fish, such as boats, water birds, sea shells.
3. Have couples whose names are not called by the whales remain in their circles.
4. Help whales to call a variety of names so that all couples are called.

SHAKE-UP [1]

NUMBER OF PLAYERS: 5-40

SPACE: Playground, gymnasium, playroom

PLAYING AREA: Letters A through J drawn two feet high on widely separated areas of the playing space

EQUIPMENT: Slips of paper giving directions to be followed by the players, and a box or covered container to hold the slips

---

[1] Adapted from a note contributed by Agnes M. Hooley to the *Journal of Health and Physical Education*, XI (September, 1940), 435. By permission.

FORMATION: Children move about the playing area, walking, skipping, running, hopping, or jumping.

PROCEDURE: Leader blows a whistle and players stop and face the leader. The latter shakes the box or can and then draws out a direction slip and reads it. Examples are "The five children nearest the letter H go to the side lines," or "The three children nearest F go to the side lines." Game continues until all players have left the area. The last to leave the area are the winners. Occasionally a last slip directs more children to leave the playing space than are on it. When this occurs all the standing children are winners.

TEACHING SUGGESTIONS

1. Vary the number of letters to be drawn and the number of written slips to be used with the size of the playing space and the number of children to participate.
2. Use cardboard letters.

SKY HIGH BALL

NUMBER OF PLAYERS: 2-16

SPACE: Playground

EQUIPMENT: Softball, volleyball, basketball, or beanbag

FORMATION: Players are divided into two teams. The players stand around informally.

PROCEDURE: Each member of Team 1 in turn throws the ball as high into the air as possible. Members of Team 2 try to catch it. When all of Team 1 have thrown, Team 2 members take their turn. Play continues until all members of both teams have thrown the ball, whereupon a round is completed. As many rounds as desired may be played.

SCORING: Each time a ball hits the ground without being caught the throwing team scores 1 point. The team with the higher score at the end of the designated number of rounds wins the game.

TEACHING SUGGESTIONS

1. Do not allow any player to interfere with the person trying to catch the ball.
2. Select some mark, such as the top of a window, top of a small tree, top of a flagpole, and require that the ball must be thrown higher than the selected point. If not thrown the necessary height the catching team may be permitted to score 1 point.
3. Even though children are grouped informally, give directions so that all may have opportunity to catch as well as to throw the ball.

STATUES

NUMBER OF PLAYERS: 4-20

SPACE: Playground, playroom, gymnasium, hallway, auditorium

PLAYING AREA: Parallel starting and finish lines some 30 feet apart

FORMATION: Players, with the exception of one, line up along and back of the starting line. The odd player, or leader, stands beyond the finish line with his back to the starting line. He gives the signals.

PROCEDURE: The leader, without turning to look at the advancing players, calls "Come on!" The players advance in any way they wish, such as walking, running, hopping, skipping, turning, or jumping. The leader signals that he is going to turn by shouting, clapping his hands three times, waving his hands high in the air, jumping into the air, or by counting loudly to ten. Upon finishing the signal he turns. The advancing players must "freeze" into the position which results from stopping suddenly. If the leader sees any player or players in motion he sends them back to the starting line to begin again. The leader again turns his back and gives his signal. Play goes on until at least half the advancing players succeed in crossing the finish line. The first player to cross the finish line is the leader for the new game.

TEACHING SUGGESTIONS

1. Encourage the leaders to vary the time of waiting so as to confuse the advancing players.
2. Play a variation of "Statues" by having the leader swing the players around and throw them gently into a position which represents some object, animal, or person. The leader then tries to guess what the statues represent. Each player gets a chance to be leader.

STOOP TAG

NUMBER OF PLAYERS: 10-20

SPACE: Playground, playroom, gymnasium, auditorium

FORMATION: One player is selected as tagger. The remaining players are scattered about in not too large an area.

PROCEDURE: The tagger may attempt to tag anyone. If the person approached can assume a squatting position he is safe. Only five squats to a player are allowed. When these are used up a player, to avoid being tagged, must resort to running. As a player is tagged he becomes the new tagger.

TEACHING SUGGESTIONS

1. Encourage children to move about energetically, since a poor game results if players are inactive.
2. Limit the length of time a person may squat.

STRIKE AND CHASE [1]

NUMBER OF PLAYERS: 8-20

SPACE: Playground, playroom, gymnasium, hallway

PLAYING AREA: Two parallel goal lines 50 feet long and 50 feet apart. If but a few children are to play, the goal lines may be much shorter in length.

FORMATION: Two teams stand facing each other behind their own goal lines. One team is designated the visiting team. The home team members stand with feet behind their goal line and with hands and arms extended.

PROCEDURE: The game is played in two innings, each team having an inning as the visiting team.

On a signal, the visiting team members advance and when and where they please strike an extended hand. The person so struck immediately chases the tagger and tries to tag him before he can cross his own goal line.

After all members of the visiting team have tagged, run, and crossed their own goal line the other team becomes the visiting team and the game is replayed.

SCORING: One point is scored by the visiting team for each successful return over the goal line without a player being tagged. The team wins which has the higher number of points at the conclusion of the playing time. Match games consist of three out of five games.

TEACHING SUGGESTIONS

1. Encourage children who are inclined to hang back to vigorous action and do not allow them to slow up the game.
2. Encourage children to make feints and false or hesitating movements in order to confuse the person whose hand is to be struck.

TELEPHONE TAG

NUMBER OF PLAYERS: 8-20

SPACE: Playground, playroom, gymnasium, auditorium

FORMATION: Players join hands and form a circle. One player, the operator, stands in the center. The players are numbered continuously, includ-

---

[1] Developed by Margaret Van Voorhees.

ing the operator, from 1 to 9 and then the circle players re-form with the numbers mixed up.

PROCEDURE: Play is started by the operator calling a number. The player (players) with that number immediately starts running around the outside of the circle in an attempt to return to his vacant place without being tagged. The operator leaves the circle through the break and tries to tag the runner. Should the operator be successful he calls out, "Hello!" to signify he got his party and he remains the operator. If unsuccessful, the operator calls out, "Wrong number!" and takes his place with the circle players, while the runner becomes the new operator.

TEACHING SUGGESTIONS

1. When the group playing is small, have the players on each side of the called number quickly join hands in an attempt to prevent the operator from following the runner immediately. If they are successful they may call out, "Busy wire."
2. If it is found to be too difficult for the operator to catch the runner, rule that the runner must take a designated number of walking steps before starting his run.
3. If the group is large, try having two or more operators, each operator chasing his own number. Players should always run in the same direction.

THREE AROUND

NUMBER OF PLAYERS: 15-40

SPACE: Playground, playroom, gymnasium, auditorium

FORMATION: One player is selected to be first tagger. Remaining players form two circles with players of the outside circle standing directly behind players of the inner circle. All players face inward.

PROCEDURE: The tagger runs around the outside circle and quickly tags a player. He continues his run. The person tagged must tag the player in front of himself *before* he can start his run. If he fails to do this he must return and tag the player and thereupon restart his run. The last player, on getting his tag and *not before*, starts running. Each of the three players strives to reach the vacant place in the circle as rapidly as possible. When the position is reached they stand one behind the other. The third player to reach the position becomes the new tagger and the game is continued.

TEACHING SUGGESTIONS

1. If the group to play is small, use a single circle with both players striving to reach the vacant place.

2. If the group is large, have several concentric circles with files of four, five, or six players.
3. Teach players to tag rapidly, avoiding long preliminary runs.

TRADES

NUMBER OF PLAYERS: 6-20

SPACE: Playground, playroom, gymnasium, auditorium

PLAYING AREA: Two restraining lines not less than 30 feet apart

FORMATION: Players are divided into two teams and each stands behind its own restraining line.

PROCEDURE: Members of Team A select some type of work on the farm or elsewhere to be demonstrated. While advancing across the field the following conversation takes place:

Team A: "Here we come!"
Team B: "Where from?"
Team A: Gives name of some town or city.
Team B: "What's your trade?"

Thereupon the members of Team A perform the action agreed upon. Team B members try to guess the trade. When a player of Team B calls out the correct answer all Team A players turn and dash to cross their own restraining line, with Team B members chasing them. The latter are privileged to tag as many Team A players as they can. Those tagged return to Team B's position and play with them. Team B selects a trade and the game continues.

TEACHING SUGGESTIONS

1. If the trade selected is too difficult to guess readily, use initials of the descriptive words as an aid.
2. Require the visiting team members to advance close to the opposite restraining line before beginning their trade actions. It may be necessary to draw a second line not more than three feet in from the restraining lines, visiting players being required to toe these lines before beginning the trade pantomime.

TWO BASE KICK

NUMBER OF PLAYERS: 6-30

SPACE: Playground, gymnasium

PLAYING AREA: Court 45 by 90 feet (Figure 96). One end line is the kicking line. Within the court, 15 feet from the kicking line and paralleling it, is the base line. Forty-five feet from the kicking line, on the two side lines, first and second bases are placed. Home base is anywhere behind the base line between the side lines.

EQUIPMENT: Soccer ball (lightweight) or large rubber ball

Procedure

The purpose of the game is for team members to kick a ball and then make as many runs as possible before being put out. The game is played in one inning and the inning is over when all members of both teams are out.

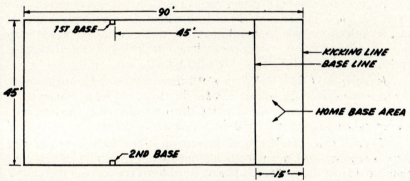

Figure 96.   Two Base Kick Court

FORMATION: One team lines up behind the kicking line. The second team goes into the field.

Kickers: Each kicker, placing the ball on the kicking line, tries to kick the ball beyond the base line and within the end and side lines of the court. Only one kick is allowed. The kicker may not stand with the supporting foot on or beyond the kicking line during the act of kicking.

Runners: The kicker becomes a runner the instant the ball is kicked. The runner tries to reach first base before the ball can be thrown across the base line by a fielder.

Runners on bases try to progress successfully from first base to second base, then across the base line at any point they may select. There may be any number of runners at the same time on either or both bases. Runners who leave a base may not return to it.

Fielders: Fielders, on securing the ball, try to throw it over the base line within the two side lines. Fielders should be encouraged to throw the ball from the place where they secure it or to throw it to a fielder who is nearer the base line.

FAIR BALL: A fair ball is (1) any ball legally kicked over the base line and within the dimensions of the court, (2) a ball which, when legally kicked within bounds, rolls or bounces outside the playing field, (3) a caught fly ball whether caught within or outside the dimensions of the playing area, or (4) a line ball.

DEAD BALL: The ball is dead or out of play either before or after the runner reaches first base or other bases (1) when it crosses the base line after being thrown by a fielder, (2) following a caught fly ball, (3) if the ball fails to enter the official area when kicked, or (4) if the kicker misses the ball when attempting a kick. Runners may not advance when the ball is a dead ball.

OUTS

Kickers are Out: (1) When the ball is kicked at but is missed; (2) when the ball is kicked but fails to land within the official playing area, that is, inside base, side, and end lines, (3) when the kicker stands with the supporting foot on or over the kicking line during the act of kicking, or (4) when a fly ball is caught by a fielder.

Runners are Out: (1) When a ball thrown by a fielder passes over the base line before the runner reaches first base, (2) when caught off a base or between bases at the time the thrown ball crosses the base line. Players when put out retire and do not return as kickers.

Team is Out: (1) When all players of a team have been put out. Players who succeed in making home runs continue kicking in turn until eliminated from the game. (2) If and when bases are full and there is no player left to kick.

SCORING: (1) One point is scored when a runner crosses the base line ahead of the ball at any point on the base line after having successfully made first and second bases. (2) One point is given the fielding team for each fly ball caught. (3) The team wins which has the larger number of points at the conclusion of the playing period.

TEACHING SUGGESTIONS

1. Use Two Base Kick to teach the place kick and the technique of catching a kicked ball.
2. Teach the fielders not to run while holding the ball.
3. Teach children to run on any kicked ball, not waiting to see if it is a fair or foul ball.
4. Permit younger children to kick the ball regardless of the position of the supporting foot.
5. Have members of the kicking team try to stop the ball after it crosses the base line, since it becomes dead on crossing the base line from the field of play.
6. Use this game to teach skills of Kick Ball and other soccer type games.

WEATHER VANE

NUMBER OF PLAYERS: 5-40

SPACE: Playground, classroom, playroom, gymnasium, hallway, auditorium

FORMATION: One player is chosen to be the wind. The remaining players are scattered about.

PROCEDURE: When the wind calls "North!" all players turn to that direction. They do the same if east or west or south is called. When "Variable" is called they move forward and backward; when "Tempest" is called they turn around three times where they are standing.

Players who fail to follow directions raise an arm to signify their error; or they may, at the conclusion of the game, have to pay a forfeit, or perform some stunt designated by the other players.

Relays

ACROSS THE ROOM RELAY

NUMBER OF PLAYERS: 6-40

SPACE: Classroom

EQUIPMENT: For each team, eraser, beanbag, or knotted towel

FORMATION: Team members are arranged so that they will be seated in rows across the room. An eraser (or substitute) is placed on the floor beside each row of players.

PROCEDURE: At a signal the player at the end of each row picks up the eraser with the nearest hand, changes it from one hand to the other while held high above his head, and puts the eraser on the floor in the aisle between him and the second player. That player repeats the action. Erasers are thus worked across the room until the last player of one row puts his eraser on the floor and raises both hands high in the air. First team to finish wins.

TEACHING SUGGESTIONS

1. Lengthen the game by requiring the return of the eraser to the original player, who on receiving it places it on the floor and lifts both hands high in the air.
2. Use additional objects to be passed successively. As the last player receives them, they are placed on the floor. If the objects are to be returned immediately, the last object to reach the end player must be placed on the floor and a different object started on the return trip.

AROUND THE ROW RELAY

NUMBER OF PLAYERS: 4-40

SPACE: Classroom

FORMATION: Children are seated with an even number of players in each row. If a team is short a player, have a child run twice, but the runs should not be consecutive.

PROCEDURE: At a signal, the last player in each row leaves his seat on the right-hand side, runs forward, continues to the left around his own row of seats and re-enters his seat from the right-hand side. The leader records which team player is first seated, and then signals the second player to run. The game continues until all have run.

SCORING: A point is given for each player who finishes the run before his opponent, and the team with the most points, after all have run, is the winner.

TEACHING SUGGESTIONS

1. See that children are careful to keep aisles unobstructed while players are running.
2. Instruct players to leave their seats from the right-hand side and re-enter them from the same side. Walk the pattern several times if necessary.
3. When played outdoors players should stand in two parallel lines. At a signal the last child in each row runs forward and continues to the left around his teammates back to his own place, whereupon the one next to him runs.

CHRISTMAS RELAY

NUMBER OF PLAYERS: 6-40

SPACE: Classroom

FORMATION: Players are seated, with an equal number of players in each row. They are numbered from front to rear. Each Number 1 player has a piece of chalk.

PROCEDURE: On a signal, Number 1 players run to the blackboard and draw a base for a Christmas tree. They return to their seats and hand the chalk to Number 2 players, who run forward and draw the tree standing in its base. Number 3 players add Christmas tree decorations (any designated number); Number 4 players attach the candles (any designated number); Number 5 players place a star at the top of their tree; Number 6 players write under their tree, "Merry Christmas!"

The team wins whose Number 1 player first has the chalk in his hand after all of the team members have played.

TEACHING SUGGESTIONS

1. Repeat the game, having players erase various parts of the completed tree.
2. Simplify the game by having the leader first draw a tree and then instruct the different numbered players as to what their job is to be.
3. Organize a relay for Thanksgiving by using the various parts of a turkey such as the head, body, legs, tail, feathers, comb.
4. If there are more than six players in each row, designate additional parts of the tree to be drawn.

CROSS OVER RELAY

NUMBER OF PLAYERS: 6-40

SPACE: Playground, playroom, gymnasium

PLAYING AREA: Two parallel lines 20 feet apart

EQUIPMENT: For each team, volleyball, basketball, soccer ball, utility ball or playground baseball, beanbag, stuffed leather ball casing, or knotted towel.

FORMATION: The teams stand in file formation behind the starting line. Each holds a ball.

PROCEDURE: On a signal, each leader runs across the farther line, faces about, and with both feet behind the line, throws the ball to the second player of his file who has stepped up and stands behind the starting line. The second player, upon catching the ball, runs across, stands behind the goal line and in front of the first player, and throws the ball to the third player. The game continues until all have crossed the farther line. If a player fumbles a ball thrown to him from behind the goal line, he must secure the ball and before beginning his run must return behind the starting line and throw the ball. If a player behind the starting line throws the ball so inaccurately that it cannot be caught, the thrower must recover the ball and return behind the starting line before throwing it the second time.

As soon as the last player of one team has crossed the goal line, the game is over, that player's team being the winner.

TEACHING SUGGESTIONS

1. As skill in throwing is gained, increase the distance between the lines.
2. If team memberships are uneven, have a player run twice but not consecutively.

HUSTLE BUSTLE RELAY

NUMBER OF PLAYERS: 6-40

SPACE: Classroom

EQUIPMENT: Beanbag, utility ball, blackboard eraser, knotted towel, or stuffed leather ball casing, one for each team

FORMATION: Children are divided into two teams. Members of one team stand in the aisle next to the windows. The other team members stand in the aisle next to the far wall. Captains stand at the rear of the room near the end of their teams. Each holds a beanbag. One aisle (or two aisles) in the center of the room is selected as the trailway for the runners.

PROCEDURE: On a signal, each captain runs toward the other, passes up the trailway to the front of the room, turns off and runs to the head of his own line, where he stops and passes the beanbag to the first man of his file. The beanbag is passed down the file of players, and the last man runs. Continue until the captain of one team receives the beanbag when standing in his former starting position. His team is the winner.

TEACHING SUGGESTIONS

1. Have each captain stand with his teammates when the signal to run is given.
2. Do not permit a new runner to leave the file position until the beanbag is received by him.
3. If a beanbag is dropped, have the runner pick it up before he can proceed.
4. Use a beanbag as more adapted to classroom use than a ball, because it does not roll.

LINE BALL RELAY [1]

NUMBER OF PLAYERS: 6-40

SPACE: Classroom

PLAYING AREA: A line drawn in front of the room two feet from and paralleling the front wall; a second line drawn between the front desks of each aisle, and paralleling the first line.

EQUIPMENT: Beanbags or utility balls, one for each row.

FORMATION: The first child in each row crosses to the front wall behind the line and faces his line of players. Each is given a beanbag. Unless there is an equal number of players in each row, one or more children should be designated to play twice for the team or teams short a player.

---

[1] Developed by Margaret Van Voorhees.

PROCEDURE: At a signal, the second child in each row stands, toes the aisle line, receives the toss from the leader, returns the ball to the leader, and sits down. Number 3 advances to the line, receives the ball, throws it back and retires to his seat. When the leader has thrown to all the members of his team he runs to cross the aisle line while holding the ball. The team wins whose captain first crosses the aisle line with the ball in his hand.

TEACHING SUGGESTIONS

1. Do not permit any player to advance to the aisle line until the previous player returns and sits with his feet and body out of the aisle.
2. Develop good sitting posture as a part of this relay.

OBJECT PASSING RELAY

NUMBER OF PLAYERS: 8-40

SPACE: Playground, playroom, classroom, gymnasium, hallway

EQUIPMENT: Beanbags, knotted towels, buckeye tree seeds, or balls, one for each team

FORMATION: Players of each team stand side by side in line formation, not more than eight players to a team. Each captain holds a beanbag.

PROCEDURE: At a signal, a beanbag is passed along the line as rapidly as possible to the foot. The last player touches the beanbag to the floor and starts it back toward the top of the line. The bag may be handled in different ways, such as using the right hand, the left hand, or both hands to pass it; by having it touched to the floor by each player before being sent on; having it passed with the feet by each player to the next player. If a bag is dropped or is not passed according to the selected method it must be returned to the head player to be restarted by him.

The team wins whose captain first receives the returned beanbag.

TEACHING SUGGESTIONS

1. If played in a classroom, have the children stand sideways in the aisles, each row of children forming a team, and with each two rows of players facing each other.

SCRAMBLE RELAY

NUMBER OF PLAYERS: 6-40

SPACE: Playground, playroom, gymnasium, auditorium, hallway

PLAYING AREA: A starting line and a goal line drawn at any desired distance from and parallel to each other

FORMATION: Teams line up in file formation behind the starting line.

PROCEDURE: At a signal, the first player in each file runs forward across the goal line, turns, and runs back, tagging the hand of the second player as he passes. He retires to the end of his file. The game continues until all have run. The first team to finish wins.

TEACHING SUGGESTIONS

1. Have file members move forward each time a runner leaves his position. The waiting player must have both feet behind the starting line while waiting to be tagged.
2. Have runners cross the goal line with both feet before returning to the starting line.
3. Teach children to tag with their right hand the right hand of the children waiting. Thus children would always return to the same side of the line and avoid accidents.

STOOP AND STRETCH RELAY

NUMBER OF PLAYERS: 6-40

SPACE: Classroom, playground

PLAYING AREA: In the aisles, between the front desks, draw lines.

EQUIPMENT: For each team, beanbag, stuffed leather ball casing, clothespin, knotted towel, or ball

FORMATION: Alternate rows of children play as teams. There should be an equal number of players in each row. Teams not playing are seated. Players stand beside desks facing forward. Leaders stand on their starting line. A beanbag is placed on the floor in front of each leader.

PROCEDURE: At a signal, each leader bends and secures his beanbag with both hands, rises, and drops it to the floor behind him, using both hands. The second player picks it up and drops it, using both hands. When the last player in each file secures the bag he runs up the vacant aisle, stops in front of his file, toes the line, and drops the beanbag over his head. While the last man is running the players move backward the distance of one desk. The first team to finish wins.

TEACHING SUGGESTIONS

1. Have all seated children keep their feet under their desks.
2. After half the teams have run, have the second group play the game.
3. If desired, have the winning team of each playing period compete to determine the final winner.
4. Have leaders standing erect when signal is given to commence playing.

Rhythmical Activities

BEAN PORRIDGE HOT [1]

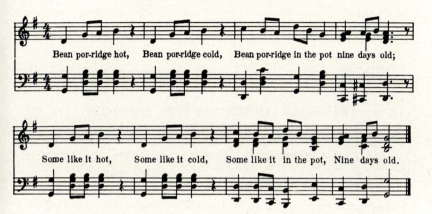

Bean por-ridge hot,   Bean por-ridge cold,   Bean por-ridge in the pot nine days old;

Some like it hot,   Some like it cold,   Some like it in the pot, Nine days old.

Victor Record No. 22761

FORMATION: Double circle with partners facing, boys on the outside.

DESCRIPTION: This is an excellent game for fun night parties or to rest a group who are weary from sitting in auditorium seats. All sing while performing the actions.

Measures 1-4. "Bean porridge hot"—all clap own hands to thighs, clap own hands together, clap partner's two hands. "Bean porridge cold"—all repeat above actions. "Bean porridge"—all clap own hands to thighs, clap own hands together. "In the pot"—all clap partner's right hand; clap own hands. "Nine days old"—all clap partner's left hand, clap own hands together, clap partner's two hands.

Measures 5-8.   All repeat above.

Chorus: Music is repeated. Partners join hands, arms extended sideways, and take 16 sliding steps counterclockwise, then 16 steps to return to place. During the last measure all move to left one place and meet a new partner.

Entire pattern is repeated with new partner.

They continue as long as desired.

Variation for Classroom: A single circle is formed, partners facing. When seats are permanently fastened to the floor, pupils may form a single circle (elongated) around a row of desks or around the outer aisles of the classroom. For a class with a large enrollment and a limited area, pupils may

[1] State of Alabama, *Manual of Physical Education*, 1923. By permission of Alabama State Department of Education.

form a single circle around a row of desks or two circles around rows of desks but with a row of desks separating the two circles. The game is played as described above, Measures 1-8. At the chorus, pupils face inward and join hands, holding them high, slide 16 steps to left or right and back to starting place. To secure a new partner, each faces partner, gives him the right hand, passes him, right shoulder to right shoulder, gives next person the left hand and passes to left, and takes the next person by the right hand as the new partner. Dance is repeated.

NOTE: See description of Grand Chain (or Grand Right and Left), page 207.

BLUEBIRD THROUGH THE WINDOW

Arranged by Anna Hermitage

Here comes a lit-tle blue-bird through the win-dow,

Through the win-dow, Through the win-dow, Here comes a lit-tle blue-bird

through the win-dow, Hur-rah for gin-ger snaps.

Verse 2. Salute your choice and rally at the window,
              Rally at the window,
              Rally at the window.
           Salute your choice and rally at the window,
              Hurrah for gingersnaps.

Verse 3. Ah, make a little bow and take her by the shoulders,
              Take her by the shoulders,
              Take her by the shoulders.
           Ah, make a little bow and take her by the shoulders,
              Hurrah for gingersnaps.

FORMATION: Single circle, boys and girls alternating, all facing center with hands joined high in the air. One or more children in the center are bluebirds.

DESCRIPTION: All sing words as they perform the action.

Verse 1. Circle players stand still. Bluebirds move in and out of the windows formed by raised arms of circle players, all going in the same direction. On last line, each center player stops in front of a circle player. Boys choose girls, girls choose boys.

Verse 2. Facing their partners, bluebirds and chosen partners do a shuffle step in place, bowing to each other twice. Girls hold skirts to side and boys grasp tops of their trousers at the sides.

Verse 3. Partners bow and place hands on each other's shoulders, turning each other around in place, using a short running step. They bow twice while turning.

Verses are repeated, the chosen players joining the other bluebirds in the center, until all become bluebirds.

CARROUSEL [1]

Arranged by Grace Van Ness

Lit-tle chil-dren sweet and gay Car-rou-sel is run-ning, It will run till eve-ning
Lit-tle ones a nick-el Big ones a dime Hur-ry up, get a mate Or you'll
sure-ly be too late Ha, ha, ha, hap-py are we
An-der-son and Pe-ter-son and Hen-der-son and me.

Victor Record No. 20432

FORMATION: Partners form a double circle, facing inward. Inside circle players, representing the machinery and animals of a merry-go-round, join hands. Outside players, representing the riders of the merry-go-round, place hands on the shoulders or around the waist of their partners. The machinery must not break down by having hands break apart, nor must the riders be thrown off during the chorus. For a strong hold, inside circle players may slide their fingers up the palms of the players on either side of them until the wrists can be grasped. They should pull in toward the center, to lessen the pull on the shoulders.

DESCRIPTION: Music begins slowly and tempo is accelerated until it doubles by the 8th measure.

Measures 1-5. Circles move to the right, taking two slides to a measure.

[1] Adapted from M. R. Wild and D. E. White, *Physical Education for Elementary Schools.* Cedar Falls, Iowa: Iowa State Teachers' College, 1924. By permission.

Measures 6-7. Slides become four stamps.

Measures 8-11. Music tempo is doubled and the carrousel is in full swing, four slides to a measure.

Measures 8-11 repeated.

Entire pattern is repeated, with inside circle players exchanging positions with outside circle players.

CHILDREN'S POLKA [1]
(Kinderpolka)

Victor Record No. 20432

FORMATION: Single circle, partners facing, boys and girls alternating. Hands are joined and extended to the side at shoulder height.

DESCRIPTION: While the dance is called "Children's Polka," the polka

[1] From C. Ward Crampton, *The Folk Dance Book.* New York: A. S. Barnes & Co., 1909. By permission.

step is not used. Slides and steps should be made lightly with plenty of spring.

Measures 1-4. All glide toward center ("slide, close, slide, close"), take three running steps in place (2 measures). They repeat, moving away from center (2 measures).

Measures 5-8. Measures 1-4 are repeated.

Measures 9-12. All clap own thighs with hands; clap own hands once in slow rhythm; clap partner's hands three times in fast rhythm (2 measures). Repeat (2 measures).

Measures 13-14. All simultaneously point right toe forward and place right elbow in left hand, shaking forefinger three times at partner (1 measure). Repeat, using left foot and left hand (1 measure).

Measure 15. All make a complete turn to the right using four jumps (1 measure).

Measure 16. All face partners and stamp three times.

Dance is repeated as often as desired. Between repetitions players may move forward one place and secure a new partner.

CSHEBOGAR [1]
(Hungarian)

Methodist Record No. 101

Victor Record No. 20992

FORMATION: Single circle, boys and girls alternating, hands joined.

DESCRIPTION

A

Measures 1-4. All take eight slides to the left, two slides to each measure; on the eighth count all raise hands and shout, "Whee!"

Measures 5-8. All take eight slides to the left and shout.

Measures 1-2 repeated. All take three steps into the center, starting with the right foot, and stamp on the fourth count.

Measures 3-4. All take three steps backward, starting with the left foot, and stamp on the fourth count.

---

[1] *We Sing.* Sacramento: California State Department of Education, 1942. By permission of C. C. Birchard & Co.

This is a dance tune, but words have been added for those who may wish to sing while they dance or while others dance.

Measures 5-8. Placing his right arm around his partner's waist, each boy holds his left arm high and partners turn together, both starting with the right foot, taking seven running steps and stamping on the eighth count.

B

Measures 9-12. Back in circle formation, each faces partner and places both hands on his or her shoulders. All take four slow slides towards the center of the circle, dragging the outside foot and looking toward the center of the circle.

Cshebogar

Ruth Harrison   Piano by Gladys Pitcher

Tra la la la, tra la la la, tra, la, la! Whee! Tra la la la,

tra la la la, tra la la! Whee! Slide once, slide twice, slide on three and
                                    Slide once, slide twice, slide us back a-

four;   Slide once,   slide twice,   slide us back once more
gain;   One, two,   three, four,   five and six and sev'n. (*stamp*)

Measures 13-16. All take four slow slides back to the outside of the circle, this time dragging the inside foot and looking towards the center of the circle.

Measures 9-10 repeated. All take two slow slides towards the center.

Measures 11-12. All take two slow slides towards the outside of the circle.

Measures 13-16. The turn is repeated as in Measures 5-8 (A).

The dance may be repeated as many times as desired.

HOT CROSS BUNS

Arranged by Anna Hermitage

1. Hot cross buns,
2. Hot cross buns,
3. One a penny,
4. Two a penny,
5. Hot cross buns.
6. If your daughters don't like them,
7. Give them to your sons.
8. One a penny, two a penny, hot cross buns.

FORMATION: Double circle formation, facing line of direction, partners with hands joined.

DESCRIPTION: All sing words as actions are performed.

1. All step forward with outside foot, swinging joined hands back; step forward with inside foot, swinging joined hands forward; step forward with outside foot, swinging joined hands back; point inside foot forward and hold.
2. All change hands, swing around and repeat 1, going in opposite direction.
3. All face partners, point right foot forward, hold up first finger of right hand to partner, and put left hand on hip.
4. All change to left foot forward, two fingers of left hand up, right hand on hip.
5. With both hands on hips, all make a quick change of right foot front, left foot front, then right foot front, pointed.
6. Girls put hands on hips and shake head, "no." Boys hold out both hands to partners, palms up, and bow.
7. Girls extend hands, palms up. Boys nod heads, "yes."
8. All repeat 3, 4, 5.

Music is repeated and, without singing, all dance face-to-face and back-to-back polka, moving in a circle as in step number 1. At the end of the dance each player moves to his own left and meets a new partner.

The whole dance is repeated with the new partner.

INDIAN WAR DANCE [1]

FORMATION: All players seated cross-legged in a single circle.

DESCRIPTION: The players go through the following pantomime, representing offering prayer to the Great Spirit and smoking the pipe of peace.

Measures 1-4. All raise the arms overhead and sway the body forward; raise the trunk again. They repeat this twice.

Measures 5-8. They repeat the action, bending to right and then to left.

Measures 9-12. All bring arms down to the side and raise them slowly overhead. This is repeated twice.

Measures 13-16. All smoke the pipe of peace four times. An imaginary pipe is passed from one to the other. On the last count all jump up, fling the arms straight up over the head and yell "Wow!" They face in counterclockwise direction so as to advance with the Indian step.

Measures 1-16 repeated. All crouch forward; leap on the right foot and swing the left up at the back; leap on the left foot, and swing the right up at the back. On the second measure all take three quick running

---

[1] Lydia Clark, *Physical Training for the Elementary Schools.* New York: Benj. H. Sanborn & Co., 1917-21. By permission.

Indian War Dance

Source Unknown

steps, right, left, right. The arms are bent at the elbows and are moved sharply up and down as the steps are taken. This is repeated for sixteen measures, alternating right and left foot.

Measure 17. All squat down, slap the floor with the right hand and then with the left hand.

Measure 18. With right hand over the mouth, all yell, "Wow, wow, wow!"

Measures 19-20. All slap the floor again, left, then right; and with left hand over the mouth, repeat the Indian yell.

Measures 21-24. The Indian step (as in Measures 1-16 repetition) is repeated twice.

Measures 25-32. Measures 17-24 are repeated, ending with "Wow!"

JOLLY IS THE MILLER [1]
(English)

Arranged by E. B. Gordon

Jol - ly is the mil - ler who lived by the mill. The wheel goes round with a right good will. One hand in the hop-per and the oth-er in the sack, The right skips for-ward and the left skips back.

Victor Record No. 20214; and No. 45-5067 (Album E 87)

Decca Record No. 18223 (Album 278)

FORMATION: Double circle, boys on the outside, partners side by side with inside hands joined and held high.

DESCRIPTION: During the singing of the verse players march forward. To secure a new partner at the end of the game, each boy steps forward to the position directly ahead of him. Game is then repeated.

[1] *Manual of Physical Education*, Part III, Folk and Singing Games. Madison: Wisconsin State Department of Education, 1924. By permission.

If desired, music can be repeated and all skip with the partner they have. Boys advance to new positions as the skip music ends. Girls slow up to permit boys to reach them.

Variations: A number of variations may be used. This is an excellent party game for fun nights. Adults may walk rapidly around instead of skipping, as may students on a limited physical education program.

1. Form circle as above, but with one player in the center of the circle. Players march forward while singing the verse, and at the last word, "back," and not before, inside circle players (girls) reverse direction and start skipping. Odd player joins those skipping on the inside. During the chorus, circle players skip forward, each circle going in the opposite direction, until music stops. The leader may stop the music at any time while skipping is in process. When music stops, everyone tries to get a partner from the opposite circle. The unsuccessful player goes to the center and game is repeated.

2. Play as in 1, but have inside players stand still while outside players skip. Repeat, having outside players stand still while inside players skip.

3. Same as 1, except that both circles skip in opposite direction, passing their partners, and joining their partners again at starting position.

JUMP JIM CROW [1]

Arranged by E. B. Gordon

[1] State of Wisconsin, *Manual of Physical Education, op. cit.* By permission.

FORMATION: A double circle, partners facing, boys on the outside.

DESCRIPTION: All sing words as actions are performed.

Measures 1-2. Partners join hands and extend them sideways. They take two slow and three quick jumps in place.

Measures 3-4. With light running steps, boys turn partners in place.

Measures 5-6. Drop hands. Members of each circle slide twice to their own right, with the three stamps being done in front of a new partner.

Measures 7-8. Join hands with new partner, turn left in place with four steps and finish pattern with three jumps in place.

Repeat entire pattern with new partner.

NIGAREPOLSKA [1]
(Swedish Nixie Polka)

Victor Record No. 21685; and 27298

FORMATION: Single circle, boys and girls alternating. All face center with hands on hips. One or more children in the center. If circle is large have one center player for every 10-12 children.

DESCRIPTION

Measures 1-2. Circle and center players, on the words, "A little while," hop on left foot and bend left knee, at the same time extending right foot forward with heel on floor and toes turned up. On "We linger here," they spring and exchange position of feet.

Measures 3-4. At "with many a joy" above action is repeated, right heel touching; at "and many a fear," they spring again, with left heel touching.

---

[1] From C. Ward Crampton and M. A. Wollaston, *The Song Play Book.* New York: A. S. Barnes & Co., 1917. By permission.

Measures 5-8. On word "Hey" all clap hands once. Circle players run in place while center players run off and select a partner from among the circle players; boys select girls, girls select boys. Center players stop in front of the partner chosen and all continue to run until end of eighth measure. Measures 5-8 may be repeated, thereby making the run longer.

Measures 1-4. While facing partners, all repeat action of Measures 1-4.

Measures 5-8. On "Hey" center players about-face, partners place hands on shoulders of person who chose them and both run off to select a third partner. This action is repeated until all have been chosen, with each line growing longer and acquiring a new leader (the end man) each time the turn is made. Game continues until all circle players have been chosen. Thereupon lines join onto other lines until one large circle is formed. Hands must remain on shoulders throughout except when the reverse turn is taken. Throughout, the action to form one large circle (the action for Measures 1-4) alternates with action for Measures 5-8. At the end the pianist can increase the tempo until the pattern cannot be maintained and the circle breaks up with laughter. This makes an excellent game for fun nights.

POP GOES THE WEASEL [1]

Methodist Record No. 104

Victor Record No. 20151

FORMATION: Double circle, with partners facing in line of direction, inside hands joined; boys on the inside.

DESCRIPTION: All sing, while performing dance.

Measures 1-2. Each, starting with outside foot, takes step, step, step, and point.

Measures 3-4. They repeat, starting with inside or pointing foot, step, step, step, and point.

Measure 5. Partners face. Boy steps to side with forward foot (left), places right foot behind and near heel of left foot, and bends both knees. At the same time, girl steps forward to side with her right foot, places left foot behind heel of right foot and bends both knees.

Measure 6. They repeat, boy stepping with his right foot and girl with her left.

Measures 7-8. Partners join right hands and girl skips under boy's right

---

[1] *Merry Music.* Edited by Peter W. Dykema and Others. A Singing School series. Boston: C. C. Birchard & Co., 1939. By permission.

arm, which is held high. All sing, "Pop Goes the Weasel." Whole dance pattern is repeated and on "Pop, etc." boy skips under girl's right arm. Each boy secures a new partner by stepping forward. Girls stand still.

Measures 9-16. (Chorus.) Entire pattern is repeated.

Variation. Every other couple faces in reverse direction; that is, Number 1 couple faces clockwise, Number 2 couple counterclockwise. Couples walk or skip four steps forward, then four steps backward (Measures 1-4). Each set of four joins hands and walks or skips to left four steps, returning to position (Measures 5-6). Couples Number 1 raise joined hands to form an arch and skip forward, four steps, while couples Number 2 skip forward under arch, four steps (Measures 7-8), and meet new couple. Repeat all as long as desired.

Pop Goes the Weasel

American Dance Song
Piano by Charles Repper

Traditional

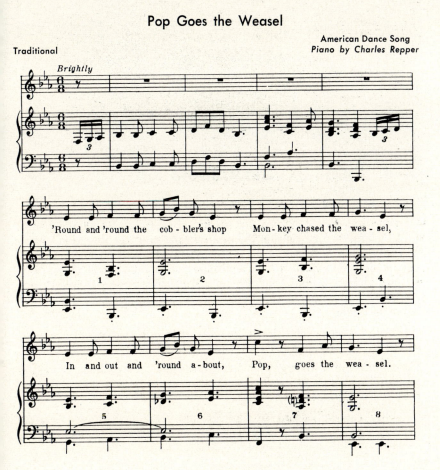

'Round and 'round the cob - bler's shop Mon - key chased the wea - sel,

In and out and 'round a - bout, Pop, goes the wea - sel.

Pen - ny for a spool of thread, Pen - ny for a need - le,

That's the way the mon - ey goes, Pop, goes the wea - sel.

Verse 2.   I've no time to wait or sigh;
            No patience to wait for bye and bye
            Kiss me quick, I'm off—good-bye,
            Pop goes the weasel!

RIG-A-JIG-JIG [1]

FORMATION: Single circle with boys and girls alternating.

DESCRIPTION: While all sing, one player, a boy (more for a large group) walks jauntily around inside the circle in the opposite direction to that taken by circle players. On the words "A pretty girl I chanced to meet" (or "A nice young man" or "A handsome man"), each center player bows to some girl in the circle, and they take hands in skating position. During the chorus the tempo of the music is increased and partners skip around inside the circle.

Dance is repeated with both players separating, walking in single file, choosing, and skipping. Continue until all are skipping.

Variation: One or more girls in the center. They choose partners and after the skip they retire to circle. Boys choose partners, skip with them and then retire. Continue alternating as long as desired.

"Rig-a-jig-jig" is fun for adult groups.

---

[1] Peter W. Dykema, *Twice 55 Games with Music.* Boston: C. C. Birchard & Co., 1924. By permission.

Rig-a-jig-jig

In leisurely walking rhythm

As I was walk-ing down the street, down the street, down the street, As
A pret-ty girl I chanc'd to meet, chanc'd to meet, chanc'd to meet, A

I was walk-ing down the street heigh o-heigh o - heigh - o.
pret-ty girl I chanc'd to meet heigh o-heigh o - heigh - o.

CHORUS *Faster: in skipping rhythm*

Rig-a-jig-jig and a - way we go, a - way we go, a - way we go;

Rig-a-jig-jig and a - way we go Heigh-o-heigh-o-heigh-o.

SKIP TO MY LOU

Decca Record No. 18224, Album 278

Victor Album E 87

FORMATION: Double circle facing counterclockwise. Boys on the inside. There should be several extra boys (or girls) in the center of the circle.

DESCRIPTION: Everybody sings.

Members of outside circle walk, skip, or step-hop around the circle. *Each* extra boy (girl) chooses a couple and takes them into the center of the circle with him. The three join hands and skip counterclockwise in own small circle as the first three lines are sung. When they sing "skip to my Lou, my darling," the girl's first partner goes under the raised hands of the girl and the extra man who chose her. These two are now partners and join the couples in the large circle. The new odd man secures a new partner for himself by selecting a couple. Action should be fast.

Continue until interest lags. There are many other verses to the game and their use should be encouraged. A boy or girl with a carrying voice might be selected to lead the singing.

Skip to My Lou

Arranged by Anna Hermitage

I've lost my gal now what'll I do I've lost my gal now what'll I do I've lost my gal now what'll I do Skip to my Lou my dar - ling.

Verse 2. Little red wagon painted blue, etc.
     3. Get me another purty as you, etc.
     4. Purty as a red bird, purtier too, etc.

SWEDISH RING DANCE [1]

Music: "Hopp Mor Annika," page 509

Victor Record No. 21618

FORMATION: Double circle, boys on inside. Partners join inside hands and face counterclockwise.

DESCRIPTION: During introduction each waits and salutes partner.

[1] Wild and White, *op. cit.* By permission of Iowa State Teachers' College, publishers.

Measures 1-4 and repeated. All walk forward around circle, arms swinging.

Measures 5-8 and repeated. All continue in same direction, but skip.

Measures 9-12. Dancers form a single circle, boys stepping backward. All join hands and slide to right, eight slides.

Measures 9-12 repeated. All slide eight slides to the left.

Measures 13-14. At the end of the slides, partners face quickly while in single circle. Partners separate by each sliding four slides to own right. Thus one partner moves in toward the center of the circle and the other moves out away from the center.

Measures 15-16. Both then slide four slides to own left, which brings them back to place, facing each other in a single circle.

Measures 13-16 repeated. Taking partner's right hand and raising left arm obliquely upward, all skip around partner with eight skipping steps, moving clockwise, and finish in double circle.

Entire dance is repeated. During introduction, boys move forward to a new partner and they greet each other.

SWISS MAY DANCE [1]

Victor Record No. 22761

FORMATION: Double circle, with boys on the outside, partners facing clockwise, inside hands joined.

DESCRIPTION: All sing while performing action.

Measures 1-3. All take nine running steps forward.

Measure 4. Partners face each other and curtsy or bow.

Measures 5-7. All face about and run nine steps back to starting position.

Measure 8. Partners face each other and bow or curtsy.

Measure 9. Partners join right hands and take three running steps, changing places with partner.

Measure 10. All face partners and bow or curtsy.

Measures 11-12. Measures 9-10 are repeated, partners crossing with left hands joined.

[1] C. Ward Crampton, *The Second Folk Dance Book.* New York: A. S. Barnes & Co., 1916. By permission.

Measures 13-14. Partners join right hands. Outside partner runs in place six steps, inside partner turns under raised arm of partner with six running steps.

Measure 15. Inside partner runs in place, three steps, outside partner runs forward three steps to next partner.

Measure 16. All bow or curtsy to new partners.

Dance is repeated from beginning.

Swiss May Dance

The cuck-oo is sing-ing "The spring it is here," On the fields and the for-est the green doth ap-pear; Then dance, chil-dren, dance, while the sky it is blue, Dance 'round and turn un-der while I go with you.

TEN LITTLE INDIANS[1]

FORMATION: Single circle, with all facing center. One player is outside the circle.

DESCRIPTION: The game is played in two parts.

---

[1] State of Wisconsin, *Manual of Physical Education, op. cit.* By permission.

Ten Little Indians

Arranged by E. B. Gordon

Chorus: Tra, la, la, la, la, etc.

2. Ten little, nine little, eight little Indians,
    Seven little, six little, five little Indians,
    Four little, three little, two little Indians,
    One little Indian boy (girl).

Chorus repeated.

I

Verse 1. During singing of verse, circle players stand still while the single player runs around outside the circle and tags ten players. Those tagged step immediately into the ring and join hands in a small circle.
Chorus. Players in the outer circle join hands and slide to the left. Those in the inner circle join hands and slide in the opposite direction.
Verse 2. Those in the center return to the outer circle in reverse order.
Chorus. All join hands and slide to the left.

II

Each child is given a number, from one to ten. They scatter about the room. Music is played without singing while all move in to form a circle with long steps, Indian fashion, crouching, shielding eyes, etc. When circle is reached all crouch down.

Verse 1. Verse is sung and as each child's number is reached he springs up and does an Indian step in place. When all are up they bend forward and do Indian step around circle, yelling as they sing the chorus.

NOTE: See American Indian Dance, page 199, and Indian War Dance, page 441.

Verse 2. As second verse is sung, all face center in a circle, and each Indian crouches when his number is reached. When all are crouched the music is played again, the Indians stealing away as their numbers are reached.

THREAD FOLLOWS THE NEEDLE [1]

The thread fol-lows the nee - dle, The thread fol-lows the nee - dle

In and out the nee-dle goes As moth - er mends the chil-dren's clothes.

Pioneer Record No. 3015

FORMATION: Single lines of about ten children each. Hands are joined. Children in each line are numbered.

DESCRIPTION: Number 10 stands in place. With a light running step Number 1 runs down the front of the line and passes under the raised arms of Numbers 9 and 10, drawing Numbers 1 to 8 after him. After they have passed under the arch, 9 and 10, keeping their hands joined, face in the opposite direction and stand with arms crossed on their chests. This starts a kind of "chain stitch." The leader runs to his former position and then, passing in front as before, runs between 8 and 9. Number 8 then turns and adds a "stitch" to the chain. This continues and the song is repeated until all the children in line have turned about in this manner. The leader, having passed under every arch in the line, then turns under his own arm, until all have faced about and all arms are crossed on the chests, making a chain.

At a signal the children all turn about and drop hands quickly, thus unraveling the chain and ripping out the stitches. The game is repeated with a new leader.

---

[1] Crampton & Wollaston, *op. cit.* By permission of A. S. Barnes & Co., publishers.

TWO-STEP

Music: Any good two-step or music in 2/4 time (Fox Trot)

FORMATION: Have group work forward in lines, then around room alone in circle formation; next with girl standing at right of partner.

DESCRIPTION: Directions apply to boy; girls use opposite foot when they are dancing as couples. Although the complete movement is done in two counts of music, there are three distinct steps plus a hold.

Measure 1. Slide left, close right, slide left, hold ("one, and, two, and"). Left foot slides forward, right foot closes to left foot, left foot slides forward.

Measure 2. Slide right, close left, slide right, hold ("one, and, two, and"). Right foot slides forward, passing beyond left foot; left foot closes to right foot, right foot slides forward. On the next measure the left foot passes beyond right foot on the first count.

Form in couples, using elbow grasp or social dancing position, and practice with boy going forward, girl backward, and then reverse. Practice turning to right and left.

The polka step evolves from the two-step when the hop is added at the beginning or end of the step.

YANKEE DOODLE [1]

1. Yankee Doodle went to town
2. Riding on a pony
3. He stuck a feather in his cap
4. And called him Macaroni.
5. Yankee Doodle, ha, ha, ha
6. Yankee Doodle Dandy
7. Yankee Doodle, ha, ha, ha
8. Buy the girls some candy.

FORMATION: A single circle is formed, all facing in line of direction; backs of hands on hips or held in front of body as if holding reins. In classroom, two rows of children play around one row of seats.

DESCRIPTION

1, 2. All take seven galloping steps forward in line of direction; at "pony," they halt and face center of circle.

3. All raise right hand and point right forefinger toward head; point forefinger upward to represent a feather; salute.

---

[1] Wild and White, *op. cit.* By permission of Iowa State Teachers College, publishers.
Music from Peter W. Dykema, *Twice 55 Games.* By permission of C. C. Birchard & Co., publishers.

4. All bow head and place tips of fingers on chest; step back on right foot and curtsy; bow well forward and extend arms sideways shoulder high.

5, 6. All join hands and circle to the right, sliding. At "Dandy," they stamp right, stamp left.

7, 8. All circle to left, sliding, and at "candy," clap hands twice.

Dance is repeated.

Yankee Doodle

ADDITIONAL RHYTHMICAL ACTIVITIES
IN THE CALIFORNIA STATE SERIES MUSIC TEXTBOOKS

New Music Horizons. Third Book. Edited by Osbourne McConathy and Others. (Copyrighted, 1944, 1949, by Silver Burdett Co.) Sacramento: California State Department of Education (1950).

Students' book and book of accompaniments and interpretation for the teacher. Page references are to the latter book.

Rhythms

Merry-Go-Round	3
Follow Me, Full of Glee	4
We Farmers Go to Market	6
Indian Lullaby	8
Marching Song	13

Singing Games and Folk Dances

List and Go	37
Seven Steps	46
The Needle's Eye	47
Polly, Put the Kettle On	59
Some Familiar Dances	70
The Bridge of Avignon	77

Rhythms

The Mill	16
Some Familiar Dances	31
Skating	63
Gavotte	68

Singing Games and Folk Dances

My Partner	92
The Lady Anne	93
Dances of Long Ago	100
Pop! Goes the Weasel	118
On the Railroad Train	155
When I Was a Water Boy	158

Merry Music. Edited by Theresa Armitage, Peter W. Dykema, and Gladys Pitcher. A Singing School series (copyrighted 1939, 1940, 1941, by C. C. Birchard & Co.). Sacramento: California State Department of Education, 1942.[1]

Students' book, teacher's manual, and book of accompaniments. Page references are to the last named book.

Rhythms

From Wheat to Bread	20
The Spinning Song	21
Meeting and Parting	25
Saturday Morning	27
Ball Games	30
Stop! Look! Listen!	40
The Fire Engine Bell	41
I'm a Duck	56
Hiawatha's Childhood	73

Singing Games

Adam's Sons	96
Button, You Must Wander	97
Sally Go Up	101

Rhythms

The Aeroplane	82
A Busy Day	95
The Jumping Rope	98
In the Parson's Yard	99
Polka	102
Hallowe'en	109
Dancing Is Fun	131
Dancing	145

Singing Games

The Minuet	152
Smoking the Peace Pipe	177
Minuet	179

SELECTED REFERENCES ON RHYTHMS[2]

Dixon, Clarice Madeleine. *The Power of Dance: The Dance and Related Arts for Children.* New York: The John Day Co., 1939.

---

[1] Former series (adoption period July 1, 1942 to July 1, 1950).
[2] Consult the bibliography and listing of phonograph records in the appendixes.

Gives data on the transition of play to art expression during the period between the ages 8 and 15. Extremely interesting reading for teachers, with helpful suggestions on how rhythm results were obtained.

Hunt, Beatrice A., and Wilson, Harry Robert. *Sing and Dance. Folk Songs and Dances Including American Play-Party Games.* Chicago: Hall & McCreary Co., 1945.

A variety of folk dances from many nations, for which there could be singing accompaniment, as well as full piano music and dance description.

Tobitt, Janet E. *Promenade All. A Compilation of Song-Dances.* New York: Janet E. Tobitt (228 E. 43d St.), 1947.

A collection of singing games and simple folk dances including melody and descriptions of the dances.

Stunts

A warm-up period or short run should precede stunt instruction. The material of previous grades should be reviewed before new stunts are introduced.

CAMEL AMBLE

SPACE: Playground or gymnasium.

PROCEDURE: Performer bends forward from the hips with back flattened. His hands reach backward and are clasped over the back with fingers pointing up to form a hump. He walks forward and, as each step is taken, pulls in and then pushes out chin, using a rhythmic motion.

DEEP SQUAT

SPACE: Playground, gymnasium

PROCEDURE: Performer should warm up with quick warm-up knee bends. With hands on hips and feet together he should go to a full squat with heels raised. He turns knees outward as body is lowered. The body must be maintained in erect position throughout the movement. A forward movement of the body should not be permitted. He returns to erect position.

DERVISH JUMP

SPACE: Gymnasium or playground.

PROCEDURE: Performer jumps into the air and makes a half-turn to the right. This is repeated, performer turning to left. He keeps this up, using arms for balance, until tired or balance is lost.

FORWARD ROLL [1]

SPACE: Playground, gymnasium

EQUIPMENT: Mat

PROCEDURE: The hands are placed flat on the floor, shoulder width apart, between the knees, with fingers pointing straight ahead. The head is tucked under, chin against neck; knees are bent and legs and heels are against the thighs. These positions are maintained throughout the rolling movement. The hands or forearms carry the weight of the body forward until shoulders or upper spine contact the mat. No direct weight should be taken by the head or neck. A beginner will take the starting position and by slowly tipping forward will roll from his hands onto his rounded back for a perfect slow-motion forward roll.

There may be enough momentum to stand after the first roll. Momentum for roll is gained through a strong push by the toes as the hands take the body weight. As roll occurs the surface area must be contacted by shoulders, rounded spine, and then the hips to the feet. The push should be strong enough to carry the body, at the finish of the roll, up over the shins in order that an erect standing position may be attained.

Person assisting tumbler should kneel at the side and place one hand on the shoulders and the other under the ankles. At the same time he MUST KEEP his own body and head ERECT so that, as assistance is given the performer through the push and lift, flying feet will not hit him in the face.

As skill is gained the roll may start from bent-knee standing position, erect standing position, following a jump, and at end of a run. The last two develop into the Dive.

Performer should be able at any time to drop into a forward roll, if balance becomes insecure while performing head or hand stands or other activities which require the inverted position.

HUMAN ROCKER

SPACE: Playground, gymnasium

EQUIPMENT: Mat

PROCEDURE: The performer lies face down, grasps his ankles, throwing the head back and elevating the chest. While the abdomen is kept rounded, he rocks back and forth from knees to chest. Action may be started by falling forward from kneeling position as the hands grasp the ankles.

---

[1] William Ralph LaPorte and Al G. Renner, *The Tumbler's Manual*. New York: Prentice-Hall, Inc., 1938. Pp. 10-17, illustrated. The techniques of the forward roll are illustrated and "don'ts" emphasized. This is excellent for the pupils to study themselves.

MEASURING WORM

SPACE: Playroom, gymnasium, playground

PROCEDURE: The body is extended along the floor in a straight line, face down, with weight on arms and toes. While arms remain stationary and legs fully extended, without body sag, performer takes very tiny steps until feet reach hands. When feet are in position, hands move forward with inching steps until the body is straight again. At no time should body be allowed to sag.

This is repeated several times without pausing.

POLE CLIMBING

SPACE: Gymnasium or outdoor playground

EQUIPMENT: Pole or rope for climbing

PROCEDURE: Performer climbs at least halfway up a climbing pole or rope and descends gradually, controlling the descent.

Figure 97. Swing Off

SEAL WALK

Space: Gymnasium or playground

Procedure: Legs are extended backward along the floor and in relaxed position from the hips down. Weight is on arms and body is pulled forward by alternating use of the arms. Legs take no part in the movement.

STAIR CLIMBING

Space: Stairway of building, indoors or outdoors

Procedure: Performers walk upstairs in best possible posture. No bend is allowed at the hips. Trunk and head must be carried over the pelvic base. Feet are not slapped down. An upward, springy step is taken.

Descent is made in a similar co-ordinated manner.

SWING OFF

Space: Gymnasium or playground

Equipment: Horizontal bar, mat if in gymnasium

Procedure: Performers hang by knees from horizontal bar and drop, landing on the feet (Figure 97).

TEACHING SUGGESTION

1. Soft landing area is essential for all work on horizontal bar.

Chapter XVII
ACTIVITIES FOR FOURTH GRADE

Activities are alphabetically arranged by title within the following four classes:

The games fall into several classes. They are indexed here by type for the convenience of the teacher.

Games

BARLEY BREAK

NUMBER OF PLAYERS: 1-40

SPACE: Playground, playroom, gymnasium

PLAYING AREA: Three continuous areas of approximately the same size, the dimensions depending on the number of children participating. A basketball court divided into three sections may be used.

FORMATION: Players are divided into two groups; a group is placed in each end area. Each player selects a partner. One couple goes into the center area or barley field. These two must always play with their arms linked. They are the wardens of the barley.

PROCEDURE: Partners in the end areas, with linked arms or singly, advance into the barley field and trample the barley. As they move about they taunt the wardens by calling, "Barley Break! Barley Break!" If partners enter the barley field with linked arms they must remain so until they re-enter their own end area.

The wardens try to tag some one. When chased, players must retire to their own end area because to enter the opposite one is not permissible. If one of a couple is tagged that player stands inactive within the barley field until his partner is caught, whereupon they link arms and join the other taggers.

The last couple to be tagged become wardens for a new game. Others in the barley field retire to their end area and the game is resumed.

TEACHING SUGGESTIONS

1. Have players venture far into the barley.
2. Encourage the timid players to be daring by helping timid children to find daring partners.
3. Do not remove tagged player from the game.

BATTLEDORE AND SHUTTLECOCK [1]

NUMBER OF PLAYERS: 1 or 2

SPACE: Playground if no wind is blowing; gymnasium, classroom

EQUIPMENT: For each player (1) a battledore (plywood paddle); (2) one or more shuttlecocks. The battledore may be one of the following: inexpensive racket found in variety stores; handmade long-handled paddle [2]; paddle-tennis paddle; or badminton racket.

---

[1] A very old game. The Chinese play the game using their feet to kick the shuttlecock.
[2] See directions for making battledore, p. 115.

FORMATION: An individual may play alone or with a partner.

PROCEDURE: The player tries to keep one or more shuttlecocks in the air simultaneously, or one or more shuttlecocks are batted simultaneously back and forth between two players. The object, in either case, is to see how long the shuttlecocks can be kept from touching the floor or other objects.

SCORING: Each time the shuttlecock is struck it counts one point. Whenever a shuttlecock falls to the floor a new count begins at one. Scores as high as 500 are possible.

TEACHING SUGGESTIONS

1. Develop eye skill in judging the direction of moving objects and the co-ordination of arm and eye to hit them successfully.
2. Pick up birdies carefully to avoid breaking the feathers. The feathers should be smoothed out each time the shuttlecock is picked up.
3. Use this game as an aid to posture habits, since players are constantly looking at a moving object high in the air.

BEARS AND CATTLE

NUMBER OF PLAYERS: 6-40

SPACE: Playground, gymnasium, auditorium

PLAYING AREA: Two goal lines are drawn, each 30 feet long and at least 50 feet apart. If the tendency of the players is to scatter too widely, connecting side lines are drawn. At one side of the playing area and halfway between the goal lines, the lines for a bear's den, 10 by 10 feet, are drawn.

FORMATION: One player, the bear, stands inside the den. The remaining players are divided into two groups and stand behind the goal lines. They are the cattle.

PROCEDURE: The cattle try to cross the opposite goal line to reach new pasture. Cattle may not return to the pasture they left. As they start running the bear leaves his den and tries to tag as many as possible. Players, if tagged, become bears and retire to the bear's den to wait for him. After all have exchanged positions the bear retires to his den. The bear and those caught join hands and form a line; the first bear is always at one end, the first player tagged at the other end. Only the two end players may tag cattle.

If, while chasing, the bears' line breaks, the end bears may not tag players and the cattle may drive the bears toward the den until the bears succeed in reforming their line. They then may give chase and continue until all the cattle are in their new pasture. The last one of the cattle to be tagged becomes the bear in the new game.

TEACHING SUGGESTIONS

1. If the group to play is small, reduce the dimensions of the field. Experience will determine the best size for a fine game.
2. If large numbers are to play, have all stand behind one goal line. This will prevent children from running into each other as they cross from opposite sides of the playing area.

THE BOILER BURST

NUMBER OF PLAYERS: 5-40

SPACE: Classroom

FORMATION: Seats are arranged so that there will be available one less seat than there are players. If seats are permanently fixed, a book is placed on those not to be used.

PROCEDURE: The player without a seat stands at the front of the room and begins a story. At its most dramatic point, the narrator says, "And then—the boiler burst!"At this all listeners must exchange seats with each other. The narrator tries to secure a seat. If unsuccessful, he continues his story. If successful, he is replaced by the person left without a seat. The new narrator may develop his own story or continue that begun by his predecessor.

TEACHING SUGGESTION

1. Play this game out of doors by having the children sit in a circle with legs crossed and almost touching, or by drawing individual circles for each player.

BOX HOCKEY [1]

NUMBER OF PLAYERS: 2 or 4

SPACE: Playroom, classroom

EQUIPMENT: (1) A wooden box frame, 3 by 9 feet, divided into three sections by cross pieces as in Figure 98. This is placed on a table. (2) 1 solid rubber ball approximately one inch in diameter; (3) 4 hardwood sticks or small croquet mallets.

FORMATION: Opponents stand on opposite sides of the box, two players opposing each other or two players on a side as partners.

PROCEDURE: The object of the game is to knock the ball with the stick through the hole at the end of the box at a player's left. The ball is placed in the center of the middle section and started by a bully or "face off."

[1] Contributed by Frank L. Thomas, Supervisor of Physical Education, Los Angeles public schools.

Players touch their sticks to the floor inside the box, then strike them together over the ball, repeating this three times. After the third tap the ball is struck with a player's stick and the game is on. The ball must be sent through the holes in the cross pieces, not over the boards. If the ball is knocked out of the box it is put into play again as at the start.

SCORING: A point is scored for each goal made. Any number of points from 1 to 5 may constitute a game, as agreed upon.

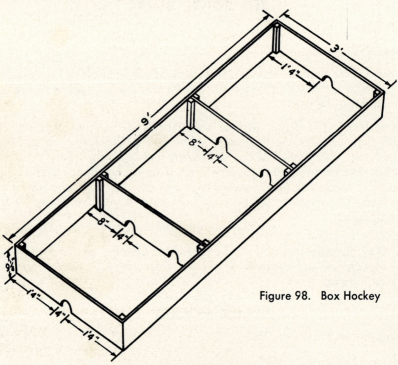

Figure 98. Box Hockey

TEACHING SUGGESTIONS

1. Have players use a short, choppy push as the most effective stroke.
2. Instruct pupils to place the hockey sticks in any of the sections of the frame in an effort to control the ball.

CIRCLE CHASE

NUMBER OF PLAYERS: 10-20

SPACE: Playground, playroom, gymnasium, auditorium

FORMATION: The group is arranged in a circle, players standing elbow distance apart, facing inward. If the group is small, they count off by twos or threes. If the group is large enough, the players stand closer together and count off by fours, fives, or sixes.

PROCEDURE: The leader calls one of the assigned numbers. All players with that number start running around the circle, each runner attempting to tag one or more players running ahead of him. As successful runners reach their starting place they stop there. Runners who are tagged are eliminated and withdraw from the game by going to the center of the circle. Another number is called and the players with that number run. Continue until all numbers have been called. Re-form the circle with the successful runners, renumber them, and repeat the pattern until only four runners remain. They are the winners. As the number of players decrease, a circle may be drawn on the ground, the runners being required to stay outside of it.

TEACHING SUGGESTIONS

1. Vary the game by having the players run two or three times around before stopping at their former positions; or by having the leader call a reversal of direction during a running period.
2. Mark a permanent circle on macadam. This will prove useful for many purposes.
3. Have children retired to the center join hands and form a circle for outside players to use.

CIRCLE DODGE BALL

NUMBER OF PLAYERS: 6-20

SPACE: Playground, gymnasium, auditorium

PLAYING AREA: Players join hands and form a circle; all then move two steps backward, and a circle is drawn on the ground in front of their toes. For tournament play and for match games, determine the size of the circle needed and use that size consistently. On asphalt or oiled surfaces, paint the necessary circle.

EQUIPMENT: Volleyball, utility ball, beanbag, knotted towel, or stuffed leather ball casing

FORMATION: Players are divided into two groups. The players of one team stand outside and around the circle. The players of the second team become dodgers and take positions inside the circle. A member of the outer team holds the ball. The game is played (1) in two or four time periods, teams exchanging positions upon the expiration of each time period, or (2) to see which team can eliminate all dodgers in the shorter time.

PROCEDURE: There are several methods of playing the game. On signal, players of the outer circle throw the ball and try to hit players within the circle. If the ball legally contacts an inside circle player he either (1) remains in the game but raises his arm immediately to signify to the scorer that he was hit; (2) joins and plays with the outside circle players; or (3) is removed from the game. The method to be used must be agreed upon beforehand.

Outside Circle Players: These players may throw directly at an inside player or they may pass the ball among themselves in order to get it in the hands of a player near an inner circle opponent. While throwing the ball they may not step on or over the circle marking. If the ball enters and remains inside the circle, an outside player may (1) enter the circle, secure the ball, and throw it to a member of his team, or (2) carry the ball outside and thereupon throw it at a player inside the circle. While inside the circle such a player may not throw the ball to hit an inner circle player.

Inside Circle Players: These players do not touch the ball at any time, their aim being to dodge, run, jump, or stoop so as to escape contact with the ball. They may not step on or over the circle marking.

Legal Hits: Any person is legally contacted whose person or clothing is hit by a fly ball, a bouncing ball, or a rolling ball. Only one player may be legally contacted by a ball. Should two players be hit by a thrown ball, the first one touched by the ball is the person legally contacted. A player so hit must (1) raise his arm immediately, (2) join the outer circle of players, or (3) leave the game immediately, according to the method agreed upon.

FOULS: The following constitute fouls:
1. For an outside player to throw at an inner circle player while he himself is inside the circle
2. For outside player to contact or step over circle marking while in the act of throwing the ball
3. For outside players to hit twice or more in succession a player who is retiring from the circle because of a legal hit.
4. For inside players to step on or over the circle marking while trying to evade the ball.

Penalty: 1 point is given the opponent team for each foul committed.

SCORING: 1 point is scored for each person legally hit. 1 point is given a team for each foul committed by opponent team. According to the agreed upon method of play, the team wins which (1) had the smaller number of hits when all players remain in the game; (2) had the smaller number of players left within the circle at the conclusion of playing periods; or (3) eliminated all opponents in the shorter time.

OFFICIALS: Officials are needed (1) to watch for foot faults by members of both teams; (2) to keep a record of hits when players remain in the game; (3) to record points for fouls committed; (4) to watch the playing time for each period of play and bring it to a close; (5) to announce the winning team.

TEACHING SUGGESTIONS

1. Make personal control a necessity to speedy play if the game is to be successful; instruction should be given in dodging, stopping, turning, and jumping.
2. Eliminate the desire to throw the ball at a player if, by throwing the ball to another player, greater success and a faster game will result for all.
3. Teach children outside the circle who are opposite the player in control of the ball to move to the most advantageous position so that, when the ball is thrown, they can prevent the ball from going out of bounds and thus speed up the game.
4. Have less skilled children throw the ball. Do not permit them to pass the ball to a team member.
5. Encourage children to enter the circle to secure the ball and throw it to a teammate.

CIRCLE RACE

NUMBER OF PLAYERS: 10-20

SPACE: Playground, playroom, gymnasium, auditorium

PLAYING AREA: Circle marked on the ground

FORMATION: Players in a single circle stretch their arms sideways to determine their starting position. Dropping their arms, all face to the left or to the right. A circle is drawn and the runners go outside the circle.

PROCEDURE: On signal, players start running around on the outside of the circle, each trying to pass the runner ahead of him on the outside. As players are passed by a runner, they drop into the center of the circle and watch the game. The last player to pass a runner wins the game.

TEACHING SUGGESTIONS

1. Add fun to the game by having the leader give a signal, while all are running hard, to reverse the direction of the run. This will change the relative positions of the runners.
2. If there are but a few players, draw a circle larger than that formed by their joined hands.

COME ALONG

NUMBER OF PLAYERS: 20-40

SPACE: Playground, playroom, gymnasium, auditorium

FORMATION: All the players but one stand in a compact circle, shoulder to shoulder, facing inward. As a player is asked to leave his place in the circle the other players *must not close in and destroy the vacant place.*

PROCEDURE: The extra player, while skipping around the inner circumference of the circle, reaches for the hand of a circle player saying, "Come along!" Keeping his hand joined with the first player, the second player invites a third, the third invites a fourth, and so on. When the leader blows his whistle, gives a call, or the music stops, all those skipping in the circle dash for a vacant space. The player unsuccessful in finding a space becomes the new leader.

TEACHING SUGGESTIONS

1. To make this game successful, use a fairly large group.
2. Use for fun night parties.

END BALL

NUMBER OF PLAYERS: 6-24

SPACE: Playground, gymnasium, auditorium, classroom

PLAYING AREA: Court 20 by 30 feet, divided into two equal half courts by a line across the center. Three feet in from each end line a second line is drawn to form end zones.

    If only a few players are available, the size of the court may be reduced, but the width of the end zones (3 feet) should remain constant. For match games or tournament play a court with agreed upon dimensions should be used throughout the periods of play.

EQUIPMENT: Basketball, volleyball, soccer ball, utility ball, or stuffed leather ball casing

Procedure

    The object is for each team to gain possession of the ball and throw it to one of their end zone players. Each successful throw scores a point.

FORMATION: Players are divided into two equal teams. A third of the players of each team are end men and take their position in their team's end zone. The remaining players are fielders and take positions in the half of the field farthest from their end zone. The ball is held by a player in one of the end zones.

PLAYING PERIOD: The game consists of two periods of an agreed upon length, with a 2-minute rest between halves. Before the beginning of the second half the teams exchange goals, the players taking positions corresponding to those held when time was called.

RULES OF PLAY: On signal, the player holding the ball tries to throw it to a fielder of his team. Players of both teams try to secure the ball and throw it to one of their end men, who must catch it without leaving the end zone.

Rotation of Players: Players of each team are numbered. Each time a team scores, members of that team rotate positions, each player moving one place. During each rotation an end man leaves the end zone and becomes a fielder, and a fielder becomes an end zone player. During the rotation the ball remains at the end where it was caught. When rotation is completed the new end zone player puts the ball in play.

Out of Bounds: If the ball is thrown or rolls out of bounds across a *side line*, the nearest fielder secures it and passes it to the nearest fielder of the team that did not send it out. Play continues immediately, the ball thrower taking his position within the court.

If the ball is thrown or knocked out of bounds over the *end lines*, the nearest end man secures it, returns it to an end man of his team, and play continues immediately. Players do not wait for the return of the out-of-court player.

FOULS: The following fouls result in loss of the ball to the opposing team:

1. For a player—fielder or end man—to step over any end line, side line, or center division line into the opponents' territory with either one or both feet.
2. For a player to carry the ball. It must be thrown from the spot where it is caught.
3. For a player to hold the ball more than three seconds.
4. For a player to push or hold an opponent.
5. For a player to snatch the ball or interfere with the ball when it is being held by another player.

Penalty: If a player on either team makes a foul, the ball is thrown to the nearest fielder of the opponent team and play continues immediately. In case of a double foul the ball is put in play from the center by opposing fielders who jump for the ball and attempt to tap it to their teammates.

SCORING: One point is scored for each successful throw. To be legal, the catcher's feet must not be touching any line of the end zone and the ball must be caught in the air without having touched a wall, window, or any other inanimate object.

The team wins which has the higher number of points at the conclusion of the playing period.

CLASSROOM ORGANIZATION: When played in a classroom with stationary desks, the opposing end men are stationed at opposite sides of the room in the aisles next to the walls. The area in the remaining aisles determines the playing area of the fielders. Indoors the rotation of players may be delayed until the number of balls caught coincides with the number of end men used by the teams, and then all end zone players become fielders and half the fielders become end zone players. It may be necessary to indicate side lines by chalk markings on the floor.

TEACHING SUGGESTIONS

1. Point out that fast, accurate throwing is desirable.
2. Have players in end zones develop the skill of jumping into the air and landing without touching any of the lines of their end zones.
3. Use as a lead-up game for distance throwing of either a soccer ball or a softball. Overhead or one-arm passes may be used.
4. Have players run to their new positions following each scoring play.

END ZONE SOCCER [1]

NUMBER OF PLAYERS: 2-40

SPACE: Playground

PLAYING AREA: Court 60 by 100 feet, marked as in Figure 99. Six feet from the end lines parallel lines called zone lines are drawn to form goal areas at each end of the field. Warning lines are drawn at the sides of the court 10 feet from the zone lines. At the center of the court a circle is drawn with a radius of 6 feet.

FORMATION: Players are divided into two teams and members of each team are numbered. Team X forwards, 1, 2, and 3, stand behind the center division line; Team X halfbacks, 4, 5, and 6, stand behind their forwards; the remaining players enter the zone area of their team and become the defenders. Team O players take corresponding positions at their end of the field.

PROCEDURE: The game is started by a kickoff on the center line; all players must be in their own half of the field and opposing players outside the center circle. Team X forwards may advance to the zone line of their opponents in an effort to kick the ball over the end goal line. Halfbacks should never get ahead of their forwards. Their duty is to follow up their forwards so as to feed the ball to them if the forwards lose it. They, like the forwards, play their own positions. Forwards, while in their own half

---

of the field, near their own goal zone, should not drop behind their warning line. The halfbacks should be there.

The defending players of each team remain in their own zone areas and may not advance beyond the zone lines. They, with the other players, *may not use their hands* while playing the ball.

If the ball is kicked for a goal and it goes over the heads of the defenders, a free kick is awarded the defenders at the spot where the ball crossed over the goal line. Out-of-bounds plays and fouls are the same as in soccer.[1] To be a legal goal the ball must pass over the line below the height of the tallest player.

Rotation of Players: Following a goal, players in each team rotate. Forwards go to the position of the highest numbered defenders; halfbacks become forwards; defenders become halfbacks.

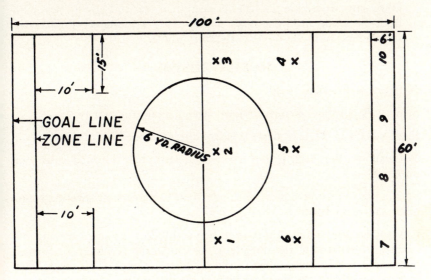

Figure 99.   End Zone Soccer Court

Playing Periods: The game is played in two halves of seven minutes each. The time periods may be increased to 15 minutes each. If Team X has the kickoff at the beginning of the game, Team O has the kickoff at the beginning of the second half. After a goal, the losing team has the kickoff. At the end of the first half, teams exchange goals.

SCORING: A goal may be scored from a free kick.[2] The team wins which has the higher total of scores for the two periods of play.

---

[1] For boys' and girls' soccer rules, see pages 775-88.
[2] For a definition of a free kick see soccer rules, page 777.

TEACHING SUGGESTIONS

1. If possible have the forwards wear a distinctive color in arm band or scarf, the halfbacks another color. Scarves may be slipped over one shoulder and under the opposite arm. Each team should wear pinnies of distinguishing color. Pinnies are apron-like garments which slip over the head and are tied around the waist. Bright colored cotton material is used for pinnies, so that teams can be distinguished by the color each member wears.
2. Teach players to play in position both in relationship to the forward players and the halfbacks and the sides and center of the field.
3. Teach the forwards to play up the field. This does not involve the complicated plays of corner and goal kicks nor the use of punting and drop-kicking.
4. Before End Zone Soccer can be successfully played, the children must know how to dribble the ball between their feet and how to pass with both the inside and the outside of each foot. Kicking a ball correctly should have been mastered in the third grade.

HUSTLE BUSTLE

NUMBER OF PLAYERS: 6-40

SPACE: Playground, gymnasium, playroom, auditorium

PLAYING AREA: Two or more separate circles formed by players

EQUIPMENT: For each group a beanbag, large ball, knotted towel, or dumbbell

FORMATION: Two groups of not more than 12 players, or several groups of equal size are formed.

PROCEDURE: On signal, Number 1 player of each group, carrying his beanbag, runs around the outside of his circle. On reaching his former position he hands the beanbag to the Number 2 player of his team. That player must thrust the beanbag high in the air and hold it there. On the next signal, Number 2 player runs around the circle and hands his beanbag to Number 3. Continue until all have run.

SCORING: A point is scored for his team by the first runner to reach his circle position and hand over his beanbag. The team wins which has the highest number of points.

TEACHING SUGGESTIONS

1. When there are more than 10 players in a circle, have a player on the opposite side of the circle run simultaneously with the Number 1 runner. For example: 1 and 6, 2 and 7, 3 and 8. Each runner must have a beanbag.

2. Have players wait for the signal to run.
3. Teach the game to the entire group and later have smaller groups organize under their own management.
4. If there are but a few players, draw two good sized circles and designate positions on the circles to be occupied by players. Runners must keep outside the circles and those to receive the beanbags must be in contact with their designated circle positions.

INNER CIRCLE BALL

NUMBER OF PLAYERS: 6-20

SPACE: Playground, playroom, gymnasium

EQUIPMENT: Several balls, not necessarily of the same size

FORMATION: Players form a double circle, all facing inward. Those in the outer circle stand some four feet distant from the players of the inner circle.

PROCEDURE: At a signal, members of the inner circle pass balls to each other or send them around the circle. Play for everyone ceases when a ball hits the floor. Players who cause another player to miss the ball because of a poor throw, or who miss balls themselves, must exchange places with the person behind them. The ball is recovered and play is continued.

As players become skillful, make the rule that members of the inner circle must not move their feet while reaching for or throwing balls. To do so retires them to the outer circle. If balls collide while being passed, the ones who threw the balls exchange places with those behind them.

TEACHING SUGGESTIONS

1. As the game is mastered, speed up the action.
2. Use to review handling of various sized balls.
3. Exchange inner and outer circles frequently.

LAST ONE UP

NUMBER OF PLAYERS: 10-30

SPACE: Classroom

FORMATION: The game is played with one row of children at a time or with alternate rows playing simultaneously, depending on the arrangement of the room. Children in the row or rows stand in the aisle to the right of their desks. An additional child is added to each row, thereby making one more player than there are seats in the row.

PROCEDURE: At a signal the children start running around their own row of desks. When the leader gives a second signal each child tries to secure a seat. The one failing to secure a seat becomes the odd player when the next run is taken. This is continued as long as seems desirable.

TEACHING SUGGESTIONS

1. Place books on the top of extra desks to signify to the children that the seats of those desks are not to be used.
2. Insist that when seated, pupils keep feet under desks.

LINK TAG

NUMBER OF PLAYERS: 8-20

SPACE: Playground, playroom, gymnasium, auditorium

PLAYING AREA: A base to which tired runners may go

FORMATION: Players are scattered about. Two players are selected to be the taggers.

PROCEDURE: The taggers link hands and attempt to tag other players with a free hand. As players are tagged they take their place between the two original taggers and the chain grows longer with each additional player tagged. Only the end players may tag. The players being chased may break the chain if pressed too closely. If they succeed in breaking the chain, the line players must unite again before tagging may be continued. Tired runners, when not being chased, may retire to the base to rest, remaining there until ready to re-enter the game. Runners may not enter the base to escape being tagged. The last two players tagged become the taggers for a new game.

TEACHING SUGGESTION

1. Do not permit the players to scatter too widely. Definite boundaries may be needed. Often the dimensions of a game area or the shadow of the building may be used to limit the running area.

LONG BALL

NUMBER OF PLAYERS: 6-20

SPACE: Playground, gymnasium

PLAYING AREA: Home plate and a pitcher's box 30 to 40 feet away from it; first and third base lines (used only to determine fair or foul balls); long base, placed to the right of home plate and 65 feet away from it. The base may be represented by a 3 by 3 foot wood or linoleum square, or a pole, tree, jumping standard, sack of sand, or chair. An extended 40-foot safety line is drawn across the playing field touching the rear of home plate.

EQUIPMENT: (1) 12-inch softball; (2) softball bats in various sizes

Procedure

Two teams alternate as batters and fielders. Each member of the batting team, in succession, bats the ball and runs to long base. If it is a fair hit, he tries to run back across the safety line before he is put out by the fielding team; if it was a foul hit, he waits at long base until a succeeding batter makes a fair hit and then tries to run to safety.

If a throwing instead of a batting game is desired, the batters throw the ball through a pitching practice frame, or between two standards placed 18 inches apart. Contact with any portion of the frame or standards constitutes a foul and the batter runs immediately to long base but no farther. A successfully thrown ball which passes through without contact is a fair ball and the batter may attempt a home run. The substitution of throwing for batting would be a good lead-up for Long Ball.

FORMATION: Players are divided into two teams and the members are numbered. Each team elects a pitcher and catcher, or players may rotate to such positions with the change of innings. Remaining members will be fielders or batters, as teams' positions are determined.

Umpires: The player of each team at bat who made the last out during the previous time at bat is the umpire for the new inning. If it becomes necessary for him to bat, the last runner of the team at bat to cross the safety line before the umpire's turn to bat takes over the umpire's duties until the official umpire returns home successfully or is put out. He then resumes his umpiring duties for the remainder of the inning. (Umpires could be elected for each game, giving each child an opportunity to have the responsibility of officiating.)

PERIODS OF PLAY: The game is played either in (1) seven innings, or (2) two equal playing periods for each team; or (3) one playing period for each team. When the first organization is used, three outs change the inning and an inning is completed when both teams have had a chance at bat. When the second or third organization is used, play continues for the team at bat regardless of outs made until the end of the time period.

BATTERS: A batter must continue at bat until a contact with the ball is made by his bat. The contact may result in (1) a foul tip (merely grazing the ball with the bat); (2) a foul ball; or (3) a fair hit. The batter may not be put out on strikes. The instant a batter contacts the ball, no matter how lightly and regardless of whether ball is "fair" or "foul," he must drop his bat and run to long base.

FOUL BALL: A ball which lands outside or behind one of the lines between home plate and first or third is a foul ball. When a foul ball is struck, the batter, if he reaches long base, must remain there until a future player of his team makes a fair hit, whereupon he and other members of his team tied up at long base may try to reach and cross the safety line.

FAIR BALL: A batted ball which lands on or inside the base lines is a fair ball. When a fair hit is made the batter should attempt a round trip to long base and home across the safety line. At the same time any players at long base should attempt to complete their run. To be a legal run each runner must cross the safety line at some point between the two ends of the line without being tagged with the ball while held in the hand of a fielder.

FIELDERS: Fielders move about as necessary. Each inning one should be assigned to remain near the long base since runners who lose contact with long base may be tagged by any fielder who holds the ball or who contacts the base with the ball in his hand before the runner reaches it.

When runners are returning from long base, fielders should go with them and be ready to receive a thrown ball in an effort to tag out one or more runners before they can cross the safety line.

OUTS: Three outs change the sides except when time periods are used. Outs for the batting team occur under the following conditions:

1. When a fly ball is caught
2. When a foul tip is caught
3. When runner is thrown out before reaching long base. In order for a runner to be thrown out, the ball must reach the fielder at long base, who must then, while holding the ball, touch long base before the runner reaches the base. Runners cannot be thrown out when trying to cross the safety line. They must be tagged with the ball while it is held in the hand of the fielder.
4. When runner going to long base or returning to safety line is tagged with the ball in the hand of a fielder
5. When a runner at long base, not in contact with the base, is tagged with the ball
6. When all players of a batting team are held at long base because only foul strikes were made by members of the team
7. When a batter slings his bat as he starts for long base

SCORING: Each time a runner reaches long base and on a fair hit returns successfully over the safety line 1 point is scored.

That team wins which has the higher number of points at the conclusion of the playing period.

TEACHING SUGGESTIONS

1. Teach that Long Ball is a game that has most of the elements of softball.
2. Because a batter may run to long base on either a foul or fair ball, point out that poor batters can enjoy the game. However, batting instruction should be given to all.

3. Have all practice underhand pitching, with both feet in contact with the pitcher's box at the beginning of the pitch.
4. Teach each child how to bat, transfer the bat to his left hand, and drop it at the home plate as he runs, thus avoiding throwing the bat.
5. Practice throwing, catching grounders and flies, and base running.
6. For older or more skillful players, require that each runner touch home plate in order to make the run legal.
7. Insist that runners run full speed toward long base or the safety line regardless of how hopeless the attempt may seem to be.

MAZE [1]

NUMBER OF PLAYERS: 2-4

SPACE: Playground, gymnasium

EQUIPMENT: (1) Maze board, 4 feet square, with 1½-inch walls, constructed as shown in Figure 100. Double lines in the diagram indicate strips ½ by ½ inches glued, nailed, or screwed to the surface of ⅜-inch plywood. The strips are painted green. Two coats of shellac are given to the entire board. The hazard areas ("Start Over," "Back to 2," "Back to 3" and so on) are painted in red; the advance areas ("Skip Over," "Advance to C," and so on) in green. The words, numbers, dots, and circles are painted with black paint. A coat of shellac and a coat of wax finish the board. (2) Four shooting cues of ⅜-inch doweling, 35 inches long; [2] (3) four disks 1¼ to 1½ inches in diameter and ¼ to ½ inch thick, numbered 1, 2, 3, and 4, painted in different colors.

FORMATION: Two, three, or four players may participate, each playing for his own score, or four players may play a partnership game, two against two.

PROCEDURE: Each player in turn shoots his disk by striking it with the cue from the starting point to the finish circle, according to the following rules.

1. Each player has an additional shot for crossing one or more hazards safely. Landing on a hazard area cancels additional shots and the penalty of the hazard is enforced when the player's next turn comes. If in the meantime another player knocks his disk free of the hazard, the first player continues his play at the point where the dislodged disk came to rest.
2. If a player in making his shot plays an opponent's disk into a hazard, the player gets an additional shot unless his own disk also remains

[1] Contributed by H. Loren Mitchell, formerly Supervisor of Physical Education, Los Angeles public schools.
[2] If cues are not available, the thumb and middle finger may be used to move the disks.

in the hazard area. In that case, both disks remain in the area until their owners' next turns occur.

3. Disks may be made to carom off maze walls or side walls.

4. If a disk lands entirely within an "advance" area, it is immediately placed at the point indicated. This completes the player's turn. An opponent's disk landing in an advance area as the result of another's play takes the benefit also.

5. All shots must be forward when considering the advance areas.

6. A disk landing in or sent to a numbered corner may be placed within the circle enclosing the number, for a satisfactory shot. In shooting from a letter, the disk must be placed upon the dot beside the letter.

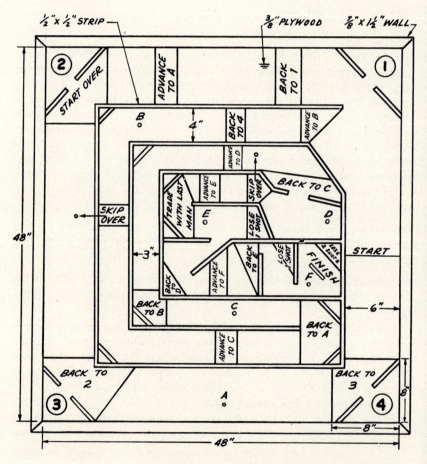

Figure 100.   Construction and Marking of a Maze Board

7. If a player's disk is crowded against a side of the frame, thereby making it difficult to shoot, he is allowed to place his disk two finger thicknesses from the frame. If a player's disk is crowded against a maze partition, he must shoot the disk from where it lies.
8. If a player makes a miscue, that is, if his cue slips on the disk and the disk does not move a space equal to its own width, the disk is replaced at the point where the miscue occurred and another shot is allowed. This does not apply, however, at the "finish" circle.
9. After each turn, disks remain where they are shot. If within a hazard, they may be released by another player's shot and not have to accept the penalty when the player's next turn occurs.
10. A disk must be entirely within the black lines outlining red hazard areas or entirely within the lines indicating the green advance areas, in order to draw the penalty or benefit. A disk contacting or resting on a line is considered a shot and carries no penalty or advantage.
11. A player's disk, shot or forced by an opponent into the wrong circle of the maze, may be placed at the entrance to his correct circle when it is again that player's turn to shoot. In the meantime the disk remains on the board until it is time for the player to use it.
12. If a disk is shot off the board or jumps to another lane, it is returned immediately to the place where it left the board and the player loses that turn. An opponent's disk thus displaced is immediately returned to the former location.

SCORING: The player or team wins who first completes the full circuit of the lanes and lands within the finish circle.

TEACHING SUGGESTIONS

1. Point out that careful easy shooting develops skill and advances the player faster than hurried hard shooting.
2. Make further rules if necessary. They should be understood and observed by all players.
3. Use in hot weather or for students who return to school following a period of illness.

MEDIEVAL GOLD [1]

NUMBER OF PLAYERS: 15-30

SPACE: Playground, gymnasium, playroom

PLAYING AREA: Court 40 by 60 feet, or a basketball court (Figure 101). The court has lines 10 feet in from the end lines and paralleling them to

---

[1] Adapted from a note contributed by Spencer C. Woolley to the *Journal of Health and Physical Education*, VI (December, 1935), 40. By permission.

form zones known as the countries of the invading enemy, such as Goths and Visigoths. A prison 10 feet long by 5 feet wide is marked at the center of and adjoining one of the side lines. The castle is a circle in the middle of the court.

EQUIPMENT: Three bags of gold—beanbags, ball casings stuffed with rags or straw, blackboard erasers, or blocks of wood—placed in the castle.

FORMATION: Players are divided into three teams with an equal number of players, each with a captain. Members of one of the teams, the defenders, occupy the territory surrounding the castle and protect the gold. The other two teams, the attackers, occupy the end zones. The attackers in each end zone are divided into five-man units.

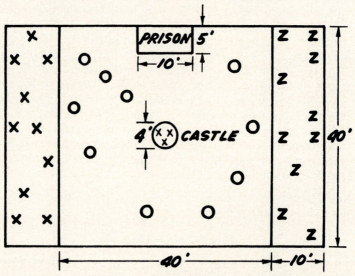

Figure 101. Court and Position of Players in "Medieval Gold"

PROCEDURE: The object of the game is to protect the gold and secure as many prisoners as possible, keeping them in prison for the four minutes of play during each period if possible. Playing time is in three 4-minute periods, each divided into 2-minute periods. At a signal, five members from each attacking country invade the castle area and try to capture and take home one or more bags of gold. Each defender of the castle attempts to capture one or more of the invaders by *catching them with his two hands*. If an attacker is so caught he must go willingly to the prison. If not caught, an attacker may return to his own territory whenever he wishes, with or without the gold. A defender may not chase an attacker into the latter's homeland. No attacker may throw captured gold from the castle into his homeland, or from within the castle to a countryman. He must attempt to carry it home himself. Once the gold reaches a country it is returned to the castle and a record is kept of the capture.

Imprisoned players of each country can be rescued by their own countrymen by (1) being tagged by an attacker before the attacker can be tagged by a defender of the castle, or (2) risking a bag of gold, if in the hands of an attacker. It may be thrown by the possessor into the prison area. If the gold is caught by a prisoner he bribes his way out by returning the gold to the castle and retires to his homeland. If the bag of gold is not caught, no prisoner is released and the gold is returned to the castle. A bag of gold may be intercepted by any defender, who immediately returns the bag to the castle before attempting to tag further invaders.

At the end of two minutes of play a signal is given. The invaders return to their country and new attackers prepare to go forth. Each country should make three rotations so that each unit of the countries may have their turn as defenders.

FOULS: Fouls may occur when any player fails to observe any of the above regulations. Violation by defenders results in the loss of one prisoner, or one bag of gold if there are no prisoners. Violations by attackers result in the imprisonment of offending member if attackers have secured no gold, or loss of one bag of gold if one had been captured.

SCORING: The team wins which retains the most gold and secures the most prisoners for the total of the three siege periods. Prisoners are valued at half the value of a bag of gold. At the end of each siege period, the castle gold and the prisoners taken are checked.

TEACHING SUGGESTIONS

1. Exercise care so that no clothing is torn. An attacker fairly caught should not resist.
2. Do not permit defending players to enter the end zones.
3. Encourage daring and strategy. The purpose of the game is to capture a bit of medieval history in game form. The game should develop alertness, dodging and guarding abilities, and team strategy.

OYSTER SHELL

NUMBER OF PLAYERS: 6-20

SPACE: Playground, playroom, gymnasium

PLAYING AREA: Two parallel center lines drawn *not more than three feet apart*. The length of the lines will depend upon the number of children playing. All but one player must toe one of the lines. Safety lines are drawn paralleling the center lines and 20 or 30 feet away from them at each end. No one may be tagged beyond these safety lines.

EQUIPMENT: The end of a wooden box 12 inches square with one side painted white, or a 4-inch wooden square with one side painted white, to represent the oyster shell.

FORMATION: Players are divided into two groups. The players of both teams toe their own center line with one foot. A leader holds the oyster shell. The leader announces which team will represent the outside of the oyster shell and which the inside. These assignments remain constant.

PROCEDURE: The leader tosses the oyster shell into the air in such a position as to have it fall within the 3-foot lane. If the white side falls face up members on the "inside of the shell" side dash across the field to cross their safety line. The opposite players give chase and try to tag as many as possible before "the inside of the shell" players cross their safety line. One player may tag several persons during the chase. Those tagged join the team of the person who tagged them and proceed to play for that team. Players line up and the game pattern is repeated.

SCORING: The game may be played (1) with the team which gets all the players on its side winning; (2) with a time limit, the team with the larger number of players on its side, when time is called, winning; or (3) a record of the number of players lining up each time at each line is kept and totaled at the end of the time limit, the team with the higher total score winning.

TEACHING SUGGESTIONS

1. Be sure that all children toe the lines.
2. Do not allow children to bunch too closely.
3. Have the leader toss the shell from both ends of the central lane.
4. Do not spoil the fun of the game by having too wide a lane.
5. Use this game to help develop the power of observation and instant reaction to the message resulting from the observation, together with the development of finer and faster co-ordinations and reactions.

Figure 102. Pateca

PATECA
(A Brazilian Game)

NUMBER OF PLAYERS: 2-8

SPACE: Playground, classroom, gymnasium

EQUIPMENT: (1) Pateca (Figure 102); (2) tennis, volleyball, or badminton net. May be played without net.

PROCEDURE: The game consists of batting the bird, or pateca, back and forth between two or more players. Only the hands are used to hit the bird. Rules vary. Players make up their own rules, or adapt rules of volleyball, net ball, badminton, or paddle tennis, depending on skill of individuals or limitations of playing space.

MAKING A PATECA. Canvas or leather is used for the base and stem of the pateca. See Figure 103. The bottom is filled with bird shot or sand, so that a good hitting surface is formed. Five or six long turkey feathers are placed in the stem. Heavy cord or string is wound around the stem of the pateca, beginning at the lower end of the stem. It is finished by tying the string securely in the last loop at the top.

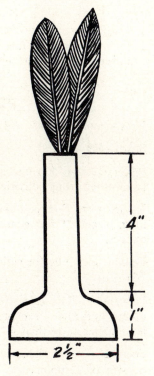

Figure 103. Dimensions for a Homemade Pateca

POISON SEAT

NUMBER OF PLAYERS: 8-30

SPACE: Classroom

FORMATION: Children, with the exception of one, sit at their desks. All unoccupied desks have a book placed on the top. Desks so marked are "poisoned" and their seats may not be occupied.

PROCEDURE: At a signal all the children exchange seats with each other, the extra child trying to secure a seat. The player who fails to secure a seat goes to the rear of the room and is no longer in the game. A book is placed on an additional desk and the game is repeated. The leader continues giving signals until all but two children are eliminated. They are the winners. The game may be played without the elimination of players, the number of desks used remaining constant.

TEACHING SUGGESTIONS

1. Clear tops of desks.
2. Give instructions that every child is to exchange seats and with a different child each time.

PONY HORSESHOES

NUMBER OF PLAYERS: 2-4

SPACE: Playground

PLAYING AREA: For one court—a level surface 10 by 40 feet, placed apart from other group activities

EQUIPMENT: For each court (1) two stakes ¾ inch thick and 2½ feet long, placed 25 feet apart; (2) four Number 2 horseshoes weighing 14 ounces.

FORMATION: The formation is described under official horseshoes, page 764.

PROCEDURE: The rules for pony horseshoes are the same as those for official horseshoes, except that the nearest shoe counts one point even if it is farther away than six inches from the stake.

SCORING: Closest shoe scores 1 point. A ringer scores 3 points. A game consists of 21 points.

SIMON SAYS

NUMBER OF PLAYERS: 6-30

SPACE: Playground, playroom, classroom, gymnasium

FORMATION: A leader stands in front of a group of people. They may be standing or sitting, preferably standing.

PROCEDURE: The leader gives commands such as "jump," "bow," "turn right." If the command is preceded by "Simon says," it is to be obeyed by all the players. If "Simon says" is omitted by the leader, the command is to be ignored. If a player fails to obey a command preceded by "Simon says," or if he obeys one not preceded by this phrase, he is eliminated.

SCORING: The last player to remain in the game is the winner. If the group is large, the last five or ten may be declared the winners.

TEACHING SUGGESTIONS

1. Have the leader give the orders in a sharp, decisive manner, and in such quick succession as to catch the players napping.
2. Use as a game for fun nights when a breathing spell is desired.
3. Have children take turns as leaders.

STEALING STICKS

NUMBER OF PLAYERS: 6-20

SPACE: Playground, playroom, gymnasium

PLAYING AREA: A 50 or 60 foot field is divided in half by a center line 25 feet long. At each end of the field a goal area, 6 feet wide by 4 feet long, is drawn; and midway between each goal area and the center line, at the left side of each team's territory, a five foot line at right angles to the center line represents a prison (Figure 104).

EQUIPMENT: Twelve sticks about one foot long and one inch in diameter. Six sticks are placed in each goal.

FORMATION: The players are divided into two equal groups. The group members stand in their own territory scattered along the center line and facing their opponents' goal. Each team selects a captain. Captains, if they wish, may appoint some of their players as runners and some as guards to protect their own goal. The guards may not stand closer than 12 feet to their goal, but may approach it if attempting to tag an opposing runner.

PROCEDURE: The object of the game is for members of a team to run to their opponents' goal and secure the sticks. Runners are allowed to take but one stick a trip. Players may be caught as soon as they have both feet in the enemy's territory. To escape being tagged they may return to their own side of the center line as often as they desire.

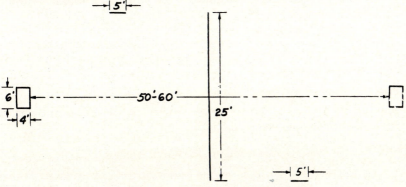

Figure 104.   Area for "Stealing Sticks"

Players, if caught, are taken to their captors' prison and must stand there until rescued by some one from their own team. While prisoners, they may reach out toward the approaching runners but they must keep both feet behind the prison lines. Runners may not take any sticks from their opponents' goal while members or a member of their team is in prison; the prisoners must be rescued first. If the runners reach prisoners without being tagged, prisoners and their rescuers return to their own side in safety. Runners may rescue but one prisoner each trip. Runners successful in reaching their opponents' goal take a stick and return to their own side in safety.

SCORING: The game is won by the team which first carries away all of its opponents' sticks.

TEACHING SUGGESTION

1. Give some distinguishing mark such as an arm band to the players belonging to one team.

STORM THE RAMPARTS

NUMBER OF PLAYERS: 4-20

SPACE: Playground

PLAYING AREA: Rectangle 100 by 200 feet divided in half at the middle

EQUIPMENT: Soccer ball, basketball, volleyball, 14-inch softball, or large beanbag

FORMATION: Players are divided into two teams. Team members stand in their own half of the rectangle. One player in the central portion of a court holds the ball.

PROCEDURE: The ball is thrown as far as possible into the opponents' field of play. Each player of a team endeavors to throw the ball over the opponents' end line without its being touched, while in the playing field, by the defenders. A member of the defending team tries to catch the ball on the fly or as soon as possible thereafter. From the place where the ball was first contacted, it is thrown back. If the ball is caught on the fly, before throwing it the catcher may take three jumping steps toward the center line.

SCORING: One point is scored by the team which succeeds in throwing the ball over the opponents' end line.

TEACHING SUGGESTION

1. Have each team try to force the opposing team away from its own end line.

THROW AROUND

NUMBER OF PLAYERS: 8-16

SPACE: Playground, gymnasium

PLAYING AREA: Softball diamond with 35-foot base lines

EQUIPMENT: 12- or 14-inch softball (called also playground softball)

FORMATION: Players are divided into two teams. One team stands at home base. The members of the second team take their places in the field, with a player at each base, including a catcher.

PROCEDURE: At a signal, a team member at home plate starts to run around the bases. At the same time, the catcher throws the ball to the first baseman, that player throws it to the second baseman, second baseman throws to the third baseman, and the latter throws the ball to the catcher. The ball must *be thrown twice around the diamond* during the time it takes the runner to return to home plate.

If the ball is fumbled it must be returned to the baseman who fumbled it and continue its journey from that person.

After all members of a team have run, that team retires to the field.

SCORING: If the base runner reaches home plate before the ball on its second trip reaches the catcher, he scores 1 point for his team. If the fielding team returns the ball to the catcher before the base runner reaches home plate, the fielding team scores 1 point.

The team wins which has the larger number of points after all players have run.

TEACHING SUGGESTIONS

1. Use this game to develop accuracy in throwing and catching.
2. If desired make the game more difficult by requiring that each baseman have a foot on his base before throwing the ball.

TIN CAN PITCH

NUMBER OF PLAYERS: 2-8

SPACE: Playground, classroom, auditorium

PLAYING AREA: A restraining line drawn 15 to 20 feet distant from a tin can board.

EQUIPMENT: (1) From three to eight empty cans (coffee cans are the best size), fastened to a foundation board approximately two feet square. A number value is painted under each can (Figure 105). Board is tilted against a wall or chair or hung on the wall. (2) Five or more small bean-bags, large buttons, rubber heels, or other suitable objects.

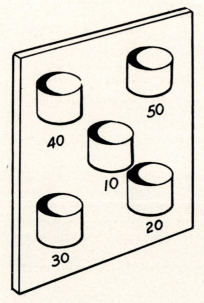

PROCEDURE: Standing behind the restraining line, players in turn endeavor to throw each beanbag into a can. A bag which remains on the edge of a can does not score.

SCORING: The number of rounds to be played and the number of points to be made are determined by participants. Each player's score is counted each time his throwing time is finished. If players add their scores incorrectly they lose 10 points from the score made during a throwing period. The player wins who first makes the required score.

Figure 105. Board for Tin Can Pitch

TEACHING SUGGESTIONS

1. Use objects which will not roll too easily.
2. Use as a hot-weather game or one for children temporarily or permanently incapacitated from more vigorous play.

TIP CAT

NUMBER OF PLAYERS: 2-4

SPACE: Playground

PLAYING AREA: A circle is drawn on the ground with a radius of 9 inches.

EQUIPMENT: A piece of broom handle 6 inches long. This is called the "cat." An additional stick is needed 18 inches long and 1 inch in diameter.

FORMATION: Two opponents or a group consisting of not more than four players, two of whom may be partners, may play. The number of innings is agreed upon before playing starts.

PROCEDURE: A player places the cat in the center of the circle and strikes one of the ends with the longer stick. He may strike it but once while it is on the ground. So struck, the cat should fly into the air. The player then tries to hit the cat again, endeavoring to send it as far as possible.

If the cat falls back into the circle the batter is out.

SCORING: If a player can bounce the cat several times in the air with the stick before knocking it away, each bounce counts 1 point.

If the cat falls outside the circle the opponent calls out how many jumps he will need, starting from the edge of the circle, in order to reach the cat. If the opponent fails to reach the cat in the number of jumps designated, the batter adds this number to his score. If the jumper succeeds he becomes the batter.

The player wins who has the highest number of points at the end of the agreed upon innings.

TEACHING SUGGESTION

1. Teach children to stand clear of and well behind the batter.

TWO DEEP

NUMBER OF PLAYERS: 10-30

SPACE: Playground, playroom, gymnasium, auditorium

FORMATION: A single circle is formed, the players facing the center and standing arm's length apart. A runner and chaser are chosen.

PROCEDURE: The chaser tries to tag the runner, who tries to escape being tagged by running around the outside of the circle *for a short distance* and then stopping in front of a circle player, where he is safe from the chaser. The runner plus the one in front of whom he has taken refuge make the circle two persons deep at that point. The player at the rear therefore becomes the runner. If the runner is caught, he becomes the chaser, and the chaser becomes the runner.

TEACHING SUGGESTIONS

1. Do not permit players to show favoritism by constantly stopping in front of certain circle players.
2. Have the runner use any tactics desired to avoid the runner except that of running through the circle.
3. With large numbers to play, use a double circle or triple circle, or form separate circles with a runner and chaser for each circle.

Relays

ARCH BALL RELAY

NUMBER OF PLAYERS: 6-40

SPACE: Playground, playroom, gymnasium

EQUIPMENT: For each team, ball, beanbag, or stuffed leather ball casing

FORMATION: Players are divided into teams with not more than six to a team. Teams are arranged in file formation. Each head player holds a ball.

PROCEDURE: On a signal, each head man, using both hands, passes the ball over his head to the player behind him, that player to the next. The end man, on receiving the ball, runs forward, faces forward, and, using both hands, passes the ball over his own head to the player behind him. This procedure continues until all have run. The team wins whose head player, with the ball in his hands, first reaches his original position.

TEACHING SUGGESTIONS

1. Have the balls or other objects of equal size.
2. Have the teams try to keep their players in as compact a file as will permit good play.

ATTENTION RELAY

NUMBER OF PLAYERS: 6-40

SPACE: Playground, classroom, playroom, gymnasium

FORMATION: Players are divided into teams with not more than six to a team. Teams line up in file formation in front of a leader. Files should be separated by a distance of at least 10 feet. Members of the teams are numbered from the front to the rear. When there are but few to play, two markers for each team should be placed a designated distance apart. The front and rear players of each team must be touching their markers when their runners are in action.

PROCEDURE: The leader brings the teams to attention and then calls out a number. The players having that number run forward around their team-mates and return to their original position. At no time may runners touch members of their team.

SCORING: The first player to return and stand at attention in his position, following his run, scores 1 point for his team. The team members are brought to attention and a new number is called. This procedure continues until all have run. The team that scores the most points wins.

TEACHING SUGGESTIONS

1. Arrange the game for a classroom by seating the pupils so that a row of empty desks will separate the rows of players.
2. If a team is short a player, have a member run twice for his team. The runs should not be consecutive.
3. Distribute teams in line formation instead of file formation, with the lines separated from one another by a distance of 10 or more feet.

The Number 1 players should be at the right end of the lines when facing the leader.
4. Have the leader scramble the numbers when calling them.
5. If there are only two teams playing, have them stand so that they face each other.

CARRY AND FETCH RELAY

NUMBER OF PLAYERS: 6-40

SPACE: Playground, classroom, playroom, gymnasium, auditorium

PLAYING AREA: A starting line is established. For each team a circle 14 inches in diameter is drawn, 15 feet from the starting line.

EQUIPMENT: For each team, one beanbag, block of wood, or blackboard eraser

FORMATION: Team members line up in file formation back of the starting line and opposite a circle. Each leader holds a beanbag.

PROCEDURE: At a signal, the first player of each team runs forward, places the beanbag in his circle, and runs back to the rear of his file, tagging the first player in the row as he passes. The second runner dashes forward, secures the beanbag, and running back hands it to the third player as he passes. The third player returns the bag to the circle. Play continues until all have run. A beanbag may not touch the circumference of a circle.

The team wins whose captain (1) first receives the beanbag from his last runner, or is (2) first tagged by the last runner, provided no fouls have been made, that is, no beanbag during the race contacted the circumference of a circle.

TEACHING SUGGESTIONS

1. Do not permit players to cross the starting line while waiting to be tagged or to be given the beanbag.
2. Play in a classroom by having the circles drawn opposite the aisles of the room.

CORNER FLY RELAY

NUMBER OF PLAYERS: 10-40

SPACE: Playground, playroom, gymnasium

PLAYING AREA: A long line is established and at a definite distance in front of it as many throwing lines as there are teams to play. Throwing lines should be two feet long and paralleling the long line.

EQUIPMENT: A ball, preferably the same size, for each team. Beanbags or stuffed leather ball casings may be used.

FORMATION: Two or more teams in line formation stand behind the long line with a space separating the teams. The leaders, each holding a ball, stand behind their throwing line facing their team.

PROCEDURE: At a signal, each leader throws the ball to the first person of his line, beginning at the right side. The ball is returned. The ball is thrown to the second player and is returned. The game is continued. As the leader throws the ball to the last player of his team he calls loudly, "Corner Fly," and immediately dashes for the right end of his team. The last player in the line dashes for the leader's former position and the game continues until all in one team have run and that team wins.

TEACHING SUGGESTION

1. Have leader and players stand behind their respective restraining lines before they throw the ball.

DIZZY IZZY RELAY [1]

NUMBER OF PLAYERS: 6-40

SPACE: Playground, playroom, gymnasium

PLAYING AREA: Two parallel lines 20 feet long drawn 30 feet apart

EQUIPMENT: For each team a baseball bat, old umbrella handle, or broom handle not less than a yard long

FORMATION: Players are divided into teams with not more than six to a team. Teams line up in file formation behind one of the lines. Each captain holds a baseball bat.

PROCEDURE: At a signal each captain runs forward. When beyond the farther line each captain places his bat in an upright position on the ground, places his forehead on the end and in that position runs around the bat three times. He then runs back to his team and hands the bat to the second runner. Play continues until all in one team have run, and that team wins.

TEACHING SUGGESTIONS

1. Have each player stand beyond the farther restraining line when circling his bat.
2. Have each player cross the starting line before giving the bat to the next runner.
3. Permit no waiting player to advance over the starting line before the bat is handed to him.

---

[1] Game developed by Margaret Van Voorhees.

DROPPING HOPPING BEANBAG RELAY

NUMBER OF PLAYERS: 8-40

SPACE: Classroom

EQUIPMENT: For each team, a beanbag

FORMATION: Children are seated at desks, an equal number in each row. Desks not in use are designated by having a book placed on them. Children decide what stunt activity is to be performed.

PROCEDURE: At a signal, each front player picks up his beanbag and, using both hands, drops it behind his head. The second player must catch or pick up the beanbag, drop it on the desk, and clap his hands. Then, and not before, and using his two hands, he drops the beanbag behind his head. The procedure continues. When the last player in a row secures the beanbag he hops down his aisle on one foot, performs the required stunt, sits down in the front seat of his row and, using both hands, passes the beanbag backward over his head in the prescribed manner. As soon as a hopping player passes a desk the person occupying that desk moves to the seat behind him.

When the starting player of one team returns to his desk, sits, places the beanbag on the top of the desk, and raises both hands high into the air, that team wins.

TEACHING SUGGESTIONS

1. See that pupils keep their feet under the desks.
2. Players will be prone to omit the hand clapping; see that it is done.
3. Sometimes allow two teams with fewer players than the other teams to compete against each other instead of against the entire group.
4. If a team is short a player, have one player run twice but not in sequence.

FARMER AND THE CROW RELAY

NUMBER OF PLAYERS: 6-40

SPACE: Playground, classroom, playroom, gymnasium

PLAYING AREA: For each team, a starting mark and a final mark 20 feet distant

EQUIPMENT: For each team, five beanbags or other small objects representing the seeds to be sown.

FORMATION: Teams line up in file formation in front of their starting marks. The first players of the teams are farmers, the second are crows, the third farmers, the fourth crows, and so to the end. The front farmers each hold five seeds.

PROCEDURE: On a signal, the farmers hop forward and plant their seeds in straight lines. The last seeds must be placed at the 20-foot mark. The farmers then turn, run back, and touch off the crows. The crows hop over each seed to the end, turn around, pick up the farthest seed, change to the other foot and hop back, picking up the remaining seeds on their way. They hand the seeds to the new farmers. Play continues. As the farmers and crows finish their play they retire to the end of their file. The first team to finish wins.

TEACHING SUGGESTION

1. Draw circles into which the seeds may be dropped, or use cardboard disks.

HOME BASE BEANBAG RELAY

NUMBER OF PLAYERS: 6-40

SPACE: Classroom

PLAYING AREA: Circles with about 12-inch diameter for home bases are drawn on the floor in front of each aisle and as far away from the desks as the room will permit.

EQUIPMENT: Beanbags, spools, buckeye seeds, or corncobs; as many for each row as there are players in the row.

FORMATION: Children are seated, with an equal number of players in each row. Beanbags are placed on the top of the front desks. Rear desks not in use should be designated by having books placed on them.

PROCEDURE: At a signal, the front players pass a beanbag backward over their heads to the next players. They in turn do likewise. When the last players receive the beanbag they run forward and place it in their own home base circle. *After the runners pass forward beyond the desks of their row*, players move one seat to the rear, thereby leaving the front seats free for the runners.

After depositing his beanbag in the circle so that no portion of the bag touches the circumference of the circle, the runner returns, sits down in the front seat and then, *and not before*, passes the second beanbag over his head to the second player. The game continues.

The team wins whose beanbags are all in the home base circle first or whose last player is first seated in the front seat with his hands held high in the air.

TEACHING SUGGESTIONS

1. Have all children keep their feet out of the aisles.
2. If one or more teams are short a player, have one child run twice.

HOPPING RELAY

NUMBER OF PLAYERS: 8-40

SPACE: Playground, playroom, gymnasium, hallway, auditorium

PLAYING AREA: Two parallel lines drawn not less than 24 feet apart.

EQUIPMENT: For each team, 10 beanbags, cardboard squares, or folded newspapers placed in rows, two feet between each. The first beanbag is placed two feet in front of one of the lines, the last on the other line.

FORMATION: Players, divided into equal teams, form files behind the starting line; the first player of each team toes the line in front of the beanbags.

PROCEDURE: At a signal the first player of each team, using his right foot, hops over each beanbag to the end of the row and then hops back on the left foot. Score is recorded and the second player of each team hops. Play is continued until all have completed the trip.

SCORING: The player in each run who first crosses the starting line after completing the trip wins 5 points for his team. One point is deducted from his team's score each time the player steps on a beanbag or touches the floor with the lifted foot. At the end of the game the team wins which has the highest score.

TEACHING SUGGESTIONS

1. Introduce variations in the methods of jumping—jumping with both feet, jumping while holding one foot, jumping backward, touching the floor with the finger tips following each jump.

PUSH OVER RELAY

NUMBER OF PLAYERS: 6-40

SPACE: Playground, playroom, gymnasium, auditorium, hallway

PLAYING AREA: Two parallel lines 20 feet long drawn 30 feet apart

EQUIPMENT: For each team: (1) a goal marker such as an Indian club, stool, stone, or block of wood placed on one line; (2) an article to be pushed on the ground such as a ball, can, beanbag (same type of article for each team); (3) a wand or pusher approximately 3 feet long and 1 to 1½ inches in diameter

FORMATION: Players are divided into teams with not more than six to a team. Teams line up in file formation behind a restraining line opposite the goal markers. The first player in each team is the captain.

PROCEDURE: On signal, captains push their article with the wand toward and behind their goal marker and back to the second player of their files. They hand their pushers to these players and retire to the rear of their file. The objects used may not be struck by the pusher. The pushers must remain close to the objects at all times, a scooping or jabbing motion being used. The first team to finish wins.

TEACHING SUGGESTIONS

1. Although the desire of the children will be to strike the ball, thereby sending it far head, do not permit this.
2. Using the same formation, have the children move the articles forward with their feet.

SACK RELAY

NUMBER OF PLAYERS: 4-40

SPACE: Playground, playroom, gymnasium, auditorium, hallway

PLAYING AREA: Two restraining lines 20 feet long drawn 30 feet apart

EQUIPMENT: Gunny sacks, one for each team

FORMATION: Players are divided into teams with not more than six to a team. Teams are divided into two sections each. Sections face each other behind the restraining lines. A gunny sack is placed on the ground behind the starting line and in front of each captain.

PROCEDURE: On signal, each captain steps into his sack, pulls it up around his waist, and then runs or hops forward to the second player of his team, to whom he gives the sack. This player steps into the sack *behind the restraining line* and runs, giving the sack to the third player. Continue until all in one team have run, and that team wins.

TEACHING SUGGESTIONS

1. Insist that runners climb into sacks while behind their restraining lines.
2. Allow the runners to run or hop.

SOCCER RELAY

NUMBER OF PLAYERS: 6-40

SPACE: Playground, gymnasium

PLAYING AREA: Three 20-foot lines paralleling each other: 12 feet between the first and second; 23 feet between the second and third

EQUIPMENT: For each team a soccer ball, stuffed ball casing, or large utility ball

FORMATION: Teams are organized in file formation, not more than six players on a team, standing behind the first line. The leader of each team holds a ball.

PROCEDURE: At a signal, each leader runs to and across the farthest line, turns, and runs back to the center line, from which point he rolls the ball along the ground to the waiting player. He must not make the return trip until he has touched both feet across the line. Each team member follows the same procedure until all in one team have finished. When the leader of that team is back in starting position with the ball in his hands, that team wins.

TEACHING SUGGESTIONS

1. Make the form more difficult by having the players control the ball with the feet: by dribbling it with the feet across the farthest line, back to the 12-foot line, and from there kicking the ball to the waiting player. When dribbling, the player should keep the ball close to the feet.
2. If the ball is so inaccurately rolled that the waiting player cannot secure it without leaving his position, have the player who rolled it recover the ball, return to the 12-foot line, and from the 12-foot line roll the ball to the waiting player.
3. Be sure that the ball is carried across the farthest line before being started on its return trip.

STUNT RELAY

NUMBER OF PLAYERS: 4-40

SPACE: Playground, lawn, gymnasium, playroom

PLAYING AREA: Two lines 20 feet long and not more than 40 feet apart

FORMATION: Teams stand in file formation with not more than six players to a file.

PROCEDURE: At a signal, each front player runs toward the farther line and on the way to it performs a stunt. After crossing the farther line each runs back and tags off the next runner in his file. The game continues until all have run.

The team wins whose leader is first tagged by the last player of the file after crossing the starting line.

TEACHING SUGGESTION

1. Use the following activities as stunts: bouncing a ball, skipping, galloping, hopping on one or both feet, using a bear walk, rabbit hop, frog hop, turning cart wheels, jumping rope, or carrying a beanbag on the head.

TOSS OVER RELAY

NUMBER OF PLAYERS: 12-48

SPACE: Playground, gymnasium

PLAYING AREA: Base line 20 feet long with parallel restraining line 20 feet distant

EQUIPMENT: For each team a basketball, volleyball, soccer ball, softball, beanbag, or stuffed leather ball casing

FORMATION: Players are divided into teams, with not more than six players to a team. Teams line up in file formation, captains in front touching the base line, last player in each file touching the restraining line. Each captain holds a ball.

PROCEDURE: At a signal, each captain steps to the right of his file and each second player steps to the left of his file. They run to the rear and, as they run, throw the ball back and forth to each other over the heads of their teammates. The balls must be passed at least four times during the run and the runners may take but one step while holding the ball.

At the rear of the file each captain stops and remains standing on the restraining line. Each second player, carrying the ball, runs around the foot of his file and goes on to the head. He is now on the right side of his file. The third player, at the left of his file at the base line, is ready to run. The ball is handed to him and the race is on again, with the second and third players tossing the ball over the heads of their teammates. The second player then remains at the rear. The play continues until all players in one team have run and the captain receives the ball again. The first team to finish wins the race.

TEACHING SUGGESTIONS

1. Impress on the players that the runner returns to the front on the opposite side of his file of players. This means that every other waiting player will step to the left or right depending on which side the runner returns to the front of the files.
2. Insist that the last player in the file, each time, stand on the restraining line when encircled by the runner.

WALKING RELAY

NUMBER OF PLAYERS: 6-40

SPACE: Playground, playroom, gymnasium

PLAYING AREA: A starting line and a goal line 20 feet long paralleling each other and 30 feet apart. Goals are designated on the goal line, one for each team, by using such articles as stools, chairs, blackboard erasers, blocks of wood, or by designating children as goals.

FORMATION: Teams are lined up in file formation with not more than six children to a file.

PROCEDURE: At a signal, the leader of each file walks forward, passes behind his goal, and walks back to tag off the second player of his team. The game continues until all have walked.

While walking a player *must place the heel of the advancing foot on the ground before the toe of the trailing foot is lifted*.

The first team to finish wins.

TEACHING SUGGESTIONS

1. Stress that walking correctly is difficult. Speed does not insure victory but careful execution of the walking step does.
2. Do not permit running and disqualify the player who runs.
3. Use this relay to teach correct walking by making the toes point straight ahead, and using the toes to push off for the next step.

WEAVERS RELAY [1]

NUMBER OF PLAYERS: 10-40

SPACE: Playground, playroom, gymnasium

EQUIPMENT: Two batons one foot long or beanbags, balls, or corncobs

FORMATION: Players stand in a circle with a four or five foot space between each player. Have the players count off by twos. The odd numbered players form one team, the evens another team. Appoint two captains who will stand side by side. Each captain has a baton.

PROCEDURE: The two captains start running around the circle in opposite directions, going behind the first person in the circle, in front of the second, behind the third, thus weaving in and out until they reach their original position, whereupon they step forward, hand the baton to the next player of their team, and drop back into their starting positions. So the game continues. Runners should pass each other at the far side of the circle. The first team to finish wins.

TEACHING SUGGESTIONS

1. Do not permit players to offer interference to any of the runners.
2. Teach accuracy in passing the baton.

---

[1] Game contributed by Margaret Van Voorhees.

Rhythmical Activities

BLEKING [1]
(Swedish)

Victor Record No. 20989

FORMATION: A single circle, partners facing each other with both hands joined

DESCRIPTION

PART I

Measure 1. All hop on left foot, bringing right heel and right arm forward, elbow straight, right hand in front of partner's shoulder, and left

---

[1] Caroline Crawford, *Folk Dances and Games.* New York: A. S. Barnes & Co., 1908. By permission.

arm well back with elbow bent ("one, and"). They hop again on right foot, extending left heel and left arm in same manner ("two, and").

Measure 2.   The same changes are made three times in quick succession, right, left, right.

Measures 3-4.   They repeat measures 1-2, beginning with the left foot.

Measures 5-8.   Measures 1-2, 3-4 are repeated.

Part II

With joined hands held straight out to the side, shoulder high, partners dance around the circle. The one with the left side toward the center starts forward with the right foot; and the partner moves backward, starting with the left foot.

Measure 9.   Both hop twice on each foot, at the same time swinging arms up and down, windmill fashion, once in each measure. Boy's right arm is down when hopping on right foot; left arm down when hopping on left foot.

Measure 10.   They use two of these steps to turn around.

Measure 11.   Hop as in Measure 9, partners in reverse position.

Measures 12-16.   Measures 9-16 are repeated.

Dance is repeated from the beginning.

Note: May be danced in double circle formation with partners facing, or with partners scattered about the room instead of in circle formation.

BROOM DANCE [1]

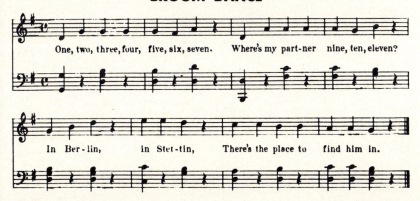

One, two, three, four, five, six, seven.   Where's my part-ner nine, ten, eleven?

In Ber-lin,   in Stet-tin,   There's the place to find him in.

---

[1] Mary Louise Curtiss and Adelaide B. Curtiss, *Physical Education for Elementary Schools.* Milwaukee: Bruce Publishing Co., 1945. By permission.

Line 1. One, two, three, four, five, six, seven;
  2. Where's my partner, nine, ten, eleven?
  3. In Berlin, in Stettin,
  4. There's the place to find him (her) in.
   Chorus: Tra la la, etc.

Victor Record No. 20448

FORMATION: Double circle, partners facing, boys on the inside; an extra person in the center with a broom in his hand

DESCRIPTION

Measures 1-8. As players march around, the center player gives the broom to someone in the circle, at the same time taking the vacated place. The one who receives the broom runs quickly to someone else and hands over the broom, and so it goes. The one who has the broom as the last word of the song is sung takes it to the center.

Measures 1-8 repeated (Chorus). Players skip while singing "Tra la la."

VARIATION: Players form two lines. Lines face each other with broom man between them. He is disgusted to be without a partner and dramatizes his disgust while marching back and forth between the lines.

Line 1. Lines advance with seven steps. Feet together on seven and hold "Seven."

Line 2. Lines retreat with seven steps "Eleven."

Line 3. Lines advance until "Stettin."

Line 4. Lines retreat until "in," whereupon all, including the broom man, rush for a partner in the opposite line. Boys select girls and girls select boys. The fun of the game is greatly lessened if players rush forward before the word "in."

Chorus: As soon as partner is secured, both skip around in a circle, thereby clearing the "mushpot" and disclosing the odd player who goes to the center of the circle.

  To re-form lines, partners separate and go to opposite lines. *They do not remain together.* It is not necessary for boys to form in one line and girls in the other. It is more fun when they are mixed up, with boys and girls in each line.

GUSTAF'S SKOAL [1]

Swedish Singing Game

[1] From Elizabeth Burchenal, *Dances of the People*. New York: G. Schirmer, Inc., 1913, 1934. Copyright renewal assigned, 1942, to G. Schirmer, Inc. Printed by permission.

Columbia Record No. D.B. 1800 (manufactured in England)
Columbia Record No. A-3046
Victor Record No. 20988

FORMATION: Children form squares, known as "sets," composed of four couples, each couple facing the center of a hollow square. Each boy stands at the left side of his partner. Couples join inside hands and place outside hands on hips.

> "Head couples"—the couple in each set whose backs are nearest the music and the couple directly opposite them
>
> "Side couples"—the remaining players, usually with their backs to the sides of the room

DESCRIPTION: The music consists of two parts, A and B, of eight measures each, repeated. The first part represents the lords and ladies of the Swedish court toasting the king on his birthday or other national holiday. Dancers display great dignity during this figure, and music is slow and dignified. Joined hands are held high during the advancing and retreating. The second part represents the general public of Sweden having their own fun while celebrating the national holidays, including the king's birthday. This figure is danced with lightness and jollity, in contrast to the formal stateliness of the first figure. The words should be sung by all dancers.

A

Measures 1-2. Beginning with right foot, head couples advance three steps toward each other. On the second count of Measure 2, they bow to the opposite couple. In bowing, the man makes the usual man's bow, a bend from the waist, with back flat and head and chest up; girl touches the left toe behind the right heel and, bending both knees, makes a bobbing curtsy.

Measures 3-4. Beginning with left foot, dancers retire to places with three walking steps, bring feet together on the second count of 4, and bow to each other.

Measures 5-6. Side couples advance (as in Measures 1-2).

Measures 7-8. Side couples retire (as in Measures 3-4).

Measures 1-8, repeated. They repeat entire figure.

B

Measures 1-4. Side couples raise inside arms and form an arch. Head couples (skipping two steps to each measure) advance toward each other, take the oncoming player as a partner, turn their backs on their former partners and pass under the arches made by the side couples. There they separate (boy to left, girl to right) and, still skipping, return to former partners.

Measures 5-8. Still skipping, the dancers clap hands on the first note of Measure 5, join both hands with partner, lean away from each other and swing vigorously in their own circle. (As pattern is learned, all four couples swing during Measures 5-8.)

Measures 1-8 repeated. Repeat figure, with head couples forming the arches and side couples performing the action.

Figure B may be repeated once more if desired.

When there are one, two, or three extra couples, they may be included in the dance by having them act as rovers. During the chorus they are free to take any couple's place in a set before that couple returns to position.

HANSEL AND GRETEL [1]

Victor Record No. 21620

FORMATION: Double circle, boys on inside, partners facing each other

DESCRIPTION

Measures 1-2. Boys bow; girls curtsy.

Measures 3-4. Partners join right hands and left hands across (4 hands joined).

Measures 5-6. Boys using left foot, girls using right foot, all point toes forward in line of direction and return to position; they repeat step.

Measures 7-8. All take four slides in line of direction.

Measures 5-8 repeated. Pointings and slides are repeated, going in reverse direction.

Measures 9-16. Joining inside hands, partners march forward around the circle counterclockwise.

Measures 9-16 repeated. Partners continue around the circle, skipping.

Measures 17-20. Partners face and pause. Each taps feet left, right, left, and pauses again. Each claps own hands three times.

Measures 21-24. Partners join crossed hands and repeat action for Measures 5-8.

Measures 17-20 repeated. Partners repeat steps for these measures except that on Measure 18 they nod the head three times and on Measure 20 snap the fingers three times instead of tapping and clapping.

[1] M. R. Wild and D. E. White, *Physical Education for Elementary Schools.* Cedar Falls, Iowa: Iowa State Teachers' College, 1924. By permission.

Hansel and Gretel

Arranged by Grace Van Ness

Lit - tle part-ner   dance with me,   Both your hands now   give to   me;

Point your toe,   away we go   Up and down the   mer - ry row.

Tra   la la la   la la la   Tra   la la la   la la la

Tra la la la   la la la la   Tra la la la   la la la

With your feet go   tap, tap, tap,   With your hands go   clap, clap, clap,
With your head go   nip, nip, nip,   With your fin - gers   snip, snip, snip,

Point your toe;   away we go,   Up and down the   mer - ry row.

Measures 21-24 repeated. Partners repeat action for Measures 5-8.
Entire dance is repeated.

VARIATION: New partners are secured when boys advance one position to their left and girls one position to their left. New lines are formed with partners facing, boys on one side, girls on the other.

HOPP MOR ANNIKA [1]
(Swedish)

Arranged by Grace Van Ness

Victor Record No. 21618

FORMATION: Double circle, boys on inside, partners facing to move counterclockwise

DESCRIPTION: During Introduction partners turn and bow to each other and then join inside hands.

Measures 1-4 and repeat. All walk forward briskly in a circle for 16

[1] Music from Wild and White, *Physical Education, op. cit.* By permission of Iowa State Teachers' College, publishers.

steps, each beginning with the outside foot (boys left, girls right). They swing the inside arms briskly and carry the outside hands on the hips.

Measures 5-8 and repeat.   All skip 16 steps and turn to face partner at the end.

Measures 9-12 and repeat.   All stamp forward with the right foot and at the same time clap their partners' right hands. Each claps his own hands. They stamp forward left and clap partners' left hands, then clap own hands. This is repeated seven times, and all end facing forward.

Measures 13-16 and repeat.   With inside hands joined, partners polka around the circle, turning first toward and then away from each other.[1]

The entire dance is repeated. During the introduction, the boys move forward to a new partner and they greet each other.

KLAPPDANS [2]

(Swedish Clap Dance)

Victor Record No. 20450

FORMATION: Double circle, facing counterclockwise, boys on the inside. All have outside hands on hips, inside hands joined.

DESCRIPTION

Measures 1-8.   Partners polka forward, starting with the outside foot.

Measures 1-8 repeated.   All do the heel and toe polka, bending backward on the "heel" and forward on the "toe."

Measures 9-12.   Each faces partner and bows, claps hands three times, and repeats.

Measures 13-14.   Each claps partner's right hand, claps own hands, claps partner's left hand, claps own hands.

Measure 15.   Each makes a complete turn to own left, striking right hand against partner's as turn is started.

Measure 16.   Each stamps three times.

Measures 9-16 repeated.   Measures 9-16 are repeated.

Entire pattern may be repeated as often as desired; players move to the left each time and so secure new partner.

---

[1] The polka step is a two-step with a hop added.
[2] C. Ward Crampton, *The Folk Dance Book.* New York: A. S. Barnes & Co., 1909. By permission.

Klappdans

LOTT IST TODT[1]

Victor Record No. 20988

FORMATION: Single circle, boys and girls alternating, partners facing. Hands joined with arms raised to shoulder height and fully extended.

[1] Based on dance in Lydia Clark, *Physical Training for the Elementary Schools.* Chicago, New York, etc.: Benj. H. Sanborn & Co., 1917-21. By permission.

DESCRIPTION: This is a Swedish dance, the title (sometimes called Ladita) meaning "Lottie is dead." The dance dramatizes the story.

Measures 1-2. (Music is played slowly.) All take four slow steps toward the center and bend bodies toward the center with each step. Outer arms rise, inner arms drop with the movement of the body. This step represents sorrow on hearing of the death of Lottie.

Measures 3-4. (Music is played faster.) All take seven rapid sliding or short hopping steps away from the center, ending with a high jump on the last note of Measure 4. This represents reaction on hearing the astonishing news that Lottie left the dancer money in her will.

Measures 1-4 repeated. Same steps are repeated.

Measures 5-8. Hopsa waltz is done around the room. Each dancer, still with arms extended, steps on the foot nearest the center of the circle and hops once on that foot. As the hop is taken, each throws his free leg up and out, with movement taking place in the hip joint. The leg should be fully extended without any bend at the knee. They continue, alternating the steps and hopping until the music ends.

Measures 5-8 repeated. Movement is continued. This represents taking a journey with the money inherited from Lottie.

The entire pattern is repeated as long as desired. As skill is gained, the boy turns the girl in one direction during Measures 5-8 and then reverses his direction for the repetition of the last four measures.

OUR LITTLE GIRLS [1]

Pioneer Record No. 3014

FORMATION: Single circle, boys and girls alternating, hands joined. Two or more boys (or girls) in the center—the more the merrier.

DESCRIPTION

I

Measures 1-16. Circle players walk 32 steps to the left, swinging arms and singing the words. Center players walk individually 32 steps in the opposite direction. Before the end of Measure 16, each center player must choose a partner, who enters the circle and they continue to walk hand in hand.

II. CHORUS

Measures 1-8. Circle players skip 16 steps, continuing to their left. Center players join hands with partners and skip 16 steps, turning in place.

---

[1] C. Ward Crampton, *The Second Folk Dance Book.* New York: A. S. Barnes & Co., 1916. By permission.

Our Little Girls

Our lit - tle girls, we know, When to danc - ing they go, Would like a girl to know With whom to dance, just so. And if thou wilt be A part - ner to me, Then take my hand in danc - ing, And sing so mer - ri - ly.

Chorus: For boomferalla, boomferalla,
Boomferalla la,
For boomferalla la,
For boomferalla la.
And if thou wilt be
A partner to me,
Then take my hand in dancing
And sing so merrily.

Measures 9-16. They reverse the direction of the skips.
Entire dance is repeated.

PASS ONE WAGON

FORMATION: Single circle, boy in front of his partner. Each puts his inside hand on the outside shoulder of the person in front of him. Players must be cautioned to work toward the center of the circle, since the return to this hand position occurs over and over again. If the circle becomes too large the rhythm and fun of the dance is spoiled. All sing the words.

DESCRIPTION: The basic movement consists of a step, followed by the heel raising and lowering of the same foot; the verse takes 16 such steps.
Measure 1-6. Each stands on outside foot with inside foot lifted from the floor; steps forward with inside foot, raises and lowers heel of same

foot. Steps forward with outside foot, raises and lowers heel of same foot. All repeat for six measures, two steps to a measure.

Measures 7-12.   Continuing step, each boy turns outward and around to the girl behind him, takes her in social dance position, turns her once around and leaves her in front of him at the end of the chorus.

If pupils are not ready for the social dancing position, have them take elbow grasp by grasping the forearm of partner, near the elbow; or hands may be joined with arms extended sideways.

Dancers again place hands on the shoulder of the person in front and continue without a break through the second verse.

Game is continued as long as desired. As each person meets a new partner each time chorus is sung, this is a very sociable game.

Pass One Wagon

Arranged by Helen C. Kranz

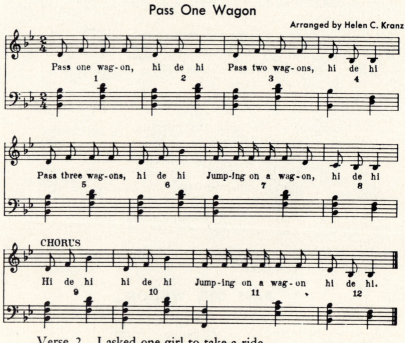

Verse 2.   I asked one girl to take a ride
She said "No, not by your side."
I asked another and she said "No,"
Jumping on the wagon, hi de hi.

NOTE: The following verses are sometimes used: [1]

[1] Mrs. L. D. Ames, "The Missouri Play-Party," *Journal of American Folk Lore,* XXIV (July-September, 1911), 311 (by permission).

Pass one window, toddy O
Pass two windows, toddy O
Pass three windows, toddy O
Pass four windows, toddy O.

Swing to the center and bow to your beau,
And all go jingle at the toddy O;
Jingle, jingle, jingle O
We'll all go jingle at the toddy O.

PAW PAW PATCH [1]
(American)

[1] M. L. Curtiss and A. B. Curtiss, *op. cit.* By permission of Bruce Publishing Co., publishers.
Music from Grace H. Johnstone, *Heel and Toe or a Do-Si-Do.* Oakland, California: Grace H.
Johnstone, 1944. By permission.

Verse 2.   Come on, boys, let's go find her,
Come on, boys, let's go find her,
Come on, boys, let's go find her,
Way down in the paw paw patch.

Pioneer Record No. 3017
Victor Record No. 45-5066 (Album E 87), a less active version

FORMATION: Sets of four or eight couples, girls in one line, boys in the other, all facing toward the foot of the set.

DESCRIPTION

Verse 1.   The girl at the head of the girls' line turns to her right and skips down behind the line of girls and up around the line of boys until she is back to her place.

Chorus.   Couples join inside hands and skip down the center of the line, led by the head couple, stooping down as if scooping up paw paws as they skip. They return to place.

Verse 2.   The same girl skips the same route as in Verse 1, followed by the entire line of boys. As the skip starts the first boy turns and beckons, urging on the other boys to help him find little "Nellie."

Chorus.   Couples skip down the center of the line, but at the end of the set the head couple raise their arms to form an arch through which all the other couples pass. The arch couple remain at the foot of the set.

The dance is repeated, this time with the second girl (now at the head of the set) leading. This is repeated until all the girls have had an opportunity to be the leader.

ROVENACKA
(Bohemian)

FORMATION: A double circle, partners facing each other.

DESCRIPTION: Accents are sharp, light, and spirited.

Measures 1-4.   Dancers stand in place for one measure, then all stamp left, right, left; pause; and each claps his own hands three times.

Measures 5-7.   Each shakes right forefinger at his partner (1 measure); shakes left forefinger (1 measure); and spins completely around to the left.

Measures 8-9.   Dancers join hands and move around the circle with the old-fashioned slide polka, turning halfway around each time ("slide, slide, step, step, step") as follows: two slides to the side, around the circle (1 measure); three tap steps, turning around in place, so that partner who was outside is now inside (1 measure).

Measures 10-11.   All repeat Measures 8-9, beginning with the other foot and moving in the same direction.

Measures 12-15.   Measures 9-11 are repeated.
All change partners and repeat the entire dance.

Rovenacka

Arranged by Anna Hermitage

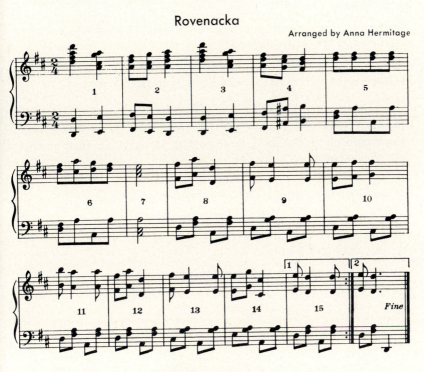

SEVEN JUMPS [1]
(Danish)

Methodist Record No. 108

Victor Record No. 21617

FORMATION: One large single circle, with boys and girls alternating. Hands joined. A number of smaller circles may be used.

DESCRIPTION

FIRST JUMP

Measures 1-8.   The circle moves around to the right with step hops, one to a measure (step on beat one and hop on beat two).

---

[1] Wild and White, *Physical Education, op. cit.* By permission of Iowa State Teachers' College, publishers.

Measures 9-16. All jump up high from the ground and come down with a stamp on both feet on the first beat of Measure 9. Then they step hop around the circle to the left.

Measure 17. All drop hands, place them on the hips, and bend the right knee upward.

Measure 18. All stamp right foot to the ground on the first note and join hands on the second note.

SECOND JUMP

Measures 1-16. Measures 1-16 of First Jump are repeated.

Measure 17. All raise right knee as before.

Measures 18-19. On the first note all stamp down the right foot; on the second note, all lift left knee; on third note all stamp left foot; on fourth note all join hands.

THIRD JUMP

Measures 1-17. Measures 1-17 of First and Second Jumps are repeated.

Measures 18-20. All stamp right foot, lift left knee, stamp left foot, place right toe backward on floor, kneel on left knee, and stand and join hands (one action to each note).

FOURTH JUMP

Measures 1-17. All repeat Measures 1-17 as before.

Measures 18-21. Actions for five notes are the same as before: stamp right, lift left knee, stamp left, place right toe back, kneel on left knee; pause; kneel on right knee (both knees down). On last note, all stand and join hands.

FIFTH JUMP

Measures 1-17. All repeat Measures 1-17.

Measures 18-22. All repeat actions as before: stamp right, lift left knee, stamp left, place right toe back, kneel on left knee; pause; kneel on right knee; put right fist to cheek, raising elbow; put right elbow on floor, with cheek resting on fist; on last note, all stand and join hands.

SIXTH JUMP

Measures 1-17. All repeat Measures 1-17.

Measures 18-23. All repeat actions as before: stamp right, lift left knee, stamp left, place right toe back, kneel on left knee; pause; kneel on right knee; put right fist to cheek; put right elbow on floor; put left fist to cheek; put left elbow on floor; on last note, all stand and join hands.

SEVENTH JUMP

Measures 1-17.   All repeat Measures 1-17.

Measures 18-24.   All repeat actions as before: stamp right, lift left knee, stamp left, place right toe back, kneel on left knee; pause; kneel on right knee; put right fist to cheek; put right elbow on floor; put left fist to cheek; put left elbow on floor; push body forward; touch forehead to floor. On last note, all stand and join hands.

Seven Jumps

Arranged by Grace Van Ness

Fine

Continue 5 times more
adding a measure each time

D.C.

SHOEMAKER'S DANCE [1]
(Danish)

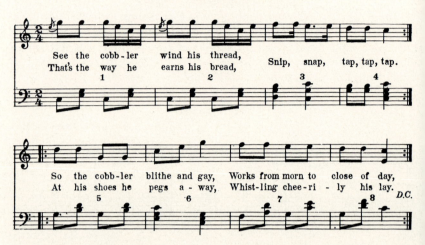

See the cobb-ler wind his thread,
That's the way he earns his bread,
Snip, snap, tap, tap, tap.

So the cobb-ler blithe and gay, Works from morn to close of day,
At his shoes he pegs a-way, Whist-ling chee-ri-ly his lay.

D.C.

Victor Record No. 20450

FORMATION: Double circle, partners facing, boys on the inside.

DESCRIPTION

Measures 1-2. With fists clenched, one in front of the other, all hold arms, bent at elbow, shoulder high. One fist is rolled over the other three times ("see the cobbler"); in reverse direction ("wind his thread").

Measure 3. Arms are pulled apart to represent breaking thread, jerking elbows outward and backward ("snip, snap").

Measure 4. All clap own hands three times ("tap, tap, tap").

Measures 1-3 repeated. All repeat actions of Measures 1-3 ("That's the way he earns his bread").

Measure 4. All double up fists and hammer one on top of the other to represent tapping in the pegs ("tap, tap, tap").

Measures 5-8 (Chorus): Partners join inside hands, outside hands on hips, and skip around the room.

NOTE: This is a good fun night activity. Older players may raise the right knee and break the thread by a vigorous downward motion of the hands and arms on Measure 3. They should polka face to face and back to back, each starting with the outside foot, on Measures 5-8.

---

[1] Based on description in *Lessons in Physical Education for Elementary Grades.* Raleigh, N. C.: Department of Public Instruction, State of North Carolina, 1926. By permission.

STRASAK [1]
(Bohemian)

Arranged by B. G.

An-nie went to the cab-bage patch, cab-bage patch, cab-bage patch,

And she pick'd the cab-ba-ges up, pick'd the cab-ba-ges up.

Lit-tle Pe-ter came a-long, came a-long, came a-long,

And he kick'd the bas-ket up, kick'd the bas-ket up.

---

[1] Elizabeth Burchenal, *Folk-Dances and Singing Games*. New York: G. Schirmer, Inc., 1909-22, 1933. Copyright renewal assigned 1938 to G. Schirmer, Inc. By permission.

Lit - tle Pe - ter came a - long, came a - long, came a - long,

And he kicked the bas - ket up, kicked the bas - ket up.

"You will have to pay for it! You will have to pay for it!"

"No, I won't! No, I won't! I'd ra - ther go to war for it!"

FORMATION: Single circle with partners facing and in position for social dancing; boy with right hand between partner's shoulders, girl with left hand on partner's shoulder, their other hands joined and held out to the side at shoulder height. The boy begins with his left foot, the girl with her right.

DESCRIPTION: The music consists of two distinct strains, A and B. The first is repeated once, making 16 measures; the second consists of eight measures. In fitting the steps to the music, each measure should be counted "one, and, two, and."

A

Couples polka around the circle from left to right, turning in the usual way. The polka is executed on the toes very lightly and breezily, as follows:

Measure 1.   Boy steps forward with the left foot ("one"), closes the right foot to the left ("and"), steps forward with the left ("two"), and hops on the left ("and"). The girl executes the same step at the same time, starting with the right foot.

Measure 2.   They repeat Measure 1, stepping forward first with the right foot (girls with left).

Measures 3-16.   They continue the polka, alternating left foot and right foot.

B

Measure 1.   With hands on hips, the dancers stand still facing each other.

Measure 2.   Dancers stamp vigorously three times, left, right, left, pause ("one, and, two, and").

Measure 3.   Dancers stand still.

Measure 4.   Dancers clap own palms together sharply three times ("one, and, two"), pause ("and").

Measure 5.   With left hand on hip, each shakes his right forefinger three times at his partner ("one, and, two"), pause ("and").

Measure 6.   With right hand on hip, each shakes his left forefinger three times threateningly at partner, and pauses.

Measure 7.   With left hand on hip, each strikes vigorously with his right hand his partner's right hand, then whirls once around in place to the left on the left foot, keeping the right foot raised from the ground.

Measure 8.   With hands on hips and facing partner, each stamps three times vigorously in place, beginning with the right foot.

The dance is repeated any number of times desired. The movements of Part A should be very light and springy, and the dancers should cover as much distance as possible while moving around the circle. During Part B, when the dancers are standing still, they should look very fiercely at one another, and all the movements should be vigorous and threatening.

WOODEN SHOES [1]

Music: "Strasak," p. 521 (repeats in music must be re-arranged to fit the steps)

Imperial Record No. 1007A
Columbia Record No. 16082F ("Polka Klumpakojis")

FORMATION: Couples in double circle, facing counterclockwise. Inside hands joined at shoulder height, outside hands on hips.

DESCRIPTION: This is an arranged version of Strasak.

A. WALKING STEP

Measures 1-4. Beginning with outside foot, partners walk forward eight steps.

Measures 5-8. Turning inward toward partner, each joins hands with partner and walks eight steps in the opposite direction.

Measures 9-12. All face partners, join right hands at shoulder height, and walk eight steps turning with partner in a small circle.

Measures 13-16. With left hands joined, partners walk eight steps in the opposite direction (in the small circle).

B. STAMP AND CLAP

Measures 1-2. Placing hands on hips, each faces partner and holds for four counts.

Measures 3-4. Each stamps right, left, right, hold.

Measures 5-6. They pause as in Measures 1-2.

Measures 7-8. Each claps own hands three times and holds for one count.

Measures 9-10. Placing right elbow in palm of left hand, each shakes right forefinger at his partner three times and holds for one count.

Measures 11-12. Actions of Measures 9-10 are repeated with left forefinger.

---

[1] *Folk Dances from Near and Far, III.* Berkeley, California: The Folk Dance Federation of California, 1947. By permission.

Measures 13-14. Swinging right hand as if to strike partner, girl takes a pivot turn to left on her left foot. At the same time the boy drops to a squat position.

Measures 15-16. The boy returns to standing position while girl stands in place.

Measures 1-16 repeated. All repeat action of Measures 1-16 (Figure B), and on last four measures boy swings at his partner and girl squats.

C. POLKA

Measures 1-16. Taking varsovienne position, all polka forward around the circle, both starting with left foot. They may use a two-step instead of a polka.

ADDITIONAL RHYTHMICAL ACTIVITIES
IN CALIFORNIA STATE SERIES MUSIC TEXTBOOKS

New Music Horizons. Fourth Book. Edited by Osbourne McConathy and Others. (Copyrighted, 1945, 1949, by Silver Burdett Co.) Sacramento: California State Department of Education (edition in preparation).

Students' book and book of accompaniments and interpretation for the teacher. Page references are to the latter book.

We Sing. Edited by Theresa Armitage, Peter W. Dykema, and Gladys Pitcher. A Singing School series (copyrighted, 1940, 1942, by C. C. Birchard & Co.). Sacramento: California State Department of Education, 1942.[1]

---

[1] Former series (adoption period July 1, 1942 to July 1, 1950).

Students' edition, teacher's manual, and book of accompaniments. Page references are to the last book.

SELECTED REFERENCES ON RHYTHMS [1]

Durlacher, E., Editor. *The Play Party Book: Singing Games for Children.* New York: Devin-Adair Co., 1945.
Thirty-seven play party games are described, with illustrations and simple piano accompaniments.

John C. Campbell Folk School. *Singing Games and Folk Dances.* Brasstown, North Carolina: The School, 1941.
Contains 23 singing games and 20 folk dances.

Johnston, Edith. *Regional Dances of Mexico.* Dallas, Texas: Banks, Upshaw & Co., 1935.
Eleven dances are described, with suggestions for a carnival.

Stunts

The materials of Grades One, Two, and Three should be reviewed before practicing the stunts in this grade. A short run or warm-up period should precede instruction in stunts.

BACKWARD ROLL [2]

Space: Gymnasium, playground

Equipment: Mat

---

[1] Consult the bibliography and listing of phonograph records in the appendixes.
[2] William R. LaPorte and A. G. Renner, *The Tumbler's Manual*, New York: Prentice-Hall, Inc., 1938. On pages 18-20, backward roll is illustrated, with suggestions of different ways to use it.

PROCEDURE: From a squatting position, the performer sits back on his heels. At the same time his hands are placed on the mat, fingers forward, to break the fall. As backward momentum is started, the hands are placed by the ears, *palms up*, fingers extended so that the weight of the body is caught on the palms of the hands as the roll is completed. When the weight of the body is on the hands, he pushes upward to prevent the weight from resting on the neck. Throughout the roll the knees are kept close to the chest and the back is rounded. The roll is continued until the body can be sent to an erect position.

CHINESE GET UP

SPACE: Gymnasium, playground

FORMATION: Two performers sit back to back with elbows locked and legs straight out before them.

PROCEDURE: The object is for both performers to reach standing position without unlocking elbows.

THE DIVE [1]

SPACE: Playground, gymnasium

EQUIPMENT: Mat

FORMATION: One performer; a spotter stands beside the performer to see that action is correct; a third person assists in the dive.

PROCEDURE: Performer begins by starting the forward roll from the erect standing position. Then he adds a jump, taking off from *both feet*. To come erect following the roll, he should throw the head forward up as an aid in gaining balance. The assistant kneels sideways to the performer with his head tucked under his arms, legs against thighs and knees close to the chest. Jumper places hands over and close to body of kneeling person and does a forward roll. The dive can become more advanced by diving over more people or by diving higher.

FROG HAND STAND
(Tip Up)

SPACE: Playground, gymnasium

PROCEDURE: Performer should squat so that hands are flat on the floor, somewhat turned in, elbows inside thighs and pressed hard against knees,

---

[1] *Ibid.,* pp. 14-17. Virginia Lee Horne, *Stunts and Tumbling for Girls.* New York: A. S. Barnes & Co., 1943. Pp. 58-65. The Dive progression is shown in pictures, and the procedure is analyzed.

e 106. Frog Hand Stand

feet close to hands. He leans forward slowly and transfers the weight of his body onto his arms and hands and at the same time lifts his toes from the floor. He holds this position for from 5 to 20 counts. Head should be held up to get good balance. (See Figure 106.)

JUMP THROUGH HANDS

SPACE: Playground, gymnasium

PROCEDURE: From prone position, the body is rested on extended arms, with legs straight back and together. The hands and the toes carry the weight of the body. Following a strong push with the toes, the performer swings his body forward between the hands so that his hips and legs are extended forward beyond the hands. He swings his feet back again to original position.

This is repeated several times.

SIAMESE TWINS

SPACE: Gymnasium, playground

FORMATION: Two performers sit back to back with arms folded and legs extended straight ahead and together.

PROCEDURE: The object is to see which performer can first stand erect with feet together while maintaining the folded arm position throughout the trial.

SKIN THE CAT

SPACE: Playground, gymnasium

EQUIPMENT: Horizontal bar

PROCEDURE: The performer hangs by the hands from a horizontal bar. He brings the legs up under the bar, at the same time turning his body over so that his feet will reach toward or contact the floor. The body is returned to starting position.

TAILOR STAND

SPACE: Playground, gymnasium

PROCEDURE: Performer sits on the floor in crossed-leg position; chest high, back flat, arms folded above chest, elbows elevated. Without unfolding arms, or changing position of legs, he rises to standing position. He then returns to sitting position.

Chapter XVIII
ACTIVITIES FOR FIFTH GRADE

Activities are alphabetically arranged by title within the following four classes:

The games fall into several classes. They are indexed here by type for the convenience of the teacher.

Games

ANTE OVER

NUMBER OF PLAYERS: 4-20

SPACE: Playground, gymnasium

PLAYING AREA: Handball backboard, shed, or low building over which a ball may be thrown

EQUIPMENT: 12-inch or 14-inch softball, tennis ball, or utility ball

FORMATION: Players are divided into two teams. The teams stand on opposite sides of the building. One player holds the ball.

PROCEDURE: The player with the ball calls loudly, "Ante Over!" and attempts to throw the ball over the building. If the ball fails to reach the top and drops back, the thrower calls loudly, "Pig's Tail!" and rethrows the ball. If the ball goes over, players on the opposing team try to catch it. If they fail, some member picks up the ball and throws it back over the building, first calling "Ante Over!" If a player is successful in catching the ball, he and his teammates dash around the building (in either direction, but all choosing the same direction) and the man with the ball attempts to hit one of the opponents. The latter try to escape around the opposite side of the building. If the thrower hits an opponent, the opponent joins the thrower's team and the ball is given to the team of the player who was hit. If the thrower is unsuccessful in hitting an opponent, he joins the opponent's team and the ball is returned to a member of the team for which he threw. Both teams take their positions and the game is resumed. The team wins which gains all the players for its side, or which has more players at the end of the playing period.

TEACHING SUGGESTION

1. When a ball is caught, have the members of that team try to confuse the players of the other team as to which player holds the ball.

BADMINTON GAMES FOR THE SCHOOLROOM

NUMBER OF PLAYERS: 2-30

SPACE: Classroom, auditorium, playroom, area out of doors protected from the wind

EQUIPMENT: (1) Shuttlecock (familiarly known as "bird" or "birdie"), or Flying Fleece balls; (2) a battledore or wooden paddle for each child [1]

---

[1] The birdie is the same as that used in badminton, made of cork and feathers. Small and large balls made of wool called Flying Fleece balls are often substituted; they may be purchased from the Oregon Worsted Company, Portland, Oregon. For construction of a paddle, see p. 115.

Procedure

The game of Battledore and Shuttlecock is a very old game. The modern version is the highly organized game of badminton. Children must learn to handle the birdie and racket before games can be played. Various methods may be used to develop skill before a game is played.

Exercises to Develop Skill with the Birdie and Paddle

1. Pupils practice holding the paddle and hitting the shuttlecock upward with short, quick strokes, remembering to keep the eyes on the shuttlecock. Paddle is picked up by grasping it with thumb around one side and fingers meeting the thumb on the other side. When bouncing the shuttlecock on the paddle, the wrist should be turned so that the palm of the hand and the fingers are turned up. This movement is not used in the game and should be practiced only to get the feel of the paddle and the necessary hand-eye co-ordination to hit the birdie.

2. Each pupil serves the birdie with an underhand stroke just as the birdie drops from the hand. To learn this skill quickly, beginners may hold the birdie by the feathers; however, advanced players hold the birdie at the throat. This skill can be practiced in couples, each partner catching the served birdie and returning the birdie by a serving stroke.

3. Pupils practice returning a served birdie. This skill can also be practiced in couples, one player tossing the bird to his partner so that he can hit it with an underhand stroke similar to the serve.

4. Pupils try to keep the birdie in the air by hitting it from any position—from below the waist, over the head, or from either side. Instruction in use of the wrist and the necessity of keeping the eyes on the birdie will be essential as the elementary strokes are mastered.

Game Forms for Competition

1. One birdie and two paddles are given to every couple. Pupils stand in the aisles, each facing his partner, with their backs to the side of the room, leaving one unoccupied aisle between the players. Partners hit the birdie back and forth until one or the other fails to return the birdie. This failure scores 1 point for the opponent. The pupil nearest the birdie returns it and play is started again. The first player to receive 11 points wins. The class may want to keep a record of winners and losers so that the winners may play the winners and losers play losers.

2. Several chalk circles with a radius of three feet are drawn on the floor. One player, with a paddle and a birdie, stands in each circle. At the sound of a whistle or the word "Go," each player bounces his birdie into the air. The players may turn or move within their circles as much as necessary. The bird should be driven eight to ten feet into the air with each stroke. Each player keeps a record of the number of times his birdie is struck successfully. The pupil who steps out of his circle or fails to hit the birdie is out of the contest.

3. Teams are organized as for Schoolroom Volleyball (see page 809). The center aisle may serve as the net, or a string may be stretched across the room, the teams standing on opposite sides. The birdie is substituted for the volleyball, and the paddle is used to strike it. Any number of players on a team may hit the birdie before it is driven into the opponents' territory, but a single player may not hit the birdie more than once in succession. Striking walls, windows, doorways, or any piece of furniture with a birdie or paddle puts the birdie out of play. Rotations are the same as for Schoolroom Volleyball. The first team to have 15 points wins, except when the score reaches 13 all, when a team must win 2 points in succession to win.

TEACHING SUGGESTIONS

1. Teach the players to smooth out the feathers of the birdie with one hand as the birdie is held by the cork end.
2. Have players take care not to hit the desks or other furniture with the paddles.
3. Teach players to play assigned positions.
4. Have players make their own shuttlecocks with cork and feathers.
5. Use aerial darts as substitutes for shuttlecocks.

BASKET SOFTBALL [1]

NUMBER OF PLAYERS: 10-18

SPACE: Playground, gymnasium

PLAYING AREA: Softball diamond with bases 35 feet apart, adjacent to basketball backstop and goal (Figure 107).

EQUIPMENT: Basketball or soccer ball

Procedure

The game combines the elements of softball and basketball. Base runners, after catching the ball, run to the basketball goal, throw for a basket, and then run as many bases as possible. Both runs completed and goals made score points.

FORMATION: Players are divided into two teams of five or more players, each team having pitcher, catcher, basemen, and fielders. One team is in the field while the other tries to make runs.

To begin the game the base runner stands with one foot touching home plate and the pitcher throws the ball to him.

Catcher: During the pitching, catcher returns ball to the pitcher.

---

[1] Adapted from a note contributed by Jessie Sheppard to the *Journal of Health and Physical Education,* V (April, 1934), 46. By permission.

Following a goal ball, the catcher may secure the ball and throw it where he wishes.

Pitcher: The pitcher is allowed three trials to throw balls accurate enough to be caught by the base runner without leaving home plate. Pitcher must be in contact with the pitcher's board or pitching line when delivering the ball.

BALLS: If the pitcher throws the ball so that the base runner cannot reach it without leaving his base, it is called a ball. Two balls thrown by the pitcher in succession allow the base runner two additional throws for the basket. (Since the runner is allowed three trials for goal on a run, the two balls will give him five trials in all.) The throws for goal are taken following the second ball.

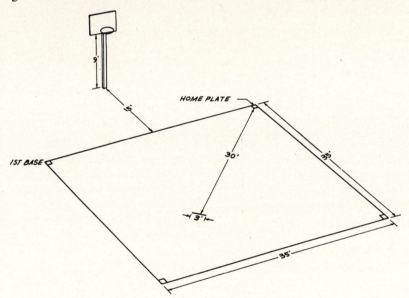

Figure 107.   Court for Basket Softball

BASE RUNNER: The instant the base runner catches the ball, he runs toward the basketball goal. At some point during the run the ball must be thrown in an effort to make a goal. The base runner is allowed three trials in the effort to make a goal, the second and third trials being taken at the spot where the ball is recovered.

If a goal is made, the base runner, leaving the ball, starts immediately to run for first base. If he can touch first, second, third, and home base without being tagged, a home run is made. At any time, a base runner may elect to remain at a base until it seems advisable to advance, or until a forced run is necessary because another base runner is advancing.

Base runners must remain on their bases while trial throws for goals are being made, as the ball is dead until it has passed through the goal. Runners may steal bases (1) during the passing of the ball between the pitcher and the base runner at home plate and (2) after the ball passes through the basketball goal.

FIELDERS: Players in the field secure the ball and try to put base runners out. No fielder may step over the boundary line between home plate and first base in an effort to secure the ball until a goal is made by the base runner. To do so is to foul. *Penalty:* (1) If the throw for the basket is successful, the base runner goes to first base. (2) If the throw is unsuccessful, the base runner is given an extra trial, making four in all.

OUTS: Three outs for each team make an inning. A base runner is out under the following circumstances:

1. When he fails to catch one of three legal balls thrown him by the pitcher
2. When he succeeds in catching a pitched ball but fails to make a goal out of the three trials permitted him
3. When, previous to the runner's arrival at a base, the baseman of that base holds the ball while contacting the base with a foot
4. When a base runner, between bases, is touched by the ball while it is held or thrown by a member of the fielding team

SCORING: One point is given for each home run whether completed in one run or in stages. Two points are given for a successful throw through the basketball goal. The team wins which has the larger number of points to its credit at the end of five innings.

TEACHING SUGGESTIONS

1. Have players rotate to the positions of catcher and pitcher.
2. Use overarm or underarm pitching.

BEANBAG TARGET TOSS

NUMBER OF PLAYERS: 2-10

SPACE: Playground, auditorium, classroom

PLAYING AREA: A restraining line drawn 10 to 20 feet from a beanbag board

EQUIPMENT: (1) Beanbag board, purchased, or constructed as shown in Figure 108; (2) three beanbags of different colors for each player

PROCEDURE: Players take turns in throwing. Each may throw three beanbags in succession or players may rotate until all three bags are thrown.

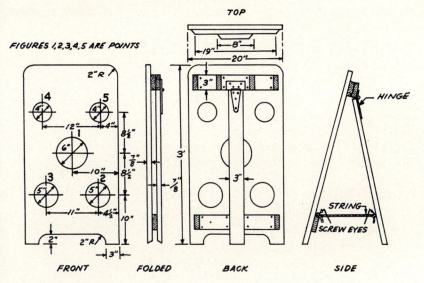

Figure 108.   Construction and Marking of a Beanbag Board

Beanbags must pass completely through the holes. One that lodges on the board does not score.

SCORING: Middle hole scores 1 point; upper right (when player faces board) scores 5 points; upper left scores 4 points; lower right scores 2 points; lower left scores 3 points.

A game may be 11 points, 21 points, or any number agreed upon by the players. Each time a player adds the total of his throws incorrectly he loses 5 points from his total score.

TEACHING SUGGESTIONS

1. Use objects other than beanbags which do not roll.
2. Use for squad play during warm weather.
3. Allow those handicapped or temporarily excused from vigorous games to use this game.

BEANBAG TARGET TOSS
(Variation)

NUMBER OF PLAYERS: 3-6

SPACE: Playground, playroom, gymnasium, classroom

PLAYING AREA: Three concentric circles drawn on the floor or ground. The inner circle has a radius of 9 inches, the second a radius of 15 inches, and the outer a radius of 21 inches. A throwing distance is established by drawing a 3-foot line 10 feet or more from the outer circle's rim.

EQUIPMENT: (1) Five beanbags, blackboard erasers, or blocks of wood; (2) score card

PROCEDURE: Players, in turn, toss the five beanbags in sequence toward the center circle. While throwing, the players must stand with the toes of one foot close to the throwing line and the other foot well back.

SCORING: A scorekeeper may be appointed or each player may keep his own score. A beanbag falling within the center circle scores 15 points; between the center circle line and the second line, 10 points; between the second and third circle lines, 5 points. Bags falling on any of the lines score only 2 points. The player who first reaches 100 points is the winner.

TEACHING SUGGESTIONS

1. When there are numerous persons to play, draw additional circles and supply additional beanbags.
2. Emphasize skill rather than speed.
3. See that every child has a beanbag of his own.

CAPTAIN BALL

NUMBER OF PLAYERS: 14-18

SPACE: Playground, gymnasium, auditorium

PLAYING AREA: Court about 15 by 55 feet, as shown in Figure 109

EQUIPMENT: Basketball, volleyball, or soccer ball

Procedure

The object of the game is for the circle players (forwards) to throw the ball to their own captains. Each time the captain receives the ball from a member of his team a point is made. After each point the game is begun again by a tossup between two opposing center players or by a toss to the center player whose team did not score.

FORMATION: Players are divided into two teams, A and B. Each has three forwards, three guards, and one or two centers. Forwards occupy the circles. Guards oppose opponents' forwards while standing outside the circles. Center players of both teams move about the court. The two circle players farthest from each other are the captains. Game is played in two 10-minute halves. At the beginning of the second half, circle men become guards and guards become circle men, and the throwing direction is changed for each team.

Circle Players. Circle players are the only players who can score points by throwing the ball to their captains. Circle players may have one foot outside their circle, but never both feet. *Penalty:* The ball goes to the opposing guard, who attempts to throw it to one of his own circle players other than his captain. The only person allowed to oppose the throw is the one guarding the circle player to whom the ball is thrown.

Guards: Guards try to prevent opponent circle players from securing the ball. If they can secure the ball they throw it to one of their own circle players. Guards may not step on the circle lines or inside circle areas, or contact circle players. *Penalty:* The ball is given to the opposing circle player, who takes an unguarded throw to his captain. The captain's guard is the only person allowed to oppose the play.

Center Players. The ball is tossed between two opposing center players at the beginning of each half. Center players move about the field of play assisting their own guards and when possible throwing the ball to their own circle players.

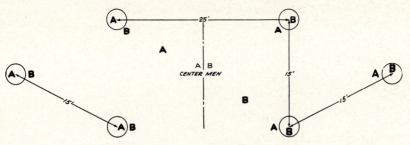

Figure 109.   Court for Captain Ball

Fouls: None of the players of either team may kick the ball, run with it, bat it out of the hands of another player, bounce it, or hold it longer than three seconds. *Penalty:* Ball is given to an opposing circle player for a free throw to his captain, the only guard being the person guarding the captain.

Scoring: One point is scored each time a captain receives the ball from one of his circle men. The team wins that has the higher score at the end of the playing period. No point is made if a guard or center player throws the ball directly to a captain.

TEACHING SUGGESTIONS

1. Teach guarding skill with this game.
2. Teach players to jump high and land correctly. Practice of the jump and reach will be helpful.
3. Add additional circles if it is desired to have more players.
4. Use Captain Ball to teach accurate passing.

CENTER CATCH TOUCH BALL

NUMBER OF PLAYERS: 6-15

SPACE: Playground, playroom, gymnasium

EQUIPMENT: Volleyball, soccer ball, basketball or utility ball

FORMATION: Players form a single circle facing in. They stretch their arms sideways until fingers touch to determine the size of the circle. A player stands in the center of the circle.

PROCEDURE: A ball is passed rapidly among the circle players. It may travel in any direction, such as across the circle, or from player to player around the circle. The center man tries to touch or catch the ball. This necessitates his moving rapidly in his effort to contact the ball. Should the center man touch or catch the ball, the person *who last touched or handled the ball before the center man did so* becomes the new center man, the former center player retiring to the circle.

The ball should not be thrown to the new center man as he enters the circle, since to do so makes the thrower center man again. As skill is gained several players should be put in the center. In this form of play the first one of the center group to touch the ball retires, the new player joining the rest of the group in the center area.

TEACHING SUGGESTIONS

1. Allow the center player to go anywhere in his effort to get his hand on the ball. Try to keep the players in circle formation.
2. Play the game using a handkerchief or knotted towel, which is known as the "hot potato." The rules are the same. In this form it is an excellent game for fun nights, the players being divided into groups of not more than eight players with a knotted handkerchief for each group.

CENTER STRIDE BALL

NUMBER OF PLAYERS: 10-20

SPACE: Playground, playroom, gymnasium

EQUIPMENT: Volleyball, basketball, soccer ball, or utility ball

FORMATION: All the players but one form a circle facing inward. One player enters the center and is given the ball. The circle players take a natural stride position with their feet touching the feet of their neighbors.

PROCEDURE: The center player tries to throw or roll the ball so that it will pass outside the circle (1) between the feet of a player, or (2)

between the bodies of two players but below their shoulders. The circle players, with feet stationary, stop the ball by using their hands.

Circle players may throw or bat the ball while endeavoring to keep it away from the center man. They may protect their own space with their hands.

If the ball passes outside between a player's feet, that player secures the ball and changes places with the center player.

If the ball passes outside between the bodies of two players, the person on whose right side the ball left the circle secures it and changes positions with the center player.

If a circle player is able to pass the ball outside by putting it between the feet of one of his two neighbors, the neighbor secures the ball and becomes the center player.

TEACHING SUGGESTIONS

1. Do not permit players to kneel down or to bring the feet close together while trying to prevent the ball from passing between the feet.
2. Avoid strides that are too wide or too narrow. There should be sufficient room for the ball to pass freely between the feet.
3. As skill is gained, increase the number of center players and the number of balls to be used.
4. If the group to play is a large one, organize two games.

CIRCLE KICK BALL

NUMBER OF PLAYERS: 10-40

SPACE: Playground, playroom, gymnasium

EQUIPMENT: Soccer ball

FORMATION: With hands joined, players form a circle. The ball is placed in front of one of the players.

PROCEDURE: The soccer ball is kicked back and forth inside the circle in an effort to send it outside the circle *under* the clasped hands of two players. The two players who permit the ball to pass under their hands are retired and leave the game. If the ball passes outside between the legs of a player, that player is retired. If the ball is kicked outside *above* the clasped hands of circle players, the kicker who sent it out is retired.

Players when not kicking try to prevent the ball from passing outside. They may use any part of their bodies to do this with the exception of their hands. These must remain clasped with the hands of their neighbors.

The game is continued until but three players remain in the circle. They are the winners of the game.

VARIATION: A line is drawn on the ground, separating the players into two teams, A and B. When so organized no players are eliminated. One-half the circle area is A's territory, the other half, B's. The teams may play in stationary positions or the circle may rotate as they try to kick the ball through. As a player crosses the line during the rotation he changes team membership. When team formation is used, 2 points are scored for kicking the ball outside the circle according to the rules. Three points are deducted if a player kicks the ball outside the circle over the arms and heads of the circle players. The team wins which first makes 12 points.

TEACHING SUGGESTIONS

1. When enough players are eliminated, give them a ball and begin a new game, playing without elimination until winners in the first circle are determined.
2. Have players avoid kicks which lift the ball high in the air.
3. Use Circle Kick Ball to teach control of the ball with the feet.

CIRCLE POLE BALL [1]

NUMBER OF PLAYERS: 14-24

SPACE: Playground, gymnasium, playroom

PLAYING AREA: Two concentric circles, one with a 12-foot radius and one with a 6-foot radius, divided in half by a line drawn across them

EQUIPMENT: (1) A pole from 10 to 15 feet high at the center of the circles. Jumping standards weighted with sandbags, giant stride pole, tether ball pole, or stool may be used. (2) Basketball, volleyball, soccer ball, or utility ball

Procedure

The game is played between two teams of from seven to twelve players. The ball is passed from one player to another, the purpose of each team being to get the ball to a baseman who tries to hit the pole and, at the same time, to prevent the other team from securing the ball or scoring. A point is made each time the pole is hit by a baseman.

FORMATION: Basemen occupy the space between the inner and outer circle, the basemen of each team playing within one half of the circle. Guards stand directly in front of the opponents' basemen. The player or players guarding the pole stand between the inner circle and the center line except during the toss when the two players taking the toss change to the other side. About half the players in each team are basemen.

---

[1] Adapted from a note contributed by L. Maude Norris to the *Journal of Health and Physical Education,* VI (December, 1935), 38. By permission.

PLAYING PERIOD: The game is played in four 5-minute quarters with a 2-minute rest between quarters and a 5-minute rest between halves. At each quarter guards and basemen rotate, and at each half teams change courts.

RULES OF PLAY: The ball is tossed up by a referee between two pole guards, one from each team. They exchange sides for the jump, returning immediately to their own court following the jump. Any guard who secures the ball sends it to one of his basemen, who may attempt to hit the pole himself or may pass to another baseman to make the attempt. If the ball goes out of bounds it is secured by the nearest baseman, who throws it to one of the opponents' guards as soon as possible before re-entering his segment. Players may not step out of their own segment while playing.

VIOLATIONS: The rule violations are those of official basketball. See p. 722.

Penalty: The ball is given to a guard of the opposing team. If personal fouls are committed, an opponent is given two unguarded throws at the pole. No guard may try to intercept the ball.

SCORING: One point is scored each time the ball hits the pole. The team wins which has the higher score at the end of four quarters.

TEACHING SUGGESTIONS

1. Encourage rapid throwing.
2. Impress those returning an out-of-bounds ball that speed is essential, since the teams are playing against time periods.
3. Require timid or unskilled players to throw the ball at the pole themselves rather than passing to another baseman.
4. Use Circle Pole Ball as an introduction to basketball rules.

DECK FLOOR HOCKEY [1]

NUMBER OF PLAYERS: 12-20

SPACE: Playroom, auditorium, gymnasium

PLAYING AREA: Basketball court or area of equal size, either a paved surface or smooth floor

EQUIPMENT: (1) Deck tennis ring or quoit; (2) wooden wands, one for each player; (3) four Indian clubs, blocks of wood, or jumping standards, placed at the center of each end line ten feet apart, to serve as goal markers; (4) stop watch; (5) whistle

---

[1] Adapted from an article contributed by Lester G. Bursey to the *Journal of Health and Physical Education,* VII (March, 1936), 194. By permission.

Procedure

The object of the game is for either of two teams to score a goal by snapping the deck tennis ring along the floor between goal markers and over the opponents' goal line with the wooden wands, at the same time defending its own goal. A referee is needed.

FORMATION: Players are divided into two teams, each having at least three forwards, two halfbacks, and one goalkeeper. Each team occupies one half of the court.

PLAYING PERIOD: The game is played in four 5-minute quarters.

RULES OF PLAY: The game is started by having two forwards "face off" as in hockey; that is, they face each other with their right sides toward their own teams, their wands crossed and at rest on the floor. The referee slides the ring along the floor and out into the middle of the court toward the two forwards. Each tries to secure it for himself or to pass it on to a teammate.

The runners advance the ring by inserting the wand in it and pushing it along the floor. The ring may be passed at any time to another player, but it may not be lifted from the floor. When passing the ring, shooting it for goal, or advancing it to a scoring position, the player must keep the ring on the floor. If a goal is made by lifting the ring from the floor, it does not count and the ring is passed out by the goalkeeper.

Each player must keep his wand in contact with the floor at all times. Players who lift the wand from the floor above their ankles lose possession of the ring to an opponent out of bounds, as in basketball. Players may intercept the ring with their feet in order to stop it from moving across the floor. When shooting the ring for a goal, or when passing to a teammate, the best method is to give a quick snap of the wrist and so let the ring slide along the floor.

If two players of opposing sides secure the ring, the referee counts ten. If by the end of that time neither one has secured the ring, the referee blows the whistle, the two in possession of the ring line up for a "face off" and the referee slides the ring toward them.

Ring Passing: The ring can be passed only to a teammate who is even with or behind the player handling the ring. When within 15 feet of the opponents' goal (basketball foul line) this requirement is cancelled.

FOULS: Players who lift the ring from the floor or their wand above their ankles lose possession of the ring to an opponent for an out-of-bounds play, as in basketball.

Tackling, roughing, tripping, or holding are not allowed. A player using such tactics is suspended from the game for one minute. Three such offenses retire the player for the rest of the game, no substitute being allowed.

SCORING: Each time the ring passes completely over a goal line between the bases, 1 point is scored. All players may score goals. The team wins which has the larger number of points at the end of the fourth quarter.

TEACHING SUGGESTIONS

1. As this game is a fast floor game, use basketball techniques such as pivots and reverses.
2. Encourage players to play their position. For example, forwards should not enter their own goal area.
3. Have the defending team play either a man-to-man defense or a zone defense as in basketball.
4. With large classes or for intramural play, after two teams have played a quarter, have two new teams take the field for the second quarter of play. This arrangement continues until all have played, whereupon the first two teams begin playing their second quarter.
5. Teach the officials how to handle the valuable stop watch.

END GOAL BALL [1]

NUMBER OF PLAYERS: 6-14

SPACE: Playground, gymnasium

PLAYING AREA: Basketball court. If basketball goals are not available, Indian clubs within circles drawn on the ground or floor may be used. With only three to five players on a team, the width of the court should be reduced to 20 feet, 10 feet on each side of the goal posts. The larger court should be used for six or more players on a team. At each end, and four feet inside the court, lines are drawn parallel to the end lines to make end zones. The court is divided in half by a center line.

EQUIPMENT: Basketball, soccer ball, or volleyball

Procedure

The game is played by two teams whose forward players try to throw the ball through the basket. Points are scored for a successful throw to a forward as well as for making goals. One official is needed.

FORMATION: Players are divided into two teams, each having one forward and two or more guards. Guards occupy the central areas farthest from their own goals; forwards occupy the end zones at their own goals. Players are numbered and take positions on the court according to number (Figure 110).

PLAYING PERIOD: The game may be played in four 6-minute quarters or in two 10-minute halves, or with a time limit of not more than 15 minutes.

---

[1] Contributed by Margaret Van Voorhees.

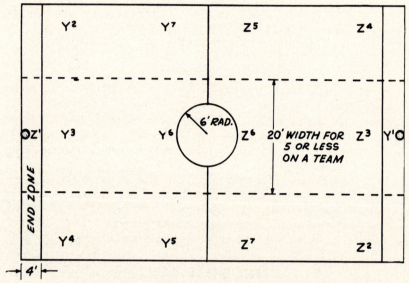

Figure 110.   Court and Position of Players for End Goal Ball

RULES OF PLAY: The game is started with a throw from out of bounds by the official to the guard then occupying the left front part of his court. The guard goes to the center circle to receive the throw. He then throws the ball to a member of his own team and returns to his playing position. That player then throws to a third member *and not until then* may a throw be attempted through the opposing team guards to the thrower's own forward confined in the opposite end zone. During play thereafter each team in possession of the ball *must make two or more passes among themselves* before attempting to score by sending the ball to their own forward. *Penalty:* For failure to observe these requirements the ball is given to an opposing guard out of bounds. A throw for goal may not be made by the out-of-bounds guard.

When the forward receives the ball he may make one attempt to shoot a goal. The forward may make the attempt from any position within his end zone. If the goal is missed, the forward attempts to throw the ball to a member of his team. If the goal is made,[1] the ball is returned to the official for a throw to the center circle. Teams alternate in taking the center throw.

Rotation of Players: After each successful goal, players of each team rotate to a new position: Forward 1 takes the place of Guard 2, Guard 7 becomes a forward, and other guards move to the position of the next higher number. Teams change courts at half time.

_____
[1] For inexperienced or younger children it may be agreed that to contact the backboard with the ball constitutes a successful scoring throw.

Violations: Violations of the rules are the same as in basketball, with the ball being given to an opponent out of bounds as the penalty. See p. 722.

Fouls: Fouls are the same as in basketball. The penalty for a foul is a free throw for goal by opposing forward from any spot within his zone area. There will be few if any personal fouls because of the segregation of opponents.

SCORING: One point is given for each successful throw to a forward. Two points are given for a goal made by the forward.

TEACHING SUGGESTIONS

1. Introduce techniques for basketball as the players learn the rules.
2. If desired, allow an additional trial for a goal to be made following an unsuccessful throw for goal.
3. While players should remain in their own areas, teach them to move about freely within that area.
4. Stress short, quick passes, as long passes are undesirable.

FREE-THROW END BALL [1]

NUMBER OF PLAYERS: 6-24
SPACE: Playground, gymnasium
PLAYING AREAS: Basketball court, divided into two courts by a center line connecting the side lines. Three feet in from the end lines of the court parallel lines are drawn to outline two end zones.

EQUIPMENT: Basketball, soccer ball, volleyball, or utility ball

Procedure

The game is played by two teams who try to throw the ball to end-zone players and, if a successful throw is made, to throw for goals. The game is similar to End Ball, p. 470.

FORMATION: The players of each team are numbered. On each team one third of the players act as end men, occupying the end zone nearest their own goal; the remaining players act as fielders, taking positions in the field farthest from and facing their end men. One official is needed.

PLAYING PERIOD: The game is played in three 5-minute periods.

RULES OF PLAY: The game is commenced by a tossup in the center of the court between opposing fielders. The fielders try to send the ball to one of their own end men. If a successful catch is made by an end man, the end man and the fielder who threw the ball to him each have the right to attempt a throw at the goal, the end man from within his zone area at

[1] Adapted from article by Frances G. Crean, *Journal of Health and Physical Education,* X (December, 1939), 594. By permission.

the spot where he caught the ball and the fielder from the free-throw line nearest his end man. Following the throw by the end man the ball is dead; following the throw by the fielder the ball is in play whether the goal is made or is missed. If an end man secures the ball following the try for goal by the fielder, it must be returned by him to one of his fielders. He may not try for a goal.

Rotation: At the expiration of each five minutes of play new end men (one third of fielders) enter the end zones, the former end-zone players becoming fielders.

Out-of-Bounds Ball: If the ball goes out of bounds over an end line, the nearest end-zone player retrieves it and throws it to an end player. If it goes out of bounds over a side line, the nearest fielder secures it and throws it to another fielder and the ball is immediately in play.

Dribble: If a fielder guarding the player in front of an end zone secures the ball, he may dribble it, if he wishes, up to the center line before attempting a throw to one of his end men.

Fouls: A fielder may not take more than two steps before beginning a dribble. *Penalty:* The ball is awarded to an opponent end man. Other fouls are the same as in End Ball.

SCORING: The team wins which has the larger number of points at the end of the third playing period. Three points are possible with each successful play. One point is earned when an end man catches the ball. Two additional points may be earned if both the end man and the fielder who threw him the ball make successful throws for goal, that is, one point for each player.

TEACHING SUGGESTIONS

1. Use Free-Throw End Ball to teach skills of guarding, shooting, passing, and dribbling.
2. Place any number of children on a team. When the group to play is small, say six to a team, draw two lines paralleling the side lines the length of the court, each line being 8 feet from the goal posts. Play must be confined within these side lines and the end lines. When the group is exceptionally large, appoint forward players to play at the center line with assisting fielder guards playing always at the rear of their forwards. Rotate in such a situation from forward to end to guard positions.

FRONT MAN

NUMBER OF PLAYERS: 10-30

SPACE: Classroom

FORMATION: A tagger and a runner are chosen. The remaining players are seated so that the rear seat of each row is occupied. If there are more seats than players, place books on the vacant desks to signify that those seats are not to be used.

PROCEDURE: The tagger tries to catch the runner. The runner may save himself at any time by stopping at the rear of any row of seats and calling loudly, "Front Man!" He is no longer the runner. The player sitting in the first seat of that row becomes the new runner and must seek safety from the tagger. If tagged, the runner and tagger change places and the game is continued.

TEACHING SUGGESTIONS

1. After the runner and tagger leave an aisle, *and not before*, have the children in the row behind which the former runner stopped move forward one seat, providing a seat for the former runner.
2. Insist that all feet of seated players must be kept out of the aisles.

HANDBALL

NUMBER OF PLAYERS: 2 or 4

SPACE: Playground, gymnasium

PLAYING AREA: Handball court (Figure 111). Smaller areas may be used, but official backstop and smooth-surfaced ground area are necessary.

EQUIPMENT: Large handball (No. 106), tennis ball, or small rubber ball

Procedure

The opponents take turns in striking the ball with the hands against the wall, a miss on the server's side resulting in a change of servers, and a miss on the receiver's side scoring a point for the server.

FORMATION: In a singles game two players oppose each other; in a doubles game two partners play against two other partners. Both players or teams stand facing the backstop.

SERVING: The server must stand within the serving area, between service line, side lines, and back lines. He must not leave this area while serving. He is permitted two preliminary bounces with the ball before serving. To serve, ball is dropped to the ground and on rebound struck with the hand so as to send the ball against the wall. It must then rebound on the fly and cross the service line, bouncing within the service area. A ball striking on a side line or on the back line is good.

There are two types of faults in serving:

1. *Foot fault:* If in serving the server steps on or over a side line or on the service line he makes a foot fault.
2. *Line fault:* There are two types of line faults, (a) a short ball, which lands after hitting the wall in the half court next the wall, on the

service line, or out of the court over a side line, or (b) a long ball, which rebounds from the wall and lands behind the back line.

After a fault, the ball is dead and a second serve is permitted. Two foot faults in succession retire the server. Two line faults (two short balls, two long balls, or a long ball and a short ball) in succession retire the server.

RECEIVING: The opponent of the server is the receiver. He accepts a properly served ball by striking it with the hand (after it has bounced once) against the wall so that it rebounds within the court or on a boundary line. Receivers (in singles or doubles) and partner of server (in doubles) must stand outside the court behind the back line until served ball, following its rebound from the wall, crosses the service line. Receiver cannot play a served ball until it has bounced once. A long or short ball, being dead, cannot be played. Except on a served short ball, all line balls are good.

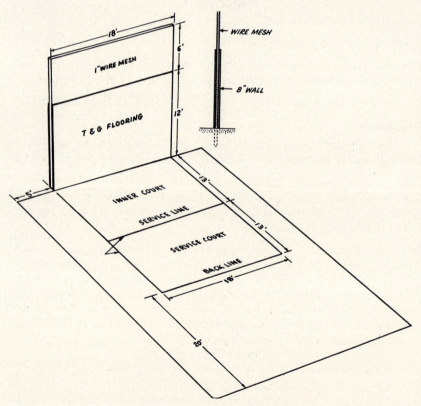

Figure 111.   Court for Handball

RALLY: After the ball is in play (after being served and struck by the receiver after the first bounce), the server and receiver alternate in striking the ball until one side or the other misses. If the receiver misses, a point is scored for the server, who re-serves the ball. *In a singles game*, if the server misses, the receiver becomes the server, but no point is made; *in a doubles game*, if the server misses he retires in favor of either his partner or a member of the other team (see Rotation of Players). During a rally in a doubles game, partners must alternate in striking the ball. After the first stroke by the receiver, ball may be played either after a bounce or on the fly. A line ball is a fair ball. A ball in play which strikes the wire above the wall area counts against the player who sent it there.

CHANGE OF SERVICE OR HAND OUT: The server loses his service under the following conditions:

1. If he makes two foot faults or two line faults in succession
2. If he serves by throwing the ball against the wall instead of using a bounce and hand stroke, or by using a toss and hand stroke instead of a bounce and hand stroke
3. If he catches or stops ball during his service
4. If he plays his own served ball
5. If he fails, during service, to strike the ball following the first bounce
6. If he touches or stops a short or long ball (or in a doubles game if server or partner touches or stops a short or long ball) before it bounces
7. If during service and before it hits the wall the ball hits the ground, wire mesh, or any other object (except when an opponent unintentionally interferes with or obstructs the flight of the ball; see Hinder)
8. If he (or in doubles his partner) fails to strike a properly returned ball so that it hits the wall and rebounds into the playing area. That is, if the ball (a) fails to hit the wall, (b) goes outside the playing area, (c) hits the wire mesh, or (d) rebounds from the wall to a position outside the boundary lines of playing area
9. If he serves out of turn during a doubles game

ROTATION OF PLAYERS IN DOUBLES: The first player of the first team serves until the serving side loses, when the receivers' side gets the ball. First player of second team serves until his side loses, when the serve goes to his partner, *not to the other team*. On the next hand out, second player of first team takes the serve, followed, on the next miss, by his partner. For example, if Team I, Players A and B, plays Team II, Players C and D, rotation is as follows: A, C, D, B, A, C, D, B, A, and so forth until one side wins.

TERMINOLOGY: The following terms are used in handball:
Ace: A service which the receiver cannot touch because the ball is so well placed

Dead Ball: A ball out of play without a penalty being imposed; usually follows a hinder or a fault

Fault: An infraction of the rules which involves a penalty

Hand out: Loss of service by a team

Hinder: A situation wherein an opponent unintentionally interferes with or obstructs the flight of the ball. Ball is replayed.

Kill: A returned ball which rebounds from the wall so close to the ground that further play is impossible. A kill is a fair stroke.

Lob: Ball lifted high in air during service or rally

Out: When server fails to serve legally, and when both partners serving in doubles have been put out, the side is out and hand out occurs.

Point: When a receiving side cannot return a legally served or returned ball

Rally: Play of ball following a successful service

Scoop: A ball that strikes the ground before hitting the wall; it counts against the player

Volley: A ball returned to the wall as a fly ball, without a bounce

Scoring: Each time receiver fails to return a correctly placed ball, 1 point is scored for serving side. A game is played for 11 or 21 points, as agreed upon. If teams are tied at 10 or 20 points, they play for game point, in which one team must make two points in succession in order to win. A match for boys consists of two 11-point games and a 21-point game in case of a tie. For girls, a match consists of two out of three 11-point games, the third game to be played only in case of a tie.

TEACHING SUGGESTIONS

1. Teach the fundamental underhand stroke, in which both hands are equally important. A full arm motion should be cultivated, with wrist snap or stiff arm action employed as needed. The hand should be held in a slightly cupped position with the point of contact the upper half of the palm near the wrist.
2. Use one backstop for eight players by having a doubles game on either side of the board.
3. Play a "threesome" game by having one player against two players.
4. Teach pupils to keep their eyes on the ball whenever it is in play.
5. Develop in the pupils balance, control, spring, and alertness.
6. Instruct players to discover an opponent's weakness and direct play toward that area.

HIT OR OUT

NUMBER OF PLAYERS: 4-8

SPACE: Playground, gymnasium

PLAYING AREA: Handball backstop, outside wall of school building, gymnasium wall, or wire baseball backstop. Draw three lines on the wall, parallel to the floor, to form four separate sections representing a one-base hit, a two-base hit, a three-base hit, or a home run, beginning at the bottom with a one-base area. If a wire backstop is used, use rope or colored string to mark the areas.

EQUIPMENT: (1) Softball bats; (2) 12-inch or 15-inch softballs. Volleyballs may be used by having the batter use his open hand instead of a bat and shortening the distance between pitcher and batter.

FORMATION: Players are divided into two teams as for softball. The pitcher stands with his back to the wall or backstop. The batter faces the pitcher, 20, 30, or 40 feet distant (depending on the ages of the players). Catcher stands behind the batter. Fielders are scattered about as needed to retrieve the balls. One or more fielders should stand behind the backstop to secure balls which pass over the top.

PROCEDURE: The game is played in general as is softball, but *no actual base running occurs*. As the ball is pitched, the batter tries to strike the ball in such a way as to hit the wall in the home-run area or one of the other areas. The number of bases credited to him is determined by the area struck by the ball. If the batter makes a successful strike (contacting the wall), he remains at bat. If he fails to hit the wall, he is out. He is also out if the pitcher catches or stops a batted ball or if a fielder catches a fly ball. Each player continues at bat until he is put out, when the next man on the team becomes the batter. When all members of the team have had a turn at bat, a half-inning is finished, and the other team has its turn. The game is played in any number of innings agreed upon by the players.

Rotation of Players: Following a team's second retirement from batting position, a rotation of players occurs at each following inning as the players go to the fielding positions. (1) Catcher goes to pitching position; (2) pitcher to fielding position; (3) fielders, in sequence, to catching position.

SCORING: Runs are credited to the batter's record according to the area on the wall struck by the ball. Runs are cumulative for as long as the batter continues at the batting position. That is, if he strikes the one-base area twice he is credited with two bases. If he strikes the two-base area twice and the home run area once, he is credited with two runs. A player's score for bases cannot be added to the next batter's score. Each home run or total of four bases counts one. The team wins which has the larger number of points to its credit at the conclusion of the game.

TEACHING SUGGESTIONS

1. Appoint a scorekeeper to keep a record of each batter's bases.
2. Use as a less strenuous game for warm days.
3. Give instruction in the relationship of body position to direction in which the ball is hit.
4. Check the grip, swing, and follow-through of the batter.

HIT PIN BASEBALL

NUMBER OF PLAYERS: 10-20

SPACE: Playground, gymnasium

PLAYING AREA: Softball diamond with bases 35 feet apart. See Figure 112.

EQUIPMENT: (1) Soccer ball or rubber ball of similar size that may be kicked; (2) four 12-inch squares of linoleum or hard wood, one placed

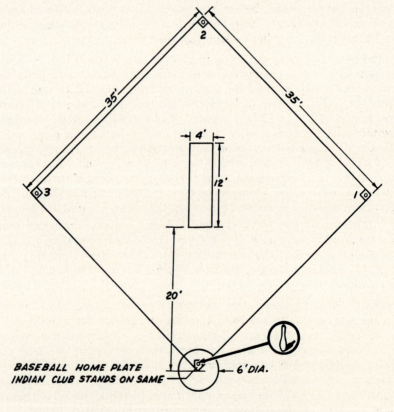

Figure 112.   Diamond for Hit Pin Baseball

at each corner of the softball diamond; (3) four Indian clubs, each one attached to a circle of wood with a radius of 3 inches. The clubs are placed on the four bases. If Indian clubs are not available, pieces of wood 3 by 3 inches and 10 inches high may be used; the bases may be 4-inch squares instead of circles. Tall, narrow tin cans may be used instead of the Indian clubs.

Procedure

The object of the game is for a kicker to score points by kicking a bowled ball and then making a home run without being put out.

FORMATION: Each team has a catcher, bowler, first, second, and third baseman, and as many fielders as are desired. One team takes position for kicking; the other team members take positions used in softball.

PLAYING PERIOD: The game is played by innings, half an inning being finished when one team has had a turn at bat. Seven innings are official unless otherwise agreed upon. When a team makes three outs, the opponents are at bat. When time for playing is limited, two time periods can be used.

BOWLER: With both feet inside the bowler's box, the bowler rolls the ball on the ground towards home plate. The bowler tries to send a ball hard to kick, and at the same time tries to knock over the Indian club standing at the center of the home base.

KICKER: Kicker must stand with his supporting foot inside the circle when attempting to kick the ball. If successful, the kicker starts a continuous run, going outside of first, second, and third bases. He must touch the ground within the circle at home plate to make the run legal.

BASEMEN AND FIELDERS: Basemen and fielders try to prevent home runs. Following a fair kick, any baseman or fielder may secure the ball. No matter where the ball is stopped, its line of travel, thereafter, is always from that spot to first base, to second base, to third base, and home in an attempt to have the ball overtake and pass the runner.

In order for a baseman to put out a runner he must receive the ball in *advance of the runner* and must knock over the Indian club at his base by use of the ball in his hands *before the runner reaches the base*. A baseman may leave his base to secure the ball or he may receive a throw from a fielder, *but before throwing the ball to the next baseman* he must have a foot contacting his base. Basemen and fielders may not interfere with a runner. To do so gives a run to the runner's team.

RUNS: A run is completed each time a player at bat, upon kicking a fair ball, makes a continuous run outside the bases and arrives at home base without having an Indian club knocked down by the baseman or a fielder ahead of his arrival at a base.

FAIR BALL: A ball is fair which (1) passes over or lands inside the small front segment of the circle at home base, (2) lands on one of the lines determining the area of the front segment of the circle, or (3) travels to the field within the base lines of home and first and home and third bases.

FOUL BALLS: The foul ball rules are the same as in softball.

DEAD BALL: A dead ball is a ball delivered by the bowler which hits a kicker. The ball must then be rebowled.

PLACE KICK: A place kick is given the kicker when four balls are called on the bowler. The ball is placed on the ground at a point inside the front segment of the circle.

STRIKES: A strike is called (1) if a kicker misses a fairly bowled ball; (2) if a kicker fails to keep the supporting foot within the circle while attempting the kick; (3) for each foul ball kicked until the kicker has two strikes. Fouls, thereafter, are not called strikes.

OUTS: The kicker is out at home base in the following circumstances:
1. Always on third strike
2. When a placed ball, awarded because of four balls, is kicked foul
3. If the Indian club at home plate is knocked down by the bowler
4. If the Indian club at home plate is knocked down by the kicker
5. If a foul fly is caught
6. If a fly ball is caught
7. If a fair ball, before it strikes the ground, knocks down an Indian club on any one of the four bases
8. If the kicker is hit by a fair ball, kicked by himself, before the ball touches the ground

The kicker is out as a runner in the following circumstances:
1. If a fly ball is caught
2. If an Indian club ahead of him is legally knocked down by a baseman or a fielder
3. If the kicker knocks down an Indian club during his run
4. If the kicker, during his run, goes inside the diamond, thereby omitting a base
5. If the kicker does not touch the ground inside the circle at the conclusion of his run
6. If the kicker interferes with any player or with the ball

SCORING: For each successful run 1 point is given. Interference with players or the ball by a player gives 1 point to the opponent team.

The team wins which has the higher number of points at the conclusion of the last inning.

Instead of innings two periods of play may be used. Members of a team play in sequence until the end of the first period, and the fielding team becomes the kicking team for the second period. The team wins which has more points at the end of the two playing periods.

TEACHING SUGGESTIONS

1. Use this game to teach base running and softball rules.
2. Teach fielders to pass the ball as rapidly as they can.
3. See that basemen touch the base before throwing the ball to the next baseman.
4. Use in the fourth grade as well as in the fifth grade.

HOOK ON

NUMBER OF PLAYERS: 9-40

SPACE: Playground, playroom, gymnasium, auditorium

FORMATION: One child is selected as a runner. The remaining players form groups of four. They stand one behind the other in file formation, each with arms clasped firmly around the waist of the player in front of him. The front players must keep their arms folded across their chests.

PROCEDURE: The runner attempts to hook on at the end of any file where he can. File members twist and swing about, trying to protect the end of their file from being caught. They must not break their arm clasps. If the runner is successful, the leader of that file becomes the new runner.

TEACHING SUGGESTIONS

1. Use additional runners after the pattern of the game is mastered.
2. Have runners dart about, not remaining too long with any one group in the effort to make a permanent contact.

INDIAN CLUB GUARD

NUMBER OF PLAYERS: 10-15

SPACE: Playground, playroom, gymnasium

EQUIPMENT: (1) Basketball, volleyball, soccer ball; (2) five Indian clubs (or sticks of wood 3 by 3 inches by 10 inches high)

FORMATION: Players form a circle. The Indian clubs are set up in the middle of the circle. A guard is selected to protect the Indian clubs.

PROCEDURE: The players in the circle endeavor to knock down the Indian clubs with the ball. The guard tries to keep between the ball and the Indian clubs. Whoever succeeds in knocking down a club or clubs changes places with the guard.

The basketball is passed swiftly across and around the circle, the players aiming at the clubs whenever the guard seems to be inattentive. The guard wins who stays longest in the center.

TEACHING SUGGESTION

1. When the group is large, organize several circles, providing players of each circle with Indian clubs and a ball.

LAST COUPLE OUT

NUMBER OF PLAYERS: 9-31

SPACE: Playground, playroom, gymnasium

FORMATION: Players stand in two files, partners being side by side. A single player stands in front of the two files, with his back to them; he must not turn his head to the right or to the left but must look straight ahead.

PROCEDURE: The odd player calls loudly, "Last Couple Out!" The two players at the ends of the files run forward and try to clasp hands with each other somewhere in front of the odd player without being tagged by him. When a runner comes within the vision of the caller he gives chase. If the tagger fails to tag a runner he remains the tagger. If he tags a runner he takes that player's partner and they go to the head of the files. The person caught becomes the new tagger.

TEACHING SUGGESTIONS

1. Discourage long runs with the partners scattering too far apart.
2. If the group is large, divide the players into two groups and have two games run simultaneously.
3. Set up definite boundaries.

NET BALL

NUMBER OF PLAYERS: 2-20

SPACE: Playground, playroom, gymnasium, classroom

PLAYING AREA: Volleyball court, 25 or 30 feet by 50 or 60 feet, or smaller if necessary. Height of net should be about 7 feet 6 inches from the ground to the top of the net. (See Figure 159, page 800.)

EQUIPMENT: Volleyball, soccer ball, utility ball, or basketball

FORMATION: Players are divided into two teams and members of each team are numbered to determine rotation of serve.

PROCEDURE: The game is a simplified form of volleyball. (See p. 801.) One side takes the serve and after the ball has been properly served it is volleyed back and forth until one side misses. Exceptions to volleyball rules are as follows: (1) The ball is thrown and caught instead of being batted; (2) players may not walk after catching the ball. *Penalty:* One point is given to the serving side if foul is committed by a member of the receiving side; loss of service occurs if foul is committed by member of the serving side. If impact in catching the ball forces the catcher to take a step, he returns the ball from the last spot occupied, whether he is inside or outside the court.

When the serving side fails to return the ball properly it loses the service to the other team. Whenever the receiving team fails to return the ball properly a point is credited to the serving team. Each time change of service occurs, service rotates to a different player, in order of their numbering.

SCORING: A game is won when either team scores a two-point lead after fifteen or more points are won. A match consists of the best two out of three games.

TEACHING SUGGESTIONS

1. Play game on time-period basis instead of point basis; in quarters or halves of agreed upon length, teams changing courts for each half or for each quarter. Suggested: Four 6-minute quarters, 1-minute rest period between quarters, 3-minute rest period between halves; or two 10-minute halves, 5-minute rest period between halves.

2. If a forward or a player in the center of the court catches the ball, have him attempt to throw the ball over the net. A player in the rear of the court should throw the ball to a center or a forward of his team. The rotation of players will eventually bring him to the position where he will be required to throw the ball over the net.

3. Encourage fast throwing.

4. Use to teach volleyball scoring rules and rotation.

5. Have play fast and vigorous.

6. Draw net tightly so that it will not sag.

7. Lower nets for small children.

NET BALL DRILLS [1]

SKILLS: Use net ball drills to teach the following:

1. Finger movement, finger spread for better striking
2. Team work
3. Rotation

---

[1] By courtesy of Oakland Public Schools.

4. Facing about to assist team members
5. Playing terms, such as ace, serve, net ball, kill [1]
6. Rules of Net Ball or Volleyball
7. Scoring technique

Formation: Divide a class according to ability and knowledge, and in order to give each the benefit of the drills rotate players as follows: (1) boys and girls together on same teams; (2) players who need more practice on one court and stronger players on the other; (3) return to practice with equal teams made up of boys and girls, weak and strong players.

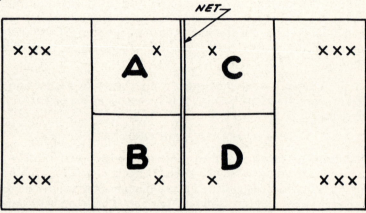

Figure 113.   Court for Net Ball Drills

Drill 1.   Using a volleyball court divided as in Figure 113, have one player in each of courts A, B, C, D; the rest of the players on teams as in diagram. Two balls are used. A and C players throw to each other, B and D to each other. Change players on a signal. Work for fast, accurate throws.

Drill 2.   With same organization of players, have A throw to D, B to C criss-crossed. This will establish the idea of throwing to other sections of the courts. It will be confusing at first because of the two balls, but this will help players to concentrate.

Drill 3.   Use the same organization and procedure as in Drill 1, except that a competitive game is played, a score being kept of throws made before error occurs. Keep players changing on signal, and play a round robin to determine the best team.[2]

Drill 4.   Have a line of three or four players in each square, with remaining players outside the court. Play regular game of Net Ball, each two teams using a half court. On a signal, front players retire, new players take positions at end of lines; players in the courts advance one position.

---

[1] See Volleyball Terminology, page 802.
[2] See Round Robin Tournament, page 183.

PADDLE BADMINTON

NUMBER OF PLAYERS: 2-20

SPACE: Playground, gymnasium, auditorium

PLAYING AREA: Court 20 by 44 feet. The court may be lengthened for a large number of players.

EQUIPMENT: (1) Two posts 6 by 6 inches by 6 feet, or jumping stand-ards, placed at the centers of the two side lines; (2) badminton or volleyball net stretched from post to post so that the top of the net is 5 feet 1 inch from the floor at the posts and 5 feet at the center; (3) for each player a long-handled paddle;[1] (4) several shuttlecocks or Flying Fleece balls.[2] If a net is not available, a rope or chicken wire may be stretched between the posts. Birds may be made by tying jackstone balls in the center of 8- or 10-inch squares of cloth.

FORMATION: Teams of from one to ten players are arranged as for volley-ball (see p. 801).

PROCEDURE: The game is played according to volleyball rules. One service only is allowed, with the exception of a let bird, which is re-served.
   Service: An underhand serve is used. A second player may not assist the bird over the net. Following service, players may use any stroke desired to return the bird, but they may not touch the net while attempt-ing to do so. A bird that strikes a boundary line is considered in court.

SCORING: The same scoring is used as for volleyball.

TEACHING SUGGESTIONS

1. Impress on children that care must be used in handling the paddle.
2. Have players use the underhand serve, holding the bird by the feathers with the left hand.

PADDLE BALL

NUMBER OF PLAYERS: 2-4

SPACE: Playground, gymnasium

PLAYING AREA: Handball court, outdoor wall, or gymnasium wall. Hand-ball wall dimensions should be 18 by 18 feet. Floor dimensions should be 26 by 18 feet. A line is drawn on the wall 2 feet above and parallel to the ground. A service line is drawn on the floor 13 feet from the wall.

EQUIPMENT: For each player, paddle-tennis paddle, old tennis ball

---

[1] See directions for constructing paddle, page 115.
[2] Flying Fleece balls are made of woolen yarn. They may be secured from sporting goods stores or from Oregon Woolen Mills, Portland, Oregon.

Figure 114. Paddle Ball Singles

FORMATION: In a singles game, two players oppose each other. In doubles, each team has two players.

PROCEDURE: To serve, player may stand anywhere within the court between the wall and the service line. If the first service is a failure, a second trial is permitted. To be fair, the served ball must strike on the wall above the 2-foot line. Thereafter any ball which strikes any portion of the wall is a legal ball. Following the serve the opponent of the server must return the ball against the wall; the next stroke is taken by the server, etc., until a miss occurs. Service changes from one side to the other whenever the server fails to hit the ball legally.

SCORING: Each time the receiver fails to return a correctly placed ball, 1 point is scored for the serving side. A game is played for 11 or 21 points, as agreed upon. If teams are tied at 10 or 20 points, they play for game point, in which one team must make two points in succession in order to win. A match for boys consists of two 11-point games and a 21-point game in case of a tie. For girls, a match consists of two out of three 11-point games, the third game to be played only in case of a tie.

TEACHING SUGGESTIONS

1. Have a match consist of three games. Omit playing for game point during match if time is limited.

2. Teach technique for holding paddle. Certain incorrect methods of handling the paddle should be avoided. A right-handed player should first grasp the playing surface of paddle in his left hand with the thin edge pointed toward the floor. This will make the playing surface parallel the line of the body. Then grip the handle at the extreme end with the right hand as though "shaking hands" with it. All fingers should be wrapped around the handle and no portion of the handle end should protrude beyond the little finger and bottom of palm. The index finger should *never extend* along the paddle handle. Thumb and forefinger should form a slight V on the side of the handle that is continuous with the thin edge of the paddle's striking surface.

PASS AND CHANGE

NUMBER OF PLAYERS: 10-20

SPACE: Playground, playroom, gymnasium

EQUIPMENT: Volleyball, basketball, soccer ball, utility ball, knotted towel, or beanbag

FORMATION: Players form a circle about 40 feet or more in diameter. Holding the ball, one player stands in the center of the circle.

PROCEDURE: At a signal, the center man calls two names and at the same time throws the ball to a third circle player. Immediately the third player returns the ball to the center player. In the meantime the players whose names were called try to exchange places with each other. The center man, upon receiving the ball from the third player, tries to hit one of the runners. If successful, he continues in the center. If unsuccessful, he retires to the circle, giving the ball to a circle player as he leaves the center.

TEACHING SUGGESTIONS

1. If the names of the players are not known, number the players, including the center man. Numbers can then be called instead of names.
2. Do not permit favoritism in the form of continually calling the names of a few players.
3. When large numbers are to play, form several circles and supply them with balls.

PIN BASKETBALL

NUMBER OF PLAYERS: 12-36

SPACE: Playground, gymnasium

PLAYING AREA: Court about the same size as that used for Nine-Court Basketball,[1] with the addition of a circle three feet in diameter drawn

---

[1] See Nine-Court Basketball, pages 662-68.

inside each middle end square. The circumference of the circles should touch the mid-point of the end line of the court.

EQUIPMENT: (1) Junior basketball, soccer ball, volleyball, utility ball, large beanbag, or stuffed leather casing; (2) two Indian clubs or lengths of stove wood, one in the center of each circle. Indian clubs or sticks should be fastened upon small wooden bases for greater stability when playing on uneven ground. Usable pins may be made of wood 1 foot long by 3 inches square fastened on bases; or 1-foot 4 by 4's unmounted; or 1-foot lengths salvaged from broken baseball bats or broom handles screwed onto bases; or old tenpins cut off at the widest part of the pins.

Procedure

Members of each team, while playing the position of forwards in the three end squares, try to knock over the Indian clubs without stepping on the circumference of or within the circles. Guards oppose their efforts.

FORMATION: The same formation is used as for Nine-Court Basketball.

RULES OF PLAY: The rules governing the game are the same as those governing Nine-Court Basketball, with the following exceptions:

1. Ball is thrown in an effort to knock down the Indian clubs instead of being thrown through basketball goals.
2. If the game is played on a basketball court, a ball which strikes the goal post and rebounds into the court is in play.
3. When a free throw for the goal is awarded, the ball is thrown, not rolled, from behind the free-throw line. If the ball touches the ground before knocking the club down, a point is not made and the ball is in play. When making a free throw the player may not step on or over the 15-foot mark until the ball enters the circle. If the throw is successful the point does not score. If unsuccessful the ball goes to the opponent of the person who made the attempt. If players step inside the circles, a free throw is awarded the opponents.

SCORING: When a pin is knocked down legally by a throw from the field, 2 points are given. When a pin is knocked down legally from a free throw, 1 point is given.

TEACHING SUGGESTIONS

1. When introducing the game, allow only the players in the middle end squares to throw to knock over the Indian clubs. As skill is gained, allow players from the three end squares to try to knock the Indian clubs over.
2. Play Pin Basketball to teach skills and rules of basketball.
3. Use a small two court basketball court to provide more freedom of movement.

RUN, SHEEP, RUN

NUMBER OF PLAYERS: 4-20

SPACE: Playground

PLAYING AREA: Designated goal and hiding areas

FORMATION: Players are divided into two teams, A and B. Each team has a captain. Team A members remain at the goal while the members of Team B hide, their captain assisting them. When all are hidden the B captain returns to the goal.

PROCEDURE: Team A members set forth to find the members of Team B. The captain sends different members of his team in different directions. The captain of Team B watches the movements of the searching party and when he feels the time is propitious for his players to reach goal and safety calls out loudly, "Run, Sheep, Run!"

Usually the captain of the hiding group gives the signal, but if the captain of the searching party, or one of his men, discovers a hiding man, he may give the signal to run. The object is for the hiding players to return to home base without being tagged by any of the hunting team members. A hunting player may tag more than one player during the run for home.

TEACHING SUGGESTIONS

1. Add fun to the game by having the captains and their teams decide on the use of signals. For example the word "lead" may mean get down; "river," to the right; "legion," to the left; "iron," go back; "diamond," hunters are near.

SCREWYLOUIE [1]

NUMBER OF PLAYERS: 4-20

SPACE: Playroom, auditorium, hallway, classroom

PLAYING AREA: End and side boundaries of court marked on floor, length and width depending on numbers to play

EQUIPMENT: (1) Bladder used in volleyball or soccer ball, or a balloon; (2) net or heavy cord, with top of net seven feet from the ground

FORMATION: Players are divided into two teams as for volleyball. [2]

PROCEDURE: The bladder is served and played as in volleyball. After service it may be sent to a teammate or over the net. The ball is played regardless of whether it hits the wall or ceiling. With practice, players

---

[1] Contributed by Edward M. Hausladen, Supervisor of Attendance and Physical Education, San Bernardino County.
[2] See Volleyball, p. 801.

learn to use walls and ceiling as an aid when playing the bladder. Rotation of players is the same as in volleyball.

SCORING: The team wins which first scores 11, 15, or 21 points. The same method is used as in Net Ball (see p. 558) or volleyball.

TEACHING SUGGESTIONS

1. When primary children are playing, have them catch and throw the bladder instead of volleying it.
2. Point out that the lightness of the bladder prevents damage to windows and light fixtures but that it is inadvisable to "smash" the bladder.
3. To accomplish rotation in a classroom with fixed seats have all net players move to the rear with other lines moving forward.
4. Teach volleyball skills, using the tips of the fingers to play a light bladder.

SOFTBALL [1]

NUMBER OF PLAYERS: 18

PLAYING AREA: Official softball diamond, with 60-foot base lines, pitching distance 35 feet; or, for intermediate grades, 45-foot or less base lines, pitching distance 35 feet (Figure 115), with an unobstructed area of 200 feet from home plate between the foul lines

EQUIPMENT: (1) Home plate, a five-sided figure made preferably of hard rubber, set flush with the ground, with dimensions as shown in Figure 116; (2) three bases 15 inches square; (3) pitcher's plate, wood or hard rubber, 2 feet by 6 inches, set flush with the ground; (4) softball bats of different weights, not more than 34 inches long and not more than 2⅛ inches in diameter at the largest part; (5) several balls, smooth seamed, not less than 11⅞ inches in circumference, weight not less than 6 ounces nor more than 6¾ ounces; (6) catcher's glove, mask, and body protector; (7) fielders' gloves

Procedure

Softball is played in general as is baseball,[2] but on a smaller diamond and with a larger and softer ball. The game is played between two teams which take turns at batting. It is suitable for boys and girls to play together. All pitching is underhand. The pitcher of the team in the field pitches to members of the batting team in order. If the batter hits a fair

---

[1] These rules are briefed. Those desiring more information should secure *The Official Softball–Track and Field Guide*. Washington: National Section on Women's Athletics, American Association for Health, Physical Education and Recreation (1201 Sixteenth St., N.W., Washington 6, D. C.), or *Official Softball Guide*. Leonia, N. J.: W. W. Wells Co.

[2] Hard baseball is not recommended as a game in elementary schools. Playgrounds are, almost without exception, too small for the game of hard baseball. The playing of hard baseball on most elementary school playgrounds is hazardous for the pupils participating as well as the other pupils in the area.

ball he runs to first base, second base, third base, and home, while the fielding team tries to put him out by catching the ball and touching him while he is off base. The base runner may stop at any base and continue his run next time the ball is fairly hit by his team. A complete run around the bases and home scores a point for the batting team. After three men on the batting team have been put out, the teams change positions and half an inning has been played. Seven innings constitute a game. Three outs retire a side at bat.

FORMATION: Nine players are on each team: pitcher, catcher, first baseman, second baseman, third baseman, shortstop, left fielder, center fielder, and right fielder. (Officially there are only nine players, but many groups add the short fielder as the tenth player.) Each position is numbered, and each player has a specific duty and a specific area to cover.

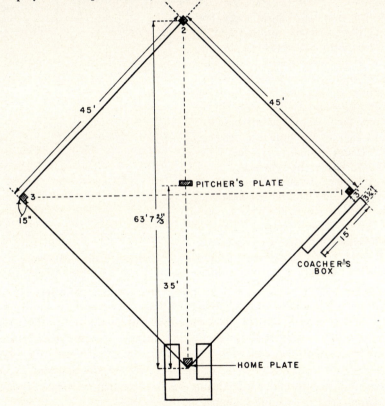

Figure 115. Softball Diamond. An official diamond has 60 feet between bases with 84' 10¼" between home plate and second base. A diamond with 55 feet between bases would have 77' 9½" between home and second base.

The pitcher, Number 1, pitches from the pitcher's plate and is responsible for fielding balls between home and the pitcher's plate. He covers first base and home plate when necessary.

The catcher, Number 2, is responsible for all plays behind home plate and balls hit in the areas within about half the distance to either first or third base. He is responsible for foul flies near home plate.

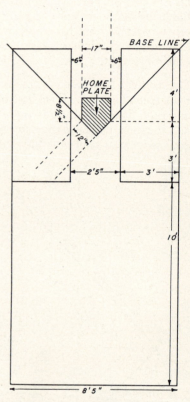

Figure 116.   Home Plate

The infield area is divided almost equally between the four infield players so that it is difficult to hit between them. First baseman, Number 3, plays back of the base line off first base about eight feet toward second base and is responsible for putting runners out on first, and for all balls hit around first base including foul flies. Second baseman, Number 4, and shortstop, Number 6, divide second base equally between them. The second baseman plays back of the base line between second and first about 12 feet from second; while the shortstop plays farther away from second on the third-base side back of the base line. The third baseman, Number 5, plays off third base toward second and is responsible for the area between that covered by the shortstop and the third base line and for foul flies.

There are three players who cover the outfield. The left fielder, Number 7, plays in the outfield about halfway between third and second bases and is always alert to back up either third base or the shortstop. Center fielder, Number 8, has the largest outfield area to cover back of second base, and backs up second base. Right fielder, Number 9, plays closer than any outfielder to cover the area between the first and second baseman in the outfield. He backs up the first baseman on some plays and situations, and the second baseman on others.

The batting order should be arranged so that a couple of average batters are followed by a strong batter. The weaker batters should be placed at the end of the lineup. There is no reason for teams to put the batters up in order of playing position, for this does not give the team its greatest scoring strength and may spoil the game.

PITCHING RULES: (1) The pitcher must, while in his box, stand with both feet on the ground and contacting the pitcher's plate. The ball must be held in front of the body with both hands. (2) The pitcher may take but one step forward while in the act of delivering the ball. This step must be taken simultaneously with the delivery of the ball forward. (3) For legal delivery the ball must be thrown underhand with hand and wrist following through past the line of the body before the ball is released. The hand must be below the hip and the wrist not farther from the side of the body than is the elbow. (4) The pitcher must not hold the ball more than 20 seconds [1] before delivering it to the batter.

Illegally Pitched Balls: If the pitcher breaks one of these pitching rules and delivers an illegal pitch, the batter is entitled to take a base, advancing any players who are on bases; the ball is dead, unless the batter hits the ball into fair territory, whereupon base runners may advance at their own risk.

BATTING: The batter may swing at a pitched ball or let it go by. If he does not swing at it, the umpire must decide whether it was a *ball* or a *strike.* If the batter swings at a ball and misses it, it is called a strike. If the batter hits the ball, it may be a *fair ball* or a *foul ball.* If a pitcher delivers four balls the batter may go to first base. After three strikes the batter is declared out. A foul ball is counted as a strike unless the batter already has two strikes. On a fair ball, the batter runs to first base, and if he gets there safely he becomes a base runner and the next batter is up.

Strikes: Legal strikes include the following: (1) pitched ball delivered over any part of home plate between the knees and shoulders of batter; (2) ball struck at by a batter without the bat's coming in contact with the ball; (3) a foul hit ball, not caught on the fly, if the batsman does not already have two strikes; (4) a pitched ball at which the batter strikes but misses, and which touches the person of the batter; (5) a foul tip caught and held by the catcher.

Balls: A pitched ball which does not pass over any portion of the home plate between the batter's shoulders and knees, or which hits the ground before passing home plate, is a ball.

Foul Balls: A legally batted ball that settles outside the foul lines between home and first base, and home and third base, or that lands in foul territory beyond first or third base, is a foul ball.

Bunted Balls: A ball that is met by the bat while the latter is horizontal to the ground in the two hands of the batter is called a bunted ball.

Foul Tip Ball: A batted ball which goes directly to the catcher is called a foul tip. If caught, a strike is called and the ball is in play as for any strike.

---

[1] A second can be measured by saying in a conversational manner, "one thousand and one."

Fair Balls: Any ball that is legally batted and settles inside the foul lines (between home and first base and home and third base), or that first falls on fair ground on or beyond first or third base, is a fair ball. A batted ball which hits foul and rolls into fair territory between home and first base or home and third base is considered a fair ball, but if this happens beyond first or third base the ball is considered a foul ball.

BASE RUNNING: A batter becomes a base runner after the following plays:
1. Instantly when a pitched ball is hit into fair territory
2. Instantly after three strikes are called, unless the first base is occupied, with less than two players out [1]
3. After four balls have been called
4. If a fairly hit ball strikes the person or clothing of the umpire or a base runner while on fair ground
5. If the catcher interferes with the batter
6. If a pitched ball, not struck at, hits the person of the batter, unless the batter did not try to get out of the way of the ball

A base runner is permitted to advance one base after the following plays:
1. When a batter becomes a base runner after four balls are delivered to him
2. When a pitched ball passes the catcher and touches an object within 25 feet of home plate (all base runners may advance one base)
3. When a pitched ball strikes the person or clothing of an umpire (runner may advance at his own risk)
4. When a ball is overthrown into foul territory (runners are entitled to one base if the ball is blocked, but may run to any number at their own risk if the ball is not blocked)

A base runner shall return to his base without being put out on the following conditions:
1. If the umpire declares a foul ball is not legally caught
2. If the umpire declares a ball illegally batted
3. If the umpire declares a dead ball, unless it is also the fourth ball, in which case the base runner is entitled to go to the next base

Base runners may try to run a base with the possibility of being put out under the following conditions:
1. After a fly ball, fair or foul, or a foul tip has been legally caught
2. After the announcement of ball four for those runners not involved in a forced play
3. When a thrown or pitched ball is not blocked, or within foul territory does not touch an obstruction

---

[1] If a team has no outs or one out, and no runner on first base, the batter must be tagged out or thrown out after the third strike.

OUTS: A batter is out after the following plays:

1. If he fails to bat in turn as his name appears on the order of players, if the error is discovered after the improper batter has completed his turn and before there has been a pitch to another batter. A player is not out for batting out of turn; the one who failed to bat in proper order is the one called "out." All acts performed while the wrong batter was up are nullified, and runners must return to bases occupied when the improper batter stepped up to bat. There is no out if the error is discovered before the improper batter has completed his turn at bat; the player who should have batted takes his turn and takes all strikes and balls called on the improper batter
2. If he fails to take position within one minute after the umpire has called for a batter
3. If he makes a foul hit, other than a foul tip, and the ball is caught by a fielder before it touches the ground
4. If after the second strike he bunts foul
5. After three strikes, if there are no outs or just one out and there is a runner on first base, or runners on first and second, or runners on first, second, and third bases, or first and third bases (batter is out even though the catcher drops the ball)
6. If on the third strike, which is struck at and missed, the ball touches any part of the batter
7. If, before two are out and while first and second, or first, second, and third bases are occupied, a fair fly is hit which the umpire judges will land within or near the base lines. (This is the Infield Fly Rule.)

A base runner is out after the following plays:

1. If a fly ball is caught that has been legally batted by the player while at bat
2. If a fair hit ball is securely held by a fielder while touching first base before the base runner arrives at first base
3. If, before reaching first base or other bases, runner is tagged by a fielder who holds a legally caught ball
4. If after a turn at bat a third strike ball is legally caught by the catcher
5. If after three strikes he is touched by a fielder holding the ball before first base is legally reached
6. If he runs outside the base line in an attempt to avoid being tagged
7. If he is caught off base and is tagged by a fielder
8. If a base runner did not hold his base when a fly ball was caught, and the baseman touches the base with the ball in his possession before the runner returns

TERMINOLOGY: The following terms are used in softball:
Block: Thrown or batted ball touched by a person not in the game. Base

Figure 117. Running to First Base. First Baseman Reaching for Throw

runners may advance one base in addition to the one to which they were going when block occurred

Wild Pitch: A ball legally delivered so high, low, or wide of the plate that the catcher cannot easily handle it

Passed Ball: A legally delivered ball that the catcher should ordinarily handle but that he fails to catch

Force-Out: When a runner is forced to leave a base because the batter becomes a base runner. To put such a player out, the next base must be tagged before the forced-off runner reaches the base, or he may be tagged off base

Scoring: One point is scored each time a runner, before three outs are made and following a fair hit, completes a run around the diamond, touching first, second, and third bases and home plate. The runs need not be continuous. If, after two outs, a run is made from third to home base on or during a play in which the runner is forced out or is put out before reaching first base, the run does not count.

TEACHING SUGGESTIONS [1]

1. Reduce base distances for beginning players. Children of different ages can be in the game at the same time if bases within bases are used.
2. Teach players to watch the ball under all conditions.
3. Point out that players should know which bases are occupied and what their individual responsibilities are under given circumstances.
4. Encourage players to take chances. Teach players to attempt to field all balls that come their way.
5. Teach fielding players to listen for their names as the captain or

---

[1] It is recommended that each school purchase a number of copies of *The Official Softball Guide* and that teachers and pupils study the general rules and consult it when specific questions on rules of play arise. Rules for boys and girls are the same.

catcher calls out which player is to try for a ball, when two players are running to secure it.

6. Create an atmosphere of helpfulness on the part of the pupils when an error is made.

7. Have enough equipment for all players to learn softball skills in a minimum of time. This includes a ball for every two players and a bat for every three players as well as gloves and catcher's equipment. See that catcher wears a mask and body protector.

8. Spend time on perfecting accuracy in throwing. Begin at short range and increase the distances. Remember that a good catch is often useless if it is not followed by a fast, accurate throw.

9. Have players take turns at pitching, catching, and fielding so that all children will have equal opportunity to learn all softball skills.

10. Encourage good players to give verbal approval when less skillful players are successful in an attempted play.

11. Stop the play often during instructional periods and have players analyze why certain plays fail.

12. Assign skillful players to assist in the coaching of less skillful players.

13. Organize pupils into squads to work on weak phases of their own game such as pitching, batting, catching, stopping grounders, controlling bunts, base running, catching fly balls, throwing from base to base and from pitcher to different bases.

14. Have each player run to first base after every hit to fair territory, even though an out seems certain.

15. Teach all children to know the number of each position as well as its name and how to keep score.

16. Provide enough bats for each child to have opportunity to learn correctly how to bat a pitched ball.

17. Watch for the following faults and have players work to correct them:
    a. Use of wrong weight of bat
    b. Incorrect handling of bat
    c. A bat held too tightly. Look for white knuckles.
    d. Movement of bat out of hitting position as the pitch is started
    e. Base runner leaving lane between home and first base. He should run at top speed for a point three or four yards beyond first base.
    f. Too long steps when starting for first base. Short digging steps should be used to start the run.
    g. Use of wrong foot when starting for first base. A right-handed batter should start with his right foot.
    h. Too great body tension. Relaxation and easy, co-ordinated movements should be sought.

i. Crouching, bending forward, or twisting of body while waiting to bat

j. Failure to carry bat parallel to the ground as it is swung

k. Failure to hit ball while it is out in front of the body

l. Failure to use arms and wrists successfully when batting

m. Dropping of rear shoulder or turning entire body toward pitcher while waiting for the pitch

n. Hitting while body weight is off balance

o. Lunging at the ball instead of waiting for it to travel to the proper position for contact

p. Throwing the bat

q. Taking too long a step when swinging at the ball

r. Failure to keep eyes on ball throughout its flight from pitcher's hand

s. Backing up to catch a ground ball

t. Basemen standing on base while waiting for the pitch so that the area out from the base is not protected from a batted ball

u. Basemen touching base with both feet while waiting for a throw, instead of having one foot on the base and the other a step in the direction of the thrower with the arms and body reaching as far out as possible toward the thrower to catch the ball (Figure 117).

SOFTBALL TECHNIQUES

The game of softball has a wide appeal to a large majority of the boys and girls in the public schools; however, during the school year

Figure 118.   Overhand Throw. Left: Ready for the throw. Right: Follow-through.

not more than a month or six weeks at the most should be spent on perfecting skill in softball. If softball skills have been acquired in lead-up games, most of the boys and girls will be ready to play softball with a minimum of instruction.

The material that follows is offered as a guide to teaching the skills that need to be included in softball instruction. It is important to include a warm-up period before a new activity is started. General body exercises or running will prepare the body for learning new skills. The players should begin actual play by throwing a softball slowly for short distances. In this way muscles will not be strained by overwork or sudden pull, and the fear of a hard thrown ball will be eliminated.

OVERHAND THROW: The overhand throw (Figure 118) should be reviewed to see that each boy and girl knows how to grip the ball, to use the entire arm, shoulder girdle, and back muscles in throwing, and to follow through with proper weight transfer. The overhand throw can be mastered by all boys and girls with both instruction and practice. This throw is used in every play in softball and baseball with the exception of the underhand pitch in softball.

UNDERHAND THROW: The underhand throw is used for pitching the ball (Figure 119). The pitcher must stand with both feet on the pitcher's plate as he holds the ball in front of him. In right-handed pitching the right arm swings downward and backward for the wind-up and as the right hand brings the ball forward, the weight of the body is carried forward and the left foot steps forward as the ball is released. The right foot must remain on the pitcher's plate until the ball has left his hand. In following through, the hand points toward the spot to which the ball is thrown.

CATCHING: The techniques of catching should be reviewed. Children should be instructed to relax their fingers and to give with the ball by bringing it toward the body to avoid hitting fingers. To catch a ball above the waist, the fingers of both relaxed hands are pointed upwards with the thumbs together. In catching a ball below the waist, the relaxed fingers are pointed downwards with the little fingers together. The ability to catch the ball is necessary for good fielding, base playing, and catching behind the batter. The catcher should help the pitcher by making a target with his hands. A glove assists greatly in catching behind the batter, and is an essential in a game. A mask and chest protector should also be a part of the catcher's equipment even in beginning games.

BATTING (RIGHT HANDED): The bat should be held with the left hand near the end of the handle and with the right hand just above the left (Figure 120). If the bat is too heavy the hands may be moved up the handle four to eight inches, which is called choking the bat. Each classroom should have bats of appropriate weights so that it is not necessary for the pupils to choke the bats. The trade-mark on the bat should always

Figure 119. Underhand Pitching. With two feet on the pitcher's plate, player begins to swing forward; carries ball forward and steps forward; follows through.

Figure 120. Batting. Good Position at Bat Waiting for the Pitch

be kept upwards so that the hitting surface is across the grain in the wood. When a batter is ready to bat, he should stand on the batter's plate in a comfortable stance with his feet slightly apart and with his left shoulder toward the pitcher. He should stand close enough to the home plate to allow the hitting part of the bat to swing completely over the plate. The bat should be held out from the right shoulder in a position of readiness to meet the pitched ball. The bat is swung in a horizontal plane, so that the ball will be met squarely. It is important that the batter keep his eyes on the ball from the time it leaves the pitcher's hand until it is hit or passes the batter. If children are instructed to keep hands and arms away from body and to swing with a full arm swing straight around, there will be no chopping motions. Left-handed batters use the same technique, with left and right reversed in the directions above. See pages 573-74, for common faults in batting.

Base Running: Children should be instructed to run the instant the ball is hit. The bat should be dropped immediately at the home plate as the runner starts for first base. If instructions are given about the importance of dropping the bat, the habit of throwing the bat will not be developed.

Figure 121. Fielder Waiting for the Ball

If a player has the habit of throwing his bat, insist that he carry it to first base until he can break the habit.

The children should learn to watch the base toward which they are running and at the same time to be aware of the whereabouts of the ball. One foot must be on the base when the pitcher is on the pitcher's plate, but the runner should start toward the next base with the pitch even if it is only to worry the pitcher and catcher, and even though he has to return to his base to avoid being put out.

FIELDING: Fielding the ball is the skill that makes the difference between a really interesting game of softball and a game which loses interest because no one is able to put the batter out when the ball is hit. A fielder should play as if he expected every batted ball to come to him, and he should know where he is going to throw the ball in case he fields it.

Fielders should be taught to watch the stance of batters so that they can judge the direction the ball is to be hit. In this way a fielder can, by anticipating the direction of the hit, get himself in position for a line drive, a long fly, or a well placed hit between his and another fielder's territory (Figure 121).

Figure 122. Fielding a Grounder

Fielding Ground Balls: When fielding a ground ball, a player should get directly in line with the ball with both feet fairly close together, knees bent, the body low and bent forward at the hips, fingers extended down with little fingers together and with eyes on the ball. A player should move forward to meet a ground ball, and be ready to throw the instant it is fielded (Figure 122).

Fielding Slow Hit Ball: A fielder should advance toward a slow-moving grounder but to receive it he should stop, catch the ball, and step in the direction of the throw. There is an exception. If the ball is coming extremely slowly he should run forward and, while running, scoop up the ball with his bare hand and make a throw.

Fielding Fly Balls: An outfielder should be taught to know about how far a ball is going to be hit by the way it is hit. He should get into position the instant the ball is hit. If, however, he misjudges and the ball is hit over his head, he should turn and run as fast as he can to get in position to catch the ball. The fielder should catch the ball, if possible, in such a position that it may be returned to the infield immediately. When returning the ball to home plate from the deep outfield, it should be thrown so that it will be received there following a first bounce. In most cases, however, if the fielder is in the distant outfield the ball should be relayed to home plate.

Figure 123.   Safety in Softball. Those waiting to bat sit at a safe distance from batter.

The palms should be upwards, with fingers relaxed but cupped and with thumbs together, when fly balls are caught above the waist. The hands should be relaxed and should give a little toward the body with the impact of the ball against the palms, or against the gloved hand.

SOFTBALL SKILLS PRACTICE [1]

THROWING AND CATCHING

1. Practice throwing (a) underhand, (b) overarm, (c) sidearm; and pitching underhand.
2. Practice catching (a) slow balls, (b) fast balls, (c) grounders, (d) high fly balls, (e) pitched balls.
3. Practice throwing to base (a) from base to base, (b) to outfield and back to infield, (c) from all points to home plate, (d) from grounder to nearest base, (e) from grounder to first base.
4. Practice pitching (a) with pitchers and catchers working together, (b) emphasizing legal delivery from a pitcher's plate.

BATTING

1. Work for correct batting position.
2. Rotate members of squads so that every player has an opportunity to hit five balls.
3. Learn to judge whether pitched balls are good or bad.
4. Practice timing and placement of balls in relation to position of fielders and base runners.

---

[1] Briefed from article by Dorothy Allen, "Coaching Hints for Softball," *Service Bulletin*, IV (February, 1940), 5, 6, 57. Used by permission of the author.

BASE RUNNING

1. Practice for a quick getaway after hitting ball. Know where ball has gone and to what point it is being returned. A ball returned behind a runner often permits the taking of an additional base.
2. Learn when to stick to a base, when to steal, when to run, when to take advantage of basemen's errors.
3. Practice touching all bases when making home runs.

FIELDING

1. Practice fielding all bases in fielder's own territory.
2. Practice throw-ins from fielding positions; there should be quick and accurate relaying of the ball in relation to positions of base runners, number of outs, and teammates' positions.
3. Practice getting into position on a long, hard, fly ball. The fielder should run toward the spot where the ball is going, and toward end of the run turn his head to look for and keep his eyes on the ball.

PLAYING POSITIONS

1. Know area to be covered by each player.
2. Learn to back up other players. Cover teammates' positions if they are pulled away from their own positions.
3. Never leave a base uncovered. Gain skill in throwing ball so that the catching of the ball and the tagging of the runner will be made easy.
4. Know where to throw ball when bases are full and there are one or two outs.

SPELLING BEE GAME

NUMBER OF PLAYERS: 2-40

SPACE: Playground (lawn), classroom, auditorium

PLAYING AREA: Open area with a restraining line some 20 feet from the packages of alphabet cards

EQUIPMENT: Two or more packages of alphabet cards. To make an alphabet set cut 31 squares, 4 by 4 inches, from sturdy cardboard. Stencil, draw, or paste large letters of the alphabet on 26 squares, and on the remaining five squares make duplicates for the letters a, e, i, o, u. Use a different colored cardboard for each set. Alphabet packages, letters mixed, are dropped on the floor some eight feet apart and in a line across the room.

FORMATION: Players are divided into as many teams as there are alphabet sets. Team members stand in file formation behind the restraining line. Three judges are appointed.

PROCEDURE: The leader announces the number of letters in a word; for example, "My word has five letters." Starting with the first player, each team counts off five players who will be the first to play. The leader then announces the word; for example, "My word is—horse." Immediately the five players in each team dash forward and each hunts for a letter that occurs in the word horse.

As soon as each player secures a letter the team members form a line, side by side, holding up their letters so that the judges may see them. The letters of the word must go from right to left, so that the rest of the players and the judges see them in proper order. Judges decide which team earns first place and then cards are returned to the alphabet sets and players retire to the end of their lines. Leader chooses another word and play continues, the next players in each line counting off.

SCORING: The first team to have the word correctly spelled and arranged wins a point. In case of a tie the teams concerned each win 1 point. At the end of the playing period the team with the most points wins.

TEACHING SUGGESTIONS

1. Have cards turned face up, but otherwise do not have them arranged for ease in discovering the desired letters.
2. Choose words that do not duplicate any letter (except the vowels), since there is only one of each letter in a set. For example, the word *proper* would require two r's and two p's.

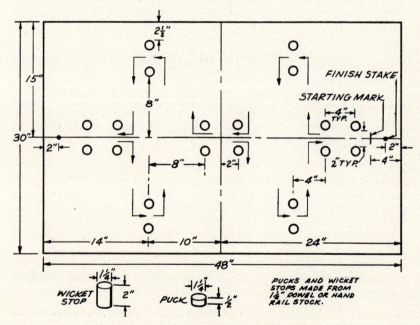

Figure 124.   Table Croquet Layout

TABLE CROQUET [1]

NUMBER OF PLAYERS: 2-4

SPACE: Playground, classroom

EQUIPMENT: (1) Table croquet board, 30 by 48 inches, constructed and marked as in Figure 124; [2] (2) 4 cues made of ⅜ inch doweling, 3 feet long; (3) 4 numbered disks of 1¼ inch doweling, ½ inch high

Procedure

The rules are the same as for garden croquet. The order of play is decided by lot. The first player places his disk on the start line and attempts to shoot it with the end of his cue through the first two wickets. If successful, he takes two more shots. If he goes through one wicket, he has one shot to get through wicket two. Play continues until he fails to go through a wicket. His disk remains at the spot where it came to rest. Other players follow in sequence. For the order of wickets see directional arrows in Figures 124 and 125.

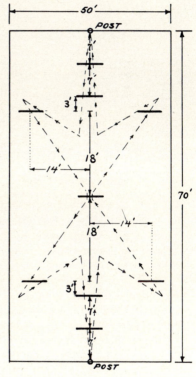

Figure 125. Official Croquet Court

RULES OF PLAY

1. If a player hits an opponent's disk, he is entitled to one additional shot. After hitting a disk the player is "dead" on that disk. That is, he cannot hit it again until he has passed through a wicket. He can, however, either (1) take the extra shot to get his own disk through a wicket or (2) place his disk in contact with his opponent's disk and, while shooting his own through a wicket, try to send the opponent's disk so that, after passing through the wicket, he will again be in position to hit the opponent's disk. Only one such shot is permissible.

---

[1] Through courtesy of Frank L. Thomas and H. Loren Mitchell, formerly Supervisors of Physical Education, Los Angeles Public Schools.

[2] Side walls are ⅞ by 1½ inches. Wooden wickets are made of two pieces of 1¼ inch doweling, 2 inches high, placed 2 inches apart. Two coats of shellac and a coat of wax should be given the board after it has been built.

Figure 126.   Outdoor Croquet Game

2. A disk shot off the board is replaced at the point where it went out of bounds. Player forfeits any further shot he may have earned.

3. A disk which comes to rest less than two inches from the edge of the wall may be moved out two inches from the wall when it is the player's turn.

4. If a disk goes through a wicket and hits an opponent's disk, two subsequent shots are allowed.

5. If a disk is moved by a cue a distance equal to double its diameter, it is counted as a turn. Otherwise player moves the disk back to its previous position and shoots again.

6. Double shots may occur only if a disk goes through the two end wickets simultaneously and through the center two wickets in like manner, except as in Rule 4.

7. The halfway mark must be contacted by a disk before return trip can be undertaken.

8. The player who first reaches the finish spot after completing the round of wickets wins the game.

TEACHING SUGGESTIONS

1. Make the construction of the game board, cues, and disks a project for members of a woodworking class or for some pupil interested in the use of tools.

2. Use for pupils temporarily incapacitated for vigorous play.
3. If game is not thoroughly understood, secure official croquet rules for reference.[1]
4. By teaching table croquet, interest pupils in playing the outdoor game of croquet both at school and at home (Figure 126). The marking and dimensions of the court can be explained at school (Figure 125).

THREE-SECTION SOCCER [2]

NUMBER OF PLAYERS: 22

SPACE: Playground, gymnasium

PLAYING AREA: Court 90 by 150 feet, marked as in Figure 127

EQUIPMENT: Soccer ball, speed ball, or ball of rubber that may be kicked

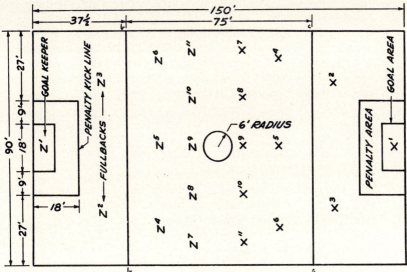

Figure 127.   Court and Position of Players in Three-Section Soccer

FORMATION: Players are divided into two teams with positions as for soccer (see Figure 127). Only the forwards may enter the end zone of the opponents. Halfbacks remain in the center area and feed the ball to the forwards if it becomes necessary. The fullbacks assist the goalkeeper in

---

[1] These may be found in *The Official Recreational Games.* Washington: National Section on Women's Athletics, American Association for Health, Physical Education and Recreation (1201 Sixteenth Street, N.W., Washington 6, D. C.), issues for 1946-48 and after 1951. Refer also to Croquet Association, Decatur, Illinois.

[2] Suggestions for this game were found in the *Service Bulletin,* IV (November, 1939), 17. By permission of the National Section on Women's Athletics, American Association for Health, Physical Education and Recreation.

defending the goal, prevent scoring, and pass the ball to one of their own halfbacks. For example,

Team X forwards should not drop back behind the middle of the field and never beyond line cc.

Team X halfbacks should not go beyond line bb.

Team X fullbacks should not go beyond line cc.

Team X goalkeeper should remain in the goal area itself.

The same arrangement holds true for Team Z.

PROCEDURE: Rules are the same as for soccer except for the restriction of the playing area.[1] Players may not touch the ball with their hands.

PENALTIES FOR FOULS:

1. For fouls committed by defenders within the goal area, a free kick for the team fouled against, all players other than the goalkeeper and kicker being outside the penalty area
2. For personal fouls committed anywhere, two free kicks without goal guard interference
3. For all other fouls, including being in the wrong areas, a free kick at the place within the goal area where the foul occurred. Opponents must be 15 feet distant. A goal may not be attempted.
4. For a foul committed by attackers, a free unguarded kick by goalkeeper or by an opponent in the area

SCORING: A field goal scores 2 points; a goal made from a penalty kick scores 1 point.

TEACHING SUGGESTIONS

1. If played indoors, use a partly deflated ball.
2. Distinguish positions by having fullbacks and goalkeepers wear red scarves, pinnies, or shirts; halfbacks, blue; forwards, white.
3. Teach passing, stopping, and dribbling ball with feet before game is played.
4. Keep rules as simple as possible.

TREASURE SMUGGLING

NUMBER OF PLAYERS: 4-20

SPACE: Playground

PLAYING AREA: A den or base in a central location. Outside boundaries are selected beyond which no players may go.

EQUIPMENT: Treasure in the form of a small ball, blackboard eraser, or block of wood

---

[1] See Boys' and Girls' Soccer Rules, pages 775-88.

FORMATION: Players are divided into two groups, the smugglers and the cops. The treasure is given to a member of the smugglers' group. His identity should not be known to the cops.

PROCEDURE: The smugglers are given an opportunity to hide. When ready, a signal is given to the cops, who thereupon go forth to find the smugglers. The smugglers try to reach the den without being tagged.

The cops, as they capture a smuggler, challenge him by "crowning" him, that is, the cop places his hand on the tagged person's head and says, "Pony-up the swag!" If the captured smuggler does not have the treasure, he goes free and the hunt continues. If the hunt continues too long without smugglers returning to the den, the leader (teacher or selected player) may sing out loudly, "Ship Ahoy!" whereupon all smugglers must race for the den. If, when challenged, the smuggler has the treasure, he must deliver it to the cop, whereupon all remaining smugglers return immediately to the den. The cops win the game and become the smugglers for the new game. If the holder of the treasure can return to the den without being caught, his side wins and he and his team go out again as the smugglers.

VIS-A-VIS

NUMBER OF PLAYERS: 7-40

SPACE: Playground, playroom, gymnasium

PLAYING AREA: Area should be no larger than a basketball court.

FORMATION: Half the players are numbered 1's; the other half 2's. An additional player is given Number 1 as his number and is the first leader. Number 1's choose partners from the Number 2's. Couples scatter over the playground within hearing of the leader's voice.

PROCEDURE: The leader stands in the center of the playing area and gives directions which the other players must follow. For example, he may say, "Face to face," "Back to back," "Kneel on knee," "Stand up," "Hands on hips." When the leader calls "Vis-à-vis" all the Number 1 players run to secure a new Number 2 partner, the Number 2 players standing still. The leader tries to secure a partner. The player who fails to get a partner becomes the leader.

TEACHING SUGGESTIONS

1. After playing for a time, have the Number 1 players stand still. Change the leader's number to Number 2.
2. Do not permit too much bunching. There should be a run in order to secure a new partner.

VOLLEY TETHER BALL [1]

NUMBER OF PLAYERS: 2

SPACE: Playground

PLAYING AREA: A tether ball pole, with surrounding area (see p. 917).

EQUIPMENT: For each pole one official volley tether ball.[2] Ordinary volleyballs may be used.

FORMATION: The shorter player has choice of courts.

PROCEDURE: The ball is always started from the south court. Players alternate in the use of the courts following the completion of each game. The object is to hit the ball with either hand in such a manner as to wind the cord attached to the ball around the pipe above the stripe which is six feet above the ground.

FOULS: The following offenses are penalized by loss of one game.

1. Hitting the ball with any part of the body other than the hands
2. Use of two hands together, open or closed, as used in volleyball
3. Use of a "set up," that is, stopping the ball to get an easy shot rather than hitting it on the fly
4. Stepping over the division line into opponent's court
5. Using pipe upright to aid in jumping for the ball
6. Catching rope and throwing rope and ball

SCORING: The player who first winds the ball into position above the scoring mark wins the game. Two out of three games make a series. Upon finishing a series the loser drops out and a new challenger from the waiting line comes into the game. When a player defeats three opponents, he automatically drops out of the game at the conclusion of the third series. In such a situation two new players take the court.

TEACHING SUGGESTIONS

1. Vary rope lengths on different poles for players of various heights.
2. Provide several poles and balls. The game is moderate in cost, the complete equipment of pole and ball approximating sixteen dollars.
3. If cement base area is provided, use game when grounds are muddy.
4. Use the official rules of tether ball (see p. 917).

---

[1] Sometimes called pol-o-ball. Directions supplied by Richard J. Cox, Willow Glen School, San Jose, California.

[2] Official balls may be purchased from sporting goods stores. If an ordinary volleyball is used, a strong leather loop should be attached to the ball by a shoemaker. The loop leather should be made of very strong soft leather, hand sewn, and backed with a leather facing inside the leather casing of the ball.

WALLOPING THE STATES

NUMBER OF PLAYERS: 10-40

SPACE: Playground, gymnasium, playroom

PLAYING AREA: A small circle in the middle of the playing area; around this circle, additional circles to hold the different groups of players

EQUIPMENT: Volleyball, softball, or beanbag

FORMATION: Players are divided into small groups of not more than three players to a group. Each group occupies a circle. One player, holding the ball, occupies the center circle. Each group is given the name of a state.

PROCEDURE: The center man calls the name of one of the states known to be present and at the same time throws the ball at the group. If the ball is caught, the one catching it calls loudly, "Ready to go. 1, 2, 3, 4, 5." All players leave their circles, dodging about because the ball holder, before calling 5, must throw the ball and try to hit someone. If the throw is successful, the person hit secures the ball, repeats the call, and tries to hit another player. Play continues as long as throws are successful.

If the ball catcher's throw is a failure, he must secure the ball and then shout loudly, "A, b, c, d, e." Before "e" is shouted all movement by other players must cease. The player holding the ball then calls loudly, "Back to your bases, 1, 2, 3, 4, 5," and again attempts to hit some one outside a circle. If the throw is successful, the person hit becomes the tagger and the game continues. If the throw is unsuccessful, the one who threw the ball remains the thrower, all enter their bases and begin again.

TEACHING SUGGESTIONS

1. Do not let the players scatter too far; it spoils the game.
2. Instead of state names, use the names of countries, animals, insects, trees, flowers, or other objects.

WORK-UP [1]

NUMBER OF PLAYERS: 6-14

SPACE: Playground, gymnasium

PLAYING AREA: Softball diamond with bases 35 feet apart; pitcher's plate 35 feet from home plate

EQUIPMENT: (1) 12-inch softball; (2) softball bats of different weights; (3) four softball bases made of boards, filled sacks, or pieces of linoleum; (4) pitcher's plate made of a strip of wood 1 by 6 inches by 3 feet placed across the diamond and flush with the ground, facing the home plate

---

[1] Rules for the game supplied by George E. Lunt, formerly Supervisor of Physical Education, Riverside County.

Procedure

Work-up is an activity which gives every player an opportunity to bat, since positions rotate each time the batter is out. There is no team score, each player keeping score for himself. Each batter tries to stay at bat for three successive runs, while those in the field try to put the runners out.

FORMATION: Official softball fielding positions are played. The umpire is included among these playing positions. The number in the batting group is determined by the number of pupils playing.

Batters: If there is only one batter, he runs between home and first base, and continues as batter until he is put out. If there are two batters, they run from home to first, to third, and home again. If there are three or more batters, all bases are used.

Batters follow each other in succession until they are put out. After a batter has made three runs in sequence he is automatically put out and goes to the right field position.

Runners: Runners are put out at bases according to official softball rules. A forced play occurs when the last batter becomes a runner and the base runner nearest home must try to reach home plate before the ball is held at home plate by the catcher. If the catcher arrives at home plate with the ball before the runner, the runner is out.

Fielders: Fielders become batters only by rotation. A caught fly *does not* entitle a fielder to become a batter. All players are fielders with special areas to cover except those who are batters and base runners. The umpire must see that all players are in position before the game begins again after rotation.

OUTS: A batter is out when a fly ball is caught, or when three strikes are called on him. A base runner is out (1) if, when off base, he is tagged by a fielder who is holding the ball; (2) if a fielder catches the ball while touching a base before the runner who is forced to run arrives at the base.

ROTATION OF PLAYERS: As a person is put out at bat or in running, he goes to right field position. The other players advance from position to position in the following order: from right field to center field; from center field to left field; from left field to shortstop; from shortstop to third base; then to second base; to first base; to umpire; to pitcher; to catcher and to a batting position. While umpiring, the player stands behind the pitcher.

SCORING: Each run scores 1 point. The player wins who has the highest number of runs at the conclusion of the playing period.

TEACHING SUGGESTIONS

1. If poor pitching spoils the game, substitute overhand throwing or a

tossed pitch for the official underhand pitching in order to provide a good hitting game.
2. Point out that this game gives players experience in every aspect of the softball game.
3. Teach batters to hold the bat so that the trademark will be on top. This helps to prevent broken and cracked bats.
4. Introduce umpiring as a regular position to aid players in mastering the rules, in making decisions, and in respecting the decisions.

Relays

ARCH GOAL BALL RELAY

NUMBER OF PLAYERS: 4-40

SPACE: Playground, playroom, classroom, gymnasium

PLAYING AREA: A basketball goal for each team. Restraining lines not less than 15 feet from each goal.

EQUIPMENT: For each team (1) an official basketball goal, peach basket nailed against wall, barrel hoop nailed to wall or tree, waste-paper basket placed on floor or hung on the wall, or bicycle tires suspended from some object; (2) volleyball, basketball, soccer ball, softball, utility ball, bean-bag, or stuffed leather ball casing

FORMATION: Any number of teams line up in file formation behind their restraining line and facing their goal. The rear players hold the balls.

PROCEDURE: At a signal the rear players, using both hands, start the balls forward by passing them over the head of the player in front of them. Those players do likewise, using both hands. When front players receive the ball they stand and throw for the goal, without stepping over the restraining line. Whether players make or miss the goal, they secure the ball, return to the rear of the file and start the ball forward, remaining at the rear. This procedure continues until all have thrown.

SCORING: Each successful throw for goal scores 1 point. The team wins which has the highest number of goal points after all have thrown.

TEACHING SUGGESTIONS

1. If played indoors with seated players, have all the players move forward one seat between the time the front players throw and secure their balls. The throwers go to the rear, *sit down*, and then start their ball forward.
2. If played in a classroom, place the baskets so that they are opposite the aisles of the room.

BULLFROG RELAY

NUMBER OF PLAYERS: 4-40

SPACE: Playground, playroom, gymnasium, auditorium

PLAYING AREA: A starting line and several designated stations equally distant from the starting line. Children, chairs, or bases may indicate the stations.

FORMATION: Teams are lined up in file formation behind the starting line.

PROCEDURE: At a signal, front players, with hands on hips and in deep knee bend position, jump forward around their given stations, then arise and run back, tagging off the waiting runners. The game continues until all the players in one team have run. The first team to finish wins.

TEACHING SUGGESTIONS

1. Do not permit waiting player to cross the starting line until tagged by the runner.
2. When players finish their runs have them go to the end of their file.
3. Have pupils warm up first with quick, easy knee bending.

KANGAROO RELAY

NUMBER OF PLAYERS: 4-40

SPACE: Playground, playroom, gymnasium, auditorium, hallway

PLAYING AREA: Two parallel restraining lines 20 feet long drawn 20 feet apart

EQUIPMENT: For each team, volleyball, basketball, soccer ball, large block of wood, large beanbag, stuffed leather ball casing, or knotted towel

FORMATION: Teams are lined up in file formation behind one line. Each leader holds a ball.

PROCEDURE: At a signal, the leaders place the balls between their knees and race forward. The hands may not be used to hold the balls in position. If the balls fall from position they must be picked up, returned to the approximate point where they fell, and replaced between the knees. After crossing the farther line with both feet, the leaders, taking the balls in their hands, race back to the starting line. They hand the balls to the waiting players, who must have both feet behind the restraining line. The leaders retire to the rear of their files. The game continues until all players in one team have run, and that team wins.

TEACHING SUGGESTIONS

1. Do not permit waiting runner to step on or over the starting line until ball is secured.
2. As skill is gained, permit returning runners to throw the ball to their teammates.

OVER-AND-UNDER RELAY

NUMBER OF PLAYERS: 6-40

SPACE: Playground, playroom, gymnasium

PLAYING AREA: A base line 30 feet long

EQUIPMENT: For each team, a volleyball, basketball, soccer ball, large utility ball, softball, large beanbag, or knotted towel

FORMATION: Captains stand on the base line and each holds a ball. Team members line up behind their captains in file formation.

PROCEDURE: At a signal, each captain passes the ball *over* his head to the player behind him. The second player passes the ball *under* or between his feet to the next player; the third player passes the ball over his head, and so on, the ball going down the line over the head of a player and between the feet of the next player. When the ball reaches the end, the last player runs with it to the front, stands on the line, and starts the ball backward *over* his head. Game continues until the captain of one team returns to his original position, and that team wins.

TEACHING SUGGESTIONS

1. Insist that the front players must be standing on the base line before they start to pass the ball backward.
2. If ball is dropped have it secured by the one who dropped it, the player returning to his position in the file. He must then pass the ball backward over his head, while facing forward, or between his feet, depending on which his position calls for. He may not hand the ball to the player behind him.

PASS AND SQUAT RELAY

NUMBER OF PLAYERS: 6-40

SPACE: Playground, playroom, classroom, gymnasium

PLAYING AREA: Two parallel lines 15 feet apart

EQUIPMENT: For each team, a ball, beanbag, knotted towel, or stuffed leather ball casing

FORMATION: Teams stand in file formation behind one of the lines. The captains, each holding a ball, stand beyond the other line, facing their teams.

PROCEDURE: At a signal, each captain throws his ball to the first player in his file. This player catches it and throws it back to his captain, immediately thereafter assuming a squatting position. This continues until all have caught the ball and passed it back to the captain, who squats after receiving the ball from the last player. The team wins whose captain first assumes squatting position after all have played.

TEACHING SUGGESTIONS

1. Have any player dropping the ball recover it and return to his position before throwing the ball.
2. If played in a classroom, have each player sit in his seat immediately following his throw.

RESCUE RELAY

NUMBER OF PLAYERS: 4-40

SPACE: Playground, playroom, gymnasium, auditorium

PLAYING AREA: Two parallel lines 20 feet apart

FORMATION: Each team stands in file formation behind one of the lines, its captain standing beyond the second line and facing his team.

PROCEDURE: At a signal, each captain runs forward, grasps the hand of the first player of his team, and then both run back to the captain's original position. The captain remains there. The player he brought over returns and brings back the second player. Play continues until all have crossed over and a new line is formed in front of the captain. The team wins which first succeeds in getting all its players across the second line.

TEACHING SUGGESTIONS

1. Insist that those to be rescued must have both feet behind their restraining line until rescuer's hand touches them.
2. Insist that the captains and others following take their runners across the second line before releasing them for the return trip.

RUN, TOSS, CATCH RELAY

NUMBER OF PLAYERS: 4-40

SPACE: Playground, gymnasium

PLAYING AREA: A net, rope, or wire stretched between two posts with the top edge 8 feet above the ground; base line marked 30 feet from, and paralleling, the net

EQUIPMENT: For each team, a volleyball, basketball, soccer ball, utility ball, softball, beanbag, knotted towel, or stuffed leather ball casing

FORMATION: Teams are lined up in file formation behind the base line and facing the net. Each captain holds a ball.

PROCEDURE: At a signal, each captain runs forward, throws the ball over the net, catches it, and runs back, *handing* the ball to the second player, who must be standing with both feet behind the base line. The second player does likewise. If a player misses his *own* throw he must secure the ball himself and continue throwing it over the net until he catches the ball. Play continues until all have played. The first team to finish wins.

TEACHING SUGGESTIONS

1. Do not permit players to be assisted in the control of the ball when receiving it or when chasing the ball because of failure to catch it.
2. Erect a temporary net by having two players hold bamboo sticks in the air with a string attached.

SHUTTLE RELAY

NUMBER OF PLAYERS: 8-40

SPACE: Playground, playroom, gymnasium

PLAYING AREA: Two parallel restraining lines, 40 feet apart

FORMATION: Members of each team are numbered and then are divided into two groups. The even numbered players in each team stand behind one line and the odd numbered players behind the second line, facing the first group. The players stand one behind the other in file formation. The Number 1 players are the captains for the teams.

PROCEDURE: At a signal, the captains run forward and tag Number 2 players as they pass them. They then go to the rear of the file. Number 2 players race across and tag Number 3 players, going thereafter to the rear of the file. Play continues until all of one team have run and exchanged positions, and that team wins.

TEACHING SUGGESTIONS

1. Have the runners carry a flag, handkerchief, beanbag, or other object to be handed to the next runner.
2. Do not have more than eight runners to a team.
3. Have waiting players keep both feet behind their restraining line until tagged.

STRIDE BALL RELAY

NUMBER OF PLAYERS: 8-40

SPACE: Playground, playroom, gymnasium

PLAYING AREA: A base line, its length depending on the number of teams playing

EQUIPMENT: For each team, a ball, beanbag, or Indian club

FORMATION: Teams stand in file formation with feet apart; the first players (the captains) stand on the base line. In front of each captain a ball is placed. •

PROCEDURE: At a signal, each captain rolls his ball between his own feet and as far as he can down the aisle made by the legs and feet of his teammates. Players may assist the ball. When the ball reaches the last player he grabs it and runs forward, *faces forward*, and, with both feet on the base line, sends the ball backward between his feet. Play continues until all in one team have run, and that team wins.

TEACHING SUGGESTIONS

1. Point out that it detracts from the game to have legs spread too far apart.
2. Insist that each runner go forward and stand on the base line before sending the ball backward between his feet.
3. Do not permit runners to face their teammates when sending the ball between the legs of the other players.
4. When there are but a few players, establish two restraining lines and have the first and last players of each team stand on these lines while the ball is being played.
5. If a player permits the ball to leave the file, have him secure it, return to his position in the file, and then, facing forward, send the ball between his legs toward the rear.

STAND 'EM UP RELAY

NUMBER OF PLAYERS: 6-40

SPACE: Playground, playroom, gymnasium, hallway, auditorium, classroom

PLAYING AREA: For each team, two adjacent circles, each not more than 12 inches in diameter, drawn on the floor or ground, and not more than 20 feet from both circles a restraining line

EQUIPMENT: For each team, three Indian clubs, sticks of wood 3 by 3 by 10 inches, beanbags, or corncobs placed in one of each team's two circles

FORMATION: Players are divided into two teams of not more than six members. They line up in file formation behind the restraining line and facing their circles.

PROCEDURE: At a signal, the captain (the last player of each team) runs up the right side of his file and with one hand changes the three Indian clubs into the empty circle. His other hand must be held behind his back. He then runs down the right side to the rear of his team and tags off the last player. He then returns to the front of his file. The second player runs forward, on the right side, and changes the Indian clubs back to the original circle. If a club falls down or if a beanbag touches a line it must be replaced before the player may return to his file. Game continues until one team finishes, and that team wins.

TEACHING SUGGESTIONS

1. If a team is short a player, have a member run twice for the team.
2. When played in a classroom, have the circles placed in front of the aisles to be used and not far from the front wall of the room.
3. If played in a classroom, have the runners go up the right side of the row of desks and back on the same side. Seated players move back one desk as the runners are working with the Indian clubs.
4. When played in a classroom, insist that all feet be kept out of the aisles.
5. If beanbags or corncobs are used, do not allow any portion of them to touch any portion of the circumference of the circles.
6. When Indian clubs are used for relays, cut them off at the thickest portion of the club, and they will stand up better.

Rhythmical Activities

THE ACE OF DIAMONDS [1]

Methodist Record No. 102
Scandinavian Album S2
Victor Record No. 20989

FORMATION: Double circle, boys on the inside. Partners face each other, hands on hips. Boy has back to center, girl faces center.

DESCRIPTION

PART I

Partners clap hands, hook elbows, and swing around and back as follows.

---

[1] From C. Ward Crampton, *The Folk Dance Book*. New York: A. S. Barnes & Co., 1909. By permission.

The Ace of Diamonds

Measure 1. They clap their own hands briskly ("one, and"); hook right elbows ("Two, and").

Measure 2. With three little running steps, they swing around to the left ("one, and, two"); free elbows ("and").

Measures 3-4. They repeat Measures 1-2, hooking left elbows and swinging around to the right.

Measures 5-8. They repeat Measures 1-4.

PART II

With arms folded and held high, partners dance with four step hops toward the center, the boy moving backward and the girl forward. With four hopping steps, they dance back to place, girl moving backward, boy forward, thus:

Measure 9. Both leaning head and shoulders sharply to the right, step with the right foot ("one, and"), hop on the right foot ("two, and").

Measure 10. They repeat, stepping with the left foot and leaning to the left.

Measures 11-12. They repeat Measures 9-10.

Measures 13-16. They repeat Measures 9-12, moving outward.

PART III

Partners face in the same direction, left sides to the center; they join inside hands at shoulder height and polka around the circle. Polka step, three short running steps and a hop ("run, run, run, hop") to each measure.

Measure 17. Each turns slightly toward partner, swinging arms well back, takes a short step forward with the outer foot ("one"), a short step forward with the inner foot ("and"), a short step forward with the outer foot ("two"), and a hop on the outer foot ("and").

Measure 18. Each turns slightly away from partner and swings the arms well forward. The step is similar to that for Measure 17, but beginning with the inside foot.

Measures 19-24. The polka is continued.

Dance is repeated from the beginning.

CIRCLE SCHOTTISCHE
(Progressive)

Standard Record No. 5013, "Balen I Karlstad"
Folkcraft Record No. F1035A, "Oklahoma Mixer (Rustic Schottische)"

FORMATION: Single circle, boys and girls alternating, boy to the left of his partner, hands joined.

DESCRIPTION

Measures 1-4. All take one schottische step to the right, one schottische step to the left, and four step hops.[1]

Measures 5-8. All repeat Measures 1-4.

Measures 9-12. Partners face each other and, each starting with right foot, take three steps, right, left, right, and clap hands (one measure). As skill is acquired, partners may turn on this step, girls moving toward the center of the circle and boys away from the center. Three steps left,

---

[1] For the schottische step, see p. 209.

right, left, back to partner (one measure). Partners hook right elbows and take four step hops around each other (two measures).

Measures 13-16. The last four measures are repeated, except that on the second measure the boy moves counterclockwise and the girl clockwise, using three steps, left, right, left, to meet a new partner. Each takes four step hops with the new partner, right elbows hooked.

The entire pattern is repeated.

COTTON-EYED JOE

Imperial Record No. 1045

FORMATION: Double circle, boys inside. Use elbow grasp or social dancing position.

DESCRIPTION

1. The boy starting with his left foot and the girl with her right foot, each takes one heel-toe and step, step, step (left, right, left; girl: right, left, right). They repeat this, boy starting with right foot and girl starting with the left foot.

    Many groups dance this step in the following manner: toe, toe, step together, step to side, and repeat to other side.

2. Turning away from partner, boy to his left, girl to her right, each takes four polka steps alone in a small circle, ending facing each other.

3. Couples, while facing each other, take four push steps counterclockwise and four back to place.

    Push-step as follows: the boy steps sideways on his left foot and then pushes away from left foot with his right foot; then takes another step sideways and gives push with right foot. Girl does the same, starting with her right foot.

4. In elbow grasp or social dancing position, partners take four polka steps in line of direction, with or without turns. The two-step may be used, which gives a smoothness to the dance which was typical of the original Negro version.

CRESTED HEN
(Danish)

Victor Record No. 21619
Methodist Record No. 108

FORMATION: A set is composed of a boy and two girls, with the boy in the middle, or one girl with two boys. Sets are scattered about the room.

Crested Hen

Arranged by Anna Hermitage

DESCRIPTION

FIGURE I

Measures 1-8. Players in each set join hands in a circle. Starting with a stamp, they move to their left, using a fast step hop.

Measures 1-8 repeated. With a high jump, players reverse their direction, moving to their right.

FIGURE II

Throughout this figure all perform the step hop continuously. Girls release their hands and dance on each side of the boy. Free hands are placed on the hip.

Measures 9-10. Girl on right step hops under arch formed by boy and girl on his left.

Measures 11-12. Boy then turns with step hops under his own right arm.

Measures 13-14.   Girl on left step hops under arch made by boy and girl on his right.

Measures 15-16.   Boy then turns under his own left arm.

Measures 9-16 repeated.   Figure II is repeated.

Entire pattern is repeated as often as desired.

DUTCH COUPLE DANCE [1]

MUSIC: "Where, Oh, Where, Has My Little Dog Gone?"

FORMATION: Double circle, facing counterclockwise. Partners join inside hands.

DESCRIPTION: Music is in two parts, A and B. The same steps are danced to each part.

Measures 1-3.   Partners take six Dutch steps forward. Dutch step: step on the inside foot with a stamp (count "one"); hop on the same foot and swing the other foot across the body, brushing foot on the floor ("two"); hop again on the inside foot ("three"). This is repeated five times, starting with opposite foot each time.

Measure 4.   Each turns away from partner and faces the opposite direction with three light jumps.

Measures 5-8.   Partners repeat Measures 1-4, ending facing partner, in double circle, girls' backs to the center.

Measures 9-10.   Each takes four step hops away from partner.

Where, Oh, Where, Has My Little Dog Gone?

¹ State of Wisconsin, *Manual of Physical Education*, Part III, Folk and Singing Games. Madison: State Department of Education, 1924-25. By permission.

Measures 11-12. Measures 9-10 are repeated, each moving forward toward partner.

Measures 13-15. Partners dance Dutch waltz six times, right and left, two waltz steps to a measure. Dutch waltz: hands joined, raised shoulder high, girl steps on right foot, boy on left; hop and raise left leg (boy, right). The body is bent toward the side on which the hopping is done.

Measure 16. Four little jumps on both feet in place, ending facing forward to repeat dance from the beginning, using B music.

FINNISH REEL [1]

(*Skvaller Ulla, "Gossiping Ella"*)

Columbia Record No. 3062

Victor Record No. 19348

FORMATION: Two parallel lines, partners facing each other, hands on hips.

DESCRIPTION

Measures 1-8. Each hops on left foot and, at the same time, touches the top of right toe at side with the leg twisted so as to raise the heel. This produces a "toeing in" position. Each hops on left foot again and touches

---

[1] From C. Ward Crampton, *The Folk Dance Book.* New York: A. S. Barnes & Co., 1909. By permission.

right heel at the side with toes turned up ("toeing out" position). Steps are repeated four times, changing each time from left to right, right to left.

Measures 9-10.   Each steps forward right and stamps left, bringing heels together. Each steps backward left and stamps right, bringing heels together.

Measures 11-12.   With three running steps, partners change positions, passing with right shoulder to right shoulder. On count four, they jump and turn to face each other.

Measures 13-16.   Measures 9-12 are repeated, each returning to starting position in line.

Entire pattern is repeated.

Finnish Reel

FIST POLKA [1]
(Finnish)

Arranged by Grace Van Ness

FORMATION: Double circle, facing counterclockwise, with boys inside. Partners join hands, right hand in right hand, left hand in left hand (skaters' position).

DESCRIPTION

PART I

Measures 1-3. Each starting with inside foot, partners do "step-together-step" and then leap onto the outside foot. The leap is similar to that made when going over a hurdle. This is repeated twice more.

Measure 4. Each stamps three times while turning in place toward partner, and finishes so as to be facing in the opposite direction (clockwise).

Measures 1-4 repeated. All repeat Measures 1-4 and finish facing partners in double circle formation.

PART II

Measure 5. With hands on hips, partners jump and turn left so that right elbows are touching. (Partners will be facing in opposite directions.)

[1] M. R. Wild and D. E. White, *Physical Education for Elementary Schools.* Cedar Falls, Iowa: Iowa State Teachers' College, 1924. By permission.

Measure 6.   They jump and turn right so that left elbows are touching.

Measure 7.   They jump so as to place right foot forward and shake right fist three times in partner's face.

Measure 8.   They jump and change feet and shake left fist.

Measures 9-10.   Partners turn outward, to own left, away from each other, with three running steps, thereby making a three-quarter turn. They run two more steps to meet their new partners, clapping hands five times as steps are taken. On the last count, each jumps and lands on both feet, facing the new partner.

GOOD NIGHT, LADIES [1]

Verse 2.   Come again, ladies, etc.

3.   Farewell, ladies, etc.

4.   Sweet dreams, ladies, etc.

5.   One kiss, ladies, etc.

[1] Music from Peter Dykema, *Twice 55 Games with Music.* Boston: C. C. Birchard & Co.. 1924. By permission.

FORMATION: Double circle, boys on the outside, partners facing. Girls stand still during singing of verses; boys travel.

DESCRIPTION

Verse 1. Boys shake hands with their partners on first "good night." Moving to their left, they shake hands with the second girl on the second "good night." Continuing to move to left, they shake hands with the third girl on the last "good night." This girl becomes the new partner. As all sing "We're going to leave you now," boys take skating position with new partners and, at the same time, face in the line of direction (clockwise). They do not advance.

Chorus. Walking rapidly or skipping, all move forward. On "O'er the deep blue sea," everyone slows down and faces his partner.

Verse 2. Boys shake hands with the new partner and game is continued, through the five verses.

HEEL AND TOE POLKA [1]

Ford Record No. 107
Victor Record No. 25-1002

FORMATION: Double circle, with boy on inside. Girl's left hand resting on boy's right forearm; or boy's right arm around girl's waist with girl's left hand resting on boy's right shoulder.

DESCRIPTION

PART I

Measure 1. Both touch outside heel forward, at same time bending backward slightly. Both touch toes of outside foot backward, at same time bending slightly forward.

Measure 2. Partners take three running steps forward, each starting with outside foot.

Measures 3-4. Partners repeat heel and toe and three running steps, starting with inside foot.

Measures 5-8. Step is repeated twice more.

PART II

Measures 9-16. Partners face, boy with hands on girl's hips, girl with hands on boy's shoulders, and they polka around the room, turning.

Parts I and II are repeated as often as desired.

---

[1] By permission of Estate of Henry Ford.

Heel and Toe Polka

MINUET [1]

Victor Record No. 20440

FORMATION: Couples scattered about the room. Partners join inside hands. Girl holds skirt with outside hand, boy places his outside hand on his hip.

DESCRIPTION: The dance is done in a slow, courtly manner. There are three minuet steps:

1. Step, step, step ("one, two, three") for one measure; point, hold ("one, two, three") for second measure
2. Step, point and hold ("one, two, three") for one measure
3. Step, step, and point ("one, two, three") for one measure.

[1] By permission of Missouri State Department of Education.

Minuet

Mozart

Measure 1. Each dancer steps on outside foot ("one"), on inside foot ("two"), points outside foot ("three").

Measure 2. Dancers repeat the step, beginning with the inside foot.

Measures 3-6. All repeat Measures 1-2 twice.

Measures 7-8. Partners face, boys bow, girls curtsy. Boy, with heels together, bows low. Girl steps in line of direction ("one"); facing partner, steps backward with inside foot, leaving the outside foot pointed forward ("two"), curtsies ("three"); steps forward on outside foot ("one"), brings inside foot up to outside ("two"), rises on toes and lowers heels ("three").

Measures 1-8 repeated.   Pattern is repeated.

Measure 9.   Facing partner, each gives partner right hand, steps forward on right foot ("one"), rises on toes and sinks ("two, three").

Measure 10.   Each steps backward on left foot ("one"), points the right foot forward ("two, three").

Measures 11-12.   Measures 9-10 are repeated.

Measure 13.   Each takes three walking steps around partner, right, left, right ("one, two, three").

Measure 14.   Each points left foot forward ("one, two, three").

Measures 15-16.   Partners bow and curtsy as in Measures 7-8.

Measures 9-16 repeated.   Couples join inside hands and take three walking steps, starting with outside foot ("one, two, three"); point ("one, two, three"). They repeat the walking steps and point twice, each time changing from outside to inside foot as the starting foot. On the last two measures they bow and curtsy.

OLD DAN TUCKER [1]

Decca Record No. 18224, Album 278

FORMATION: Any number of couples join hands in a single circle, with one odd man (Dan Tucker) in the center.

DESCRIPTION: The usual country-dance step (running walk step) and galop are used. When a large number are dancing, or when there are more men than women, several Dan Tuckers can be in the center.

Measures 1-2. "BALANCE ALL." Dancers in the circle "balance" to Dan Tucker. Either (1) take a step forward with the right foot, swing the left foot forward, then step backward with the left foot and swing the right foot slightly forward; or (2) beginning with the right foot, take two walking steps forward and two back.

Measures 3-8. "TURN LEFT AND RIGHT" (or "ALLEMANDE LEFT"). Each man takes the right hand of the woman on his left in his right hand, and turns her once around, then with his left hand turns his partner once around.

[1] Dance from Elizabeth Burchenal, *Folk Dances from Old Homelands.* New York: G. Schirmer, Inc., 1922. Copyright renewal assigned, 1945, to G. Schirmer, Inc. Printed by permission.

Old Dan Tucker

Measures 9-16. "Right hand to partner, and grand right and left." All give right hands to partners and dance Grand Right and Left (or Grand Chain), in which Dan Tucker joins. They continue the chain until the leader calls the next figure.

Measures 1-8. "Promenade all." Each man secures the woman nearest him as a partner. The man left without a partner is the next Dan Tucker. Joining crossed hands, all couples promenade with the usual country-dance step around the circle counterclockwise, while the new Dan Tucker takes his place in the center.

Measures 9-12. "Forward and back." All couples join hands in a circle, and go four steps toward the center and four steps back.

Measures 13-16. "ALL HANDS AROUND." With hands still joined, they go around the circle clockwise, with the usual country-dance step (or galop step).

When the dance has been continued as long as desired, it is brought to a finish with "BALANCE AND SWING PARTNERS," and "PROMENADE AROUND THE HALL."

POLLY-WOLLY-DOODLE [1]

Old College Song
Piano by Gladys Pitcher

Traditional

Oh, I went down south for to
Oh, my Sal, she am a —
see my Sal, Sing Pol-ly-wol-ly-doo-dle all the day!
maid-en fair,
My
With
Sal - ly am a spunk-y gal,
curl - y eyes and laugh-ing hair, Sing Pol-ly-wol-ly-doo-dle all the

[1] *Music Everywhere.* A Singing School series. Sacramento: California State Department of Education, 1945. By permission of C. C. Birchard & Co.

FORMATION: Double circle, boys outside, partners facing, both hands joined and extended sideways, shoulder high. All sing.

DESCRIPTION

Measures 1-2. All take four slides clockwise.

Measures 3-4. With five light stamps, partners turn away from each other and make a complete turn in place. (Boy starts with left foot; girl starts with right foot.) Hands on hips.

Measures 5-6. All take four slides counterclockwise back to place.

Measures 7-8. They repeat Measures 3-4.

Measures 9-10. Boys make one slow, low bow to partner with hands on hips, and girls curtsy.

Measures 11-12. Each faces right and, starting with right foot, skips eight steps forward around the circle, away from partner.

Measures 13-14. Both face inward and about and take eight skip steps back to partner.

Measures 15-16. Partners join right hands and skip around each other, making two turns with eight skip steps. Each player moves to his own left and secures a new partner.

The dance is repeated as often as desired.

PRACTICE POLKA

Ford Record No. 107B (slow tempo)
MacGregor Record No. 400 (average tempo)
Victor Record No. 24090B (fast)

Music: See Heel and Toe Polka, p. 607

FORMATION: Double circle, boys on the inside; inside hands joined, free hand on hip; facing counterclockwise.

DESCRIPTION: A polka step is a two-step with a hop added, danced as follows: With a preliminary hop on the left foot (count "and"), step forward with right foot ("one"), close left foot to right foot ("and"), step forward again with right foot ("two"), hop on right foot ("and").

Step 1. Partners polka three times forward, starting with outside foot. They stamp three times and hold. They repeat the three polka steps and stamp and hold, moving around the room.

Step 2. Partners repeat above; with a half turn, they face each other, then they turn back to back, then face to face. At the same time, the inside arms swing well back and up, forward and up, back and up. Partners face and clap hands three times and hold.

Step 3. Partners take elbow grasp position or social dancing position and polka around the room, while turning continuously.

PUSH THE BUSINESS ON [1]

FORMATION: Double circle, facing counterclockwise, boys on the inside.

DESCRIPTION

Measures 1-8. All march around circle, hands joined, singing.
Measures 9-10. All face partners, clap partner's hands three times.
Measures 11-12. All take one step to right, and clap next person's hands three times.

---

[1] A slight variation is given in *We Sing*. A Singing School series. Boston: C. C. Birchard & Co., 1940, p. 144.

Measures 13-16. All join hands with new partner, and skip around in place.

The pattern is repeated as often as desired.

Push the Business On

Arranged by Anna Hermitage

TROIKA [1]

David Stevens

Russian
Piano by Gladys Pitcher

Hear the mer - ry sleigh - bells ring - ing, See the hors - es step - ping high. See how they're pranc - ing, See how they're danc - ing Un - der - neath the blue and win - try sky Hi! hi! hi! and ho! ho! ho! As o - ver hill and dale we go;

---

[1] *We Sing, op. cit.* By permission of C. C. Birchard & Co., publishers.

Hi! hi! hi! and a ho! ho! ho! For what care we for ice and snow!

Kismet Record No. 104
Methodist Record No. 105

FORMATION: Sets of threes, a coachman (preferably a boy) in the middle, with a pony (girls) on either side of him. These sets now arrange themselves in a circle facing clockwise; the pony on the right of the coachman should be nearest the center of the circle.

DESCRIPTION: This is a gay little dance imitating the Russian sleighs drawn by spirited, prancing ponies. The step used throughout is a running step, very well marked, bringing the knees up high as though prancing.

Measures 1-4. Coachman holds the two "ponies" by their inside hands very close to him. Starting with right foot, all take sixteen running steps forward, two steps to each beat.

Measures 5-8. Outside pony (left), still holding coachman's hand, takes sixteen running steps around coachman and other pony back to place, while they mark time in place.

Measures 9-12. The two ponies now join their free hands (each set forming its own small circle). All take fourteen running steps around to the left and stamp, stamp.

Measures 13-14. All take eight running steps around to the right.

Measures 15-16. The two ponies of each set now raise their joined hands, forming an arch, and "shoo" or swing their coachman under their arch and on to the set in front of them. Each set of ponies now has a new coachman and the dance continues without interruption. Dance may be repeated until coachman returns to his original ponies, or as long as desired.

TURN AROUND ME [1]

(Czechoslovakian)

Victor Record No. 21620

FORMATION: Double circle, girls on outside, boys on the inside, partners facing.

[1] M. L. Curtiss and A. B. Curtiss, *Physical Education for Elementary Schools.* Milwaukee: Bruce Publishing Co., 1945. By permission.

Turn Around Me

DESCRIPTION

Measures 1-3.   Partners do right elbow turn, taking small steps.

Measure 4.   With arms at sides, all stamp right foot.

Measures 5-8.   Hooking left elbows, partners repeat Measures 1-4.

Measures 9-10.   Partners join right hands high over head and each boy turns girl once around under her own arm.

Measures 11-12.   Each girl turns boy once around under his right arm.

Measures 13-16.   Partners hook right elbows and turn.

Measures 9-12 repeated.   Boy turns girl under raised arm and girl turns boy under his raised arm.

Measures 13-16 repeated.   Taking girl in social dancing position, boy swings girl rapidly in place, using the pivot step; that is, keeping right foot in the same place, he gives a rapid pushing action with the left foot as the turn is made.

VIRGINIA REEL[1]

Victor Record No. 20447 (without calls)
Victor Record No. 35771 (with calls)

FORMATION: This is a longways dance pattern. Form sets with not more than six couples to a set. Each set forms two lines, partners facing, boys in one line, girls in the other.

DESCRIPTION: There are three parts to the dance. A light, springy step is used, not a hop or a skip. Noise should be controlled in deference to the caller, whose directions must be heard.

PART I

Measures 1-4. "FORWARD AND BACK." Players in each line join hands, holding them high. Lines walk forward four steps and greet each other. Lines walk backward four steps. "DO IT AGAIN." Step is repeated.

Measures 5-8. "RIGHT HAND TO OPPOSITE." Partners turn each other, using right hands and then backing into their own positions.

Measures 9-12. "LEFT HAND TO OPPOSITE." Repeat Measures 5-8, using left hands.

Measures 13-16. "TWO HANDS TURNING LEFT." Partners join both hands, turn each other to their own left and then back up, returning to their own line positions.

Measures 1-4 (music repeated). "TWO HANDS TURNING RIGHT." Repeat above, turning to right.

Measures 5-8. "DOS-A-DOS LEFT." With arms folded and held high, partners advance and, without turning, pass back to back, left shoulder to left shoulder, and then back into their positions.

Measures 9-12. "DOS-A-DOS RIGHT." Repeat, partners backing around, right shoulder to right shoulder.

Measures 13-16. "HEAD COUPLE DOWN THE CENTER AND BACK." Partners nearest the music (always the head couple) join hands and slide (chassé) down the center of their lines for eight slides and return to position with eight slides.

PART II. THE REEL

In this figure the boy is to dance with all the girls in the opposite line and the girl is to dance with all the boys. If only girls are in the dance, half the group might wear some distinctive color (arm band, handkerchief, scarf, etc.) and take the place of boys. The reel takes 32 measures of music.

Measures 1-16 and repeat. "HEAD COUPLE REEL" (or "RIGHT ARM TO PARTNER AND REEL"). Head couple hook right arms and turn each other

---

[1] "Good Morning"; *After a Sleep of Twenty-five Years Old Fashioned Dancing Is Being Revived by Mr. and Mrs. Henry Ford.* Dearborn, Mich.: Dearborn Publishing Co., 1926. By permission of Estate of Henry Ford.

once and a half around. This brings girl in position to dance with boys. Girl then turns first boy in the line by hooking his left elbow with her left elbow. At same time, head boy is turning first girl in the line with his left elbow hooked into her left elbow. Head couple then return to the center, hook right elbows and turn each other; then, using left elbows, they turn second person in their line (boys turning girls, girls turning boys), and so on to the end. Always partners turn each other with right elbows, the line players with left elbows. At the end of the line, boy turns girl halfway around so that she is on the same side as her line and they slide or chassé to the head of their set.

Virginia Reel (Sir Roger de Coverly)

Larry O'Gaff

Part III. The March

Measures 1-8 and repeat. "Head couples lead off." Leaders turn away from each other and lead their lines to the foot of their set, where they stop, face, join hands and form an arch. Those following them pass under the arch and march up to their starting positions (Figure 128). Former head couple remain at the foot of the set, leaving a new couple in head position, and dance is repeated until every couple has had a chance to be at the head.

TEACHING SUGGESTIONS

1. Considerable practice will be necessary before all grasp the pattern of the reel. Have practice periods in which head couple start the reel, and when they begin the reel with the three couples (Part II), have the second couple in the line start to reel, etc. Those finishing the reel remain at the foot of the set and continue to turn with oncoming players.

2. The traditional form of the Virginia Reel calls for the head lady and and the end gentleman of a set, and the head gentleman and the end lady of a set to alternate in Part I, while other players stand still. This is a somewhat inactive form and, therefore, less desirable for children and adolescents.

Figure 128. Under the Arch in the Virginia Reel

3. The caller must time each call so that it will be finished just before a new figure is to commence, and so that no break in the rhythm occurs. Practice giving calls during the last two counts of each four measures.

4. Whenever one set finishes ahead of other sets, the dancers must stand still until all the sets are ready for the next figure.

ADDITIONAL RHYTHMICAL ACTIVITIES IN CALIFORNIA STATE SERIES MUSIC TEXTBOOKS

New Music Horizons. Fifth Book. Edited by Osbourne McConathy and Others. (Copyrighted, 1946, 1949, by Silver Burdett Co.) Sacramento: California State Department of Education (edition in preparation).

Students' book and book of accompaniments and interpretation for the teacher. Page references are to the latter book.

Our Land of Song. Edited by Theresa Armitage and Others. A Singing School series (copyrighted, 1942, 1944, by C. C. Birchard & Co.). Sacramento: California State Department of Education, 1946.

Students' book and teacher's manual (with accompaniments). Page references are to the latter book.

We Sing. Edited by Theresa Armitage, Peter W. Dykema, and Gladys
Pitcher. A Singing School series (copyrighted, 1940, 1942, by C. C.
Birchard & Co.). Sacramento: California State Department of Educa-
tion, 1942.[1]

Students' edition, teacher's manual, and book of accompaniments. Page references are to the last book.

SELECTED REFERENCES ON RHYTHMS [2]

Czarnowski, Lucile. *Dances of Early California Days*. Palo Alto, California: Pacific Books, 1950.

A presentation of music and explanation of dance steps of early California days,
classified as before 1849 and after 1849. Many of the more simple dances will be
enjoyed by children in their California Festivals.

Manners, Zeke. *American Square Dances*. New York: Robbins Music
Corp. (799 Seventh Ave.), 1948.

Simple American square dances, with calls, illustrations, and music.

Wilson, Harry Robert. *Songs of the Hills and Plains. Early American
Songs Arranged for Modern Use*. Chicago: Hall & McCreary Co., 1943.

Songs of early America, including mountain songs, cowboy songs, Negro songs,
pioneer songs, play party songs, and children's songs, with descriptions for the play
party games.

Stunts

Figure 129.   Cart Wheel

A warm-up period of exercise or running should precede each
instruction period. Review of materials given in other grades will give
each pupil a background of stunt experiences.

---

[1] Former series (adoption period July 1, 1942 to July 1, 1950).
[2] Consult the bibliography and listing of records in the appendixes.

re 130. Crab Run

CART WHEEL

Space: Gymnasium or playground (grass)

Procedure: Performer stands erect with left hand raised over head, elbow extended, fingers spread. He bends body directly to the left. As the left hand touches the ground, he flings the right leg high with knee and foot fully extended. He continues the sideward movement with the right hand contacting the ground, then the right foot, the left foot, and then to the upright position. The body is extended throughout, with no bend at the hips. The movement must be continuous. As skill is gained, cart wheels may follow each other without a pause. The sideward movement should be in a straight line. Arms and legs should be in Y positions and fully extended throughout the stunt. Side abdominal muscles will need to be strengthened before complete success is experienced.[1] (Figure 129.)

CRAB RUN

Space: Gymnasium or playground (grass)

Procedure: Performer squats and reaches backward until hands are on

---

[1] William R. LaPorte and A. G. Renner, *The Tumbler's Manual.* New York: Prentice-Hall, Inc., 1938. Pp. 42, 43. Virginia Lee Horne, *Stunts and Tumbling for Girls.* New York: A. S. Barnes & Co., 1943. Pp. 71-73, 74-75, 107-8.

the ground. He straightens his back and walks or runs forward or backward as desired. There should be no sag of the body. (Figure 130.)

DOUBLE ROLL

SPACE: Gymnasium, playground

EQUIPMENT: Mat

FORMATION: Two tumblers of about the same size are needed. Number 1 lies down and grasps the ankles of standing Number 2.

PROCEDURE: As Number 1 is raising his feet from the mat, Number 2 grasps his ankles. The forward roll is performed without breaking grasps of the hands.[1] The weight for the body at the beginning of the forward roll is taken with the hands on the ankles of the person lying down, just as it would be taken with the hands on the mat for a single forward roll.

FOREARM BALANCE

SPACE: Playground (grassy), gymnasium

EQUIPMENT: Mat (if in gymnasium)

PROCEDURE: Performer kneels and places forearms and hands parallel on the mat, shoulder width apart. Shoulders should be in front of the elbows. He starts "walking" the hips upward while looking ahead and then throws the legs upward in an effort to get and keep them in the air, close together. The toes are pointed upward directly overhead to keep the feet well balanced. The lowering or raising of the head will control the arch of the back. Performer returns to the floor by bending the hips and lowering the legs.[2]

FROG DANCE

SPACE: Gymnasium, playground

PROCEDURE: Performer squats on a heel with other heel extended to the side. He pulls in extended leg until it is under the body and at the same time extends the opposite leg to the side. He changes position of feet in rapid succession. Body must be maintained in an erect position. Arms are used to maintain balance.

---

[1] LaPorte and Renner, op. cit., p. 20. Illustrated. Horne, op. cit., "Eskimo Roll," pp. 106, 108.
[2] LaPorte and Renner, op. cit., pp. 28, 29.

HAND PUSH

SPACE: Gymnasium, playground

FORMATION: Two players face, standing toe to toe, with hands clasped at chest height.

PROCEDURE: Opponents try to make each other lose balance by pushing with the hands. Three out of five trials determine the winner.

HEEL KNOCK

SPACE: Gymnasium, playground

PROCEDURE: Performer springs into air, knocks heels together once, twice, or three times and lands with feet apart and knees bent.

HUMAN BALL

SPACE: Gymnasium, playground (grassy)

EQUIPMENT: Mat (if in gymnasium)

PROCEDURE: Performer sits with feet together, knees bent and turned out. He thrusts arms under knees from inside and locks fingers over ankles. Fingers must be locked together. He starts a swaying motion either right or left while keeping the above position, and continues the roll onto the thigh and shoulder, onto the back, then to opposite thigh and shoulder and so to erect sitting position. Momentum to return to erect position is given by knees and shoulders as they touch the floor. Rolls may be continued without interruption.

INDIAN WRESTLING

SPACE: Gymnasium, playground (grassy)

EQUIPMENT: Mat (in gymnasium)

FORMATION: Two players lie on their backs, side by side but facing in opposite directions, with right elbows locked.

PROCEDURE: On count, each swings inside leg up, hooks opponent's knee, and tries to move him. Three out of five trials determine the winner.

JUMP FOOT

SPACE: Gymnasium, playground area near a wall or fence or side of building

PROCEDURE: Performer places one foot about 12 inches from the floor against a wall or other stationary object. He jumps over the high foot without removing it from the wall. If able to do this with either foot, he tries jumping backward over the high foot. He places foot higher and jumps over it. He runs, places foot against wall, and jumps over it. In order to make a successful jump, he must not have any weight on the high foot.

JUMPING JACK

SPACE: Gymnasium, playground

PROCEDURE: Performer drops to the squat position, knees spread, body erect, arms crossed in front of body, with weight of body over the toes. He springs to erect position, knees straight, feet about eighteen inches apart, weight on heels, toes pointing upward, knees extended and with arms flung sideward-upward. Movements are repeated in rapid succession without losing balance or erect position of the body.

JUMPING THE STICK

SPACE: Gymnasium, playground

EQUIPMENT: A light, pliable stick about three feet long

PROCEDURE: Performer holds the stick in front of the body, using the tips of the fingers. He tries to jump over the stick without letting go and without touching the stick with the feet. He jumps back. He should practice going back and forth rapidly. To gain initial skill, the legs should be exercised to limber them, then one knee at a time should be brought high against the chest; at the same time, the performer steps over the stick with the raised foot. On the jump from both feet, the knees are raised as high up toward the chin as possible.

NECK SPRING

SPACE: Gymnasium, playground area near wall or side of building

PROCEDURE: Performer stands facing a wall at a distance that is one-half his height. He bends forward from hips and places his forehead against wall. Without using hands, he returns to standing position by bending knees and using neck and body muscles. Feet must not be moved. As skill is gained, performer may move feet farther from the wall.

TWIRLING TOP

SPACE: Gymnasium, playground

PROCEDURE: Performer springs upward and at the same time tries to make a complete turn while in the air. Balance must be maintained when landing. Arms should be used to help the twist. He should practice right and left turns.

WHEELBARROW WALK

SPACE: Gymnasium, playground

FORMATION: Two players perform the stunt. Number 1 stretches out with weight on arms, elbows extended. Number 2 grasps ankles of Number 1 and holds them against his own hips.

PROCEDURE: Number 1 walks forward with his hands, Number 2 walking after him. Prone person must keep body extended straight, not bending hips. Action can be completed by Number 1 doing a forward roll, Number 2 following.

Chapter XIX

ACTIVITIES FOR SIXTH GRADE

Activities are alphabetically arranged by title within the following four classes:

The games fall into several classes. They are indexed here by type for the convenience of the teacher.

Games

ALLEY SOCCER [1]

NUMBER OF PLAYERS: 16-30

SPACE: Playground, gymnasium

PLAYING AREA: Court 30 by 60 feet, divided into three lengthwise, equalized courts or alleys. The short lines of the court are known as the end or goal lines. Fifteen feet from the goal lines in the center alley a restraining line 8 feet long is drawn at each end of the field.

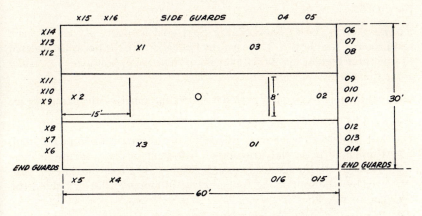

Figure 131.   Court and Position of Players in Alley Soccer

EQUIPMENT: Soccer ball. For indoor play the ball may be deflated so that it cannot be kicked farther than the length of the room.

Procedure

The game is played between two teams, each of which tries to kick the ball over the opponents' end line. Each team has a player in each of the three alleys and the other players are guards, two or three end guards for each alley and two or more side guards on each side. Players must remain in their own alleys and guards must remain outside the field.

FORMATION: Players are divided into two teams and each player has a number, from 1 to 8 or more in each team. They are distinguished by scarves or pinnies. For the kickoff, the ball is placed in the center of the field and the alley players take positions in the three courts. See Figure 131, where players O-2 and X-2 are behind the restraining lines, O-1 and X-3, O-3 and X-1 are in the outer alleys. Guards are outside the court.

---

[1] Suggestions for the game were found in a note contributed by Esther L. French to the *Journal of Health and Physical Education,* V (April, 1934), 45-46. By permission.

RULES OF PLAY: At the starting signal all the players within the lanes advance toward the ball. The center alley players try to secure the ball in order to dribble it and attempt to kick a goal, or they try to pass the ball to a teammate. The end guards try to prevent points from being made. The side guards attempt to keep the ball in the field of play and within the control of their own team players. They may kick the ball into the court or catch the ball and drop it to the ground for a kick. Players may not advance the ball by the use of the hands. Guards should try to kick the ball to one of their own forwards within the alleys.

A field goal is made when the ball crosses completely over the end line on the ground or in the air not higher than the reach of the hands of the guards.

ROTATION OF PLAYERS: Each time a field goal is made, players of each team rotate: Numbers 1, 2, 3 leave the field and take the positions vacated by the three highest numbered players of their team; Numbers 4, 5, and 6 enter the court.

PLAYING PERIOD: A playing period is agreed upon before the game begins.

FOULS: The following are fouls:

1. For runners to leave their own alley or for guards to enter the field. Runners may reach across with a foot in an effort to secure or control the ball. End and side guards may swing a foot into the playing area but the supporting foot must be in contact with or behind the end or side lines.

2. For runners to use hands or forearms in an effort to control the ball.

3. For players to push, hold, or shove other players.

4. For alley players to kick the ball over the side lines.

   Penalty: For each foul, a free kick from behind the restraining line in front of the opponents' goal is awarded to the team which did not make the foul. The kick may not be guarded. Center runner takes the kick.

SCORING: Points may be scored by any one of the six runners: 2 points for a field goal; 1 point for a successful free kick. The team wins which has the higher number of points at the end of the playing period.

TEACHING SUGGESTIONS

1. If possible, use fifteen on a side, as this number makes an excellent game, although teams smaller or larger may be used.

2. Reduce the length of the court if but few players are available.

3. Teach the runners to stay even with the ball at all times. For example, if the ball is at one end of the field all the runners should be near that particular end. They may run the full length of their alleys.

BALL STAND

NUMBER OF PLAYERS: 3-20

SPACE: Playground, playroom, gymnasium

PLAYING AREA: (1) A portion of a building against which a ball may be thrown; (2) definite ground area limitations beyond which players may not pass. Experience and the numbers of players available will determine what the dimensions should be.

EQUIPMENT: Volleyball, soccer ball, or utility ball

FORMATION: Players are numbered and stand in a line about three feet from and facing the wall. One player is given the ball or the teacher holds it.

PROCEDURE: When ready, the leader throws the ball high against the building and at the same time calls loudly a number.

Immediately all the players, except the one whose number is called, start running as far away from the ball as possible but at the same time keeping within the designated boundary lines of the playing area.

The player whose number is called secures the ball and, *standing still at the spot where he picks it up,* calls loudly, "Ball Stand!" Each runner must stop immediately when he hears the call and *without turning his head* must stand with his back to the player holding the ball. The player with the ball, after taking time to aim, throws the ball and tries to hit the back of a player. If the player is hit, he calls out loudly, "Ball Hit!" and goes after the ball; the other players run away from him. When he picks up the ball he stands still and calls loudly, "Ball Stand!"

This play continues until a player aimed at is not hit by the ball, whereupon the call "missed" is given and the players return to the wall. The person who failed to hit a player secures the ball, throws it against the wall, and calls a new number. After stopping their run, players should not move their feet until the ball is declared dead. If the ball rolls along the ground and touches a player's foot that player becomes the thrower and the game continues.

TEACHING SUGGESTIONS

1. Keep the playing area somewhat restricted. Often the shadow thrown by the building will supply a large enough area.
2. Insist that players shall not look over their shoulders until they hear the cry, "Ball Hit!"
3. If the ball leaves the playing area, have the thrower secure it and return to a boundary line and throw it from there.

BOMBARDMENT

NUMBER OF PLAYERS: 4-40

SPACE: Playground, gymnasium

PLAYING AREA: A court 20 by 40 feet, divided into two equal-sized courts by a line across the center. The area may be wider or narrower depending on the number to play. The length remains constant.

EQUIPMENT: (1) For each player one Indian club, block of wood 3 by 3 inches by 1 foot, or other substitute that will stand erect. These are placed about three feet apart on the end lines. (2) Soccer ball, volleyball or basketball. If large numbers are to play several balls should be used.

FORMATION: Players are divided into two teams. Each player stands in front of the Indian club he is to guard. The referee gives the ball to a player. If two or more balls are used they are divided between the two teams. There should be two playing periods of five minutes' duration. Teams exchange courts at half time.

PROCEDURE: By throwing the ball a player attempts to knock down the opponents' Indian clubs. At the same time each player is responsible for guarding his own club. Players may move to any position in their own court to secure and throw the ball but they may not advance into the opponents' territory.

The player with the ball may (1) advance to the center line and throw the ball; or (2) throw the ball from the spot where he picked it up. Each player must throw his own ball and may not pass it to a team member. A club may be legally upset by a fly ball, a rolling ball, a bouncing ball, or by a player other than the one guarding it. As soon as a club is upset, it should be replaced immediately in order to keep the game going.

When a ball rolls over an end line without knocking down a club the nearest member of that team secures the ball and throws it to a member of his own team, who in turn puts the ball into play as rapidly as possible. When the ball rolls over a side boundary line the nearest player of either team secures it and throws it as soon as possible to a member of his own team, who thereupon puts it into play.

FOUL: It is a foul for a player to step over the center line into the opponents' court, or to upset his own club. *Penalty:* 1 point is awarded to the opponents for each foul committed.

SCORING: Each club upset by a ball scores 2 points, and each foul committed by the opposing team counts 1 point. The team wins that has the higher score at the end of the playing periods.

TEACHING SUGGESTIONS

1. If the teams are small, reduce the width of the courts.
2. When the game is played with definite time periods, do not permit time-out for a ball out of bounds.
3. As skill is gained, use two or three balls during the game.

BOTTLE CAP GOLF [1]

NUMBER OF PLAYERS: 2-4

SPACE: Playground, classroom, playroom, hallway

PLAYING AREA: Nine 3-inch pasteboard circles scattered in a shady area, or marked on a floor, from four to eight feet apart in an irregular formation. The holes are numbered.

EQUIPMENT: A tin bottle cap for each player. Jackstones, buttons, or marbles may be substituted.

FORMATION: Two to four persons play together. They follow each other in sequence.

PROCEDURE: Each cap is started from within Hole 1 by a snap of a finger and a thumb. The course is completed when a player's cap re-enters Hole 1. A bottle cap which rests on a circle circumference line requires another snap. Each player to enter the next highest circle snaps his bottle cap again. He tries to use as few snaps as possible. After all players have entered a circle, play begins for the next highest circle. The winner is the player who makes the nine holes in the fewest strokes.

TEACHING SUGGESTIONS

1. Make the course more difficult by the introduction of various obstacles to be overcome, or by reducing the size of certain holes.
2. Use as a hot-weather game.

BOWL BALL

NUMBER OF PLAYERS: 8-20

SPACE: Playground, gymnasium

PLAYING AREA: (1) Home plate; (2) pitcher's plate placed 15 feet from home plate; (3) field base not less than 40 feet from home plate and placed 15 feet to the left of pitcher's box as pitcher faces home plate. This is the only base used.

---

[1] Adapted from a note by Teckla M. Petersen, *Journal of Health and Physical Education,* XI (January, 1940), 43. By permission.

EQUIPMENT: (1) Soccer ball; (2) Indian club, tall tin can, or block of wood placed on field base.

FORMATION: The same team formation is used as in softball: pitcher, catcher, one baseman, and fielders.

PROCEDURE: The object of the game is for players to make as many round trip runs as possible before being put out.

Periods of Play: The game is played by innings. Three men put out constitutes one half an inning. Five or more innings constitute a game. Instead of innings, four time periods of five minutes each may be used, each team being at bat during alternate periods. As many runs as possible are made by the team at bat during each period of play regardless of outs made by team members.

Pitcher: The pitcher bowls the ball toward the catcher, using an underarm throw that rolls the ball on the ground. If the pitcher bowls four "balls," that is, the balls do not go over home plate, the kicker places the ball on home plate and tries to kick it.

Kicker: Kicker stands in front of the catcher and directly behind home plate. The kicker must run if the ball, when kicked, rolls a distance equal to its circumference. As soon as his kick is made the kicker tries to reach field base and return to home plate without being put out. If and when the kicker makes a successful round trip run, he remains as kicker.

Fielders: Fielders must throw the ball from the place where they secure it. The ball may not be passed more than once between any two members of the fielding team. It must pass to a third player who may or may not return the ball to one of the previous players. The more desirable play is to throw the ball to a fourth player if the runner cannot be contacted.

There are no out-of-bounds restrictions.

Fouls: For a fielder to run with the ball is a foul. *Penalty:* One point for kicker. Kicker continues his run.

Outs: A kicker is out under the following circumstances:

1. If he fails to kick the ball on the third strike. First two unsuccessful kicks count as fouls.
2. If a fly ball is caught
3. If, while running and before he reaches the field base or home plate, a fielder knocks over the Indian club, or home base is tagged with the ball
4. If, while running to and from field base, he is tagged with or hit by a thrown ball which contacts him below the shoulders and above the knees
5. If he misses the place kick given after four balls
6. If he stops at the field base

7. If he runs out of the lane between home plate and the field base
8. If he fails to touch the field base or home plate during his run

SCORING: A successful run scores 2 points for the kicker. For each foul committed by fielders, 1 point is scored for the kicker. The team wins which has the higher score at the end of the playing time.

TEACHING SUGGESTIONS

1. See that runners touch both the field base and home plate.
2. Teach that the ball when pitched should roll along the ground.
3. See that two or three proficient players do not keep the ball passing between themselves. Call a foul for doing so.

BOWLING AT INDIAN CLUBS

NUMBER OF PLAYERS: 2-6

SPACE: Outdoors, a cement or wooden floor, playroom, gymnasium

PLAYING AREA: One or more 6-inch triangles are drawn on the ground with apex toward the bowlers. A bowling line is drawn 20 feet from apexes of the triangles.

EQUIPMENT: (1) Three Indian clubs or sticks of wood 2 by 2 by 8 inches; a set for each triangle to be used. Clubs are placed on the corners of the triangle. (2) Softballs; at least one for each triangle used.

FORMATION: Each player, in turn, stands with his feet behind the bowling line.

PROCEDURE: Without stepping over the bowling line each player bowls by sending the balls along the ground and tries to knock over all the Indian clubs. The ball may not be thrown. Three trials are permitted unless all the Indian clubs are knocked down with the first bowl.

SCORING: One point is scored for one club knocked down; 3 points for two clubs; and 5 points if all the clubs are overturned.

TEACHING SUGGESTIONS

1. Use as a good game for warm weather. A tournament can be run off between individuals or between teams.
2. Have players awaiting their turn help retrieve the balls and replace the Indian clubs following the final bowl of a given player.
3. If additional balls are available, a faster game will result.
4. Instruct players to bowl with ankles, knees, and hips bent, so that the ball is very close to the ground at the beginning of the bowl.
5. Explain the importance of pointing the bowling hand directly toward the target, not only during but following the bowling motion.

CENTER SQUARE BALL [1]

NUMBER OF PLAYERS: 10-30

SPACE: Playground, gymnasium

PLAYING AREA: Court 30 to 60 feet by 60 to 90 feet, depending on the number of players (Figure 132). There are 8-foot end zones at both ends of the field and a rectangle, 10 to 20 by 15 to 30 feet, in the center of the field.

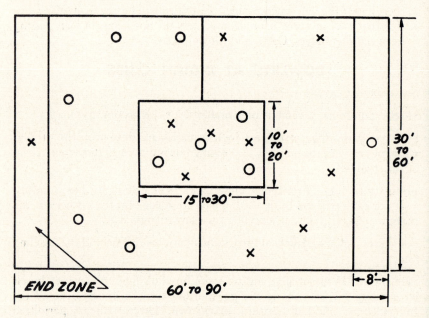

Figure 132.   Court and Position of Players in Center Square Ball

EQUIPMENT: Basketball, soccer ball, or volleyball

Procedure

The game is played in four 6-minute quarters. Teams exchange courts at half time. The object of the game is to complete a pass from a field area player or a center player to his own end man.

FORMATION: Players are divided into two teams who take places on the court as shown in Figure 132: four of each team in the center rectangle, one player in his team's end zone, and the rest in the field area opposite their end zone.

---

[1] Game contributed by Miss Virginia Covey, Supervisor of Physical Education, Pomona Public Schools.

Center Court Players: Four or fewer players for each team may be in the center area simultaneously. If four players are permitted, there should be two jumpers and two guards, with jumpers alternating in the jumps. When so organized, only center players may pass to end men after receiving the ball from a teammate outside the center court. Players may enter the center court and leave if they desire, and may move about in their own field area. They may not enter the end zone of the opponent team.

When less than four players to a team are permitted in the center court, passes to the end men may be made by players from center court or field area.

Jump Ball (Tossup): The ball is tossed between two opponents at the center of the small rectangle (1) at start of the game; (2) at the beginning of each quarter; (3) following a scoring play by either team.

Tie Ball: Tie balls are to be called by the players themselves and a jump ball used at the point where the tie ball occurs.

Out-of-Bounds Ball: When the ball goes out of bounds it is put in play by a throw-in, from the point where the ball left the field, by a member of the team whose field area it left. No score can be made from a throw-in. A throw-in may not be a direct throw to an end man.

Fouls: All personal fouls recognized in basketball such as pushing, holding, or charging are to be called. *Penalty:* All players in the center court and field area of the team fouled against step off the court. The person fouled against stands in the center area and attempts two passes to his end player. The team which fouled is allowed one guard in its field area to try to intercept the throw. If the second throw is intercepted, the ball is in play.

Violations: The following are violations:
1. Walking with the ball, using a double dribble, or delaying the game
2. Traveling over any of the division lines of the playing area
3. End men leaving the end zones at any time
4. Field area player stepping into an end zone

Penalty: Opponents gain possession of the ball out of bounds at the point on their own boundary corresponding to the point where the violation occurred in the opposite territory.

Scoring: Each successful pass to an end man counts 1 point. Passes caught from a wall rebound do not score. Play is resumed by a center toss. The team wins that has the higher score at the end of the fourth quarter.

TEACHING SUGGESTIONS

1. Rotate end players following each scoring play.

2. Do not permit certain players to remain always in the center section.
3. Encourage players to move about actively.
4. Teach several types of passing.
5. Teach the players how to dodge and to run to meet the ball as it is passed.
6. Encourage straight, quick passes instead of high, looping passes.

CIRCLE STRIKE

NUMBER OF PLAYERS: 12-20

SPACE: Playground, gymnasium

PLAYING AREA: A circle not less than 60 feet in diameter

EQUIPMENT: (1) Bats; (2) several softballs

FORMATION: Players are divided into two teams and members of each team are numbered. Players on Team A are scattered around the circumference of the circle. Members of Team B form in line outside the circle. Number 1 player of Team A acts as catcher. The player on the circle directly opposite the catcher serves as pitcher. The pitcher steps into the circle and takes a position about 30 feet from the catcher. Number 1 of Team B becomes the first batter. He steps into the circle and stands in front of the catcher facing the pitcher.

PROCEDURE: Five balls are pitched to the batter and he attempts to bat each of them outside the circle. Rotation occurs when a batter has had five trials. The play shifts one place to the right or left. Number 2 player of Team A becomes the catcher; the player opposite him becomes the pitcher. Batter Number 2 of Team B then has his five trials.

Play continues until all members of a team have batted, whereupon the teams exchange positions and the second team tries to score points. Players of Team A field the balls inside or outside the circle, returning the balls to the pitcher as rapidly as possible. Members of the batting teams, while awaiting their turn, join in the fielding of balls.

SCORING: Each batted ball that lands on the ground outside the circle scores 1 point for the batter's team. A fly ball caught by any player prevents the batter from scoring for that pitch. He continues batting until he has hit five balls.

The total points for the members of each team are tallied, the team with the higher total winning the game.

TEACHING SUGGESTIONS

1. Use several softballs to speed up the game.
2. Point out that this is an excellent game to develop batting, fielding, pitching, and catching skill.

3. Insist that batters swing at every ball which comes anywhere near them. This trains eye and muscle co-ordinations.
4. Check on player's grip of the bat, right hand above left, both hands in the middle of the bat handle.
5. Show how foot position changes the direction of a batted ball.
6. Teach batters to move body weight into a thrown ball—never backward—when batting.
7. Teach batters to swing parallel to the ground.

CLUB SNATCH

Number of Players: 4-30

Space: Playground, playroom, front of a classroom, gymnasium

Playing Area: Two goal lines some 20 feet apart

Equipment: At a point nearer one of the goals is placed an object such as an Indian club, wastepaper basket turned upside down, or block of wood. A handkerchief is hung or placed on this object.

Formation: Players are divided into two equal groups, each group lining up back of its own goal line.

Procedure: On a signal, the first player in each team runs forward. The player nearest the object tries to snatch the handkerchief and return across his goal line uncaught. The runner from the other team tries to tag the snatcher before he can cross his goal line. If tagged, both runner and snatcher return to the goal of the tagger. If the tagger is unsuccessful he joins the team of the snatcher. The same thing is repeated, with the second and succeeding runners of each team having a turn. The team wins which first brings all of the opponents to its own goal area, or which, at the end of a specified time, has the larger number of players.

TEACHING SUGGESTIONS

1. Select a distance for the placing of the object in keeping with the skill of the players. Experience will soon determine the most advantageous point for a lively game.
2. Teach that a snatcher may delay his attempt to secure the handkerchief if the tagger is faster than he is in reaching the object. This adds fun and develops alertness and the ability to get away fast once the handkerchief is secured.
3. Teach a second method of play by having the tagger run and cross the opponents' goal line before the snatcher can secure the handkerchief and cross the same goal line.
4. Use this game in warm weather.

CROSS TAG

NUMBER OF PLAYERS: 4-20

SPACE: Playground, playroom, gymnasium

PROCEDURE: The player who is "it" tries to tag a member of the group while all are running. If another runner crosses between the chaser and the one he is chasing, the chaser has to change his direction and chase the new runner. Thus a tired runner may save himself. Any one tagged becomes "it."

TEACHING SUGGESTIONS

1. When a tagger becomes weary, send in a new tagger.
2. Restrict the area in which the game is to be played.

DARE BASE

NUMBER OF PLAYERS: 4-20

SPACE: Playground, gymnasium

PLAYING AREA: Two goal lines 30 feet long and 60 feet apart are drawn. A line drawn through the center of the outlined area and paralleling the goal lines is the dare base line.

FORMATION: A player stands at each end of the dare base line. These are taggers. The remaining players are divided into two groups, members of which stand behind their own goal line.

PROCEDURE: Players try to pass from one goal line to the other, while the taggers try to catch them. If caught, the players retire from the game. Runners are safe when they are beyond the goal lines or are in contact with the dare base line. They may not return from the dare base line to the goal line they left but must go forward toward the opposite goal area.

The player wins who is the last one to be caught. He becomes the tagger for the new game and chooses his assistant.

TEACHING SUGGESTIONS

1. Encourage the players to run frequently. It slows up the game if the players are too cautious.
2. Use longer distances between goal lines for older players.

DUCK ON THE ROCK

NUMBER OF PLAYERS: 3-15

SPACE: Playground, gymnasium

PLAYING AREA: (1) A rock or other elevated object upon which a smaller stone or beanbag may be placed; (2) a base line 20 feet long drawn not less than 20 feet from the rock

EQUIPMENT: For each player a beanbag or "duck." Each player's duck should be easily recognized; a stone not smaller than the size of a lemon nor larger than an orange may be used instead of beanbags.

FORMATION: To discover which player will be the first drake, players line up behind the base line and toss their ducks toward the rock. The player whose duck is farthest from the rock becomes the drake. Placing his duck on the rock, the drake takes a position some yards from the rock. The remaining players line up behind the base line.

PROCEDURE: In turn, each player throws his duck in an effort to knock the drake's duck off the rock. If unsuccessful in his aim he may (1) stand and wait until another player knocks off the duck, whereupon he may run in and try to recover his own duck; or (2) immediately after his throw he may venture across the base line and try to recover his duck without being tagged by the drake, who has tagging power as long as his duck remains on the rock. After entering the playing area he may acquire safety in two ways: (a) if he reaches his duck and places his foot on it; (b) if he picks up his duck and returns beyond the base line without being tagged by the drake.

When a player succeeds in knocking off the duck, all those who have thrown their ducks may run forward in an effort to pick up their ducks and return beyond the base line, or if this is not possible place a foot on their duck. *The drake may not tag anyone until he has replaced his duck on the rock.* If the drake succeeds in tagging a player before that player reaches one of the two points of safety, the drake must run, take off his own duck, and dash for safety, since the one tagged now becomes the drake and, after placing his duck on the rock, may chase the former drake or another player as he wishes.

TEACHING SUGGESTIONS

1. If stones are used as ducks, exercise care to see that the following conditions are met:
   (a) That the drake stands far enough away from his duck to avoid being hit
   (b) That players do not run into the field of play until all the ducks have been thrown
2. Do not permit a duck to be moved once a foot is placed on it.
3. Do not allow a player to pick up his duck and, because of danger, place it on the ground again while within the playing area.
4. Have a player, on reaching the base line after rescuing his duck, begin throwing again in an effort to dislodge the duck that is on the rock.

EIGHT OUT[1]

NUMBER OF PLAYERS: 6-8

SPACE: Gymnasium, hallway, playroom, wooden sidewalk

PLAYING AREA: Bowling alley of regulation length or shorter, depending on grade placement of players (Figure 133). Ten pin spots are made, 12 inches apart. Center of spots 7, 8, 9, 10 should be three inches from pit edge or drop if possible. A wooden frame may be used for marking pin spots rapidly (see directions for making frame, page 116).

When played indoors, balls may be controlled by the following methods: (1) hang a gymnasium mat on wall and place pin spots 5 to 6 feet distant; then roll two mats lengthwise and place in relation to wall hanging so that a spreading U-shaped catch basin will be formed for control of balls; (2) use cage shown in drawing for School Bowling (Figure 177, p. 889); pad inner face of three sections so as to deaden the sound of the balls.

EQUIPMENT: For each alley (1) ten duckpins; (2) two official duckpin balls.[2]

Procedure

The object of the game is to knock over as many pins as possible with two balls bowled in succession.

FORMATION: Players are numbered and line up in file formation behind the foul line. Numbers 1 and 2 will serve as first pin setters.

Pin Setter: The first bowler to fail in knocking over eight pins with two balls becomes a pin setter and takes the place of Number 1. The second player to fail to knock down eight pins with two balls releases Number 2 as pin setter. Released players take their place at the end of the file. Each player bowls until he fails to knock down eight or more pins with the two bowls.

SAFETY MEASURES: To prevent injuries to players and avoid damage to equipment and floor, observe the following rules:

1. After the first ball is rolled, a pin setter picks it up and holds it.
2. Any dead pins are removed from the floor by the second pin setter before the second ball is delivered. Pin setters keep the score and announce it following each roll.
3. After the second pin is rolled and secured, balls are rolled back *one at a time* with sufficient interval to permit the new bowler to secure both balls.

---

[1] A duckpin bowling game. Rules adapted from an article by Patrick A. Tork, "Bowling as a Recreational and Physical Education Activity in the School Program," *Journal of Health and Physical Education,* XVI (January, 1945), 43-4. By permission.

[2] Often owners of bowling alleys who handle duckpin games will donate used pins and balls.

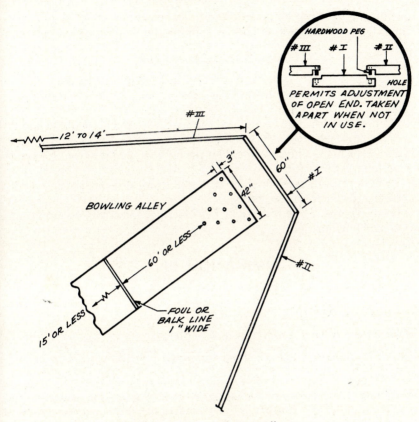

Figure 133.   Eight Out Alley

4. Balls must be first stopped by a bowler stepping on them with a forward movement of the foot in order to retard the forward motion of the ball.

5. Lofting of the ball at the start of the roll must not be permitted, as the ball will dent the floor. A player who lofts a ball loses his next bowl.

6. No ball may be bowled while a pin setter is working or is stooping to secure a ball.

Any other safety rule that seems necessary may be instituted.

FOULS: The bowler may not permit any part of his foot or his person to rest on or beyond the foul line before the delivered ball reaches the pins.

Penalty: No count is made and any pins that are knocked down are set up again. It counts against the bowler as a rolled ball, however.

SCORING: One point is scored for each pin knocked over. Official scoring for bowling need not be used in lead-up games for bowling. The player wins who has the highest number of points at the end of the playing time.

TEACHING SUGGESTIONS

1. Teach players to release the ball when the hand is near the floor.
2. Teach pupils to take four walking steps, beginning with the right foot, and to deliver the ball when the left foot is forward.
3. Do not allow the bowler to bend the arm or back. He should bend his knees and make delivery when his hand is not higher than 12 inches above the floor. The ball should hit the floor beyond the front foot and within two feet of it.
4. Point out that duckpin bowling is almost identical to the bowling pitch of kick ball and similar games.
5. Be sure pupils know that Eight Out does not use scoring methods of official bowling.

ELIMINATION PASS

NUMBER OF PLAYERS: 3-40

SPACE: Playground, playroom, gymnasium

EQUIPMENT: A ball for each circle of 10 players

FORMATION: Players stand in their circle, 4 to 10 feet apart and facing inward

PROCEDURE: At a signal, the ball is passed rapidly from one player to the next one in the circle. The players may pass the ball in any manner desired, but they should pass it with speed and accuracy. Any pass which the receiving player can touch with both hands is considered a fair pass. When the leader says, "Change direction," the direction of the ball is reversed.

Players dropping the ball are eliminated, as well as players making throws which cannot be caught with two hands.

The last player to remain in the circle wins.

TEACHING SUGGESTIONS

1. Review all types of passing before playing the game.
2. Instruct pupils to give with the catch and to follow through on the pass with a rhythmical motion.
3. Show how important it is to have the entire body help throw the ball, not just the hands.
4. Play the game without eliminating players. Each time a player makes a poor throw or catch, it is scored against him personally. At the end of the playing period the player with the fewest failures is the winner.

FLOOR CHECKERS

NUMBER OF PLAYERS: 2

SPACE: Playground, classroom, auditorium

PLAYING AREA: Checkerboard pattern is painted on floor, sidewalk, or cement area. Thirty-two black and thirty-two white squares are needed. Black and white alternate so that there will be four black and four white on each of the four sides of the square. The squares are one foot in size.

EQUIPMENT: Twenty-four checkers made from coffee cans. Fill them with cement and insert in each a 16-inch handle made from old broom handles. Paint half of the checkers red and half of them blue. Each checker will weigh about six pounds. Checkers are placed on the white squares of the first three rows on each side.

FORMATION: Players take positions so that each has a vacant square at his lower right-hand corner. This is known as the double corner because two men are located in the white squares immediately adjacent to it. The left hand, or the single corner, is occupied by only one man.

PROCEDURE: Moves are made the same as in the usual game of checkers.[1] Children must bend the knees to lift the checkers. They must not be permitted to push them with the feet.

TEACHING SUGGESTIONS

1. Point out that this is also an interesting game for grownups.
2. Use for children on a modified program.

GLENDALE BALL [2]

NUMER OF PLAYERS: 6-32

SPACE: Playground, gymnasium

PLAYING AREA: Large free area with a circle three feet in diameter located in the center

EQUIPMENT: (1) One 14-inch or 12-inch softball; (2) a bat for each pair of players. A softball bat is best, but a wooden paddle, shovel handle, or pole cut from a tree branch makes an acceptable substitute. (3) A base for each pair of players. The base may be regulation. An acceptable substitute may be a linoleum square, a chunk of wood, gunny sack, handful of sawdust, or large flat stone. Each base is placed not less than 10 feet

---

[1] Rules may be obtained when purchasing checkerboards or in game books. See Kenneth M. Grover and Thomas Wiswell, *Chess*. New York: A. S. Barnes & Co., 1941.

[2] Game was developed by the pupils of the Glendale School in Humboldt County, Lyle Alison, teacher.

from other bases but a 30-foot distance is preferable. Each base should be 40 feet from the pitcher's circle.

FORMATION: Players are divided into pairs. Equality of skill is not required. Each batter stands beside his base with his catcher behind him; thus two circles of players are formed around the pitcher. The game may be played with a pitcher and three pairs of players, one of whom is a batter, the other a catcher. Any number of pairs of players may be used; from three to sixteen pairs being the best number. As children arrive they equip themselves with a base and a bat, choose a catcher, locate themselves between any other two bases, and are immediately part of the game. The pitcher holding a ball stands inside his circle.

PROCEDURE: The pitcher starts the game by throwing the ball towards one of the bases. He must use an underhand throw.

Batters: If a batter succeeds in hitting the ball, he and every other batter drops his bat and runs counterclockwise to the nearest base. Only one base may be run on any one hit.

Catchers: Each catcher, as well as the pitcher, attempts to field the ball. When the ball is secured, the catcher tries to tag any one of the runners himself or he may throw the ball to some catcher closer to a runner. The second catcher should then attempt to tag out the runner. If the ball goes afield, the nearest catcher secures it and throws it to the pitcher. The batter tagged and the one who tagged him exchange places.

Pitcher: The pitcher becomes a batter if he catches a fly. When this occurs all runners continue to the base toward which they were running. Then, and only then, the pitcher and the man he caught out exchange places.

The pitcher is not required to pitch to any one batter but may change at will, delivering the ball to several batters in turn, if he so desires, until cumulatively they score three strikes, whereupon the batters become catchers and the catchers, batters.

Balls and Strikes: Balls and strikes may be called as in regular softball. For less skilled players it will be worthwhile to continue the pitching until a hit is made.

Outs: Any batter may be put out when struck out by the pitcher, tagged out by a catcher, or when the pitcher catches a fly ball. When a batter is out, all batters become catchers and all catchers become batters. The exchange of positions takes place after each runner reaches the base toward which he is running when the out occurs.

Walks: Since all bases are always full, all batters walk to the next base when a walk is awarded. A walk is awarded after four balls have been pitched.

SCORING: Each player keeps his own score. Each base legally reached counts one point. The person with the highest number of points wins.

GOAL-HI BASKETBALL [1]

NUMBER OF PLAYERS: 10-20

SPACE: Playground, gymnasium, auditorium

PLAYING AREA: Three concentric circles drawn on the floor or ground. The inner circle should have a four-foot radius, the outer circle a radius of from 20 to 30 feet (if indoors, it may be 15 to 25 feet), and the center circle should have a radius of half the outer one. The inner line is the restraining line, the second the free-throw line, and the outer the out-of-bounds line. At the center of the circles the Goal-Hi standard is placed.

EQUIPMENT: (1) Basketball, soccer ball, speed ball, volleyball, or utility ball; (2) one Goal-Hi basket and standard. The height of the circle of the basket from the floor should be eight feet for elementary school children. The basket consists of a ring 18 inches in diameter, inside measurements, supported by three curved braces that join and become a part of the basket base or cone. A three-way chute is formed which serves as a runway for the ball when leaving the basket through one of the three exits, and which causes the ball to arch away from the vertical standard supporting the basket so that it will strike the floor or ground outside of the innermost or restraining circle of the playing court. Each of the three exits is fitted with a swinging gate that prevents the entrance of a low ball from the outside when it strikes any part of the basket below the ring.

Procedure

Game is played according to basketball rules, with certain modifications to meet the special needs resulting from the use of but one goal and a circular playing court. The ball may be passed, batted, bounced, thrown, or dribbled in any direction. Following a goal from the field or after a free throw, whether made or missed, the ball remains in play and play is interrupted only by the referee's whistle calling attention to a violation or to a foul.

FORMATION: The same formation is used as for basketball; [2] five or six players for each team, though as many as 10 on a team may be used.

PLAYING PERIOD: For players in the sixth grade or lower the game consists of four quarters of four minutes each, with a 2-minute intermission between quarters and a 10-minute intermission between halves. Seventh and eighth grade players use four 5-minute quarters with a 1-minute intermission between quarters and a 10-minute intermission between

---

[1] Contributed through the kindness of Dr. Forrest C. Allen, Director of Physical Education and Varsity Basketball Coach, University of Kansas, inventor of the game, and the Fred Medart Manufacturing Company. The rules have been briefed. Full rules may be obtained from the Fred Medart Mfg. Co., St. Louis, Mo.

[2] See Basketball, p. 720.

halves. Each quarter and overtime period must begin with a jump ball inside the inner court, six feet from the free-throw line.

JUMP BALL: The ball is put in play by a jump ball in the inner court in the following instances: (1) at the beginning of each quarter and of each extra period; (2) after held ball on or inside of free-throw line; (3) after the last free throw following a double foul; (4) after a free throw following a technical foul, or after the last free throw following a technical foul if more than one technical foul has been called.

The referee may choose any advantageous area in the inner court to toss the ball and each jumper stands with both feet in the inner court six feet from the free-throw line, facing each other and an equal distance from the goal. The ball is thrown between the jumpers to a height greater than either of them can jump and so that it will drop between them. The ball must be tapped by one or both of the jumping players after it reaches its highest point. Neither jumper may tap the ball more than twice, after which neither may touch the ball again until it has touched one of the other players, the floor or ground, or the basket.

Inner Court Jump Ball: When a jump ball takes place in the inner court, jumpers must be inside the inner court and all other players on both teams must remain in the outer court until the ball has been tapped. *Penalty:* Infraction of this condition is a violation. The ball is awarded to an opponent out of bounds after a violation.

Outer Court Jump Ball: When the ball is tossed up between two players in the outer court all players except the two jumpers remain in the inner court until the ball has been tapped.

OUT-OF-BOUNDS PLAY: When a ball goes out of bounds not more than five seconds is permitted in getting the ball into play. An opponent to the one who sent the ball out of bounds is designated by the referee to return the ball into court. The designated player throws or bounces the ball to another player within the court from a point out of bounds near where the ball left the court.

When the referee cannot determine which player touched the ball last, before it went out of bounds, the ball is put in play by a jump ball at the spot where it was last touched inside the court, but not less than six feet from the boundary line. If on a jump ball, in either the inner or outer court, the ball is tapped out of bounds by both players simultaneously, it is put in play again at the same point by a jump ball.

A player is out of bounds when any part of his body touches the boundary line or area outside the boundary line, or when a player on the *team in possession* of the ball strikes the Goal-Hi standard.

If the standard is touched by a player on the *team not in possession* of the ball, play will continue unless in the opinion of the referee play has been interfered with, in which case a technical foul may be called.

Ball is out of bounds when any part of it touches the out-of-bounds line, the floor outside the out-of-bounds line, any object on or outside the out-of-bounds line, or when it is touched by a player who is out of bounds. The ball is caused to go out of bounds by the last player touched by it before it crosses the line.

GOAL-HI WITH PENALTY-BOX PROVISION: When a penalty-box is to be used the rules continue the same but no free throws for personal or technical fouls are awarded. Fouls are called on the offending player. The referee orders the offending player to the penalty box for the duration of one minute. An assistant timekeeper has control of the penalty box and after the 60 seconds the offending player is sent back into the game by the assistant timekeeper without notifying the referee.

If a player is disqualified for unsportsmanlike conduct or unnecessary roughness and must leave the game, a substitute may be sent into the game to take his place after 1 minute and 30 seconds.

SCORING: A field goal from within the outer court scores 3 points. A field goal from within the inner court scores 2 points. A successful free throw scores 1 point.

If a player shoots a field goal while any part of his body is touching the free-throw line the goal counts only 2 points.

The winner of the game is the team scoring the greater number of points in the playing time.

TEACHING SUGGESTIONS

1. Use the Goal-Hi equipment at the official height of eight feet for elementary school boys and girls.
2. Use distinctive colors or shirts to distinguish players.
3. Use in schools with enrollments too small for playing official basketball, or to teach skills found in basketball.

GOAL-HI—THREE SEGMENTS

NUMBER OF PLAYERS: 6-30

PLAYING AREA: The same area is used as described for Goal-Hi Basketball. It is divided into three equal segments by three lines drawn from the center to connect with the out-of-bounds line. The segments are called A, B, and C.

EQUIPMENT: Basketball, soccer ball, volleyball, or utility ball

Procedure

The game of Goal-Hi Basketball is played, except that there are three teams instead of two, each playing within its own segment.

FORMATION: Players are divided into three teams, each team having one or more players in each segment. Players may not leave the segment in which they are to play.

PLAYING PERIOD: Playing time should be divided into thirds instead of quarters and halves. The length of playing time should be determined by the physical condition of the players.

RULES OF PLAY: At the beginning of the game or each one-third period the ball is put in play by being tossed to a player in segment A. The player receiving the ball may pass or dribble the ball laterally or backward, or he may try for a goal.

During each period of play the players on each team remain in their own court and do not enter the territory to the right or left of them. If any part of a player's body touches a division line or enters an adjacent court he commits a violation. The penalty for stepping into another territory is an out-of-bounds play by an opponent opposite the place where the violation occurred.

During play children should not step over or on the out-of-bounds line nor cause the ball to leave the playing area. If a player steps over the line or causes the ball to go out of bounds, the ball is given to the nearest opponent within the segment where the foul was committed or, if only 3 persons are playing, to the opponent in the court which is nearest the point where the ball or player went out of bounds.

When the ball is over a division line any player in either adjoining segments may try to secure the ball or may jump and tap the ball, if in so doing he does not enter the adjacent territory. All rules which apply to Goal-Hi Basketball control the play in this game.

ROTATION OF PLAYERS: Players of each team rotate from one segment to the next at the end of each one-third period of play. For example, Team Number 1, starting the game in segment A, begins the second period of play in segment C with Team Number 3 moving into segment A and Team Number 2 in segment B.

SCORING: A field goal made from the outer court scores 3 points. A field goal made from the inner court scores 2 points. A goal made from a free throw scores 1 point.

If a player makes a field goal while any part of his body is touching the free-throw line, the goal scores only 2 points.

TEACHING SUGGESTIONS

1. Use Goal-Hi-Three Segments as a basketball type game for children whose activity must be limited.
2. Play with a small ball and with the goal in its lowest position.

GOAL TAG

NUMBER OF PLAYERS: 4-20

SPACE: Playground, playroom, gymnasium

PLAYING AREA: A goal base for each player: a beanbag, a chalk mark, or a square of linoleum.

FORMATION: Each player occupies or contacts his own goal base. One of the players is selected to be the tagger.

PROCEDURE: When the tagger leaves his base all the others must leave their base and seek a new one. The tagger attempts to tag any one of the players while the players are seeking a new base. No player may return to the base he has previously occupied until he has occupied a third base. No two players may occupy the same goal area at the same time. The person tagged becomes "it" and the game continues.

TEACHING SUGGESTIONS

1. Do not have the playing area too extensive in size.
2. Encourage rapid playing.
3. See that all move from the base they occupy when the taggers move away from their bases.

HAND TENNIS

NUMBER OF PLAYERS: 2-8

SPACE: Playground, gymnasium

PLAYING AREA: Court 16 by 40 feet running north and south. Short lines are service or base lines. Restraining lines are drawn across the court 17 feet from and paralleling the base lines. The area between the net and the restraining line is neutral territory.

EQUIPMENT: (1) Two posts extending 3 feet above the ground; or two jumping standards weighted with sandbags, placed at the center points of the side lines; (2) tennis net, volleyball net, chicken wire, gunny sack net, or rope stretched across between the posts so that the upper edge at the center of the court is 2 feet 4 inches from the ground and at the posts, 2 feet 5 inches; (3) large or small rubber ball with plenty of resilience.

Procedure

The game is played according to the rules of lawn tennis, the ball being struck with the hand rather than with a racket.

FORMATION: One player on each side of the net; or two teams with two members each as in tennis; or two teams with three members each, two near the base line, the third playing in the area just back of the restraining line; or two teams with four members each, two near the base line and two behind the restraining line.

Server: The server, standing outside the base line on the right-hand side, drops the ball to the ground and strikes it with his hand following its first rebound. He tries to send the ball over the net into the opposite area beyond the restraining line. He continues to serve, alternating from right to left side of his court, until the game is finished. An underhand stroke is necessary when serving, but the use of either hand is permitted. During the rally any type of stroke is permissible.

Receiver: The player to receive a served ball must be in the side of the court diagonally opposite that occupied by the server. He must try, following the ball's first bounce, to return it into the opposite court in such a manner as to make it impossible for the opponents to return it.

Receivers do not change positions when served to; server's partners move across the court each time server moves.

Let Service: Server has but one service after each point is made or lost unless served ball hits the top of the net and drops into the opposite court. This is a let service, and the ball is served again from the same position.

Rally: After the receiver returns the ball it may thereafter be played by any member of either team while using either hand. It may be played on the fly as well as following a first bounce. During the rally, if the ball at any time hits the top of the net and drops into the opposite court it is still a good ball and should be played. If more than two persons are playing on a side, those near the restraining line maintain their relative positions until rotation brings them to the rear section of the court.

Rotation of Players: When three or four players are on a team, the service rotation is to the left, Number 2 taking the place of Number 1 and Number 1 taking the place of Number 3 or 4.

Fouls: Fouls occur in the following circumstances:

1. When a server steps on or over the base line while serving
2. When a player steps on a restraining line or into neutral territory
3. When a receiver returns a served ball on the fly

Penalty: Opponents are given 1 point for each foul. A point so earned may or may not conclude the game.

Scoring: Scoring is the same as for lawn tennis, which is 15, 30, 40, game. See Tennis, page 915.

TEACHING SUGGESTIONS

1. Have pupils study the method of scoring from the blackboard. Draw

a court and with a pointer illustrate plays that may occur and have pupils call the score.
2. Assign pupils to watch for foot faults or other errors.
3. Permit a fifth player to enter the game. As the server finished he would leave the game and return later as rotation brought him back. Thus ten pupils could be kept interested in a game.

HIGH BALL

NUMBER OF PLAYERS: 4-40

SPACE: Playground, playroom, gymnasium

EQUIPMENT: A volleyball for each group playing. If but one ball is available, divide the players into two groups and have the groups play alternately for two minutes each. If several balls are available the game may continue for five minutes.

FORMATION: Divide the players into two equal groups and number the players in each group. Each group stands informally by itself, the members facing each other in an irregular circular grouping.

PROCEDURE: The object of the game is to keep the ball in the air by batting or volleying it. On receiving the signal for play, Number 1 of each group sends the ball into the air by volleying it with the fingers of both hands, trying to direct the ball to a member of his group. Players must move about in the effort to bat the ball and thus keep it in the air. Passing is continued from player to player until one of the following errors is made:

1. The ball is struck by a player using but one hand.
2. The ball is hit with the fist.
3. The ball hits some object other than the hands of players.
4. The ball falls to the ground.
5. The ball is handled twice in succession by the same player.

When an error is made the next higher numbered player of the group puts the ball into play as rapidly as possible. See Volleyball, p. 801.

SCORING: Each time the ball is successfully batted from player to player a score of 1 point is made for each successful pass. The instant an error is made that score is terminated. A new score begins with each renewal of play. A continuous match may be played by keeping the highest daily score of each group and totaling these scores each week or season.

TEACHING SUGGESTIONS

1. Encourage the players to move about, to go to the ball and get directly under it for the hit.
2. As skill is gained, have the ball sent higher into the air.
3. Teach the children to use their fingertips to volley the ball.

HINDOO TAG

NUMBER OF PLAYERS: 5-40

SPACE: Playground, playroom, gymnasium

FORMATION: Players are scattered about within a restricted area.

PROCEDURE: One player is chosen tagger. He attempts to tag another player. That player is safe only if he is on his knees with his forehead touching the floor. After the tagger has passed, the kneeling players *must rise* and move to new positions.

TEACHING SUGGESTIONS

1. As the tendency will be for the players to stand in one spot, see that they move about.
2. Keep the playing space small in proportion to the number of players.

IN-AND-OUT BASKETBALL [1]

NUMBER OF PLAYERS: 15-18

SPACE: Playground, gymnasium

PLAYING AREA: Basketball court

EQUIPMENT: Basketball, volleyball, soccer ball or utility ball

FORMATION: Players are divided into three teams, five or six on a team. Two teams play, the third team remaining on the side lines until a point is made. The losing team then retires and the third team plays the winners.

PROCEDURE: The game is played with simple basketball rules. See Boys' or Girls' Basketball, pages 720, 723.

SCORING: A field goal scores 2 points. A free throw scores 1 point. Each team keeps its own score. The game is played for a certain period of time such as three minutes, or for two out of three field goals, whichever happens first. In case of a tie, play until one team scores.

TEACHING SUGGESTIONS

1. Teach basketball skills.
2. Use this game in situations where there are more players than there are courts. The odd team plays the winners.
3. If girls play, use girls' rules, and if boys play use boys' rules. For mixed teams use girls' rules.

---

[1] Contributed by J. Ted Chism, Principal, Williams School, Bakersfield.

INDIAN BALL [1]
(Sometimes called Infield)

NUMBER OF PLAYERS: 4-20

SPACE: Playground

PLAYING AREA: Field about 50 by 75 feet, adjusted to space available and number of players (Figure 134).

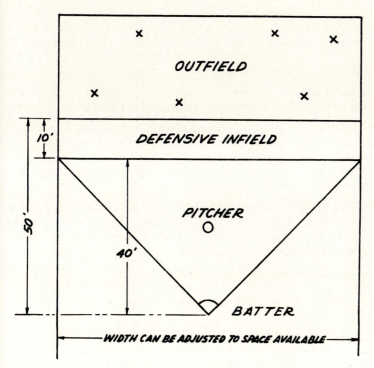

Figure 134. Field for Indian Ball

EQUIPMENT: (1) Bat; (2) softball

FORMATION: O team, the offensive, at bat, with their own pitcher on the pitcher's plate; X, the defensive, fielding. All the players of the defensive team must be beyond the defensive infield area while a batter is at the plate.

PROCEDURE: Indian Ball is played like softball, except that no base running occurs. Defensive play is stressed.

---

[1] Adapted from description found in *Leisure,* III (May, 1936), 45.

Pitcher: The member of team at bat does not oppose a fielding team pitcher but bats against his own pitcher, that person being the *only person* between the batter and the defensive infield area. The pitcher serves as a buffer for his own team. Besides pitching he tries to stop weakly hit ground balls from entering the defensive infield area. The pitcher has only to touch the ball to make a "save" and the batter is then safe even if the ball continues on to a player in the defensive infield area.

Batter: A batter cannot strike out. He remains at bat until he is retired by (1) a fly ball caught in the outfield (a fly ball caught elsewhere does not retire the batter); (2) a cleanly fielded ground ball which passes the pitcher and is secured by an opponent *within* the boundaries of the defensive infield area; (3) four foul balls; (4) four "balls" delivered by the pitcher.

Fielders: While batter is up fielders may not be within the defensive infield area. After the ball is contacted by bat, fielders may enter this area.

Base Running: As there is no base running, each safe hit by a player makes him a mythical "man on base" who moves up with each succeeding hit and "scores" a run when enough hits by himself or succeeding batters advance him. Under these circumstances he might make more than one run while at bat.

Hits: The batter is credited with a hit (1) if a ground ball is fielded by an infielder in back of or in front of the boundary lines of the defensive infield area; or (2) if the ball is caught as a fly in area between "home plate" and front line of defensive infield area.

Fly Balls: A fly ball which falls to the ground in the outfield is considered a hit. A fly ball falling to the earth in the defensive infield area and then properly fielded as a ground ball *before* it rolls outside the defensive infield area retires the batter.

Batted Balls: If the ball is driven past the pitcher toward the defense team it must, if a ground ball, be fielded without a fumble *within* the 10-foot width of the defensive infield in order to retire the batter.

SCORING: Scoring is similar to softball except as shown in the rules.

TEACHING SUGGESTIONS

1. Use underhand or overhand pitching.
2. Have a player bat fly balls for other players to catch as a good practice procedure.
3. Use as a hot weather game, since no base running occurs.
4. Point out that this game is an excellent set-up for batting and fielding practice.

KICK FOOTBALL [1]

NUMBER OF PLAYERS: 30

SPACE: Playground

PLAYING AREA: Rectangular field with two end zones 10 yards wide; a set of goal posts on each goal line; a mid-field line halfway between each goal; and two kickoff lines 10 yards on each side of the mid-field line. In addition, there should be a restraining line 5 yards inside and parallel to each side line.

EQUIPMENT: (1) Junior size football; (2) pinnies or uniforms to distinguish players

Procedure

Two teams of 15 players each try to obtain possession of the ball and advance it across the opponents' goal line by kicking, passing, or running with the ball. After the kickoff the receiving team runs or passes the ball up the field as far as it can before the player with the ball is touched or the pass is incomplete. The last player on a complete play, the passer of an incomplete pass, or a runner who is touched returns to the point of touch or to the point from which the incomplete pass was thrown and punts the ball to his opponents. The ball must be punted unless the kicker has passed the defensive team's kickoff line, in which case it may be drop-kicked. If the ball becomes dead too close to the goal line, the kicker may back up to make his kick, but he may not improve the angle of his kick if he is within the restraining side lines.

The ball carrier may be stopped when a defensive player touches him with one hand between the knee and shoulder.

When the ball is passed or carried over the goal line it counts as a touchdown; when it is drop-kicked over the crossbar between the goal posts it counts as a field goal; when a runner is tagged behind his own goal line, it counts as a safety.

FORMATION: The captains of the two teams meet with the official and toss a coin to decide which is the kicking and which is the receiving team for the kickoff. The winning captain has his choice of kicking or receiving and choice of goals. The ball is kicked off by a place kick from the kickoff line 10 yards back of mid-field. The receiving team must have 7 men not closer than 10 yards nor farther than 20 yards from the ball. The other players are any place back of the 10-yard line.

PLAYING PERIOD: A game consists of two halves, each 15 minutes in length, with a 10-minute rest period between halves.

---

[1] Contributed by Robert D. Widger, Supervisor of Health and Physical Education and Recreation, elementary schools of Visalia.

RULES OF PLAY

Onside: The kicker must wait until his teammates are onside before kicking the ball or an offside penalty will result. Players are onside if, when lining up for a kick, all players are on a line with or behind the kicker when he starts his two steps to kick.

Offside: Any opposing or defensive player who is closer than 10 yards to the kicker's line is declared offside, as well as an offensive player who is ahead of the kicker's line.

Punted Ball: The kicker is allowed not more than two steps in getting his kick away. If a punted ball is caught by the receiving team in the end zone or on the playing field, its members may advance the ball by running or passing. A ball caught in the end zone must be advanced beyond the goal line by running, or by a completed pass. Otherwise a safety is awarded the other team. If a punted ball touches the ground, it is put into play from the spot in which the first person has complete control of the ball. The ball must be punted, and cannot be run if it has touched the ground.

Out of Bounds: Any ball which goes out over the side lines is put in play by the nearest player of the team which did not cause the ball to go out of bounds. The ball is put in play on the spot from which it went out, by a punt.

Touchback: A touchback occurs when the ball is caught in the end zone or when the ball rolls dead in the end zone, or rolls out of the end zone. After a touchback the ball goes into play by a kick from the goal line by the person who retrieves the ball.

Interference: When there is deliberate interference on a pass play, the pass is considered completed at the spot of the foul. If the foul occurs over the goal line it is counted as a touchdown.

FOULS: The penalty for all fouls is a 10-yard penalty from the spot where the foul occurred or where the ball becomes dead, whichever is the most severe penalty. The following are fouls: (1) tripping, (2) pushing, (3) holding, (4) unnecessary roughness, (5) pass interference, (6) being offside, (7) unsportsmanlike conduct, (8) clipping and leaving the feet for a block or a tag.

SCORING: A touchdown scores 6 points. A field goal counts 3 points. A safety scores 2 points. A touchback does not count.

After a touchdown, field goal, or safety the team scored against has its choice of kicking or receiving. The team with the higher score at the end of the playing time wins.

TEACHING SUGGESTIONS

1. Teach the players to cover the entire playing field from side to side and back as far as the opposing team is able to return the kick.
2. Teach the players to kick the ball high when close to the scoring area in

order that the offensive team may have time to advance down the field; kick low when team is backed up against its own goal.
3. Teach the players to throw more short, accurate passes instead of a few long desperation passes.
4. Instruct the best passers and runners to play in the backfield, and the best receivers and blockers to play in the front line.
5. Work out a few fundamental play patterns for older children to add interest to the game.

NET BASKETBALL [1]

NUMBER OF PLAYERS: 16

SPACE: Playground, gymnasium

PLAYING AREA: A basketball court properly marked with free-throw circles and lanes as for boys' basketball.

EQUIPMENT: (1) Basketball, soccer ball, or volleyball; (2) volleyball or tennis net, or rope, stretched taut the long way of the court, dividing the court into two equal alleys. The top of the net should be 7 feet from the ground. Lower the net if players are small.

FORMATION: Players are divided into two teams of eight players each, four of each team, on one side of the net and the remaining four on the other side. Players of the two teams move the entire length of their half of the court. Each team is assigned a basketball goal. Members of teams should wear some distinguishing mark such as a sash, arm band, or pinnie. The game is played in 10-minute halves.

PROCEDURE: A member of one team takes the ball out of bounds opposite the center of the court. The ball is thrown over the net to a teammate and the thrower re-enters the court. The ball is then tossed back and forth over the net in order for it to reach a player within a free-throw circle and lane area, from which area *only* a try for goal may be made. After a goal is made the ball is taken out of bounds opposite the center of the court by a member of the team scored against, and play is resumed.

Players are not allowed to dribble the ball or stop with the ball. All fly balls and those hitting the floor within bounds and bouncing may be caught and thrown. The ball is out of play if tossed under the net. Basketball rules are used to cover points not mentioned herein.

FOULS: Players committing personal fouls, technical fouls, or violations found in basketball rules are retired from the game for from 1 to 5 minutes depending on the severity of the offense in the judgment of the

[1] Suggestions for the game found in an article on "Volley Basketball" by Raymond Welsh in the *Journal of Health and Physical Education*, IV (November, 1933), 50. By permission.

referee. *Substitutes may not be used* for those so removed from the game. The person fouled against takes the ball out of bounds.

SCORING: Two points are scored every time a player makes a goal. The team wins which has the higher score at the end of the playing period.

TEACHING SUGGESTIONS

1. Encourage rapid passing.
2. Encourage timid players to throw the ball over the net themselves and to shoot for goal if they are in the correct position to do so.
3. Teach the guarding techniques of intercepting a pass and guarding as the ball leaves an opponent's hands.

NINE-COURT BASKETBALL

NUMBER OF PLAYERS: 14 to 36

SPACE: Playground, gymnasium

PLAYING AREA: Court 36 by 60 feet, divided into nine small courts, each 12 by 20 feet (Figure 135). The courts are numbered from 1 to 9, beginning with the corner and proceeding clockwise, ending with the center rectangle. A basketball goal is placed in the center of each end line, with the goal nine feet from the ground. A free-throw line is drawn 15 feet from each basket.

EQUIPMENT: Junior basketball or soccer ball

Procedure

Nine-Court Basketball is a simple basketball type game which can be played by boys and girls together. A player from each team plays in each of the nine courts. Passing is the basketball skill which is emphasized because neither a dribble nor juggle may be used. For this reason players must be taught to be always on the move to receive a pass in their little square; unless they do this Nine-Court Basketball will teach the poor habit of standing to receive a pass. The skills of guarding and shooting for goals are also taught as well as familiarity with the usual fouls and violations.

FORMATION: Players are divided into two equal teams, A and B, and numbered from 1 to 9 in each team. Each player takes his position in the court corresponding to his number, so that there will be a player from each team in each rectangle (see Figure 135). The position of the rectangle determines the playing position of each player. The players in the three courts near their own basket are forwards, those near their opponents' basket are guards, those in the center rectangle (Number 9) are jumping centers, and those in the two side rectangles at the middle of the court are side centers. If there are but seven players to a team, Number 7 covers the entire center court (rectangles 8, 9, 4); if there are eight to a team, Number 8 plays in courts 8 and 9.

ROTATION: After each goal made, players rotate to the next higher position, Number 9's to Number 1 position. At the end of the first half teams change goals.

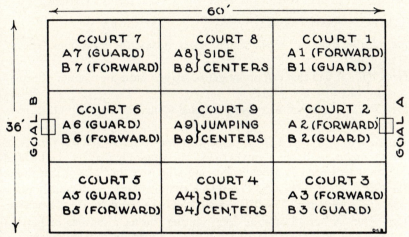

Figure 135. Court and Position of Players in Nine-Court Basketball

RULES OF PLAY: The rules for girls' basketball [1] apply with the following exceptions:

1. The ball is put in play by being tossed up between opposing centers.
2. No bouncing of the ball is allowed.
3. No juggling of the ball is allowed.
4. Only forwards in the three end rectangles may attempt to make goals.
5. When a free throw is awarded a team, a member of that team who is standing in rectangles 2 or 6 at the time of the award attempts the throw. All other players within rectangles 2 or 6 leave the rectangle and stand in rectangles 1 or 3, 5 or 7 until the ball has left the forward's hands. The forward making the free throw may not take a step over the free-throw line until the ball has left her hands. The ball is not dead after one free throw. It is dead only following a second free throw awarded for a double foul whether the ball entered or missed the goal.

[1] See p. 723, or consult *Official Basketball Guide*. Washington: National Section on Women's Athletics, American Association for Health, Physical Education and Recreation (1201 Sixteenth Street, N.W., Washington 6, D. C.).

6. If the ball travels from one end of the court to the other it must go through one of the center players. Long passes are undesirable because an opponent may get possession of the ball. Short, quick passes make for a faster game.

PERIODS OF PLAY: Four 5-minute (or 6-minute) quarters is the recommended time for contest games. There should be a 2-minute rest between quarters and a 5-minute rest period between halves. Time may be called by the official in charge of the game whenever it seems advisable.

TERMS AND RESTRICTIONS

Ball Out of Bounds: A ball which passes outside the legal boundaries of the court

Dead Ball: A ball that can no longer be played until the manner of replay is indicated by the referee

Free Throw: The act of trying for a goal while standing behind the free-throw line

Tossed Ball or Jump Ball: A ball thrown into the air by the referee at right angles to the floor and between two opposing players. To be legal it must be tossed to a height beyond which neither player can jump.

Tie Ball or Held Ball: A ball on which two players simultaneously place one or both hands. The ball is tossed up between them by the referee.

Time Out: A period of time taken during the legal periods of play in which the game may be stopped without detriment to either team

TOSSUP: The ball is put in play by a tossup between the two opposing jumping centers (1) at the beginning of each period of play, (2) after a legal goal is made, (3) after the last free throw for goal following a double foul. Each jumping center tries to tap the ball to a teammate. Neither one may touch the ball again until it has touched the ground or some other player has handled the ball. Two completed passes are required before a forward may try for a goal.

As soon as the ball has been put in play by the centers, each team tries to get possession of the ball and direct it toward the forwards of their team so that the forwards can throw for their basket.

VIOLATIONS AND FOULS: There are three types of errors carrying penalties: (1) violations, (2) technical fouls, (3) personal fouls.

1. *Violations:* Kicking the ball intentionally; holding the ball more than three seconds in court or five seconds out of bounds; striking, rolling, juggling, bouncing the ball, traveling with it, or handing the ball to another player.[1] *Penalty:* The ball is given to the opponent of the player committing the violation on the sideline nearest the spot where the violation occurs.

---

[1] Juggling and bouncing the ball are not violations in official basketball.

2. *Technical fouls:* Fouls that do not involve personal contact, such as: (a) delaying the game; (b) keeping one or both hands on ball after it has been secured by an opponent; (c) snatching or batting ball from hands of an opponent; (d) waving hands in front of eyes of player who holds the ball; (e) guarding in such a manner as to box-up an opponent. *Penalty:* Opponent is awarded a free throw for goal. Five technical fouls automatically disqualify a player and he must leave the game.

3. *Personal fouls:* Fouls in which personal contacts occur, such as obstructing, blocking, charging, holding, tagging, or tripping an opponent, or making personal contact with or pushing an opponent. *Penalty:* (a) If a forward is fouled while throwing for a goal and the goal is successful, one free throw is awarded; if unsuccessful, two free throws are awarded; (b) if a center is fouled against, a forward takes the free throw. Personal fouls which are intentional may disqualify a player immediately, and four personal fouls automatically remove him from the game. A combination of five technical and personal fouls puts a player out of the game.

TOSSED BALL: The ball is tossed between two opponents when:

1. A tie-ball occurs.

2. A double violation occurs. The ball is brought three feet into the court opposite the spot where the violation occurred and is tossed between two opponents selected by the official in charge.

3. When the ball lodges on the supports holding the goal. The ball is put in play at the free-throw line between two players in rectangle 2 or 6.

4. When a spectator interferes with the progress of the ball. The ball is put in play between two opponents three feet in from the boundary line where interference occurred.

5. When the official is in doubt as to who last touched the ball before it went out of bounds. A tossup is taken three feet inside the side line opposite the point where the ball went out of bounds.

6. When the official is in doubt about an out-of-bounds ball over the end lines and under a basket, or when the need for a tossup occurs under a basket. The ball for the tossup is taken to the free-throw line or at a point paralleling the free-throw line.

TOSSUP LIMITATIONS: There are certain things players may not do while taking the tossup:

1. Players may not tap ball until it has begun its descent

2. Players may not catch the ball as it descends

3. Players may not, after tapping the ball, play the ball again until it has touched the floor or has been handled by another player.

Penalty: The ball is given to an opponent for an out-of-bounds play over the side line at the approximate spot where the ball was when the whistle was blown. In case of a simultaneous violation by a member of each team, the ball is tossed up between opponents who were nearest the ball when the foul occurred.

LINE VIOLATION: Players may not touch with any part of the body the floor or ground beyond the dividing lines of the rectangles in which they are playing nor beyond the outside boundary lines of the court. Players may reach over division lines to pick up or receive the ball. Players are not penalized if they step on a dividing line and immediately remove the foot from the line. If the foot remains on or over the line a violation occurs.

Penalty: An out-of-bounds play is awarded to a member of the team not making the violation, on the side line opposite the point where the violation occurred.

FREE THROW: The following are violations if committed during a free throw:
  1. Crossing the free-throw line before the ball has left the player's hands
  2. Entering the free-throw area of rectangles 2 and 6 before the ball has left the hands of the forward making the free throw
  3. Interfering with the shooting of the ball
  4. Attempting to disconcert the thrower

Penalty: (a) If a forward makes the violation and the goal is made it does not count and the ball is given to a guard out of bounds at the side line. (b) If a guard makes the violation and the goal is made it counts and the ball is awarded to a forward out of bounds at the side line. (c) If a double violation is made by members of opposite teams, the goal, if made, does not count and the ball is put in play by a tossup at the free-throw line between a forward and an opponent.

ILLEGAL GOAL: The following are illegal attempts for goal:
  1. Trying for goal from an out-of-bounds play
  2. Trying for goal while playing position of guard, side center, or jumping center
  3. Trying for goal when ball is dead. *Penalty:* The goal, if made, does not count and the ball is given to an opponent out of bounds. If the goal is not made, the ball is still in play.
  4. Trying for goal before two completed passes have been made following a tossed ball at the center. *Penalty:* Whether goal is made or missed the ball is awarded to an opponent out of bounds.

VIOLATIONS OR OUT-OF-BOUNDS PLAYS: The following are violations for which an out-of-bounds play is taken:
  1. Causing ball to go out of bounds

2. Advancing into court carrying the ball
3. Touching the ball after putting it in play from an out-of-bounds play until it is touched or played by another player
4. Holding the ball more than five seconds in an out-of-bounds play
5. Failure to return into court at the point where the ball was thrown into court.

Penalty: The ball goes to an opponent and an out-of-bounds play is made at the point opposite where the violation occurred. If members of both teams violate this rule simultaneously, the ball is tossed up between two opponents at a spot three feet inside the court nearest to the spot where the violation occurred.

SCORING: Each successful field goal thrown by a forward in rectangle 1, 2, 3, 5, 6, or 7 counts 2 points. Each successful goal thrown from the free-throw line counts 1 point. The team wins which scores more points during the total playing time. A tie score stands.

OFFICIALS: [1] For match games there should be the following officials: referee, umpire, two timekeepers, two scorers.
Referee: The referee, who is in charge of the game, has the following duties:

1. To put the ball in play at the center of the court
2. To announce penalties for fouls or violations committed
3. To watch players on free-throw lane and at free-throw line during free-throw plays
4. To disqualify players for committing more than permitted fouls or violations
5. To announce goal made, by whistle and arm signal
6. To announce score at end of each quarter
7. To sign scorebook at end of the games

Umpire: The umpire assists the referee. He watches that part of the court to which the ball is going. He watches the players rather than the ball. He has the following specific duties:

1. To help the scorers by announcing the type of foul committed
2. To call fouls which the referee cannot see, especially blocking, tagging, and holding
3. To watch for out-of-bounds balls and to toss the ball between players who are near him if the offender is not known
4. To call line violations
5. To recognize substitutes and get them into the game
6. To toss the ball after tie-ball

---

[1] See *Official Basketball Rules, op. cit.*

Scorers: Working together, the scorers keep a record of goals made and fouls committed.

Timekeepers: The two timekeepers have control of time-out periods, give signals for starting and terminating the quarters and halves and for completion of the game.

TEACHING SUGGESTIONS

1. Teach players to keep their eyes on the ball.
2. Teach players to guard without touching an opponent.
3. Practice for skill in starting and stopping, pivoting, jumping, goal shooting and passing. See basketball techniques, page 727.
4. Teach players to move to receive the ball from a pass, so that a fast passing, fast-moving game results.
5. Use lead-up games for this and previous grades before teaching Nine-Court Basketball.

NIP NOP [1]

NUMBER OF PLAYERS: 2

SPACE: Surfaced playground area, gymnasium, auditorium, playroom

PLAYING AREA: Court 6 1/3 by 12 feet, divided into two courts by a net or center board ten inches high

EQUIPMENT: For each player (1) a table tennis paddle, or battledore; [2] (2) celluloid ball or table tennis ball

FORMATION: A player at each end of the court. Neither player may at any time step within the court.

PROCEDURE: The rules of Table Tennis are followed. See page 789.

Service: In order to decide who is to start the game, either player serves the ball and both play until one or the other wins the point. That player starts the game. To be a fair service the ball must be struck into the near court so that it will bounce over the net into the far court before being struck by the receiver. The service changes from one side to the other at every 2 points. A service which hits the top of the net and goes over into the proper court is a "let" service and the ball is served again. Following the service, play continues until one or the other player misses the ball or knocks it out of bounds.

Fouls: A player is not permitted to have any part of his body or his paddle touch a line or the ground inside his court. *Penalty:* Loss of point or service.

---

[1] Adapted from article by Ray B. Singer in the *Journal of Health and Physical Education,* XI (May, 1940), 314-15. By permission.
[2] See directions for constructing paddles, p. 115.

Scoring: A point is gained each time an opponent makes a mistake. Game: 11, 15, or 21 points. Deuce game: 10-all, 14-all, or 20-all. To win a deuce game one player must make two points in succession. A match consists of two out of three games. When playing a match the loser of the preceding game serves first.

TEACHING SUGGESTIONS

1. Teach forehand and backhand table tennis or paddle tennis strokes.
2. Point out that the hand-eye co-ordination is not as difficult as that for table tennis, but the same game elements are provided.

PADDLE TENNIS

Number of Players: 2-4

Space: Playground, gymnasium

Playing Area: Court 18 by 39 feet, divided at the center by a net. (Figure 136.) See directions for laying out a court, page 96.

If possible, use cement or asphalt surface larger than actual size of court; if this is impracticable, the dirt surface should be leveled at the edges of the court. One official tennis court will permit the laying out of four paddle tennis courts if put crosswise, thereby accommodating 16 players instead of four.

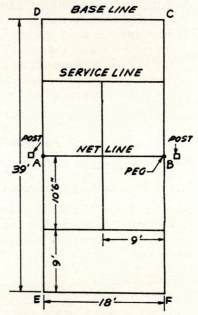

Figure 136. Paddle Tennis Court

For elementary school pupils the top of the net should be 2 feet 4 inches from the ground near the posts and not less than 2 feet 2 inches at the center. For older pupils and adults the height should be 2 feet 9 inches and 2 feet 6 inches. The use of commercial posts and ratchets to control the height of the net is recommended. In the absence of an official net, chicken wire may be used, the top being bound with heavy durable material to save balls from being damaged by the wire. Gunny sacks sewn together, or rope, with white strips of cloth tied to it at intervals along its length, are usable substitutes for an official tennis net.

EQUIPMENT: (1) Two or more sponge rubber balls about 2½ inches in diameter; or dead tennis balls; (2) wooden paddles, either official paddle tennis paddles [1] or homemade ones. See construction directions, page 115.

FORMATION: When two persons play, the official game area for each is between the long inner side lines and the base lines of the court. When three persons play, the partners play inside the entire court up to the net, and the third person plays between the long inner side lines up to the net. When four persons play, the entire court is used, the long inner side lines being ignored except during service.

PROCEDURE: The playing rules for both age groups are the same as for lawn tennis (see page 911), with the exception that advanced players are permitted but one serve. If the serve is a fault, the server loses that point. The rule for foot faults should be rigidly enforced. A bounce serve could be substituted for the official overhead service, if the overhead service proves too advanced for eleven-year-olds.

TEACHING SUGGESTIONS

1. Encourage big arm sweeps. Insist that elbow must not remain close to the body. Strokes should be made with extended arm. See: Skills Developed Through Intermediate Grade Activities, pages 320-21.

2. If during service, before the ball is contacted, a player permits a foot to touch the base line or the foot passes over the base line into the court, whether in the air or on the ground, point out that a foot fault occurs and the server loses the point. This bad habit is a serious one to acquire and will be disastrous during tournament play as the server will lose the point even if point is earned. Therefore instruct those keeping score to watch for and call all foot faults.

PRISONERS' BASE [2]

NUMBER OF PLAYERS: 6-40

SPACE: Playground, gymnasium, auditorium

PLAYING AREA: Agreed-upon boundaries, with a line dividing the area into two equal parts. The end lines serve as restraining lines. At each end designate definite prison areas which in size are not more than 4 by 4 feet.

---

[1] Official rules designate junior and senior courts. For junior players (under 16 years of age), paddles should not be more than 15 inches in length, and on a senior court paddles should not be more than 17 inches long.

[2] Additional forms of Prisoners' Base are to be found in Jessie Bancroft, *Games*. New York: The Macmillan Co., 1937.

FORMATION: Two teams are scattered along the center line in their own half of the playing area.

PROCEDURE: Players try to run through the opponents' territory in order to enter the opponents' prison or in order to rescue a teammate who may be in the prison. As players are tagged they must go to the prison of the tagger.

A tired runner may rest in safety behind an opponent's end restraining line but once he returns across the line he may not recross it; neither may he enter the prison area or rescue a teammate until he has returned to his own territory. He may be tagged while trying to reach his own playing area. Members of each team guard their own prison. A rescuer may take only one prisoner with him. Both may be tagged while returning to their own area. Prisoners are not permitted to make a chain in order to approach an oncoming runner. They may not step outside the prison area.

The team wins (1) which first makes prisoners of all the opponents or (2) when an untagged runner enters the opponents' prison while it is free of prisoners.

TEACHING SUGGESTIONS

1. Allow players who enter the enemy's territory to return to their own territory as often as they can accomplish it without being tagged.
2. Encourage players to be venturesome.

PUNT BACK

NUMBER OF PLAYERS: 4-12

SPACE: Playground

PLAYING AREA: Two goal lines not less than 200 feet apart

EQUIPMENT: One or more soccer balls or junior size footballs

FORMATION: Players are divided into two teams. The ball is given to a member of a team who stands on his own goal line; the rest of the players of that team are scattered between the two ends of the goal lines and onside (which means players must be on a line with or behind their own kicker). The game may be played in two halves with definite time limits.

PROCEDURE: The object of the game is for players by punting the ball to get close to the opponents' goal line, and then by drop-kicking over that line to score points.

The player having the ball punts it toward his opponents' goal line. (Punting is kicking the dropped ball just before it touches the ground, using the instep or top of the foot.) Any field player on the opposing team may secure the ball. The player endeavoring to secure the ball may not be interfered with by any other player. The player who secures the ball kicks it from the point where he gained possession of it, the other members of his team coming to the onside position.

A player who catches the ball on the fly is allowed to advance three steps before attempting to kick the ball; a player who catches the ball while "marking" it (which means he has extended one foot and placed the heel on the ground) is allowed five steps before attempting to kick the ball.

If the ball is not caught on the fly it is punted from the place where it is first touched by a player, or where the ball rests when recovered, providing the resting place is between the goal lines. If secured out of bounds, the ball is brought to the side line and is played from there by the person who secured it.

In order to earn a point a player must drop-kick the ball over the goal line at a height at least equal to the height of the tallest player. To drop-kick the ball, the player drops the ball and kicks it as it bounces on the ground.

Fouls: Any player who contacts another player while the latter is attempting to catch the ball commits a foul. *Penalty:* Three yards from spot of collision or spot of touch, whichever is the most severe.

SCORING: Each ball drop-kicked over the goal line counts 1 point. The team wins which has more points at the end of the playing period.

TEACHING SUGGESTIONS

1. Review the skills of punting and drop-kicking before playing this game. See pages 798-99 for teaching suggestions.
2. If two soccer balls or footballs are used, have a player from each team begin the play simultaneously, each standing on his own goal line.

SOCCER KICK BALL [1]

NUMBER OF PLAYERS: 10-30

SPACE: Playground, gymnasium

PLAYING AREA: Area 36 by about 60 feet, depending on the space available (see Figure 137). A semicircle 12 feet in radius is marked at one end of the field and a goal line 12 feet long is marked within the half circle area. A post is placed at a corner of the field at the end opposite the semicircle.

EQUIPMENT: (1) A soccer ball, either of rubber or leather; (2) a post, chair, or stool; (3) goal line ends designated by jumping standards, chairs, stones, Indian clubs, or baseball bases.

---

[1] Game contributed by George Ormsby, Consultant in Audio-Visual Education, California State Department of Education.

Procedure

The game is played between two teams who alternate as kickers and fielders. The object is for the members of the kicking team, in succession, to kick the ball from the goal line and then to run down the field, around the post, and back to the goal line before the fielding team can put them out.

PLAYING PERIOD: The game is played in any number of innings agreed upon. An inning is completed when all members of both teams have run.

FORMATION: Team O (kicking team) stands behind the goal line; Team X (fielding team) is scattered about the field outside of the half circle.

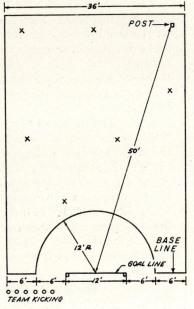

Figure 137. Area for Soccer Kick Ball

Runners: Team O members in turn place the ball on the goal line and kick it into the playing field. They run forward around the post, and in returning try to cross the goal line between the end markers before the ball can be kicked over the goal line by the fielders.

Fielders: Using only their feet, fielders try to advance the ball by short passes toward the semicircle, and while outside the semicircle endeavor to kick the ball over the goal line. If the ball stops inside the semicircle, a fielder must enter, kick the ball out to another fielder, and immediately leave the semicircle. A goal kick must not be attempted until the fielder has left the semi-circle.

FOULS: The following fouls committed by a fielder give the running team 1 point:

1. Touching the ball with the arms or hands. If this happens, fielder must raise an arm and call loudly, "Safe." This signifies that the runner's team is to be credited with the point. The runner continues his run and may or may not complete it.
2. Being inside the half circle when the ball is kicked into the field from the goal line
3. Being inside the circle when a teammate attempts to kick the ball

OUTS: Kickers are out under the following circumstances:
1. If they fail to cross between the ends of the goal line before the ball crosses it
2. If they fail to include the post in their run

SCORING: Each successful run scores 2 points. If the ball is kicked over the base line of the court but outside the goal line area by the fielders, the runner's team is credited with 1 point.

The runner's team is credited with 1 point if a fielder commits a foul.

The team which has more points at the end of the agreed upon number of innings wins.

TEACHING SUGGESTIONS

1. Point out that Soccer Kick Ball, besides being a good game in itself, is an introduction to soccer techniques.
2. Make this game as elementary or as advanced as the ability of the group indicates.
3. If the ball is kicked far afield, have the player who recovers it run with it to the boundary of the field and kick it in from there to a fielder of his team.
4. Establish the distance of the post from the goal line depending on the ability of the team in the field to return the ball.
5. Decrease the length of the goal line and increase the radius of the semicircle as the ability of the players increases.
6. Adapt this game to large or small numbers, and to large or small areas.
7. When played in a gymnasium, use a somewhat deflated soccer ball.
8. If the group is skilled in soccer, make the game more challenging by having a goalkeeper from the kicking team whose duty it will be to prevent fielders from kicking the ball over the goal line and thus to assist the runner to get home.

SUCTION-CUP DART BASEBALL [1]

NUMBER OF PLAYERS: 2-18

SPACE: Playground, auditorium, classroom, hallway

PLAYING AREA: A pitching line 15 to 20 feet from a dart board

EQUIPMENT: (1) A dart board 3 feet square constructed as in Figure 138, painted as in Figure 139, and lettered as in Figure 140. Any smooth, hard-surfaced, glossy fiberboard may be used. Quarter-inch plywood is usable but needs much attention, as it tends to crack and must be shellacked often. The diagram of the game is painted with enamel. When sufficiently dry a coat of varnish should be applied. If plywood is used several coats of shellac should be applied before painting the diagram. The recommended

---

[1] Contributed by Albert A. Pilvelis, Director of Health and Physical Education, Public Schools of New Haven, Connecticut.

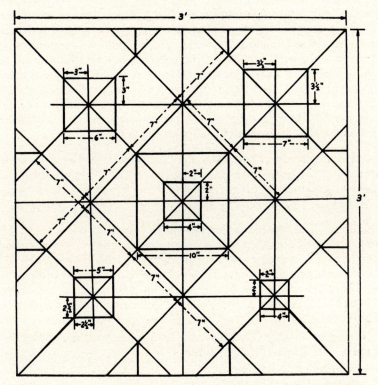

Figure 138.   Construction of Board for Suction-Cup Dart Baseball

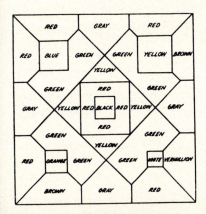

Figure 139.   Chart for Painting Suction-Cup Dart Baseball Board

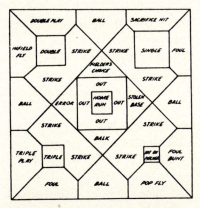

Figure 140.   Chart for Lettering of Suction-Cup Dart Baseball Board

colors are red, yellow, blue, white, and black. The additional colors needed may be obtained by mixing colors as follows: gray (black and white); brown (black and yellow and red); green (yellow, blue, and white); vermilion (two parts of red, one of yellow); orange (yellow and red). Scoring directions should be lettered in after spaces have been colored. The board should be hung or placed with a slight backward slant to compensate for the arc taken by the darts during their flight. (2) Three to six suction-cup darts made of wood about six inches long with feathers at one end and a 1¼-inch rubber suction cup at the other.

FORMATION: Players choose sides and take turns at pitching the suction-cup darts at the board, one side being the "batting" team until it makes three outs, and then the other side being at bat. There may be any number of innings.

PROCEDURE: The first player pitches until a play or an out is made. Three outs are allowed one team before teams exchange sides. A dart failing to hit the board counts as an out. A dart failing to stick long enough for an account of the pitch scores as an out. The play is made according to the spot where the greater part of the dart lands. If the dart is equally divided between two areas, the heaviest penalty counts; that is, if the dart lands equally between the "ball" and "strike" areas, the pitch counts as a strike.

The rules of baseball apply, and the play is made according to the area in which the dart lands, as follows:

Home Run—a run is scored

Out—batter is out

Error—batter is safe at first

Stolen Base—all base runners advance one base; batter continues throwing

Sacrifice Hit—batter is out; base runners advance one base

Hit by Pitcher—batter takes first base

Pop Fly—batter is out

Ball—four balls entitle batter to take first base

Foul—except on last strike counts as a strike

Triple Play—three outs are scored. It is necessary to have two men on base to score a triple play. If only one man is on base, two outs are scored.

Double Play—two outs are scored

Single—batter takes one base

Double—batter takes two bases

Triple—batter takes three bases

Foul Bunt—on third strike batter is out

Strike—three strikes make an out

Infield Fly—batter is out; base runners cannot advance

Fielder's Choice—if there are no runners on base batter is out. If there are runners on base, captain of team not batting decides on play. For example, if there is a runner on first base, captain would declare runner on first base running to second base out, and the batter safe on first base. Or, if all bases are occupied captain would declare runner on third base running home out, thereby preventing a score against his team.

SCORING: As in baseball, a home run scores a point for the batting team.

TEACHING SUGGESTIONS

1. Choose an umpire and let his decisions be final.
2. Show that this is not only a quiet social game for home and school but also a good means of teaching softball and baseball rules and strategy.

SWING SWAT [1]

NUMBER OF PLAYERS: 2

SPACE: Playground, gymnasium, playroom, auditorium

PLAYING AREA: Court 6 1/3 by 12 feet, with a net across the center. On each side of the net and 18 inches from it, parallel lines. The area inside these lines is neutral territory. Starting with these lines, each court is divided lengthwise into two sections.

EQUIPMENT: (1) For each player a paddle, either a paddle tennis paddle or battledore; [2] (2) net, its top three feet from the ground; (3) shuttlecocks or badminton birds

FORMATION: A player stands at each end of the court, *outside* the boundary lines.

PROCEDURE: The game is played much as is badminton. Only upward or sideward strokes are permissible.

Service: One player serves by holding the bird by the feathers with the rubber tip toward the floor, and hitting with an upward stroke of the paddle. Service is first to the right court and then into the left, changing from one side to the other every two points.

The Rally: After the service, the bird is sent back and forth across the net until a player fails to make a legal return. Server loses his serve when he makes a mistake; a point is scored for the server when the receiver makes a mistake. A line bird is good. A bird which enters the neutral area counts against the player who last touched it. No downward stroke is permitted; hence the hand must at all times be higher than the blade of the paddle.

---

[1] Adapted from an article by Ray B. Singer in *Journal of Health and Physical Education,* XI (May, 1940), 315. By permission.
[2] See construction of paddle, p. 115.

Fouls: The following fouls result in loss of point when committed by the receiver, and loss of service when committed by the server:
1. Stepping on the line or into the court during play
2. Touching the paddle or any part of player's body to the floor within the court during play
3. Using a downward stroke

SCORING: A point is scored by the serving player when the opponent makes an error or foul. A game is 11, 15, or 21 points, as agreed upon.

TEACHING SUGGESTIONS

1. Use this game in preparing for the game of badminton.
2. See Nip Nop, a similar game, p. 668.

THREE-MAN BASKETBALL [1]

NUMBER OF PLAYERS: 6

SPACE: Playground, gymnasium

PLAYING AREA: One half of a basketball court

EQUIPMENT: (1) Basketball backstop and goal; (2) basketball, soccer ball, volleyball or utility ball

FORMATION: Players are divided into two teams of three players each; a forward, a center, and a guard. Each team attempts to score points while using the same goal.

PROCEDURE: The rules of basketball govern the game, with exceptions noted below. The game begins with a jump at the center, the jumpers (centers) facing the side lines.

Centers and guards attempt to send the ball to their forward. When the ball is advanced for a scoring play, and an opponent secures the ball from the backboard before a successful play can be completed, the opponent may attempt to score immediately. (If greater skill in passing is desired, the rule may be that the opponent securing the ball must pass to a teammate before a scoring play may be attempted.) When a successful play is completed, an opponent takes the ball immediately out of bounds at the end of the half court opposite the goal and play is resumed.

Fouls: When a player is fouled, instead of being awarded a free throw, he puts the ball in play at the nearest out-of-bounds region. For a personal foul, two free throws may be awarded or the player may be removed from the game, his team continuing to play without a substitute.

[1] Adapted from article by Harold J. Weekley, *Journal of Health and Physical Education*, X (December, 1939), 593, 594. By permission.

SCORING: One point is earned for each successful goal. The game may be played for points or for a time period. If played for points, a game is 40 points. If played in time periods, four 6-minute quarters are played.

TEACHING SUGGESTIONS

1. Use 8- or 9-foot goals and a light ball for smaller boys and girls.
2. Present goal shooting and passing techniques to the class before the game is played.
3. Use in schools having small enrollments or schools having only one basketball backstop and goal.

TWO OLD CAT

NUMBER OF PLAYERS: 4-12

SPACE: Playground, gymnasium

PLAYING AREA: Open area with two bases placed 35 feet apart

EQUIPMENT: (1) One or more 12- or 14-inch softballs; (2) two or more softball bats; (3) two softball bases. Gunny sacks, or squares of linoleum or wood may be used for bases.

Procedure

The object of the game is for each batter to remain at bat and make as many runs between bases as possible before being retired.

FORMATION: One batter and one pitcher-catcher [1] stand at each base. The remaining players are fielders and are scattered about the playing area. Each player keeps his own score.

Pitcher-Catcher: The ball is thrown back and forth between the players back of each base. When a player pitches he is the pitcher; when he catches behind a base, he is a catcher. An overhand or underhand throw is used, as agreed upon before the beginning of the game. When a pitcher throws four balls to a batter, both batters, without interference, exchange bases, the one fouled against earning half a point. To put a runner out a pitcher-catcher must have a ball in his hand and a foot in contact with his base before the advancing runner reaches the base.

Batter: As the ball is pitched in his direction each batter tries to strike a fair ball. If successful, both runners, carrying the bats with them, run to exchange bases.

Fielders: Each fielder tries to catch fly balls or return ground balls to the nearest pitcher-catcher since either base runner can be put out.

---

[1] At each base a player both pitches and receives the pitch from the player at the opposite base.

FAIR BALL: A ball is fair that strikes the ground or is caught by a fielder or pitcher-catcher within the area between the bases or beyond the base farthest from the batter who contacted the ball.

FOUL BALL: A ball is foul which, when struck, falls behind the batter or the goal where he stands. The first two foul balls count as strikes.

OUTS: A batter is out after the following plays:
1. When a fly ball is caught by a fielder or pitcher-catcher
2. When a third foul is caught
3. When a first or second foul ball, sent higher than the head of the batter, is caught by the pitcher-catcher
4. When 3 strikes are called against a batter
5. When a batter, while running between bases, is tagged with the ball while it is held in the hand of a fielder or pitcher-catcher.
6. When a pitcher-catcher, while holding the ball, is able to place a foot on a base previous to the arrival of the batter

EXCHANGE OF PLAYER POSITIONS: When a fair fly ball is caught, the batter who struck the ball and the player who caught the ball exchange positions on the field. Each other player continues to hold the same position he held before the fly was caught.

ADVANCEMENT OF PLAYERS: Fielders advance in the following order:
1. Fielders, in sequence, to pitcher-catcher positions
2. Pitcher-catcher to batter positions
3. Previous batters to fielding positions

SCORING: Each batter earns 1 point whenever he succeeds, after a fair hit, in reaching the opposite base. Each is given one-half point when four balls are called on the catcher-pitcher serving him. The player wins the game who makes the most points during the period of play.

TEACHING SUGGESTIONS

1. Insist that the batters carry their bats with them when running bases.
2. Have additional balls available to speed up the game.
3. Use Two Old Cat to teach batting, fielding, and accurate throwing to many at the same time.

WHOOPLA BALL [1]

NUMBER OF PLAYERS: 10-40

SPACE: Playground, gymnasium

PLAYING AREA: The field may be of any size, depending upon the age of the players. It should be rectangular in shape with side lines and end

---

[1] Game supplied by L. R. Stewart, Saticoy, California.

lines marked. A speed ball field is suitable for upper grade players. One end line is known as the home base; the other as the far base line.

EQUIPMENT: Volleyball, utility ball, or softball and bat

Procedure

The object of the game is for team members to score as many runs as possible between the home and far base lines and back to home again. The game is played with an agreed upon time period. The batter may throw the ball into the air and hit it with his hand, or a pitcher may throw the ball toward the batter, who tries to hit it. If a softball is used, it is struck with the bat. Teams may elect in which manner the game is to be played.

FORMATION: Players are divided into two teams. A pitcher and a catcher are chosen for each team. One team is at bat, the other team is in the field. Fielding team members do not have to stay within the boundaries of the field. They play wherever there is the likelihood of a ball being struck. Members of the batting team, while running, have to remain within the side boundaries of the field of play.

RULES OF PLAY: All balls hit in a forward direction are fair. A ball which, when struck, goes behind the batter is a foul ball. The first two foul balls count as strikes. A foul ball caught retires the batter. There are no walks allowed as in softball.

OUTS: A player is out as a result of the following plays: (1) on three strikes; (2) when a foul ball is caught; (3) on being tagged with a ball held in the hand of the catcher, pitcher, or a fielder; (4) on being tagged by a fielder when standing off the base line or home line while waiting a chance to run; (5) when he steps on or over a side line during a run.

Three outs change the team at bat.

BATTING ORDER: There is no precise batting order for either team. Players at the far base, knowing when their turn at bat is to occur, should make an effort to get across the home base line before their turn at bat arrives again, otherwise the next batter in line takes the turn.

BATTER: A batter has two choices after successfully hitting the ball. He may (1) attempt a run, or (2) delay his run by lining up on the home base line beyond the batting position and wait there in the hope that a future batter of his team may make a longer hit than he made. The batter so deciding may not return to bat until his run is attempted. Once a batter starts his run no turning back is permitted. Because of this privilege several previous batters may be lined up waiting for an advantageous hit before running to the far base line. The batter, as a runner, must remain within the limits of the side boundary lines.

RUNNER: A runner may dodge or double back and forth as he sees fit, to escape being tagged, but he may not return to the base that he left. He may not step on or over the side boundary lines; to do so puts him out.

If a runner reaches the far base line he may (1) return immediately, or (2) wait there until some one at bat hits a fair ball, whereupon he may attempt the completion of his run. More than one runner may be on the far base line waiting to return home. Several runners may be in action at the same time.

FIELDLRS: The duties of the fielders, the catcher, and the pitcher are to catch foul and fly balls and to tag out runners while holding the ball in the hand. A member of the fielding team may (1) tag out any player caught off the base lines, or (2) tag as many runners as he can, or (3) throw the ball to another fielder nearer a runner than he is.

A fast runner should be stationed near the far base line. Hit balls, when retrieved, should be thrown to him if a runner or runners are attempting to reach home base line.

RETIREMENT OF BATTING TEAM: Three methods of retiring the batting team are possible: (1) When a third foul strike is caught; (2) when three outs occur; (3) when a fair fly ball is caught.

Fair Fly Catch: When a fair fly is caught the ball is placed immediately on the ground at the spot where the fielder caught it and all *fielders* dash to cross the home base line before a member of the batting team can run out and secure the ball. Thereafter the player of the batting team who secures the ball tries to tag one fielder with the ball before all the fielders succeed in crossing the home base line. If fielders cross successfully that team becomes the batting team *immediately*, regardless of how "outs" stand for the team at bat. If one fielder is tagged the teams remain as they were.

When a fair fly ball is caught and a fielder is tagged before all members of his team can cross the home base line, the runs made by the batting team returning home score points.

If the fielding team succeeds in exchanging places with the batting team, any runs made by members of the latter team during the fielders' run do not score points. Previous runs do score.

SCORING: One point is scored for each successful round trip to the far base line and home. The team wins which has the higher score at the end of the agreed upon time period.

TEACHING SUGGESTIONS

1. Make special ground rules if the playing field is not very good. For example: Over the fence is out.
2. Try having the players toss and bat their own balls without using a pitcher and catcher.

3. When a volleyball is used, strike it with the heel of the open hand or partially closed hand as in volleyball. In lower grades a utility ball could be hit with a bat to teach batting an object larger than a softball.

ZONE DODGE BALL [1]

NUMBER OF PLAYERS: 6-10

SPACE: Playground, gymnasium, playroom

PLAYING AREA: A field divided into two equal areas, each one having an end zone four feet wide. See diagram 99 (End Zone Soccer). For large numbers of players basketball or volleyball courts may be used by adding the end zones.

EQUIPMENT: Volleyball or soccer ball, utility ball or beanbag

Procedure

The object of the game is for a team to gain possession of the ball and to throw it at a member of the opposing team. Players so struck retire to an end zone. The team wins which has the fewer players sent to the end zone.

FORMATION: Players are divided into two equal teams; each team occupies one of the two center areas. Each team selects one player to occupy the end zone farthest from its own center area and a player to be jumping center.

RULES OF PLAY: The game is started by a tossup between the jumping centers. Each center faces his own team, while standing in the opponents' court. When the jump is finished each returns to his own court. If a jumper succeeds in tapping the ball and a member of his team secures the ball on the fly, from a bounce, or while it is rolling, that member throws the ball to hit a player of the opponent team. A player is considered to be legally struck by a ball (1) if he is struck by a fly ball thrown by an opponent, or (2) if he catches a fly ball instead of dodging it. A player is not legally hit if a rolling or bouncing ball touches him. The ball may be passed not more than three times between players of a team before a throw at an opponent is attempted, or the ball may be passed between end zone players and their court players as needed in an effort to contact an opponent player.

End Zone: A player legally hit by a ball leaves his center area immediately by passing over a side line. He then goes to his team's end zone and continues to play within that zone. Only one player at a time may be retired from a center to an end zone. The ball may not be handled by

---

[1] By permission of Miss Amy Howland, Director of Physical Education, public schools of Mt. Vernon, New York.

members of a team whose territory the ball enters until the ball has contacted the floor or the body of a player.

A player in the end zone may secure the ball by catching it on the fly, from a bounce, or while the ball is rolling. He then attempts to hit a player on the opposing team in the area directly in front of the end zone which he occupies. If a zone player is contacting any line of his zone area when he gets the ball, he is not permitted to throw at a player in front of him but must give the ball to a member of that team.

FOULS: Players are not permitted to run with the ball, or to step forward over the center line, backward into an end zone, or over a side boundary line. An end zone player may not step into a center playing area. *Penalty:* The ball is given to an opponent when a foul occurs; play continues.

BALL OUT OF BOUNDS: When the ball leaves the playing field by passing over the zone end lines or the side lines, the player nearest to the ball runs to secure it. When within throwing distance, the player throws the ball to a player within the playing area who is nearest to the spot where the ball left the field of play. Following the throw, the player returns immediately to his playing position.

SCORING: When time is called the team which has the fewer players in its end zone wins the game.

TEACHING SUGGESTIONS

1. After skill is gained, increase the fun by adding a second ball.
2. Depending on the size of the available space, use any number of players on teams.
3. Point out that the advantage of this game is that players are not eliminated from the game when legally hit by a ball.
4. Encourage timid or less skilled players to attempt to throw the ball themselves at opponent players.

Relays

BLACKBOARD RELAY

NUMBER OF PLAYERS: 6-40

SPACE: Classroom

EQUIPMENT: A piece of chalk placed on the front desk of each row used

PROCEDURE: The players are numbered from the front to the rear in each row. At a signal, each Number 1 player runs to the blackboard, makes a mark, returns and sits in his seat, and then hands the chalk to the player behind him. That player runs. This continues until the last player makes his mark, returns to his seat, and after being seated holds the chalk high in the air with both hands. The row to finish first wins.

TEACHING SUGGESTIONS

1. Do not permit the runner to hand the chalk to the next player before he is seated, since the aisle must be clear for the new runner.
2. Insist that all feet be kept under the desks.
3. Require players to make a cross, a capital letter, question mark, or write a word.
4. Organize the group so that there will be an equal number of players seated in each row. When necessary appoint a player to run twice for a team, but his two runs should not be consecutive.

CAP TRANSFER RELAY

NUMBER OF PLAYERS: 8-40

SPACE: Playground, playroom, gymnasium

PLAYING AREA: Two parallel lines 30 feet apart

EQUIPMENT: (1) For each file of players a cap or a 6 by 6 inch square of cloth. (2) For each file three sticks not more than 12 inches long with rounded ends. Broom handles may be cut in suitable lengths.

FORMATION: Players line up in files, not more than six players to a file. The players in each file are numbered beginning with the first player. A stick is given to the first three players in each file. Number 1 of each file takes his position beyond the far line and opposite his file. Number 2 player of each file is given a cap which he places on the end of his stick.

PROCEDURE: On signal, Number 2 runs forward, transfers his cap to the stick of Number 1 player, and takes Number 1's place. Number 1 runs across, transfers the cap to the stick of Number 3, gives his stick to Number 4 and then retires to the end of his file.

Number 3 runs forward, transfers the cap to the stick of Number 2, and takes Number 2's place. Game continues until all have transferred the cap. The first team to finish wins.

TEACHING SUGGESTIONS

1. See that the runners remain outside the two lines when receiving the caps.
2. If a cap is dropped to the ground have the runner stop and put it on the end of a stick without any assistance from the hands.

CIRCLE PASS BALL RELAY

NUMBER OF PLAYERS: 10-40

SPACE: Playground, playroom, auditorium, gymnasium

EQUIPMENT: For each circle of players a ball, knotted towel, beanbag, dumbbell, or stick of wood. Objects to be used should be the same size.

FORMATION: Two or more circles formed by equal numbers of players. Each circle plays independently. A captain is selected for each group. A ball is given to each captain.

PROCEDURE: Players agree upon the number of trips the balls are to take. On a signal, each captain passes the ball to the player on his right, who passes it to the right around the circle. When the ball is returned to the captain he calls loudly "One," signifying that one trip has been made. The second time he calls out "Two." The game continues until the agreed number of trips are accomplished by one team and that team wins.

TEACHING SUGGESTIONS

1. Have the players stand 10 to 12 feet apart.
2. If a player misses the ball, have him secure it, return to his position in the circle, and then proceed to pass the ball.
3. Have the players vary the game by one of the following:
   (a) Changing the direction taken by the balls
   (b) Passing the ball with the right or the left hand
   (c) Passing the ball by rolling it on the floor
   (d) Bouncing the ball between players

EGGSHELL RELAY

NUMBER OF PLAYERS: 6-40

SPACE: Gymnasium, auditorium, classroom

PLAYING AREA: Two restraining lines, A and B, eight feet apart. On line B, about four feet apart, place Indian clubs, bottles, or tin cans, one for each team.

EQUIPMENT: (1) Six or more eggshells with contents blown out. Eggshells are placed on line A, opposite the Indian clubs. (2) Fans made of stiff pieces of cardboard, 8 by 11 inches or smaller, or pie pans.

FORMATION: Players are divided into teams of equal size, not more than than six to a team. They line up behind the eggshells and the leader of each team has a fan.

PROCEDURE: On a signal the leader of each team must, by fanning his shell and without touching it, drive it across line B, around the Indian

club, and home again across line A. The player who finishes first earns
a point for his team. The second player in each line takes the fan and
repeats the race. Touching the eggshell with the fan disqualifies the
player from further competition in that game. The team which wins the
most points wins.

TEACHING SUGGESTIONS

1. Use this relay as an amusing stunt night event.
2. Stress carefulness, as this game is quickly ruined if contestants break
   the shells by careless play or excessive enthusiasm.

IN-AND-OUT RELAY

NUMBER OF PLAYERS: 6-40

SPACE: Playground, playroom, gymnasium

PLAYING AREA: Two parallel lines 30 feet apart serve as restraining lines
and goal lines. Their length will depend on the number of teams playing.

EQUIPMENT: For each team three Indian clubs, tin cans, or beanbags,
which are lined up, two feet apart, in front of the goal line.

FORMATION: Players are divided into teams of six players or less. They line
up in file formation behind the restraining line and opposite their row of
Indian clubs.

PROCEDURE: On signal, the first player of each file runs forward and zigzags in and out between the clubs. Passing behind the third club he turns
and zigzags back until he tags the outstretched hand of the second player
in his file. He then retires to the end of the file while the second player
runs across and back. Play continues until all the players have run.

The player to be tagged must stand with hand outstretched and with
the forward foot toeing the starting line until his hand is touched by the
runner. To advance beyond the starting line without being touched is
a foul.

If an Indian club is knocked down the runner must stop, replace
the club, and continue his zigzag run from that club.

The teams win in order of finishing unless fouls are committed. If
fouls are made, the team with the fewest fouls wins. Thus a team finishing
fourth with no fouls would get first place if one or more players of the
teams finishing first, second, and third committed fouls.

TEACHING SUGGESTION

1. Have the players standing second in line act as linesmen to determine
   whether fouls are made by the person waiting to be tagged.

ODD-AND-EVEN RELAY

NUMBER OF PLAYERS: 8-40

SPACE: Playground, playroom, gymnasium

EQUIPMENT: Two balls, beanbags, blackboard erasers, knotted towels, or stuffed leather ball casings

FORMATION: Players stand in a single circle with a spread of the arms between each. Players are numbered around the circle by ones and twos. A captain for each team (1 and 2), go to the center of the circle. Each captain is given a ball.

PROCEDURE: At a signal, each captain starts throwing his ball in sequence to the members of his team. Each player returns the ball to his captain. If a player misses the ball he must secure it, return to his position, and from there deliver it correctly. Team members must be alert to help the captain distinguish members of the team as the ball is thrown from captain to player.

SCORING: The team wins 1 point whose ball first completes the circle. Two out of 3, 3 out of 5, or 4 out of 7 circuits may be selected as the number of circuits that must be made to determine which team has the largest number of points and is the winner.

TEACHING SUGGESTIONS

1. As skill is gained, increase the distance between the circle players and the captains.
2. Encourage the players to throw the ball as rapidly as possible.

SIDEWARD PASS RELAY

NUMBER OF PLAYERS: 6-40

SPACE: Classroom

EQUIPMENT: For each team, a beanbag, ball, knotted towel, blackboard eraser, or other object.

FORMATION: Players are seated at their desks. Those sitting in the front row, across the room, form Team A; those in the second row, Team B, and so on. One or more beanbags are placed on the floor at one side of the room opposite each player occupying a seat.

PROCEDURE: On signal, those next to the beanbags pick them up with the nearest hand, pass the beanbags to the opposite hand, and with that hand place the beanbags on the floor in the next aisle. The process of picking up, changing from hand to hand, and placing the beanbags on the floor is continued across the room. The players in the farthest rows of desks, as they receive the beanbags, touch the bags to the floor and immediately start the beanbags on their return trip. As the original aisle players receive the beanbags they touch them to the floor and then lift the beanbags high into the air, as a signal that the relay is completed. The first row to complete the game wins.

TEACHING SUGGESTIONS

1. Increase the number of times an object is passed before determining the winner.
2. Reverse the direction of the first passing.
3. Pass the beanbags while using only one hand.
4. Have all players sit facing the side wall of the room. Beanbags are passed backward over their heads, those behind having to stretch to secure the beanbag.

SKIP ROPE RELAY

NUMBER OF PLAYERS: 4-40

SPACE: Playground, playroom, gymnasium, auditorium

PLAYING AREA: A starting line 20 or more feet long (depending on the number of teams), and a goal line 40 feet distant and paralleling the starting line.

EQUIPMENT: (1) Goals, designated by the use of chairs, Indian clubs, tin cans, blocks of wood, baseball bases, for each team, placed on the goal line; (2) an 8-foot jump rope for each team.

FORMATION: Players are divided into any number of teams, not more than six players to a team. Players stand in file formation opposite the team's goal. A distance of 10 feet should separate the relay files. A jump rope is given to the front player of each file.

PROCEDURE: On signal, each front player skips forward, jumping rope as he skips. Passing behind his goal he skips rope back toward the starting line. After skipping over the starting line each player hands his rope to the Number 2 player of his file; this player begins rope skipping immediately. The game continues until all in one team have finished. The first team to finish wins.

TEACHING SUGGESTIONS

1. Have any player who stops skipping and starts to run, halt, return 5 steps, and again begin his rope skipping.
2. Watch to see that front players do not advance across the starting line while waiting for or receiving the jump rope.

ZIGZAG BOUNCE BALL RELAY

NUMBER OF PLAYERS: 8-40

SPACE: Playground, playroom, gymnasium, auditorium

PLAYING AREA: Two parallel restraining lines 10 feet apart. The length of the lines needed will depend upon the number of teams to play.

EQUIPMENT: Balls of equal size that bounce, one or more for each team

FORMATION: Players of each team are divided into two groups and stand opposite each other in line formation behind and paralleling the playing area lines. A captain for each team, holding a ball, stands at the end of one of his team's lines.

PROCEDURE: On signal, each captain passes the ball by bouncing it to the first player of his team in the line opposite him. That player passes it by bouncing it back to the player standing next to the captain. Play is continued until the end player of the opposite line receives the ball by a bounce pass. For a successful bounce pass, the following should be observed: (1) The player should have one foot in front of the other in a forward stride position; (2) The start of the bounce should begin from a waist high position; (3) The ball should hit a spot about halfway between the passer and the receiver.

SCORING: The team whose last player first receives the ball scores 1 point. The winning score may be 10 points or any number agreed upon by the captains.

TEACHING SUGGESTIONS

1. If a poorly bounced ball is delivered, have the person for whom it was intended secure the ball, return to his position, and then send the ball across with a bounce.
2. Use more than one ball for each team.
3. Have each captain introduce balls of various sizes.
4. Point out that the bounce pass is a necessary basketball skill.

Rhythmical Activities

ACROSS THE HALL

MUSIC: "The Girl I Left Behind Me"

FORMATION: One large circle made up of small circles with not more than six couples in each small circle. Active couples in each circle are any two couples directly opposite each other, designated by a chosen leader within each circle.

DESCRIPTION: The dance is done to the following calls.

Measures 1-2. "STRAIGHT ACROSS THE HALL TO THE OPPOSITE LADY." Active couples advance toward each other.

Measure 3. "SWING HER BY THE RIGHT HAND." Active boys turn the opposite girls by joining right hands with them and turning them once around.

Measure 4. "THEN YOUR PARTNER BY THE LEFT, AND PROMENADE THE GIRL BEHIND YOU." Using left hands, all boys turn their own partners. The boys then take for their new partner the girl who is behind them, and in skating position promenade counterclockwise around the set while the music is repeated once. The active boys remain active and start the game again, selecting the next couple to the right of the original couple. They continue active until each boy returns to his original partner. Immediately the next two boys to the right of the original active boys become active. The dance continues until all boys have had their turn.

The Girl I Left Behind Me

Arranged by Anna Hermitage

Oh that girl, that pret-ty lit-tle girl, That girl I left be-hind me.

I went and cried the day I died, For the girl I left be-hind me.

CAPTAIN JINKS

Decca Record No. 18222, Album 278
Methodist Record No. 103

FORMATION: Single circle, each girl in front of a boy. Boy places hands on shoulders of the girl in front of him, his partner.

DESCRIPTION

Measures 1-4. All march forward. On the word "beans," girls turn, face partners, and they join hands.

Measures 5-8. Both skip in own small circle.

Measures 9-16.   Joining inside hands, side by side, with boys on the inside, partners skip forward around the circle.

Measures 1-8.   Salute your partner, turn to the right,
And swing your neighbor with all your might,
Then promenade with the lady right,
For that's the style in the Army!

Measures 1-4.   Partners face and salute each other with right hand (1 measure). Each then makes a quick military turn, one-eighth to the right (1 measure). Each takes a new partner (girl or boy diagonally right, facing him or her). They turn once around in place (1 measure).

Measures 5-8.   Each walks forward with new partner.

Entire pattern is repeated, with each boy slipping behind his new partner. He stays with her until the words "Swing your neighbor."

Captain Jinks

American

I'm Cap-tain Jinks of the Horse Ma-rines, I feed my horse good corn and beans, I

swing the la-dies in their teens, For that's the style in the arm-y!

I teach the la-dies how to dance, How to dance, how to dance, I

teach the la-dies how to dance, For that's the style in the arm-y!

VARIATION I [1]

FORMATION: A quadrille, four couples in a square. The dance is done to calls.

Measures 1-4. "Now it's DOS-A-DOS WITH YOUR CORNERS ALL, YOUR CORNERS ALL, YOUR CORNERS ALL." The "corner" girl is the girl to the left of the boy (his partner being the girl to the right). Boy and his corner girl pass each other with right shoulder to right shoulder, back to back, and return to place without turning around.

Measures 5-8. "AND IT'S DOS-A-DOS WITH YOUR PARTNERS ALL, FOR THAT'S THE STYLE IN THE ARMY." Partners pass each other, right shoulder to right shoulder, back to back, and return to place.

Measures 9-12. "ALLEMANDE LEFT WITH YOUR CORNERS ALL, YOUR CORNERS ALL, YOUR CORNERS ALL." Boy gives left hand to the girl at his left, walks around her, and returns to place.

Measures 13-16. "ALLEMANDE RIGHT WITH YOUR PARTNERS, AND SWING THEM ALL AROUND." Boy gives right hand to partner, walks around her, and returns to place.

Measures 1-4. "BALANCE TO YOUR CORNERS ALL, CORNERS ALL, YOUR CORNERS ALL." Boy faces girl on his left, points right toe over in front of left, puts right foot back in place; points left foot and replaces it; repeats ("right, in place, left, in place").

Measures 5-16. "SWING THE CORNER LADY, ALL, AND PROMENADE THE HALL." Boy swings the girl on his left, and then, in skating position, they march around the square in a counterclockwise direction.

VARIATION II

Victor Record No. 22991

FORMATION: Single circle, boys and girls alternating, boy's partner on his right.

DESCRIPTION: The dance is done to calls.

Measures 1-2. "CAPTAIN JINKS CAME HOME LAST NIGHT." All join hands and take two steps into circle and two steps out.

Measures 3-4. "GENTLEMAN PASSES TO THE RIGHT." Each faces partner, gives right hand to partner, and walks on to meet a new partner (the next advancing girl or boy).

Measures 5-8. "SWING YOUR PARTNER SO POLITE. FOR THAT'S THE STYLE IN THE ARMY." Each joins hands with new partner and swings around

---

[1] The World of Fun Series. Produced by the Audio-Visual Department of the Methodist Church, Nashville, Tennessee, 1947. By permission. May be purchased with records from the Methodist Publishing House, 85 McAllister St., San Francisco 2, and 125 E. Sunset Blvd., Los Angeles 12, California.

once, finishing so that all will be in a single circle with boy's partner on his right.

Measures 9-16.   "ALL JOIN HANDS AND CIRCLE LEFT,
    CIRCLE LEFT, CIRCLE LEFT,
    ALL JOIN HANDS AND CIRCLE LEFT,
    FOR THAT'S THE STYLE IN THE ARMY."

All join hands and circle to the left until end of the music.

    Entire pattern is repeated.

CIRCLE ALL or PAUL JONES
(A Mixer)

MUSIC: Two-step or any popular 4/4 rhythm.

FORMATION: Couples are scattered about the room dancing.

DESCRIPTION: Leader calls "Circle All." All drop into a big single circle with girls on the right of their partners. Leader calls "Grand Right and Left" (see page 207). Girls turn to their left, boys turn to their right and begin the figure. After five or six persons have been passed, leader calls "Everybody Dance." Each boy takes the girl facing him for his new partner. Those who failed to get a partner go immediately to the center, get a partner, and start to dance. Boys should hurry to the center and secure a partner.

    Call, "Circle All," is repeated several times after partners have been together for an appreciable period of time.

COME, LET US BE JOYFUL [1]
(German)

Victor Record No. 20448
Methodist Record No. 102

FORMATION: Circle in sets of six, three opposite three. Each three consists of a boy in the middle, with a girl on each side, holding inside hands. If girls are fewer in number than boys, put a girl in the middle of the lines.

DESCRIPTION

Measures 1-2.   Two lines advance toward each other with three walking steps, ending with a bow by boy and a curtsy by the girls.

Measures 3-4.   Two lines then walk backward to place, bring their feet together on the fourth count.

---

[1] State of Wisconsin, *Manual of Physical Education*, Part III, Folk and Singing Games. Madison, Wis.: State Department of Education, 1924-25. By permission.

Come, Let Us Be Joyful

Arranged by E. B. Gordon

Measures 5-8. All advance and retire again.

Measures 9-16. Each boy, with his right elbow, hooks right elbows with girl on his right and turns her with two hop steps. (Four walking steps or 2 skips may be substituted.) Releasing the right-hand girl, boy hooks his left elbow with the left elbow of girl on his left and swings her. Repeat, turning right-hand girl. Repeat, turning left-hand girl. Finish in two original lines. Girls when not turning step hop in place.

Measures 1-8 repeated. Two endings are possible. In Ending A, the boy remains with the same two girls, all three advancing around the circle. In Ending B, boy travels while girls remain where they are.

A. Measures 1-8. Both lines advance and retire as is done at the start of the pattern, except that the second time they advance, instead of bowing, all three pass through the advancing line (passing left shoulders) and meet a new set which is advancing from the opposite direction.

Entire pattern is repeated with the new set of players.
Repeat as long as desired.

B. Measures 1-8. In this figure the boy moves on and meets two new girls. During the last eight counts girls face and back away from each other for four steps, thereby clearing the lane for advancing boys. Girls then advance toward each other for three steps and face in the line of direction on the fourth step. *At the same time* boys march forward for eight steps passing through the line they were facing and stop with the two girls whose backs are toward them as they advance.

This is a useful game for fun nights and for use with adult groups.

DUCK THE OYSTER, DUCK THE CLAM [1]

Music: "Bully of the Town"; "Allen's Favorite"; "Two Rows of Corn"; "Arkansas Traveler," or any good quadrille music
Square Dance Associates Album II (with instructions and calls)
Victor Record No. 20592 ("Soldier's Joy")

FORMATION: Four boys and four girls form a square.

DESCRIPTION: The step is an easy, springy walk, no skipping or hopping. The dance is done to calls.

1. "FIRST COUPLE BALANCE AND SWING." The first couple (with their backs to the music), balance and swing. Balance: partners face each other, each takes two short steps forward and two steps backward. Swing: partners turn with a country-dance walking step, making two complete revolutions.

2. "LEAD OUT TO THE RIGHT OF THE RING, FOUR HANDS UP AND HALF AROUND." First couple walks to second couple and they form a ring by joining hands. The two couples then move clockwise until the first couple is facing the center of the set.

3. "DUCK THE OYSTER." With all four persons retaining joined hands the second girl and boy form an arch by raising their joined hands, and the first couple dive under this arch. They do not pass completely through the arch, but merely under it, and then retreat, back to place.

4. "DUCK THE CLAM." The first couple now form an arch for couple two, who "duck" under the arch and then back to place.

5. "DUCK THE OYSTER AND ON YOU GO." Second couple form an arch as before. This time the first couple drop the hands of the second couple, pass completely through the arch and walk to the third couple.

[1] Based on description in Chicago Park District (W.P.A. Project), *The Square Dance.* Chicago: Chicago Park District, 1940. By permission.

6. "FOUR HANDS UP AND HALF AROUND, DUCK THE OYSTER AND THEN THE CLAM, AND NOW THE OYSTER AND ON YOU GO." First couple repeat, with couple Number 3, movements in 2-5.

7. "FOUR HANDS UP AND HALF AROUND, DUCK THE OYSTER AND THEN THE CLAM, AND NOW THE OYSTER AND HOME YOU GO." First couple repeat, with couple Number 4, movements in 2-5.

8. "AND EVERYBODY SWING. ALLEMANDE LEFT, GRAND RIGHT AND LEFT, MEET YOUR PARTNER AND PROMENADE HOME." All swing their partners, then perform Allemande Left and progress around the circle with Grand Right and Left (see p. 207, Chap. VIII) until they meet their original partners and promenade home again.

Entire dance is repeated, with second couple performing the figures, then again with third couple active, and finally with fourth couple leading.

FUN ON THE GREEN

Composer Unknown

FORMATION: Two lines of three face and make a set of six. Lines stand about four feet apart. Inside hands are joined and held high. Outside hands at waist. Boy is in the center of each line or girl is in center with a boy on each side. Sets radiate from the center of the room like spokes in a wheel.

DESCRIPTION

Measures 1-2. Beginning with the right foot, all touch right toe in front, then touch right heel in same place. Starting with the right foot, all take three running steps forward.

Measures 3-4. Measures 1-2 are repeated, all moving backward, beginning with left foot; toe, heel, and three running steps.

Measures 1-4 repeated.

Measures 5-8. The first figure is repeated, with the following variations: During the first two measures of this figure, the player on the left of the leader (center person in line) passes under the arch made by the raised arms of the other two. During the third measure, the leader turns under his own arm. During the fourth measure, the one on the right of the leader turns under his own left arm.

Passing under the arches is done by each in turn, not simultaneously. The step used throughout is three running steps and a pause. All do the step in place while awaiting their turn. No one stands still.

Measures 5-6. Part II of the music is repeated, using the second ending. All lines take two glides to their own right and three light running steps in place (2 measures).

Measures 7-8. Returning to their left with two glides and three running steps they pass *back to back* the three they have been facing and meet a new line.

Dance is repeated from the beginning as many times as desired. The action throughout should be very light and gay because of the fast tempo of the music and the use of the running step.

THE MERRY-GO-ROUND
(A Mixer)

MUSIC: Any good tune in 6/8 time

FORMATION: Single circle, girl to right of her partner. All face center, with hands joined. A player without a partner stands in the center of the circle.

DESCRIPTION: This is a traditional North Carolina play party game.

1. All take eight slides to the left.

2. All take eight slides to the right.

3. Each faces partner and joins both hands. All take four slides toward the center and four slides away from the center.

4. Giving right hand to partner, all do the Grand Right and Left around the circle (see p. 207, Chap. VIII). The center player joins in this movement. Whenever the music is stopped by the leader or musician, each player tries to secure an oncoming player as a partner.

The unsuccessful person then goes to the center and the game is played again.

THE PEDDLER'S PACK [1]
(Korobushka)

Kismet Record No. 106
Imperial Record No. 1022
Methodist Record No. 108

FORMATION: Any number of couples form two lines facing each other, boys in one line and girls in the other. Partners join both hands.

DESCRIPTION: Dance directions are by Michael Herman. When danced, music is in strict tempo. Although this is an old song, the dance originated among Russian exiles in America near the close of World War I.

FIGURE I

Measures 1-2. Beginning with the left foot, boy takes three walking steps forward; beginning with right foot, partner does same backward (count "one, two, one"). Boy hops on left foot, girl on right (count "two").

Measures 3-4. Beginning with right foot, boy takes three walking steps backward; beginning with left foot, partner does same forward (count "one, two, one"). Boy hops on right foot; partner on left (count "two").

Measures 5-6. Measures 1-4 are repeated.

Measure 7. Boy takes step backward with right foot, partner forward with left (count "one"). Each points free foot to the side ("two").

Measure 8. Each brings heels together (count "one"); pauses on count "two."

FIGURE II

A. *Measures 9-10.* Partners drop hands. All fold arms. All beginning with right foot, moving in straight lines, take three steps to right, away from partner ("one, two, one"), hop on right foot, and swing left forward over right ("two").

Measures 11-12. Beginning with left foot, all return to place ("one, two, one"); hop on left foot, and swing right forward over left ("two").

Measure 13. Partners join right hands, balance forward toward each other with right foot, raising joined hands ("one"). They pause on count "two."

Measure 14. All balance backward with left foot, lowering hands ("one"); they pause on count "two."

Measure 15. Partners take two steps forward, changing places.

Measure 16. Partners face each other, bringing heels together, pause, and drop hands.

B. *Measures 17-24.* Figure is repeated, all ending in original position.

---

[1] *Music Highways and Byways.* By special permission, Silver Burdett Co., copyright, 1936.

The Peddler's Pack

Translated from the Russian   Russian Folk Song

Full to the brim is my fine ko-ro-bush-ka Pack'd with co-ton, silk, and lace; Glad am I to be young and lust-y, Shoul-ders strong and stur-dy pace, Glad am I to be young and lust-y,

Verse 2. Much have I paid, for the goods are costly,
Bargain not nor stingy be;
See, my dove, all that I can offer,
Closer come and sit by me,
See, my dove, all that I can offer,
Closer come and sit by me.

Verse 3. I shall be standing upon the highway,
Till the nightfall I shall wait;
When you come, then before your dark eyes
Spread my wares and learn my fate,
When you come, then before your dark eyes
Spread my wares and learn my fate.

POP GOES THE WEASEL [1]
(Longways Version)

Methodist Record No. 104

FORMATION: Longways set for six or more couples, boys in one line and girls in the other.

DESCRIPTION: The usual country-dance step is used, and a caller gives the signal for each figure.

Measures 1-8. "DOWN THE OUTSIDE AND BACK." The first girl and first boy turn outward and go eight steps down the outside of their respective lines toward the foot of the set. They return up the outside of their lines to the head of the set.

Measures 9-16. "DOWN THE CENTER AND BACK." the first couple join inside hands and go eight steps down the center toward the foot of the set. Releasing hands, they face about, join hands again, and return up the center toward the head.

Measures 1-8. "THREE HANDS AROUND WITH LADY." The first couple join hands in a ring with the second girl and swing once and a half around

[1] Elizabeth Burchenal, *American Country Dances.* New York: G. Schirmer, Inc., 1918. Copyright renewal assigned, 1945 to G. Schirmer, Inc. Printed by permission.

Pop Goes the Weasel

to the left, so that at the end of the sixth measure the circle arrives at a point at which the second girl is facing her original position. On the first note of the seventh measure ("Pop"), the first couple raise their joined hands and release the hands of the second girl, who at the same time passes under the arch to her original position in the girls' line, and immediately moves up one place to the head of the set.

Measures 9-16. "THREE HANDS AROUND WITH GENTLEMAN." The first couple now join hands in a ring with the second boy, and dance once and a half around to the left. On the first note of the fifteenth measure, the second boy "pops" through the arch formed by the first couple, to his original position in line, and immediately moves up one place to the head of the set.

The first couple now repeat the whole dance, but this time swinging the girl and boy next lower in line.

All the other odd couples (third, fifth, etc.) are "active" also, and begin dancing with the next couple below at the same time and in the same manner as described for the first couple.

They progress down the set, one place lower each time. When an inactive couple reach the head, they stand idle during one repetition of the dance as described for the first couple. When an active couple reach the foot, they become inactive.

When the dance has been continued as long as desired, it is finished with "Forward and swing partners," and "Promenade around the hall."

RUSTIC REEL

Music: "Rustic Reel," *Our Land of Song.*[1] Any good reel music in 6/8 time
Columbia Record No. 37646
Victor Record No. 36403A

FORMATION: Triple circle, with every six players facing—three in each line. Sets are made up of a boy with a girl on either side, facing a similar group, or a girl in center with a boy on either side.

DESCRIPTION

Measures 1-8. The center player in each line takes the hands of the opposite girl on his right and they slide eight slides out to the right and eight slides back to place.

Measures 1-8 repeated. The center player takes the hands of the opposite girl on his left, and they slide eight slides to the left and eight slides back to place.

Measures 9-16. Joining hands in their lines, all move four steps forward, four steps backward.

Measures 9-16 repeated. All move forward again, pass through (right shoulders to right shoulders), meet a new line of players, and pause.

Entire pattern is repeated with a new group of three.

NOTES: If space is limited, substitute four slides out, four slides in, four slides out, four slides in.

Insist that all take eight slides, no matter how small the slides, before reversing the direction.

This is an excellent game because boys meet new girls each time.

---

[1] A Singing School series. Sacramento: California State Department of Education, 1945. Page 191 in Book of Accompaniments.

SCHOTTISCHE [1]

Arranged by G. H. Johnstone

Decca Record No. 25062 (Album A-525), "Military Schottische"

FORMATION: Double circle, partners facing counterclockwise, boys on the inside. Inside hands joined, outside hands on hips.

DESCRIPTION

Measures 1-2.   Starting with the outside foot, all run three steps and hop; starting with inside foot, all run three steps and hop.

Measures 3-4.   Partners face each other and take four step hops in place.

The pattern is repeated as long as desired. The schottische pattern is usually eight measures of the same step, instead of alternating steps every two measures as this dance is written. The following steps are variations of

---

[1] Grace H. Johnstone, *Heel and Toe or a Do-Si-Do.* Oakland, California: Grace H. Johnstone. 1944. By permission.

the step hops suggested in Measures 3 and 4 and may be introduced as the leader wishes.

1. Partners drop hands and turn away from each other with four step hops, making a complete turn in place.

2. Partners join both hands and together make a complete turn with four step hops, left arms leading.

3. The boy takes four step hops in place while the girl turns under the boy's arm. This is repeated, with the girl step-hopping in place and the boy turning under her arm.

4. Partners take skating position (left hands joined, right hands joined, boy's right arm under girl's left, both facing forward). The boy takes four step hops in place while the girl crosses over in front of the boy to his left side, with four step hops. The step is repeated, the girl crossing back to the boy's right side. They do not drop hands.

5. Partners join hands in skating position and both turn under raised arms and then come back to position (this is the figure called "wringing the dish cloth").

SICILIAN CIRCLE [1]

Columbia Record No. 556D
Methodist Record No. 104
Victor Records No. 22991 and 20369

FORMATION: Double circle. In each set, every two couples face each other, their backs being toward the couple in the next set. Each boy's partner stands at his right. Dancers and music begin together.

DESCRIPTION: This is an early American dance pattern which is a good introduction to the more complicated quadrille patterns. The caller should give call just before the new figure is to occur.

Measures 1-4. "ALL FORWARD AND BACK." Joining inside hands, couples advance four steps toward each other, bow on fourth step, and retire to position by walking backward four steps.

Measures 5-8. "CIRCLE FOUR HANDS AROUND." Both couples join hands and, moving in a small circle to the left, complete the circle and return to positions (eight steps).

Measures 9-16. "LADIES CHAIN." Boy stays where he is and turns first the visiting girl (the one opposite him), then his own partner. Each girl gives her right hand to the other girl; they pass each other and each gives the left hand to the left hand of the boy opposite. Putting his right hand at the girl's back, boy backs up and turns in place, handing the girl around, thereby completing a small circle (eight steps). Girl, again taking right hand of the

[1] *"Good Morning"; After a Sleep of Twenty-five Years Old Fashioned Dancing is Being Revived by Mr. and Mrs. Henry Ford.* Dearborn, Mich.: Dearborn Publishing Co., 1926. By permission of Estate of Henry Ford.

Sicilian Circle

girl opposite, offers left hand to her partner, who turns her in place (eight steps).

Measures 17-24. "Right and left." Taking skating position, partners move slightly to the right on the diagonal, passing the opposite couple (four steps). Each boy turns his partner in place with four steps. (Girl never walks backward during the turn.) Repeat, moving to left, and return to place.

Measures 25-28. "Forward and back." Couples walk forward four steps and backward four steps. (Be sure this is not done with only six steps.)

Measures 29-32. "Forward again and pass through." Couples advance and, passing each other, meet a new oncoming couple (eight steps). Each boy should step far enough from his partner to permit the oncoming girl to pass between him and his partner. Hands are not joined during this figure.

Dance is repeated from the beginning as often as desired.

THREE-STEP [1]

Music: "Air from *Rigoletto*"
Decca Record No. 25061 ("Moon Winks")

Formation: Couples in social dancing position or elbow grasp. Music is slow 3/4 tempo.

Description

Measure 1. All take three slides, the boy to the left starting with the left foot, the girl to the right, starting with the right foot (1 measure).

---

[1] Adapted from Alice Jameyson. *Old Time Ballroom Dances that are Fun to Dance Today.* Berkeley, California: The Professional Press, 1941. By permission of author. Music is from Grace H. Johnstone's *Heel and Toe or a Do-Si-Do.* Oakland, California: Grace H. Johnstone, 1944. By permission.

Air from "Rigoletto"
(La donna e mobile)

Giuseppe Verdi
Arranged by G. H. Johnstone

Measure 2. All turn half about to the boys' left and take three slides to the boys' right, starting on the right foot (girl left).

Measure 3. All take three walking steps turning in a pivot turn, with the boy moving forward.

Measure 4. All dip on count "one" of Measure 4. The boy steps backward with right foot, girl forward with left. All return to erect position and step twice in place to finish measure.

Measures 5-16. Action of Measures 1-4 is repeated three times.

TWO LITTLE LADIES FORM A RING [1]

Music: "Hinky-Dinky, Parlee-Voo" [2] or "Captain Jinks," p. 692. Any good quadrille music may be used.

FORMATION: Four couples in a quadrille set

DESCRIPTION: The calls are given at the beginning of each step.

1. "FIRST COUPLE BALANCE AND SWING." For Balance and Swing, see p. 696.

2. "FIRST LADY LEAD TO THE CENTER OF THE RING.
   TWO LITTLE LADIES FORM A RING,
   ONCE AROUND AND HOME AND SWING."

First and second girl walk into the center of the set, where they meet and face each other. They join hands at arm's length and walk around in a circle to the left (clockwise) for one complete turn. Then girls drop hands, return to home position and swing with their partners.

3. "THREE LITTLE LADIES TO THE CENTER OF THE RING,
   THREE LITTLE LADIES FORM A RING,
   AND WHEN YOU GET HOME YOU BREAK AND SWING."

First, second, and third girls walk into the center of the set, join hands, forming a ring, and move around in a circle to the left (clockwise), for one complete turn. The girls then drop hands, return to their home stations, and swing with their partners.

4. "FOUR LITTLE LADIES TO THE CENTER OF THE FLOOR,
   ONCE AROUND AND THEN NO MORE,
   WHEN YOU GET HOME YOU BREAK AND SWING."

All four girls walk into the center of the set, join hands, and move around in a circle to the left for one turn. They drop hands and return to their home stations, where they swing their partners.

5. "NOW SWING YOUR PARTNERS ALL,
   ALLEMANDE LEFT, GRAND RIGHT AND LEFT,
   MEET YOUR PARTNER AND PROMENADE."

All swing partners, perform Allemande Left, progress around the circle with Grand Right and Left (see p. 207, Chap. VIII) meet original partners and promenade home.

Entire pattern is repeated, with second couple balancing and swinging, and second girl leading through the figures, then once again with third girl leading, and finally with fourth girl leading.

---

[1] Reproduced by permission of the Recreation Division, Chicago Park District.
[2] Music from Grace H. Johnstone's *Heel and Toe or a Do-Si-Do.* Oakland, California: Grace H. Johnstone, 1944. By permission.

Hinky-Dinky, Parlee-Voo

VARSOVIENNE [1]
(Mazurka)

---

[1] *"Good Morning," op. cit.* By permission of Estate of Henry Ford.
    Music also found in *We Sing.* A Singing School series. Boston: C. C. Birchard & Co., 1940,
Book of Accompaniments, p. 134.

Coast Record No. 225
Decca Record No. 25060 (with waltz)
Globe Record No. 5002
MacGregor Record No. 10-398-3
Methodist Record No. 107

FORMATION: Varsovienne position, with boy slightly behind and to the left of the girl. In this position, partners' hands are held high, with right hand in right hand, left hand in left hand. Boy's right arm goes behind girl's right shoulder. The waltz position may be used, with both partners moving sideward.

DESCRIPTION

I

Measures 1-4. Both start with left foot and perform step as follows: left slide, right close, left raise (swing foot out and in over supporting foot, a "cut step"); left slide, right close, left raise; left slide, right close, left step; turn, and point right foot to right side. They make a half turn on the "steps."

Measures 5-8. Measures 1-4 are repeated, both moving to the right.

II

Measures 9-10. Starting with the left foot, raised to the left side, both make a half turn with the following steps: Swing left foot over right supporting foot, slide it left, close right to left, step left, and point right foot and hold.

Measures 11-12. They repeat, starting with right foot and moving back into position.

Measures 13-16. They repeat all.

In the 3/4 rhythm, called "Put Your Little Foot," the step is swing, close, step; swing, close, step; swing, close, step, turn and point, instead of the Mazurka step. This makes a very smooth rhythm.

Some recordings add the waltz to the "Varsovienne" step which more often is danced with the swing instead of the raise of the Mazurka step.

Varsovienne is also danced as a mixer. Couples are in a circle and on Measures 9-10 the girl only turns in toward the center of the circle with a half turn, and on Measures 11-12 she returns to her partner who has danced in place. On Measures 13-14 the girl again makes a half turn into the center of the circle, but on Measures 15-16 she lets go the hand of her partner and turns the second half of her turn to arrive in front of the boy behind her, with whom she begins the dance again. This is continued as long as the group is interested.

ADDITIONAL RHYTHMICAL ACTIVITIES
IN CALIFORNIA STATE SERIES MUSIC TEXTBOOKS

New Music Horizons. Sixth Book. Edited by Osbourne McConathy and Others. (Copyrighted, 1946, 1949, by Silver Burdett Co.) Sacramento: California State Department of Education (edition in preparation).

Students' book and book of accompaniments and interpretation for the teacher. Page references are to the latter book.

Rhythms

At the Dance	25
Polka	26
Mazurka	36
Walking Song	50

Folk Dances

The Minuet: A Dream of Long Ago	58

Folk Dances

Dancing	103
The Wind Among the Trees	176
A Village Dance	203
The Irish Washerwoman	54
Captain Jinks	104
Weevily Wheat	144
Gathering Peascods	227

Music Everywhere. Edited by Theresa Armitage and Others. A Singing School series (copyrighted, 1943, 1944, by C. C. Birchard & Co.). Sacramento: California State Department of Education, 1945.

Students' edition and teacher's manual (with accompaniments). Page references are to the latter book.

Folk Dances

Polly-Wolly Doodle	17
Old Brass Wagon	151
Lead Through That Sugar and Tea	151
Arkansaw Traveler	170

Folk Dances

The Waltz of the Broom	204
La Cucaracha	207
Si, Señor	222
Huyanó (invocation for a good harvest)	226

Our Land of Song. Edited by Theresa Armitage and Others. A Singing School series (copyrighted, 1942, 1944, by C. C. Birchard & Co.). Sacramento: California State Department of Education, 1946.

Students' book and teacher's manual (with accompaniments). Page references are to the latter book.

Gavotte (1743)	183	Lady 'Round the Lady	188
Brown-Eyed Mary	186	King and Queen	192

Music of Many Lands and Peoples. Edited by Osbourne McConathy, John W. Beattie, and Russell V. Morgan. The Music Hour series (copyrighted, 1932, by Silver Burdett & Co.). Sacramento: California State Department of Education, 1942.[1]

Folk Dances

Christmas Dance (dance directions only)	258
Goddesses (dance directions only)	258

Folk Dances

Old Dan Tucker (dance directions only)	258

Music Highways and Byways. Edited by Osbourne McConathy, John W. Beattie, and Russell V. Morgan. The Music Hour series (copy-

---

[1] Former series (adoption period July 1, 1942 to July 1, 1950).

righted, 1936, by Silver Burdett Co.). Sacramento: California State Department of Education, 1942.[1]

We Sing. Edited by Theresa Armitage, Peter W. Dykema, and Gladys Pitcher. A Singing School series (copyrighted, 1940, 1942, by C. C. Birchard & Co.). Sacramento: California State Department of Education, 1942.[1]

Students' edition, teacher's manual, and book of accompaniments. Page references are to the last book.

SELECTED REFERENCES ON RHYTHMS[2]

Linson, Ellen, and Smith, Jacqueline. *All Join Hands: First Steps for Recreation Leaders.* Chicago, Ill.: Co-operative League of the United States, 1946. (343 S. Dearborn St., Chicago 4, Ill.)

Mason, Bernard S., and Mitchell, Elmer D. *Party Games for All. Social Mixers, Games and Contests, Stunts and Tricks.* (Everyday Handbook Series.) New York: Barnes & Noble, Inc., 1946.

A comprehensive handbook for parties, including a few dances suitable for all ages. No music is given.

Stunts

A warm-up period or short run before instruction begins will insure safety in performance of stunts. Materials of previous grades should be reviewed at the beginning of the season.

BACK-TO-BACK STICK PULL-AWAY

SPACE: Playground, gymnasium

EQUIPMENT: A stick or pole from a foot to a yard long

FORMATION: Two opponents stand back to back and hold the stick high in the air over their heads.

PROCEDURE: Each performer tries to get the stick by pulling it forward and across his own chest. Neither should let go of the stick.

---

[1] Former series (adoption period July 1, 1942 to July 1, 1950).
[2] Consult the bibliography and listing of phonograph records in the appendixes.

BACK SPRING

SPACE: Playground, gymnasium

EQUIPMENT: Mat

FORMATION: Two performers take turns in acting as a hurdle for the other

PROCEDURE: Number 1 (the hurdle) takes a position on hands and knees, with side of body toward Number 2. Number 2, taking a short run, places his hands on the floor near body of Number 1 and turns a flip over his body.

While learning the stunt, the ground man should raise his back as he feels the runner going over. This will help the performer to land on his feet.

CAMEL WALK [1]

SPACE: Playground, gymnasium

FORMATION: Two performers stand close together, while facing in the same direction, Number 1 with his back to Number 2.

PROCEDURE: Front contestant (Number 1) jumps and locks his legs high up under the arms of Number 2. Number 1 then crawls through the legs of 2 and extending his arms grasps the heels of 2. Head is carried high. At the same time Number 2 falls forward onto his hands and walks on all fours.

ELEPHANT WALK

SPACE: Playground, gymnasium

FORMATION: Two contestants stand facing each other.

PROCEDURE: Number 1 grasps the waist of Number 2. Number 2 jumps and locks his legs high up under Number 1's arms. He lowers his body backward and swings between the legs of Number 1. In this position he grasps the heels of Number 1, straightens his arms, arches his back and holds his head high. At the same time Number 2 falls forward on his hands and walks on all fours. (Figure 141.)

GRECIAN WRESTLE

SPACE: Gymnasium, playground

FORMATION: Several teams form a horse and rider, the lighter weight boy of each team being the rider.

[1] William Ralph LaPorte and Al G. Renner, *The Tumbler's Manual.* New York: Prentice-Hall, Inc., 1938. Page 21.

PROCEDURE: The teams try to dismount the riders of other teams. Three out of five trials determine the winners.

HAND STAND

SPACE: Gymnasium or playground where a wall is available

EQUIPMENT: Mat

PROCEDURE: Performer stands facing a wall or a partner, and places his hands on the floor about shoulder width apart. Arms and legs should be fully extended, head thrown well up. He should try to throw the feet so that they contact the wall or are caught by the partner. Position is held by pointing toes, as feet balance over raised head. The hand stand may be taught first from a position of both hands and one foot on the floor. The free leg then by a swing pulls both legs up into the air. Many children can do a hand stand easily from a standing position.

HEAD STAND

SPACE: Gymnasium or playground where a wall is available

EQUIPMENT: Mat

PROCEDURE: Performer stands facing a wall or a partner, and places his hands on the floor about shoulder width apart. He drops the top of his head to the floor eight or ten inches in front of the hands, thereby forming a triangle. He tries to throw the feet so that they contact the wall or are caught by the partner. The position is held. As skill is gained the performer may push the feet along the wall until the body is fully extended. He tries the same without using the wall or partner as a support.

The head stand is often taught by putting the head on the mat next to the ankle of a "spotter." Both legs may be brought up slowly with great lower back control, or one leg at a time may be swung up over the supporting head and hands.

POLE PULL AND PUSH

SPACE: Playground, gymnasium

PLAYING AREA: A base line is drawn on floor or ground.

EQUIPMENT: A pole three to five feet long

FORMATION: Two contestants stand on either side of the base line, back to back, grasping a pole at either end.

PROCEDURE: The stunt is to pull the opponent over the dividing base line. Contestants may then stand facing each other and try to push each other across the line.

ROOSTER FIGHT

SPACE: Playground or gymnasium; two or more circles are drawn, five or six feet in diameter

FORMATION: Two contestants stand within each circle. Each grasps his own left foot with the right hand behind his own back, while with his left hand he grasps his right forearm behind his own back.

PROCEDURE: At a signal, each rooster tries to force the opponent to go out of the circle or to lose his balance. The one who is forced out of the circle or who loosens the grasp of either hand is the loser. Three out of five trials determine the winner of the match.

STICK WRESTLE

SPACE: Playground or gymnasium

EQUIPMENT: A short stick or pole

re 141. Elephant Walk

PROCEDURE: Two opponents face each other and grasp the stick. Each tries to take the stick from the opponent.

TWISTER [1]

SPACE: Playground or gymnasium

FORMATION: Partners stand about three feet apart with right hands grasped; this grasp must not be broken.

PROCEDURE: Number 1 swings his left leg, straddles hands, and ends with back to Number 2. Number 2 lifts and swings right leg, straddles hands, and ends with back to Number 1.

Number 1 swings right leg over body of Number 2 and faces him. Number 2 swings left leg over body of Number 1 and finishes facing him.

This is repeated in quick succession a number of times.

---

[1] Virginia Lee Horne, *Stunts and Tumbling for Girls*. New York: A. S. Barnes & Co., 1943. Page 98.

Chapter XX

ACTIVITIES FOR SEVENTH GRADE

Activities are alphabetically arranged by title within the following four classes:

The games fall into several classes. They are indexed here by type for the convenience of the teacher.

[719]

Games

BASKETBALL FOR BOYS [1]

NUMBER OF PLAYERS: 10

SPACE: Playground, gymnasium

PLAYING AREA: Rectangular court 40 by 60 feet, minimum, to 50 by 84 or 94 feet, maximum, marked as shown in Figure 142. A basketball goal is placed 4 feet from the end lines at each end, the rim of the basket being 9 feet from the ground or floor.

EQUIPMENT: Basketball or junior basketball

Procedure

Basketball is a team game played on a court by two teams of five players each. The object is to throw the ball into the team's own goal and to prevent the opponents from securing the ball or scoring. The ball cannot be carried or kicked but must be advanced by passing or dribbling.

FORMATION: There are two teams of five players each: right and left guards, right and left forwards, and center. At the beginning of the game, two guards of one team stand between the opposing forwards and the forwards' goal, while the two forwards of the same team are guarded similarly at the opposite goal. The two opposing centers take the tossup or jump ball. After the jump ball is completed the ten players may play anywhere within the court boundaries.

PLAYING PERIODS: For players fourteen years old and younger, the game is played in four quarters of six minutes each, with a 2-minute rest period between quarters and a 10-minute rest period between halves. During the half time players may leave the court. Time out is taken after a foul is called or when injuries occur or in other cases of a dead ball. Each team may have five time-outs charged to it without a penalty.

RULES OF PLAY: The game is started by the referee's tossing the ball up between the centers in the center circle. The two centers must stand with both feet inside the center circle and they must not tap the ball more than twice after it has reached its highest point.

When a team has the ball in its back court, that team must advance the ball to its front court within 10 seconds, or lose the ball to the opposite team on an out-of-bounds play.

After a goal from the field, any member of the team not making the goal may put the ball into play from any point out of bounds at the end of the court where the goal was made.

---

[1] Based on *Basketball Rules.* Chicago: National Federation of State High School Athletic Associations, 1950.

DEFINITIONS AND PLAYING REGULATIONS

Blocking: Hindering the progress of a player who does not have the ball. Blocking is a foul.

Dead Ball: The ball is dead after (a) whistle is blown, (b) goal is made, (c) time-out is called, (d) held ball is called, (e) ball goes out of bounds.

Dribble: Advancing the ball by bouncing or batting the ball and touching it again before it touches another player.

Foul: An infraction of the rules for which one or more free throws are given.

Held Ball (or Tie Ball): When two or more opposing players have one or both hands firmly on the ball. Put in play by a jump in the center of the restraining circle closest to the spot where the held ball occurred.

Jump Ball: A play in which the official tosses the ball between two opposing players. Called "Tossed Ball" in Girls' Basketball and in Nine-Court Basketball.

Own Basket: The basket in which a team tries to throw the ball to score a goal.

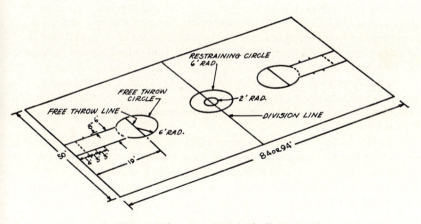

Figure 142.   Boys' Basketball Court

Running with the Ball: Traveling while holding the ball beyond the following limits: (a) A player may pivot with either foot if he received the ball while standing still. (b) A player who receives the ball while moving may take only one step before the ball leaves his hands.

Violation: An infraction of the rules for which the opponents are awarded the ball out of bounds.

OUT OF BOUNDS: The last player to touch a ball which goes out of bounds causes the ball to go out of bounds. The opponent of the player causing the ball to go out of bounds is awarded the ball outside of the court at the point where the ball went out, and within five seconds after he is given the ball he must pass the ball to a player within the court. If two players at the same time cause the ball to go out of bounds, the ball is put in play by a jump between the contending players at the nearest circle.

VIOLATIONS: Minor infractions of the rules are called violations, for which a member of the opposing team is given the ball out of bounds nearest the point where the violation occurred. Common violations are as follows: (1) infraction of rules governing free throws; (2) causing the ball to go out of bounds; (3) running with the ball or kicking it; (4) making a second dribble after completing a dribble before the ball has been touched by another player or has hit the backboard; (5) infraction of rules governing a jump ball.

FOULS: Fouls are major infractions of basketball rules for which one or more free throws are awarded. There are two kinds of fouls: personal and technical.

Personal fouls include the following: (1) pushing; (2) tripping; (3) blocking the progress of an opponent with any part of the body; (4) charging into a player with the ball; (5) shifting the body position into the pathway of an opponent to prevent him from reaching a desired position (similar to blocking in Girls' Basketball). A player is disqualified after five personal fouls or a single disqualifying foul which in the judgment of the referee is a willful foul.

Technical fouls include the following: (1) delaying the game; (2) using unsportsmanlike tactics, such as using profanity or disrespectfully addressing officials; (3) being illegally substituted, or leaving the court without permission.

For each foul, either personal or technical, one free throw is awarded. An additional free throw is awarded to a forward who is fouled in the act of shooting. If the field goal is made it counts, and then only one free throw is given in addition, unless the foul was judged by the official to be a deliberate one.

FREE THROW: A free throw for the goal is awarded a player for a foul committed by a member of the opposing team. When a personal foul is called, the player that was fouled takes the throw. The opposing players must line up alternately on the sides of the free-throw lane. When a technical foul is called the free throw may be attempted by any member of the opposing team.

The free throw must be taken within 10 seconds after the ball has been placed on the free-throw line. No player may move into the free-throw lane until the ball has touched the basket rim or backboard. If during the free throw a violation is made by the free thrower or his team, no point can be made, but the ball is awarded out of bounds to the opponents on the side near the center circle (after a technical foul) or on the side near the free-throw line (after a personal foul). If during the free throw a violation is made by the free thrower's opponent, any goal made counts and the violation is disregarded, but if no goal is made another free throw is attempted. If both teams violate the rules, the ball is dead, no score can be made, and play is started by a jump between centers at the nearer free-throw line.

After a successful free throw caused by a personal foul is made, the ball is thrown in from out of bounds by an opponent of the free thrower; if the free throw is for a technical foul, whether or not it was successful, the ball is thrown in by any player of free thrower's team from out of bounds at mid-court. Play continues after an unsuccessful throw after a personal foul.

SCORING: A goal made from the court is called a field goal and counts 2 points; a goal made from a free throw counts 1 point. That team wins which has the greater number of points at the end of the playing period.

TEACHING SUGGESTIONS

1. Introduce basketball skills through simple games before attempting to play basketball. See Basketball Skill Drills, p. 744.
2. Study the section on Basketball Techniques (page 727-44) before teaching the game.
3. Use a current edition of *Basketball Rules*.

BASKETBALL FOR GIRLS [1]

NUMBER OF PLAYERS: 12

SPACE: Playground, gymnasium

PLAYING AREA: Rectangular court 40 by 60 feet, minimum, or 50 by 84 feet, maximum, marked as for boys' basketball with the exception of (1) two parallel center lines (one foot apart) or one solid line twelve inches wide dividing the court into two equal parts, and (2) one center circle with a 3-foot radius instead of two circles (Figure 143).

EQUIPMENT: Basketball or junior basketball

Procedure

Girls' basketball is played much as is boys' basketball, with a few exceptions. There are six players to a team, rather than five. No player may cross the center division line; forwards play only in the half of the court nearest their goal, and the guards play only in the half of the court nearest their opponents' goal.

[1] Based on *Official Basketball Guide*. Washington: National Section on Women's Athletics, American Association for Health, Physical Education and Recreation (1201 Sixteenth St., N.W., Washington 6, D. C.).

FORMATION: Each team has six players, three forwards and three guards. The right and left guards stand between the opposing forwards and the goal toward which they are shooting. The center guard stands outside the center circle between the center forward and her goal. If the opposing team receives the center throw, the center guard guards the player in the circle, but if the forward of the center guard's team receives the center throw, the guard plays farther back in the court.

PLAYING PERIOD: The game consists of four 8-minute quarters with a 2-minute rest between quarters and a 10-minute rest between halves. For elementary school girls 5-minute or 6-minute quarters are recommended. At the beginning of each quarter the center throw is awarded alternately to the two teams. After each goal, the team not making the goal receives the center throw.

Time-out is taken only when the ball is dead or in case of injury. It must be called by the referee or umpire. A team is allowed three time-outs during a game.

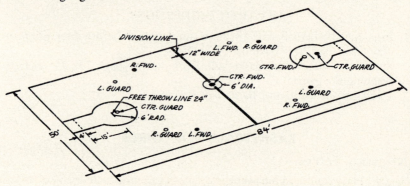

Figure 143. Girls' Basketball Court

DEFINITION OF TERMS AND RESTRICTIONS

Blocking: A personal foul in which a player, using her arms or body, interferes with the progress of a player who does not have the ball.

Bounce: Legally advancing the ball by bouncing it on the ground and taking as many steps as possible before catching the ball. The 1949-50 rules make legal a limited dribble, allowing two bounces in succession with no pause between each bounce. Some schools are trying out a continuous dribble.

Bounce Pass: A play in which the ball is passed to another player by bouncing the ball.

Boundary Lines: All lines are out of bounds. A player may not step on any line with the exception of the neutral territory in the center division line.

Dead Ball: The ball is dead when play ceases and it must be put into play by an official.

Goal: The basket toward which team is throwing is its own goal.

Guarding: Covering an opponent who has the ball. Guarding may be done with both arms in any plane, providing the guarding player does not touch her opponent's body or the ball held by her opponent.

Juggle: A legal play in which a player advances the ball by throwing it or tapping it into the air and catching it again before the ball has touched the ground or another player.

Pivot: A play in which a player who has the ball in her hands steps once or more in any direction with the same foot, the other foot (called the pivot foot) touching the floor at the original spot of contact. The pivot foot may be lifted from the floor when the ball is thrown, if the ball has left the player's hands before the pivot foot touches the floor again. The pivot foot may be dragged up to the other foot when releasing the ball after a pivot.

Tie Ball (called Held Ball in boys' rules): When two players place one or both hands on the ball simultaneously. A foul is called on the player who places her hand on the ball after her opponent has legally secured it. A tossed ball is used after a tie ball. If two players on opposite sides of the center line have a tie ball, they may temporarily cross the division line for the tossed ball.

Tossed Ball: The play in which the ball is tossed between two opponents who may tap it after it has reached its height if they stay within their own half of the circle. Neither player may catch the ball until it has touched the floor or another player has touched it. Jump Ball is the name given to this play in the boys' rules. The opponents stand with both feet in own half of the center of imaginary circle (nearest opponent's goal, so that players face own goal) when they jump for the ball tossed between them. The ball must be tossed to a greater height than either player can reach when jumping and must be tossed vertically so that it will drop between them.

RULES OF PLAY: The game is started with a center throw by the referee to a center forward. (Any forward, however, may take the center throw.) The choice of center throw or basket is made by the toss of a coin.

On the center throw all players must be outside the center circle except the forward receiving the throw. The forward may face in any direction to receive this throw. The center who receives the center throw must pass the ball within three seconds in any direction to another player; she may not touch the ball again until it has been touched by another player. Two completed passes are necessary after the center throws, before a forward may shoot for the goal, unless the ball is intercepted or tied by an opponent.

The ball may be legally caught and thrown with one hand, but must be thrown within three seconds. If a player falls down, this three seconds is counted from the time she is back on her feet.

A player may not combine a dribble and a juggle. The ball must be passed, not handed to another player.

OUT OF BOUNDS: A player with the ball in her hands is out of bounds if any part of her body touches the boundary line or any object outside the boundary. Whenever the ball goes out of bounds it is put in play at the side lines by the opponent of the person who last touched the ball at a spot opposite where it went out.

VIOLATIONS: Minor infractions of the rules for which an out-of-bounds play is awarded an opponent is called a violation. The following are common violations: (1) stepping over a boundary line; (2) holding the ball for more than three seconds in the court; more than five seconds on an out-of-bounds play; (3) traveling with the ball while it is in player's hands; (4) taking more than one bounce unless a limited dribble is used; (5) kicking or handing the ball; (6) violating free-throw rules.

FOULS: Fouls are major infractions of the rules for which one or more free throws are awarded. There are two kinds of fouls, personal and technical.

Personal fouls are those that involve body contact and blocking, which may not involve body contact. Personal fouls are as follows: (1) obstructing a player who is advancing with the ball; (2) charging with the ball into a player; (3) blocking the progress of a person without the ball; (4) holding a player by contact with body; (5) using unnecessary roughness; (6) tripping.

Technical fouls are those that do not involve body contact, and they are as follows: (1) overguarding the ball by keeping the hands on ball after opponent has legally secured it; (2) boxing-up a player by two players guarding one opponent; (3) waving hands before eyes of player who has the ball; (4) delaying the game in any way; (5) committing a team foul, which is charged to the team.

A player is automatically disqualified for making five technical fouls, four personal fouls, or five technical and personal fouls combined.

For each foul, either personal or technical, time-out is taken and one free throw is awarded. Two free throws are awarded if a forward is fouled upon while in the act of shooting, if the goal is not made. If the goal is made, in spite of the foul, only one free throw is awarded.

FREE THROW: A free throw for a goal from the free-throw line is given a team when one of its members has been fouled against. When a foul has been called, the referee immediately gets the ball and places it on the free-throw line of the team entitled to shoot. The forward fouled against must take the free throw within 10 seconds but any forward may take the free throw if a guard is fouled against. All players must remain outside the free-throw lane and circle until the ball has left the free thrower's hands. For such a violation by a forward, the goal if made does not count, and the ball is put in play by a guard out of bounds opposite to the free throw line. If a guard makes a violation, the goal counts if made, and a forward puts the ball in play from the side lines. If the goal is made or missed the ball is put in play by the player taking the free throw on an out-of-bounds play at the side lines opposite the free-throw line. After a double foul, the ball is put in play by a tossed ball in the center circle.

SCORING: A goal from the field counts 2 points. A goal from a free throw counts one point. The team wins which has the higher score at the end of the playing time. A tie score stands.

TEACHING SUGGESTIONS

1. Teach basketball skills through relays, simple games, and coeducational basketball type games.
2. Adapt the section on Basketball Techniques to help teach skills to the girls.
3. Use a current edition of the *Official Basketball Guide*.

BASKETBALL TECHNIQUES [1]

A good game of basketball for either boy or girl depends on individual skills and team play. A primary requirement is the ability of each player to handle the ball effectively. This means not only accurate passes and shots for the basket but also the ability to move quickly and speedily. The ball should be handled with the tips of the fingers and thumbs, with hands cupped, not flat handed. The ball should be held firmly between the hands, and the fingers should be relaxed at all times. A player cannot pass or shoot with accuracy without the ability to control the ball.

CATCHING THE BALL: In catching a basketball the player should move to meet it and "watch it into his hands." The player must, in addition to catching the ball, watch the movement of players in preparation for a pass. The ability to watch the fringe of a movement is peripheral vision.

The fingers should be relaxed and cupped and extended either upward or downward to receive the ball. The fingers, wrists, and arms should be relaxed until the instant the ball is caught. The shock of the catch is taken by the recoil of the arms and the grip of the fingers. At the instant of contact the arms and hands should give with the ball in such a way that the movement prepares one for the next pass.

---

[1] Briefed from *Lessons in Basketball*, by William A. Moore, Supervisor, Division of Recreation, Central Park, Louisville, Kentucky. By permission of the author. Reviewed and edited by Aubrey R. Bonham, Director of Physical Education for Men and Varsity Basketball Coach, Whittier College, Whittier, California.

PASSING: Skill in passing is a fundamental ability of extreme value. It ranks in importance with accuracy in goal shooting. From *two to three hundred passes* are made during a game while usually only forty to eighty attempts are made to throw for a basket. Furthermore, passing techniques can be improved with comparatively much less effort than can goal throwing.

Passing from Position of Reception: The passer can assist the receiver greatly by delivering the ball so that it is easy to catch. Under normal conditions the ball should travel approximately parallel with the floor. When a ball arrives two feet above the head of a player and that player passes from that position, there is a tendency for the ball to be passed at a downward angle. Likewise, a ball thrown from a low position usually travels upward. Passes moving with an upward or downward angle are difficult to receive. If timing is not a factor, it is better to move the ball to a more advantageous position before passing.

Types of Passes: Various special passes are used by players in particular areas for specific purposes. Following are descriptions of some of these passes.

Two-Handed Underarm Pass: The ball is held in both hands waist high at the side of the passer near his hips. The elbows are bent and held slightly away from the side of the body. The delivery is made with a snap of the wrists. The fingers and arms follow through behind the ball. As the weight shifts, the rear leg follows through into the next step.

Chest Pass: The feet may be in parallel position or they may be in a running stride position. The body is approximately in an erect position. The ball is held in both hands at chest level. The elbows are kept close to the body. The thumbs are widely spread on the ball from the index fingers. The ball is delivered by a sudden push forward of the arms and hands. The arms and hands follow through with weight shift from rear to front foot.

Shoulder Pass: The ball is moved by both hands to a point over the shouder at the side of or above the head, at which point the passing hand assumes complete control of the ball. The ball is propelled by a straight forward movement of the arm and hand, with the body and legs following through.

Hook Pass: The ball to be thrown may be held in either hand. It is held between the hand and elbow on the forearm. The ball is thrown by means of a full swing directly over the head. The ball should leave the hand at the highest point of the swing. While this arm action is occurring, the passer should spring upward and away from the defensive guard. Finger tips should be kept above center line of ball for good control.

Skip Pass: For fast break or moving passes, a skip pass should be executed. The receiver takes a skip just before the ball reaches his fingers. This lowers the center of gravity for the stop, hesitation, and execution of any pass, followed by a quick start.

Bounce Pass: The ball is held in the same position as for the chest pass and is delivered in the same way by being pushed forward to strike the floor three feet or more in front of the receiver. The ball should bounce at least waist high for most successful catching.

Overhead Pass: The ball is held overhead in both hands, feet slightly apart. Player bends knees slightly and lowers ball slightly to the back of the head. He then straightens knees and arms and releases the ball. Usually the pass is considered advantageous only when ball is received overhead, or when the passing team has a height advantage.

Other Special Passes: Many other passes may be developed, depending upon the special abilities of a player, or his size or speed. Among these passes are (a) the one-hand underhand, (b) the two-hand over-the-shoulder, (c) slow looping bounce passes, and (d) false passes or passes thrown in any fashion while the passer is looking in some other direction.

DRIBBLING: The start of the dribble must be legal; that is, the ball must leave the hand before, or as, the rear foot or pivot foot leaves the floor. The first bounce is started with both hands but one hand directs the final delivery of the ball. Either hand may be used to bounce the ball. The palm of the hand should never slap or spank the ball to the floor. The force is applied to the ball with the cupped fingers and the thumb while the source of the force lies in the fingers, wrist, and the slight flexing of the arm at the elbow. The hand should follow through behind the ball, giving the player the "feel" of where next to put his hand to continue the dribble. The bounce or limited dribble for girls has the same skill principles.

SUGGESTIONS TO PLAYERS IN DRIBBLING

1. Do not spank the ball to the floor. Get the touch by following through behind the ball with the fingers. Press or knead ball with arm, wrist, and finger tips with enough force to bring ball up from floor to meet the hand. No sound should come from hand action on ball.

2. Keep the head up. Keep the eyes just above the ball so that it can be seen at the highest point of the bounce. Do not focus eyes directly on any definite object. Wide vision is essential so that the player is able to see all floor action and not handicap the offense.

3. Protect the ball with the body when an opponent approaches. Dribble with the left hand if attacked from the right. Dribble at side when under defensive pressure.

4. Remember to dribble only when a pass is not possible.

BODY MOVEMENT AND FOOTWORK: A player, to be successful, must develop clever footwork and body movements. When it can be said of a player, "He is hard to guard," then that player is effectively handling his body and feet. It is essential that each player know the technique of starting, stopping, turning, pivoting, and changing pace and direction, in order that he may protect the ball from the opponents. The same techniques are necessary also to free a player from a guard even if the player does not hold the ball. It is of great importance that a player's center of balance be low to the ground when the player suddenly starts, stops, or changes direction.

Quick Starts: It is of utmost importance that the offensive player be able to execute sudden starts in order to elude the guard. If the player executing the quick start *is able to gain a full running stride in his first step*, the guard will not be able to follow the movement soon enough to stop the intended play. Timing is of great importance in quick starting. The technique to be used is rather indefinite in that it varies with different types of players. As a general rule (1) the weight of the player should be low to the floor, (2) the feet must be in such a position that they will enable the player to start quickly in any direction, and (3) the whole soles of the shoes should be in contact with the floor to give the greatest possible traction. To this physical technique must be added the desire to get away quickly. No player ever learns sudden starts without this mental attitude.

SUGGESTIONS TO PLAYERS IN STARTING

1. To start suddenly, get low to the floor.
2. Put effort into the first step. Taking a long step for the first step will put the player closer to the floor so that the next steps can be short and fast to build momentum which allows the player to get free from his opponent.
3. Be sure that the rear foot will not slip as start is made. The shoe should hold if enough rubber is in contact with the floor surface.
4. Feint as if to go in one direction but actually go in another. A head and shoulder rock to left, with center of balance moving to right, is the best fake.

Sudden Stops: The use of sudden stops to elude a guard is equally important whether an offensive player has the ball or does not have the ball. A defensive man, in full running stride, will always over-run an offensive player who executes a sudden stop. Two methods have been developed for effecting a quick stop: (1) the jump stop, and (2) the running stride stop. Frequently a combination of jumping into the stop is used, with the feet and legs in the position for the running stride stop.

Jump Stop: The player leaves the floor with a jump from either foot, jumps forward with the feet only one or two inches from the floor, and plants both feet in a parallel position. The knees are bent to take up the shock of the stop, the body is held erect, and the weight is distributed on both feet. The whole surface of the soles of both shoes must be in contact with the floor. The toes should be pointed straight ahead. Slipping or loss of balance are thus eliminated. The jump stop is extremely sudden and effective, but the player should bend his knees to absorb the body jar.

Running Stride Stop: To execute this type of stop the direction of the feet must not be changed. The player merely plants his forward foot firmly on the floor surface with the toes pointing forward. The entire soles of the shoes must contact the floor to prevent slipping. The rear leg bends deeply at the knee and the weight is thrown slightly backward, resulting in excellent balance. At the same time the body becomes more erect from the hips upward while the center of weight remains low by tucking the hips under. The running stride stop is not as sudden as the jump stop and is not as hard on the muscles of the feet and legs.

SUGGESTIONS TO PLAYERS IN STOPPING

1. Stop suddenly. Do not take another step after deciding to stop.
2. Keep the toes of the shoes pointing forward, for if this is done the shoes are less apt to slip. Thrust great toes at the floor, using inside edge of shoe for the fast stop.
3. Shift the weight backward as stop is made, because otherwise balance will be lost.

Pivots: There are several types of pivots that players use. Each one is important and skills in each must be cultivated.

Full Pivot: The full pivot is used by a player in possession of the ball who desires to change his direction and at the same time protect the ball with his body from an opponent. The full pivot can be used after either the jump or running stride stop. It must be remembered in particular that the ball must come into the hands of the pivoter as, or after, the stop is made. If the ball comes into the hands before the stop, the pivoter may commit a violation for traveling with the ball.

When the pivot is made to the right, the weight of the pivoter should be shifted to the right or pivot foot. At the same time, the left leg provides the force for the whirl. Before the pivot a slight movement of the body to the left or a feint pass to the left will often draw the defensive player out of position. The left foot is raised from the floor and may be placed instantly at the correct position for the maintenance of balance. The heel of the right or pivot foot is not in contact with the floor. The whirl is made on the ball of the pivot foot.

The body is crouched and the ball is held away from the defensive player. The head is up and the eyes are gazing over the field to where the ball is to be passed. The ball must be held at arm's length from the body as the pivoter begins to whirl. The whirl must be executed with great speed.

The major teaching points of the pivot may be summed up as follows: (a) the pivot foot may not be changed after the ball is in the hands of the player; (b) the body must be whirled suddenly; (c) the body must be crouched in order to hold the ball away from the guard; (d) the hips of the pivoter, through the pivot, should be in line between the ball and the near hip of the opponent; (e) every pivoter should turn far enough around to make a forward pass; (f) pivot must be made away from the guard, not into him; (g) the ball must be in act of being thrown as the pivot foot leaves the floor; (h) a player should be able to pivot equally well in either direction.

Forward Pivot: A dribbler who is being closely followed by an opponent may suddenly stop and execute a forward pivot. The moving foot passes in front of the pivot foot. This causes the pivoter to end his pivot facing in the opposite direction from that at the start of the pivot. When pivoting to the left, the weight is shifted to the left foot. The left shoulder is dropped slightly, while the right foot provides the speed of the whirl.

Reverse Pivot: A reverse pivot may be used when an offensive player receives the ball while he and a guard are moving to meet the ball. The reverse pivot is similar to the movement in military drill known as, "To the rear march!" A running stride stop is executed at the time the ball comes into the hands with the reverse whirl following almost simultaneously. The ball receiver executes a reverse pivot by crouching, shifting his weight to the rear foot, and forcing his whirl with the right leg. The right foot is carried back in front of the left. The hips protect the ball. This pivot can be made from a jump stop in either direction.

The reverse pivot may be used by a player who does not have the ball to elude his opponent or to guard a player who does not have the ball, in boys' basketball.

SUGGESTIONS TO PLAYERS IN PIVOTING

1. Keep the opponent guessing as to whether a reverse pivot or change of direction will be used during a dribble.
2. Always place the leg nearest the guard in the front position when using a reverse pivot.
3. Cover as much area as is possible with the pivot step.
4. Do the reverse pivot suddenly and with plenty of power.

Reverse Turn: This turn is usually employed at the sideline by an offensive player who has been forced there by a closely guarding opponent. The offensive player who holds the ball comes to a running stride stop. The body is twisted at the hips in such a way that the ball is protected by the body. The pass should be made forward to a teammate. During this action the foot must turn slightly in the direction of the pass.

SUGGESTIONS TO PLAYERS IN TURNING

1. Make the stop, twist, and pass of the reverse turn at the same time.
2. Turn away from the direction of the pass after performing a reverse turn. Since the opponent player usually watches the direction of the pass, a new position may be taken by the offensive player.
3. Use a one-hand follow-through pass.

Change of Direction: A basketball player is more difficult to guard, whether he has the ball or not, if he moves in one direction for a few strides and then suddenly changes direction at a positive angle. A player desiring to change his direction to his left from a definite pass should place his right foot forward at the point where he desires to change direction and move his left foot across the angle he wishes to make. Players who move in curved paths are more easily guarded.

SUGGESTIONS TO PLAYERS IN CHANGING DIRECTION

1. Do not run in curved paths. Run in zig-zag lines. Make every change of direction a positive one.
2. If desiring to turn to the left, make the right foot the corner of the change of direction. If turning to the right, the left foot should be forward.
3. Use change of direction while dribbling.

Change of Pace: The ability to change one's pace is a valuable asset to any offensive player. The player with the ball should learn to hesitate slightly in an attempt to cause the guarding player to adjust his speed to the slower rate. After this adjustment takes place, a quickened speed will cause the play to be more effective. A player without the ball may use a change of pace to aid him in getting into position to receive a pass.

Three Speeds Used: Three speeds are necessary for change of pace. In general each player should have the following abilities: (1) He should have a slow jogging speed for offensive adjustment, (2) He should speed up the adjustment pace just before he is to receive a pass, (3) He should be able to suddenly burst into full speed to grasp an opportunity to shoot for goal. Such skills must be developed during playing periods.

SUGGESTIONS TO PLAYERS IN CHANGE OF PACE

1. Do not run at the fastest speed all the time.

2. Trot or jog about the court when there is no need to hurry.

3. Meet the ball at a fast pace when about to catch it.

4. Break away as fast as possible when an opportunity to score occurs.

5. Slow pace down if it is seen that you will reach the position for receiving the ball ahead of time. Slow up, then speed up to meet the ball.

6. Use a slower pace to bring an opposing guard out and then pass to a teammate who has gone in behind the guard.

Footwork for Player Without Ball: It is most important that all players on the team which is in possession of the ball should be alert to receive the ball at any moment from the player with the ball. The footwork of these players is of great importance, because they must be in position to receive the ball at any time and to get free for a shot at the basket.

SUGGESTIONS TO PLAYERS IN FOOTWORK

1. When without the ball, start, dart, and stop rapidly. Worry the defensive players all the time.

2. Play just as hard without the ball as one does with it.

3. Get into position by a quick start; do not depend on speed alone to get into position to receive the ball.

INDIVIDUAL DEFENSE: The success of the defense of a team rests upon the ability of each player on that team to guard effectively. Too often guards are the only players who play successfully on defense. The forwards and center must have the same skill. Each and every player must be drilled in defense tactics until every movement becomes automatic.

The body of the player who is guarding must be in such position that he can move in any direction, including jumping upward and squatting, to meet the movement of the opponent. A defense player must never give away his intended action in any of his movements. If he does, and if the play does not occur as anticipated, he will be unable to recover in time to prevent the play which actually does occur. Then too, defensive players must realize that it is just as important that they hurry, prevent, or intercept passes as it is for them to prevent shots at the basket. It is essential that a defensive player be located at all times in a position between his opponent and the basket and in such a position that he can see both his opponent and the ball.

The Defensive Stance: The stance of a guard or defensive player is similar to that of the wrestler: (1) The feet should be spread. (2) The weight of the body should be equally distributed on the balls of the feet. (3) The knees should be bent. (4) The body should be held in a crouched position; when moving in a circular pattern, hold elbows close, as this lets you pivot or change directions faster. (5) The arm nearest the side-line should be extended well in the air to prevent a shot at the basket. Against hard outside drivers use inside hand up and inside leg up on sidelines. (6) The other arm should be extended at a height which is even with the shoulder to prevent a pass out into the court. The position of the arms may be switched to meet the need. (7) The head should be held up with the eyes gazing at the opponent.

This stance will vary somewhat with movement, but in no case should the feet be brought close together. The stance of the guard is the key to all defense work. The player will be able to move in any direction with the quickest possible action if this body position is maintained as nearly as possible at all times. The maintenance of the stance, furthermore, will prevent the player from completely giving away his intended movement.

Guarding Procedures: The guarding of opponents may be divided into three general classifications: (1) guarding an opponent who has the ball; (2) guarding an opponent who does not have the ball; and (3) guarding two opponents, one of whom has the ball.

Guarding an Opponent Who Has the Ball: Often an offensive player receives a pass while some five or six feet in front of an advancing defensive player. In this position the offensive player may decide to dribble to either side of the guard, shoot for goal, pivot, and then dribble or pass to a teammate. The guard's duty is to prevent any of these movements. He should move forward quickly, maintaining his stance. As the guard advances he should attempt to fake the opponent into the movement the guard desires. When the attacker begins his movement the guard should attempt to get his hand in contact with the ball and deflect its flight if he is unable to get complete control of the ball. The guard must not move his feet if the offensive player makes a feint to pass, shoot, or dribble. The feet should move only as, or after, the feet of the opponent move. A good guard makes the offensive man move forward toward him. He should not be caught moving away from the basket and toward the offensive man.

The guard must be careful not to watch the flight of the ball to the neglect of the passer when the latter passes to a teammate. If the guard changes his eye direction, the offensive player may move around him and so be open to receive a return pass. Watching the flight of the ball is the primary weakness of all defensive players. A good guard never waits for offensive feints but starts his own feint to guide the offensive player's actions.

The guard should never jump from the floor in an effort to block a shot, except when the shot is being taken close to the basket and the offensive player has no chance to dribble. The direction of the ball must be judged for rebound by the thrower and he must try to get the ball. The guard must prevent the thrower's rebound play. The guard may best do this by turning his back to the forward player as soon as that offensive player has indicated the direction he is to take. When the guard is able to whirl into a position in front of the rebound play, the forward is legally blocked. The guard should jump forward and upward and gain possession of the ball at the time the ball comes off the backboard. As the guard completes his jump he should whirl and be prepared to pass the ball out to a teammate in the safety area.

Opposing Dribbler's Technique: When a dribbler advances down the court and meets a defensive player the dribbler may attempt: (a) to dribble around the guard; (b) to bounce pass; (c) to pivot and pass to a teammate; (d) to try for a goal; or (e) to swerve his dribble toward the side line. The guard must attempt to prevent the execution of any of these possibilities. He should advance in his crouching stride toward the dribbler. Defensive fakes are a necessity in order to cause the dribbler to attempt the action which the guard player desires.

A guard should pick up a dribbler slowly and drive him away from the basket and hold him on the sidelines if possible. If the dribbler attempts to go around the guard the latter must play low to the ground, shift in front of the dribbler, and play the ball as it nears the floor, since the ball is out of control of the dribbler when it hits the floor. The guard should advance rapidly if the dribbler attempts to bounce pass, pivot and pass, or shoot for goal.

When the dribbler swerves toward the sideline it is an advantage for the guard, since the offensive player at the sideline has but one direction in which to pass the ball. The progress of the guard should be a half-forward and half-sideward stride with knees held far apart. The center of guard's body should be directly opposite the shoulder of the dribbler.

At the sideline the offensive player may: (a) change the direction of his dribble and continue toward the basket; (b) hook pass back to a teammate; (c) execute a forward pivot and pass or shoot; or (d) execute a reverse turn and pass. The defensive player must guard against action in front of and behind the offensive player. Frequently an offensive player is forced to hesitate while waiting for a teammate to get in position for a pass. During this period the guard may close in. The offensive player will naturally turn his back to the guard. The guard should take such a position that the median line of his body is opposite the median line of the opponent's body. If the offensive player tries to pass in one direction, the guard should shift and maintain the same relation with his opponent. If the offensive player attempts to pass in the other direction, the guard should shift and prevent the attempt. Each time the guard must attempt to get his hand on the ball by reaching for it. The chief objective of the guard is to secure the ball or cause a jump ball.

SUGGESTIONS FOR GUARDING PLAYER WHO HAS THE BALL

1. Dominate the opponent. Convince him that you can and will prevent the successful completion of every move he attempts.
2. Go after an offensive player aggressively when he is undecided what to do.
3. Do not be afraid of being fouled by the official. The defensive man who does not foul occasionally is not aggressive.
4. Take the ball away from an opponent by a slight push downward and quick twist to rotate the ball. Usually it cannot be taken away by sheer strength. (This technique applies only to Basketball for Boys; it is illegal for girls.)
5. Be especially aggressive in taking defensive rebounds. Be sure that no one takes the ball away from you or that you do not step out of bounds when you get your hands on the ball.

SUGGESTIONS FOR GUARDING PLAYER WHO DOES NOT HAVE THE BALL

1. Keep close to the player. Anticipate his every move. Usually the passer has but one logical pass. Anticipate that pass.
2. Do not let your player get behind you.
3. Be sure to gaze between the ball and the player that you are guarding if they are on different sides of the court. By this gaze you see both out of the corners of your eyes.
4. Do not move when a player feints in any direction except to take a half step backwards.

Guarding Two Men, One of Whom Has the Ball: The situation is entirely in favor of the offensive player, when a player is advancing rapidly toward his basket on one side of the court while his teammate is dribbling toward the basket on the other side. The whole responsibility of the defense rests upon the guard. The defense objective in such a situation is: (a) To retard the speed of the offensive players until a defensive teammate is able to aid the guard; (b) to feint at the dribbler in order to make him stop his dribble as far out in the court as possible and then cover the man without the ball. The defensive player should go back within six or eight feet of the basket if the offensive players are passing the ball between themselves, thereby protecting the basket from a possible shot by forcing an offensive player to shoot from as far out in the court as possible.

When two players are attacking, the dribbler should be made to think that the ball is to be taken from him. A guard should slide back toward the second offensive player to intercept the pass when the dribbler takes up the ball.

There are two kinds of attacking systems. A fast breaking system results in a player being forced to be on the move while he is attempting to score; whereas a slow breaking attack tends to give the player more time for set shots. The defensive players try to break the shooting rhythm of a player.

GOAL THROWING: Skill in throwing goals is extremely important. Some players seem to have natural ability to make goals in spite of all conditions. Others must acquire the skill. Each player must have: (1) the desire to put the ball in the basket; (2) confidence in his ability to do so; (3) poise that keeps him cool and unhurried; and (4) a physical condition allowing efficient use of his body in shooting. Players must develop confidence, concentration, balance in the air or on the floor, relaxation and easy follow-through in order to develop accurate shooting.

Paths the Ball May Travel: On leaving the thrower's hands the ball may travel in a high arc or loop; it may be a beeline shot; or it may be between these two types.

High Arc Loop: High loop shots become relatively inaccurate because of the great distance through which the ball must go before it arrives at the basket. This element of inaccuracy is somewhat equalized by the entrance angle of the ball into the basket. The rebound of the ball from this shot is usually high and close to the basket.

Beeline Shot: In this throw the ball travels the minimum distance from the shooter's hands to the basket. Greater accuracy of direction and distance is possible but the entrance angle into the basket is less advantageous.

Medium Shot: This represents a loop shot which combines excellent accuracy of direction with some advantage in the entrance angle. A medium rebound of the ball in height and distance from the basket results, if the goal is missed. It must be concluded, after studying arc angles of shots for the basket, that neither an exceedingly high arc nor the exceedingly low one will have the efficiency of the medium arc.

Thrower's Eye Position: Some instructors believe that the player who is shooting should imagine a spot above the basket ring and attempt to throw the ball through that spot. Others teach their players to toss the ball to an imaginary spot on the backboard. The majority of instructors and players prefer to make the near rim of the basket the target for the shot. This should be done not only because the rim makes a better target for the shot, but because careful attention centered on the rim makes for better concentration in the execution of the shot. It seems advisable, therefore, to tell throwers to fix their eyes on the rim and toss the ball to the basket. The eyes should remain fixed on the target until after the ball has left the player's hands. After the ball has left the player's hands he should proceed to an advantageous position for the rebound if the basket is not scored.

Thrower's Head Position: The position of the head is important in the development of goal throwing skill. Since the eyes are located in the head, most of the body movements revolve about the head as a pivotal point. During the act of shooting, the eyes, through the brain, estimate distance and direction, the muscles of the body making final and accurate adjustments to these factors. The head should be kept in the same position from the moment a player looks at the basket until the ball is delivered. Developing muscle pressures for spot shooting on concentric circles 15, 22, and 26 feet from the basket aids greatly in learning to shoot.

Types of Shots Used in Goal Throwing: The technique of shooting for goal varies with the different areas from which the shots are taken.

Underhand Loop Shot: This shot is the most natural throw for the basket. A person who has never before attempted to make a throw will toss the ball underhanded on his first attempt. The ball leaves the hands about the height of the shoulders after the hands carry the ball from the knees upward. The shot is often blocked, not because the movement is slow but rather because the ball is in a low position when it leaves the hands. The feet are in regular running stride position, the body is inclined forward, the head is up with the eyes focused on the rim of the basket. The ball is held chest high by use of the tips of the fingers and thumbs of both hands. The ball is tossed by first dropping it to a position even with the belt line and rather close to the body. The elbows must be moved outward slightly to permit a true drop of the ball. The ball is then tossed upward and forward by a simultaneous action of the legs, arms, wrists, and fingers. As the ball moves upward in the hands it should travel as close to the body as possible. The use of leg pressure to propel the ball will let arms relax through the shot and act as guides. As the ball is delivered the body should be stretched in a complete follow-through behind the path of the ball. The player must remember not to drop the ball lower than the waist, to bring the ball up in front of the face close to the body, and to follow through with hands and body behind the shot.

Poised Chest Shot: This shot has been developed through the improved aggressive play of guards. The ball passes upward and away from the reach of the defensive player. The shot is delivered from a running stride position while the player is momentarily stationary. The forward foot points in the direction of the basket while the rear foot points also, as nearly as possible, toward the basket. At the start the player bends his knees, squats three or four inches, with weight equally distributed on both feet. This foot and leg position gives the thrower added poise. The body should be crouched forward somewhat, with the head erect, the chin over the ball, and the eyes focused on the rim of the basket. The ball should be held chest high with the fingers and thumbs (palms free) slightly behind the axis of the ball. The angle formed by the thumb and forefinger should not be greater than fifteen degrees. The wrists should be straight and the elbows in a normal position at the sides of the body. Again use leg pressure to propel the shot and keep arms, wrists, and fingers relaxed.

The player, before the ball is thrown, may relax his arms and body by a slight settling movement. The ball is delivered by the simultaneous action of the legs, body, arms, and hands in a push upward and toward the basket. When the ball leaves the hands, the fingers should be pointed in the line of flight of the ball, palms away from the face. The arms, body, and legs should be extended in the path of the ball in such a way as to result in a complete follow-through. The weight is on the front foot while the rear foot is being carried forward into the next step.

Wide latitude should be granted players in developing the poised chest shot. It may be made with both heels together in such a position that the player may shoot, dribble, or make a sudden pass. The head is held very still in space with only a slight movement being made forward and upward toward the basket. Occasionally the player may jump with the shot as a part of the follow-through.

SUGGESTIONS TO PLAYERS IN SHOOTING

1. Secure body balance before attempting a shot at basket.
2. Relax before starting the throw.
3. Always have both feet pointed toward the basket. Make the knees work as hinges.
4. Hold the ball lightly but firmly between fingers and thumbs.
5. Move the arms some before shooting.
6. Get a good follow-through. Keep the hands up and pointing toward the path of the ball for a short time after the throw.
7. Keep thumbs three or four inches apart on the follow-through.
8. Remember that most players shoot more quickly than is necessary.

The Push Chest Shot or Wrist Snap: The technique for this shot varies somewhat from the poised chest shot. The position of the feet has no particular bearing upon the shot, but the body, legs, and hands are held in the same position as when a push pass is being thrown. The tips of the fingers of both hands hold the ball behind the axis, while the thumbs are at right angles to the forefingers. The ball must be adjusted according to the size of the hands. Small hands should hold the ball on its axis; big hands move toward the top side of the ball. The head is held erect and the eyes are fixed on the rim of the basket.

The ball is propelled toward the basket by a sudden push or snap of the fingers, wrists, and arms, the thumbs providing the major part of the force that gives the ball a spin called a "reverse English." The legs may add to some of the force in the case of shots from long distances. It is only necessary that the hands and arms follow through, but many players follow through with the entire body.

SUGGESTIONS TO PLAYERS IN CHEST SHOT

1. Learn the position for a push pass and then shoot a push chest shot from the same position.
2. Snap the ball to the basket with a sudden flip of the wrists and hands. Get the thumbs behind the ball as it is thrown.
3. After the ball leaves the hands, attempt to obtain an advantageous rebound position.

One-Hand Pivot Shot: A regular two-hand shot proves impractical in many defensive situations. These situations frequently occur in the vicinity of the free-throw circle. A player, therefore, has need for a shot which is difficult to guard because of body position and quickness of delivery. The one-hand shot answers this need. The attacking player makes a complete pivot to the right, the left being used as the pivot foot. He turns his head to locate the basket and has his left hand freed from the ball. The head, after the turn, is held practically still while the judgment of direction and distance is being made for a very quick delivery of the ball. This shot is to be made only within the vicinity of the foul circle.

SUGGESTIONS TO PLAYERS IN ONE-HAND SHOT

1. Try to pivot suddenly and shoot with one hand when near the free-throw circle.

2. Make the shot the finish of the pivot.

3. Make a feint in the opposite direction before pivoting if player can shoot only with the right hand.

4. Carry the ball up past the chin before the shot is made.

5. Keep the head still and eyes on the basket until after the ball leaves the hand, then recover and advance to good rebound position.

6. Let the shooting hand follow through behind the ball.

One-Hand Short Shot: Many shots attempted by a team are taken at the side of the basket when the shooter is moving toward the basket. Such attempts follow a dribble to the basket, or a pass to a player as he darts to the scoring position. This particular shot is commonly known as the "set-up" or "crip-shot." One form or technique seems to dominate this type of shot, irrespective of the plan of attack. It becomes necessary for the player to convert his forward momentum into upward momentum after the 1-2 count or one-step is taken in the delivery of such a shot, in order that the ball will have the shortest possible distance to travel. A maximum distance toward the basket before shooting will be gained if the shooter takes off with the left foot, receives the ball while in the air, hits the floor with the right foot, then with the left foot for the 1-2 count, jumps, and delivers the ball into the basket with the right hand. A left-handed player should reverse the footwork. This method of take-off and delivery enables the player to secure excellent body balance, the greatest elevation of the body from the floor, and the delivery of the ball from the highest possible point because of the cross-body stretch. The ball, going up in both hands, is transferred from the control of both to that of the right hand alone. As the body reaches the highest point, the right leg is snapped downward and the right arm is fully extended toward the basket. The ball should contact an imaginary point on the backboard some twelve inches above the near rim of the basket. The palm of the hand may be facing the backboard or be open toward the court. The body must follow through in a direct line behind the shot. Occasionally a right-handed player is found who cannot jump from his left foot. Such a player should be taught to deliver the ball against the backboard with both hands.

California One-Hand Outside Shot: The California one-hand shot is used not only in elementary schools but also in California high schools. The base of the right hand shot varies from a position with the right foot forward to one with feet together or with left foot forward. The body weight is shifted forward with knees easy. The shoulders are relaxed with the head balanced. The ball is shifted to the right hand and pushed toward the basket. Some players swing the arm out and up, pushing the ball toward the basket in a low arc. Some execute a shot by having the ball travel in a high arc with the delivery simulating a shot-put off the shoulder. Others take a medium overhand delivery.

The follow-through action of the body in all shots is similar. There is a slight variation in the hand and finger release. Some carry the palm straight forward toward the basket, releasing the ball from the three middle fingers, with the wrist relaxed to give the hand a complete follow-through. Other shooters turn the palm in a quarter turn to the right, releasing the ball of the thumb and the middle fingers.

This shot can be taken with feet on the floor or with feet in the air. Short players use the jump shot, adding height to the release.

SUGGESTIONS TO PLAYERS IN ONE-HAND SHORT SHOT

1. Have the ball hand as close to the target as possible when delivering the ball to the basket or backboard.

2. Attempt to lay the ball up as softly as possible.

3. Always deliver the ball from a point directly in front of the eyes.

4. Jump high on every attempted shot.

5. Learn to know your own personal effective take-off distance. Adjust the foot position to the take-off spot by lengthening, rather than shortening, the stride.

6. Shoot the same way from either side of the basket.

The Hook Shot: This shot may be delivered as is the hook pass, with the basket as the target instead of a teammate. A player moving toward either sideline and away from the basket may employ this type of shot most effectively. In all cases the player's body must protect the ball from the guard. Never cross the basket to make a hook shot when it is possible to shoot from the front side.

Free Throw for Goal: The ability to free-throw for goal is a very important skill. The underhand loop shot or the chest shot is used.

Underhand Loop Shot: The technique for this shot is indefinite. Some players place their toes on a line parallel with the free-throw line and their feet about 24 inches apart. From this position players assume a position represented by a short walking stride. A complete leg follow-through is possible with this foot position. The arms should be slightly bent at the elbows, the ball should be held by the tips of the fingers and thumbs at the axis of the ball. The head should be erect, and the eyes should be focused on the rim of the basket with the head still. The entire body must be relaxed. The player must squat slightly and bend the knees to gain force for the toss. The ball should be made to follow a medium arc toward the basket when it is tossed by flexing the hands, wrists, and arms. The legs, body, arms, and hands should follow through completely in the path of the ball. Player must develop a fixed point of release in order to be consistent.

RELAXATION SUGGESTIONS FOR PLAYER MAKING A FREE THROW FOR GOAL

1. Assume a position two short steps from the free-throw line, fix the ball properly in the hands, step forward in a natural walking rhythm, and deliver the ball as the second step is taken.

2. Use a wind-up before tossing the ball. This may be accomplished by slightly dropping the hands, or by extending the ball toward the basket before the actual tossing movement begins.

3. Adopt a throwing pattern. Have physical control and confidence before stepping up to line. The ball is balanced on finger tips around ball axis. Take a deep breath, let it out, and with a slumped body, drop the ball with the hands between the knees as the serving is started. The eyes should concentrate on the rim of the basket. The hands and

body should follow through. Practice will make these actions mechanical.

4. Focus eyes on the ball or on a certain spot on the floor until the upward movement of the ball is begun. Then focus upon the rim of the basket or other desired spot.

Technique for Developing Free-Throwing Skill: The player should be relaxed; have confidence; always use the same delivery; never hurry; and should practice frequently.

Two general methods of delivering the ball from behind the free-throw line are used: (1) underhand shot from between the knees, and (2) the chest or overhand shot. Each player should try out the two methods until each has determined his own best throw and should then cultivate that particular skill.

During the underhand shot the seams of the ball should run crosswise in the hands. The latter are spread over the ball's surface, thumbs on top, with the fingers and thumbs doing the holding.

For the chest throw, thumbs and the palms of the hands do the work. The seams of the ball should run crosswise.

Neither foot may touch the free-throw line before, during, or following the throw until the ball makes or misses the basket in Basketball for Boys, but as soon as the ball leaves the thrower's hands, players are free to move in Basketball for Girls. The player throwing for free throw should have a good balance and feeling of security, however, for either game.

BASKETBALL SKILL DRILLS

Because of the complexities of basketball, several drills are presented that may be used as games in earlier grades and also during the period of instruction in basketball. In such drills, it is important to use the ball that is used in the game itself; therefore, the players should not run with it, nor should it ever be kicked.

Passing and Catching: [1] It is important to teach the proper technique of passing and catching. There are three important passes: (1) The chest or push pass, in which the ball is propelled forward from the chest by a quick extension of the arms; (2) the underarm, in which the ball is passed with one hand or two hands from below the waist and to one side of the body; (3) the bounce pass, in which the ball is bounced to another player by using either one or two hands.

In catching the ball the catcher receives the ball with the hands, and, at the moment of impact, bends his elbows and wrists slightly. This

---

[1] The material in this section is adapted from George W. Ayars, *Skill Drills and Other Physical Activities.* Dover, Delaware: Department of Public Instruction, State of Delaware, 1944. By permission.

receiving action is the proper beginning of a movement that may be continued into the passing of the ball.

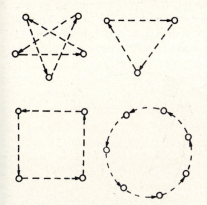

Pass and Catch Drills: The class may be arranged in any one of several geometrical patterns for passing and catching the ball. Three players may form a triangle, four a square, five a star, or a larger number a circle, as shown in Figure 144.

The ball may be passed as indicated by the arrows. The distances between players should depend upon the ability of players.

Figure 144. Positions for Ball Passing

Pass and Move Drills: Ten to twelve players are arranged in two rows facing each other (Figure 145). A passes the ball to B and B to C. As soon as A passes, he moves to take B's position and B, after his own pass, moves to take C's position. The others do likewise as the ball comes to them. When the ball reaches J, he makes a long pass to A, who is in the position B, and then J moves up to take A's place, since after his own pass A will move to position C. The line may be lengthened by adding players and more than one ball may be used. Emphasis should be placed upon accuracy in the pass.

Three-Player Pass: In this drill three players pass and move to new positions. It requires good passing and quick starts and change of direc-

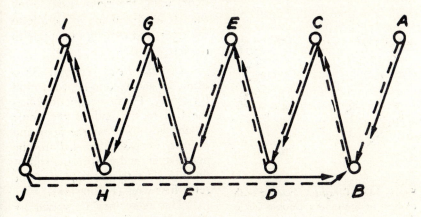

Figure 145. Diagram Showing Players in Pass and Move Drill

tion. The movement of the ball is indicated in Figure 146 by dotted lines and that of the players by solid lines. A starts the play, and B moves forward to catch the ball at X. B then passes to C who has moved to XX while A quickly runs behind B and takes up position XY where he will receive the ball from C. After passing to C at XX, B runs quickly behind C to take up position XZ. The drill is continued as shown in the diagram.

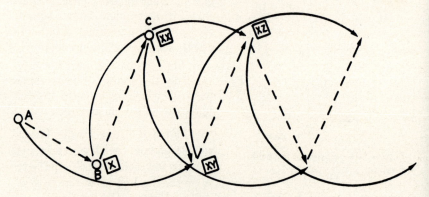

Figure 146.   Diagram of Three-Player Pass

Double-Circle Pass: Two circles with four players inside and eight outside face each other. The ball is passed between the players of the two circles, or in any direction desired by the teacher. Later the two circles may be in motion, first both moving in the same direction, then in opposite directions (Figure 147).

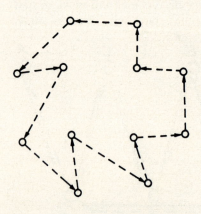

Figure 147.   Diagram Showing Path of Ball in Stationary Double-Circle Pass

Dribble Pass (Boys): Players dribble (bounce) the ball on the floor, using the right hand; using the left hand; moving in a circle to the right; and moving in a circle to the left.

Dribble Relay (Boys): Two teams are arranged in file formation for a relay. The first runner dribbles the ball to the end of the court around an object on the floor and returns; he passes the ball to the next player, and goes to the end of the file. The team completing the relay first wins (Figure 148).

This relay may be varied by changing the line from which the pass to the next player is made, by using a chest pass, an underarm pass, and a bounce pass.

Further variation may be secured and additional skills developed by requiring the dribbler to weave around objects placed on the floor, such as Indian clubs (Figure 149).

Situations similar to game situations may be used by arranging the group in a circle with players about four to five feet apart. The dribbler weaves around the other players and when he returns to his starting place he passes the ball to the player on his right who then continues the drill.

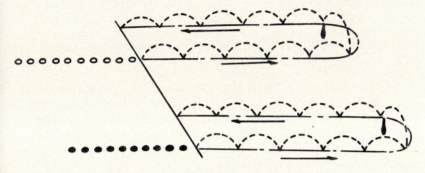

Figure 148.   Diagram of Dribble Relay

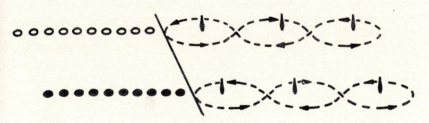

Figure 149.   Diagram of Dribble Relay Around Three Indian Clubs

Goal Shooting: [1] The player stands near the basket and at the signal "go" tries to shoot as many goals as possible in 20 seconds. Each goal scores two points for the player's team.

This may be varied by combining it with a dribble from a starting line and shooting for the goal until one is made, and then passing the ball to the next player at the starting line. If, however, the goal is not made in three trials, the player passes the ball to the next player. A great many variations of this drill may be arranged by the teacher.

[1] Contributed by Aubrey R. Bonham, Director of Physical Education for Men and Varsity Basketball Coach, Whittier College, Whittier, California.

Pivoting: Pivoting may be taught in such drills as the following: (1) The player steps forward on one foot as he shoots for goal. (2) The player steps, takes one dribble and shoots. (3) Next, he stands with his back to basket, pivots right, and as he leaps forward, he shoots. Various combinations are possible.

Reverse Pivot: The defensive players are stationed about 30 feet ahead of the line of players. Each of these players takes a turn at dribbling the ball up to the stationary defense man, at which point the dribbler must change direction. He changes direction by executing a jump step and by pulling either the left or right foot to the rear and making a 90° to 180° turn. As he turns, the ball is passed back to the next boy in the squad line. This is repeated by each boy in turn. After the rear pivot has been learned, the defense man can move into the dribbler to make the situation more game-like.

Front or Forward Pivot: The players should be arranged in pairs down the side lines. The guard is on the inside and the dribbler next to the side line. The guard tries to take the ball away from the dribbler. To avoid the guard, the dribbler stops, steps in front and across the foot next to the side line and, turning at a 180° angle, passes the ball to the dribbler in back of him. The play is continued.

Ball off Backboard: The players should be grouped in pairs with one shooting as an offensive player and one player trying to block the shot. As the offensive player shoots, the defensive player pivots into a position to put his body between the shooter and the goal. The defensive player must be taught to watch the rebound and to jump high, reach for the ball, squeeze it firmly and move the ball for a pass as he hits the floor. The players should be instructed to make one effort for the ball and to get it.

This drill could be varied by adding two defensive players against three offensive players, and then three players against three players. A defense player must always be in position between the offensive player for whom he is responsible and the basket. The offensive player, on the other hand, tries to get in the best position to receive the ball according to the position of the ball, basket, and defensive player.

Defensive Drill Game: The players are lined up at the end of the court and numbered so that there are two 1's, two 2's, two 3's, two 4's, two 5's. The leader starts on one side line about 20 feet from end line. He rolls the ball slowly across the floor parallel to the end line as he calls a number. Both players with the number respond, and the first one to get the ball starts shooting. The other player immediately becomes a defensive player and tries to get possession of the ball. If distinguishing colors or shirts are given the players, more than one number could be called at once. In this situation, all the players wearing the color of the player who obtained the ball first would be on the offensive and the other players would be on the defensive. The ability to change from defensive to offensive playing is a needed skill in boys' basketball.

These drills can be adapted to the girls' game by substituting the limited dribble for the dribble.

CHAIN TAG

NUMBER OF PLAYERS: 5-20

SPACE: Playground, playroom, gymnasium

FORMATION: One player is the tagger, the remaining players the runners.

PROCEDURE As soon as a runner is tagged he joins the tagger. With inside hands joined, the two continue trying to tag with their free hands. Each person tagged joins the taggers by taking places in the middle of the line, but only the two outside members may tag others. If the line breaks, no one may be tagged until the line is re-formed. Runners may dodge under the arms of players in the tagging line. If trapped they may be detained until an end man can tag them. The last person to be tagged wins.

TEACHING SUGGESTIONS

1. Limit the area over which the players may move, depending on the number of players. The playing field may be determined by the dimensions of a court, the shadow of a building, or a combination of several court areas.
2. Keep the action lively. If a large number is to play, use two taggers, each building up his own line.

FLAG FOOTBALL [1]

NUMBER OF PLAYERS: 14

SPACE: Playground

PLAYING AREA: A field 40 by 80 yards, divided by two cross stripes in the middle of the field. Two thirty-yard lines should be marked. Goal posts are not necessary.

EQUIPMENT: (1) Official football for the older age group, or junior regulation football for the younger age group; (2) for each player, two flags, 24 inches long, with a knot in each 4 inches from one end and 16 inches from the other. The short ends are pulled up under the player's

---

[1] Seven-man Flag Football was developed by the Recreation Department of the City of Alhambra.

belt so that the knots are snug against the lower edges of the belt and the longer ends hang down each hip. (3) Jerseys or other distinguishing markings for each team. Rubber-soled shoes should be worn. Metal cleats or spikes of any kind should not be allowed, nor any hard-surfaced padding such as shoulder pads, hip pads, or helmets. Only soft basketball knee pads and baseball sliding pads may be used.

Procedure

Flag football is played according to official football rules [1] except that there is no tackling; a ball carrier is downed when the flag is pulled from his belt. Other exceptions to the official rules are listed below.

FORMATION: Players are divided into two teams of not more than seven players. There must be three offensive players on the line at the kickoff. The receiving team must have three players not more than 20 yards or less than 15 yards from line of kickoff.

PLAYING PERIOD: The game consists of four 10-minute quarters, counted as straight time, including all time-outs and suspension of play excepting the last two minutes of the first half and last five minutes of the second half, when the clock should be stopped for all time-outs.

There should be a 2-minute rest period between quarters and a 10-minute rest period between halves.

RULES OF PLAY

Kickoff: The ball is kicked off from the offensive team's 20-yard line and should travel at least 20 yards towards oponent's goal, unless touched by the receiving team, in order to continue in play.

If the ball goes out of bounds on the kickoff it must be kicked again from the same line. After a second out-of-bounds kickoff, the receiving team puts the ball in play at midfield.

Out of Bounds Ball: When putting the ball in play, after having gone out of bounds, it should be placed 13 yards in from the side line, opposite the spot where it went out of bounds.

Downs: A team has four downs to advance the ball from wherever they receive it to the next zone. If they fail to reach the next zone in four downs, their opponents gain possession of the ball at the spot where the ball is declared dead on the fourth down.

Downed Ball: In order to down a ball carrier, either flag must be pulled from the belt. The ball carrier is declared downed at that point.

[1] *Official Football Rules.* Chicago: National Federation of State High School Athletic Associations. Edited, published, and copyrighted by the Association annually and obtained from the Association headquarters, 7 S. Dearborn St., Chicago 3, Ill.

It is illegal for a ball carrier to deliberately touch his own flag. *Penalty:* 15 yards from point of foul and loss of down.

Fumble: A recovered fumble *may be advanced* by either team.

Passing: All players of the offensive team are eligible to receive passes. A forward pass may be thrown from any point behind the line of scrimmage. A distinct lateral pass should precede every running play. The penalty for the failure to lateral is five yards from spot of preceding down and loss of a down.

Hacking: It is a foul to hack [1] or straight-arm [2] another player. However, a ball carrier may, with his open hand, attempt to push a potential tagger's hand away. The penalty for hacking is 15 yards from the point of the foul and first down.

Tackling: It is a foul to tackle. This is considered the same as any other unnecessary roughness. The penalty is 15 yards from spot of foul and loss of down. The offender may be excluded from the game at the discretion of the official.

Blocking: Line blocking is the same as in regulation football. In open field blocking, it is illegal for the blocker to leave his feet. The block should be more of a "bumping-screening" block, with the blocker retaining his balance. The penalty for an infraction on the part of an offensive player is 15 yards and the loss of a down from the spot of the foul. The penalty for an infraction on the part of the defensive team is 15 yards and the ensuing down is first down for the offensive team.

PLAYERS AND SUBSTITUTES: Any combination of players for line or backfield may be used. The free substitution rule prevails; substitution may be made any time the ball is dead, but must not delay the game. Substitutes are permitted to talk immediately after entering without the necessity of waiting one play. It is not necessary for substitutes to report to an official. Sportsmanlike conduct is expected of all players at all times and offenders should be immediately suspended from the game.

SCORING: A touchdown counts 6 points. A try for point after a touchdown counts 1 point and may be made by running or passing only. A safety counts 2 points. In case of a tie, the game remains a tie and each team is credited with a half game won and a half game lost in ranking teams on a percentage basis.

---

[1] Hack, *verb transitive*, to kick the shins of (an opposing player).
[2] Straight-arm, *verb transitive*, to ward off (an opponent) with the arms held straight.

FLOOR HOCKEY [1]

NUMBER OF PLAYERS: 12

SPACE: Playground, gymnasium

PLAYING AREA: Two adjacent tennis courts or hard-surfaced area similar in size, or gymnasium marked with boundary lines.

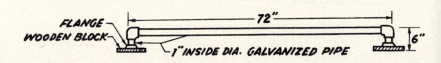

Figure 150.   Construction of Goal for Floor Hockey

EQUIPMENT: (1) Two goals constructed as in Figure 150. The goals should be placed in the middle of the end zones of the playing area, at north and south ends of court, and five feet inside the end lines or the walls of the gymnasium. (2) Two pair of hockey shin guards for the goal guards. (3) Floor hockey practice puck.[2] It should be the same size as an ice-hockey puck but with a hole in the middle simulating a doughnut to lighten its weight and make it more resilient. (4) For each player a hockey stick. Purchase additional sticks for a reserve in case of breakage. Light ash sticks or junior size ice-hockey sticks are desirable. If ice-hockey sticks are used, tape the ends to prevent splintering. (5) Stop watch.

FORMATION: Players are divided into two teams: goalkeeper in front of goal; right and left guards in the middle of their own half of court; right, center, and left forwards in the front position of their half of court.

PROCEDURE: The game resembles shinny. Two, three, or four periods of play of equal duration may be used. The rules should be kept as simple as possible with adequate safety precautions during play.

The Bully: The game is started by "bullying off," in which the puck is placed on the ground at the center of the playing area. The sticks of the center forwards are placed firmly against the puck before attempting to pass it. A second method of bullying is to place the sticks against the puck and on signal cross them above the puck three times before trying to gain possession. Those taking the bully stand with their left side toward their opponents' goal. No other players may be within 10 feet.

---

[1] An adaptation of ice-hockey techniques. The general plan for the game was adapted from a note by C. F. Gucker and D. F. Loebs contributed to the *Journal of Health and Physical Education,* III (September, 1932), 46. By permission.

[2] Floor hockey practice pucks may be purchased from sporting goods stores.

At the sound of the whistle those bullying try to gain possession of the puck or try to pass it to a teammate. No bully should be made for any reason within 10 feet of the goals either from the front or from side positions.

The Puck: The puck may be stopped by a stick or by any part of the body of a player. It may not be propelled by being pushed, held, carried, or kicked by a player. The stick is the only means whereby the direction and propulsion of the puck may be controlled. The goalkeeper is the only player who may kick the puck as he removes it from his goal area.

Players may pass behind the goals when controlling the puck in an effort to score or in an effort to protect their goal. A goal may not be attempted until three different players of a team have handled the puck.

Out-of-Bounds Play: If a puck goes out of bounds over a side line it is brought into the court five feet, at the point where it left the court; the two nearest opponents take the bully. If the puck goes out of bounds over the end line, other than through a goal, it is brought in five feet at some point between a goal post and the side line. Two opponents take the bully.

If the puck goes under gymnasium apparatus it is brought out five feet and a bully occurs between two opponents.

Time Out: If play is stopped by the referee for any reason the game is resumed by a bully between opponents at the place where the puck was when time was called.

FOULS: Because of the danger inherent in any vigorous game, rules regarding foul should be strictly enforced. The person in charge has more than usual responsibility, as he has to determine the length of time by which the offender is penalized. It is a foul in Floor Hockey for a player to commit the following: (1) to raise his stick above his hips; (2) to throw his stick along the floor; (3) to charge, trip, or push another player; (4) to lie, sit, or kneel on the floor in front of his goal or elsewhere on the court; (5) to kick the puck (except for the goalkeeper); (6) to place his stick full length in front of his goal; (7) to carry, hold, or push the puck with any part of his body. *Penalty:* For committing any foul the referee should remove the player or players from the game for a period of from one to five minutes, or for the entire game, according to the seriousness of the offense. No substitute is permitted when players are so removed. The referee signals with his fingers how many minutes the player is penalized for the foul committed. A closed fist signifies that the player is out for the remainder of the game. The timekeeper keeps a check on the time by use of a stop watch.

SCORING: Each goal made counts 1 point. The team wins that has the higher point score at the completion of the playing period.

TEACHING SUGGESTIONS

1. Teach such techniques of ice hockey as handling the stick, maneuvering the puck, position play, and team co-operation. As skill is gained, additional ice-hockey rules may be introduced, but not before the group masters the fundamentals outlined above.
2. Do not allow play to stop when penalized players re-enter the game.
3. Drill on safety measures. There should be no need for calling fouls because of careless playing.

FOOT BASEBALL [1]

NUMBER OF PLAYERS: 8-40

SPACE: Playground, gymnasium

PLAYING AREA: Baseball diamond with bases 25 feet apart and pitcher's box 20 feet from home base (Figure 151).

EQUIPMENT: (1) Soccer ball or regulation football; (2) regulation soccer posts or two jumping standards placed 40 feet from home plate and 12 feet apart. These serve as goal posts. Indoors the goal posts may be indicated by chairs or by chalk marks on the gymnasium wall.

Procedure

Softball rules are used, with a few exceptions as indicated below. Seven innings constitute a game.

FORMATION: Players are divided into two teams of equal numbers. One team is up for kicking; the other team in the field. One to four fielders, scattered beyond the pitcher and some 25 feet from home plate, are known as rushers. The remaining fielders may be located as desired but may not "rush" the ball.

Pitcher: The pitcher, turning his back to the kicker, snaps the ball between his legs as does the center in football.

Kicker: The kicker, while in contact with home base, tries to make a legal catch. If successful he endeavors to make a drop-kick between the goal posts. A punt is allowed in case the kicker does not desire to drop-kick with thin shoes. If a successful kick is made anywhere between the two foul lines the kicker runs bases as in softball.

Rushers: The rushers, as soon as the ball is snapped by the pitcher, run in and try to block the kick. They may not run into or touch the kicker. Other fielders remain in the approximate positions held before the kick is made or try to secure the ball if it goes beyond the position of the rushers.

---

[1] Suggestions for game were found in a note contributed by C. R. Warthen to the *Journal of Health and Physical Education*, I (January, 1930), 55. By permission.

RULES OF PLAY

Blocked Balls: A blocked ball, from any position on the field, must be thrown to the pitcher who must be inside his pitcher's box to receive it. He immediately throws the ball to home plate, where, to make the catch legal, a fielder must be in contact with home plate when he receives the ball. If the throw is successfully completed the kicker is out regardless of his position on bases.

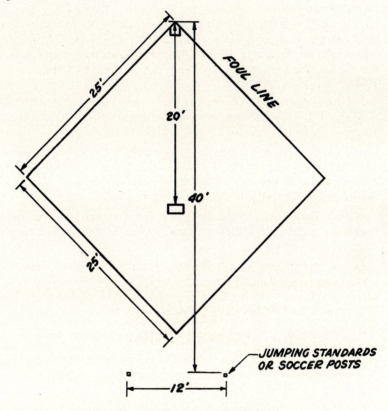

Figure 151.   Diamond for Foot Baseball

Balls: The ball must be snapped within reasonable reach of the kicker; otherwise a ball is called. Two balls give the kicker a base on balls.

Fly Balls: A fly ball caught puts the kicker out.

Strikes: (1) If the kicker fumbles the ball or fails to kick it, or (2) if the ball is touched by a rusher before it can be kicked, it is a strike. Two strikes retire the kicker.

Stealing Bases: A base runner may not steal home from third on a ball or strike, nor when the pitcher is in his box. Other bases may be stolen at any time.

Foul Balls: The ball is foul which is kicked behind or across and outside the foul lines between home and first or home and third bases. The ball is foul, regardless of where it lands, if the kicker fumbles the ball and, picking it up, kicks it. Two foul balls retire the kicker. A foul fly caught retires the kicker.

Drop-kicked Balls: If the kicker drop-kicks the ball so that it goes between the goal posts, he is credited with a field goal. A drop-kicked ball caught on the fly by a fielder behind the goal posts reduces the score for the kick one point. The ball may not be caught on the rebound for scoring purposes.

Offside Play: Rushers must remain behind the pitcher until the ball is snapped. If they advance beyond the pitcher they are offside; that is, ahead of the ball. Credit for a "ball" is given to the kicker.

Outs: A player is out following: (1) a caught fly ball; (2) two strikes; (3) a caught foul fly ball; (4) two fouls; (5) successfully blocked ball which reaches a fielding player at home plate by way of the pitcher before runner arrives at home; (6) illegal run home.

Personal Fouls: It is a personal foul for a rusher or other fielder to touch the person of a kicker. *Penalty:* Kicker is awarded two unobstructed place kicks.

Scoring: A field goal scores 3 points. Each run scores 1 point. A drop-kicked ball caught behind the goal posts by a fielder scores 2 points. Each place-kicked ball which passes between the goal posts scores 2 points. The team wins that has more points at the finish of the game.

TEACHING SUGGESTIONS

1. Teach the kicker to work fast to avoid interference from rushers.
2. Rotate players occupying the rushers' positions at frequent intervals.

FOOTBALL LEAD-UP GAMES [1]
(Boys)

While it is very undesirable to have teams play American football in elementary and junior high schools (the State Department of Education most emphatically and earnestly recommends no use of the game below the tenth year of senior high school), the fact remains that there are some elements and techniques in American football that greatly interest younger boys.

---

[1] Suggestions for these activities were found in an article by D. K. Brace in *Pentathlon,* II (October, 1929). By permission of the author.

Tackling *should never be permitted.* The first and most important reason is the incomplete physiological development of boys in the elementary and junior high schools; second, the lack of proper protective clothing. Innumerable games develop the physical strength and mental reasoning that will prepare younger boys to be excellent football players later in their school life.

The games which follow may be played with soccer balls or footballs. A ball for at least every four boys is needed for adequate participation and instruction.

FOLLOW THE LEADER: A leader performs a stunt, while the others, following in single file, imitate the stunts: running, skipping, running on all fours, hopping, turning around left or right while running, and other conditioning exercises.

KEEP AWAY: A limited area of about 60 feet square is needed. Two teams are organized. The ball is passed between members of one team while members of the other team try to secure it.

Each time a pass is completed the first player to catch it calls out, "One." The next successful catcher calls, "Two," and so on. If an opponent gets the ball the count must start again at one. The ball must be passed with but one hand and from over the head.

FORWARD PASS DRIVE: Two end lines are established 200 feet apart. Members of one team put the ball in play at a point 70 feet from an end line by a pass. The opponents try to intercept it. At the point where the ball is touched or caught, it is thrown back. If a player catches the ball he may take five steps toward the opponents' goal before throwing it.

The game is won when a pass which is not caught is made over an opponents' goal line. A ball caught behind a goal line is thrown back from the goal line. A player may not pass the ball twice in succession.

PUNTING DRIVE: The game situation is the same as Forward Pass Drive except that players try to send the ball over the opponents' goal post by punting the ball (kicking a dropped ball before it hits the ground).

DROP-KICK DRIVE: The game set-up is the same as Forward Pass Drive except that players try to send the ball over the opponents' goal post by drop-kicking the ball (kicking a dropped ball after it bounces).

CENTER NUMBER PASS: Squads of four or more boys line up in semicircle formation. All players are numbered. Each squad has a ball. One boy from each squad, acting as a center, stands three yards in front of the other players. Another member, acting as a quarterback, calls out the numbers. The center must throw the ball between his feet to the boy whose number is called. Playing positions should be rotated after a number of passes are attempted.

Scoring: One point is given for each completed pass.

BALL SNATCH: Members of one team line up in two rows about three feet apart and facing each other. Members of the other team, one at a time, run down the lane carrying the ball. Lane players try to snatch the ball or cause the runner to drop it.

Scoring: One point is given for each ball carried through successfully.

CHANGING BALL RELAY: Players are divided into teams and line up in file formation with some 15 feet between each player. All the players stand in a crouched position. The leader of each file, carrying a ball, runs toward the end of his file, zig-zagging in and out around each player. He must carry the ball on the side that is away from the player he is running around, hence the ball must be changed frequently. When the runner passes the last man of his file he throws the ball back to the head of his file and remains at the foot of the file.

Scoring: The first leader to receive the ball from his last runner wins and the team is credited with 10 points. One point is deducted for each foul. A foul consists of not changing the ball or of dropping it during the run.

FOLLOWING THE BALL: Two squads line up in a crouching position beside each other in a continuous line. A leader takes his position on the line between the two squads. The ball is on the ground in front of him. The leader sweeps up the ball and at the same time charges a short distance directly forward or on the diagonal, and then grounds the ball. Members of both squads charge forward as the ball is snatched up and they line up again when the ball is placed on the ground.

Scoring: One point is credited to the squad whose members first form a straight line in crouched position with no members offside (that is, ahead of the ball).

PIVOT PASS RELAY: Teams line up in file formation with approximately 15 feet between players and files. The leader of each file runs to the boy behind him and places the ball against that player's abdomen. He in turn grasps the ball, pivots, and runs to the third player. Play is continued until the last man receives the ball and carries it to the head of his file. Runners remain at the position where they got rid of the ball.

The team wins whose leader first receives the ball from the last player of his file.

CHARGING: Two parallel goal lines are drawn 20 feet apart. An equal distance between the two a third line is drawn. The time period for play is one to two minutes.

Teams line up on the center line facing each other and crouching shoulder to shoulder. On a signal, players of each team try to push the opponent players across the line behind them. *Hands may not be used.*

Players once pushed back across their own goal line and the players who forced them over cannot return to the game.

The team wins that forces more opponents out of the playing area.

FORWARD RUNNING WITH BACKWARD PASSING: Teams line up in file formation. On signal, members of each file start running forward. The leader carries the ball until the player behind him overtakes him, whereupon he passes him the ball. Play continues until the ball is given to the last player of the file.

The team wins whose last player gets across the field first and receives the ball.

CENTER PASS SNATCH: Two teams of from five to seven players form parallel lines three feet apart and face each other. One player stands at one end of and between the two lines. Turning his back, he snaps the ball between his legs so that it passes between the two lines of players.

Scoring: A player who catches the ball without moving from his line position scores one point for his team.

DODGING: Two base lines are established 40 feet apart. Team A lines up behind one of the lines; Team B members are in the area between the two lines. On a signal, Team A players run across to the other line and Team B players try to tag them. To catch a runner officially, a tagger must, while using both hands, tag the runner on one of his thighs. One-hand tagging has provided players better balance than two-hand tagging and may be substituted here.

Scoring: One point is credited to a team for each player tagged. Each team has five trials as the tagging group.

BOUNCING BALL CONTEST: Players of each team are each given a number and all are stationed on a given line. Each team selects a thrower who alternates with the opponents' thrower in throwing the ball. As the ball is thrown into the air the thrower calls a number. The player with that number runs out and tries to catch the ball *after* the first bounce.

Scoring: One point is allowed for each successful catch. The team wins whose players score more points.

TARGET KICK: Two target areas about 30 feet square are marked diagonally opposite each other and 90 feet apart. Both teams line up on a center line and, taking turns, try to punt a ball so that it will land within the boundaries of their own target.

Scoring: One point is scored for each kicked ball which hits the target.

ELIMINATION KICK: A referee is needed for each team. Two lines are drawn 40 yards apart. The Number 1 player of team A kicks the ball as far as he can. Then Number 1 player of team B, from the place where the ball first hit the ground, kicks the ball back. If the B player kicks the ball past the mark from which the A player kicked the ball, the A player is eliminated. If B's kick does not reach the point from which A kicked, then B is eliminated.

Play continues until all of one team are eliminated.

KICK 'ER OVER: This is Punting Drive with the exception that if the ball is caught on the fly it may be kicked in any manner desired. If not caught it must be drop-kicked from where it first touched the ground.

In order to win, a member of one team must drop-kick the ball over the opponents' goal.

KICKOFF BALL: A regular soccer field is used. A member of one team kicks the ball on the 40-yard line. An opponent secures the ball and runs it toward the kicker's goal line. The ball is down, or out of play, where the runner is tagged by a member of the team whose player kicked the ball. This is repeated twice and then the other team has three turns at kickoff.

Scoring: The team which secured the kicked ball scores points according to the area the runner is able to reach while carrying the ball before being tagged. Sections of the field count as follows: between 10- and 20-yard lines, 1 point; between 20- and 30-yard lines, 2 points; between 30- and 40-yard lines, 3 points; between 40- and 50-yard lines, 5 points.

PASS NEWCOMB: A rectangular area 45 by 120 feet is marked off. At the center, lines to form a neutral area 15 feet wide are drawn. Teams of from five to ten players are placed back of the neutral area in the end zones. Members of each team try to throw the ball into the opponents' court so that it will land on the ground without being touched by the opponents. If the ball enters the neutral area the nearest player to it secures the ball and throws it to a member of his own team before re-entering his area of play.

Scoring: Each time a team member fails to catch the ball or drops the ball when attempting a catch the opponents score 1 point. Fifteen points constitute a game.

KNOCK 'ER DOWN: A rectangular area 45 by 120 feet is marked off. At the center lines are drawn to form a neutral area 15 feet wide. Team A has half its members in the two end zones back of the neutral area, as does Team B. The object is for members of a team in one end zone to pass the ball to teammates on the other side of the neutral area. Opposing team members try to knock the ball to the ground before it can be caught.

Scoring: If the ball is caught by a member of the team making the pass no points are scored and the person catching the ball puts it into play immediately.

If the ball is knocked to the ground by opponents, the opponents score 1 point.

The game may be played by time periods, the team making the most points winning the game. Or teams may play for an agreed upon number of points.

DROP-KICK CONTEST: Goal posts and a crossbar are necessary. One team is spread out behind the goal area, the second team in front of the goal area. Teams alternate in kicking. The ball must be drop-kicked from beyond a five-yard line. Teammates must take their turn in kicking, for no one player may do all the kicking for a team. Each team tries to kick the ball over the crossbar and between the goal posts and members of each team try to catch a successfully kicked ball.

Scoring: One point is scored for the team whose player drop-kicks the ball over, and if opponents fail to catch the kicked ball an additional point is earned.

DROP-KICK FOOTBALL: This game is played on a soccer field. The ball can be put in play and continued in play only by use of drop kicks. Play starts at the center of the field with a drop kick. Each team is allowed four downs (or kicks) in succession. The ball then goes to the other team. If a kick is intercepted the ball must be taken back and be put in play at the place from which the intercepted kick was taken.

Scoring: A point is made when a team player can drop-kick the ball across the opponents' goal line.

FOX AND GEESE

NUMBER OF PLAYERS: 5-20

SPACE: Playground, playroom, gymnasium

FORMATION: A player is chosen to be the fox and another to be the gander. The remaining players are geese. The geese line up in single file back of the head player in the file, the gander. Each goose grasps the shoulder or the waist of the goose in front of him.

PROCEDURE: The goose at the end of the file is the only goose that the fox may capture. He tries in every way possible to reach and tag the end goose. The gander, with his arms folded across his chest, protects his end goose from the fox by trying to keep in front of the fox. As the gander moves about, his line of geese must move with him. It is poor play for the geese to break their hold. When the fox succeeds in tagging the end goose, that goose becomes the fox and the old fox becomes the new gander and takes his position at the head of the file.

TEACHING SUGGESTIONS

1. Form separate groups of not more than 10, each file having its own fox, when there is a large number of players.

2. Put boys and girls in each file.
3. Teach the players to use a firm hand grip to prevent the files from breaking.

FRAME BASKETBALL [1]

NUMBER OF PLAYERS: 3-20

SPACE: Playground, gymnasium

EQUIPMENT: (1) Basketball backstop and goal or Goal-Hi; [2] (2) basketball, soccer ball, or volleyball

FORMATION: Players line up behind a free-throw line or area some fifteen feet from the basket.

PROCEDURE: This is a basketball shooting game, in which scores are made individually in groups. Each contestant throws the ball through the basket, but in order to score it is necessary that three consecutive players make the goal. If a player misses, he is eliminated and the next player starts a new "frame" of three. Thus if Numbers 1 and 2 make baskets but Number 3 misses, no score is made for 1 or 2 but they remain in the game while 3 steps out. Next time Numbers 1 and 2 throw they may be in a group of three who make their goals and each will score 1 point. When but two players remain, the player first missing his throw is eliminated and the last player scores one point. A new game is then started, in which all the players may again participate.

SCORING: An agreed upon number of games may be played, and the player who makes the most points when that number of games has been played wins. Or a certain number of points may be agreed upon and the first player to score that many points wins.

TEACHING SUGGESTIONS

1. Use as a good basketball practice drill, or as a less technical variation of Knock-Out Freeze-Out Basketball (see p. 768).

HALF-COURT BASKETBALL [3]

NUMBER OF PLAYERS: 12 to 18 on half court

SPACE: Playground, gymnasium

---

[1] Suggestion for this game secured from *Recreation*, XXXV (January, 1942), 622. By permission of the National Recreation Association, publisher.
[2] See page 649.
[3] Adapted from a note contributed by Martha J. Leonard to the *Journal of Health and Physical Education*, X (February, 1939), 108-9. By permission.

PLAYING AREA: Any basketball court that is available may be used. A neutral area four feet wide parallel to the center line is established. The center circle is moved from the center line of the court to this new neutral area line. If both half courts are to be used, a second neutral area will be needed.

EQUIPMENT: (1) Basketball backstops and goals; (2) junior or official basketball

Procedure

In general, with but few exceptions, the rules of basketball govern fouls, penalties, and general playing situations.

FORMATION: Two teams on each half court. Six or more players for each team. Each team has three forwards and three guards if six players make up a team. All move about the dimensions of the half-court.

PERIODS OF PLAY: The game is played in four 6-minute quarters, with a 2-minute rest period between quarters, and a 5-minute rest period between halves. The ball is given to the player who had it when time was called except at the end of the half time when a throw-in restarts the game.

RULES OF PLAY: The ball is thrown, alternately, to a forward of each team by the referee while he is standing near a side line some 10 feet from the center circle. The forward taking the throw-in must be standing in the center circle with one foot in the neutral area of the half-court. The forward taking the throw-in is unguarded. A throw-in is used to start the game and following each scoring play.

Out-of-Bounds Play: On an out-of-bounds play it is not necessary to return the ball to the neutral area before a goal can be attempted. However, two completed passes must occur before a goal can be attempted.

Rotation of Players: Following each successful scoring play, members of both teams rotate positions, a guard becoming a forward and a forward a guard.

VIOLATIONS: The violations and their penalties are as follows: (1) A forward may not throw for a goal when the progress of the ball to the basket was not started by a member of the forward's team while standing with one or both feet in the neutral area. *Penalty:* The goal, if made, does not score and the ball is awarded to an opponent out of bounds at a side line. (2) A player may not try for a goal, following a free throw missed by a member of opponent team, until the ball has been returned by passing to the neutral area. *Penalty:* The goal, if made, does not score and the ball is awarded to an opponent team member out of bounds at a side line. (3) A player may not carry or cause the ball to go over the center line into the adjoining half-court. *Penalty:* The ball is awarded to an opponent out of bounds at a side line of the neutral area. All other violations and fouls may be found on pages 720-23, Basketball for Boys, and pages 723-27, Basketball for Girls.

SCORING: A field goal scores 2 points and a free throw 1 point. In order to score a field goal, the progress of the ball must have originated from within the neutral area and must meet the following conditions: (1) The ball must not have been touched by an opponent. (2) Not less than two completed passes must have occurred. (3) A forward of the team must make the successful throw.

TEACHING SUGGESTIONS

1. Have forwards of each team wear different colored arm bands, pinnies, or shirts to distinguish teams.
2. Teach the forwards to remember which one is to take the throw-in at the center circle. A cardboard, with each side a distinctive color to represent each team, can be given to a non-player. As soon as a team's forward completes a throw-in play the cardboard is flipped and the color of the other team is shown until a forward of that team completes a throw-in, whereupon the card is flipped again.
3. Teach the two forwards of the throwing team, when a free throw is awarded, to remain away from the goal area, leaving to their guards the responsibility of securing the ball. One forward should stand in the center circle in position to start the ball legally toward the goal.
4. Use as a basketball type game.
5. Use in schools with small enrollment.

HORSESHOE PITCHING [1]

NUMBER OF PLAYERS: 2-4

SPACE: Playground, unless rubber horseshoes are used, when the game can be played indoors

PLAYING AREA: Level surface 10 by 50 feet, running north and south and placed apart from other group activities (Figure 152).

EQUIPMENT: (1) Two stakes of soft steel or iron, 1 inch in diameter, so placed in the ground as to allow a 3-inch pitch of the pegs toward each other, and extending 10 to 12 inches above the ground surface. Stakes for men's official games should be 40 feet apart, measured from the front of each stake where it enters the ground. Stakes for women and children

---

[1] For further information about court construction and official rules write to the National Horseshoe Pitchers Association of America, 912 Melrose Avenue, Santa Cruz, California. Teaching suggestions and rules are found in the *Official Recreational Games—Volleyball Guide.* Washington: National Section on Women's Athletics, American Association for Health, Physical Education and Recreation (1201 Sixteenth St., N.W., Washington 6, D. C.), issues for 1946 to 1948. Refer also to the Diamond Calk Horseshoe Company, Duluth, Minnesota.

under 16 years of age should be 30 feet apart. (2) Four horseshoes. Official horseshoes shall not exceed the following dimensions: Length, 7½ inches; width, 7 inches; weight, 2½ pounds. No toe or heel calk shall project more than ¾ inch; the opening between the heel calks shall not exceed 3½ inches, inside measurements; on the inner circle of the shoes no projection shall be allowed beyond the heel calks.

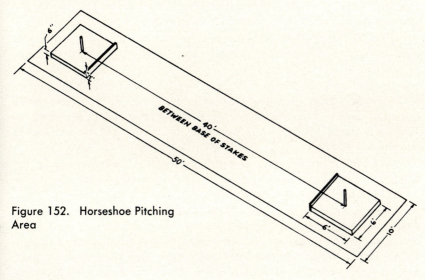

Figure 152. Horseshoe Pitching Area

Procedure

The game is played between two persons or between two partners and two opponent partners. The object is to throw the horseshoe so that it will encircle the stake or, failing that, will land closer to the stake than any shoe thrown by an opponent.

FORMATION: Two players for a singles game; four players for a doubles game. When a *singles game* is played the two players stand at the same stake, pitch their two shoes in turn, and afterward walk to the farthest stake, where the score is determined and where play is resumed. When a *doubles game* is played a team consisting of two players stands at each end of the court. When a player is pitching, the second player must stand away from and behind the stake and must not move or speak while the opponent is throwing his shoes. A player may not walk across to the opposite stake and examine the position of shoes until he has made his final pitch.

PLAYING PERIOD: Each game is divided into innings. In *singles* each inning constitutes the pitching of four shoes, two by each player. In *doubles* each inning constitutes the pitching of eight shoes, two by each player.

RULES OF PLAY: A coin is tossed (a shoe would be a good substitute) to determine who shall pitch first. The winner has choice of whether to pitch first or to follow his opponent. At the beginning of the new game or games the loser of the previous game shall have the first pitch.

When cement slabs or pitcher's boxes are not provided, the players when throwing must have the instep of the rear foot not farther forward than the stake position. The thrower may stand on either side of the stake. Each player throws his two shoes in sequence.

Foul Shoes: A shoe pitched while the contestant is not standing in legal position is a foul shoe; although successfully pitched, it shall not be scored.

Interfering With Pitched Shoes: A player may not touch his own or his opponent's shoes after they are pitched until the final decision is made as to the scoring value of each shoe. If a player does touch a shoe, his shoe is declared foul and the opponent is entitled to the new score determined by the position of his shoes in relation to the stake.

"Ringer" Horseshoes: A ringer is a shoe that encircles a stake far enough to permit the straight edge of a rule, pencil, or straight stick to touch both heel calks simultaneously.

Moving Pitched Shoes: When a thrown shoe moves a shoe already at a stake, all shoes are scored in their new positions. When a player knocks out of position his own or his opponent's ringers, the removed ringers do not score. When a player knocks an opponent's shoe or shoes from a non-ringer position to a ringer position, the changed shoes have scoring value.

SCORING: In practice games the regulation game consists of 21 points. In tournaments and matches a regulation game consists of 50 points. Shoes which are foul are not scored or credited. All shoes must be within six inches of a stake to be eligible for scoring points. All equals count as ties and no points are scored. A shoe leaning against a stake in a tilted position has no advantage over a shoe lying flat but touching the stake. All such shoes are ties and the scores are cancelled. A shoe which leans against a stake shall count only as a "closest shoe."

The scoring possibilities are as follows:

1 point for closest shoe to stake.

2 points for two shoes closer than opponent's shoes.

3 points for one ringer.

6 points for two ringers.

4 points for one ringer and closest shoe of same player.

3 points if a player has 2 ringers and his opponent has 1 ringer.

1 point, if each player has a ringer, for the next closest shoe (if within six inches of stake).

Figure 153. Begin-
ning the Pitch

In case there is a tie because all four shoes are ringers, or four shoes are an equal distance from the stake, no scores are recorded. The player who made the last pitch is entitled to first pitch on the next throw.

The winner of points calls the results. In case of a tie the player pitching last calls the score.

Measurement Technique: Measurements to determine which shoe is the closest to the stake shall be made by calipers, the straight edge of a ruler, or a straight stick.

How to Record Results of Play: The recording of scores is done with the following symbols: W=games won; L=games lost; P=points; R=ringer; DR=double ringer; SP=shoes pitched; OP=opponent's points; PCT=percentage of ringers.

TEACHING SUGGESTIONS

1. Teach this game not only to children incapacitated for more vigorous types of play but also to all the boys and girls as a recreational game.
2. Teach the players to pitch a shoe by the following method (Figure 153):
   a. Grip the shoe so that it is held by the thumb and finger
   b. Release the shoe with the calks down

c. Sight with shoe toward stake
d. Stand with right foot slightly ahead of the left foot
e. Shift the weight to the back foot as the serving is made
f. Twist the wrist toward the left as the shoe is swung down and backward so that as it passes the leg it is perpendicular to the ground
g. Hold the shoe in a perpendicular position until the shoe is released with a flip of the wrist to make the shoe flat as it leaves the hand with the palms up.

KNOCK-OUT FREEZE-OUT BASKETBALL [1]

NUMBER OF PLAYERS: 3 or more

SPACE: Playground, gymnasium

EQUIPMENT: (1) Basketball backstop and goal, or Goal-Hi; [2] (2) basketball or soccer ball

FORMATION: Players line up behind a free-throw line some fifteen feet from the basket.

PROCEDURE: This is a goal-shooting game with a premium put on quickness and accuracy. Players number themselves for their turn at shooting. The first player, in each playing period, throws the ball from behind the free-throw line. Thereafter each player in turn must throw the ball from the spot where he secures it after the throw of the preceding player. If a player fails to make the goal, the next player may secure the ball from a bounce or on the fly.

Knock-Out: If the previous player throws the ball through the basket, the next in turn must catch the ball before it hits the ground. If he fails he is automatically "knocked-out" of that particular playing period.

Freeze-Out: The next higher numbered player secures the ball and must make it go through the basket. If he does not he is a "freeze-out" and he too must wait for a new playing period to start.

At the conclusion of each playing period the next higher numbered player from the one starting that period starts the new playing period.

SCORING: A definite number of points to be worked for are decided upon before play begins.

If the first player makes his goal while throwing from behind the free-throw line, he is credited with one point. When all players but one are eliminated through knock-out and freeze-out plays, the last player is

---

[1] Suggestion for this game secured from *Recreation*, XXXV (January, 1942), **622**. By permission of National Recreation Association, publisher.
[2] See page 649.

credited with one point. The player who first earns the agreed-upon number of points wins the series.

All eliminated players re-enter the play at the beginning of each new playing period. Each player in turn tries to secure the ball and make his goal. A point is credited to each player as it is earned until the winner is determined.

TEACHING SUGGESTIONS

1. Use Knock-Out Freeze-Out Basketball as a skill game to teach shooting accuracy and quick recovery from the backboard.
2. Have the pupils practice particular shots with this game.
3. Help all pupils to overcome their shooting errors by analyzing their faults.

LABYRINTH TAG [1]

NUMBER OF PLAYERS: 15-40

SPACE: Playground, playroom, gymnasium

FORMATION: A runner and a tagger are selected. The remaining players stand in parallel files. There should be as many files as there are players in a file, so that when all players turn to right or left they form new files of the same length. Facing forward, the players grasp the hands of their neighbors.

PROCEDURE: The runner, in order to escape from the tagger, runs up and down the aisles formed by the rows of players. The fun of the game consists in sudden aisle changes brought about by a leader who, in rapid succession, gives such commands as "Face Right!" "Face Front!" "Face Left!" "Face Rear!"

When the players hear a command they drop hands, face in the given direction, and quickly join hands with new neighbors. The runner and tagger must adjust to the new direction. The runner may not break through hands that are clasped. The tagger may not reach across grasped hands in order to tag the runner.

Play continues until the chaser tags the runner or until a time limit expires. The previous runner and chaser choose successors and play is resumed.

TEACHING SUGGESTIONS

1. Make commands snappy with frequent shifts.
2. Teach the leader to watch the position of the runner and tagger and to give a command when capture seems imminent.
3. Prevent the game from dragging by changing the tagger and the runner frequently.

---

[1] This tag is also known by such names as Streets and Alleys and Maze Tag.

NOSE TAG

NUMBER OF PLAYERS: 5-20

SPACE: A restricted area within which the players must remain

FORMATION: A tagger is chosen; remaining players are runners.

PROCEDURE: The tagger tries to touch a runner. A runner, when in danger of being tagged, must stand on one foot, pass a hand under the raised knee of the other foot and with fingers of that hand grasp his nose. As soon as a player is tagged he becomes the tagger.

TEACHING SUGGESTIONS

1. Do not permit the runners to remain in one spot. At the same time insist that the runners stay near enough to each other to make a lively game.
2. When the group to play is large, form two or more groups, each with its own tagger.

OLD PLUG TAG

NUMBER OF PLAYERS: 10-40

SPACE: Playground, playroom, gymnasium

EQUIPMENT: Volleyball, 12- or 15-inch softball, beanbag, or knotted towel

FORMATION: Two thirds of the players form a circle. The remaining players form files of three to five members inside the circle. They are known as "old plugs," the front players being the heads, the end players the tails. Each player of the plugs puts his arms around the waist of the one in front and clasps his own hands firmly.

PROCEDURE: Using a ball, circle players may attempt to hit the tail of a plug or they may pass the ball to a player who may be in a better position to throw at a tail. The plugs try to avoid being hit on their tails by keeping their heads always facing the ball. This will necessitate rapid movement by all the players who form the body and tail of the plugs.

The head men of the files use their hands to knock the ball toward the circle players. In so doing they protect the tails of their plugs as well as speed up the game. No players within the circle except a front player of a file may touch the ball with his hands. When a circle player succeeds in hitting a plug's tail he becomes the head of that particular plug and goes to the front of the file. As new heads join the plugs the tail players drop off and join the circle players. The game is then resumed.

POISON TAG

NUMBER OF PLAYERS: 5-40

SPACE: Playground, playroom, auditorium, gymnasium

PLAYING AREA: A circle is marked on the ground approximately one third the size of the circle formed by the players when extending their arms and touching each others' hands.

EQUIPMENT: Safety spots for all but one player. Beanbags or sticks of wood can be used for safety spots. They are scattered some distance from the ground circle.

FORMATION: The players form a circle outside the ground circle by clasping hands.

PROCEDURE: At a signal each player attempts to push or pull his two neighbors over the ground circle into the center but struggles himself to stay out. The first player to touch the ground within the circle is said to be poisoned and becomes the chaser. The cry goes up, "Poisoned!" Players dash for a safety spot to avoid being tagged by the poisoned player. No one can be tagged while standing on a safety spot.

If the chaser succeeds in tagging players before they can reach a safety spot, they too become chasers and assist the first chaser. Whenever, during the running, the first chaser or the teacher in charge calls, "Change Your Safety," players on safety spots must exchange with each other or find a new safety spot. While so doing they are of course in danger of being tagged.

When all have been caught, the ground circle is once more surrounded and the game is repeated. The last player to be tagged is winner of the game.

TEACHING SUGGESTIONS

1. Do not permit the players to scatter too widely when seeking safety.
2. Mark safety spots with chalk when playing on a wood floor.

SIDE-LINE BASKETBALL [1]

NUMBER OF PLAYERS: 20-50

SPACE: Playground, gymnasium

PLAYING AREA: Basketball court

EQUIPMENT: Basketball, soccer ball, or volleyball

FORMATION: The players are divided into two groups, lined up on oppo-

---

[1] Adapted from a note contributed by Helen M. Reily to the *Journal of Health and Physical Education*, VII (March 1936), 193-94. By permission.

site sides of the basketball court. The players are numbered according to the size of the class, so that there will be a total of 10 players (5 for each team), having the same number. For example, with 20 players on each side, the lines would number off by twos; a class of 40 would number by fours; 70 by sevens.

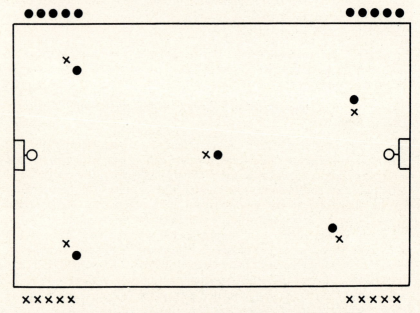

Figure 154. Position of Players in Side-Line Basketball

PROCEDURE: On a signal, Number 1 players of both teams step into the court and take basketball positions as opponents (Figure 154). Following a scoring play Number 2's step into the court, the former players retiring to the side lines. After the next scoring play Number 3's enter the court, and this continues until all have had a turn in the court.

The game is played as is regulation basketball, with the exception that no player within the court may pass the ball directly to another court player but must each time pass to a side-line player. In case of successive throws for the goal, however, this rule is waived. The ball may not be dribbled. Line players may not lose contact with the ground outside of the court or with the court line itself.

Violations: The following violations cause the offending team to lose the ball: (1) failure to pass to side-line players each time; (2) side-line player taking more than one step off the side line; (3) side-line player passing to another side-line player; (4) dribbling the ball; (5) other violations as in regulation basketball.

Penalty: Ball goes to the side line of opponent.

Fouls: Personal and technical fouls are the same as in official basketball, either boys' or girls' rules. The penalty for a foul is a free throw for the opponents.

Playing Time: The playing time should be so divided that each player has the same amount of time within the court area.

SCORING: The same scoring is used as for official basketball.

TEACHING SUGGESTIONS

1. Use as a game for large numbers of players with limited basketball facilities.
2. Teach basketball passing skills, team play, or rules with Side-Line Basketball.

SIX-MAN SOCCER

NUMBER OF PLAYERS: 12

SPACE: Playground, gymnasium

PLAYING AREA: Field 90 by 150 feet. Goal areas 61 by 27 feet marked from the center of the end lines. A circle with diameter of 9 feet at center of field.

EQUIPMENT: (1) Soccer ball; for gymnasium play a slightly deflated ball; (2) two goals made of two 2 by 4 inch uprights 7 feet high placed 10 feet apart at the center of each end line, with crossbars at the top.

FORMATION: Players are divided into two teams. Center forward, right inside forward, left inside forward, right halfback, left halfback, and one fullback take their positions as in official soccer. The fullback has the duties of a goalkeeper, as well as the goalkeeper's privileges while he is playing within the penalty area.

PROCEDURE: The procedure is the same as for soccer, with the exception that offside is not called.[1]

SCORING: Official soccer scoring methods are used.

TEACHING SUGGESTIONS

1. Rotate players after each goal made.
2. Give students a digest of soccer rules in order that they may more easily master rules of the game.
3. Use as a lead-up game for soccer because skills are learned faster with fewer players on a team.

---

[1] See Soccer for Boys, p. 775.

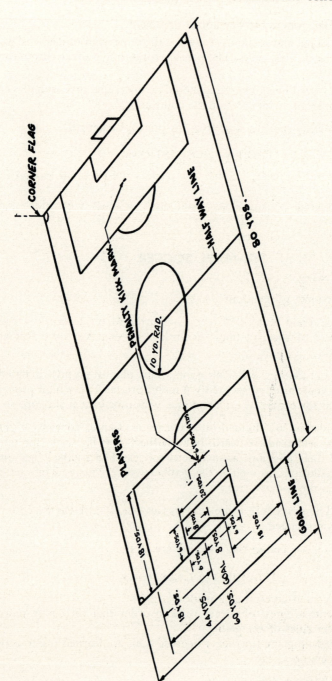

Figure 155.   Field for Boys' Soccer

SOCCER FOR BOYS [1]

NUMBER OF PLAYERS: 22

SPACE: Playground

PLAYING AREA: Field with a maximum dimension of 60 by 80 yards (Figure 155). Center circle is 10 yards in radius from center of the field of play; the penalty area is 44 by 18 yards; the goal area is 20 by 6 yards and is within the penalty area. The goal is 8 yards wide and 8 feet high to the crossbar; penalty kick mark is midway between goal area and penalty area lines. A flag is often used to mark clearly the course of the field.

EQUIPMENT: (1) Soccer ball; (2) goal posts with crossbars; (3) whistles for use of officials; (4) pinnies or other distinguishing marks for teams

Procedure

Soccer is a field game played between two teams of eleven players. The purpose of the game is to make goals by dribbling, heading, or volleying the ball over the opponents' goal line between the goal posts and under the crossbar, while defending the team's own goal from opponents. The attacking team tries to advance the ball toward the opponents' goal without use of hands or arms. In addition to carrying the ball with the feet, a player may use head, shoulder, hip, legs, or chest in an effort to control the ball.

FORMATION: Players are divided into two teams of 11 players: 5 forwards, 3 halfbacks, 2 fullbacks, 1 goalkeeper. Forwards take positions along and on their side of the center line, the forwards of the team not taking the kickoff standing back of the center line. Center halfbacks stand behind and not far from their own center forwards. The two outside halfbacks take positions behind and to the right of their own center halfback. Fullbacks stand behind their own outside halfbacks. Goalkeepers stand in front of the goals and within the goal areas.

PLAYING TIME: For seventh grade, the recommended playing time is four 6-minute quarters, with a maximum of four 8-minute quarters. [2] There should be a 1-minute rest between quarters, and a 10-minute rest between halves. Shorter playing periods may be used by mutual agreement.

START OF GAME: To start the game the official flips a coin and the captain of the team winning the toss has first choice as to end of field and direction of kickoff. The game is started with a place kick from the center of the

---

[1] See official rules in National Collegiate Athletic Bureau, *Soccer Guide*. New York: N. C. A. B. (P. O. Box 757, Grand Central Station, New York 17), 1950.
[2] Official playing time is four 22-minute quarters.

field. A center forward usually takes the kick. Until the ball is kicked the opponents may not be closer than 10 yards, nor may any players of the kicking team pass the halfway line before the kick. The ball must travel not less than its circumference to be legally kicked. The player taking the kick may not touch the ball again until another person plays it. After a goal is made, game is again started with a kickoff by the losing team.

TERMINOLOGY: Information about certain terms used in soccer will help to clarify the rules.

Attacking Team: The team which has possession of the ball and which attempts to put the ball over the opponents' goal line.

Defending Team: The team not in possession of the ball and which attempts to keep the ball from crossing its goal line.

Drop Kick: A kick made when a player, with or without one or two preliminary steps, drops the ball and just as it strikes the ground kicks it. Only goalkeepers within their own penalty area may drop-kick the ball.

Place Kick: A kick made when a stationary ball is kicked by a player, who may or may not take preliminary steps before kicking.

Punt: A kick made when a player drops the ball and kicks it before it strikes the ground. Only goalkeepers within their own penalty area may punt the ball.

Blocking: Intercepting the progress of the ball by use of any part of the body other than arms and hands.

Dribbling: Slight and frequent kicks which propel the ball forward and, at the same time, keep it near to the feet of the dribbler.

Heading: Meeting the ball with the sides or the front of the head.

Juggling: Juggling the ball forward by throwing or tapping it in the air and then catching it before it can touch the ground. Only the goalkeeper may juggle the ball.

Shouldering: Using front, back, or top of shoulder to meet the ball, provided no section of the arm contacts the ball.

Trapping: Stopping the ball's progress by use of a foot on top of it, by use of both feet, or by use of the front of the legs and the ground. Knees must be bent.

Touch Line: Side lines of the playing area.

Goal Line: End lines of the playing area.

DEAD BALL OR BALL OUT OF PLAY: A ball which has left the playing area either by rolling or traveling through the air, or which for other reasons is declared out of play is a dead ball.

BALL IN PLAY: The ball is in play until a goal is made, or the ball passes over goal line outside the goal scoring area or over a touch line; or until an official blows his whistle. Following each goal made, the losing team kicks off from the center of the field. Teams change goals at the end of the first, second, and third quarters. After a temporary suspension of the game, in which no goal, foul, or touch was involved, the game is started when the official drops the ball to the ground at the spot where play was suspended.

FOULS: Fouls in soccer are as follows:

1. Intentional touching of the ball with any part of hands or arms by any player other than a goalkeeper
2. Unnecessary roughness against other players, such as: (a) charging an opponent from behind; (b) pushing, holding, tripping, or jumping at an opponent
3. Technical evasion of rules by players, which include: (a) playing ball second time before it has been contacted by another player following a throw-in, penalty kick, or free kick; (b) touching ball before it touches the ground after it has been dropped by an official; (c) not facing field of play and keeping both feet on the ground when taking a throw-in; (d) goalkeeper carrying the ball, or taking more than four steps while holding the ball; (e) being offside; (f) failure to kick ball forward when awarded a penalty kick; (g) improperly charging a goalkeeper. *Note:* Goalkeeper may be charged while he holds the ball if he is obstructing an opponent and if he is not within the goal area. Such play must not be intentionally rough.

OFFSIDE: When a player kicks the ball and any player of his team is nearer to the opponents' goal than is the kicker, that second player is offside. While offside a player may not touch the ball himself or interfere with the play of an opponent until he is put onside.

A player once offside cannot put himself onside. It must be done for him in one of the following three ways: (1) if an opponent next plays the ball; (2) if he is behind the ball when it is next played by a member of his own team; or (3) if there are two opponents between him and their goal line when the ball is played by a member of his own team while that player is farther from the opponents' goal than himself.

A player cannot be offside if he is in his own half of the field; if he is behind the ball when it is being played; if he is in advance of the ball and there are two opponents between him and the opponents' goal line; or while a goal kick or corner kick is being made.

FREE KICK: There are two kinds of free kicks; (1) a direct free kick from which a goal can be scored; and (2) an indirect free kick from which a goal cannot be scored until it has been played by another player. A free kick is a place kick and the kicker must not play it again until it has been played by another player. All opponents must be at least 10 yards away.

A direct free kick is given for the following fouls committed against an opponent: (1) tripping, (2) kicking, (3) striking, (4) jumping, (5) handling the ball, (6) pushing, or (7) charging, using hands or arm. If the goalkeeper carries the ball outside the penalty area a direct free kick is given.

An indirect free kick is given for the following fouls: (1) offside, (2) carrying ball by goalkeeper more than four steps without bouncing it within the penalty area, (3) charging the goalkeeper when he does not have the ball, (4) playing the ball a second time before it has touched another player after a throw-in, free kick, corner kick or penalty kick, and (5) dangerous play.

PENALTY KICK: A penalty kick is awarded to the opponents when a player of the defending team, while *within* his own penalty area (1) commits a foul by tripping, kicking, striking, holding or pushing an opponent; or (2) controls the ball by use of hands or arm. Goalkeepers while within their own penalty area may use their hands.

In a penalty kick the ball is placed on the penalty-kick line in the penalty area where the foul occurred, and it must be kicked forward toward the goal. All players except the goalkeeper and the kicker must remain outside the penalty area until ball is kicked. The goalkeeper may not advance over the goal line until the ball is kicked. The person kicking may not touch the ball again until another player has done so.

If goal is made 1 point is scored. If goal is not made the ball remains in play.

CORNER KICK: A corner kick is awarded to attacking team if member of the *defending* team, intentionally or not, kicks ball over a goal line but not between the goal posts.

The ball is placed on the ground within the quarter circle nearest the point where the ball left the field of play. Members of defending team may be no nearer than 10 yards until the ball is kicked. The kicker may not touch the ball again until another person has played it. A goal may be scored from a corner kick.

GOAL KICK: A goal kick is awarded to a member of the defending team (usually the goalkeeper or a fullback) when a member of the *attacking* team kicks the ball over a goal line but not between the goal posts.

The ball is placed on the goal line at the point where it passed over the goal line. No opponent may be within 10 yards of the ball until it is kicked. The kicker may not touch the ball again until a second player has touched it.

TOUCH: A touch occurs when the ball, while in the air or on the ground, passes out of the field of play over a touch (side) line.

THROW-IN: A throw-in is awarded when a touch occurs. An opponent (usually a halfback) of team which sent ball into touch takes the throw-in.

The thrower must stand outside but facing the field at the place where the ball left the field. The feet must be together and both arms fully extended over the head while holding the ball. The feet must not leave the ground while the throw is being made. The ball may be thrown in any direction. A goal *may not* be attempted during a throw-in. The thrower may not touch the ball again until a second person has played it. Infraction of these regulations requires that the ball be given to the opponents for a free kick at the place where the infraction occurs.

SCORING: Each goal made counts 1 point.

A goal does not occur in the following circumstances:

1. If ball is thrown through the goal area
2. If ball is knocked through; that is, struck or sent forward by action of arm or hand
3. If ball is carried through by member of attacking team
4. If passage of ball through goal results from a kickoff, goal kick, or indirect free kick

The team wins that has the higher number of points at the conclusion of the fourth quarter. During tournaments, there should be no extension of playing time in an effort to break a tie score.

TEACHING SUGGESTIONS

1. Each school should have the current official rules of soccer so that pupils can refer to them.
2. Refer to the section, Soccer Players and Their Responsibilities, page 783, Soccer Techniques, p. 784, and Soccer Skill Drills, p. 787.

SOCCER FOR GIRLS [1]

NUMBER OF PLAYERS: 22

SPACE: Playground

PLAYING AREA: A field with a maximum dimension of 60 by 80 yards, marked as in Figure 156.

EQUIPMENT: (1) Soccer ball; (2) costumes of distinguishing colors for the two teams. Shoes may be only cloth with rubber soles and rubber or leather toe protectors. Light shin-guards may be worn.

Procedure

Soccer for girls is similar to the game for boys in general team play

---

[1] Rules based on *Official Soccer-Speedball Guide*. Washington: National Section on Women's Athletics, American Association for Health, Physical Education and Recreation (1201 Sixteenth Street, N.W., Washington 6, D. C.).

and manner of scoring. The rules for girls' soccer, however, permit no body contact without a penalty involved.

FORMATION: Players are divided into two teams of 11 players each: (forward line) center, left wing, left inner center, right inner center, and right wing; left, center, and right halfbacks; left and right fullbacks; and goalkeeper. When a team takes the kickoff the five members of the forward line must stand back of the halfway line, the halfbacks behind the restraining lines, the fullbacks, dividing the field between them, behind the halfbacks, and the goalkeeper in front of her goal. Members of the defending team are in similar formation in their half of the field, but all players must be behind their restraining line.

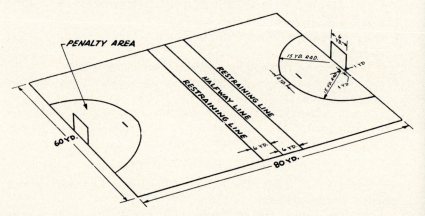

Figure 156.   Field for Girls' Soccer

PLAYING TIME: A game consists of four quarters with a maximum of eight minutes each, and with a rest period of two minutes between quarters and ten minutes between halves. Time-out may be taken only when the ball is out of play, or in case of injury. Two time-outs will be allowed each team during a game.

START OF GAME: The captains decide which is to have the choice of goal and kickoff by tossing a coin. After the first quarter the kickoff alternates. Goals are changed at half time.

The game is started with a place kick from the center of the field. The ball is kicked toward the opponents' goal. The ball must be kicked into the opponents' territory at least the difference of its own circumference. The player who takes the kickoff may not play the ball again until it has been touched by another player. No opponent may cross the restraining line and no member of the team taking the kickoff may cross the halfway line until the ball has been kicked.

The attacking team members, by passing, dribbling, kicking with the feet, or advancing the ball with any part of their bodies except their hands and arms, try to take the ball down the field to make a goal across the opponents' goal line.

TERMINOLOGY: A brief description of terms used in soccer will make the rules more understandable. Refer also to terms used in Boys' Soccer, p. 776.

Attackers: The team in possession of the ball, attempting to make a goal

Defenders: The team which does not have the ball and which attempts to stop a goal from being made across their goal line

Own Goal: Members of a team stand at the kickoff with their backs toward their own goal. Each goal guard protects his own goal.

Own Half of Field: That half of the field between the halfway line and the goal line on which the team's goal is located

Dribbling: Carrying the ball forward with slight successive kicks so that dribbler keeps control of the ball.

ADVANCING THE BALL BY MEANS OF THE BODY: The ball may be advanced by heading, which is allowing the top or side of the head to meet the ball, and by shouldering, which is meeting the ball with the front, top, or back of the shoulder. The arm must not strike the ball unless it is touched with the upper arm while in total contact with the body.

Another way to advance the ball with the body is volleying. A volley is a play in which some part of the body sends the ball into the air from another player.

The ball may be stopped by blocking or trapping. Blocking is intercepting the progress of the ball with the body, whereas trapping the ball is stopping its progress with the feet or legs.

GOAL GUARD's PRIVILEGES: A goal guard within her own penalty area may use her hands on the ball. She, therefore, is the only player who may use the punt.

OUT-OF-BOUNDS BALLS: When a ball goes entirely over the side lines, a player from the team which did not send the ball out kicks the ball in from the spot where it went out. The kicker may not play the ball again until it has been played by another player. All opponents must be six yards away until the ball has been kicked. A goal may not be scored from the kick-in. If the ball does not roll its circumference, or is played by the kicker before another player touches it, a kick-in is awarded the opposing team.

When the ball is sent over the crossbar or over the goal line outside the goal posts by a player of the attacking team, it is kicked in with a place kick by a member of the defending team, anywhere on the line marking the penalty area. The ball must roll its circumference and may not be played by the defense kicker until it has been touched by another player. All opponents must be six yards away.

A corner kick is taken when any player of the defending team sends the ball over the crossbar or outside the goal posts. A corner kick is taken by a player of the attacking team on the 5-yard mark at the corner of the field. Halfbacks, fullbacks, and the goalkeeper of the defending team must stand on or behind the goal line until the ball is kicked. No opponent may play closer than six yards until the ball is kicked. A goal may be scored from a corner kick. For not kicking the ball its circumference, or for kicking it the second time, a free kick is awarded the opponents.

If the ball goes over the side line or goal line outside the goal posts off the feet or body of two opposing players, a roll-in is taken. For a roll-in the umpire rolls the ball at a spot two yards in from the side or goal line where the ball left the field of play. The opposing players taking the roll-in must stand six yards apart and may move to kick the ball as soon as it leaves the umpire's hands. All other players must be six yards away.

Fouls: A player may not trip, push, kick, hold, strike, charge, or jump at her opponent. A player (except the goalkeeper within her own penalty area) may not handle the ball. The goalkeeper may not take more than two steps while holding the ball.

Offside is a foul in which a player is nearer her opponents' goal line than the ball is, at the moment the ball is played by one of her own team members (unless she is in her own half of the field or there are three of her opponents nearer their own goal than she is). A player is not penalized for being offside unless she has gained some advantage by doing so. She is put back onside if she is behind the ball when it is next played by one of her own teammates, or if there are three opponents between her and their goal line when the ball is played by one of her own teammates further from her opponents' goal than she is.

Penalties: Free kicks are awarded as penalties for any fouls committed outside a team's own penalty area. A free kick is also awarded for an illegal defense kick in the penalty area by the defending team, and misuse of the goalkeeper's privileges. When a free kick is awarded, a place kick is taken at the spot where the foul occurred. All opponents must be six yards away, and the kicker must kick the ball its circumference and not play it again until it has been touched by another player.

A penalty kick is awarded for the following fouls committed by the defending team in its own penalty area: (1) tripping an opponent, (2) kicking an opponent, (3) striking an opponent, (4) jumping at an opponent, (5) charging an opponent, (6) holding an opponent, (7) pushing an opponent, (8) handling the ball. A penalty kick is awarded also for the following: (1) carrying the ball by the goalkeeper, (2) taking a defense kick incorrectly, and (3) taking a free kick incorrectly. A penalty kick is also given to the opponents for a team taking more than two time-outs; for a player re-entering the game more than once; and for a substitute entering the game without reporting. When a penalty kick is awarded, a place kick is taken on the penalty kick mark 12 yards from the goal line. Any attacker may kick but it must be an attempted goal. All players, with the exception of the kicker and the opposing goalkeeper, must be outside the penalty area and in the field of play until the ball has been kicked.

SCORING: A field goal counts 2 points and a penalty kick counts 1 point. A field goal is scored when a ball has been kicked or legally hit by the body so that it passes over the goal line between the goal posts and under the crossbar. A field goal may be scored from any spot within the field by any player who is onside.

A penalty kick is scored when the ball passes over the goal line between the goal posts and under the crossbar, if the ball was kicked at the penalty-kick mark by a player taking the penalty kick.

The team that scores more points during the playing period wins the game.

SOCCER PLAYERS AND THEIR RESPONSIBILITIES

A brief description of the necessary skills and duties of the players is given to provide a better understanding of the game of soccer (boys' and girls').

GOALKEEPERS: Goalkeepers need courage, cool heads, and patience, since often they have long periods during which they stand idle. They should have special skill in handling the ball with their hands as they are the only players who, under certain conditions, may use hands in an effort to control the ball. Goalkeepers may use any part of the body in any position while trying to prevent passage of the ball through the scoring areas. Experienced goalkeepers stand some two feet in front of their goal line, never directly over it. When handling a ball they endeavor to send it toward a touch line (side line)—never directly forward.

Goalkeepers should not go far from their goal area and should have the support of the fullbacks of their team when defense of the goal area becomes necessary.

Goalkeepers may, while within a penalty or goal area, do the following:

1. Catch the ball
2. Pick up the ball
3. Throw the ball
4. Bounce the ball
5. Juggle the ball once by throwing or tapping it into the air before throwing it

6. Tap or throw ball above and over the crossbar
7. Fist the ball with one or both fists
8. Punt the ball
9. Drop-kick the ball
10. Combine a bounce or a juggle with a punt, drop kick or a throw
11. Take not more than four steps while holding the ball

FULLBACKS: The main responsibility of the fullbacks is to defend the goal area. They should practice accurate kicking with either foot. They should work for speed and endurance. Time should be spent in practicing quick starts and short dashes. They are responsible for taking the ball away from the inside forwards (inners in girls' game).

HALFBACKS: Much running is the lot of halfbacks, since in one minute they are attackers and in the next they have to become defenders. Center halfbacks are considered to have one of the most vital positions on a team, because they back up their own forward line and also defend their own goal. Right, left, and center halfbacks have to learn to attack. They must be able to endure sustained running as well as sprinting when necessity arises.

The main duty of halfbacks is to feed the ball to their own forwards, following up their forwards as they advance by receiving passes from their own fullbacks. They should not enter the opponents' goal area nor their own goal area.

FORWARDS: The forwards have different names in the girls' and boys' games, but they have the same responsibilities. All need speed in running, accuracy in managing the ball, and endurance. Their main duty is to carry the ball into their opponents' area and thus score points. They should enter the opponents' goal area but not their own. All need practice in dribbling and accuracy in passing to either side while moving rapidly. Each forward should learn to play in his own part of the field so that the entire width of the field is used and there is no bunching in the center.

SOCCER TECHNIQUES

The following material should assist teachers when presenting activities requiring the use of a soccer ball, when hands and arms may not be used. It is recommended that other source materials be made available so that students may study technique and strategy.

KICKING: The top, heel or side of a foot should be used in kicking. The end of the toes should never come in direct contact with the ball.

Use of Inside of Foot When Kicking: The weight should be on the ball of the nonkicking foot. The entire leg of the kicking foot should swing from the hip with the knee slightly bent. The swing should be forward toward the direction the kick is to be made. After a kick the leg follows through, ending with a step in the direction of the kick.

Use of Outside of Foot When Kicking: The weight should be on the ball of the nonkicking foot. The kicking foot should first swing in a short arc across and in front of the nonkicking foot. Then, with a snap, the foot should move away from the supporting foot. At the same time the ankle should be sharply extended as impact with the ball occurs. After the kick the leg should follow through, ending with a step in the direction of the kick.

Use of Top of Foot When Kicking: The body is balanced on the non-kicking foot. The kicking leg should swing back easily, then forward with speed, with the knee slightly bent. The ball should be met with the top of the foot and the knee straightened as contact is made with the ball. The supporting leg should start the weight of body upward on the toes as the swinging leg starts forward; the supporting foot should leave the ground with a spring as the free foot contacts the underside of the ball.

Use of Heel When Kicking Backwards: Much practice is needed to perfect this skill. Care should be exercised that the kicker does not fall backward. As the leg is swung forward over the oncoming ball, the body weight should be well forward and over both the supporting leg and the ball. The knee of the swinging leg should be bent sharply as the backward swing of the leg occurs. The ankle should be extended sharply as the heel kicks the ball. See Figure 13, p. 39.

DRIBBLING: Dribbling is a very essential yet difficult technique. Much time should be spent in acquiring this skill. Dribbling is executed by the feet alternately tapping the ball while the body is moving forward. The ball should not be permitted to get more than a foot in advance of the player. It is necessary to develop a rhythm while performing the foot action, such as:

Slow Run: Kick right, step right, kick left, step left
Fast Run: Kick right, run right, left, right; kick left, run left, right, left

The control and direction of the ball is secured by manipulation of the feet and flexing of the ankles.

VOLLEYING: Volleying the ball involves kicking or contacting the ball with hip, shoulder, head, or chest before ball touches the ground. Girls, when preparing to chest a ball, should fold their arms close to the chest with elbows down. During a half-volley the ball is contacted just as it starts upward from a bounce. During a volley, the player should always move to meet the ball and endeavor to redirect it to a teammate.

In volleying with the knee or thigh, the player should spring toward the ball and at the same time swing the contacting leg up, with the knee bent. The ball should make contact near the outside of the knee or on the inside or front of the thigh. In volleying with the hip, the player should move into the ball, spring, and at the same time turn slightly sideward, thereby meeting the ball with the side of the body or the hip. In volleying with the shoulder, the player should spring and meet the ball with the front or top of the shoulder. The arms should be held away from the body and in a downward position in order to avoid touching the ball with them.

HEADING: Practice in heading should be delayed until players have become skillful in handling their bodies and in the execution of other forms of volleying. *Partially deflated balls should be used until skill and confidence are developed.* Players should get under the ball, keep their eyes on it, and contact the ball at the highest point of the jump, taking the blow on the front and top of the foreheads. As the contact is made, the spine and neck muscles should be tensed, the head giving slightly at the instant of impact.

TRAPPING: Several trapping methods are used to stop and keep possession of the ball.

Single Foot Trap: The weight remains on one foot. The heel of the other foot is lowered, with the toes elevated so that the sole of the foot meets and slows the action of the ball.

Ankle Trap: The weight remains on one foot. The other leg is turned in from the hip, the knee is bent and the foot turned in, so that the ball is trapped between the leg and the ground. This particular technique is used on fast-rolling or low-bounding balls.

Single Knee Trap: The weight remains on one foot while the other foot is moved forward. Both knees should be bent with the forward knee dropped over and on the ball.

Double Knee Trap: The double knee trap is similar to the single knee trap, with both knees contacting the ball lightly.

BLOCKING: The ball itself may be blocked—that is slowed down—by any part of the body except arms or hands; or a player may be blocked by another player without body contact. Such a play may prevent the ball from being received or the execution of the block may prevent a person from reaching the ball. The body or a segment of the body taking the block should give slightly in the direction in which the ball is traveling as contact occurs.

RUNNING: Every player should cultivate the ability to run fast for long or short distances; to change direction easily; and at all times to be on balance. Running relays and warming up by running around the field will develop endurance.

PASSING: Passing is an important skill that requires much practice. Players should study the position of other players before passing the ball. Passes may be made by using the inside, or the outside, or the top of the foot, never by use of the ends of the toes.

TACKLING: This is the art of securing the ball by the use of the feet. Bodily contact should not occur. Tackling should be practiced first in slow motion, so that kicking the feet of the players is avoided.

GOAL KICKING: The ball should be kicked forcibly while the performer is running. Angle shots are difficult.

SOCCER SKILL DRILLS

FOOT SKILLS: Several soccer balls should be made available for the squad which is practicing.

Kicking for Goals: Four or six players should be placed in front of the goal, with the goalkeeper in front of the goal area and two assistants in back of the goal area. Each player should kick an approaching ball while it is (1) rolling or bouncing directly toward him; (2) approaching him from different angles while rolling or bouncing; or (3) while a fly ball. The goalkeeper should attempt to stop every shot, scooping the ball up and throwing it out toward the kicker. Assistants return the ball to the goalkeeper. Contacts should be made with a sweep of the leg as the ball is contacted with the instep. When a ball is approaching on a direct line from the goal to the kicker, the kicker should rotate the leg and point toe in so that the instep strikes the ball. Playing positions are rotated.

Kicking Practice for Backs: Four to six players are placed 20 to 30 yards apart. Each is directed to kick a ball to an indicated player who stops the ball with his feet and kicks it to another designated player.

Kicking Practice for Goalkeeping: Players are placed 20 to 30 yards apart. While the ball is on the ground the players, in turn, take a short run and kick the ball to an opposite player, who stops the ball through the use of arms, feet, legs, and body.

Place Kick: Either with partners or in squads, pupils practice kicking a stationary ball. The player should use the upper instep of the foot and never the end of the toes.

Punt: In couples or in groups of four, pupils should practice the punt. The kicker, using two hands, holds the soccer ball extended outward and downward, a little below waist level. The lacing of the ball should be on top and nearer the kicker's body with ends of laced area near the hands. In balls without lacing, the air holes should be on top. The ball should be gripped with both hands and when ready to drop the ball, the hands are just slightly separated.

A punt should always be made in a straight line. It is best to kick low balls when practicing to reach a given point. Low balls are difficult to catch and an added roll is often obtained.

Drop Kick: The drop kick should be first practiced in couples or in groups of four across the field and later over the crossbar of the goals.

DRIBBLING AND PASSING SKILLS: Dribbling and passing should be taught together. Three to five players should be spread across the field, with 10 to 15 yards between them. Each player dribbles the ball a short distance and then passes the ball to the next player. A dribble consists of a series of very short kicks which keep the ball *close to the foot* and *under the control* of the dribbler. Each player must learn to pass sideways, while using the inside and outside of the foot. To pass with the inside of the foot, the player must learn to sweep the leg in front of the body. To pass with the outside of the foot, the player must point his toe in and at the same time give his foot a fling away from the body.

HEADING SKILLS: In couples or in squad formation heading is practiced first from a bouncing ball. After skill in contacting the ball is acquired, players should learn to jump into the air to head the ball.

TRAPPING SKILLS: In couples or in squad formation, the four types of trapping are practiced, first from a rolled ball and later from a kicked ball.

TACKLING AND DODGING SKILLS: The term "tackling" in soccer does not mean the same as it does in tackle football. In boys' soccer a player may charge an opponent to knock him away from the ball as long as the charger does not do so from the rear. The opponent is touched through use of the shoulder and at the same instant by a lift to the attacker's body.

In couple formation, with the opponents traveling in the same direction, the attacker practices putting his body across the path of an opponent in order to tackle. This is done by the attacking player's stepping with his near leg and bracing himself to get on the near hip the impact of the opponent's rush, which thereby breaks the opponent's stride and makes for greater ease in gaining control of the ball.

No body contact is allowed in girls' soccer, but all tackles are made by taking the ball away from the feet only. Couples facing each other should practice tackling: the girl without the ball puts her foot on the ball between taps of the dribble or the pass of the attacking player.

Dodging is the skill which must be taught to players in order for them to outplay a tackle. This is done by changing direction in dribbling, by passing to another player, or by changing the speed of the dribble or pass.

As couples, either facing each other or running side by side, practice tackling they will also practice dodging. Players carrying the ball should first learn the skill of changing direction before the opposing player tries to gain possession of the ball. The formation to use for a passing dodge is a double file line facing a single line. The couples in the double line dribble and pass as the player from the single line attacks.

SPONGE BALL

NUMBER OF PLAYERS: 2-20

SPACE: Classroom, playroom, gymnasium, area out of doors protected from wind

PLAYING AREA: Volleyball court with the dimensions adjusted to number of players if necessary

EQUIPMENT: (1) Volleyball net, rope, wire mesh, or gunny sacks fashioned into a net; (2) one ball formed from a large sponge (not sponge rubber). Shape the sponge with scissors until the circumference is approximately the same size throughout. (3) For each player a paddle-tennis paddle,[1] table-tennis paddle, or tennis racket

FORMATION: One to ten players form a team, as in volleyball or badminton.

PROCEDURE: The sponge is played like a volleyball, paddles propelling it through the air. Volleyball rules are used.[2] The sponge is very light and has an action that is different from other balls. It remains in the air longer and therefore gives the players a better opportunity to strike it. The game is most successful when played within doors. If paddles are not available the hands may be used.

SCORING: The same scoring is used as in volleyball.

TEACHING SUGGESTIONS

1. Use as a recreational game at socials.
2. Use to teach either volleyball or badminton rules.

TABLE TENNIS [3]

NUMBER OF PLAYERS: 2-4

SPACE: Playground, gymnasium, hallway, classroom, auditorium

PLAYING AREA: Table top 5 by 9 feet, placed 30 inches from the floor. Top may be made of ⅝-inch plywood supported by wooden horses. Top should be painted dark green. A ¾-inch white strip should be painted down the center and around the edges of the table top (Figure 157).

---

[1] For description of paddle-tennis paddle see page 115.
[2] See Volleyball, p. 801.
[3] Refer to *Rules of Table Tennis*. Free on request to General Sportcraft Company, 215 Fourth Avenue, New York 3, N. Y.

Helpful material may be found in *Official Recreational Games—Volleyball Guide*. Washington: National Section on Women's Athletics, American Association for Health, Physical Education and Recreation (1201 Sixteenth Street, N.W., Washington 6, D. C.).

EQUIPMENT: (1) Two adjustable posts for holding net in position, placed at the center of the table at each side; (2) net 66 inches long stretched across the table from post to post, with the top edge 6¾ inches from the table top; (3) wooden rackets for each player; (4) celluloid balls

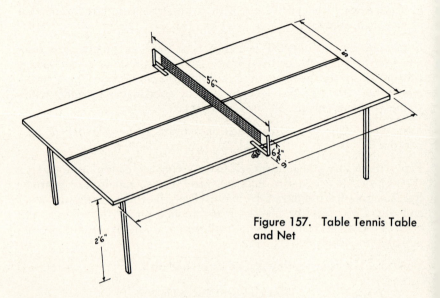

Figure 157.   Table Tennis Table and Net

Procedure

Table tennis is much like lawn tennis on a small scale. A small ball is batted back and forth over a net on a table top.

FORMATION: Players stand at each end of the table and may play a singles or a doubles game.

SERVING: The server, standing behind the end of the table, must keep his ball and racket behind the end line of the court and between the side lines as if they were extended. The ball is dropped or tossed by the server and is then so struck that it will hit the table on the side of the server before bouncing over the net. Each server serves the ball five times.

RECEIVING: Taking the ball following the first bounce, the receiver endeavors to return the ball to the server's side in such a way that the latter cannot return it and so he cannot make the point. The ball is never taken on the fly. Play continues until one side or the other misses the ball.

Singles: In singles the ball may hit anywhere on the opposite half of the table.

Doubles: In doubles the ball must be served to the diagonally opposite court, but following the service, doubles partners must alternate in hitting the ball.

The order of service in doubles is different from that in singles. The server serves five times. The second five serves are made by the receiver of the first five serves. The third five serves are delivered by the partner of the first server, and the fourth by the partner of the first receiver, who is called a striker-out in table tennis.

Let Ball: A let ball is a ball which strikes the top of the net as it goes over. The first let ball is served again. A let serve must hit into the proper court on the receiver's side after hitting the net. A let return is a legal return.

SCORING: A player makes points each time an opponent makes an error, whether he is the server or the receiver.

Points: An opponent wins a point each time a player makes one of the following errors: (1) fails to make a good service, (2) fails to make a good return, (3) permits free hand to touch surface of court while ball is in play, (4) permits clothing or racket to contact an opponent's ball before it crosses the net, (5) returns to opponent's court a ball which goes over a side line without touching the court.

A score of 21 points is a game. If the score is tied at 20 points, service changes after each point and the side wins which first gets two consecutive points. A match is two out of three games.

TEACHING SUGGESTIONS

1. Teach players the proper grip for the racket. Two methods of hand grip are generally accepted:

   (a) The pencil-holder grip, in which paddle handle is held between the thumb and index finger with the back of the racket supported by the remaining fingers. With this grip all strokes are taken on the face of the racket.

   (b) The tennis grip, in which the paddle is held in the "hand-shaking" position and both forehand and backhand strokes are used. Nearly all experts use the tennis grip.

2. Teach players to "cut" the ball, thereby giving different spins to the ball.

3. Teach the players to move toward the ball as they strike it.

4. Teach players to play away from the table.

5. Demonstrate the importance of wrist action.

6. Instruct the children to keep their eyes on the ball.

7. Teach the players to be ready to move in any direction at any time.

TOUCH FOOTBALL [1]

NUMBER OF PLAYERS: 14

SPACE: Playground

PLAYING AREA: For elementary school boys and girls a field 30 by 60 yards, including end zones of 10 yards each; maximum field 40 by 70 yards (Figure 158). For junior high school boys and girls, field should be 40 by 80 yards, including end zones of 10 yards each; maximum field should be 53 1/3 by 120 yards.

The field is marked at intervals of 20 yards with lines parallel to the goal lines. These lines are called dividing lines. The scoring zone at each end is 10 yards deep. This depth remains constant with various sized fields. Goal posts with crossbars should be placed in the middle of the end lines. Soccer goal posts will serve. The game could be played without goal posts.

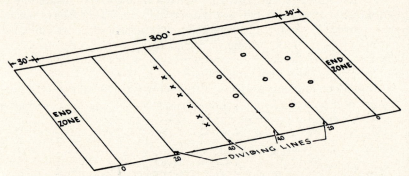

Figure 158.   Touch Football Field with Players in Position to Start Game

EQUIPMENT: (1) Junior official football or soccer ball; (2) jerseys, sweatshirts, or pinnies so that members of teams may be distinguished easily.

Players must wear only rubber-soled tennis or basketball shoes. Spiked or cleated shoes and special protective devices such as shoulder pads or helmets may not be worn.

Procedure

Touch football is a field game in which two teams of seven players each try to obtain and retain possession of the ball and advance it across the opponents' goal line. A team's own goal line is always the goal line it

[1] These rules have been worked out and presented by H. A. Applequist, Supervisor of Physical Education, Sacramento City Schools. For official football rules each school should purchase *Official Football Rules*, Chicago: National Federation of State High School Athletic Associations. Edited, published, and copyrighted by the Association annually and obtained from the Association headquarters, 7 South Dearborn St., Chicago 3, Illinois.

is defending. This game involves most of the basic skills, strategy, and elements of team play found in American football and eliminates the safety hazards of wedge formations, diving interference, and tackling.

The offensive team (team in possession of the ball) may advance the ball forward by a running play, forward pass play, or kicking play. The center must make a backward pass or snap to a teammate in his backfield before the ball or any other player may advance beyond the line of scrimmage. A scrimmage line is an imaginary line across the field from the spot where the center passes the ball.

The defensive team has the right to intercept passes, return kicks, and gain possession of the ball through a fumble or a blocked kick by the offensive team. On the defensive team only the ends and center may attempt to block a kick. Roughing of a player who kicks from behind his scrimmage line is not permitted.

FORMATION: On kickoff plays, the seven players of each team stand in their own half of the field with their backs toward their own goal. The players of the kicking team must be behind the imaginary line drawn through the ball before the ball is kicked. The players of the receiving team may line up in any formation they wish if they form no group interference and are behind a line 10 yards away from where the ball is put in play. (See diagram: X is the kicking team; O is the receiving team.)

On scrimmage plays, the offensive team must have three players on the line of scrimmage and four players at least one yard back of the line of scrimmage when the ball is put in play. The defensive team is not restricted as to the position of the players while on defense, except when the offensive team goes into a kicking formation and then only three players may be on the line of scrimmage and attempt to block the kick.

The positions on each team are as follows: left end, center, right end, left halfback, fullback, right halfback, and quarterback.

PLAYING PERIOD: The game is played in 8-minute quarters, with a 2-minute rest between first and second and third and fourth quarters. There is a 5-minute rest period at half time, at which time players may leave the field.

Time-Out: Time is taken out (1) after a touchdown, (2) after a safety or touchback, (3) during try for point, (4) when a ball goes out of bounds, (5) when play is suspended by referee, (6) for enforcement or declination of penalties. Time is not taken out for an incomplete forward pass as it is in American football.

SUBSTITUTES: A player may be substituted for another at any time without penalty, providing the substitution is made after the ball has been declared dead and before the expiration of 25 seconds allowed to put the ball in play.

PLAYING TERMS AND RESTRICTIONS: Most of the terms used in touch football are identical with those used in interscholastic or intercollegiate football. The restrictions and variations in interpretation are related to mass play, blocking or screening, and tackling.

Blocking: Blocking is obstructing an opponent by use of the blocker's body. Any player on the offensive team may interpose his body between an opponent and the ball carrier to prevent a "touch." No part of the blocker's body except his feet or feet and hands should touch the ground before, during, or after contact is made with the defensive player. Both feet must be on the ground while blocking. The forearms should be held against the chest when contact is made with defensive player.

Defensive Team: The team which does not have the ball is designated as the defensive team.

Downed Ball: A player is downed and the ball is dead when a defensive player touches the ball-carrier below the neck with both hands.

Downs: The team is allowed four downs or four tries to advance the ball from wherever they got possession of the ball to or beyond the nearest dividing line in the direction of the opponents' goal. If in four downs this is not accomplished, the ball goes to the opponents at the spot where the ball is declared dead after the fourth down.

Forward Pass: A forward pass may be made by the offensive team from any point behind the line of scrimmage. Any player of either team is eligible to receive a forward pass.

Fumbled or Muffed Ball: Any time a ball is fumbled or muffed, the ball is dead at the spot where it touched the ground, and belongs to the team in possession of the ball when the fumble or muff occurred. A muff is an attempted catch of a ball that is unsuccessful.

Huddle: When players in possession of the ball group together to call a play, it is called a huddle.

Incomplete Pass: It is an incomplete pass when a legal pass is thrown forward and hits the ground before it is caught by a player of either side. The ball is brought back to spot of the previous snap. The penalty is loss of a down.

Line of Scrimmage: This term is used to designate an imaginary line across the field as wide as the length of the football and at the point where the ball is to be put in play by scrimmage.

Interference: This is a term used to designate the action which occurs by blocking or screening to clear a path for the ball carrier.

Offensive Team: The team in possession of the ball is designated as the offensive team.

Offside: A player is considered to be offside when any part of his body is ahead of the ball when it is put in play. Examples are: (1) when a player of either team is ahead of the ball before the kickoff occurs;

(2) when a player of either team infringes upon or crosses into the neutral area (ground area separating two lines of players or scrimmage line) before ball is snapped.

Out of Bounds: The ball is out of bounds when the ball carrier steps on or outside of a side line, or when the ball is fumbled or muffed and hits the ground on or outside a side line.

Reverse: A reverse is a play in which a back receives the ball from center, starts toward a side line, and hands the ball or makes a lateral pass to another player coming around and running in the opposite direction.

Running Play: An attempt to carry the ball through or around the defensive team is a running play. A wide sweeping play which attempts to advance the ball outside the defensive end is an end run.

Safety: A safety occurs when a player of the team attempting to advance the ball is touched behind his own goal with the ball in his possession; when a player of the team attempting to advance the ball causes it to go over his own goal line by a kick, muff, fumble, or pass, and is touched in his own end zone with the ball in his possession; or when a player of either team is responsible for the ball's being back of his own goal line and he is unable to get it out without being touched in the end zone. The team making the safety puts the ball in play by a free kick anywhere on the nearer 20-yard dividing line.

Snap: Throwing or passing the ball between the legs to a player in the backfield is called a snap. It is used by the player occupying center position when scrimmage play starts.

Touchback: When a kick which does not score a goal is punted, drop-kicked, or place-kicked and crosses the defending team's goal line, it is a touchback. The ball is taken to the 20-yard dividing line where the team which has been on the defense puts it in play by scrimmage. When a forward pass becomes incomplete on the end zone on the fourth down, it is also considered a touchback.

Touching: Touching takes the place of regular football tackling. It results when the ball carrier is touched or tagged below the neck by a defensive player *with both hands simultaneously*. Ball is declared dead at the point where touch occurs. No part of the toucher's body, except his feet, may be in contact with the ground throughout the touch; defensive player may not, while lying or kneeling on the ground, touch the ball carrier. Pushing or striking the ball carrier is penalized as unnecessary roughness. After a ball carrier is touched, the toucher should bring his arms directly above his head to indicate that a touch has occurred.

Use of Hands: Defensive players may use their hands to protect themselves from offensive blockers and to get to the player with the ball. They are restricted in the use of their hands to touching the shoulders and body of attacking blockers. Offensive players may not use their hands in blocking or screening defensive players.

RULES OF PLAY: The game is started with a kickoff from any point on the 40-yard line. All players of the kicking team must be behind the imaginary line through the ball when the ball is kicked. The ball may be punted or elevated one inch for a free kick by a place kick. Players of the receiving team may line up in any formation they may choose but may not form group interference. All players for the receiving team must be behind a line parallel to and 10 yards in advance of the kicking team's restraining line. The ball must be kicked at least 10 yards or be touched by a player of the receiving team prior to going 10 yards to be considered in play. If the receiving team, after having had the ball in its possession for four consecutive downs, shall not have advanced the ball to the nearest dividing line in the direction of the opponents' goal line, it shall go to the opponents at the spot of the fifth down and the procedure is reversed. To keep possession of the ball, the offensive team (team in possession of the ball) must advance the ball to the nearest dividing line in four consecutive downs.

If on a kickoff the ball goes out of bounds between the goal lines without being in possession and control of a player of the receiving team, it must be kicked over again. If the ball goes out of bounds a second time, the receiving team puts the ball in play by scrimmage on the yard line from which it was last kicked. Any kicked ball from scrimmage which goes out of bounds is put in play by a scrimmage by the receiving team at the in-bounds spot from the point where the ball went out of bounds. If a kicked ball from scrimmage or a free kick which has traveled the necessary 10 yards is muffed, fumbled, or touched, it is dead where it first touches the ground and belongs to the receiving team at this spot. A blocked kick is dead where it touches the ground and belongs to the team blocking the kick at the spot.

FORWARD PASSING: The offensive team is permitted to make one forward pass during a play from any point behind the line of scrimmage. A forward pass made by a player in advance of his line of scrimmage is a violation, the penalty for which is 5 yards and loss of a down from the spot of the illegal pass. Forward passes are not allowed on a kickoff, a punt, a pass interception, or by the defensive team on any play. All members of both teams are eligible to receive a forward pass. Any forward pass caught by a player of either team is considered to be a completed pass regardless of the number of players on either side touching the ball. If a forward pass is incomplete, the ball is put in play at the spot of previous down.

FOULS AND PENALTIES: When a foul occurs, the captain of the team fouled against may decline a penalty if he so desires, whenever the yardage gained on a play is greater than that received by a penalty.

The following fouls are penalized by 5 yards from the spot of the foul and a first down for the team fouled against: (1) tripping, (2) clipping, (3) tackling, (4) leaving the feet when touching a player carrying the ball, (5) forming mass interference on the return of a kickoff, (6) rough play, (7) unsportsmanlike conduct. The referee may bar a player for unsportsmanlike conduct or talking back at any time.

Offside: It is a foul for a player to be offside just before or as the ball is put into play. It is considered offside when any part of a player's person is ahead of the end of the ball nearest to him when the ball is put in play. The play is not called back until the ball is dead. The penalty is the loss of 5 yards from the spot of the snap.

Fouls Committed by the Defensive Team: All fouls committed by the defensive team are ruled as first downs with either the dividing line or the goal line to be crossed before the fifth down, except on offside, extra time-outs, or delay in the game, in which cases the down remains the same as when the ball was put in play. In all cases where it is not otherwise stated, regular football rules should be followed.

SCORING: The scoring is the same as in football. Running plays, forward pass plays, and lateral plays which result in carrying the ball over the goal line into the end zone for a touchdown score 6 points. The team scoring a touchdown may score an additional point by successfully making a place kick or drop kick, or by carrying the ball across the goal line from a scrimmage on the 2-yard line. After each touchdown score the team scored upon has the choice of kicking off or receiving.

A safety scores 2 points. After a safety the ball is put in play by a kick from the 20-yard line by the team scored upon.

If a tie exists at the end of the regular playing time, the winner may be determined through an extra series of eight plays. To begin the extra period, the ball is placed in midfield and a coin tossed to see which team starts the offensive play. The play continues with teams alternating in possession of the ball until each team has had its four plays. The team which has advanced the ball into the other's territory at the end of the eight-play series is awarded one point and declared the winner. If at the end of the eight-play series the score is still tied, an additional extra series of six plays may be awarded.

No kicking, except the try for point after a touchdown, is allowed in extra-period games. After each play the ball is put in play halfway between the side lines in line with the spot where the ball was declared dead.

OFFICIALS: Four officials may be needed when official games are played. The officials necessary for touch football have the following duties:

Referee: The referee is the chief official. He has the major responsibility for the conduct of the games. He takes his position behind the offensive team and follows the ball. He introduces the captains and before the start of the game he tosses a coin to determine which team kicks off, receives the kickoff, and the goals each team defends. He checks the field to see that it is marked properly. He calls any fouls which he observes and exacts all penalties for violations observed by himself and by other officials.

Linesman: This official takes his position on the line of scrimmage. He is responsible for calling offsides; he watches the out-of-bounds line on the nearest side line; and he announces the down to be played after each play. He observes and calls all violations he sees; and assists in determining whether the ball carrier was legally tagged on any play.

Timekeeper: The timekeeper keeps the game time and notifies the referee two minutes before time expires each quarter. The referee notifies team captains.

Scorer: There are two scorers. They keep a record of scores made, the play used, and the name of the player who scores.

TEACHING SUGGESTIONS

1. Teach the following points in connection with passing:
    (a) Gripping ball above the middle, with the fingers just overlapping the middle seam line
    (b) Delivering the ball with a full overarm throw
    (c) Guiding the ball by the index finger
    (d) Swinging the weight of the body from back to front as the ball is thrown, with the full weight forward as the ball leaves the hand
    (e) Knowing where the player is to throw the ball and taking plenty of time to do it in good form
    (f) Passing laterally with a swinging side motion, in which two arms are used. The ball must be thrown so that the receiver catches it while he is still behind the thrower.

2. Teach the following running techniques:
    (a) Backfield players running at top speed in advancing the ball
    (b) Backfield players going into action the instant the ball is snapped
    (c) Defense players anticipating plays
    (d) Linesmen avoiding offside errors and refraining from making personal fouls
    (e) Linesmen blocking out an opponent by placing themselves between opponent and the ball carrier
    (f) Linesmen getting away fast the instant the ball is snapped

3. Instruct in the techniques of three kinds of kicks: (a) punt; (b) drop kick; (c) place kick.

(a) Punt: Hold ball with right hand at the rear, and with left hand along its side as it is tilted slightly downward and to the left front. Extend the leg and just as the hands let go of the ball, take the kick. Kick with the instep instead of the toes. Keep the eyes on the ball until the kick is made.

(b) Drop kick: Hold the ball with a hand on each side, the long axis of the ball being nearly perpendicular with the ground. Extend arms about knee height or a little above knee height. Drop ball, and just as it bounces from the ground kick it. Work for accurate placing of the ball. Follow through by pointing the foot in the exact direction in which the ball is supposed to go.

(c) Place kick: Have another player hold the ball on the ground, with his finger on top of the long axis and with the body of the ball leaning slightly backward from perpendicular. Stand far enough away from the ball so that the weight-bearing foot is placed alongside the ball, about six to twelve inches lateral to it. Kick with the upper area of toes of rear foot just below the midline of the ball. Keep eyes on the spot of contact for a count of two following the "boot." Work to gain accuracy in sending the ball to desired areas within the field.

4. Teach players the following points of tactics and strategy:
   (a) Understanding the positions and the responsibilities of each position
   (b) Organizing the huddles so that only the quarterback talks
   (c) Practicing forward and lateral passes to gain speed and accuracy
   (d) Working out planned plays and calling signals
   (e) Diagramming plays and learning them so that each player knows his responsibility
   (f) Trying out the following plays with signals: (1) various end runs; (2) reverse runs to right and left; (3) passing while running.

TWENTY-ONE [1]

NUMBER OF PLAYERS: 4

SPACE: Playground, gymnasium

PLAYING AREA: A basketball court with free-throw line 15 feet from goal post

EQUIPMENT: (1) Basketball backstop and goal; Goal-Hi;[2] (2) basketball, soccer ball, or volleyball

---

[1] Suggestions for this game secured from *Recreation*, XXXV (January, 1942), 622. By permission of National Recreation Association, publisher.
[2] See Goal-Hi, page 649.

FORMATION: There are four players with two players on each team. The Number 1 man of each team throws from behind the free-throw line. The Number 2 man of each team throws from underneath the basket.

PROCEDURE: Number 1 of Team A shoots first. If he makes the basket he continues shooting until he misses, whereupon Number 2 player of B Team, from under the basket, tries to make a goal. Whether successful or unsuccessful in his trial, he throws the ball to his teammate, Number 1 of Team B, at the free-throw line, who in turn throws for the goal and continues until he misses. Thereupon Number 2 of Team A (who is starting near the basket) receives the ball and tries for the goal.

When 10 or 11 points are scored by either team, the Number 1 and 2 players of each team exchange places and play continues.

Variation: Each time the player behind the foul line is successful in his throw, his partner shoots immediately and then returns the ball to his partner, who shoots again. Play continues until the player behind the free-throw line misses, whereupon the ball passes to the player of the other team who is shooting from the free-throw line.

SCORING: Twenty-one points constitutes a game. Each time a goal is made from behind the free-throw line 2 points are credited to the player's team. Each time a goal is made from under the basket 1 point is credited to the player's team.

TEACHING SUGGESTIONS

1. Teach players under the basket to make angle shots.
2. Use as a game to develop shooting skills.
3. Simplify game by giving one point for each goal, regardless of position from which it was shot.

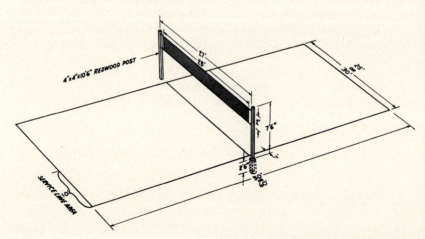

Figure 159. Volleyball Court and Net (size suitable for seventh-grade pupils)

VOLLEYBALL [1]

NUMBER OF PLAYERS: 2-18

SPACE: Playground, gymnasium, auditorium, stage

PLAYING AREA: A court 25 or 30 by 50 or 60 feet, located when possible on a cement, macadamized, or other firm surface, on which dimension lines can be painted.[2] A center line paralleling the end lines should be drawn dividing the court into two equal-sized courts (Figure 159). Ten feet from the right back corner of each court a line three feet long should be drawn at right angles to the end lines. This is the service line area. For inexperienced players, a service line should be marked inside the court, 5 to 15 feet from the end line and between the end line and the net, parallel to the end line.

EQUIPMENT: (1) Two redwood posts 4 by 4 inches by 12 feet, sunk into the ground 2½ feet at points at least 1 foot outside of the court dimensions opposite the ends of the center line. The posts should be planed and painted to prevent splinters. Heavy wrought-iron or 3-inch galvanized pipe may be used. Jumping standards, their bases weighted down with bags of sand, may be used. (2) Two ring eyelets or hooks so placed on the posts that they will permit the top of the net throughout its length to be 7 feet 6 inches from the ground; a maximum height of 6 feet 6 inches is recommended for elementary school children. Two cleats should be placed lower on the posts to permit the net to be drawn tightly at the four corners. No sag should be permitted in the net. (3) Regulation volleyball net, 25 feet long, 2 feet wide; or as a substitute, chicken wire, grain sacks sewn together, or a length of rope. If wire is used, the top edge should be wrapped or bound with strips of cloth to prevent the sharp edge from cutting the casing of the ball. If a rope is used pieces of white or colored cloth should be tied along it at intervals to make it more visible. For players who are learning the game white tapes may be tied on the top of the net immediately above the two side lines of the court, to determine fair and out-of-bounds balls. (4) A volleyball. The balls with white leather casing should be used only if there is no moisture. A lightweight rubber volleyball is more serviceable on rough and damp surfaces.

Procedure

Volleyball is played across a high net by two teams made up of from one to nine players. The purpose of the game is to control the ball by volleying (batting with the fingers) on one side and to return it to the

---

[1] Teachers should be familiar with the *Official Recreational Games—Volleyball Guide*. Washington: National Section on Women's Athletics, American Association for Health, Physical Education, and Recreation (1201 Sixteenth Street, N.W., Washington 6, D. C.).

[2] Out of doors the length of the court should run north and south. Dirt playing areas may be outlined with lime, with narrow, V-shaped trenches, or with 2 by 6 inch redwood boards sunk level with the ground, the exposed surfaces painted white.

opponents' court in such a way that the latter team cannot return the ball. Points are won only by the serving team. A player is required to serve the ball from behind the right end line without assistance from teammates.[1] Each member of each team serves in turn as numbered. Following each successful service, the server steps into the court and helps with the volleying. The server continues her serve until her side makes a mistake and loses the serve.

FORMATION: Players are divided into two teams. There are six on an official boys' team, eight on an official girls' team. For boys the three forwards, left, center, and right, play near the net and the three backs, left, center, and right, play in the back part of the court. For an official girls' game, there are in addition to the three forwards and three backs the two centers, left and right, who play between the forwards and backs. The game can, however, be played with any number on a side.

TERMINOLOGY: The following terms used in volleyball will clarify the rules:

Serving Team: Team that serves the ball over the net at the beginning of the game and after each point thereafter until it loses the serve

Receiving Team: Team that endeavors to return the ball over the net after service or after a return by the serving team

Serving or Service: Act of striking the ball so as to send it across the net and into the opponents' court at the beginning of the game and after each point

Side Out: When serving team loses its service and the ball goes to the receiving team (no point is scored)

Volley: The process of batting the ball back and forth over the net after service and before an error is made (sometimes spoken of as the rally)

Let Ball: A ball that clips the top of the net and falls into the opponents' court

Net Ball: A ball that strikes into the net

Dead Ball: A ball that because of some violation of the rules or because of its flight out of the court becomes out of play and has to be returned to the server

Line Ball: A ball which strikes any boundary line of either court (a fair ball)

Spiking the Ball: Striking the ball over the net into the opponents' court so close to the net that it cannot be returned

Setting Up the Ball: Playing the ball so that it will be in position for a forward to drive over the net

SERVICE: Serving, for skilled players, occurs at the right back position outside the rear boundary line. For inexperienced players a service position may be used from 5 to 15 feet from the net at the center of each court.

---

[1] By mutual agreement one assist may be permitted.

The server must stand within the official serving area and with both feet outside the court. A foot fault is made if the server steps on or over the rear boundary line into the playing court during the act of serving.

The server must strike the ball with the hand, open or closed, or with the forearm. A server may touch the ball but once until it has been returned to his court by an opponent.

The server continues to serve until retired by (1) failure of his own service; (2) loss of the ball caused by failure of his team to return the ball successfully within the court of the opponents; or (3) fouls made by himself or by members of his team.

SERVED BALL: The value of a served ball is determined by one of three conditions that may prevail following the service:

Fair Ball: A serve is a fair ball if the ball is (a) correctly served and it clears the net and falls to the ground within or on a boundary line of the opposite court, or (b) it is legally contacted by a member of the opposing team.

Let Ball: In official girls' rules a let ball is served again, but in boys' rules it loses the service. After the service a let ball is a fair ball.

Dead Ball: A ball is dead under any of the following circumstances:

(1) If it is served against the mesh of the net and falls within the server's court, or having crossed the net it falls to the ground outside the receiving team's court. In this case the server is retired and the ball goes to the opponents.

(2) If a member of the receiving team sends the ball into the net on his side. In this case one point is given to the serving team.

(3) If a member of the receiving team fails to return the ball over the net. In this case one point is scored by the serving team.

(4) If a member of the receiving team returns the ball over the net but outside the opponents' court. In this case one point is scored for serving team.

(5) If the ball rests momentarily on the hands of a player.

(6) If the ball hits any object other than the hands of a player within the boundary lines—ceiling, wall, or person of a player.

(7) If more than three players hit the ball on one side before returning it over the net.[1]

THE VOLLEY OR RALLY: Following the service the ball may be played back and forth over the net, the players attempting to send the ball so that it will hit the ground within the opponents' court. A line ball is a good ball. A ball is good which during the rally clips the top of the net and falls into the court of the opponents. A ball which during the rally is

---

[1] This rule should be ignored during the learning of the volleyball game by elementary school boys and girls.

batted into the net may be played by a team member who volleys it as it falls from the net. The person playing it, however, may not (1) touch the net, or (2) step on or over the center line.

It is official in girls' rules for the ball to be hit twice in succession while the ball is being volleyed. This means that there would be a maximum of six hits on one court before the ball was dead, providing three different people each volleyed it twice in succession. Many elementary schools find it advantageous to allow all pupils this volleying privilege. In official boys' rules only one volley is allowed to a player.

SPIKING THE BALL: Players who occupy positions next to the net are in position to spike the ball. These players without touching or reaching over the net, and by jumping for a high ball, endeavor to drive the ball over the net and into the court of the opponents. One hand, usually the one farthest from the net, should be used by spikers. Forwards try to rescue the ball as it rebounds off the net or as it drops toward the floor after contacting the net. They endeavor to get the ball in position so that another forward may send the ball over the net with a spike.

FOULS: If the server (or members of the serving side) makes a foul, the ball is given to the opponents.

If a member of the receiving side makes a foul, the serving side receives a point for each foul made.

If a double foul is committed (one by each team), the play is taken over again.

The following fouls cause change of service or score point for the server, depending on which side offends:

1. Touching the net
2. Stepping on or over the center line
3. Holding, pushing, scooping, or lifting the ball
4. Volleying the ball more than twice (in official boys' rules, more than once)
5. Stepping on or beyond the service line when serving
6. Touching the net while reaching over it in a follow-through stroke
7. Pushing or holding ball against net
8. Playing the ball with other parts of body beside the hands (in girls' game only; boys' rules allow the player to use any part of the body above and including his knees)

ROTATION OF PLAYERS: In official girls' and boys' volleyball, rotation is clockwise, with the right center in a girls' team serving second; and with right forward on a boys' team serving second. In games where there are more than eight players, rotation is in a zig-zag formation instead of a circle. The second server, with nine or more players, is the center back. The server, at the conclusion of his serve, crosses diagonally across the court to take the left forward position. The forward line moves from left to right; the center line from right to left; and the back line left to right. Players should be numbered in order of service. There is also provision for a girls' game in which no rotation takes place except the original server. This is caller a non-rotation game.

SCORING: In official boys' volleyball, a game is won when either team scores a two-point lead after fifteen or more points are won. A girls' game, however, is played in two 15-minute halves, so that at the end of the playing time the team with the higher score wins. Beginning and practice games may be played for an agreed upon number of points, or by time periods.

The serving team scores one point each time the server or a member of the serving team succeeds in volleying the ball so that it crosses the net and the receiving team fails to return the ball legally to the server's court, or when a foul is made by the receiving team. No point is scored and "side out" is called when the serving team fails to win the point or plays the ball illegally.

OFFICIALS: Volleyball affords excellent opportunity for pupils to officiate. It is desirable to have officials, especially when match games are played. Those needed are the following:

Referee: The referee is in charge of the game. He calls "point" or "side out." The referee decides when the ball is in play or when the ball is dead and out of play. The referee's position is near a post.

Umpire: The umpire assists the referee by calling any fouls for which the referee may wish him to watch. It is the umpire's duty to watch the center line. He stands across the court from the referee's position.

Scorer: The scorer keeps the official record as points are made and are called by the referee. Before the game starts, the scorer secures the names and numbers of the players of each team and sees that each serves in sequence and plays the position that should be his at a given time. The scorer stands on the same side of the court as the referee.

Linesmen: Two linesmen stand at opposite ends of the court, each watching one back line and one side line of the court. When the ball lands on the ground near their lines they call "good" or "out." Linesmen watch for service or foot faults made by the server and notify the referee.

TEACHING SUGGESTIONS

1. Use the game High Ball, page 655, to teach volleyball skills.
2. Teach the players to keep their eyes on the ball at all times, since it may be necessary to send the ball forward while standing with one's back to the net.
3. Encourage the players to stand with knees slightly bent, arms at about waist height and fingers spread, so that they may move instantly.

4. Instruct players to try to get directly under the ball and, as contact is made, straighten the knees so that the weight of the body is put into the drive of the ball.

5. Teach the players to hit the ball with the fingers relaxed and spread.

6. Teach players to look for the uncovered space in opponents' court toward which the ball should be directed.

7. Insist that players learn to meet the ball *with fingers of both hands* when volleying.

8. Insist that a server get his own ball over the net. Reduce the distance for service rather than permit the server's ball to be assisted over the net.

9. Teach net players to stand about an arm's distance from the net with their bodies sideways to it.

10. Teach the following techniques for serving the volleyball:

(a) *Sidearm:* The server (right handed) stands with the left side of his body toward the net and with both feet outside the court. The ball may be held on the palm of the hand that is nearest the net. Preliminary to contacting the ball, with wrist and elbow held in fixed position, the entire arm sweeps down and backward and then forward and upward across the front of the body in a line paralleling the side line of the court; the power of the stroke comes from the shoulder. The ball is struck with the heel of the swinging hand with the fingers open and somewhat separated from each other. The weight of the body is carried through onto the left foot. This is a difficult serve for beginners.

Figure 160.   Corecreational Volleyball

(b) *Underarm:* A second method of serving is the underarm serve. The server stands facing the net with the left foot somewhat advanced but outside the court. The server's weight is on the rear foot and the ball is held in the palm of the left hand. The striking right arm is swung from the shoulder with the wrist and elbow straight, to hit the ball from the left hand with the right hand. The weight of the body is transferred to the forward left foot. The hand follows through to point to the spot where the ball is to go. Beginners can learn the underarm serve most easily.

(c) *Overhand:* A third method of serving is to toss the ball into the air with the left hand and bat it with the right hand just as the ball starts down, while it is above the server's head. This is an advanced serve and is, of course, comparable to the tennis serve.

CORECREATIONAL VOLLEYBALL

Because the game of volleyball has two sets of rules, one for boys and one for girls, the following suggestions are made for games in which both girls and boys play.

1. A team should have an equal number of boys and girls, four and four.
2. The game is played for at least 21 points, or by 15-minute halves.
3. Each player has only one service if fault or error is made.
4. If there is a let service, it is re-served.
5. The ball may be played three times before it is returned. If a girl plays the ball twice in succession, that team has only one more hit before the ball must be returned. Boys have only one hit. This rule could be relaxed for beginners.
6. All other rules are similar to official girls' and women's volleyball.

VOLLEYBALL SKILL TESTS

The following tests should prove useful as guides in determining volleyball skills of boys and girls in the seventh and eighth grades. The tests can be scored on a five- or ten-trial basis. The former is more easily administered where space and equipment is limited and classes are large.

Pupils should be divided into squads, with not more than three to five persons in a squad, and with a score-keeping leader in charge of the squad. Two such squads can work simultaneously in each half of a court while remaining squads play other games until it is their turn to be tested. The greater the number of volleyballs available the faster the scoring will proceed. Exchange of positions should be taken on the run to speed up numbers taking the test during a given period.

Test 1. Service: The pupil being tested stands behind the serving line and serves the ball as in a game. The scorer stands near the server to watch for foot faults and illegal serves. Squad members stand in the opposite court and return balls *after the ball has bounced.* They announce whether the ball was good, out, or a line ball. The latter is scored as good. Each ball successfully served within the boundary of the half court on the opposite side of the net counts one point.

Test 2. Placement: One half court is divided into six equal spaces and each space is numbered. The player taking the test stands on the opposite side of the net and six feet from the net. *Before starting each ball* the player states toward which space he is trying to send the ball. All spaces need not be used in the placement tests, but one area may not be played twice during the trial. A helper stands near the player and tosses a high arched ball, thereby setting up the ball for a return over the net. A line ball is not a good ball. Each ball falling within the designated space counts one point.

Test 3. Spiking the Ball: A line is drawn four feet from the net and paralleling it. The person being tested stands three feet from the net in the opposite court. An assistant, standing to one side of the player, throws a high arched ball. The player jumps to spike or drive the ball within the four-foot area beyond but next to the net. If the set-up is poor a retrial may be permitted. With skilled players a real set-up may be performed with the use of a third player. The ball must be permitted to bounce before being returned to the assistant. A line ball is a good ball. Each ball that is driven within the four-foot area counts one point.

Test 4. Ball Recovered from Net: The net must be drawn very tight. The person being tested stands four or five feet from the net. An assistant stands beside but some four feet distant from him. The object of the assistant is to throw the ball directly in front of the contestant so that it will roll down the net rather than bounce from the net. The player squats low and endeavors to bat the ball higher than his own head when standing and within his own court. The ball must be permitted to bounce before being returned. A miss is recorded if the ball goes over the net, if the ball does not go higher than the height of the contestant or if the ball lands outside his own court. A point is scored each time the ball which went higher than player's own height falls within the court where the player stands.

VOLLEYBALL DOUBLES

NUMBER OF PLAYERS: 4

SPACE: Playground, gymnasium

PLAYING AREA: Court 15 by 40 feet or smaller. Two courts can be made on a standard volleyball court. Out-of-doors courts should run north and south.

EQUIPMENT: (1) Volleyball; (2) two jumping standards 8½ feet high, weighted down with sandbags at their bases; (3) net or rope stretched tightly between standards. Height of net at the top should be 8 feet from the ground at center of court. The net may be lowered to 7 feet 6 inches or to 6 feet 6 inches at the center depending on age and ability of players.

FORMATION: Two partners stand side by side on each side of the court.

PROCEDURE: Members of a doubles team alternate for service as in the game of volleyball. In doubles, players change positions each time one receives the ball following a "side out."

Service: While serving, players stand with both feet outside the court behind the back or service line. Following service, however, the server may go to any area within the court. The server continues serving until "side out" occurs. Volleyball rules govern the game with one exception: A player may recover his own or his partner's ball which is sent into the net during a rally following service. Such a recovery counts as one hit, and the ball, to be correctly played, must cross the net not later than the third hit.

SCORING: The scoring is similar to that of volleyball. A game is won when either team scores a 2-point lead with 15 or more points. When the score is tied at 14-all, a team must make two consecutive points to win unless otherwise agreed upon. A time game could be played in doubles also.

Matches: Two out of three games constitute a match. If three 15-point games seem to be too strenuous, the first two games should be played for 11 points each without using the required 2-point lead in case of a tie, and the third or deciding game should be played for 15 points.

TEACHING SUGGESTIONS

1. Reduce the size of the court for a singles game.
2. Use in small rural schools which have only a few upper-grade students.

VOLLEYBALL FOR THE SCHOOLROOM

NUMBER OF PLAYERS: 2-40

SPACE: Classroom

EQUIPMENT: (1) A net if possible. Otherwise string or rope can be used. The net should be stretched across the center of the room with the top of the net taut. The top of the net should measure 7 feet 6 inches from the floor if the ceiling height will permit, otherwise 6 feet from the floor. (2) A ball bladder. The best bladder to use is a volleyball bladder. It should be placed in a covering made from the end of an old stocking and then inflated; or the bladder may be protected with a thin cotton covering. Bladders which fold into a pointed ellipse are the best ones to buy.

FORMATION: Players are divided into two teams. When *seats and desks can be moved*, clear the room and establish a playing court, the size depending on the number to play. Players should be able to cover ground space equal to the spread of their two arms.

When *seats and desks cannot be moved* the players stand in the aisles, the two teams facing each other.

PROCEDURE: Persons of all ages may take part in the same game. Children in the first six grades catch and throw the ball while children in the seventh and eighth grades should strike the ball with open hands and may not catch the ball.

The serving team attempts to keep control of the ball, thereby continuing its opportunity to make points. The opponents, known as the receiving team, try to stop the service of the members of the serving team.

Volleyball rules are used with the following adjustments to meet schoolroom conditions. (1) The ball may not be played off the walls or the ceiling, nor from a bounce off a desk or from the floor. Out-of-bound areas should be determined and markings made on the floor to signify the court dimensions. (2) The rotation of players is as follows when rows of desks cannot be moved: the rear members of the files for each team take their turn at service, the players serving from their own aisle position. After all the members of the team in the rear of the room have served they move to the front of their file, next to the net, the other players moving back one position. The new servers are then in position to play. SCORING: The team wins which first makes 11 or 21 points, as agreed upon, or which scores the highest number of points within a given time.

The serving team scores one point whenever a member of the opponent team allows the ball to touch floor, wall, or desk on his side of the net; does not return the ball within the boundaries of the serving side's court; or permits the ball to hit the ceiling.

The receiving team becomes the server if the ball is served incorrectly; if players on the serving side fail to send the ball over the net and within the confines of the opponents' court; or if they permit the ball to hit the ceiling. Upon taking the serve the opponents have the opportunity to score points. No point is made when the serving team loses its serve and "side out" is called.

TEACHING SUGGESTIONS

1. Use care not to puncture the bladder when sewing or pinning the covering in place.
2. Do not tolerate extreme roughness in handling the ball.
3. Teach children to use two hands when attempting to catch or bat the ball.

VOLLEYBALL MODIFIED

NUMBER OF PLAYERS: 12-24

PLAYING AREA: A volleyball court modified in size for the number to play. For teams of 6, court should be 20 by 40 feet; for teams of 9, court should be 25 by 50 feet; for teams of 12, court should be 30 by 60 feet.

EQUIPMENT: (1) Net, its top 6½ feet from the floor; (2) large ball, 31 to 32 inches in circumference, weighing not less than 9 nor more than 10 ounces, its air pressure not less than 7½ pounds nor more than 8 pounds. Or a ball corresponding in size to the official volleyball, 26 to 27 inches in circumference, weighing not less than 6 nor more than 7 ounces, its air pressure not less than 7½ pounds and not more than 8 pounds.

FORMATION: Six, nine, or twelve players form a team. They are arranged in lines of three or four on each side of the net.

PROCEDURE: A regulation volleyball game is played, with the following modifications in the rules.

1. The server may serve from a position in the center of the court.
2. Two or more service trials may be allowed. An assisted serve is permissible, which means that a teammate may play a ball which has been served in an effort to send it over the net.
3. During the rally there is no limit to the number of players who may bat the ball before it goes over the net.
4. The requirement of position play may be disregarded although position play should be encouraged.
5. The ball may be hit not more than three times in succession by the same player.
6. The rotation of playing position may be eliminated.
7. The ball may be played from a bounce instead of from the air.

TEACHING SUGGESTIONS

1. Play until each player has accomplished some volleyball skill.
2. Teach the players to use both hands during the rally.

WHIP TAG
(Boys)

NUMBER OF PLAYERS: 10-40

SPACE: Playground, playroom, gymnasium, auditorium

EQUIPMENT: Knotted towel, or a number of newspapers rolled together to form a stick 12 to 15 inches long

FORMATION: Holding the towel, one player stands outside a circle formed by the remaining players. The circle players stand with their hands clasped behind them with the palms facing upward in position to receive the whip.

PROCEDURE: The player who holds the towel runs around the outside of the circle and, without pausing, drops the towel into the up-turned hands of a circle player. Continuing his run some 10 or 12 steps he drops between any two players. This clears the field for the runners who are following him.

The player into whose hands the towel is dropped is known as the beater. The beater is not concerned with the person who gave him the towel, but, turning, he begins immediately to beat his right-hand neighbor. The neighbor, to escape further beating, runs around the outside of the circle and returns to his former position. The beater follows and continues beating his victim unless the neighbor can outdistance the beater by use of greater speed. If the neighbor is outrunning the beater, the latter should, while running, quickly place the towel in the hands of a new circle player and thereupon drop into the circle a short distance farther on. The game is continued with the new beater.

TEACHING SUGGESTIONS

1. Do not permit the runner, after giving the whip to another player, to continue around the circle for any great distance.
2. Play with several circles if many children are to play simultaneously.
3. Do not permit three or four players to monopolize the game by continually choosing each other.
4. Do not permit long runs.

Relays

CHARIOT RACE RELAY

NUMBER OF PLAYERS: 6-42

SPACE: Playground, gymnasium

PLAYING AREA: (1) A line is marked on the ground that will serve as the starting and finish line. Its length will be determined by the number of players competing. (2) A goal for each file around which players must pass before returning to starting position

EQUIPMENT: Colored streamers or rope reins for each group of three players. For goals, children, chairs, jumping standards, Indian clubs, bottles, or sandbags may be used. The goals are placed 10 feet apart and 20 feet distant from the starting lines.

FORMATION: Children are divided into two or more teams and within each team they are arranged in groups of three. Two players of each group stand with inside hands joined, each holding a rein with his outside hand. These players represent the horses. The third player of each group (the driver) stands behind the starting line holding both reins; or the horses and drivers may be placed in file formation. Sets of three stand with their reins in their hands, but not running until a horse is tagged by the driver of the returning chariot.

PROCEDURE: At a signal the horses and drivers first in each team race forward around their own turning point and home across the finish line, where they tag off the horse of the second chariot of their team. Drivers must pass over the finish line before they may tag the horse of the waiting chariot. Each chariot thus runs in turn until all of one team have finished, and that team wins the race.

TEACHING SUGGESTION

1. If the group is small, play as a straight race rather than as a relay. In this case, the chariots all run at once and the one crossing the finish line first wins.

DOZEN-WAYS-OF-GETTING-THERE RELAY

NUMBER OF PLAYERS: 4-40

SPACE: Playground, gymnasium, auditorium, hallway, playroom

PLAYING AREA: A starting line and a second line paralleling it 30 feet distant, the length of the lines to be determined by the number playing

EQUIPMENT: Children, bottles, Indian clubs, or sandbags should be used to indicate turning points on the line 30 feet distant from the runners. The turning points should be placed 10 or 15 feet apart, with one for each file.

FORMATION: Players are organized into files with not more than six players to a file. The players are numbered in each file from the front to the rear. Files stand 10 feet apart and behind the starting line facing their own turning point. Players are then told the manner in which they are to race. Number 1 may hop; Number 2 may skip; Number 3, run, etc.

PROCEDURE: On a signal, Number 1 players race forward in the manner assigned to the group. Passing behind their turning points, they hop back and touch off the next player in their file. After tagging the waiting player, the hoppers retire to the rear of their files. Number 2 players race in the manner assigned them. The game continues until all in one team have raced, and the team finishing first wins.

TEACHING SUGGESTIONS

1. Have a player race twice but not in sequence if a file is short a player.

2. Let children select actions to be performed.
3. Insist that both feet be kept behind the starting line while awaiting the touch-off from an approaching runner.
4. Do not permit a participant to retire to the end of his file until he has actually tagged the waiting player.

GOAL THROWING RELAY

NUMBER OF PLAYERS: 4-40

SPACE: Playground, gymnasium, auditorium

PLAYING AREA: Basketball court or practice field with basketball backstops; starting lines 5 feet long placed 20 feet distant from each basketball backstop post

EQUIPMENT: A junior basketball, volleyball, soccer ball, or beanbag for each team

FORMATION: Players are formed into as many teams as there are basketball backstops, goals, and balls available. Team players line up in file formation behind the starting line. The front players of the files hold balls.

PROCEDURE: On a signal, the front player of each file runs forward and tries to throw his ball through the basketball goal. He continues throwing until successful, whereupon he secures the ball and throws it to the second player in his file, after which he passes to the rear of his file. The second player repeats the process of running and throwing. Game continues until all players in one team have finished and the file which finishes first wins.

TEACHING SUGGESTIONS

1. Teach the players to throw the balls quickly.
2. Instruct the children to recover the ball before it touches the floor.
3. Insist that the waiting players have both feet behind the starting line when receiving the ball.

HOOP OR TIRE ROLLING RELAY

NUMBER OF PLAYERS: 4-40

SPACE: Playground, gymnasium

EQUIPMENT: (1) Starting line, its length depending on the number of players; (2) for each file a steel hoop or automobile tire casing; (3) for each file an Indian club, block of wood, chair, or child placed 40 feet from the starting line and 8 feet from each other.

FORMATION: Two or more teams in file formation behind the starting line, each leader having a hoop or tire casing. Not more than six players should be in each file.

PROCEDURE: At a signal, the first player in each file rolls his hoop around his Indian club and back across the starting line, which thus becomes the finish line. After the hoop crosses the finish line it is secured by the second player in the file. Play continues until all in one file have run, and that file is the winner.

TEACHING SUGGESTIONS

1. Teach the players to replace an Indian club before proceeding if a runner knocks over an Indian club.
2. Insist that the hoop be rolled, not carried in the hand.

JACK RABBIT RELAY

NUMBER OF PLAYERS: 8-40

SPACE: Playground, playroom, gymnasium, auditorium

EQUIPMENT: (1) A starting line long enough to accommodate all files; (2) for each team a strong wand five feet long. Discarded broom handles may be used.

FORMATION: Players are divided into two or more teams of equal number. Each team lines up in file formation behind the starting line. There should be about 10 feet between the files and an arm's distance between the players in each file. A captain stands at the head of his file facing forward. Each captain holds one end of a wand with the other end resting on the ground behind the starting line.

PROCEDURE: At a signal, each captain turns, hands the free end of the wand to the second person in his file and both, stooping, race to the rear of their file while members of the file jump over the wand as it reaches them. The captain remains at the rear of the file after the last member jumps; the Number 2 player races to the front, hands the free end of the wand to Number 3 and they race to the rear, causing all the file members to jump in turn. Number 2 remains at the rear. The racing is continued until the captain of one team is again at the head of his file behind the starting line with the free end of his wand on the ground beyond the starting line. His team is the winner.

TEACHING SUGGESTIONS

1. Instruct players how to jump with ankles and knees relaxed.
2. Teach players to keep the wand close to the ground.

SKINNING THE SNAKE RELAY

NUMBER OF PLAYERS: 6-40

SPACE: Playground, lawn, playroom, gymnasium, auditorium

FORMATION: Divide players into equal teams. Members of each team stand in file formation. Each player extends his left hand backward between his legs and at the same time grasps, with his right hand, the left hand of the player in front of him.

PROCEDURE: At a signal, members of each file start moving backward. The rear player of each file, as the backward movement commences, lies down on his back, retaining the hand grasp with the player in front of him. The second rear player, after moving backward by straddling the last player, lies down, still maintaining the grasp with his two hands. The backward movement is continued, each player lying down after he passes over the other players by straddling them. When all are lying on their backs, the one at the rear of the file (the captain) arises and, straddling the prone players, moves forward, pulling the second player from the rear to his feet. This player pulls the third player. Action continues until all are on their feet once more. The team wins whose captain first returns all the members of his file to the standing position, provided no hand grasps were broken.

TEACHING SUGGESTIONS

1. Instruct each player, as he lies down, to keep his legs close against the body of the player in front of him, at the same time turning his toes in.
2. Teach the players who are moving backward to move with their legs well apart while straddling.
3. Practice in slow motion before using as a race.

SQUARE RELAY

NUMBER OF PLAYERS: 6-40

SPACE: Playground, playroom, gymnasium, auditorium

PLAYING AREA: A 10- or 20-foot square marked out by four Indian clubs, baseball bases, blocks of wood, beanbags, chairs, or children. The four bases are placed at each corner of the square. The bases are named, counterclockwise, A, B, C, D. Each two teams of players will require a square.

EQUIPMENT: For each file a ball, beanbag, knotted towel, stone, or stick. The objects used should be of the same size and weight.

FORMATION: The children are organized into two, four, or six teams, with not more than six players on a team. Team 1 lines up in file formation behind base A. Team 2 lines up back of base C. There should be sufficient space between the base and the front player of a file so that runners may pass between them.

PROCEDURE: At a signal, the leader of Team 1 runs around outside of bases B, C, D, and back to A, hands the ball to the second runner of his file, and retires to the end of his file. At the same time the leader of Team 2 runs around outside of bases D, A, B, and back to C and hands the ball to the second runner of his file. Play is continued until all have run. All players run in the same direction, counterclockwise. The team wins whose leader first receives the ball after all members of his team have run.

VARIATIONS: (1) A runner of Team 1 may throw the ball to the next runner of his file at any point between bases D and A after passing base D. The runner of Team 2 may throw the ball from any point between bases B and C after passing base B. (2) Players, while carrying the ball, may walk, skip, or walk backward. (3) If it seems advisable, one square may be used by four teams, but this game formation is not as desirable as having two teams to a square.

TEACHING SUGGESTIONS

1. If a wild throw is made by a runner and the ball rolls into the center of the square or beyond a line that, if drawn, would connect bases A and B, and bases C and D, teach the runner toward whom the ball was thrown to secure the ball, return to his starting point, and include base A or C as one of the four bases in his run.
2. Do not permit player to omit a base by cutting across the square. To do so constitutes an error and the runner must rectify the error before continuing the race.

STRADDLE, PASS, AND KNEEL RELAY

NUMBER OF PLAYERS: 6-40

SPACE: Playground, playroom, gymnasium, auditorium

EQUIPMENT: For each file of players, ball, beanbag, knotted towel, stick of wood, or rocks of equal size

FORMATION: Players are divided into teams of not more than six members. They stand in file formation, in stride position.

PROCEDURE: On a signal, the front player of each file passes the ball between his legs to the player behind him, who in turn passes it on. As soon as the ball leaves the hands of a player, that player kneels down with feet and legs close together, his head resting in his hands, which are on the ground, and his elbows held close to his body. As the last man in each file receives the ball, he runs forward, straddling the kneeling players. Kneeling players stand and take stride position as soon as the runner has passed them. Reaching the front of the file, the runner, facing forward, passes the ball backward between his legs and immediately kneels. Play is continued until all have run forward carrying the ball. The team wins the race whose front player, while carrying the ball, first reaches his original position in the file.

TEACHING SUGGESTIONS

1. Have players run in place for knee warm-up before playing this kneeling relay.
2. See that feet and elbows are not an accident hazard.

Rhythmical Activities

BROOM DANCE
(A Social Dance Mixer)

Music: Two-step, fox trot, waltz or march

Formation: Double circle, girls and boys in each circle, partners facing and standing a few feet apart. An odd player is supplied with a broom.[1]

Description: Circle players advance toward each other with four walking steps (4 counts) or they waltz forward two steps (6 counts) and then retire. Continue the forward and backward steps until the broom is given away.

Broom man walks between the two circles sweeping. At the same time he looks the players over for a "sweetheart." Making his choice, he drops the broom and grabs the partner. Immediately all others take partners and two-step (or waltz), with turns, while progressing counterclockwise. The circle formation is maintained. The player left without a partner secures the broom and dances with it until the leader calls for the re-forming of the double circle. The dance is repeated.

TEACHING SUGGESTIONS

1. Have both circles make a quarter turn and continue to move forward in opposite directions until broom man makes his selection. This procedure will correct the situation when couples seem unwilling to change partners.
2. When there are more girls than boys, have the extra girls take the part of boys. Provide them with pinnies, armbands, or other distinguishing

---

[1] Use Raggedy Ann doll, old teddy bear, or small pillow as substitute for the broom.

insignia. See that this group is changed frequently. When class membership is even in numbers, the instructor should participate.

HOL-DI-RI-DI-A [1]

Music: The Weggis Dance [2]

Methodist Record No. M101

FORMATION: Double circle, boys inside, all facing counterclockwise.

DESCRIPTION: This is a walking song. It is not a traditional folk game but was composed by a Swiss folk-dance group in New York, using Swiss steps and authentic Swiss music. It is sometimes called Swiss Walking Song, Weggis (pronounced Vā-gus), or Alpine Song. A few measures of the music should be played as an introduction between the figures to allow partners to get ready for the next figure.

FIGURE I. HEEL AND TOE

Measures 1-8. Partners take skating position and start with outside foot, the boy with the left and the girl with the right. They touch heel of outside foot to floor and then touch the toe of the same foot to the floor. Step forward with outside foot; take half-step with inside foot, then step again with outside foot. (Count "heel, toe, step, step, step"; 2 measures.) Next starting with inside foot, they do heel and toe, step, half-step, step (2 measures). Figure is repeated (4 measures).

CHORUS. TYROLEAN STEP

Measures 9-16. In the Tyrolean step, the boy moves toward the center of the circle, the girl away from the center. The boy takes one step toward center on left foot, slides right foot to left and a little behind it; again steps toward center and kicks right foot slightly over the left foot. (Count "step, slide, step, kick"; 1 measure.) Moving back to his partner, he places the right foot one step toward partner, sliding left foot to right and slightly back; he takes another step toward partner and kicks left foot slightly over right (1 measure). The girl takes the same steps, beginning with opposite foot.

By this time the partners are together. They take each other's hands or arms and do four step hops around in a circle, the boy beginning the hop step with his left foot and the girl with her right (2 measures).

This is repeated, moving into center (girl away from center) and back, and step hops (4 measures).

---

[1] The World of Fun Series. Nashville, Tennessee: Methodist Publishing House, 1947. May be purchased from the Methodist Publishing House, 85 McAllister Street, San Francisco 2, or 125 E. Sunset Boulevard, Los Angeles 12, California. By permission.

[2] *We Sing.* A Singing School series. Boston: C. C. Birchard & Co., 1940, Book of Accompaniments, pp. 132-33.

The Tyrolean step is repeated after each movement or figure.

FIGURE II.   The WINDMILL

Measures 1-8.   Partners face one another with arms outstretched, boys facing clockwise, bodies bent and inner arms pointing down toward the center of the circle. They repeat the heel and toe step of Figure I, moving in toward the center and back to the original place (4 measures). As they come back the outer hands are pointing downward toward the outside of the circle. Repeat (4 measures). The movement of the outstretched hands represents the turning of a windmill.

Measures 9-16 (Chorus).Tyrolean Step repeated.

FIGURE III.   LEFT AND RIGHT

Measures 1-8.   Both partners, in skating position, step forward on the left foot and then cross the left foot with the right, making an arc. The right foot forward, cross with the left, making an arc. (Count "left, and, right and"; 1 measure). Then step, half-step, step, half-step ("step, step, step, step"; 1 measure). Repeat (2 measures), beginning with opposite foot. Repeat entire movement (4 measures).

Measures 9-16 (Chorus). Tyrolean Step repeated.

FIGURE IV.   LEFT AND RIGHT,
FACING PARTNERS

Measures 1-8.   Partners face one another, boys with backs to center, holding right hands. The left and right movement of Figure III is repeated, beginning with left foot ("left, and, right, and, step, step, step, step"; 2 measures). On the last four steps the partners exchange positions, moving in a semicircle, so that the boy is on the outside and the girl on the inside of the circle. The 2 measures are repeated, boy and girl returning to their original positions.

Repeat entire figure (4 measures).

Measures 9-16 (Chorus). Tyrolean Step repeated.

FIGURE V.   THE PIVOT

Measures 1-8. Partners face each other at a three-quarter angle, the boy lightly holding the left hand of the girl in his right hand. They raise hands backward, then swing them down and forward, letting go hands at bottom of swing but following through in circular movement so that the player completes a semicircle with his arms, thus giving momentum to both players in the pivot. The step is as follows: boy moves to the left one step as the girl moves to the right one step. They turn away from each other, the boy stepping with his right for the second step (pivoting on left). He takes the third step with his left (pivoting on right) so as to face partner again. As he turns outward, the girl steps forward (the second step) with her left and for the third step with her right, also turning away from her partner on the second step and back to face him on the third. On the fourth count the players close by drawing their feet together, the boy drawing his right to the left and the girl drawing her left to her right. (Count "step, step, step, close"; 2 measures.) As the players finish the pivot, they take hands in order to balance one another. Thus in the pivot the positions are face to face, back to back, and face to face. Repeat, beginning with boy's right (2 measures). Repeat entire figure (4 measures).

Measures 9-16. (Chorus). Tyrolean Step repeated.

KOHANOTCHKA [1]

Kismet Record No. A101

FORMATION: Couples in large circle, moving counterclockwise

DESCRIPTION: Version I, as described by Nadine Ermalova, a Russian dance instructor:

A. *Measure 1.* Partners face and join inside hands. Each performs a *Pas de Basque* on outside foot, turning back to partner.

> A description of a *Pas de Basque* (in 3/4 time): leap sideward, or diagonally forward, on right foot (count "one"); step with left foot in front of right foot ("two"); step backward in place with right foot ("three"). For 2/4 rhythm, count "one, and, two, and."

Measure 2. Each performs a *Pas de Basque* on inside foot, facing partner.

Measures 3-4. Both drop hands and turn completely around forward and away from partner with three walking steps and stamp.

Measures 5-8. Measures 1-4 repeated.

B. *Measures 1-4.* Each faces partner, drops hands, and walks three steps away from partner to own right and swings left leg forward; returns to partner walking left, right, left; swings right.

Measures 5-8. Facing partner, both *Pas de Basque* right, then left, turn completely around to right with three walking steps, and stamp.

C. *Measures 1-4.* Both clap own hands twice, with two polka steps cross into partner's place, passing right shoulders (without turning), stamp three times.

Measures 5-8. They repeat, backing to place.

Measures 1-8 repeated. Measures 1-8 are repeated both forward and back.

VARIATION (as danced by several folk dance groups)

[1] Adapted from description in **Folk Dances from Near and Far**, Volume I. Berkeley, California: Folk Dance Federation of California, 1945. By permission.

A. *Measures 1-8.* Dancers perform the *Pas de Basque* and turn, as in first version, A.

B. *Measures 1-2.* Couples take Russian (or varsovienne) position: girl in front and slightly to the right of the boy, with her back to him. The boy holds the girl's left hand in his left hand at shoulder height. His right arm extends across behind the girl's shoulder and he holds her right hand in his right hand. Girl and boy polka forward on left foot, back on right foot (like a rocking horse) in Russian polka.

Russian polka step omits the hop; thus it is danced step, close, step, hold ("one, and, two, and").

Measures 3-4. Couples polka left and right forward, counterclockwise.

Measures 5-8. Measures 1-4 are repeated.

C. *Measures 1-4.* Partners face each other in double circle. Each claps own hands twice, takes three Russian polka steps backward away from partner.

Measures 5-8. They repeat claps, take two Russian polka steps and three stamps forward, passing each other with right shoulders.

Measures 1-4. They repeat claps, taking three Russian polka steps backward, passing each other with right shoulder.

Measures 5-8. They repeat claps, taking two Russian polka steps and three stamps, moving one place to left at end of dance to face new partner.

Entire pattern is repeated with new partner.

MAYPOLE DANCE [1]

Music: "Bluff King Hal"
Victor Record No. 20990

FORMATION: Double circle around the Maypole, all facing clockwise, boys inside

Bluff King Hal

[1] Based on dance as described by Elizabeth Burchenal, *Folk Dances and Singing Games*, New York: G. Schirmer, Inc., 1909-22. Copyright renewal assigned, 1938, to G. Schirmer, Inc. By permission.

DESCRIPTION: This is a traditional English dance. The Maypole, dedicated to the Goddess of Flowers, stands some twelve feet high, its top dressed with flowers, and long streamers (one for each dancer) of various light spring colors hang from the top. Each movement of the dance should be free and joyous, expressive of the sunshine and the new life that comes with spring. The step used is a vigorous skip with high knee-action and swaying of the head from side to side, except where the polka is introduced. (Review polka step, p. 208.)

The music has an Introduction, followed by three parts, lettered A, B, C, of eight measures each. The Introduction is played once, the rest of the music four times, ending with A and C (B omitted). The third and fourth figures consist of winding the pole.

INTRODUCTION

Measures 1-4. Partners join inside hands at shoulder level, girls holding skirts diagonally outward with outer hand, boys placing free hand on hip. All stand with right foot pointed forward and hold this position throughout Introduction.

FIGURE I

A. *Measures 1-6.* All skip around circle, beginning with right foot, two skips to each measure.

Measures 7-8. With four skipping steps, couples swing in facing the pole, and form a single circle, hands joined.

B. *Measures 1-2.* With four skipping steps, all advance toward the pole.

Measures 3-4. With four skipping steps, all move back from the pole.

Measures 5-8. Measures 1-2, 3-4 repeated.

C. *Measures 1-8.* Partners join hands, girl lifting skirts with left hand and boy with free hands on hip; beginning with right foot, they turn partners, making two skipping steps to a measure. They finish with girl on inside, back to pole and facing partner.

FIGURE II

A. *Measure 1.* Girls' lifting skirts with both hands and boys with hands on hips, and beginning with the right foot, all polka to the right. (Count "one, and two, and.")

Measure 2. All hop on right foot and point the left foot forward and slightly to left ("one, and"); hop on right foot and at the same time touch the left toe behind the right heel ("two, and").

Measures 3-4. Measures 1 and 2 are repeated, beginning with the left foot and moving toward the left.

Measures 5-8. Measures 1-4 repeated.

B. *Measures 1-7.* Partners join right hands and turn each other, beginning with the right foot and making one polka step to a measure (seven steps, counting each "one, and, two, and"). During step, girls hold skirts out as before.

Measure 8. All swing into a single circle, with one more polka step.

C. *Measures 1-8.* All dance around the circle, beginning with the right foot and make two skipping steps to a measure.

Figure III

A. *Measures 1-2.* With four skipping steps, all advance to the pole.

Measures 3-4. With four skipping steps, all move back from the pole.

Measures 5-8. Same as measures 1-4.

B. *Measures 1-2.* With four skipping steps, the first couple advance to the pole, and each grasps a ribbon with the right hand.

Measures 3-4. With four skipping steps, couple move backward from the pole to place and face each other, right foot pointed forward, girl turned slightly toward the pole, boy turned slightly away from the pole.

Measures 5-8. Second couple repeat Measures 1-4.

C. *Measures 1-4.* Third couple repeat Measures 1-4 (B).

Measures 5-8. Fourth couple repeat Measures 1-4 (B).

If there are four couples, this will bring them to the last measure of C. If there are more couples, repeat A until all have taken ribbons.

Figure IV

A-B. *Measures 1-16.* With thirty-two skipping steps, or longer if desired, all make a grand chain, girls moving around the circle clockwise, boys in the opposite direction, weaving the ribbons alternately over and under as they pass each other. This will wind the Maypole and is continued until the ribbons are plaited as far down the pole as desired. The streamers should be held firmly so that there will be no sag as the weaving is done.

C. *Measures 1-2.* With four skipping steps all advance to the pole and drop ribbons.

Measures 3-4. All join hands, and with four skipping steps move back from the pole.

Measures 5-8. All advance and retire again.

Figure V

A. *Measures 1-8.* Still in a single circle, with sixteen skipping steps all dance around pole.

C. (B is omitted). *Measures 1-8.* Girl of first couple releases the hand of the dancer in front of her. All continue skipping and girl leads the dancers in a string away from the pole.

MONEY MUSK [1]

Ford Record No. 118
Victor Record No. 20447

FORMATION: This is a longways dance, six couples in a set, boys in one line, girls in the other.

DESCRIPTION: A caller gives directions for each movement, giving the first call before the music begins.

Measures 1-8. "FIRST COUPLE SWING ONCE AND A HALF AROUND." First couple (the two nearest the music) advance, grasp each other's right hands, and turn once and a half around and stop, the boy between the second and third girls, and his partner between the second and third boys. Both are now in opposite lines.

Measures 9-12. "FORWARD SIX." First boy, who is standing between two girls, takes their hands, while his partner, between two boys, takes their hands, and all move forward four steps and back four steps.

Money Musk

---

[1] The tune of "Money Musk," which is about a century old, took its name from the village of Moneymusk on the River Don in Aberdeenshire. It is published in *"Good Morning": After a Sleep of Twenty-five Years, Old-Fashioned Dancing is Being Revived by Mr. and Mrs. Henry Ford.* Dearborn, Michigan: Dearborn Publishing Company, 1926. By permission of Estate of Henry Ford.

Measures 13-16. "SWING THREE-FOURTHS AROUND." First boy and girl join right hands and turn three-quarters around, so that they finish between the lines (opposite second and third couples), the girl facing toward the head of the set, her partner facing her and toward the foot of the set.

Measures 17-20. "FORWARD SIX." The girl joins left hand with the boy on her left and right hand with the girl on her right, forming a straight line facing the head of the set. The boy joins right hand with the boy on his right, left hand with the girl on his left, all facing the opposite three. All step forward four steps and back four steps.

Measures 21-24. "SWING THREE-QUARTERS TO PLACE." The first couple join hands, swing three-quarters round to their own side of the set, one couple below where they started. This leaves the two girls of couples 1 and 2 together, and two boys of couples 1 and 2 together.

Measures 25-32. "RIGHT AND LEFT." The two head couples pass through to opposite side of set, each gives left hand to boy or girl of other couple, turns, and returns to place.

The pattern is repeated, the head couple progressing each time one couple lower, until they reach the foot of the set. After the first couple have danced by three couples, the couple then at the head begin, so that there are now two couples leading at the same time. Continue until all couples have gone through the movements. To end the dance, call "ALL JOIN HANDS FORWARD, TURN PARTNERS, PROMENADE TO SEATS."

NORIU MIEGO [1]
(Lithuanian)

FORMATION: Two couples form a small square, all four dancers facing in toward the center of the set. The girls put their hands on their hips, with palms and fingers in front. The boys fold their arms high in front.

DESCRIPTION

A

Measure 1. With a little spring all place right feet forward toward the center of the square (count "one, and"); pause in this position (count "two, and").

Measure 2. With a little spring, all exchange the position of their feet, so that the left feet are placed forward (count "one, and") pause in this position (count "two, and").

Measures 3-4. In the same manner all make three quick changes, putting forward first the right foot (count "one, and"), then left foot (count "two, and"), then right foot (count "one, and"); pause in this position (count "two, and").

Measures 5-8. Measures 1-4 are repeated.

B

Measure 9. All clap own hands twice (count "one, and, two, and").

Measures 10-12. The four dancers form a right-hand star and move

[1] Elizabeth Burchenal, *Folk Dances From Old Homelands.* New York: G. Schirmer, Inc., 1922. Copyright renewal assigned to G. Schirmer, Inc., 1945. Printed by permission.

around to the left with six walking steps, beginning with the left foot. Right-hand star: The four dancers join right hands across the center, the two girls grasping hands and the two boys doing the same.

Measures 13-16.   All clap hands twice, form a left-hand star by turning and joining left hands, and move around in the opposite direction.

The dance is repeated in the same manner as often as desired. At each repetition, the music may be accelerated until at the close it is played as quickly as possible, with the dance at top speed.

Noriu Miego

Arranged by Anna Hermitage

OH! SUSANNA[1]

Victor Record No. 20638 ("Oh, Susanna" and "Arkansas Traveller" Medley)

FORMATION: Single circle, girls and boys alternating, facing center.

DESCRIPTION

Measures 1-4. Girls skip forward into circle and skip backward into place.

Measures 5-8. Boys do the same.

Measures 1-4. Girls repeat.

Measures 5-8. Boys repeat.

Measures 9-16. On the chorus, partners face each other in a single circle, and do Grand Right and Left (page 207).

Measures 9-16. On repeat of chorus, each boy takes the girl approaching him and turns her around into promenade position. With this new partner, each boy skips or walks around the circle counterclockwise.

Oh! Susanna

Stephen C. Foster

Stephen C. Foster
Piano by Gladys Pitcher

[1] *We Sing.* A Singing School series. Boston: C. C. Birchard & Co., 1940. By permission.

going to Lou'- si - a - na, My Su- san - na for to see.
sun so hot I froze to death, Su - san - na don't you cry.

Oh! Su - san - na, Oh! don't you cry for me, For I

come from Al - a - ba - ma With my ban jo - on my knee.

2. I had a dream the other night
When ev'rything was still,
I thought I saw Susanna dear
Acoming down the hill.
The buckwheat cake was in her mouth,
The tear was in her eye;
I said I'm coming from the south,
Susanna, don't you cry.

The dance may be repeated many times, with a new partner at the beginning of each repeated chorus. If some are without partners at the end of the Grand Right and Left, they should be instructed to step into the center, secure a partner, and rejoin the promenading circle.

ROAD TO THE ISLES[1]

Music: *Partners All—Places All*, p. 110.[2]
Imperial Record No. 1005A

FORMATION: Couples in double circle facing counterclockwise in varsovienne position (see p. 205).

DESCRIPTION: In tracing the origin of this dance, Mr. Phil Aldrich has found that the music stems from an old Scottish pipe tune. It is presumed that the dance is relatively modern and in pattern is similar to the Scottish Douglas Schottische.

The dance is in two parts, the second of which uses the schottische step (see p. 209).

I

Measure 1. All point left toe forward slightly to the left and hold.
Measures 2-3. All take three steps, starting with the left foot, as follows: left foot slightly in back of right foot (count "one"); right foot to right ("two"); left foot forward in front of right foot and hold ("one, two").
Measure 4. All point right toe forward and slightly to right and hold.
Measures 5-6. All take three steps, starting with right foot, as follows: right foot slightly in back of left foot (count "one"); left foot to left ("two"); right foot forward in front of left and hold ("one, two").
Measure 7. All point left toe forward and hold.
Measure 8. All place left toe back and hold.

II

Measures 9-10. All schottische forward slightly to the left, beginning on left foot.
Measures 11-12. All schottische forward slightly to the right, beginning on the right foot. On hop (count 2 of measure 12), all half turn to the right, facing opposite direction. Hands remain joined.
Measures 13-14. All schottische, beginning on left foot. On hop, all half turn to left, facing original direction.
Measures 15-16. All step in place right, left, right, hold.

---

[1] From *Folk Dances from Near and Far*, Volume III. Berkeley, Calif.: Folk Dance Federation of California, 1947. By permission.
[2] Miriam H. Kirkell and Irma K. Schaffnit, *Partners All—Places All!* New York: E. P. Dutton Co., 1949.
"The Border Trail," a song set to the tune of "Road to the Isles," is in *Sing Along the Way*. Delaware, Ohio: Cooperative Recreation Service, no date. Available from The Woman's Press, 600 Lexington Avenue, New York 22, N. Y. The song is also found in *Joyful Singing*, edited by Lynn Rohrbough, by the same publisher, bound in "HANDY TWO."

RYE WALTZ[1]

[1] *"Good Morning," op. cit.* Permission of Estate of Henry Ford.

Decca Record No. 25058A
Imperial Record No. 1044
MacGregor Record No. 10-399-2

FORMATION: Partners take social dancing position or elbow grasp position

DESCRIPTION

Measure 1.   Boy extends left foot to side and touches toe to floor (count "one"), brings left foot just behind right heel and touches floor with toe (count "two"), touches left toe to side again (count "three"), and touches left toe in front of right toe ("four"). Girl does the same step simultaneously, but with the right foot.

Measure 2.   Partners slide (chassé) four slides to the boy's left.

Measures 3-4.   Partners repeat Measures 1-2, boy starting with right foot and sliding to right.

Measures 5-8.   Partners repeat Measures 1-4.

Measures 9-24.   Partners waltz around the room, moving counterclockwise.

SHE'LL BE COMING 'ROUND THE MOUNTAIN

Arranged by Anna Hermitage

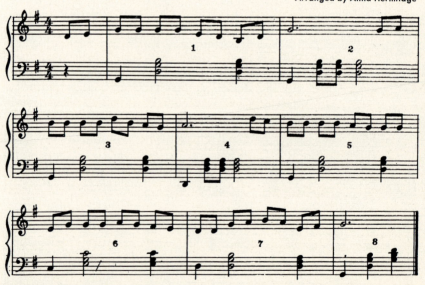

Imperial Record No. 1012

FORMATION: Triple circle facing counterclockwise. Boy in middle with girl on each side, or vice versa. Inside hands joined and held high.

DESCRIPTION

I

Measures 1-2.   All walk forward eight steps.

Measures 3-4.   All take eight steps in place, while outside girl marches under arch made by inside girl and left arm of boy. Boy or center person follows outside girl by turning under his own arm. Eight counts are allowed for this figure. All finish facing in line of direction—counterclockwise.

Measures 5-6.   All walk forward eight steps counterclockwise.

Measures 7-8.   Inside girl goes under arch formed by outside girl and boy's right arm. Boy follows by turning under his own arm. All finish facing in line of direction, counterclockwise.

II

Measures 1-2.   All join hands, forming circles of threes, and turn eight steps clockwise.

Measures 3-4.   All take eight steps in place while boy goes under arch formed by two girls, and they, in turn, turn under their own arms, finishing in circle of threes with all backs to the center.

Measures 5-6.   Circle walks eight steps *clockwise.*

Measures 7-8.   They take eight steps in place, while boy backs under arch formed by arms of the two girls, and they then turn under their own arms. Girls drop hands and all finish in original lines of three facing counterclockwise.

Dance is repeated from the beginning.

SPANISH CIRCLE DANCE [1]

Folkcraft Record No. 1045
Imperial Record No. 1043
Methodist Record No. 105

FORMATION: Two couples, partners standing side by side and holding right hands, face each other.

DESCRIPTION: This is a simplified version, in a casual ballroom formation, of the Spanish Circle.

Measures 1-2.   All balance forward on outside foot and backward on inside foot.

Measures 3-4.   Boys balance forward and backward again as they swing partner's hand high, and drop it as girl takes two waltz steps across to opposite girl's place, taking opposite boy's right hand in her right.

---

[1] Alice Jameyson, *Old Time Ballroom Dances That Are Fun to Dance Today.* Berkeley, California: The Professional Press, 1941. By permission of the author.

Spanish Circle Dance

The version most frequently used in California: Balance forward and back and change places with opposite lady with two waltz steps—whole pattern takes four measures. Three more repetitions bring partners back to original position.

Measures 5-8. All repeat back to own partner (Measures 1-4).

Measures 9-16. All repeat both patterns (Measures 1-8).

Measures 17-24. All join right hands in a star formation and take four waltz steps clockwise, turn, join left hands and take four waltz steps counterclockwise.

Measures 25-32. In closed waltz position with partner, all dance eight waltz steps around the room. Dance may be repeated with another partner or with the same one.

Another version: Holding inside hands, balance forward and back, then taking right hand of opposite person with two waltz steps, change back with two waltz steps. Next the girls pass between opposite partners to continue the entire dance.

SWING THE MAN FROM ARKANSAS [1]

Music: "Arkansas Traveler," "Soldier's Joy" (p. 942), "Mrs. McLeod's Reel" (p. 620), or any good quadrille music

FORMATION: Four couples form a square.

DESCRIPTION: A caller calls the directions as the dancers perform the figures. Action is slow and easy, not skipping or hopping but an easy springy walk.

"FIRST COUPLE BALANCE AND SWING." First couple (the two nearest the music) face each other, take a step swing by boy stepping left and swinging right foot and then stepping right and swinging left foot while the girl steps on the opposite foot. The couple then swings around each other.

1. "THE LADY LEAD OUT TO THE RIGHT OF THE RING. SWING YOUR MA, SWING YOUR PA." First girl walks to second couple, where she swings the second girl, then the second boy. Meanwhile her partner steps into the center of the set and stands there.

2. "NOW SWING THE MAN FROM ARKANSAS."
First girl swings her own partner.

3. "AND ON YOU GO AND SWING YOUR MA, THEN SWING YOUR PA, AND NOW SWING THE MAN FROM ARKANSAS." First girl walks to third couple and repeats, with members of this couple, movements described in 1 and 2.

---

[1] Based on description in Chicago Park District (W.P.A. Project), *The Square Dance.* Chicago: Chicago Park District, 1940. By permission.

4. "AND ON YOU GO AND SWING YOUR MA, THEN SWING YOUR PA, AND NOW SWING THE MAN FROM ARKANSAS." First girl walks to fourth couple and repeats, with the members of that couple, the movements described in 1 and 2.

5. "AND EVERYBODY SWING. OH! SWING YOUR PARTNERS ALL." First couple returns to home position and every boy swings his own partner.

6. "ALLEMANDE LEFT, GRAND RIGHT AND LEFT, MEET YOUR PARTNER AND PROMENADE HOME." Each couple performs Allemande Left and all progress around the circle with Grand Right and Left (see p. 207), until they meet their own partners, and promenade home again.

Entire dance is repeated, with second couple performing the figures, then with third couple, and lastly with fourth couple.

TAKE A WALK
(A Mixer)

Music: Two-step (fox trot)

FORMATION: Couples in social dancing position scattered about the room.

DESCRIPTION: Everyone starts dancing with the beginning of the music.

When leader calls "Take a walk" two couples link arms and march around the room four abreast.

When all are in fours, leader calls "Circle to the right." Each four form a small circle walking to their right. When call is given, "Circle to the left," all circle left.

The final call is "Dance with the opposite lady." Each boy takes the other girl in his set of four for his new partner.

Repeat as many times as necessary to mix up the group.

TANTOLI [1]
(Swedish)

Victor Record No. 20992
Scandinavian Folk Dance Record No. 1120, Album S-2 [2]

FORMATION:. Double circle, boy's and girl's inside hands joined. Outside hands on hips. Face to move counterclockwise around circle.

DESCRIPTION

FIGURE I

Measures 1-8. All do heel and toe polka forward around circle, beginning with outside foot. A heel-toe polka is done to two measures of 2/4

---

[1] From M. R. Wild and D. E. White, *Physical Education.* Cedar Falls. Iowa: Iowa State Teachers' College, 1924. By permission.
[2] A more extended version is found on cover of this album.

time as follows: Touch heel of outside foot forward, lean body slightly
backward (count "one"); touch outside toe backward, lean slightly forward (count "two"); slide forward with outside foot, bring inside foot
up to it (count "one"); slide forward, outside foot (count "two"). This
is repeated, using inside foot (2 measures). It is repeated with each foot
again (4 measures).

FIGURE II

Measures 9-16. Partners, side by side, step-hop forward around circle
until last measure. A step-hop is done to one measure of 2/4 time as
follows: Step on outside foot (count "one"), hop on this foot, lifting the
other knee high in front (count "two"). On the last measure, partners
jump from both feet, high in the air, landing on both feet, ready to start
dance again.

Variation 1.   During Figure I, boy puts right arm around partner's waist,
who puts left arm on boy's right shoulder. The steps remain the same.

Variation 2.   During Figure II, partners face each other. Boy puts hands
on waist of partner, who puts hands on shoulder of boy. Beginning with
forward foot (left for boy, right for girl), they hop with the free leg
raised sideways instead of up in front. A polka may be substituted for
the step-hop. On the last measure, boy jumps his partner high in the air
and puts her down on his right, ready for the repetition of the dance.

Tantoli

Arranged by Grace Van Ness

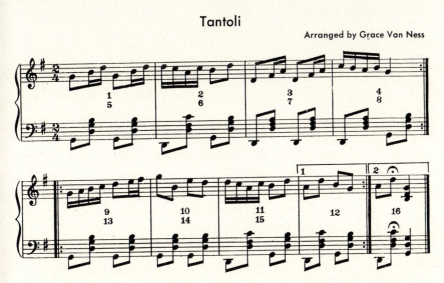

THE WALTZ

Music: "Merry Widow Waltz" [1]

Columbia Album C-136, "Waltz Time" by Abe Lyman

FORMATION: Couples in social dancing position. For instruction purposes, individuals may stand in a line in front of the teacher.

DESCRIPTION: Waltz rhythm is a 3/4 rhythm with the accent on count one. In learning the waltz, attention should be given to the Balance, the Pursuit Step, moving in a straight line, and turning.

The Balance [2]

Count 1. Step back on left foot.
Counts 2-3. Lift (swing) right foot in front and hold (1 measure).
Count 1. Step forward on right foot.
Counts 2-3. Raise (swing) left foot in back and hold (1 measure).
(Each count has the same value in time).

Repeat all six times, to waltz music—8 measures in all. Then reverse, by starting back with the right foot. The full weight of the body is transferred to the foot that takes the first step (accented note) in each measure.

The Pursuit Step (Figure 161)

Execute it directly forward for many steps, or backward, without turning.
Count 1. Slide right foot forward.
Count 2. Slide left foot forward, beyond right foot.
Count 3. Bring right foot to left foot and transfer weight to right foot—1 measure.
Count 1. Slide left foot forward.
Count 2. Slide right foot forward beyond left foot.
Count 3. Bring left foot to right foot and transfer weight to left foot (1 measure).

Repeat many times, going forward.

Repeat many times, moving backward.

Moving Backward and Forward in a Straight Line
Use simple walking steps.

[1] From Grace H. Johnstone's *Heel and Toe, or a Do-Si-Do.* Oakland, California: Grace H. Johnstone, 1944. By permission.
[2] Lesson plans for teaching the waltz are from *"Good Morning,"* op. cit. By permission of the Estate of Henry Ford, by Mr. L. J. Thompson, who wrote as follows: "Our early American Dance Books and Records were not the usual commercial project, but just one of the many things Mr. Ford enjoyed and shared throughout his life. The manuals were compiled and descriptions written by Mr. Benjamin B. Lovett, during the many years he was with us and the recordings were by our own Early American orchestra, which has been disbanded."

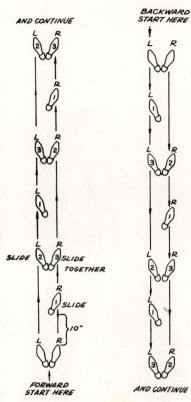

Figure 161.   The Pursuit Step

Count 1.   Step back on left foot.

Count 2.   Step back on right foot, *passing by* the left foot.

Count 3.   Close left foot to right and transfer weight to left foot (1 measure).

Count 1.   Step forward on right foot.

Count 2.   Step forward on left foot, *passing by* the right foot.

Count 3.   Close right foot to left and transfer weight to right foot (1 measure).
Continue to repeat until control of the movement is mastered.

Dancing in a Square

First, have each student draw a 15-inch square on the floor, or hang up a large diagram so all can see it (Figure 162). Stand in first position (heels together) on numbers 5 and 6 of the diagram.

Count 1.   Slide left foot directly back.

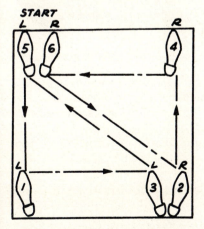

Figure 162.   Dancing in a Square

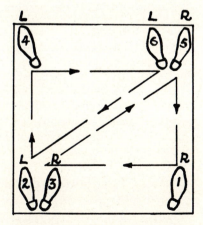

Figure 163.   Reverse in the Square

Count 2.   Slide right foot to lower right-hand corner.

Count 3.   Close left foot to right foot and transfer weight to left foot (1 measure).

Count 1.   Slide right foot directly forward, 4.

Count 2.   Slide left foot to upper left-hand corner, 5.

Count 3.   Close right foot to left foot and transfer weight, 6 (1 measure).

Practice above 20 times or more.

The Reverse of the Square
(Figure 163)

Using the same square, stand in positions 5 and 6.

Count 1.   Slide right foot directly back.

Count 2.   Slide left foot to lower left-hand corner.

Count 3.   Close right foot to left foot, transfer weight (1 measure).

Count 1.   Slide left foot directly forward, 4.

Count 2.   Slide right foot to upper right-hand corner, 5.

Count 3.   Close left foot to right and transfer weight, 6 (1 measure).

Practice above 20 times or more.

Couple Waltz Step [1]

Couples take social dancing position: girl's left hand on right shoulder of her partner, her right hand in his left hand. Boy's right hand is at the girl's back somewhat below her shoulder blades (Figure 164). The shoulder or elbow grasp position may be used until pupils are ready to accept the social dancing position.

Figure 164.   The Waltz Position

The boy's part is described. The girl's part is the same except that she starts with the opposite foot. Boys generally begin couple dances with the left foot.

Count 1.   Step forward (or slide forward) with left foot (girl backward with right foot).

---

[1] Chicago Park District (W.P.A. Project), *The Square Dance*. Chicago: Chicago Park District, 1940. By permission.

Count 2.   Step forward (or slide) with right foot which *passes* the
   left foot.

Count 3.   Close in the left foot, bringing it even with the right foot,
   and transfer weight to the left foot.

Repeat same three movements starting with the right foot (step, slide
past, close) to give the required six counts to complete the figure. When
the boy starts backward with his right foot the girl starts forward with
her left.

Waltz Turn [1]

The waltz turn is one in which the boy and girl use the same steps.
The following are descriptions of the waltz turn done to the right and
to the left.

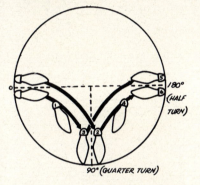

Figure 165.   Waltz Turn Right

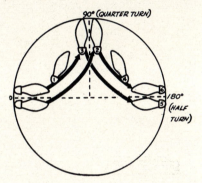

Figure 166.   Waltz Turn Left

Waltz Turn Right (Figure 165)

(Boy's part is described).

Count 1.   Step forward with right foot.

Count 2.   Bring left foot forward, *passing* the right and transferring
   the weight to left foot. At the same time turn one-quarter to the right.

Count 3.   Close the right foot up to the left and transfer the weight to
   the right foot. This completes a quarter turn.

Count 1.   Step directly back with the left foot, 4.

Count 2.   Bring the right foot back, passing the left and shifting the
   weight to the right foot. At the same time turn one-quarter to the
   right, 5.

Count 3.   Close the left foot to the right, transferring the weight to
   the left foot, 6. This completes another quarter turn.

To complete the full turn repeat the entire movement of six counts
just as described. A complete turn requires 12 counts.

[1] From *The Square Dance.*

Merry Widow Waltz

Franz Lehar   Arranged by J. B. Ocken

Waltz Turn Left (Figure 166)

This is the reverse of the right waltz turn. Again the couples take the same steps but start with opposite feet.

(Boy's part is described).

Count 1. Step forward with the left foot.

Count 2. Bring the right foot forward, *passing* the left and shifting the weight to the right foot. At the same time turn one-quarter to the left.

Count 3. Close the left foot to the right, transferring the weight to the left foot. This completes a quarter turn.

Count 1. Step directly back with the right foot, 4.

Count 2. Bring the left foot back, *passing* the right and at the same time turn one-quarter to the left, shifting the weight to the left foot, 5.

Count 3. Close the right foot to the left, transferring the weight to the right foot, 6.

To complete the full turn repeat the entire movement of six counts just as described. A complete turn requires 12 counts.

WAVES OF TORY [1]
(Irish)

Music: "Galway Piper"
Methodist Record No. 102

FORMATION: Longways line of couples, the men opposite the women as in the Virginia Reel. While six or eight couples are usually used, Waves of Tory is impressive when there are long lines of couples. It takes longer to complete the action, however. About six feet separates one line from the other. Dancers are paired into sets of two couples, numbered 1, 2, 1, 2, and so on down the line.

DESCRIPTION

Waves. Holding hands, girls up and down their line and boys up and down theirs, the two lines advance toward each other with three steps, raising joined hands high into the air on the fourth count. They retire to place with four steps. Forward and back again. (8 measures.)

Whirlpools. The lines come together again, and each boy of a Number 1 couple gives his right hand to the girl of the opposite (Number 2) couple, Number 2 boys give right hand to Number 1 girls, to form a right-hand star. They walk around in star formation eight counts, then shift to left hands across (left-hand star) and walk around eight steps, ending in line in place. (8 measures.)

---

[1] *World of Fun Series.* Nashville, Tennessee: Audio-Visual Department, Methodist Church, 1947. By permission of the Methodist Publishing Co., 85 McAllister St., San Francisco. May be purchased with records.

Galway Piper

Arranged by Anna Hermitage

Waves repeated. (8 measures.)

Whirlpools repeated. This time they start with left-hand star and conclude with right-hand star. (8 measures.)

Waves sweep out to sea. All face front. Girl takes partner's right arm and head couple promenade down beside the girls' line toward the foot, all couples following behind. The head couple return to original place, the others following.

Whitecaps. The waves do an "over and under." First couple turn and face toward the foot of the line, joining inside hands. All others face toward the head and join inside hands with partners. Making an arch with their joined inside hands, the head couple move down the line toward the foot, going with their arch over the heads of the second couple, passing under the arch of the third couple, etc. As the head couple approaches each other couple, the new couple join the action, and with over and under motion progress to the head, then to the foot of the line, and back to original position. When any couple reach the head or the foot position, they drop hands, turn themselves about, and join inside hands to move back in the opposite direction. All of this figure is done with the over and under arches. (Head couple start over and foot couple start under.)

Waves part. The head couple "cast off," and the girl leads down her line, all the girls following; the boy leads his line to the foot. At the foot the head couple make a double arch by joining both hands and raising them high and all of the others (1) go through the arch and (2) return to place in the line.

The pattern is repeated as often as desired. The head couple stay at the foot. Therefore, the right-hand and left-hand stars change. If Waves of Tory is to be repeated, the group should check their stars to see who will be in each newly-formed pair of couples.

ADDITIONAL RHYTHMICAL ACTIVITIES IN CALIFORNIA STATE SERIES MUSIC TEXTBOOKS

Sing Out! Edited by Peter W. Dykema and Others. A Singing School series (copyrighted, 1946, 1947, by C. C. Birchard & Co.). Sacramento: California State Department of Education (edition in preparation).

Students' edition and teacher's book. Page references are to the latter book.

Music Everywhere. Edited by Theresa Armitage and Others. A Singing School series (copyrighted, 1943, 1944, by C. C. Birchard & Co.). Sacramento: California State Department of Education, 1945.

Students' edition and teacher's manual (with accompaniments). Page references are to the latter book.

We Sing. Edited by Theresa Armitage, Peter W. Dykema, and Gladys Pitcher. A Singing School series (copyrighted, 1940, 1942, by C. C. Birchard & Co.). Sacramento: California State Department of Education, 1942.[1]

Students' edition, teacher's manual, and book of accompaniments. Page references are to the last named book.

A Gay Waltz	61	Polka and Waltz	106
Little White Dove	92	Varsovienne	134
Molly, My Dear	100	Raatikkoon	143

Music Highways and Byways. Edited by Osbourne McConathy, John W. Beattie, and Russell V. Morgan. The Music Hour series (copyrighted, 1936, by Silver Burdett Co.). Sacramento: California State Department of Education, 1942.[1]

Buxom Lassies	10	Leather Breeches	91
The Peddler's Pack	26	Maddalena (music)	174
Krakowiak	36	Maddalena (dance directions)	242
Hurry Up, Fellows	37	Tarantella (dance directions)	242

SELECTED REFERENCES ON RHYTHMS [2]

Ethel Bowers. *Parties Plus: Fun for Threesomes.* New York: National Recreation Association, 1943.

Contains Grand March figures, musical mixers, songs and song contests, folk games and modern adaptations, square sets for twelve people, and suggestions for adapting other activities to three.

Thomas E. Parsons. *Popular Ballroom Dances for All.* New York: Barnes and Noble, Inc., 1947.

Describes the fox trot, the waltz, the rumba, the samba, the tango, and the Lindy. Diagrams show steps.

Stunts

A stunt instruction period should be started with exercises or a short run. It is usually wise to review material presented in previous grades so that all pupils will have the same stunt background.

Numerous individual athletic events, such as baseball throw for accuracy, goal throwing, jump and reach, and the shuttle broad jump (see Chapter VII) may be used as part of the stunt program.

Apparatus stunts should include chinning, climbing, ladder traveling, and turning body over horizontal bar.

---

[1] Former series (adoption period July 1, 1942 to July 1, 1950).
[2] Consult the bibliography and listing of phonograph records in the appendixes.

BALL WRESTLE

SPACE: Playground, gymnasium

EQUIPMENT: Soccer ball, basketball, or other large ball

FORMATION: Two opponents stand facing each other. Each places both hands on the ball, held at chest height.

PROCEDURE: The object is for one contestant to take the ball away from his opponent. Three out of five trials determine the winner.

BULLDOG FIGHT

SPACE: Playground, gymnasium

EQUIPMENT: A leather belt or wide strap with ends fastened together

FORMATION: Two contestants drop to their hands and knees facing each other on opposite sides of a three-foot line drawn on the floor or ground. A belt is placed over their heads at the neck level.

PROCEDURE: Each contestant tries to pull the other over the line by pushing backward and so pulling the belt toward him. Three trials out of five determine the winner.

CENTIPEDE

SPACE: Playground, gymnasium

FORMATION: Any number of performers may join in this stunt.

PROCEDURE: Number 1 jumps onto the back of Number 2, locking his legs around Number 2's body. Number 2 leans forward until both participants can place hands on the floor, and both begin to walk (four hands, two feet). They practice until the movement becomes easy. Number 3 then mounts on Number 1 and clamps his knees against 1's waist with feet along the hips. Hands are placed on the floor ahead of the hands of Number 1 and 2. Six hands and two feet now walk. Participants can be added one by one in the same fashion.

CORKSCREW

SPACE: Gymnasium, playground

EQUIPMENT: A button or small wad of paper

PROCEDURE: The button is placed on the floor beside the outside edge of the performer's right foot. The feet are placed a few inches apart. To pick up the object, the performer passes his left hand in front of his body, around the outside of the right leg to the rear, forward between the legs and around in front of right leg. When the object has been picked off the floor, it is put down again on the outside edge of the left foot and picked up again by repeating stunt on the opposite side.

HEAD AND HAND BALANCE

SPACE: Gymnasium, playground (grassy)

EQUIPMENT: Mat if in gymnasium

FORMATION: A single performer, with a spotter to assist him while learning.

PROCEDURE: Performer forms a triangle on the floor with head and two hands. He walks slowly forward with his feet and raises the hips high. He then raises one leg after the other until hips and knees can be held straight in vertical position, with legs, feet, and toes in a straight line. He returns to the ground by bending hips and lowering legs.[1] This is a controlled head stand.

NECK PULL

SPACE: Playground, gymnasium

EQUIPMENT: A belt, towel, or broad band with ends fastened together

FORMATION: Two contestants sit on the ground back to back and about one foot apart, an equal distance from a line drawn between them. The strap or band is placed across the foreheads, from one to the other.

PROCEDURE: Each tries to pull his opponent over the line by leaning forward against the band. A point is made when one is pulled over the line or the strap slips off his forehead. Three out of five trials determine the winner.

---

[1] W. R. LaPorte and A. G. Renner, *The Tumbler's Manual.* New York: Prentice-Hall, Inc., 1938, pp. 26-37.

Chapter XXI
ACTIVITIES FOR EIGHTH GRADE

Activities are alphabetically arranged by title within the following four classes:

The games fall into several classes. They are indexed here by type for the convenience of the teacher.

[851]

Games

ATTACK

NUMBER OF PLAYERS: 4-20

SPACE: Playground

PLAYING AREA: Two goal lines 200 feet apart (or less if desired)

EQUIPMENT: Soccer ball or football. Soccer posts may be used if greater accuracy in kicking is desired, but their use is not mandatory

Procedure

The object of the game is for each team to drop-kick the ball over the opponents' goal line, advancing the ball by means of place kicks or punts until a drop kick is possible. To the game of Punt Back (Grade VI), Attack adds the possibility of catching a kicked ball from a teammate rather than just an exchange of kicked balls between opponents.

FORMATION: Players are divided into two teams. Members of each team are distributed over the field between the two goal lines. A coin is tossed to decide which team will have the kickoff from the center of the field, and the player to take the kick is designated by the referee.

PLACE KICK: A place kick (kicking the ball from position on the ground) is used to put the ball in play. If the ball during its flight is touched but not caught by a player, it is returned to that player at the spot where it was touched and is then put in play by a place kick. If the ball is completely missed by a player, the person successful in securing it puts it in play with a punt (kicking the ball with the top of the instep after it is dropped from the hands, before it hits the ground) or with a place kick, unless he is near enough to the goal to attempt a drop kick (kicking the ball on the rebound after it has been dropped from the hands).

FLY BALL: After any kickoff, if the ball is caught on the fly, the catcher may advance ten steps or leaps toward the opponents' goal line while carrying the ball before he attempts to punt or drop-kick over the goal.

FOULS: When the ball is caught, the other players must retire 10 feet or more from the person with the ball. *Penalty:* Three steps toward the goal line awarded to the kicker.

A player may not be tackled, rushed, or interfered with when attempting to secure the ball, while striding forward following the catching of a fly ball, or while preparing to kick. *Penalty:* Five steps forward awarded to kicker.

A player, while attempting to intercept the ball, may not step on or over his own goal line. *Penalty:* Three steps forward awarded to next member of opposing team who secures the ball.

SCORING: One point is awarded for each drop kick which passes as a fly ball over the goal line. No score results if the ball, kicked over a goal line by a drop kick, is touched by an opponent who is in the field of play and not touching a goal line. The ball, in this case, goes to the player who touches the ball.

The team first making 10 points wins.

TEACHING SUGGESTIONS

1. Teach the players to play far apart in order to intercept kicks and avoid player contacts.
2. Avoid long waits by keeping the play continuous.
3. Use as a football or soccer lead-up game on a warm day.
4. Use distinguishing clothes or colors for the different teams.

BACKBOARD TENNIS [1]

NUMBER OF PLAYERS: 2

SPACE: Playground, gymnasium

PLAYING AREA: Handball backstop (or wall of gymnasium or side of building). If the size of the backboard and space before it permit, the court marked on the ground, asphalt, or floor may be half the size of a regulation tennis court, 36 by 39 feet. (Figure 167.) The service line should be 21 feet from the backboard. On the backboard two lines should be drawn 4 feet apart; the lower line, 3 feet 6 inches from the ground, represents the top of a tennis net.

EQUIPMENT: (1) Two tennis rackets; (2) three tennis balls

FORMATION: The server stands outside the court behind the base line, to the right of the center. His opponent, the receiver, stands inside the court, near the base line, to the left of the center. (See diagram.) At each service the players alternate sides of court.

PROCEDURE: The rules of lawn tennis are followed.

The server sends the ball diagonally across the court, endeavoring to have it strike the backboard in the 4-foot area between the two lines on the left side. In the rebound from the backboard the ball must land inside the left service court. On the second serve, the server stands in the left court and serves to the right court, alternating thereafter for each serve.

After one bounce of the ball, the opponent returns the ball against the backboad. The next stroke is taken by the server, and thereafter strokes are taken alternately by the two players until a miss occurs. After the service the ball may be played on the fly or after one bounce, and it

---

[1] Rules contributed by Daniel Scott Farmer, Associate Professor of Physical Education, San Francisco State College.

must be kept within the side and base lines but not within the service courts. Balls against the backboard must strike within the 4-foot area. Line balls are fair balls. The ball is dead if it strikes the wall outside the 4-foot area.

When a miss occurs, the server serves again, using the opposite court. He continues to serve until a game is won, whereupon the receiver becomes the server.

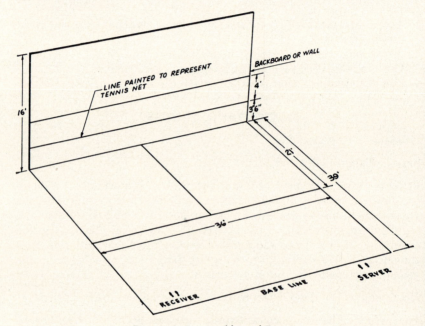

Figure 167.   Backboard Tennis

SCORING: When the server fails to serve or to return a ball properly, the receiver wins a point. When the receiver fails to return the ball properly, a point is scored by the server. Points are counted as in lawn tennis: 15 for the first point, 30 for the second point; 40 for the third point; and game for the fourth point. If both sides have 40, or deuce, one must make two points in succession in order to win the game.

TEACHING SUGGESTIONS

1. Practice against a backboard to give players more strokes per minute than tennis practice on a court affords.
2. Use substitutes for painted net dimensions on walls, such as stakes driven into the ground at the ends of the area, or adhesive tape used to indicate net height.

BADMINTON

NUMBER OF PLAYERS: 2-4

SPACE: Playground when no wind is blowing, or gymnasium; a modified game may be played in the classroom.

PLAYING AREA: Court 44 feet long, divided in the center by a net; for a singles game, 17 feet wide; for a doubles game, 20 feet wide. Posts, placed at the center of the side boundary lines, should be 5 feet 1 inch high, and the net, 2 feet 6 inches wide, should be hung from the top of the posts and tightly stretched so that it is 5 feet from the ground at the center. For markings of court, see Figure 168. If desired, fine-mesh wire fencing may be substituted for the net.

The side boundaries and length are different for singles and doubles games; if two players use a court marked for doubles to play a singles game, they play within the inner side line and the back boundary line, using the full length of the court. A singles court is long and narrow; a doubles court is short and wide.

EQUIPMENT: (1) Two shuttlecocks (familiarly known as "birds" or "birdies") or Flying Fleece balls [1]; (2) a badminton racket or wooden paddle [2] for each player

Procedure [3]

The game consists of volleying the bird with the racket back and forth over the net without allowing it to hit the ground. Points are made only when the side has the service. The game is started by an underhand stroke, but after the service, the bird may be hit underhand, overhead, or from the side.

FORMATION: Two players, one on each side of the net, for a singles game; four players, two as partners on each side of the net, for a doubles game. When three people wish to play, the partners may play in the doubles court dimensions but play to the singles court. For each game there is a serving player or team and a receiving player or team, sometimes known as the "in" side and the "out" side.

Before the game begins, a toss decides which side has the choice of courts and first or second service.

SERVICE: The game is started by a serve from the right-hand court. The server holds the bird in his left hand below his waist and out from his body at the right side. He stands in a stride position, facing his opponent,

---

[1] "Flying Fleece" balls are small balls of wool, cheaper and less perishable than shuttlecocks. They may be obtained from sporting goods stores or from Oregon Worsted Company, Portland, Oregon.

[2] See diagram for making paddles, p. 115.

[3] The rules are given in brief here. For official rules consult *The Official Tennis-Badminton Guide*. Washington: National Section on Women's Athletics, American Association for Health, Physical Education and Recreation. Obtainable from the Association, 1201 Sixteenth Street, N.W., Washington 6, D. C.

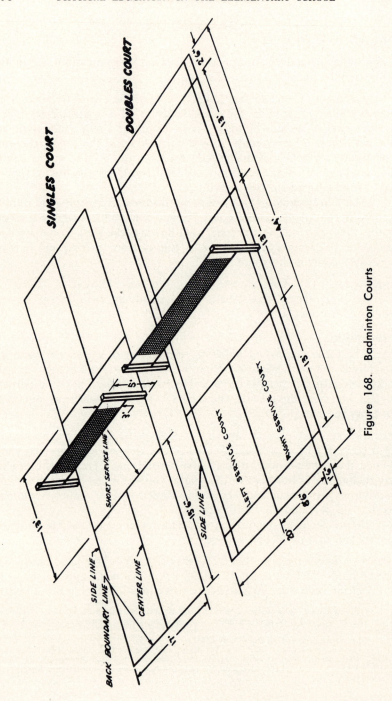

Figure 168. Badminton Courts

in his service court near the short service line. The racket is swung in a a pendular swing backwards and under the bird just as it is dropped from the hand. The racket and hand must be no higher than the player's waist before contact with the bird is made. The served bird must fall beyond the short service line and inside the boundary lines of the diagonally opposite service court to be a legal serve. After the service, the bird may be sent to any part of the opposite court within the boundary lines.

Change of Service: In a *singles game*, each server moves back and forth from right to left court on his side of the net as he wins each point. The service is always from the right-hand court at the start of the game and for even points thereafter. If the server's score is 0-2-4-6-8-10 the service is from his right-hand court. Service will be from the server's left-hand court when his score is uneven (1-3-5-7-9). When the server makes a mistake he loses the serve and it goes to his opponent. Only one trial is given in serving.

In a *doubles game* the rotation of serving is from partners A to B, to opponent partners C to D and back to A, except the service following the first service error, which goes immediately across the net to opponent C. Player D then follows C in service, and when D loses the service it comes back to the opponent in the right-hand court, which may be either A or B. Both A and B serve and the play continues with partners following each other in service before the bird goes across the net to the opponents. In a doubles game the service always occurs from the right-hand side at the beginning of the game and after each side out, which means that A may serve twice before B serves.

Let Service: If the bird while being served touches the top of the net but otherwise would have fallen in the proper service court, it is called a "let service" and is played over. A returned bird is in play if it touches the top of the net, however.

FAULTS: The following faults award 1 point to the serving side if made by their opponents, or lose the service for the serving side if made by the servers.

1. If during service the bird, at the instant of being struck, is higher than any part of the hand which holds it

2. If the head of the racket, at the instant of contacting the bird, is higher than any part of the hand which holds it

3. If the bird does not fall within the official service court. The serve is good if the bird hits a boundary line composing part of the official dimensions of the receiver's court.

4. If a bird is struck before it crosses the net. The striker's racket may follow over the net after the bird is struck fairly.

5. If a player touches the net or posts with racket, clothing, or person

6. If at the time of service one of the feet of either server or receiver is touching a line, is out of court, or is off the floor. In doubles the respective partners may take up any position, provided they do not ˙obstruct an opponent.

CHANGING COURTS: Players change sides of net at the beginning of the second game and at the beginning of the third game if there is one. *During the third game* players change courts when the leading score reaches 6 in a game of 11 aces or points; 8 in a game of 15 aces; 11 in a game of 21 aces.

SCORING: Men's singles, men's doubles, and mixed doubles games consist of 15 or 21 points or aces. Women's singles games are played for 11 aces. A set consists of the best of three games. A match consists of the best of three sets.

In doubles, when the score is 13-all in a 15-point game, the first team to reach 13 aces may choose to set the game to 5 (to play until one side has 18 aces instead of 15). When the score is 14-all, it may be set to 3 (with the final score 17 aces). In women's singles the first player to reach 9 when the score is 9-all may set the game to 3, and when the score is 10-all, the first player to reach 10 may set it to 2.

TEACHING SUGGESTIONS

1. *How to Hold the Racket:* In contrast to the "handshake" paddle tennis grip, take the grip which is natural in picking up the racket from the floor. The end of the racket handle should not extend beyond the heel of the hand. The fingers are closed comfortably around the handle with the thumb on the left side.

2. *How to Balance:* In order to maintain good balance while playing badminton, the use of the feet is very important. When a player waits for the bird his feet should be apart the width of the shoulders with the weight carried over the ball of the feet. When waiting for the bird the basic position for a singles player is astride the center line and from 3 to 6 feet back of the short service line.

3. *Forehand Strokes:* The left foot is the pivot foot, the right foot moving with the stroke. This forehand stroke is similar to that for paddle ball and tennis except that the wrist bends to allow the racket to be "whipped" as it hits the bird.

4. *Backhand Strokes:* The left foot is the pivot foot, the right foot moving with the stroke. During forehand or backhand shots while in the stride position, the weight of the body should be carried on the weight-bearing foot until after the bird has been struck. The backhand stroke is identical to the forehand except that the bird is hit on the player's left.

5. *Overhead Strokes:* The left shoulder should be toward the net, the feet being approximately side by side and pointing toward the net to be ready for an overhead stroke. From this position the right foot can be swung forward or the left foot backward to be in position to strike the bird. The racket is swung backward and up over the head to reach the bird just as it is directly over the player's head. The follow-through of the racket may be to the right or to the left of the body.

6. *Use of the Legs:* Long, lunging steps, with some bend in the knees, should be used when reaching for the bird. When turning or pivoting, both the knees and hips should be used as well as the foot and leg.

7. *Form While Playing:* A player should try at all times to take strokes sufficiently far from the body so that the arm may be fully extended. When strokes are taken close to the body, weak and poorly directed strokes are the result.

8. *Service:* Players may improve service ability by serving six to eight birds, one after the other, for placement in various parts of the court. A player should be able to serve the bird just over the net and into the service court near the short service line, and also to make a deep serve just inside the back service line. The badminton serve is similar to the volleyball serve, with the exception that the racket hits a slow-moving bird.

ure 169.   Badminton Doubles

9. *Six Players:* If the class is large, the instruction should begin with the different types of strokes or shots to be used. Six players could use a court while they are learning the different shots.

10. *Eyes on Bird:* Players should be taught to keep their eyes on the bird. A player in the fore-court should not turn around to see what his partner is doing with the bird. He should learn to judge where the bird will land in the back court by its position overhead as it passes him.

BASE SOCCER [1]

NUMBER OF PLAYERS: 12-24

SPACE: Playground, gymnasium

PLAYING AREA: Soccer field or softball diamond (Figure 170). If played in a gymnasium, use the whole floor. Home base is placed on the goal line and field base 8 feet from the goal line. On a soccer field a regular goal is used, with posts 24 feet apart and a crossbar 8 feet from the ground.

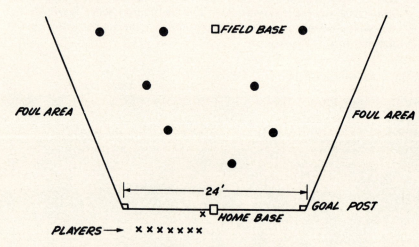

Figure 170.   Field for Base Soccer

The number of players, their age, experience, and size all combine to determine the width of the field of play and the length of the base line. For a strong defensive team, aid the offense by shortening the length to base, by increasing the width of the field of play, or by allowing them to

[1] Adapted from an article by Robert Berry in *The Journal of Health and Physical Education* XI (November, 1940), 560-61. **By permission.**

use a fullback to defend the goal. To aid the defense, narrow the playing field, or lengthen the field and distance to field base.

EQUIPMENT: Soccer ball. If played in a gymnasium, use a slightly deflated ball.

Procedure

The object of the game is to score runs. Each kicker in turn kicks the ball into the field of play, runs around the field base, and tries to get back to the home base before the fielders can kick the ball between the goal posts or hit the runner with the kicked ball.

FORMATION: Players are divided into two equal teams. Kicking team members stand behind the goal line and fielding team members are scattered over the field inside the boundary lines.

RULES OF PLAY

Kicking: The kicker stands four or five steps behind the ball, which rests on home plate. He puts the ball in play with a place kick. He then starts his run.

Base Running: The kicker does not have to touch the field base so long as he goes around it. To score a run legally, the kicker must touch home plate.

Fair and Foul Balls: A ball is fair or foul depending on the place where it first touches a surface after being kicked off. To be a fair ball it must land inside the side lines leading from the goal posts.

A foul ball retires the kicker; three foul balls retire the side.

Fielding: Fielders are not permitted at any time to touch the ball with their hands. Fielders (excepting the one handling the ball) may not interfere with the runner.

When endeavoring to make a goal, the ball must go under the crossbar of the goal posts. Where there is no crossbar, the height of the kick should be limited to the reach of the tallest player.

Fielders must return the ball through the goal by kicking, heading, or other methods approved in official soccer play.

OUTS: Three outs retire the team that is kicking. An out occurs in any of the following ways:

1. When the kicker kicks a foul ball
2. When the runner is hit by a fielded ball
3. When the ball is returned legally under the crossbar and over the home goal line before the kicker completes the circuit from home base to field base and home

SCORING: Each run scores 1 point. A run is scored (1) when a runner reaches home base safely before the ball crosses the goal line; (2) when a fielding team member touches the ball with a hand or arm; and (3) when a fielder *not* playing the ball interferes with a runner.

The team wins which has the most runs at the end of seven innings. The game may be played against time, in which case each team has a designated number of minutes in which to make as many runs as possible; or the first team to score 21 runs wins. In the latter the outs are recorded and each three outs changes the positions of the teams.

TEACHING SUGGESTIONS

1. Use as a game to introduce a season of soccer.
2. Instruct the girls to fold their arms over their breasts when blocking a ball.
3. Change dimensions of playing area to meet the degree of skill of the players.

BASKET SPEED BALL

NUMBER OF PLAYERS: 24-60

SPACE: Playground, gymnasium

PLAYING AREA: A basketball court divided into two equal sections by a line across the center

EQUIPMENT: Soccer ball, slightly deflated

Procedure

The game is played between two six-man teams, with two new teams entering the field after each scoring play, so that a large number of players can be used. The elements .of basketball and speed ball are combined, since the ball must be played with the feet until it is raised into the air by a kick, when it may be thrown for a basket. A score is made each time a basketball goal is made and each time the ball is kicked over the goal line.

FORMATION: The players are numbered off by sixes. The first two groups of six enter the court as opposing teams. Inside the court Numbers 1, 2, and 3 of each team line up near the center line, taking the positions of left wing (1), center forward (2), and right wing (3); Numbers 4, 5, and 6 take the positions of right fullback (4), center back (5), and left fullback (6). The center back players stand midway between the center line and the goal line, and directly behind their own center forwards. The fullbacks stand near the end line and behind their center forwards (Figure 171).

The remaining players, in groups of six, are assigned to one or the other team as goalkeepers. They line up in sequence outside the court and behind their own goal lines.

Rules of Play: The ball is placed at the mid-point of the center dividing line. Each center forward places a foot on the ball. At the signal each tries to pull the ball with his foot so that it can be sent backward toward his center back. As soon as the ball is in play and has passed from the center forward, he, with his wings, advances toward the opponents' goal. The center back tries to pass the ball forward to one of his wings or to his center forward. The ball is played as in soccer, as long as it remains on the ground and is not raised into the air by a foot. If the ball is raised into the air by a foot it may be caught and thrown as in basketball until missed by a player. No ball that has bounced, no matter how high, may be touched with the hands.

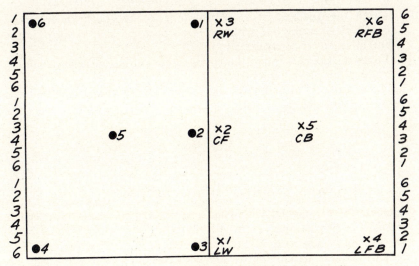

Figure 171. Position of Players in Basket Speed Ball

Wings and center forwards attempt to shoot goals if fly balls are caught from a kick; or to kick the ball over the end goal lines if the ball is being played as a soccer ball. Goalkeepers may block a ground ball or catch a fly ball and may either kick the blocked ground ball forward into the field of play to a teammate, or attempt to throw the caught fly to one of their own backfield players, who should then attempt to send it to a wing or center forward of his own team. These forwards then attempt to make a goal at the other end of the court. No out-of-bounds rules are used.

Each time a scoring play is made two new six-man teams (who have acted as goalkeepers) enter the court and play is continued. Those leaving the court take positions as goalkeepers and await their re-entrance into the court.

FOULS: Fouls are the same as for soccer and basketball. The penalty for a soccer foul is a free unguarded kick toward a team member at the place where the foul occurred. The penalty for a basketball foul is a free unguarded throw towards a team member where the foul occurred. A pass must be completed between two players before a goal can be made, so that no scoring occurs directly from an awarded ball.

SCORING: One point is awarded for each basketball goal made. One point is awarded for each ball kicked over the goal line

TEACHING SUGGESTIONS

1. Teach the goalkeepers to remain outside the court, though they may kick over the line with the lifted foot and may reach over the line in an effort to catch a fly ball.
2. Teach the backs to guard the opposing forwards, especially when the ball is being played as a basketball.
3. Use as a review of basketball and soccer techniques and rules and as a lead-up game to speed ball.

BOCCIE

NUMBER OF PLAYERS: 2 or 4

SPACE: Playground, gymnasium, hallway, auditorium

EQUIPMENT: (1) A box with sides and flooring made of 2- or 3-inch boards. The size may vary from 24 to 36 inches in width and from 8 to 16 feet in length. The sides of the box should be 8 or 9 inches high. The floor of the box should be covered with carpeting. The game may be played with the box on the floor or on a table. (2) Nine golf balls, four painted red, four blue, and one—the pallino—white

FORMATION: For a singles game, two opponents stand at the same end of the box; for a doubles game, two players as partners play against two opponents. In a singles game, each player uses two balls; for a doubles game, each player uses two balls, or four for each side.

PROCEDURE: The game is based on the Italian bowling game, *boccie*. Each player tries to bowl his balls so that they will stop closer to the pallino than his opponent's balls did; he may strike the latter with his ball in order to send them farther from the pallino. Balls are delivered by the player while he stands behind the end of the box. They are rolled, not thrown. Balls must be banked off a side of the box before reaching the pallino or the opponent's ball.

A tossed coin decides who is to play first. The player who wins the toss rolls the pallino toward the opposite end of the box. He then rolls his own ball in such a way that it will hit the side of the box and roll back as close to the pallino as possible. His opponent then rolls his first ball in such a way as to have it strike the side of the box and then land close to the pallino or knock the opponent's ball farther from the pallino.

After these two balls have been played, the player whose ball is closer to the pallino takes the next shot.

When each player has bowled his two balls, the player whose ball lies closest to the pallino is given one point and the balls are played again, the winning player rolling the pallino out following it with his first ball as before. Thereafter, when a new game is played the player with the highest score rolls the pallino.

SCORING: The player or team which first scores 12 points wins, unless the game is tied at 11 to 11, in which case the game is continued until one player has a 2-point lead.

BRONCO TAG

NUMBER OF PLAYERS: 6-40

SPACE: Playground, playroom, gymnasium

PLAYING AREA: A basketball court or area of similar size (the shadow made by a building may sometimes be used)

FORMATION: A runner and a chaser are chosen. The remaining players are scattered about within the playing area; they stand in couples, one in front of and with his back to his partner. The front player represents the head of a bronco; the second player represents the tail. The front player must fold his arms across his chest, as he may not use them in the game. The second player puts his arms around the waist of his partner and clasps his own hands firmly.

PROCEDURE: The purpose of the game is for the runner to escape being tagged by seizing the tail of a bronco. Each bronco twists and turns in any direction to prevent a runner from seizing his tail. If the runner is successful in clasping his arms around the waist of a bronco's tail, the front man has to leave his tail and become the chaser, the original chaser becoming the runner. If a chaser succeeds in tagging a runner before he can attach himself to a bronco's tail, the positions are reversed, the runner becoming the chaser and the chaser the runner.

TEACHING SUGGESTION

1. Instruct the players to try to keep head and tail of bronco from separating, in order to keep the game going at a fast speed.

BUST THE LEATHER

NUMBER OF PLAYERS: 10-40

SPACE: Playground, gymnasium

PLAYING AREA: Two parallel lines are drawn 20 to 25 feet apart. These are known as "driver lines." To determine their length, allow 3 feet for each player on a team but do not have the lines less than 30 feet long. Goal lines 5 feet back of the driver lines and paralleling them should also be drawn.

EQUIPMENT: Soccer ball; if played in a gymnasium use a somewhat deflated ball.

Procedure

The players of two opposing teams, standing (with clasped hands) in front of their own goal, attempt to defend that goal and also to kick the ball over their opponents' goal line. To keep the ball in motion a "driver" from each team occupies the center of the field (between the driver lines) and kicks the ball toward his teammates.

FORMATION: Each member is given a number. The Number 1 players of each team are the drivers to start the game. Each team has one or more drivers, depending on the number playing. When large numbers are to play it would be better to have four drivers, one from each end of each team. Drivers occupy the central zone between the two driver lines. When starting the game they stand so as to face their own team members and yet face each other. The remaining players, the goal guards, occupy the space between their goal and driver line. They stand with hands joined facing their opponents.

RULES OF PLAY: The referee puts the ball in play by rolling it between the drivers. This is done (1) at the beginning of the game, (2) whenever the ball rolls out of bounds, and (3) following each scoring play.

Drivers: These players may not attempt to kick the ball over the opponents' goal line, but, using their feet, must try to advance the ball to their own goal guards.

Goal Guards: Their responsibilities are to prevent the ball from passing over their own goal line and to kick the ball over their opponents' goal line within the ends of the line. No score can be made if handclasps are broken, even though the ball is kicked legitimately. Guards may extend the kicking foot over the goal line above the ground in order to contact the ball, but they may not step outside the goal area with both feet.

Players may obstruct the ball by using their heads, shoulders, arms, hips, legs, and feet, providing they do not use their hands and do not break the line by letting go their neighbors' hands.

When a goal is made by either team, Number 2 players become the drivers. The former drivers retire to the middle of their respective lines.

PLAYING PERIOD: A game consists of four innings. An inning is terminated when a team makes 5 points. At the end of each inning teams exchange goal areas, the new drivers take their positions, and play continues. If desired, a game may terminate when all players of each team have served as drivers.

FOULS: The following are fouls: (1) stepping on or over the driver line; (2) obstructing the ball while the team's line is broken; (3) touching the ball with the hand (except to protect the face); (4) stepping out of the goal area with both feet. *Penalty:* For each foul, 1 point is awarded to opponents.

SCORING: For kicking the ball across opponents' goal line above the heads of the opponents and within the two ends of the goal line, 1 point is scored.

For kicking the ball across the opponents' goal line below the hands and under the arms of the opponents and within the two ends of the goal line, 2 points are scored.

For each foul committed by opponents, 1 point is scored.

CATCH AND PULL TUG OF WAR

NUMBER OF PLAYERS: 6-40

SPACE: Playground, playroom, gymnasium

PLAYING AREA: A line drawn on the ground, its length depending on the number of players (the edge of a shadow thrown by a building may be used)

FORMATION: The players are divided into two teams as nearly matched in weight as possible. The teams stand on opposite sides of the line.

PROCEDURE: On a signal, the players reach over the line in an effort to catch and pull an opponent over the line. Any part of a player's body such as the hand, arm, or foot may be grasped. A player is not captured until his entire body has been pulled over the line. When captured the player joins his captors in trying to secure members of his former team. Any number of players on a team may try to secure an opponent and any number of the opponent's teammates may come to his rescue. They may try to keep him in his own territory or they may try to secure holds on his opponents and pull them over the line.

SCORING: The group wins which first pulls all of their opponents into their own territory or has the largest number of players on their side at the end of the time limit.

DECK TENNIS

NUMBER OF PLAYERS: 2-4

SPACE: Playground, gymnasium

PLAYING AREA: For a singles game, court 12 by 40 feet; for a doubles game, court is 18 feet wide and divided into two 9-foot courts. Three feet from the net on each side a line is drawn across the court to set off a neutral area. (Figure 172.)

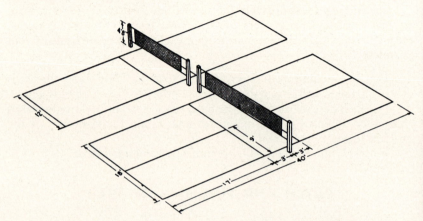

Figure 172.   Deck Tennis Courts (for singles and doubles)

EQUIPMENT: (1) Two posts, 3 by 3 inches by 7 feet, placed 2 feet 4 inches in the ground at the center of the two side lines.[1] Four eyelets are attached to the posts, through which ropes of the net are drawn. (2) Net stretched tightly across between the posts so that its top is 4 feet 8 inches from the ground for its entire length. (3) Deck tennis ring, sometimes called a "tenikoit." The ring may be made of spliced rope, of rubber with air vents to permit a give when caught, or of rubber hose length with wooden stopper at both ends.

Procedure

The ring is thrown back and forth over the net in an effort to prevent an opponent from returning it. The ring must be caught with but one hand, either right or left, and must be returned immediately with the same hand. The ring must travel in an upward direction, for a down stroke is a foul either on the service or a rally stroke.

---

[1] See diagram for erecting a tether ball post, page 100.

FORMATION: For a singles game, one player plays on each side of the net. For a doubles game, two persons play on each side of the net as partners.

SERVICE: The server, standing outside of the right-hand court, tries to throw the ring with an upward toss beyond the neutral area and into the diagonally opposite half court. If the server or his teammate makes the point, the ring is thrown again by the server from the left-hand court. Server continues to alternate from left to right courts until his side makes an error or a foul.

RALLY: Following service, the ring is thrown back and forth over the net until a player misses or fouls. If the serving side misses or fouls, no point is made but the serving side loses the serve. If the opponent or his partner misses or fouls, 1 point is credited to the serving side. The entire area of the court from net to back line and both side lines may be used for rally play. The neutral area is disregarded except for the service.

In a doubles game, the retiring server takes his position in the right-hand court and becomes the first receiver; his partner takes the next service sent by the opponent; the partner of the first server takes the third service, and so on until the game is won or lost.

FOULS: The following plays are fouls: (1) catching the ring with both hands; (2) changing the ring from the catching hand in order to throw

re 173. Deck Tennis Doubles

more successfully; (3) while serving, stepping on or over the rear boundary line; (4) making a downward stroke when throwing the ring; (5) permitting the ring to touch any part of the body other than the catching hand. If a foul is committed by the server or his partner a loss of service occurs and the ring is given to an opponent player. No score is made on the loss of a serve. If a foul is committed by a receiving side player, one score is credited to the serving team and the ring continues in service.

SCORING: The serving side scores a point whenever the receiving side misses a play or makes a foul. A game consists of 15 points. If a game reaches 14-all, it is a deuce game and one player or team must win 2 successive points in order to win. A match consists of two out of three games.

TEACHING SUGGESTIONS

1. Use volleyball or net ball rules when more than two play on one side.
2. Teach players to let hand give in toward the body when catching the ring.
3. Practice catching the ring at short distances.
4. Instruct the players to catch the ring between the thumb and fingers.
5. Teach the players to catch equally well with both hands.

EIGHT-MAN TENNIS [1]

NUMBER OF PLAYERS: 8

SPACE: Playground, gymnasium

PLAYING AREA: Tennis court, with net [2]

EQUIPMENT: (1) Eight tennis rackets; (2) three tennis balls

FORMATION: Players are divided into two teams of four players each, who take positions as in Figure 174. Each team has two members who play net positions and two who take care of the back court, remaining near the base line. The server and partner change back and forth for service in their playing area as is done in the official tennis game. At the beginning of a game, and previous to each service, net players of the serving team stand in the alleys near the net. As the game progresses, net players move into position, halfway between the center line and side line. As the games are played, all persons play each position on the court.

PROCEDURE: The rules are the same as for lawn tennis. Each player covers his own area and should not reach into his partner's area.

Example of Net Procedure: Player A-1 is to serve B-1 player, A-3 and A-4 standing in the alleys of the court. After a successful service to

---

[1] The rules were provided by Daniel Scott Farmer, Associate Professor of Physical Education, San Francisco State College.
[2] See Tennis Court, Figure 182, p. 912.

B-1, A-3 steps into position in the main part of the court as B-1 attempts to return the ball. As B-1 strikes the ball over the net, B-3 steps into position. On service to B-2, A-4 will step in and then B-4. Naturally, if there is a continuous rally following A-1's service, all net players will have to move about their own area. Players remain in the alley until service is successful, to lessen the danger of a served ball hitting a net player.

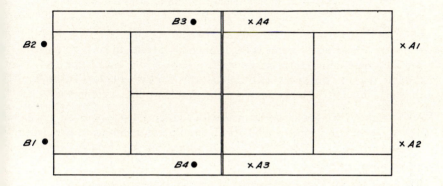

Figure 174. Position of Players in Eight-Man Tennis

Rallying the Ball: The ball is rallied back and forth until the serving side or the receiving side scores a point. On the return strokes each player tries to return the ball to score a point by returning it between the net players or over the net players' heads, or by passing the net players with a well-placed drive or backhand stroke.

Rotation of Players: The shift of players is clockwise. A-1 takes A-2's position; A-2 takes A-3's position; A-3 takes A-4's position; A-4 becomes server. Two methods of rotation may be used. Both teams may rotate positions after a single game has been completed, or after two games have been played.

SCORING: The scoring is the same as for lawn tennis: 15, 30, 40, game.

TEACHING SUGGESTIONS

1. Use eight-man tennis to provide more players with tennis instruction than the official tennis game.
2. Teach net players to be quick and well-balanced to return ball at the net.
3. Substitute a bounce serve for an overhead tennis serve for a beginning game.

FIELD DODGE BALL

NUMBER OF PLAYERS: 6-40

SPACE: Playground, gymnasium

PLAYING AREA: A home base line not less than 30 feet in length; in line with the center point of the home base line and 60 feet distant, a field base

EQUIPMENT: Volleyball, basketball, soccer ball, large rubber ball

Procedure

The object of the game is for runners of a team, in turn, to encircle the field base and return across the home base line within the ends of the line without being hit with the ball thrown by a fielder. To be legal the ball must hit the body between the shoulders and the knees.

FORMATION: Two teams are formed with two or more players on a team. The members of the team who are to run line up behind and parallel to the home base line. Members of the fielding team are scattered over the playing area. The fielding team should not bunch up.

RULES OF PLAY: The game is played by innings. Half an inning is completed when all members of a team have run. As many innings may be played as are desired. If one team is short a player, one pupil may run twice, but not in sequence.

To start the game, an official rolls or throws a ball into the field of play from a side line. Immediately *two runners* try to encircle the pole and return home without being hit with the ball. They do not have to keep together while running but *there always must be two runners in the field*. As soon as a runner is legally hit he must raise an arm high into the air, thereby signalling the next man of his team to begin his run. The tagged runner then returns to the end of his line as rapidly as possible without interfering with other runners or fielders. The instant a runner crosses the home base line it is a signal for the next player of his team to start his run. *Prospective runners should not begin their run until* the active runner crosses the base line or is hit while still in the field.

The fielders try to hit each runner with the ball before the runner can cross the base line. Fielders while *standing still* may try to hit a runner or pass the ball to another fielder who may be in a better position to throw at a runner. A fielder may run to get the ball but, once the ball is in his hands, he must stand still while throwing the ball.

FOULS AND PENALTIES: The fouls in field dodge ball are as follows:
1. A fielder may not walk or run while holding the ball. *Penalty:* 1 point is given to the runner's team and the runner continues to run. He may or may not make his run.

2. Fielders may not "bottle up" a runner. That is, two fielders may not close in on a runner while passing the ball back and forth several times between themselves; a third person must be involved. *Penalty:* 1 point is given to the runner's team as well as 2 points for the run.
3. A runner must include the field base in his run. *Penalty:* 1 point is given to the fielding team and the runner fails to score a run. Runners may approach the field base from either side and must pass behind it.
4. A runner, when hit legally, must signal by raising an arm high in the air and, thereafter, leave the field of play as rapidly as possible. *Penalty:* 1 point is given to the fielding team. No pause in the game should occur.

SCORING: A run scores 2 points. A foul scores 1 point for the opponents. A run is made each time a runner encircles the field base and returns home, crossing the home base line within the ends of the line, without being hit.

The team wins which has the higher number of points at the end of the designated number of innings.

VARIATION: A game may be played in two or more time periods. When so played the members of a team continue to make as many runs as possible within the time limits. Members must run in sequence.

TEACHING SUGGESTIONS

1. Use game in cool weather.
2. Teach the pupils to watch for two types of outs and so be ready to start their run immediately.

FIVE-MAN BADMINTON [1]

NUMBER OF PLAYERS: 10

SPACE: Gymnasium, auditorium, playground (if no wind)

PLAYING AREA: Court 20 by 54½ feet, marked as shown in Figure 175

EQUIPMENT: (1) Ten paddles [2] made of three-ply fir wood, 9 inches long, 7¼ inches wide and ¼ inch thick, with handle 6 inches long; (2) rubber-base shuttlecock ("bird" or "birdie") or homemade one of cork, or rubber ball; (3) net 17 to 20 feet in length. The top of the net should be 6 feet from the ground.

FORMATION: Players are divided into two teams of five each, occupying positions as shown in Figure 175.

---

[1] Suggestions for game found in a note by Stephen Harrick, *Journal of Health and Physical Education*, X (March, 1939), 174. By permission.
[2] See construction of paddle, page 115.

PROCEDURE: Official badminton rules are used,[1] with the following exceptions: (1) Wooden paddles are used instead of badminton rackets; (2) the
net height is 6 feet; (3) the bird may be hit twice in succession by the
same side but not by the same player.

The service is taken by player Number 1 from inside the right-hand
court to the front line opponent in the diagonally opposite right-hand
court. If a point is made, service is made from inside left-hand court to
front player in diagonally opposite court. Service continues until serving
side makes an error. The server and his front line partner exchange courts
with each service.

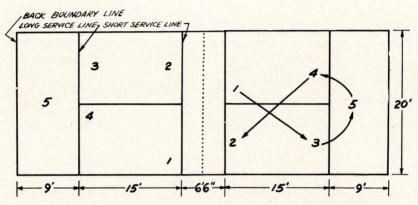

Figure 175.   Position and Rotation of Players in Five-Man Badminton

ROTATION OF PLAYERS: See Figure 175. Rotation takes place after the
service changes. The players of the team to serve rotate. Should Number 1
finish serving while in the left half of the court, originally occupied by
Number 2, Number 1 goes immediately to Number 3's position and
Number 2, who will be the next server, is in position to serve from the
right half of the court. Serving takes place in numerical order.

FOULS: Fouls are called in the following circumstances:
  1. If service is overhand. A serve is considered overhand if the birdie,
     when struck, is higher than the server's waist.
  2. If the bird, during service, fails to land in diagonally opposite court.
  3. If server's or receiver's feet are contacting a line of their court when
     service occurs.
  4. If the bird, during the rally, is struck before it crosses the net. The
     striker may, however, follow the birdie over the net with his paddle.
  5. If a player touches the net or its supports with paddle, person or
     dress while birdie is in play.

---

[1] Refer to Badminton, page 855.

Penalty: Any of the above fouls made by any player of the serving side puts the server out; if made by a player of the receiving team, it counts as a point for the serving side.

SCORING: Scoring is the same as for badminton doubles; 15 or 21 aces or points constitute a game.

In tournament play 15 points constitute a game for girls and 15 or 21 for boys.

In a 15-point game when the score is 13-all the side first reaching 13 has the option of setting the game to 5; that is, continuing to play until one side gets 18 points. When the score is 14-all, the side which first reached 14 has the option of setting the game to 3. After a game has been set the team wins which first scores 5 or 3 points, according as the game was set at 13 or 14 all.

With a game calling for 21 points the same method of scoring will be used, substituting 19 and 20 for 13 and 14.

A rubber or match is the best of 3 games.

Players change courts at the beginning of the second game and also when third game starts, if a third game is needed to decide the rubber. In the third game, players exchange courts when the leading score reaches 8, in a game of 15 aces, or 11 in a game of 21 aces or points.

TEACHING SUGGESTIONS

1. Teach players to play their positions and not to play each other's bird.
2. Teach players to use wrist action in order to get quick, sure strokes.

FLY CASTING

NUMBER OF PLAYERS: 1-15

SPACE: Playground, gymnasium

PLAYING AREA: (1) Restraining line; (2) circles three feet in diameter on ground or floor placed at different distances from the restraining line.

EQUIPMENT: Fishing rods, lines, reels, leaders, and plugs

FORMATION: One or more players behind a restraining line cast individually for a given circle.

PROCEDURE: Fly casting provides opportunity to acquire a recreational skill. Individually or in small groups children can learn the techniques of casting and acquire accuracy. The four events which provide this opportunity are (1) casting dry for accuracy, (2) ⅝-ounce plug casting for accuracy, (3) distance fly, and (4) distance plug casting. The two accuracy events are the two styles practiced by anglers who fish for trout and black bass.

TEACHING SUGGESTIONS

1. Discuss selection of good equipment: rods, lines, rules, flies, leaders.
2. Teach tying of leaders and flies.
3. Use any available water for fly casting: a pond, an irrigation ditch, a stream.
4. Include game laws and their observance in class discussion.
5. Write to Weber Fly Casting Co., Stevens Point, Wisconsin, for full information on various steps in fly casting.
6. Use such references as the following: (1) *Angling*. New York: Boy Scouts of America (200 Fifth Ave.), 1925; (2) Gilmer G. Robinson, *Bait Casting*. New York: A. S. Barnes & Co., 1942.

GALLOP THE PUCK [1]

NUMBER OF PLAYERS: 10-30

SPACE: Playground, gymnasium, playroom

PLAYING AREA: Basketball court or hard-surfaced area similar in size. At each end of the court free-throw lines and a circle should be drawn. The free-throw lines are continued to touch the circles at each side. The portions between the extended line and the arcs of the circles form the goal areas (Figure 176).

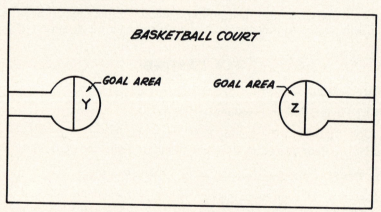

Figure 176. Court for "Gallop the Puck"

EQUIPMENT: (1) For each player a regulation field hockey stick, wooden wand, or broomstick; (2) one round puck made from wood, 2 inches wide by 1 inch thick, ice hockey puck, or large rubber shoe heel. The puck is placed at the center of the court.

FORMATION: Players are divided into two teams. Three guards only defend each goal area. They patrol outside the goal area but may not enter the area. Before the game begins the remaining team players stand in their own half of the court with their backs toward their own goal area. No player may be nearer the puck than five feet.

PROCEDURE: At a signal, two opponent players at the center of the court try to push the puck to a teammate or try to shove it toward the opponents' goal area. A player may not swing at or strike the puck but may *push* it only. Once the puck is in motion, players may go anywhere within the court; the goal areas may be approached from any angle. If the puck leaves the playing area, the nearest opponent places it on the line at the point where it left the court and tries to push it to a teammate. A goal may not be attemped from an out-of-bounds play. A second player must receive the puck before a goal may be attempted. All other players must be at least 10 feet distant on an out-of-bounds play. The sticks must be in contact with the floor *at all times*. Blocking with the body or stick is permissible once the puck is in play.

A goal is accomplished when the puck comes to rest on the lines of or inside a goal area. A puck passing through a goal area does not score.

Playing Periods: The game is played with 8-minute quarters. At the beginning of the 3d quarter teams exchange playing areas. Two halves of five minutes each may be used.

SCORING: The team wins which at the end of the playing period has the largest total of points. Score is made in the following ways: (1) Five points for a goal made by any player; (2) one point for the opponents each time a player lifts his stick point from the floor; (3) two points for the opponents each time a player swings at the puck.

TEACHING SUGGESTIONS

1. For a small number of children, use one goal and one-half the basketball court.
2. Play "Gallop the Puck" in a large open classroom in the absence of a gymnasium or playroom.

GRID BALL [1]

NUMBER OF PLAYERS: 14-30

SPACE: Playground

PLAYING AREA: Field similar to a touch football field, 50 by 80 yards, with minimum dimensions of 30 by 50 yards, on surface of grass if possible.

---

[1] Used by permission of author, Paxton Jordan, Redlands Junior High School, Redlands, California.

Asphalt surfaced area is not recommended but if it is the only surface available, the ball must be somewhat deflated. Use field markings, goal areas, and goal posts as for touch football (see p. 792).

EQUIPMENT: (1) Soccer ball; (2) goal posts or jumping standards

Procedure

This game combines elements of speed ball, soccer, and football; the ball cannot be handled while it is a ground ball, but players may run while holding the ball as in football. Two teams compete, each trying to put the ball across the opponents' goal line by passing, kicking, throwing, or running with the ball.

FORMATION: Two teams of 11 players each are formed. It is permissible to have from 7 to 15 players on a team. Two players are elected captains. Goal guards are the only players who must play a particular position in the game.

Substitutions: Substitutions may be made following scoring plays and at no other time. Substitutes must report to the referee. Failure to do so will give the other team 1 point.

Referee: The referee has full charge of the game and may expel a player for unnecessary roughness or unsportsmanlike conduct.

PLAYING PERIOD: The game consists of two periods of play, 10 to 20 minutes long, with a 3- to 5-minute rest between the halves.

RULES OF PLAY: The ball is placed on the 40-yard line [1] or 10 yards back of the center line for a place kick, or the kickoff may be a punt. All players of the kicking team must be behind the line where the ball rests. Opponents receive the kickoff from behind their 40-yard line. Ball must be kicked to the opponents.

Out-of-Bounds Ball: Any kickoff ball which goes out of bounds beyond the middle line of the field (50-yard line) is brought in at the point where it crossed the side line.

A kickoff ball going out before reaching the middle line of the field is placed in play at the middle line. The ball is returned with the use of a throw-in as in soccer.

Goal Guard: These are the only players who can pick up a ground ball.[2] They may advance as far as the 20-yard line to pick up the ball but may not so handle it beyond the 20-yard line.

---

[1] Whenever the term "40-yard line" is used in these rules, the line 10 yards from the center line is meant; the term "50-yard line" indicates the center line, and "20-yard line" indicates a line 20 yards from the goal.
[2] See Speed Ball, page 904.

Once the ball is secured, across the 20-yard line, a goal guard may run with, toss, or kick the ball down the field in an effort to score. As soon as a goal guard gives up the ball, he returns immediately to his goal guarding position.

Ground Ball: Players cannot pick up a ground ball. It may be dribbled, kicked, or picked up by the feet as in speed ball.[1] On a kick-up to one's self or to a teammate the ball may then be passed with the hands in any direction as in speed ball, but in addition a player may run with the ball, *when at all possible.*

Pass: There is no limit to passes, forward or lateral or backward. Any direction is legal. Any member of the team is eligible at any time to receive the ball from a pass any place on the field.

Pivot: The pivot is used the same as in basketball (keeping one foot on the ground). If a man carrying the ball is about.to be touched he may avoid loss of the ball by stopping before the opponent catches him and pivoting, keeping the ball clear for a pass out to a teammate. Should the man guarding him be faked away by a fake pass, the man with the ball may continue toward the goal again, using a run, a kick, or a pass.

Heading: The ball may be headed (struck with the head) when on the fly (when raised into the air directly from a kick) or when bouncing. Also, it is legal to shoulder the ball but at no time may the arms or fists be used on the ball, except when receiving a pass, fly ball, or kick-up.

Touching: A touch occurs whenever an opponent touches a ball carrier with either hand between shoulders and hips.

The ball is declared dead at the point where the touch occurs and is placed on the ground for the other team. An opponent will have 10 seconds to put the ball in play by a kick, run, or pass. All other players must take a position 10 yards away, in back, front, or in a circle.

If the referee is unable to see whether or not a runner is touched, then the word of the tagger must be taken.

Fumble: A fumbled ball is a free ball and is to be played.

Held Ball: If a ball is held for more than 3 seconds, the ball must be thrown up between two opponents as in basketball.

Ball in Play Following Scoring Play: After each score the team scored upon takes the ball and puts it in play from behind its own goal line. The ball may be put in play by use of a throw-in, a kick-in, or a run into the playing field.

Fouls and Penalties: The following plays are fouls:

1. Pushing, tripping, holding, tackling, or using unnecessary roughness on another player.

---

[1] See converted ground ball, Speed Ball rules, page 906.

2. Touching with the hands or forearms a ground or bounce ball, either intentionally or unintentionally.
3. Forming interference at any time, using hands, elbows, forearms, or feet in an attempt to block an opponent.
4. Using a straight arm, set elbow, hand, or arm when warding off an opponent. Penalty for 1, 2, 3, 4: Loss of ball at point of foul.
5. Body contact. The penalty for body contact is the loss of the ball, but after five offenses the player is removed from the game, and no substitute is allowed.

SCORING: A pass over goal line into any part of goal area or end zone to a teammate scores 5 points.

A run while carrying the ball over goal line into any part of goal area or end zone scores 4 points.

A drop kick over the goal crossbar scores 3 points.

A soccer kick through goal posts and under the crossbar scores 2 points.

A throw of the ball with the hands through the goal posts scores 1 point.

After each score, the team scored upon takes the ball and puts it in play from behind its own goal line. The ball may be put in play by a throw-in, a kick-in, or by a run into the playing field.

TEACHING SUGGESTIONS

1. Have players wear distinguishing jerseys, armbands, or caps.
2. Do not permit spikes, cleats, headgear, or padding of any kind to be worn. Long trousers help to minimize abrasions.

GYMNASIUM SOCCER [1]

NUMBER OF PLAYERS: 12-18

SPACE: Gymnasium, playground

PLAYING AREA: A court the size of a basketball court, divided into two equal areas by a line through the middle meeting the side lines. Basketball free-throw lines and circles should be marked on the court.

The goal and penalty areas are identical. The area defined by the free-throw circles, lane lines, and the goal lines at the end is both the goal and penalty area. Penalty marks are the free-throw lines.

A circle 3 feet in diameter at the center of the court should be drawn for the "center-off."

EQUIPMENT: (1) Soccer ball *inflated only enough* so that a kick will cause it to travel not more than the length of the court; (2) four jumping

[1] Suggestions for the game found in a note by Roger Gray contributed to the *Journal of Health and Physical Education*, VI (April, 1935), 42. By permission.

standards, two being placed 9 feet apart at each end on the end lines and an equal distance from the side lines; (3) two crossbars or rope lengths placed on the jumping standards 6 feet above the floor.

Procedure

Members of each team, by contacting the ball with their feet, head, or any part of their bodies, except arms below the elbows, endeavor to send the ball between the opponents' goal posts and under the crossbar. Goal guards, while in the goal area, are the only persons who may use their hands on the ball.

FORMATION: Players are divided into two teams of nine players or fewer: center, left and right inside-forward, left and right outer-forward, left and right halfback, fullback, and goal guard. To start the game, players of each team must be between the middle line and their own goal lines in their proper positions. The captain who wins the toss may choose the goal to defend. Teams exchange goals at half time.

START OF PLAY: The ball is "centered-off"; that is, the ball is dropped between the two centers while they are in the center circle. The ball may not be kicked until it has struck the floor. After the ball leaves the center circle neither center may touch it again until it has been played by a third person.

PERIODS OF PLAY: The game consists of four 6-minute quarters with a two-minute rest period between quarters and a 5-minute rest period between halves. Periods of play may be reduced to meet needs of the players. No time-outs are allowed except in case of an injury, when a new player may enter the game. In this case the ball is centered-off at the spot where the ball was when play was stopped.

PLAYING PRIVILEGES: Following the center-off, players may move over the entire court area but it is advisable to instruct forwards not to drop back into their own half-court, halfbacks not to back up behind their own fullbacks, fullbacks not to cross the center line, and goal guards not to leave the goal areas.

Any player may charge another player who is playing the ball with the exception of the goal guard unless the goal guard has the ball. By charging is meant pushing with shoulders or body or upper arms but not with forearms and hands. Players within 10 feet of the ball may be considered as playing the ball. Charging does not permit unnecessary roughness. No player should intentionally use his hand or hands on the ball. Goal guards are the only exception.

OUT-OF-BOUNDS BALL: When the ball goes out of the court *over a side line*, the player who last touched the ball is considered to have caused it to go out of bounds. The ball is awarded to a player of the opponent team at the point on the side line where it passed out of the court. The thrower must stand on both feet outside the court and facing the middle of the court directly in front of him. The throw-in is made from overhead while using both hands. During the throw-in the feet may not leave the floor.

A ball that passes over an end line but not between the goal posts and under the crossbar is out of bounds at the end lines. If last touched by a member of the *defending team* the ball is awarded to a member of attacking team at the corner where end and side lines join, from which place it must be place-kicked into the court. If last touched by member of *attacking team* the ball is awarded to a goal guard of defending team who puts it in play by placing it on the floor within six feet of the goal line and then kicking it. Attacking team members must be not nearer than 15 feet until the ball is kicked.

When the official in charge is not sure as to the cause of an out-of-bounds play, the ball is centered-off three feet inside the line at the place where the ball passed out of bounds.

PENALTY KICK: For a penalty kick the ball is placed on the penalty mark. The goal is guarded by the goal guard only. Members of the defending team must remain behind the goal line outside the court, or on the field of play at least three yards from the lines of the free-throw lane. Members of the team taking the kick must be stationed behind the kicker and outside the circle.

PERSONAL FOULS: The following are personal fouls: (1) Kicking, holding, striking, tripping, or jumping at a player; and (2) kicking at or kneeing upward at a descending ball when two or more players are within touching distance of each other.

For a personal foul committed by a member of a team (1) he may be removed from the game and no substitute allowed, or (2) the opponents shall be awarded two unobstructed penalty kicks with only the opposing goal guard attempting to stop the kicks. The goal guard may not use his hands during the trials. Following the second penalty kick the ball shall be centered-off.

TECHNICAL FOULS: Intentional use of forearms or hands against the ball while the ball is within bounds of the court, is a technical foul. The goal guards are the exception to the rule.

When a technical foul is committed by a *defending member* while *within* his own goal area, one penalty kick is awarded to opponents.

When a technical foul is committed by a *defending player outside* his own goal area the ball is awarded to an opponent for an out-of-bounds throw-in at the nearest side line opposite the spot where the foul occurred.

When a technical foul is committed by an *attacking player within* the goal area of the defending team an unobstructed place kick by the defending goal guard is awarded. All other players must not be nearer than 15 feet.

When a technical foul is committed by an *attacking player within* the defenders' half of the court but *outside* the defenders' goal area, a corner kick is awarded. The ball is taken to nearest corner where end and side lines join and placed on the ground. A member of the defending team takes the place kick. All members of the attacking team must be not nearer than 15 feet.

SCORING: A team scores 1 point each time the ball goes through the opponents' goal. Goals are made by the following methods: (1) by a direct kick; (2) by contact with head of a player; (3) by contact with body of a player; or (4) as the result of a penalty kick. A ball thrown through a goal during a throw-in from out of bounds does not score a point.

OFFICIALS: It will be well to have two officials. One should keep the score, have general supervision of the game, and referee on one half of the court; the second one should keep the time and referee on the second half of the court. If but one official can be used, a timekeeper and a scorekeeper should be appointed in addition.

TEACHING SUGGESTIONS

1. When it is only possible to use six players on a team, use a center, left and right halfback, left and right forward, and goal guard.
2. Use distinguishing colors for the team members.
3. Do not permit bunching, with many players kicking at the ball.

KICK OVER BALL

NUMBER OF PLAYERS: 10-40

SPACE: Playground (lawn); gymnasium

PLAYING AREA: A goal base is placed 20 feet distant from the end players of each team. A finish line 20 feet long is drawn at right angles to and five feet from the head players of the teams.

EQUIPMENT: Soccer ball

FORMATION: Two teams sit on the grass or floor in parallel lines facing each other, feet extended. A distance of one foot should separate the feet of the players. Players extend their arms backward to support their bodies. Two officials are needed, one standing at each end of the two lines of players.

PROCEDURE: By kicking and running, each team tries to outscore the other. An official rolls the ball on the floor between the two rows of feet.

The players of each team try to kick the ball over the heads of their opponents. When this occurs the two end players, one from each team, jump up, run around the goal base (either side) and race back to the finish line. After crossing the line, the two runners sit down at the head of their lines nearest to the finish line, the players in each having moved one space toward the goal base.

Out of Bounds: If the ball goes out of bounds but not over the heads of the opponents, it is secured by the player nearest to it. It is then put in play by the official at the end of the line nearest the player who secured the ball.

Fouls: The following are fouls: (1) Touching the ball with the hands except to protect face; (2) batting the ball with the hands over the heads of the opponents; (3) running before the ball is successfully kicked; and (4) kicking an opponent on any part of the body above the knees. *Penalty:* For each foul committed, 1 point for the opponents.

SCORING: One point is scored for the team whose player succeeds in kicking the ball over the heads of the opponents. One point is scored for the team whose runner first crosses the finish line after encircling the goal base, and 1 point is scored each time an opponent commits a foul.

TEACHING SUGGESTIONS

1. Protect pupils who wear glasses with glass protectors, or do not permit glasses to be worn while playing Kick Over Ball.
2. Have girls wear slacks or jeans.

MASS DECK TENNIS

NUMBER OF PLAYERS: 6-30

SPACE: Playground, gymnasium

PLAYING AREA: Court 18 feet wide by 40 feet long

EQUIPMENT: (1) One deck tennis ring made of pliable rubber or a ring 6 inches in diameter made of ½ inch manila rope; (2) two jumping standards; (3) net placed so that top edge is not less than 5 feet from the ground. As the group numbers increase, the height of the net should be raised to not more than 7 feet 6 inches. Rope may be used if a net is not available.

FORMATION: Players are divided into two teams and are placed on the court as for volleyball.

PROCEDURE: Mass Deck Tennis is played as is deck tennis with many pupils on one side instead of just one or two as in singles or doubles. Service is taken from behind a line 15 feet from the net. Players may not walk or run while holding the ring nor make service feints. The deck tennis ring must be sent *always* with an upward movement. A down stroke is not permitted. It must be returned as soon as received. The ring may not be batted. Either hand may be used in receiving the ring and it must be returned by the hand which caught it.

Rotation: Rotation is the same as that used in volleyball.

SCORING: Volleyball scoring method is used.

TEACHING SUGGESTIONS

1. Use Mass Deck Tennis to practice techniques of deck tennis.
2. Refer to deck tennis rules on page 868.

MASTER OF THE RING

NUMBER OF PLAYERS: 4-20

SPACE: Playground, playroom, gymnasium

PLAYING AREA: A circle drawn to enclose the feet of all the players

FORMATION: Players stand within the circle in a compact group with their arms folded and held close to their bodies.

PROCEDURE: At a given signal each player tries to push his neighbor out of the circle but endeavors to remain inside it himself. If any player unfolds his arms, falls down, or gets both feet outside the circle, he is out of the game.

The player who is finally left alone in the circle is master of the ring and wins the game.

TEACHING SUGGESTIONS

1. Teach players to keep arms folded.
2. Use this game in the classroom when activity must be indoors.

PIG IN THE HOLE

NUMBER OF PLAYERS: 6-20

SPACE: Playground, playroom, gymnasium

EQUIPMENT: (1) For each player a stick about 3 feet long; (2) a ball, small tin can, or other object to be the pig; (3) a depression in the ground somewhat larger than the pig used but not wider than two inches. The pig is placed in this depression.

FORMATION: All the players, with the exception of one, form a circle some 12 feet distant from the pig with six or eight feet between each of the players. Each player makes a shallow hole in front of his feet a little larger than the end of his stick but never more than three inches in diameter. On a processed or wooden floor, chalk may be used to draw small circles.

PROCEDURE: To determine who shall be the first driver all the players place the ends of their sticks under the pig, which is resting in the center depression. They count, "one, two, three." On count "three" in unison they lift the pig into the air. Immediately each player rushes to place the end of his stick in any one of the small holes. The player who fails to secure a hole becomes the driver of the pig.

The purpose of the game is for the driver, using only his stick, to push or knock the pig into the center hole so that it comes to rest in the depression. Circle players try to prevent the driver from doing this. If the driver is successful the game is ended. A new game is started as described above. The circle players, using only their sticks, try to do three things: (1) steal each other's holes by placing their own stick in a vacant hole; (2) keep the pig inside the circle by hitting it with their sticks; and (3) prevent the driver from driving the pig into the center depression by hitting the pig with their own sticks.

The driver may attempt at any time to release himself from being the driver by placing the end of his stick in an unoccupied hole. If the driver is successful in doing this the player left without a hole becomes the new driver. The circle players may advance into the circle to strike or push the pig with their sticks and, at the same time, should protect the hole they left or steal the hole of an unwary neighbor.

TEACHING SUGGESTIONS

1. When the surface is hard, use a somewhat deflated ball.
2. Use in the classroom on days when outdoor play is impossible.

POISON STAKE

NUMBER OF PLAYERS: 8-40

SPACE: Playground, playroom, gymnasium

PLAYING AREA: Place Indian clubs near enough together so that players will have difficulty in stepping or swinging between them.

EQUIPMENT: 5 to 15 Indian clubs or substitutes

FORMATION: Players form a circle outside the clubs by clasping each others' hands.

PROCEDURE: On signal each player tries, by pushing and pulling, to make his neighbors knock over an Indian club and at the same time tries not to do so himself. Players who overturn clubs or who break their grip must leave the game immediately. Clubs are replaced and the circle is re-formed. When enough players are eliminated they may start a new game.

When several circles play simultaneously a time limit is agreed upon. At the conclusion of the playing time persons remaining in the different games join forces and again play until a winner or winners are determined.

TEACHING SUGGESTIONS

1. When a large number are to play, form two or three circles with an equal number of players in each. Provide the same number of Indian clubs for each circle.
2. Substitute blocks of stove wood or paper milk cartons for Indian clubs.

PROGRESSIVE END BALL

NUMBER OF PLAYERS: 10-50

SPACE: Playground, gymnasium, playroom

PLAYING AREA: A court 25 by 50 feet, divided into two equal courts by a line across the center. At each end and four feet inside the court, lines paralleling the end lines are drawn. The two small areas formed are known as end zones. If large groups are to play, the size of the court should be increased, the width of the end zones remaining the same, four feet.

EQUIPMENT: Volleyball or large beanbag

Procedure

The game is played between two teams who try to retire members of the opposing team by hitting them with a fly ball. Players struck by a ball must retire to their end zone, where they continue to play.

FORMATION: All the players of one team, with the exception of one member, take positions in the field on one side of the center line. The odd player goes to his team's end zone, at the far end of the field. Members of the other team take positions on the opposite end of the field and place one member in their end zone. No player may leave his own court.

RULES OF PLAY: To start the game, the ball is tossed up between two opponents at the middle of the court. Each jumper crosses the center line and faces his own team during the jump, then returns to his own playing area. The player who catches the ball throws it and tries to hit a player of the other team. If the player aimed at is hit he goes to the end zone where his team's end man is stationed. Thereafter, that player must remain in the end zone but he continues in the game, trying to hit the opponents in the area directly in front of him. Only a fly ball tags a player, thereby retiring him to the end zone. Only one player at a time may be hit with the ball.

Once the ball touches the floor it is any man's ball so long as the player does not leave his own area while attempting to secure it. The ball may be passed between players, if desired, before being thrown at an opponent. Players may reach over, but not step over, boundary lines in an effort to secure the ball.

When the ball leaves the field of play the nearest player to it runs to secure the ball, throws it to a teammate, and then, and not before, returns to position on the court.

Hits: A player is tagged by two methods: (1) if he catches a ball thrown by an opponent and (2) if he is struck by a ball thrown by an opponent.

Fouls: The fouls are as follows: (1) No player may run while holding the ball. *Penalty:* The ball is given to an opponent. (2) Players may not step over the boundary lines of their court. *Penalty:* The ball is given to an opponent. (3) Players may not be hit on the head though they may be hit on any other part of the body. *Penalty:* The ball is given to an opponent and player is not tagged.

Periods of Play: Any length of playing time may be agreed on.

SCORING: When time is called the team wins which has the smaller number of players in its end zone.

TEACHING SUGGESTIONS

1. If certain players continually pass the ball instead of throwing it at an opponent, discontinue the privilege of passing.
2. Adapt for classroom play if outdoor space is unsuitable.

SCHOOL BOWLING

NUMBER OF PLAYERS: 2-10

SPACE: Bowling surface (hard surface), playground, gymnasium, hallway

PLAYING AREA: Painted pin spots 12 inches apart in a triangle arrangement, as used in an official bowling game.[1] The apex is toward the player (pin Number 1). Number 2 and 3 are in the second line, 4, 5, 6 in the third, 7, 8, 9, 10 in the last. At least 30 feet from the front pin a 3-foot foul line is drawn, the distance from the pins depending on the age and skill of the player.

EQUIPMENT: (1) Cage constructed of 2 by 2-inch wood and half-inch wire mesh (Figure 177) with a mat over the wire to absorb the force and noise of balls and pins. (2) Ten duckpins. Pins with rubber band or

---

[1] See Eight Out, p. 644, for regulation bowling alley dimensions. Figure 41, p. 116, shows a frame for marking pin spots with chalk.

inner tubing around them will be less noisy (Figure 177). Discarded pins can sometimes be secured from local bowling establishments. Home-made pins may be constructed from tapered cylindrical milk containers partly filled with sand (Figure 178). (3) Two or more duckpin balls, ladies' weight, or two-pound 14-inch balls of hard red rubber in size similar to a baseball. (Black rubber balls leave black marks on the floor.) (4) Bowling score sheets.

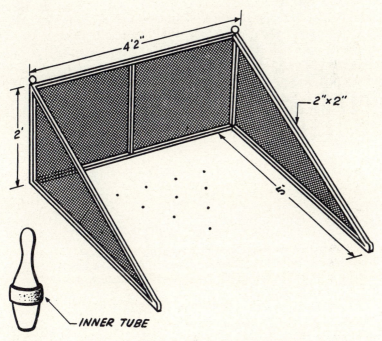

Figure 177.   Cage for School Bowling and Pin Protected by Strip of Rubber

FORMATION: A singles game can be played between two opponents or a doubles game between two sets of partners, or teams with as many as five members may compete. Balls are bowled from behind the foul line, two for each player each turn. Players take turns in setting up pins.

PROCEDURE: The object is to roll the ball toward the pins and knock down as many as possible. A game consists of *frames* corresponding to squares on the score sheet into which the score is written. A bowler bowls twice in each frame unless he makes a strike (knocks down all ten pins)

with the first ball, in which case he does not bowl a second. Official ten-pins rules are followed.[1]

Figure 178.   Homemade Bowling Equipment

SCORING: The score is kept cumulatively on a score sheet marked for ten frames (see page 891). Each pin knocked down counts 1 point. When one ball knocks down all ten pins, that is called a *strike;* when ten pins are knocked down with two balls, it is called a *spare;* when less than ten pins are knocked down, it is called a *break.* When a strike is made, the bowler gets 10 points plus the points made on the next two balls. He therefore does not enter his score until two more balls have been bowled, but instead puts an X in the right-hand corner of the frame. When a spare is made, the bowler adds to the 10 points the number of points he makes on the next ball. He enters a diagonal stroke (representing half of an X) in the corner of the frame and does not add the total until after the next ball is bowled.

---

[1] Rules are found in *The Official Individual Sports Guide with Archery, Bowling, Fencing, Golf, and Riding.* Washington: National Section on Women's Athletics, American Association for Health, Physical Education and Recreation (1201 Sixteenth Street, N.W., Washington 6, D. C.).

NAME	1	2	3	4	5	6	7	8	9	10	Total
John	9	16	32	38	56	70	77	82	87	91	91
Jane	8	13	23	24	30	48	56	60	68	71	71

Bowling Score Sheet

Example of Scoring: On the first frame John made 9, on the second he made 7. The total for the two frames was entered in the second frame. On the third frame he made a strike, so the X was entered in the corner. On the next two balls he made 6. This was added to the 10 points for frame three and the total of 16, plus the previous 16, made 32 to enter in the third frame. In the fourth frame the 6 points were added. On the fifth frame he made a spare and entered the stroke in the corner. On the sixth frame, with the first ball he knocked down 8 pins. These were added to the 10 for the spare, giving him 18 points to add in frame five. On the second ball of frame six he knocked over the other two pins, giving him another spare, for which he entered a stroke in the corner. On the seventh frame he made 4 on the first ball, 3 on the second. The 4 was added to the 10 for his sixth frame, and the 7 points were added for frame seven. On the next three frames he made 5, 5, and 4 which were added each time to make his score for the ten frames 91.

Jane made the following points: first, 8; second, 5; third, a spare; fourth, 1 (on the second ball, so that only 10 counted in the third frame); fifth, 6; sixth, a strike; seventh, 4 on each ball (adding 8 to the strike for frame six); eighth, 4; ninth, 8; tenth, 3; making a total for the ten frames of 71.

If a strike or spare is bowled in the last frame, the two or one extra balls are bowled.

The highest possible score for a game is 300 points.

SEAT TAG

NUMBER OF PLAYERS: 6-40

SPACE: Usual classroom distribution of pupils at their desks

FORMATION: A runner and a tagger are chosen.

PROCEDURE: At any time a runner may prevent himself from being tagged by sitting in a seat with another player. The person with whom he sits becomes the new tagger and the former tagger becomes the runner. If a runner is tagged while running he becomes the tagger and the tagger the runner.

SHUFFLEBOARD

NUMBER OF PLAYERS: 2 or 4

SPACE: Sidewalk, playroom, auditorium, or gymnasium

PLAYING AREA: Court markings may be painted on a surfaced area or an official shuffleboard court may be constructed and marked as in Figure 179. Out of doors the court dimensions should run north and south. The official court for adults is 6 by 52 feet, but a better size for elementary schools is 6 by 44 feet. If the length is reduced the space is taken away from the area between the dead lines, not from the scoring sections. An added space of fifteen feet is needed at each end. One end of the court is called the head, the other the foot.

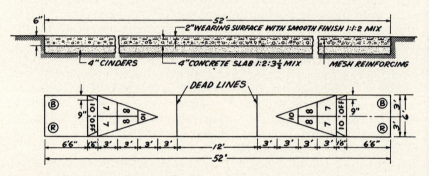

Figure 179.   Construction and Marking of Shuffleboard Court.   Upper: Longitudinal section; no expansion joint to show.   Lower: Court marking; B=black, R=red, when playing doubles.

For concrete surfaces, a high quality black paint made with an oil or varnish base is satisfactory for marking the court. When new cement courts are built, a zinc sulphate wash, consisting of three pounds of crystals to a gallon of water, should be applied and allowed to stand for at least 48 hours before painting. Any crystals that appear should be brushed off before painting lines. Lines used should be three-quarters of an inch wide. All dimensions are measured to line centers.

When wooden flooring is used, floor wax should be sprinkled over the surface before playing games.

EQUIPMENT: (1) Four cues. Cue handles measure from 5 feet to 6 feet 3 inches in length. The handles are round to within a few inches of the lower end, where they broaden into a blade 3 inches wide, curved to fit the disk. (2) Eight disks: 4 painted red, 4 painted black. Disks are circular, made of hard wood, 1 inch thick and 6 inches in diameter.

Procedure

Each player tries, during alternate turns, to push his disks so that they will remain within the scoring area until the end of the round of play. To count for a score, a disk must be inside but not touching any line of the scoring area at the end of the round. A player may move his own disk to a better position by striking it with a second disk, or he may move his opponent's disk to a less favorable position in the same way.

FORMATION: Two players are opponents in a singles game, four players, in opposing teams of two each, play a doubles game.

Determination of Team Colors: When a singles game is played each contestant places a disk in the 10-off area at the head of the court and pushes it toward the farthest dead line with a cue. The player whose disk rests nearer to the dead line has choice of color. For a doubles game, one player of each team pushes a disk for choice of color. Distances are measured from the center of the disk to the center of the dead line.

Singles Game: Both contestants play from the same end of the court, one playing from the right half of the 10-off area, the other from the left half, depending on the color of their disks, red playing first from the right side, then black from the left, and alternating thereafter until all eight disks have been played. When the round is over they walk to the foot of the court and count the scores. Play is resumed from the foot with a black disk leading from the left side.

Doubles Game: Two opponents play side by side at one end of the court, red disk leading off. These two alternate playing their disks until all eight have been played. The score is determined, and the other two players resume the play from the foot of the court, the red disk leading. The partners' scores are added together.

Sequence of Disks: Red disks are always played from the red half of the 10-off area at the head of the court and always from the left half of the 10-off area at the foot of the court. When, during a doubles game, play is to begin at the foot, a red disk is played first, colors alternating thereafter.

RULES OF PLAY: Each contestant places his disks within the correct half of the 10-off area at the head of the court in such a way that his disks do not touch each other or any boundary line. All disks must be played from within these areas. Five points are deducted from a player's score for a violation of this rule. If the played disk touches the side line or lines of the 10-off triangle, the penalty is 10 points off, the offender's disk is removed, and the opponent is credited with any disks that were moved.

No hesitation shots are allowed. The forward motion of the disk must be continuous. A balk occurs when a disk passes over the diagonal or front line of the scoring section without continuous motion. The penalty for a noncontinuous motion is 10 points off and removal of offender's disk; the opponent is credited with the former score of any disk if displaced by the offender's disk.

A player, while propelling his disk, may not step on or over the line of the 10-off area. The penalty is 5 points off his score. A player may stand beside the alley when "sighting" a play on his own or an opponent's disk, but he may not stand on an adjoining court if courts are side by side. The penalty for violation is 5 points off.

Interference: Players may not stand in the way of, nor interfere with, an opponent while the opponent is executing a stroke. A player may not touch live disks at any time. The penalty is 5 points off.

Dead Disks: A disk is dead and must be removed under the following conditions: (1) If it remains on or returns to the court after having struck any object other than a live disk; (2) if it enters a court from an adjoining court; (3) if it stops before crossing the farthest dead line. A disk that stops just beyond a base line must be moved at least eight inches way from the base line in the direction it was traveling.

Round of Play: A round of play is completed when both contestants or pairs of contestants have played all their disks.

Scoring: A disk scores the value of the area in which it finally rests after all eight disks have been shot. The score cannot be determined until the eight plays have been made. A disk originally may be shot to space 8 but if a later disk sends it to 10-off and it remains there at the close of the play, 10-off is the score for that disk. In order to score, a disk must be within the scoring area and not touching any line.

A game consists of 50, 75, or 100 points, as agreed upon by the contestants. A tie is settled by shooting the eight disks twice from each end. The winner of a game is the first one to play in the new game.

Match Play: The winner of two out of three games wins the match. The second game in match play is started by the black at the end of the court where the preceding game was finished.

TEACHING SUGGESTIONS

1. Instruct the players to keep the cue in constant contact with the floor when shooting.
2. Teach the players to hold the cue in one hand.
3. Teach the players to stand facing opposite court, to bend to sight and get ready to shoot, and finally to shoot by taking a long step forward.
4. Watch for foot faults on or over the base line.

SIX-MAN TENNIS

Number of Players: 6-8

Space: Playground, gymnasium

PLAYING AREA: Tennis court

EQUIPMENT: (1) Four tennis rackets, (2) two tennis balls

FORMATION: Four players on the court. The fifth player during the first game watches for and calls out foot faults; the sixth player umpires the game and keeps the score.

PROCEDURE: A regulation tennis doubles game is played. At the end of the game, the server, or Number 1 player, takes over Number 6's duties; Number 6 takes over Number 5's responsibilities; Number 5 enters the court to play in the second game. Number 2 player takes Number 1's position. Rotation takes place at the end of each game. The rules are those for tennis.

SCORING: Tennis scoring is used.

TEACHING SUGGESTIONS

1. Have pupils hand in their calls on foot faults, giving the names of those who made the error, also their scoring results for the game they umpired.
2. Have those umpiring call aloud the score before each service.
3. Have those watching foot faults call aloud the name of offender. Umpire will then change the score if necessary.
4. Use eight players, the two additional ones watching the side lines. Rotation occurs after one game, four players retiring to officials' duties, and the others playing.

SOCCER BALL TAG

NUMBER OF PLAYERS: 6-40

SPACE: Playground, gymnasium

PLAYING AREA: A limited play area such as a circle, the shadow cast by a building, a volleyball court, half a basketball court, or other small unit, the size being dependent upon the number of players.

EQUIPMENT: A soccer ball

FORMATION: One player is chosen to be the tagger. Other players are scattered inside the playing area.

PROCEDURE: No restrictions are made as to how the players move about inside the playing area. The ball must be played by the feet and may not be controlled by the hands except to protect the face. Players try to secure the ball with their feet and to tag any other player with it. At the same time they try not to be tagged. Players may not kick the ball into the air higher than the chest height of players. Each time a player is touched by the ball, no matter how lightly, he becomes the tagger. If a player sees that a ball is going out of bounds he may run outside the playing area and stop it with his feet or hands. If the ball passes out of bounds without being stopped, the nearest person at the point of departure goes after it, returns the ball as rapidly as possible by kicking it or by carrying it to the boundary line. He may dribble the ball in himself without losing a point.

SCORING: Each player starts with 5 points to his credit. Every time a player is tagged with the ball, he has 1 point deducted from his score. Whenever a kicker sends the ball higher than the chests of players 1 point is deducted for each offense. To use the hands, other than to protect the face, causes the loss of 1 point for the offending player. When a player's 5 points are exhausted he is retired from the game. If he is the kicker when the 5th point is lost he remains as kicker in the game until he tags another player. As fouls are made, the offending player calls "One," "Two," "Three," according to the number of points he has had deducted. The player remaining in the game longest wins.

TEACHING SUGGESTIONS

1. Teach the players to approach the other players by dribbling the ball.
2. Do not use too large a playing area.
3. Drill the players in the art of keeping the ball within bounds.

SOCK-A-BALL [1]

NUMBER OF PLAYERS: 22

SPACE: Playground, gymnasium

PLAYING AREA: Softball diamond, with 60-foot base lines, pitcher's plate 43 feet from outside corner of home plate. (Shortened base lines of 40, 45, or 50 feet, with a pitcher's distance of 40 feet, may be used.) A circle 8 feet in diameter, called the pitcher's zone, surrounds the pitcher's plate, the front of the plate being 2 feet from the rear of the circle. A rectangle 4 by 8 feet, directly behind home plate and with the 4-foot front line parallel to and touching the back section of home plate, is the catcher's box.[2] A circle 24 feet in diameter, centered on home plate, is the batter's zone. Batter's and coacher's boxes are the same as in softball.

EQUIPMENT: (1) One or more regulation 12-inch smooth-seamed softballs (for use on diamond with shortened bases, 14-inch softballs); (2) one or more regulation softball bats

---

[1] Invented and copyrighted by Walter L. Scott, Supervisor of Physical Education, Long Beach, and Director of Municipal and School Recreation. Used with author's permission.
[2] This box may be increased in size if it seems desirable.

Procedure

The game is played according to official softball rules, except as modified by the following regulations. A game consists of eleven innings, with eleven players. Teams expert in fielding technique may by mutual consent require 4 outs each inning instead of 3.

FORMATION: Players are divided into two teams of eleven players each: (1) catcher, (2) short fielder, (3) first baseman, (4) second baseman, (5) shortstop, (6) third baseman, (7) left flyer, (8) right flyer, (9) left fielder, (10) center fielder, (11) right fielder. It is recommended that the short fielder play directly behind the pitcher until the pitched ball has left the hand of the pitcher. It is also recommended that the three outfielders play in the deepest zones of the field and that the two flyers play midway between them and the right infielders. Each team elects a captain.

UMPIRE: It is suggested that the umpire not take a position directly behind the pitcher, as the short fielder usually plays there. Since all pitched balls are called strikes there is no need for the umpire to judge each pitched ball.

RULES GOVERNING THE PITCHER: Each team must designate two and only two pitchers, each of whom acts as part-time pitcher in the team's regular line-up. Each pitches only to his own teammates, and acts as a pitcher only when his side is at bat. When in the field they play any two of the eleven fielding positions assigned by their captain. They are known by the positions they play in the field.

When their team is at bat pitchers alternate between pitching and batting. When pitching they are known as Number 1 and Number 2 pitchers. The Number 1 pitcher is the one whose name appears second as a batter in the batting order. They should be listed thus in the batting line-up so that there will be little conflict with their pitching, batting, and baserunning responsibilities.

Number 1 pitcher must go to the pitcher's plate first. He must continue pitching to his own teammates until it is his turn to bat. When he goes to bat, Number 2 pitcher takes the mound until it is his turn to bat, when he is relieved by Number 1 pitcher. They continue to alternate in this manner throughout the game.

Pitcher Relieved of Baserunning: If a pitcher is baserunning when his time comes to pitch, another player of his team must be substituted by the captain to run bases so that the pitcher will be free for pitching.

Ball in Play: After the ball leaves the pitcher's hand it is considered as being in play until (1) delivered again to the pitcher, or (2) declared dead by the umpire.

Pitcher Confined to Pitcher's Zone: A pitcher while on mound duty must stay inside the pitcher's zone until his side is retired at bat. The pitcher may go, without permission, to take his turn at bat or he may get permission from the umpire to leave for any other reason. No penalty can be inflicted should a pitcher, at any time he is in the pitcher's zone, take his position on the pitcher's plate without the ball in his possession. No illegal pitch may be declared for such act.

Pitcher Offering Interference to Player: A pitcher may not intentionally interfere with the play of any fielding team member (1) by touching or catching a thrown ball that is in play, (2) by yelling or blocking, or (3) by making false motions or feints.[1]

Pitcher's Zone Rights:[2] After the ball is dead and in the hands of the pitcher, no fielding player may step on, over, or inside the circular line which designates the pitcher's zone before the ball has left the pitcher's hand for the batter.

Pitcher's Right of Way: After the ball is dead and in the hands of the pitcher, no fielding player may place himself between the pitcher's zone and the batter or home plate before the pitched ball has left the pitcher's hand.

Player Interference with Pitcher: When a pitcher is in the pitcher's zone, no player of the fielding team may, under any circumstance, interfere with the pitcher. They may not (1) yell at him, (2) make false motions or feints, (3) touch him, (4) run into him, (5) hit him with a thrown ball, or (6) interfere with him intentionally or accidentally in any other way.

Illegal Pitching: In all cases where the pitcher makes an illegal pitch (as described in official softball rules) the batter is out, the ball is dead, and the baserunners cannot advance unless otherwise specified in these rules.

Inaccurate Pitching: No balls are called, therefore no walks are allowed, when pitcher fails to throw the ball accurately over home plate When a wild pitch is thrown a strike is called on the pitcher. Umpire judges and declares wild pitches. When uncertain, umpire shall call ball a wild pitch.

Wild Pitch: Any ball thrown too high or wide of home plate which catcher cannot reasonably be expected to catch with ordinary effort without stepping on or over the line which designates the boundaries of the catcher's box is a wild pitch. Following a wild pitch the ball is dead and baserunners cannot advance.

---

[1] Note: Pitcher must clearly make an honest effort to avoid all interference. If there is accidental interference the team at bat cannot be penalized if the incident occurred while the pitcher was within the pitcher's zone. Exception: Pitcher hit by batted ball, or catching a batted ball. See *Fouls.*

[2] Note: If this rule is violated the ball becomes dead immediately, whether thrown or not thrown, unless the batter makes a hit. If the batter hits the ball in such a play he may advance to whatever base he thinks he can reach safely; if he is put out on the play he is allowed to return safe to first base.

Short Pitch: A short pitch is any pitched ball which hits home plate or ground in front of the plate before it is touched by the bat. The ball is dead and baserunners cannot advance.

Stalling Prohibited: A strike is called each time the pitcher delays the game by failing, for a period longer than 10 seconds, to deliver the ball to the batsman. At the beginning of each inning or when any pitcher relieves another, the pitcher may occupy 30 seconds in delivering not more than 3 balls to the catcher, during which time play is suspended.

If pitcher and batter are ready but game is delayed more than 30 seconds because of action of fielders, the batter is allowed a walk to first base.

RULES GOVERNING THE BATTER: The batter may not use more than 30 seconds to take his position.

Safety in Batter's Zone: Special permission must be secured from the umpire for a person associated or identified with the team at bat to walk inside the batter's zone while batter is in the batter's box ready to bat or is actually batting.

Practice Throws: At the beginning of an inning the pitcher may not throw the ball to any member of the fielding team other than the catcher after the umpire gives the call, "Play Ball!"

Passed Ball: A passed ball is a legally delivered ball that could have been held or controlled by the catcher with ordinary effort without the catcher being forced to step on or over the line which designates the boundaries of the catcher's box. Baserunners may advance one base only on a passed ball if they can make it without being put out on the play; therefore, baserunners can score a run from third base if not put out.

Hit or Pitched Ball: A strike is called on a batter when he is hit or touched by a pitched ball. Ball is dead whether struck or not, and baserunners cannot advance. Pitcher puts ball in play with his next pitch.

Bunts: [1] A team is allowed only 1 bunted ball in each inning.

Thrown Bat: A batter may not throw his bat so that it hits any player or so that it lands outside the boundary of the batter's zone. If a player is hit by a thrown bat and it is clearly not the fault of the batter, the latter should not be called out by the umpire.

Short Fielder's Position: The short fielder may not play closer to the batter than the pitcher plays until after the pitched ball has reached the batter.

RULES GOVERNING THE BASERUNNER: A baserunner must be in contact with the base he is entitled to occupy while the pitcher has the ball in his possession and until a legally pitched ball leaves the hand of the pitcher.

---

[1] Bunt, to bat or tap (the ball) lightly within the infield by meeting it with a loosely held bat and no swing.

With bases less than 60 feet apart a baserunner may not lose contact with his base while the pitcher has the ball in his hand and until a legally pitched ball crosses home plate or is hit by the batter.

Under the following conditions base runners may not advance:

1. When pitcher is hit by a batted ball
2. When pitcher makes an illegal pitch
3. When person associated with team at bat walks into batter's zone without permission from umpire
4. When pitcher makes a wild pitch
5. When pitcher makes a short pitch
6. When batter is touched or hit by a pitched ball
7. When second bunt is attempted during any given inning
8. When thrown bat strikes a player or leaves batter's zone
9. When pitcher throws ball to a fielder other than the catcher after the umpire calls, "Play Ball"
10. When person associated with fielding team walks into batter's zone without permission from umpire

STRIKES: All pitched balls are called strikes.

On the Pitcher: Strikes are called on the pitcher in the following situations:

1. When the pitcher delays the game, for a period longer than 10 seconds, by failing to deliver the ball to the batsman
2. When pitcher makes motion to pitch without immediately delivering ball to the batter

On the Batter: Strikes are called on the batter in the following circumstances:

1. When the batter is touched or hit by a pitched ball
2. When pitcher makes a wild pitch

Batter is allowed only 3 pitched balls, unless the third strike results in a foul tip by the batter. The play which follows is governed by regulation softball rules.

WALKS: The batter may walk to first base after the following plays:

1. When fielders interfere with the pitcher while the ball is dead and in pitcher's hand before wind-up is started. Batter to whom pitcher would next throw ball is given a walk to first base
2. When fielding team delays game for more than 30 seconds when pitcher and catcher are ready to play
3. When fielder places himself between pitcher's zone and batter or home plate while ball is dead in the hands of the pitcher and before it is thrown
4. When fielder gets on, over, or inside circular line which designates pitcher's zone before ball leaves pitcher's hand

5. When short fielder plays closer to the batter than the pitcher plays before ball is pitched

6. When catcher moves outside the catcher's box before the ball leaves the pitcher's hand

7. When any person associated or identified with the fielding team, other than the catcher, enters batter's zone. If batter makes a hit he and other baserunners may advance to any bases they think they can make on the play.

DEAD BALL: Under certain circumstances a ball is declared dead and is out of play.

The Pitcher Causes the Ball to be Dead

1. When ball is in the hands of pitcher while he stands in the pitcher's zone

2. When pitcher intentionally interferes with a fielding team member (a) by making false motions or feints; (b) by yelling; (c) by touching or catching a thrown ball that is in play, or (d) by other unsportsmanlike action

3. After a legally pitched ball when all baserunners have been held at their bases by the fielding team and play for that occasion is clearly finished (The pitcher must not handle the ball if he is in doubt for whom a thrown ball is intended.)

4. When pitcher touches or catches a ball thrown by a fielder

5. When pitcher leaves his pitching zone illegally

6. When pitcher touches a batted ball

7. When pitcher throws a wild pitch

8. When pitcher throws a short pitch

9. When pitcher makes an illegal pitch (Batter is out whether batter hits ball into fair or into foul territory.)

10. If pitcher throws a ball to member of fielding team other than catcher after the umpire calls, "Play Ball!"

The Batter Causes the Ball to be Dead

1. When a batter makes a second attempt to bunt during an inning

2. When batter throws bat so that it strikes a player or lands outside the batter's zone

3. When batter is touched or hit by a pitched ball

The Fielder Causes the Ball to be Dead

1. When fielder enters the pitcher's zone before the pitcher delivers the ball

2. When fielder gets between pitcher's zone and batter at home plate before the pitcher delivers the ball

3. When short fielder plays closer to the bat than the pitcher does before pitched ball reaches the batter [1]

OUTS: Several errors made by members of the batting team result in outs for the players making the error. Three outs must be made by each team before an inning is over. Outs occur following these plays:

1. When pitcher touches a batted ball, batter is out, and ball is dead.
2. When pitcher touches or catches a ball thrown by a fielder, batter and all baserunners are out.
3. When pitcher makes an illegal pitch, batter is out whether batter hits ball into fair or into foul territory.
4. When pitcher leaves his mound illegally while on duty, person to whom next pitch would have been made is declared out by the umpire.
5. When pitcher, after umpire calls "Play Ball" at the beginning of the inning, throws ball to member of fielding team other than the catcher, baserunners cannot advance, and batter to whom ball would be next pitched is declared out by the umpire.
6. When pitcher intentionally interferes with play of any fielding team member (a) by making false motions or feints, (b) by yelling, (c) by touching or catching a thrown ball that is in play, or (d) by other unsportsmanlike action, batter and all baserunners are out immediately.
7. When batter fails to take position within 30 seconds when called by umpire, batter is out.
8. When a batter attempts a second bunt during a time at bat, batter is out.
9. When a batter throws the bat so that it hits a player or it lands outside the boundary of the batter's zone, batter is out. If a player is hit by a thrown bat and it is clearly not the fault of the batter, the latter shall not be called out by the umpire.
10. When baserunner, 60-foot base line being used, leaves or fails to keep contact with the base he is entitled to while ball is in hand of pitcher and until legally pitched ball leaves hand of pitcher, he is out.
11. When baserunner, playing on less than 60-foot base lines, leaves or fails to keep contact with his base while ball is in hand of pitcher and before a legally pitched ball crosses the home plate or is hit by the batter, he is out.
12. When person associated with or identified with the team at bat, without permission from the umpire, walks inside the batter's zone while batter is in batter's box ready to bat or actually batting, the batter to whom ball would be next pitched is declared out by the umpire.

---

[1] NOTE: If batter hits the ball he may advance to whatever base he thinks he can reach safely. If batter is put out on the play, he is allowed to return to his first base.

Fouls: Members of the batting team or the fielding team may make errors which carry with them certain penalties. These fouls and penalties are as follows:

1. When pitcher yells at a fielder, touches or blocks a fielder, makes a false motion or feint toward fielder, or touches or catches a ball thrown by a fielder, the ball is dead, all baserunners are declared out by the umpire, and no score can be made.

2. When pitcher makes a wild pitch, the ball is dead and baserunners cannot advance.

3. When pitcher leaves pitcher's box while on mound duty, ball is dead and teammate to whom he would send the next ball is declared out by the umpire.

4. When pitcher throws a ball to a member of fielding team other than the catcher after the umpire calls, "Play ball!" ball is dead, baserunners cannot advance, and batter to whom pitcher would normally have thrown ball is declared to be out.

5. When short fielder plays closer to the batter than the pitcher until after the pitched ball has reached the batter, batter walks to first base.

6. When a fielder interferes with the pitcher while the latter is in the pitcher's zone, the penalty is as follows: While ball is dead and in hands of pitcher, a fielder may not step on, over, or inside of pitcher's zone before ball leaves the pitcher's hands for the batter. If a violation occurs while ball is dead in pitcher's hands, and before the wind-up is started, the batter to whom pitcher would have thrown the next ball is given a walk. If violation occurs after the wind-up or delivery is started but before the play is completed and ball is again returned to the pitcher, the batter is entitled to a walk if he does not make a safe hit. If the batter makes a safe hit on the play, he and all base runners are allowed to reach the bases safely for which they were running when violation occurred and they may run beyond these bases at their own risk.

7. When fielder delays game more than 30 seconds when batter and pitcher are in position ready to play, batter is allowed a walk to first base.

8. When fielder gets between pitcher's zone and batter or home plate before pitched ball leaves hand of pitcher, batter walks to first base.

9. When a batter attempts a second bunt during an inning. The ball is dead, baserunners cannot advance, and the batter is out.

10. When batter throws his bat so that it strikes a player or lands outside the boundary of the batter's zone, the ball is dead, baserunners cannot advance, and the batter is declared out.

11. When catcher moves out of his box previous to time ball leaves the pitcher's hand, the batter is allowed a walk to first base.

12. When any person associated with or identified with the team at bat, without permission from the umpire, walks inside the batter's zone while batter is in batter's box ready to bat or is actually batting, the ball is dead, the baserunner cannot advance, and the batter is out.

13. When any person associated with or identified with the fielding team, without permission from the umpire, enters the batter's zone, the ball is dead, baserunners may not advance, and the batter is given a walk unless he makes a hit. If hit is made batter and other baserunners may advance to any bases they think they can make.

SCORING: Each successful run scores 1 point. The team wins which has the higher score at the end of the playing time.

SPEED BALL

NUMBER OF PLAYERS: 22

SPACE: Playground

PLAYING AREA: Field 40 by 80 yards (Figure 180). If field must be smaller, the end zones remain the same, 6 yards. The shorter lines are the goal lines, the longer lines the side lines. The length of the field should run north and south. The playing area includes all the space between the goal lines and the side lines. Twelve yards from the goal lines short penalty lines are drawn. In a beginning game, play will be aided if a line divides the court lengthwise into two equal parts, all players but the centers and goalkeepers being required to remain in their half of the field.

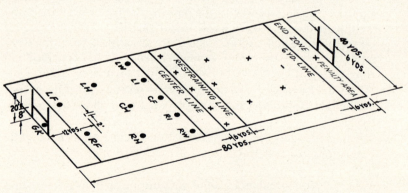

Figure 180.   Field for Speed Ball

EQUIPMENT: (1) Soccer ball; (2) four goal posts 20 feet high at ground level, placed 18 feet apart at each end of the field at the exact center of the goal lines (jumping standards may be used); (3) crossbars 8 feet from the ground; (4) different colored armbands or pinnies to distinguish players and their positions.

Procedure [1]

Speed ball is a combination of soccer and basketball, and uses some of the techniques of both. It is played between two teams who may score either by kicking or passing the ball over the opponents' goal line.

FORMATION: Each team has 11 players: 5 forwards (left and right wing, left and right inner and center forward); 5 backs (left, center, and right halfbacks, left and right fullbacks); and 1 goalkeeper. The forward line of the team having the kickoff is scattered along and behind the center line. Opponents' forward line is scattered along and behind their restraining line. Halfbacks stand midfield behind their forwards and are scattered across the field. Fullbacks stand behind halfbacks. They assist the goalkeepers. The goalkeeper remains near the goal and adjacent area. The goalkeepers have no special privileges as in soccer.

PLAYING PERIOD: The game is played in four quarters of 6 to 8 minutes each, with a 2-minute rest between quarters and a 10-minute rest between halves.

RULES OF PLAY: The captain who wins the toss of a coin has choice of goal to be defended and of taking the kickoff.

The game is started by a kickoff at the center of the field. The center forward of the kicking team takes a place kick. No player of the kicking team may cross the center line until the ball is kicked and no opponent may cross his restraining line until after the ball is kicked. This rule holds good after each kickoff. After each scoring play the team which was scored against takes the kickoff, always at the center of the field.

ADVANCING THE BALL: The ball may be advanced in two ways.

A Ground Ball (one that touches the ground and bounces, rolls, or remains stationary) may be kicked, headed, or bounced off the body, but *it may not be played with the hands*. The use of the body against a ground ball does not convert it into a fly ball. The ball must be kicked by the foot to make it an aerial ball. A bouncing ball may be headed (struck with the side of the head) or volleyed with the hip or shoulder.

An Aerial Ball (one that has been raised into the air directly from a kick) may be caught and passed with the hands or blocked with the body,

---

[1] These rules are briefed. Those desiring fuller information should consult *The Official Soccer-Speedball Guide.* Washington: National Section on Women's Athletics, American Association for Health, Physical Education and Recreation (1201 Sixteenth St., N.W., Washington 6, D. C.).

or it may be knocked to the ground to become a ground ball. It may be kicked or kneed also.

OUT-OF-BOUNDS BALL: When the ball passes over a side line it is put in play by an opponent by a throw-in. The player stands outside the field at the point where the ball went out of bounds and throws the ball with any kind of one-hand or two-hand pass into the field. The ball may be played as an aerial or as a ground ball. All players must be six yards away. No score can result from a throw-in. When it goes over the end line without scoring it is put in play by an opponent from outside the field of play, using either a punt, drop kick, place kick, or pass. Defenders usually punt, attackers or offense players usually pass.

If two opponents kick the ball out of bounds it is put in play with a tossup 1 yard in from the spot where the ball crossed the line. A tossup is also used when the referee is uncertain as to who caused the ball to leave the field of play.

HELD BALL: If the ball is held simultaneously by two opponents the ball is tossed up between them as in basketball.

All opponents must be at least 6 yards away from all free-kick, tossup, or out-of-bounds plays.

CONVERTED GROUND BALL: A ground ball may be converted into an aerial ball by one of the following methods:

1. By placing the instep of the foot under the ball and lifting it into the air so that it may be directed to another player who may catch it.
2. By a kick-up to one's self in which the sole of the foot is placed on the top of the ball and it is rolled rapidly toward one's self until it rolls on top of the instep, when it can be lifted higher by knee action. This motion is similar to the pick-up used by tennis players when retrieving a ball from the ground with the racket.
3. By use of both legs, the ball being held between the ankles. A quick jump is taken from both feet and at the same time the ball is released with an upward twist so that it may be caught by the two hands of the kicker. (This is a dangerous play if other players are near because if they attempt to kick the ball also, the player with the ball will probably lose his balance and may fall.)
4. By permitting an approaching rolling ball to roll onto the instep of the foot and then with an upward action of the knee elevating the ball into the air high enough so that it can be caught by two hands.

FOULS: All infractions of the rules are called fouls and are grouped as individual, team, and disqualifying fouls. They are as follows:

Individual Fouls: (a) Kicking, tripping, charging, pushing, holding, blocking an opponent who does not have the ball; (b) unnecessary roughness, including knocking the ball out of a player's hands; (c) running with the ball; (d) touching a ground ball with the hands; (e) juggling the ball more than once; (f) holding the ball more than 3 seconds on the field; (g) boxing up players, and (h) drop-kicking for a goal while within the penalty area.

Team Fouls: (a) Making an illegal substitution; (b) taking more than 3 time-outs in a game; and (c) having more than 11 players on the field.

Disqualifying Fouls: Rough and dangerous play or continued unsportsmanlike conduct.

Penalties: For an individual foul made outside the player's own penalty area, a free kick is awarded to the opponents. The ball is placed on the ground at the point where the foul occurred and a place kick is taken. If the foul is made within or behind the player's own penalty area, a penalty kick is awarded to the opponents.

For a team foul, the opponent is awarded a penalty kick.

For a disqualifying foul, the player is removed from the game and a free-kick or penalty kick is awarded to the opponents.

The game is started after a double foul by a tossup where the foul occurred.

Penalty Kick: When a penalty kick is awarded to a team, the ball is placed on the penalty mark (12 yards from the goal line) and a drop kick is taken. To be legal the ball must pass between the goal posts and over the crossbar. Only the goalkeeper is allowed to guard the goal until the ball is kicked. All players must be 6 yards away from the kicker and out of the penalty area until the ball has been kicked.

TERMINOLOGY: The following terms are used in speed ball.

Dribble: The use of the inside and outside of the feet and the instep to control and direct the ball (identical to the dribble in soccer)

Drop Kick: A kick made when a player, with or without preliminary steps, drops the ball and kicks it just as the ball touches the ground

Aerial Ball: A ball that has been lifted into the air by a foot; it may be played as in basketball, with the exception of bouncing it

Ground Ball: A ball that is in contact with the ground, as a bouncing, rolling, or stationary ball

Kick-up: The act of converting a ground ball into a fly ball by lifting it (see "Converted Ground Ball" above)

Juggle: Throwing the ball into the air and catching it again to gain better playing position; same player must catch the ball; one juggle is allowed on each play

Place Kick: A kick made when ball is placed on the ground and the kicker, with or without preliminary steps, kicks the stationary ball

Punt: A kick made when the ball is dropped to the instep and the player kicks the ball before it strikes the ground

SCORING: *A drop kick* scores 3 points. A drop kick is scored when a player drop-kicks the ball from outside of a penalty area and it goes between the goal posts *above* the crossbar.

A *field goal* scores 2 points. A field goal is scored when a ground ball is kicked or legally pushed with the body between the goal posts *under* the crossbar.

A *touchdown* scores 2 points. A touchdown is made when a forward pass is completed across the opponents' penalty area by a player outside of the penalty area throwing the ball to a player of his own team who is *behind* the goal line.

A *penalty kick* scores 1 point. The ball must pass between the goal posts and over the crossbar.

TEACHING SUGGESTIONS

1. Keep the game simple in the beginning, adding information about new fouls as the general understanding of the game increases.
2. Use running relays to develop running endurance and quick foot action.
3. Insist that players play their positions.
4. Teach girls to fold their arms over the chest when blocking the ball with the chest.
5. Teach forwards to attack and score goals. Do not permit them to drop behind their own restraining line.
6. Teach the halfbacks that they are the first line of defense and that they seldom enter an end zone.
7. Instruct the fullbacks that they are the second line of defense and must be able to get the ball away from their own goal area.
8. Impress upon the goalkeepers that they are the last line of defense and that they should seldom, if ever, leave their end zone but should stay near their goal while depending on their fullbacks to assist them.

TABLE SHUFFLEBOARD [1]

NUMBER OF PLAYERS: 2-4

SPACE: Playground, playroom, gymnasium, hallway

EQUIPMENT: (1) Table and frame constructed and marked as in Figure 181; (2) eight wooden checkers, four red, four black. The table, 17 by 72 inches, rests on a frame about 2½ feet high. Playing top is of three-ply board, with a ¼ by 1 inch strip to catch the checkers across both ends

---

[1] Suggestions for game found in *The American Home,* XXVII (December, 1941), 23. By permission.

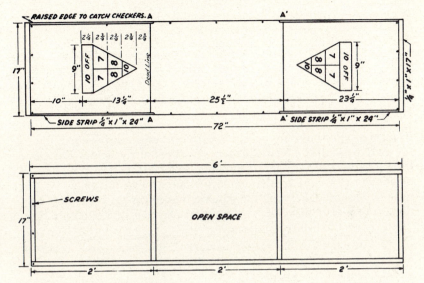

Figure 181. Construction and Marking of Board for Table Shuffleboard. Lower: Wooden frame for table.

and extending along 24 inches from the ends at both sides. It is fastened to the frame with 18 brass screws, 1 foot apart on the sides and 2 at each end. The board is sanded and then the playing diagram is drawn with a ruling pen and India ink. It is varnished with two coats of spar varnish, and then sanded again.

FORMATION: The same formation is used as for shuffleboard, page 892.

PROCEDURE: The general procedure of shuffleboard is followed. Checkers are snapped toward the far end of the board with the fingers. When sliding the checkers, the hand must not pass over the nearest line of the minus-10 area. If checker hits the end strip, it is dead. If checker rests on a black line, the score does not count. If checker lands between dead lines AA and A'A', it is removed from the board before the next play.

SCORING: The scoring is similar to that for official shuffleboard. A game consists of 25 points.

TARGET BALL[1]

NUMBER OF PLAYERS: 12-24

SPACE: Playground, gymnasium, playroom

[1] Adapted from a note contributed by Louie Gratch to the *Journal of Health and Physical Education*, X (February, 1939), 109. By permission.

PLAYING AREA: Court approximately 36 by 60 feet

EQUIPMENT: Volleyball, soccer ball, basketball, or large beanbag

FORMATION: Two teams are formed, from 6 to 12 players on a team. The players are given numbers. Two players of each team are known as the targets. They are distinguished by arm bands or other insignia. Players are placed as for basketball.

PROCEDURE: For boys, the rules for boys' basketball and for girls the rules for girls' basketball govern the general phases of the game. The game is started with a tossup between opposing centers. Players may pass, dribble, or use any tactics to hit the opponents' target with the ball. This target must be hit not higher than the shoulder nor lower than the knee. Target players of a team may throw at a target player of the opposing team if they receive the ball from teammates.

Following a scoring play a member of the team scored against puts ball in play with an out-of-bounds throw at point nearest to position target occupied when scored against.

Two halves or four quarters of playing time are used.

Rotation of Target Player: At the end of each quarter, or halfway between the time allowed for a half, target players in each team are changed.

Fouls: The same fouls as are found in boys' basketball or girls' basketball rules are called by the players themselves or by the referee. The player who fouls is removed from the game until the opposing team scores, or until a member of the opposing team commits a personal foul. The suspended player does not have to report to the official when re-entering the game.

If a target player fouls, a temporary target player is appointed to play until original target player re-enters the game.

SCORING: Two points are scored each time a target player is hit by the ball when thrown by a player, or tagged by the ball when held in the hands of a player.

The team wins that has the highest score at the end of the playing period.

TEACHING SUGGESTIONS

1. Do not use regulation boundary lines if it seems more desirable to use a smaller or larger space.
2. Teach players to seek positions near one or the other opponent targets when they do not have the ball.

TENNIS

NUMBER OF PLAYERS: 2-4

SPACE: Playground, gymnasium

PLAYING AREA: The court dimensions and run-back area are shown in the diagram (Figure 182). The area should be surfaced to the backstops and sidewalls of the fence, with lines painted for permanency. Wire fence should enclose the court or courts. The height of the fence should be from 8 to 12 feet, with the ends placed 18 feet back from the base lines of the court, and with the side fence 10 feet out from the side lines of the court.

EQUIPMENT: (1) Two tennis posts either of wood or iron. Posts with ratchets to control the tension and height of the net will prove valuable. Wooden posts should be 4 inches by 4 inches by 6 feet 6 inches set 2 feet 6 inches into the ground. See diagram.[1] (2) Tennis net. Nets vary as to strength and wearability. A high-grade net will more than pay for the greater expense. The top of the net at the center of court should be 3 feet and at the posts 3 feet 6 inches from the ground. (3) Tennis balls in quantity. (4) Six or more tennis rackets. Rackets should be purchased for instructional purposes. Children should be encouraged to purchase their own rackets for use during periods other than instructional.

Procedure

Tennis is a net game played between two or four players with a tennis ball and rackets on a hard-surfaced court. The ball is put into play with an overhand serve (Figure 183), and must land in a diagonally opposite service court before it can be legally returned. After the service the ball is hit back and forth across the net until it is missed, goes into the net, or hits outside the court lines. One person serves until the game is won.

FORMATION: For a singles game, two players compete, one on each side of the net; for a doubles game, four players take part, two partners on each side of the net.

During a *singles* game the play is confined within the base lines of the court and the two inner side lines which extend to the base lines.

During a *doubles* game the entire area of the court is used.

The choice of court or the right to be first server is usually determined by spinning a racket. If the rough side of stringing (the side the knots are tied on, next to the stem of the handle) comes up, the player who chose "rough" has choice of court or service.

---

[1] See also diagram for erecting tether ball posts, page 100.

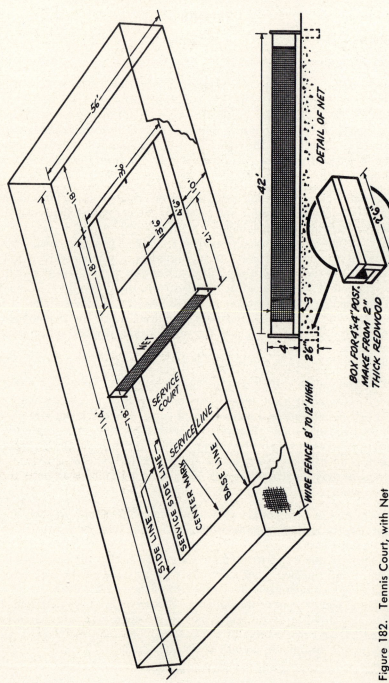

Figure 182. Tennis Court, with Net
Elevation and Ground Box Detail

Figure 183. Tennis
Serve

TERMINOLOGY: The following terms are used in a game of tennis: (1) The player is known as the *server* who, at the beginning of a game and following each point made or lost during the game, serves or strikes the ball to the opponent in a diagonally opposite service court. The act of putting the ball in play by the server is known as the *service*. (2) The player to whom the ball is directed by the server is known as the *receiver*. (3) The act of sending the ball back and forth over the net following a successful service stroke is known as *rallying* the ball. (4) The winning of six games with a two-game lead over the opponents is called a *set*.

SERVER: The server begins a game always from the right-hand court, alternating thereafter, following each point made or lost, until the finish of the game. When serving, the server must stand outside the base line, but within the area between the right-hand limits or left-hand limits of the service line and the imaginary continuation of the center line which divides the service courts. When serving, the server *must not step on or over the base line until after the ball has been struck*. If he does so a foot fault is called. If the server commits two foot faults in succession, the opponent is given the point even if the server has earned it, and the server moves to the opposite serving position. When striking the ball the server must not touch the ball with any part of his body, or anything worn or carried, except his tennis racket. The server must delay service until his opponent is ready to receive the ball.

Faults: If the server swings at the ball and misses it, if the ball goes out of bounds or into the net, or if the server steps on or over the line too soon, a fault is called and the server is permitted one more serve. (See Figure 184.) A second trial is allowed with each service if the first service is a fault. If the receiver fails to return a ball legally, the server receives one point.

Let Ball: If the server hits a let ball on his first service, which means that the ball hits the top of the net and falls over into the opponent's service court, he is allowed two more serves. If he strikes a let ball on his second serve, he is permitted one more trial.

Figure 184. Correct Procedure in Serving for Tennis, Volleyball, or Paddle Tennis. Begin service with feet back of base line. During act of serving, both feet must be back of base line until ball is struck.

RECEIVER: The person to whom the ball is served is known as the receiver. He may play any position within his court or outside of it in his endeavor to return the served ball following its bounce. He should stand so that he is always behind the ball. Following the service play, the receiver and the server may take balls from a bounce or on the fly. A served ball hitting the receiver before it hits the ground scores a point for the server.

BALL IN PLAY: To be a legal service the ball must go over the net and must strike the ground in the service court diagonally opposite to the server. If the first ball served is a fault the ball is re-served. If the second ball is a fault, the server must change to the other side of the court and the point is credited to the receiver. A served ball that hits in the diagonally opposite service court is a good ball. A served ball that contacts a line of the service court is a good ball.

RALLY: When the ball is hit back and forth by the players following the service it is known as the rally. The ball may be taken on the fly or from a bounce. If it is taken on the fly the term volley is used. Either player may leave the boundaries of the court in his effort to control the ball. During the rally a let ball is good. A ball that hits a player, however, causes that player to lose the point. A fair return of a ball is made when a player strikes it over the net within the boundary lines of the opposite court. A ball which strikes a line during the rally is a good ball.

Doubles Game: In a doubles game players of the two teams alternate in service. Each team decides which partner is to serve first, and thereafter the partners alternate in serving throughout the set.

At the beginning of a new set, either partner of the pair who received in the last game of the previous set may serve. The same privilege is given to their opponents in the second game of the new set.

The first server of a new set, when served to, is not required to receive service in the right-hand court. He may elect either side of the court at the beginning of the set but must continue on the side chosen until the end of that set.

SCORING: Each ball missed scores 1 point for the opponent. The first point is 15, the second 30, the third 40, and the fourth 50, or game. The score is called deuce if each player has three points. One player must then win two points in succession to win. The first point after deuce is called "advantage" for server or receiver, as the case may be. The server calls the score before each service, giving his score first. "Love" means nothing, and "nothing" is often substituted for the older term. For example, "love-all" means neither side has a point; "love-thirty" means the server has nothing, the receiver has 2 points; "thirty-all" means that both sides have 2 points.

re 185.   Tennis Doubles Game

The first player to win six games wins the set, except that if both players have five games it is a deuce set and one player must win two games in succession to win the set.

A match consists of two out of three sets.

TEACHING SUGGESTIONS

1. Give great attention to foot faults. (See Figures 184 and 186.) The habit of faulting, once formed, is disastrous for future participation in tournament play.
2. Organize individuals or squads for practice against handball backstop, wall of school building, garage wall, or tennis practice backstop. On the wall draw a line the height of the net (three feet) from the ground

Figure 186.   Common Foot Faults in Tennis, Paddle Tennis, and Volley-ball.   If your foot just touches the base line, it is a foot fault. Stepping on the base line is a foot fault.

Swinging a foot over the base line and into the court before ball is hit is a foot fault. A jump is a foot fault. Maintain contact with the ground with at least one foot.

and two feet above it draw a second line. Have players endeavor to send all balls between the two lines. Establish a service line the official distance from the wall.

3. When there are many to play, and but one court, eliminate the use of deuce play for determining game and set outcomes. One point will decide the winner when both sides reach 40.

4. Teach players to call their own game and concede points or take replays if necessary.

5. Teach the following tennis strokes: (a) forehand, (b) backhand, and (c) serve.

6. Analyze the elements of each stroke for the pupils.

TETHER BALL

NUMBER OF PLAYERS: 2

SPACE: Playground, gymnasium, playroom

PLAYING AREA: Level area free from all obstruction for a distance of 9 feet from the center. Circle with 3-foot radius; foul line 20 feet long drawn through the center of the circle. A pole in the center of the circle; [1] a mark is made on the pole 6 feet from the ground. Two service areas 6 feet from pole on each side.

EQUIPMENT: (1) Official tether ball or homemade substitute; (2) 2 wooden paddles or tennis rackets

FORMATION: Players stand on opposite sides of the circle. Players may not step into the area within the three-foot circle next to the poles. This is known as the neutral area.

PROCEDURE: The object of the game is to wind the cord in the desired direction by hitting the ball with the paddle. The opponent tries to hit the approaching ball in the opposite direction. Both players try to wind the ball completely around the pole above the 6-foot winding mark. To begin the game, the server stands on the service area, and hits the ball.

Fouls: Fouls include the following: (1) Allowing cord to wind around paddle or hands; (2) touching pole with hands or paddle; (3) reaching into opponent's court. The penalty for a foul is a free hit for the opponent. The free hit is taken like the serve, with the exception that the cord may not be unwound more than one half turn before the hit is taken.

SCORING: In order to score, a player must strike and, if necessary, continue to strike the ball until the cord is wound around the pole in such a manner that the ball rests against the pole above the painted mark. The point is awarded to the player in whose direction it is wound, regardless

---

[1] See Chapter V, p. 100.

of which player completed the winding. After a point is scored, the serve goes to the loser.

A game can be set to any number of points or played within a time limit.

TEACHING SUGGESTIONS

1. If pupils wish to hit the ball with their hands, substitute a larger ball now manufactured specifically for such games. See Volley Tether Ball, page 588.
2. Teach players to serve and hit the ball with a rhythmical motion, using their leg, back, and shoulder muscles, as well as their arm muscles.

VOLLEY TENNIS [1]

NUMBER OF PLAYERS: 6-20

SPACE: Playground, gymnasium, playroom

PLAYING AREA: Maximum size 30 by 60 feet. Size may be adjusted to meet the needs of the players.

EQUIPMENT: (1) Two tennis posts, volleyball posts, jumping standards, or chairs; (2) tennis net or rope stretched tightly between posts, the top of the net being 3 feet 6 inches at the posts and 3 feet at the center of the court; (3) volleyball or large rubber ball.

FORMATION: Six players are on each team for match games. Teams form circle or hollow square within the boundary of their own court. More than six players may be used on each team for instruction or practice.

PROCEDURE: Each team tries to send the ball into the opposite court over the net, as in volleyball.

Service: The server stands with both feet outside the rear boundary of his court. The server may serve underhand or overhand. The server tries to strike the ball causing it to bounce within his own court in such a position that the player occupying the center front of the court, next to the net, will be able to bat the ball over the net following its bounce; this player may use one or both hands. No other player may assist the server. The served ball must not bounce over the net unassisted. It must not touch the net in its flight.

Rally: Following the service, the ball may bounce once inside the opponents' court before being returned, or may be batted back over the net without being allowed to bounce. During the rally the ball may bounce and go over the net unassisted. The ball may be played with one or both hands by any player, with the exception of the server who, when

---

[1] Game developed by R. F. McLeod, Director of North Park Recreation Area, San Diego, California, and included by his permission.

serving, may use only one hand to bat the ball. A ball that strikes a player with a direct and not a rolling contact, and then bounces off, may be continued in play as though that player had used his hands against the ball. No player may contact the ball twice in succession. More than one player may strike the ball at the same time. A ball that during the rally is struck into the net may be re-batted into the net to gain speed and distance providing the player does not touch the net. The ball may not be held or pushed. A ball during the rally may be bounced and, thereafter, go over the net with its own momentum.

Fouls: The following are fouls in volley tennis: (1) The ball during service bounces over the net by itself without being assisted by the server's teammate occupying the front net position. (2) The served ball touches the net. Let balls [1] and net balls are not re-served. (3) The ball touches the ground outside a court. (4) The ball is touched twice in succession by one player. (5) The ball is caught or held, juggled, or the hand contacting the ball follows along with the ball. (6) The ball bounces more than once inside a court before being sent over the net. (7) The ball is kicked or is bunted with the knee, accidentally or intentionally. (8) Any part of a player's body extends over the net during a play.

Immediately after a foul the ball is declared dead. If the *serving side* committed the foul, that side loses the ball. If the foul is committed by the *receiving side*, the serving side is given 1 point for each foul committed.

Rotation of Players: Rotation occurs whenever a team wins the right to serve. Rotation is clockwise.

Scoring: When the serving side sends a legally served or returned ball that the receiving side fails to return into the serving side's court, the serving side makes 1 point. The server continues his play.

When the serving side fails to serve correctly or fails to return the ball during the rally, the serving side loses the ball, a change of service occurs and the opponents then have their opportunity to try to make points. No points are awarded when the serve is changed.

The team wins which first makes 15 points. When the teams tie with 14 points each the referee calls, "Game Point." Thereafter, in order to win, a team must make 2 points in succession. After 8 points are scored, teams should change courts.

TEACHING SUGGESTIONS

1. Stretch the net tightly at the four corners to permit successful play of the ball against the surface of the net.
2. Allow experienced players only one service attempt, but permit beginning players two trials at service.
3. Use volley tennis in the sixth grade as a lead-up to volleyball.

---

[1] For description of let ball, see Tennis, page 914.

Relays

AROUND THE CIRCLE RELAY

NUMBER OF PLAYERS: 10-40

SPACE: Playground, playroom, gymnasium

PLAYING AREA: Two circles formed by players

EQUIPMENT: For each team a ball, beanbag, knotted towel, or stuffed leather ball casing. Objects should be the same size and weight for each team.

FORMATION: An even number of players form a double circle and stand facing each other. Members of each circle then number off by twos. Number 1's in each circle form one team and Number 2's a second team. Captains are chosen. They face each other and each holds a ball.

PROCEDURE: On a signal, a ball is thrown forward and back in a zigzag manner between Number 1 players until it reaches the Number 1 captain. Number 2 players do likewise. A player who misses the ball must get it and return to his position before throwing it. Game continues until one team's captain receives the ball, and that team wins.

VARIATIONS: Game may be varied in the following ways: (1) Having balls thrown around circles a designated number of times before winner is determined; (2) using more than one ball for each team; (3) having players reverse direction of ball after it has been once around; (4) having players bounce ball back and forth.

TEACHING SUGGESTIONS

1. Increase the distance between players as skill improves.
2. Use this type of formation to practice various types of passes in a small space.

BANG 'EM DOWN SHUFFLEBOARD RELAY

NUMBER OF PLAYERS: 6-40

SPACE: Wide sidewalk, cemented area, gymnasium, playroom

PLAYING AREA: Set up Indian clubs in clusters of six, on 1-foot triangles, for as many teams as are needed. Twenty feet distant from the Indian clubs the teams are lined up.

EQUIPMENT: For each team (1) six Indian clubs; (2) four shuffleboard disks; (3) one shuffleboard cue, with a handle. Balls may be substituted for cues and disks.

Disks and cues may be homemade in the following manner. Take 10-inch squares of hard wood 1 inch thick. Eight-inch disks are cut, starting across the grain of the wood. The crescents that remain will make part of the cue. Opposite the crescent's opening (the grain should run crosswise and not parallel to the pushing surface of the cue) a handle is attached at a 45-degree angle. Handles may be made of yellow or white pine 1 inch square and 5 feet long. Broom handles are often used. The disks, in sets of four, are painted different colors.

FORMATION: Players are divided into teams of equal numbers. Each relay team faces its own Indian clubs. The last member of each team is sent down to the Indian club area. His duty is to set up the clubs.

PROCEDURE: At the signal, each Number 1 player pushes his four disks in succession, trying to knock over as many pins as possible. As soon as all the pins are down or the last disk has been sent, the player runs to the pins, picks up the disks as rapidly as possible, and carries them back for Number 2 to use, thereafter going to the rear of his relay line. Play continues as long as desired.

Fouls: The following plays are fouls: (1) striking the disk instead of pushing it; (2) stepping over the starting line while pushing. One point is taken from the player's score as a penalty.

SCORING: A point is gained for each pin knocked down. Play may be for total points made by each team at the end of a definite number of games. A game is finished when all persons have pushed the four disks. Play may be to see which team will first reach a designated number of points, in which case the game becomes a relay and the play is continuous.

TEACHING SUGGESTIONS

1. Appoint a scorekeeper and have a blackboard which all the players can watch, or use large sheets of manila paper on which to keep the score.
2. Use standard equipment if possible, since it will serve in the official shuffleboard game as well.

CRAB RELAY

NUMBER OF PLAYERS: 6-40

SPACE: Playground (lawn), gymnasium, playroom, auditorium

PLAYING AREA: As many 3-foot circles (or bases) as there are teams to play, placed in a parallel line and five feet apart. A line 10 to 15 feet distant from and paralleling the row of circles should be drawn.

FORMATION: Players are divided into teams of equal number, not more than six players to a team. They stand in file formation. Number one of each team steps over the starting line and, with his back to his circle and while facing his teammates, drops to his hands and feet with his heels contacting the starting line, and the front of his body upwards, crab-fashion.

PROCEDURE: On a signal, each Number 1 player runs backward to reach his circle. On entering his circle, contestant stands and runs back, touching off the Number 2 player, who is in position with heels touching the starting line. Number 1 goes to the rear of his file. Game continues until all the players of one team have run, and that team is the winner.

VARIATION: Number the players in each team and have Number 1's run first, record a point for the winner, and then signal Number 2's to run. The team wins that has the most points.

TEACHING SUGGESTIONS

1. Build up strength in the abdominal wall muscles with this relay.
2. Use the school lawn for relay races.

HOP HOLD RELAY

NUMBER OF PLAYERS: 6-40

SPACE: Playground, gymnasium, playroom, auditorium

PLAYING AREA: Two parallel lines, not more than fifteen feet apart, length depending on number of players

FORMATION: Players are divided into teams, not more than six to a team, and stand in file formation behind one of the parallel lines.

PROCEDURE: On signal, the first player in each file, holding one foot by the hand, hops forward until he crosses the farther line. He changes to the other foot, grasps it, and hops back across the starting line to tag the second player in his team. Players may change feet once on the way down and once on the way back. As soon as second player is tagged, he hops across and back, tagging off the third player. Game continues until all players in one team have run, and that team wins.

VARIATION: Team members may be numbered from front to rear. As soon as Number 1's have made the run, points are recorded for first, second, and third places, and then Number 2's are given the signal to start. The team wins that has most points (one for each first, second, or third places) after all have run.

TEACHING SUGGESTIONS

1. Do not have too great a distance between lines.
2. Teach pupils that if a foot slips out of a player's hand he must grasp it again before he can continuing his hopping.

HUMAN HURDLE RELAY

NUMBER OF PLAYERS: 10-40

SPACE: Playground, gymnasium, auditorium

FORMATION: Divide players into two equal teams and number players in each team. Members of each team sit in a circle, facing outward, legs extended forward and close together, with about two feet of space between each player.

PROCEDURE: On a signal, Number 1 of each team stands and runs around the circle clockwise, jumping over the legs as he goes. When he reaches his own place, he tags off Number 2 player, who runs in the opposite direction around the circle. Each player, as his turn comes, goes in the opposite direction from his predecessor. Last player raises his right arm in the air as he seats himself after the run, and the team wins whose last player is first to do this.

VARIATIONS: Each team may wait until Number 1's complete the run, when a point is scored for the winner. Then, on signal, Number 2's run. Team with highest score after all players have run is the winner. Or as soon as Number 1 has jumped over the feet of Number 2, the latter immediately stands and follows Number 1; Number 3 follows 2, and so on until all have run. Team wins whose last player is first to sit down with his arm raised in the air.

TEACHING SUGGESTIONS

1. Insist that players be seated before next runner rises.
2. Teach players to keep legs together and fully extended.

LAME DOG RELAY

NUMBER OF PLAYERS: 6-40

SPACE: Playground (lawn), gymnasium, playroom

PLAYING AREA: Two lines 15 feet apart

FORMATION: Teams with no more than six members are formed; they stand in file formation behind one of the lines.

PROCEDURE: On a signal, Number 1 player of each team drops forward so that his body is supported by his hands and feet. Lifting one foot off the floor he races in lame-dog position across the restraining line. The first Number 1 player to cross the line wins a point for his team. He must have the supporting foot across the line to score. On a second signal, Number 2 player runs, and game continues until all have run, when the team with most points wins.

TEACHING SUGGESTIONS

1. Have players established at the finish line to help judge the first to cross.
2. Use this relay to help develop leg muscles and general body flexibility and co-ordination.

LEAPFROG RELAY

NUMBER OF PLAYERS: 10-40

SPACE: Playground, hallway, auditorium, playroom

FORMATION: Players, divided into teams of equal numbers, stand in file formation. Enough space is left between players so that each can reach his hands easily to the hips of the player in front.

PROCEDURE: Number 1 of each file bends over by supporting his hands on his knees and ducks his head. Number 2, placing his hands on Number 1's back, jumps over him and immediately bends forward. Number 3 follows, jumping over the backs of Numbers 1 and 2 and then bending forward.

As soon as Number 1 is the end man he jumps forward over all the backs and then steps to one side. Number 2 follows and steps aside. Play continues until one team has no more players to be jumped over, and that team wins.

VARIATIONS: Leapfrog relay may be varied as follows: (1) Players crawl under the spread legs of teammates, the end man in each file beginning the crawl. When end man reaches the head he stands and signals the next man to start. (2) The end man runs forward, weaving in and out while passing players. When he reaches the front he remains there. Under both variations, the team wins whose Number 1 player is first back in his original position.

TEACHING SUGGESTIONS

1. Teach players to keep heads ducked until leap has been made.
2. Teach jumpers to place hands between shoulders of persons over whom they are jumping.
3. Point out the importance of jumping from both feet, instead of pushing the supporting person.

OBSTACLE RELAY

NUMBER OF PLAYERS: 6-40

SPACE: Playground, gymnasium

PLAYING AREA: Two parallel lines 20 feet or more apart, or stationary apparatus or equipment to determine the length of the race

EQUIPMENT: Automobile tires or hoops, horizontal rings, skip ropes, Indian clubs, bean bags, or other objects, depending on stunt chosen

FORMATION: Players are divided into teams with not more than six players to a team. Each team, in file formation, stands behind the starting line.

PROCEDURE: The procedure is the same as for a simple running relay, except that each runner must perform a chosen activity during the race before tagging off the next runner. Before the game begins the activity is decided upon. It might be one of the following: perform a forward roll or somersault; hop on one foot for ten hops; run around a chair; climb through an automobile tire casing; swing forward and back on rings for five swings; climb through rungs of a ladder; run in and out between Indian clubs; or carry a beanbag on the head throughout the race without using the hands. Game continues until all players of one team have run and that team wins.

VARIATION: Number 1 players may compete against each other, then Number 2's, and so forth. The team wins that has the highest number of first-place winners.

TEACHING SUGGESTIONS

1. Have the performer count aloud where hopping and rope skipping are used.
2. If an object is dropped, have the runner retrieve it and return to the place where the object was dropped before continuing his race.
3. Encourage the players to think up obstacles or stunts themselves.

ROCKING RELAY

NUMBER OF PLAYERS: 4-40

SPACE: Playground, auditorium, playroom

PLAYING AREA: Two restraining lines three to five feet apart

FORMATION: Teams with not more than six players to a team are organized. Each team is divided into two sections whose members are placed on opposite sides of the restraining lines, facing each other, in file formation.

PROCEDURE: On a signal, Number 1 players facing the line step forward on their left foot and rock forward onto the toes of the left foot. At the same time they swing the right foot behind the left foot and reach as far forward beyond the toes of the left foot as they can. The rocking motion is repeated with the right foot, the left foot being swung behind the right foot. The weight is carried forward onto the toes of the rear foot each time a step is taken. An advance of only a few inches can be made with each step. If contestant steps forward to prevent a fall the foot must be replaced on spot formerly occupied.

Reaching the opposite line the contestant tags off the second member of his team, who moves back in the same manner. Play is continued until all members of one team have covered the distance, and that team is the winner.

If played by individuals rather than teams the individual wins who first crosses the farther restraining line.

RUN AND PASS RELAY

NUMBER OF PLAYERS: 6-40

SPACE: Playground, gymnasium, playroom

PLAYING AREA: Two restraining lines are drawn 15 feet apart, with cross lines 1 foot long drawn at each end of the restraining lines. The length of the lines will depend on the number of players assigned to the teams. If there are enough players for four or six teams, draw more restraining lines.

EQUIPMENT: For each team a ball, beanbag, or stuffed leather ball casing

FORMATION: Two teams stand facing each other, members of each team toeing their own restraining line, head and end players touching the cross lines, head players holding the ball.

PROCEDURE: On signal, each head player runs forward, behind and around the opposite team and hands or throws the ball to the end player of his own team. The ball is then passed up the line of players to the top player. All players are required to hand or throw the ball to the next higher player. The runner remains at the end of his line, all others moving up one place. As top and end players receive the ball they must have one foot contacting the cross line of their restraining line. If a throw is missed or ball fails to reach the end man, he must secure it, return to his position, and, with foot touching the cross line, pass the ball up his line.

Pause after the end man receives a ball and record first, second, and third winner. After all have run tally the results. Or have members of teams run consecutively without pause, in which case the game is over as soon as all players of one team have run, and that team wins.

TOSS, CATCH, AND PASS RELAY

NUMBER OF PLAYERS: 6-40

SPACE: Classroom

PLAYING AREA: A restraining line marked in front of each aisle two feet from the wall

EQUIPMENT: For each team, a beanbag, ball, knotted towel, or stuffed leather ball casing

FORMATION: Even rows of seated teams. Captain, in the front seat of each row, holds a ball.

PROCEDURE: On a signal, all team members stand in their right-hand aisle and face forward. At the same time captains run forward, stand behind their restraining line with both feet and throw the ball to first players in their teams. As the first player catches the ball, he throws it back to his captain and sits down. The captain throws to the second player. He returns the ball and sits down. Game continues until last player in the row returns the ball to the captain. The captain runs to the rear of the room calling as he runs, "Stand up and face rear!" All players in his team do so. When the captain reaches the rear of the room he faces the rear wall and passes the ball over his head to the next player. He sits down in the rear seat, all other players moving one seat forward. Game continues until each player has served as captain. Two methods of scoring are possible: (1) determine relative position of each team as the new captain receives the ball, or (2) have action continuous until all members of one team have served as captains, and that team is declared the winner.

TEACHING SUGGESTIONS

1. Impress on all players that when seated the feet must be kept out of the aisles.
2. Instruct players to make fast throws.
3. Have one player throw twice but not consecutively, if the number playing is uneven.

WALKING RELAY

NUMBER OF PLAYERS: 4-40

SPACE: Playground, gymnasium, auditorium

PLAYING AREA: Two lines 15 to 20 feet apart paralleling each other

FORMATION: Players are divided into two or more teams with not more than six to a team. The leader of each team toes the starting line, and the other members line up behind him.

PROCEDURE: On a signal, first man in each team walks as rapidly as possible to the farther line. The heel of the advancing foot *must be* on the ground *before* the toes of the rear foot leave the ground. As soon as the first player is completely across the line, the second man of his team starts across. This continues until one team has all its members on the farther side of the field, and that team wins. If desired, Number 1 players of each team may compete against each other, Number 2 players, etc., and the team with the highest number of first places wins.

TEACHING SUGGESTIONS

1. Instruct the players to use their shoulders and arms to help the forward movement of the walker.
2. Watch that heels and toes are on the ground simultaneously during a portion of each step.

WHEELBARROW RELAY

NUMBER OF PLAYERS: 4-40

SPACE: Playground (lawn), gymnasium, playroom

PLAYING AREA: Two restraining lines 10 feet apart, length of lines depending on number of teams

FORMATION: Divide players into equal teams and teams into couples, as far as possible of equal size and strength. The first person in each couple (the wheelbarrow) walks on his hands, knees stiff, legs extended, and back straight. His partner grasps his feet.

PROCEDURE: On a signal, the first couple of each team, starting from behind the restraining line, walk forward and cross the farther line. When *both* have crossed the line, they exchange positions and walk back to the starting line. When *both* have crossed, they tag the second couple, which is in position to start. The game continues until all members of one team have completed the run, and that team is the winner. Both members of the couple must cross the line before game is over.

VARIATION: First couple in each team may compete, the winner gaining a point for his team. Second couples are then given a signal to start. Team wins that has most points.

TEACHING SUGGESTIONS

1. Instruct the players holding the feet not to push the "wheelbarrow" too strenuously or the "wheel" may collapse.
2. Increase the distance between restraining lines as arm strength is gained.

Rhythmical Activities

BADGER GAVOTTE [1]

Decca Record No. 25062 ("Trilby")
Ford Record No. 110
Pioneer Record No. 3010

FORMATION: Partners in open dance position, side by side, inside hands joined

DESCRIPTION: The step in the first part is a walking step, a smooth, gliding movement, the ball of the foot touching the floor first, and the heel last. In the second part the two-step is used.

Badger Gavotte

---

[1] *"Good Morning": After a Sleep of Twenty-five Years Old Fashioned Dancing is Being Revived by Mr. and Mrs. Henry Ford.* Dearborn, Mich.: Dearborn Publishing Co., 1926. By permission of Estate of Henry Ford.

Part I

Measures 1-2. All walk forward four steps, beginning with the outside foot (boy's left and girl's right); facing partner, hands joined, waist high, all chassé or slide four steps in the same direction.

Measures 3-4. They turn and repeat in opposite direction, beginning with outside foot.

Part II

Measures 5-8. In social dance position, all take eight slow two-steps, starting with boy's left foot, girl's right.

Both patterns are repeated from the beginning until the music ends.

BUFFALO GLIDE [1]

Music: Any 2/4 rhythm minstrel type of dance
Decca Record No. 91706 ("Swinging at the Hoedown"—fast tempo)
Decca Record No. DLA 1423 ("Tuxedo"—slow tempo)

FORMATION: Couples in social dance position

DESCRIPTION: This dance is typically American and should be done with a great deal of stamping and flourish. Several steps are used. (1) Step draw, step stamp: Boy steps to the left (girl uses opposite foot); draws right foot up to left and changes weight; steps left again; brings right foot up to left and stamps on right. (2) Cakewalk: The walking step is done in an exaggerated manner, with the knees brought high and ankles limber. (3) Two-step or polka (see p. 208). (4) Rocking pivot turn: In social dance position couples turn in place by placing right insteps against each other. Boy steps back on left foot while girl steps forward on right, then boy steps forward on right while girl steps back on left, in a rocking movement, turning clockwise.

Measures 1-2. Boy steps left (girl right), draws right foot up and changes weight; steps left again, brings right foot up and stamps on right ("step, draw, step, stamp").

Measures 3-4. They repeat 1-2, beginning with right, stamping left (girl beginning left, stamping right).

Measures 5-6. Boy steps left, draws right foot up to left and stamps on right ("step, stamp"); repeats, starting right, stamping left ("step, stamp"). (Girl does the same, using opposite foot.)

Measures 7-8. Boy moves partner to his right until their right shoulders are in line. He moves forward, left foot, she backward, right foot, with four exaggerated steps—cakewalk or strut.

Measures 9-14. In social dance position, partners do six two-steps or polka steps.

Measures 15-16. Partners do four pivot (rocking pivot turn) steps in place.

CALIFORNIA SCHOTTISCHE [2]

Music: Any good old-fashioned schottische

FORMATION: Couples in varsovienne position, facing counterclockwise around the room

DESCRIPTION: Herb Greggerson of the Texas "Blue Bonnets" suggests we call this form of the schottische the California schottische since

[1] *Folk Dances from Near and Far*, Volume III. Berkeley, Calif.: Folk Dance Federation of California, 1947. By permission.
[2] *Folk Dances from Near and Far*, Volume II. Berkeley, Calif.: Folk Dance Federation of California, 1946. By permission.

Spanish soldiers learned it in California during the Gold Rush and took it to New Mexico. It is sometimes called the military schottische. It is a smooth dance with none of the usual schottische steps and step-hops, and the variations do not necessarily follow in a certain order. Other steps besides the two given here are danced in New Mexico and Texas.

I

Measure 1. Both start left, point left toe forward (count "one, two"); point left toe to left side ("three, four").

Measure 2. Both step on left back of right ("one"); step sideward right on right ("two"); close left to right ("three"); hold ("four").

Measures 3-4. Partners repeat action of Measures 1-2, starting right.

Measures 5-8. Partners repeat Measures 1-4.

II

Measure 1. Partners walk forward left (count "one, two"); right ("three, four").

Measure 2. They half turn in place to right with three steps and hold, backing around so as to end facing clockwise. Boy now has his partner on his left, hands still held.

Measure 3. Both walk backward (counterclockwise), right, left.

Measure 4. They half turn in place to left with three steps and hold, backing around so as to end facing counterclockwise. Boy now has his partner on his right again.

Measures 5-8. Measures 1-4 of Figure II are repeated.

Both figures are repeated as many times as desired.

FIREMAN'S DANCE [1]

Decca Record No. 18221, Album A275 (with calls)
Methodist Record No. 107 (without calls)

FORMATION: Sets of four couples in two lines facing, forming a long column according to diagram.

(head couples)	G-1	B-1		G-3	B-3	(foot couples)	SET I
	B-2	G-2		B-4	G-4		
(head couples)	G-1	B-1		G-3	B-3	(foot couples)	SET II
	B-2	G-2		B-4	G-4		

[1] *Folk Dances from Near and Far*, Volume I. Berkeley, Calif.: Folk Dance Federation of California, 1945. By permission.

DESCRIPTION: This is a traditional American longways dance.

A

Measures 1-8. Head girl and head boy (G-1, B-2) move back a step and chassé (slide) down the outside of their respective lines to the foot and return the same way. At the same time foot boy and girl (B-3, G-4) join hands and chassé between the lines to the head and return.

Measures 1-8. The movement is repeated with head couple going down the inside of the lines, foot couple on the outside of the lines.

B

Measures 1-8. Couples 1 and 2 execute a Ladies Chain, while couples 3 and 4 execute a Right and Left.

Couples 1 and 2 face each other; girls advance, giving each other right hands in passing, and give left hand to opposite boy. Boy, with girl's left hand in his left, puts his right arm around her waist and takes her right hand in his right. In this back-hand promenade position, they wheel about (to the left) in place to face opposite couple. They repeat until each is back in his own place.

Couples 3 and 4 advance toward each other, girls passing between opposite couple. Each couple then takes back-hand promenade position (as above), and wheel about in place, boy backing around, so that couples have changed places and boys still have own partners on their right sides. They repeat until couples are back in places.

C. "FIRE, FIRE"

Measures 1-8. The dancers in each line join hands and walk four steps forward to the opposite line and back four steps. They walk forward again four steps, drop hands and the two lines pass through each other (girls between opposite couple). Each line now faces a new line of couples (from another set) and the whole dance is repeated. When a line reaches either end of the room and is facing no other line, it turns around (girls on right of partner) and waits for a repetition of the dance to bring a new line facing them.

FOR HE'S A JOLLY GOOD FELLOW

(A Mixer)

Music: *New Music Horizons*, Fifth Book, Accompaniments and Interpretation, page 165.[1]

FORMATION: Triple circle, facing counterclockwise, one boy between two girls.

---

[1] Edited by Osbourne McConathy and Others. Copyrighted 1949. Silver Burdett Co. Sacramento: California State Department of Education (edition in preparation).

Line 1. For she's a jolly young lady.
    2. And she's a jolly young lady.
    3. And he's a jolly good fellow.
    4. Which nobody can deny
    5. Which nobody can deny
        Which nobody can deny
    6. For we are jolly good fellows
        Yes, we are jolly good fellows
    7. Yes, we are jolly good fellows
    8. Which nobody can deny.

DESCRIPTION: Boys sing lines 1-2, girls sing line 3, all sing the remainder.

Line 1. Boy bows to girl on his right and girl makes a curtsy.

Line 2. Boy bows to girl on his left, and she makes a curtsy.

Lines 3-4. Members of each line join hands, forming a circle of three. Circles turn clockwise and finish with girls dropping each other's hands and all forming a large single circle, players facing in.

Line 5. Girls take three steps toward center and point toe; girls walk backward and bring feet together.

Line 6. Boys repeat above action.

Line 7-8. Boy turns girl on right once around, hooking right elbows. Boy turns girl on left once around, hooking left elbows. Finish in single circle.

Lines 5-8 repeated. All join hands and advance toward center and retreat. Forward and back again. All drop back into line formation, boy between two girls. Boys move forward to new set while girls face forward ready for the advancing player.

Entire dance is repeated.

GENTS TO THE CENTER [1]

Music: Any square dance music; "Captain Jinks," page 692 (grade 6), "Arkansas Traveler"
Imperial Album FD-8.

FORMATION: Four couples form a square

DESCRIPTION: The calls for this dance describe the movements:

1. All gents to center with right-hand cross,
    Ha! da di diddle a dum
    Form a star with left hand back
    Take your partner as you go round.

Chorus: Gents swing out, and ladies swing in
Hold your "holts" and circle again,
Break the swing and promenade
Promenade with a waltzing swing.

2. All gents to the center with right-hand cross,
Ha! da diddle do dum
Form a star with left hand back
Skip your partner and take the next.

Chorus repeated.

3. All gents to the center and form a ring
And when you have formed, go balance and swing
And when you have swung, remember your call,
Swing the next lady and run away all.

Chorus repeated.

4. Up and down the railroad track
Half a swing around
Back to the center with the same old swing
And swing four hands round and swing four hands
around.

Chorus repeated.

GOOD NIGHT, LADIES

(A Mixer)

Music: See page 606.

FORMATION: Triple circle, with each boy facing two girls or vice versa. Boys face counterclockwise. Girls stand slightly apart and back from the boys. Girls face clockwise.

DESCRIPTION: During the singing of the verse the following action takes place:

Line 1. Boy shakes hands with girl on his right.

Line 2. Boy shakes hands with girl on his left.

Line 3. He bows to both as they curtsy to him.

Line 4. Boy passes between girls and joins two girls of the set ahead of him. As boys move forward girls face counterclockwise.

Lines 1-3. On the chorus boy links elbows with new partners and they skip counterclockwise for first three lines of chorus.

Line 4. All stop skipping and boy nods a greeting to each girl as he swings them in front of him.

The entire pattern is repeated.

HELLO—GOODBYE [1]

(A Mixer)

Music: Any music in 4/4 time may be used. "Glow Worm" or "Yankee Doodle" are recommended.

FORMATION: Partners in a double circle facing counterclockwise, boys on the inside.

DESCRIPTION: The music should be played slowly at first and the tempo increased as participants learn the figure. It adds greatly to the fun if participants do each figure simultaneously. The tendency is for some to go faster than the music or the crowd.

Measure 1.   Partners march forward together four steps.

Measure 2.   Partners face and march backward away from each other four steps.

Measure 3.   Each faces diagonally left forward, points finger at the person opposite (boy is thus pointing to girl of couple ahead), marches four steps forward to this new partner, and grasps other's outstretched hands.

Measure 4.   Boy turns new partner with a four-step turn.

Pattern is repeated as long as desired. There is no pause in the music between the turning and the marching.

HONEY, YOU CAN'T LOVE ONE

Arranged by Anna Hermitage

---

[1] Suggested by Dr. Bernice Moss, former Director of Health, Physical Education and Recreation, State of Utah.

Verse 2.   Honey, you can't love two,
            Honey, you can't love two,
            You can't love two, and still be true,
            Oh! Honey, you can't love two.
Succeeding Verses:
            Three—and still love me
            Four—and love any more
            Five—and come out alive
            Six—and not be in a fix
            Seven—and still get to Heaven
            Eight—and pass the pearly gate
            Nine—and love 'em all the time
            Ten—'cause you can't have all the men.

FORMATION: Large single circle, facing counterclockwise. A leisurely strolling walk is used.

DESCRIPTION

Verse 1.   All promenade alone.

Verse 2.   All take partners and promenade.

Verse 3.   All form into threes, link arms, and promenade

Verses 4, 5, etc.   All promenade in fours, fives, and so on, with arms linked. Extra players who cannot join a line stand in the center.

LITTLE MAN IN A FIX

Victor Record No. 20449

FORMATION: Two couples dancing together form a set. Boys hook left elbows, which means they will face in opposite directions. Their partners stand beside them. Each boy places his right arm around his partner's waist; girl places her left hand on her partner's right shoulder and her right hand on her hip.

DESCRIPTION:

Measures 1-8.   In above position, members of each set run forward in a circle, using small steps. Girls may have to lean backward if tempo becomes too fast.

Measures 1-8 repeated.   Without pausing in their run, lines of players begin to spread apart until boys have left hands joined and at the same time have partner's left hand in their right. Simultaneously girls increase their speed and run under the boys' joined hands, then turning left toward their partners, they face each other. They extend their right hands, joining them above the boys' joined left hands and run until the finish of the 8th measure.

Little Man in a Fix

Arranged by Anna Hermitage

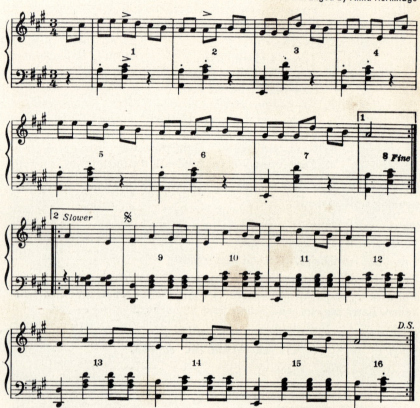

Measures 9-10. Boy takes opposite girl's left hand in his right and, standing side by side, they dance the Tyroler waltz step, which is as follows: Beginning with his left foot, and girl with her right foot, they balance away from each other (3 counts) and toward each other (3 counts).

Measures 11-12. The Tyroler waltz step is repeated.

Measures 13-16. In social dancing position, couples perform four waltz steps, turning.

Measures 9-16 repeated. Players may waltz continuously if desired.

At the end of the figure, each couple seeks a new couple with whom to repeat the pattern. If there is an odd number of couples, one will be unable to find another to dance with, so that with each repetition there will be one "little man in a fix" who dances alone with his partner. There is no pause in the music as new lines of four are organized.

POLSTER DANCE

(Jewish Wedding Dance)

Music: Slow waltz

FORMATION: An even number of dancers join hands in a single circle. One person, holding a pillow, is in the center.

DESCRIPTION: This game has been used since the beginning of the nineteenth century. It is a good "mixer." Circle players waltz forward continuously, counterclockwise. Center player dances alone, making faces and imitating selected dancers. When he so desires, he selects the girl of his choice by placing the pillow on the floor in front of her and kneels on it. The person selected has to kneel rapidly, or the pillow-holder may withdraw it and seek another partner. Those who, because of slowness, kneel on the bare floor, have to remain kneeling there until the end of the dance.

If chosen partner succeeds in kneeling on the pillow, she arises and waltzes together with the center player inside the circle. After a short time boy joins circle of dancers and girl, using the pillow, selects a new partner.

VARIATIONS: (1) Have partners continue dancing in the center, with girl handing the pillow to a new boy in the circle. He then seeks a partner. (2) When there are extra men, try giving each a pillow.

LA RASPA [1]

(New Mexican)

Music: Mela C. Sedillo, *Mexican and New Mexican Folk Dances* [2] Methodist Record No. 106

FORMATION: Couples, facing in opposite directions, left shoulder to left shoulder, boy's left hand in girl's right hand in front of her chest, boy's right hand in girl's left, in front of boy's chest.

DESCRIPTION: This is a popular Spanish Colonial dance of New Mexico, danced as a ballroom dance in Santa Fe and other cities.

I

Measure 1. Both slide right forward and left backward (count "one"); slide left forward and right backward ("two").

Measure 2. Both slide right forward and left backward ("one"); hold ("two").

---

[1] *Folk Dances from Near and Far*, Volume II. Berkeley, Calif.: Folk Dance Federation of California, 1946. By permission.
[2] Albuquerque: University of New Mexico, 1939 (2d ed., 1946). A slightly different version of the dance, with words and music, is found in *Music Everywhere*, A Singing School series. Sacramento: California State Department of Education, 1945. Book of Accompaniments, p. 229.

Measures 3-4. Measures 1-2 are repeated, sliding left foot forward first.

Measures 5-8. Keeping hands joined, each turns toward partner and faces in the opposite direction, right shoulder to right shoulder, and they repeat Measures 1-4.

Measures 9-16. Measures 1-8 are repeated.

II

Measures 1-4. With right elbows hooked, left hands held high, partners turn with eight running steps (two to a measure).

Measures 5-8. Reversing direction, with left elbows linked, partners turn with eight running steps, clapping hands on eighth measure.

Measures 9-12. Reversing direction again, partners repeat the running steps. It is characteristic of this step to continue running without pause on changes of direction.

SCHOTTISCHE FOR FOUR

Music: Any good schottische. See Schottische, p. 704; "Barn Dance," *Let Music Ring.*[1]
Decca Record No. 25062

FORMATION: Double circle facing counterclockwise. Boys on the inside. Each two couples form a set. Partners join inside hands. Front couple of each set reach back and take the ouside hands of the rear couple.

DESCRIPTION: All, starting with the outside foot, run forward three steps (3 counts); on the fourth count each hops on the outside foot. They repeat, starting with the inside foot.

During the four step hops, head couple of each set, *retaining* the hands of rear couple, let go of partners' hands, turn outward and move to the rear of their set where they join hands again. Runs are repeated, with the former rear couple the leader of its set.

Pattern is repeated as often as desired. This is an excellent dance to introduce the schottische step.

SCHOTTISCHE FOR THREE

Music: Any good schottische
Victor Record No. 260001

FORMATION: Groups of three facing counterclockwise. Each boy has two girls immediately behind him who are his partners. Or a girl may be the leader with two boys behind her. The boy folds his arms and the girls

---

[1] *Let Music Ring!* A Singing School. Sacramento: California State Department of Education, 1951. Teacher's Book, p. 67.

place their hands on the shoulders of the boy in front of them. The dance uses the schottische step and step hops.

DESCRIPTION: The schottische pattern is as follows: Step forward with the right foot ("one"); bring the left foot to the rear of the right, transfer weight ("two"); step forward on the right ("three"); hop on the right foot and at the same time swing the left foot forward ("four"). This step takes one measure.

I

All take two schottische steps forward and four step hops, and repeat. On the first step hop of the repetition, the leader claps his hands and holds them out to the side. The girl immediately behind the leader moves to the right side; the second girl moves to the left side. They join hands with the leader and during the last two step hops turn once under the leader's arms.

II

All take two schottische steps forward and four step hops and repeat. On the first step hop of the repetition, still holding hands, the girl on the right passes on the outside of the girl on the left who is passing in front of the leader; they take each other's positions. The leader, on the last two step hops, turns under his right arm. At this time the girls turn once in place. Three are now facing in the opposite direction.

III

All repeat Figure II and return to the line of direction.

IV

All take two schottische steps and four step hops forward. During the first two step hops girls, hands still joined with boy's, cross and stand shoulder to shoulder facing the boy; they take the last two step hops moving backward while the boy moves forward.

Continuing above position, all take two schottische steps in the line of direction (the boy moving forward, the girls backward). During the four step hops, the girls surround the boy and turn once under his arms. They are now back in starting position.

V

The boy folds his arms and takes two schottische steps (one backward and one forward). At the same time the girls join hands and with one schottische step cross in front of the boy, exchanging positions. Turning and joining left hands they return to position during one schottische step.

All clap hands once, place hands on each other's shoulders, forming a small circle, and take four step hops to the right, turning half a circle so that they will be facing away from the line of direction.

The above is repeated, with the boy and the girls returning to the line of direction position. All drop hands, and as music starts again, the boy passes in front of the girls. They drop behind, place their hands on his shoulders, and the entire dance is repeated.

SOLDIER'S JOY

Arranged by Anna Hermitage

Decca Record No. 18214 (without calls)
Victor Record No. 20592 and 36403 from Album C-036
Black and White Record No. 6000

FORMATION: Double circle, each circle alternating boys and girls. Girl stands to right of boy, every two couples facing.

DESCRIPTION: Call is given before music for new figure is to begin.

Measures 1-4. "ALL FORWARD AND BACK." Couples, joining inside hands, walk toward opposite couple four steps and back four steps.

Measures 5-8. "TURN THE OPPOSITE." Taking waltz position with opposite girl, each boy turns her, using pivot step; that is, revolving on one foot with no transfer of weight.

Measures 1-4. "ALL BALANCE." Partners face and join right hands. Each executes a step-swing: Step on left foot and swing right foot up and across left; step on right foot and swing left up and across right. Repeat.

Measures 5-8. "ALL SWING PARTNERS." Taking waltz position, boys turn partner in place, using buzz step: One foot remaining in place while the other foot pushes him around.

Measures 9-16. "LADIES CHAIN." Girls advance and give right hand to opposite girl; they give left hand to opposite boy, who turns the girl in place. Girls return, giving right hands to each other, left hands to partners, who turn them in place.

Measures 9-16. "FORWARD AND BACK." Joining inside hand with partner, couples walk forward four steps and back four steps. They turn slightly and greet each other as last step is taken.

Measures 1-8. "FORWARD AND PASS THROUGH." Partners advance, pass through advancing couple (boys should be on the outside), and meet a new couple.

Figures are repeated as often as desired. The following call may be used to end the dance: "FORWARD AND BACK, BALANCE PARTNERS, PROMENADE TO SEATS." Partners face each other, take three short steps backward and pause; then take three steps forward and pause; join hands waist high and turn around once. Then each boy walks with the girl to her seat.

TO TUR [1]
(Danish)

Imperial Record No. 1038

FORMATION: Single circle, with hands joined. Girl stands at right of partner.

DESCRIPTION
INTRODUCTION
Measures 1-8. All walk clockwise 16 steps.

Measures 1-8 repeated. All turn and walk counterclockwise 16 steps.

I

Measure 9. Partners face each other and take social dancing position. They move forward toward center of circle as follows: boy steps forward on left foot (count "one"), brings right foot up to left (count "and"), steps forward again on left foot (count "two"), pauses ("and"). Girl uses opposite foot, starting right.

---

[1] Pronounced "Toe-Toor," meaning two dance.

To Tur

Arranged by Anna Hermitage

Measure 10. Partners take two walking steps forward, continuing in same direction. Boy steps left, right; girl steps right, left.

Measures 11-12. Repeat 9 and 10, moving backward to starting position. Boy steps right back, close left, right back and pause ("one, and, two, and"); and two walking steps. Girl uses opposite foot.

Measures 13-16. Partners do four polka steps, turning clockwise while circle moves counterclockwise.

Measures 9-16 repeated. Figure is repeated.

II

Measures 1-8. Partners, facing, give right hands to each other. Using a walking step or polka, they swing into Grand Right and Left. Girls move to right, boys to left, the girl taking the second boy by the left hand, third boy by the right, and so on around the circle.

Figures I and II are repeated as many times as desired. If there is a player without a partner, he or she can join in the Grand Right and Left in an effort to find a partner.

VALETA WALTZ

Decca Record No. 25060
Imperial Record No. 1045

FORMATION: Couples stand side by side, girl on right, inside hands joined.
(In second figure, social dancing position is used.)

DESCRIPTION

I

Measures 1-2.   Starting with outside foot (boy's left, girl's right), couples waltz forward two steps.

Measures 3-4.   Facing partner and changing hands (boy's left holding girl's right), couples execute two draw steps, continuing in same direction.
    Draw step (boy's part): Facing partner, he steps in line of direction with left foot, rotates right leg so that toes, while touching floor, point directly away from body, then pulls heel toward left foot.

Measures 5-8.   Measures 1-4 are repeated, moving in the opposite direction, boy starting with right foot, girl with left.

II

Measures 1-2.   Starting with left foot, couple takes two waltz steps, turning.

Measures 3-4.   Couples take two draw steps. Boy, stepping with left, draws right foot to left; girl, stepping with right, draws left foot to right; and each looks over the shoulders at right and left foot.

Measures 5-8.   All take four waltz steps, turning.
Figure II is repeated.
Dance is repeated from the beginning.

ADDITIONAL RHYTHMICAL ACTIVITIES
IN CALIFORNIA STATE SERIES MUSIC TEXTBOOKS

Let Music Ring! Edited by Peter W. Dykema, Gladys Pitcher, and
    Lillian Vandevere. A Singing School series (copyrighted, 1949, by
    C. C. Birchard & Co.). Sacramento: California State Department of
    Education (edition in preparation).
        Students' edition and teacher's book (with accompaniments). Page references
    are to the latter book.

Music of Many Lands and Peoples. Edited by Osbourne McConathy John W. Beattie, and Russell V. Morgan. The Music Hour series (copyrighted, 1932, by Silver, Burdett & Co.). Sacramento: California State Department of Education, 1942.[1]

Music Highways and Byways. Edited by Osbourne McConathy, John W. Beattie, and Russell V. Morgan. The Music Hour series (copyrighted, 1936, by Silver Burdett Co.). Sacramento: California State Department of Education, 1942.[1]

We Sing. Edited by Theresa Armitage, Peter W. Dykema, and Gladys Pitcher. A Singing School series (copyrighted, 1940, 1942, by C. C. Birchard & Co.). Sacramento: California State Department of Education, 1942.[1]

Students' edition, teacher's manual, and book of accompaniments. Page reference is to the latter book.

SELECTED REFERENCES ON RHYTHMS [3]

Burchenal, Elizabeth. *Folk Dances of Germany.* New York: G. Schirmer, Inc., 1938.

Twenty-nine dances are described. Except for a few couple dances (*kleine bunte Tänze,* as they are sometimes called) commonly known and danced throughout most of Germany, the dances are, in the main, the characteristic "bunte Tänze," group dances for four couples in quadrille formation.

---

[1] Former series (adoption period July 1, 1942 to July 1, 1950).
[2] Also found in *Folk Dances from Near and Far.* Volume I. Berkeley, California: Folk Dance Federation of California, 1945. Page 22.
[3] Consult the bibliography and listing of phonograph records in the appendixes.

Folk Dances from Near and Far. Berkeley, California: Folk Dance Federation of California, Volume I, 1945, Volume II, 1946, Volume III, 1947, Volume IV, 1948.

An excellent collection of dances and some music, with a large glossary and bibliography.

Folk Festival Handbook. Prepared by Evening Folk Festival Association, Philadelphia 5, Bulletin Bldg.

Book contains old and new songs and dances helpful for leaders in the presentation of community folk festivals.

Glass, Henry. "Social Dancing for Junior High Schools," *The Journal of Health and Physical Education*, XVI (March, 1945), 130-31, 148.

Discusses procedures used when social dancing was introduced as a functional part of California junior high school program. Student responsibilities, class organization, desirable types of music, and teaching procedures receive attention.

Rogers, Julia Anne. *Parties and Programs for Parents' Days*. New York: National Recreation Association, 1939.

Contains suggestions for parties, banquets, community center programs.

Stunts

A warm-up period or short run before instruction begins will insure less muscular strain. Materials of previous grades should be reviewed before stunts at this age level are taught.

Clown programs can be easily worked out by putting together in sequence many of the previously learned stunts with those for this grade.[1] Help in such programs can be found in McClow's *Tumbling Illustrated*.[1]

ARM LOCK WRESTLE

SPACE: Playground, gymnasium

FORMATION: Two contestants sit on ground back to back. Each locks his right arm inside opponent's left arm. Legs are spread.

PROCEDURE: As a signal is given, each tries to pull opponent over the side so that left arm or shoulder touches the ground. Match consists of five trials. Three successful tries determine the winner.

---

[1] L. L. McClow, *Tumbling Illustrated*. New York: A. S. Barnes & Co., 1931. Pp. 167-77.

Figure 187. Hand Knee
Shoulder Stand

BACK TO BACK AND OVER

SPACE: Playground, gymnasium

EQUIPMENT: Mat if in gymnasium or on hard surface

FORMATION: Two performers stand back to back, hands above head.

PROCEDURE: Number 1 grasps partner's hands from inside, bends forward and rolls partner over his back and brings him to standing position. Both will be facing each other. Number 1 should be careful not to pull on Number 2's arms during the roll.[1]

BICYCLING

SPACE: Playground (grassy), gymnasium

EQUIPMENT: Mat if on hard surface

PROCEDURE: Performer lies on his back with legs high over hips. He holds hips up by placing elbows on the ground and hands under hips. He makes slow, complete bicycling movements with the legs, increasing speed as long as he can maintain the upright shoulder stand position.

---

[1] *Ibid.*, p. 72.

BOUNCING BALL

SPACE: Playground, gymnasium

PROCEDURE: Performer stoops with feet apart, knees straight, hips high, arms at shoulder width, with hands on the ground. He travels forward in this position by a series of short upward springs from feet and hands simultaneously.

CHEST STAND

SPACE: Playground, gymnasium

FORMATION: Two performers take positions, Number 1 on hands and knees with hands directly under shoulders and knees directly under hips. His head is erect and back is flat, never humped. Number 2 places one hand on the arm and the other hand on the thigh of Number 1 so that his chest is resting easily on the back of Number 1. A spotter stands beside the performers.

PROCEDURE: By keeping his head raised and swinging one leg up, Number 2 lifts both legs over his head as he balances on the back of Number 1. If there are clothes to grasp on the arm or leg, it makes the chest stand easier for beginners. The spotter is stationed so as to catch the feet of Number 2 if he forgets to keep his head raised.

HAND KNEE SHOULDER STAND

SPACE: Playground (grassy), gymnasium

EQUIPMENT: Mat if on hard surface

FORMATION: Two performers are chosen. Number 1, or bottom man, must have strong shoulder muscles. He lies on his back with his knees bent. Number 2 stands between his knees and as close to the bent hips of Number 1 as he can. Three spotters should be used while this stunt is being learned, one to stand at each side and one at the head of Number 1.

PROCEDURE: Number 2 places his hands either on the knees or thighs of Number 1, according the length of his arms, as he leans forward to allow his shoulders to be caught by the hands of Number 1. The elbows of 2 must not bend and 1 must be careful to get a comfortable grasp on 2's shoulders. Number 2, by swinging one leg upward, raises both legs over his head. If Number 2 remembers to point his toes and keep his head raised, he will have a perfect balance on the hands and knees of 1 (see Figure 187).

MOUNTAIN CLIMBER

SPACE: Playground, gymnasium

PROCEDURE: Performer squats with right leg extended to the rear and left leg up under the chest. He extends left leg back and brings right leg to chest. This is repeated rapidly a number of times.

PULL-UP [1]

SPACE: Gymnasium, playground

EQUIPMENT: Horizontal bar

PROCEDURE: With outward grasp of hands, more than shoulder width apart, performer pulls chin to bar as many times as possible.

ROCKING CHAIR

SPACE: Gymnasium, playground

FORMATION: Two performers sit on each other's feet, facing each other, with knees bent. Each grasps his partner's arm just above the wrist.

PROCEDURE: Partners rock back and forth, getting as much height as possible and still keeping a controlled movement.

STANDING BROAD JUMPS [2]

SPACE: Playground, gymnasium. A base line is established on the floor or ground.

PROCEDURE: With feet together and toes touching the base line, performer takes two successive forward jumps and in each case lands on both feet. There is no pause between jumps.[1] (This is a double broad jump.) For a triple broad jump, performer takes three successive forward jumps.

STANDING THREE HOPS

SPACE: Playground, gymnasium. A take-off line is established; eight feet beyond this line and every four feet thereafter additional lines are added until the 20-foot mark is reached. Each space made by the lines beginning with the take-off line is numbered.

EQUIPMENT: A 50-foot steel tape or a yardstick

[1] N. P. Neilson and Frederick W. Cozens, *Achievement Scales in Physical Education Activities*. Sacramento: California State Department of Education, 1942, pp. 24, 62.
[2] *Ibid.*, pp. 35-36, 96-97, 104-5.

PROCEDURE: Contestant stands on one foot toeing the take-off line. On a signal, he makes three consecutive hops forward on the same foot without pausing between hops. The free foot must not touch the ground until the jumps are finished. The score for each contestant is determined by the number of the space in which he lands.

THIGH STAND OR FLYING MERCURY [1]

SPACE: Playground (grassy), gymnasium

EQUIPMENT: Mat if on hard surface

FORMATION: Two performers stand one in front of the other, both facing the same way. The top man should be lighter and shorter than the base man. A spotter stands at each side to assist the stunt.

PROCEDURE: The rear man (base), keeping his back and head erect, stoops down, weight on both feet, and places his head between the legs of the front man (top). With his hands on his own thighs to assist him, the base man straightens his legs and at the same time lifts the front man from the ground. The weight of the body must all be lifted from the thighs. Grasping the ankles of the top man, the base man bends his knees and at the same time places the top man's feet on his own thighs just below the hip joint as the base man removes his head from between the legs of the top man. He then slides his hands up to the knees of the top man. The top man, while keeping his knees straight and back arched, leans backward and extends his arms sideward. The bottom man stands with his weight thrown backward to balance the forward pull of the top man.

---

[1] William Ralph La Porte and Al G. Renner, *The Tumbler's Manual*. New York: Prentice-Hall, Inc., 1938. Page 60.

APPENDIXES

Appendix A

STATE LEGAL PROVISIONS IN CALIFORNIA RELATING TO HEALTH EDUCATION, PHYSICAL EDUCATION, AND RECREATION

In the material that follows, section numbers apply to the Education Code unless otherwise designated. References to the Health and Safety Code are so indicated. The Rules and Regulations of the State Board of Education, here included, are designated by the abbreviation, R. & R., and are from Subchapter 1, Chapter 1, Title 5, Education, of the California Administrative Code.

MAINTENANCE OF SAFE AND HEALTHFUL CONDITIONS

Supervision of Play and Other Activities

R. & R. 18. Where playground supervision is not otherwise provided, the principal of each school shall provide for the supervision, by teachers, of the conduct and direction of the play of the pupils of the school or on the school grounds during recesses and other intermissions and before and after school. All athletic or social activities, wherever held, when conducted under the name or auspices of any public school, or of any class or organization thereof, shall be under the direct supervision of the authorities of the district.

R. & R. 24. Principals and teachers shall exercise careful supervision over the moral conditions in their respective schools. Gambling, immorality, profanity, frequenting public pool rooms, the use of tobacco, narcotics and intoxicating liquors on the school grounds, or elsewhere on the part of pupils shall not be tolerated.

Sanitary Premises and Facilities

R. & R. 19. Governing boards of school districts, superintendents, principals, and teachers are responsible for the sanitary, neat and cleanly condition of the school premises.

18009. The governing board of every school district shall provide, as an integral part of each school building, or as part of at least one building of a group of separate buildings, sufficient patent flush water closets for the use of the pupils. In school districts where the water supply is inadequate, chemical water closets may be substituted for patent flush water closets by the board.

This section shall apply to all buildings now existing or to be constructed after its effective date.

R. & R. 72. Adequate separate toilet facilities shall be provided for each sex and all buildings and grounds shall be maintained according to the Regulations of the Board of Health having jurisdiction over the school district.

Health and Safety Code Section 3700. No person conducting, having charge of, or control of, any hotel restaurant, saloon, soda fountain, store, theatre, public hall, public or private school, church, hospital, club, office building, park, playground, lavatory or washroom, barber shop, railroad train, boat, or any other public place, building, room, or conveyance, shall provide or expose for common use, or permit to be so provided or exposed, or allow to be used in common, any cup, glass, or other receptacle used for drinking purposes.

Health and Safety Code Section 3702. No cask, water cooler, or other receptacle shall be used for storing or supplying drinking water to the public or to employees unless it is covered and protected so as to prevent persons from dipping the water therefrom or contaminating the water. All containers shall be provided with a faucet or other suitable device for drawing the water; except that jugs, cans, buckets, and similar receptacles without faucets, or other devices for withdrawing water may be used if the water is protected against contamination and is withdrawn by pouring only.

Health and Safety Code Section 3800. No person conducting, operating, or having charge or control of any hotel, restaurant, factory, store, barber shop, office building, school, public hall, railroad train, railway station, boat, or any other public place, room, or conveyance, shall maintain or keep in or about any such place any towel for common use.

Cafeterias

19301. The governing board of any school district may establish cafeterias in the schools under its jurisdiction whenever in its judgment it is advisable to do so.

19302. The cost of housing and equipping cafeterias is a charge against the funds of the school district. The governing board of a school district may by resolution make the cost of maintenance of the physical plant used in connection with cafeterias, the cost of replacement of equipment, and the cost of water, electricity, gas, coal, wood, fuel oil, and garbage disposal a charge against the funds of the school district.

19303. The governing board may provide for the general supervision of the cafeterias and if provided the cost of the said general supervision may be a charge against the funds of the school district. The governing board may by resolution make the salaries of any or all employees of cafeterias a charge against the funds of the school district.

19304. The food served shall be sold to the patrons of the cafeterias at such a price as will pay the cost of maintaining the cafeterias, exclusive of the costs made a charge against the funds of the school district by this chapter, and items made a charge against the funds of the school district by resolution of the governing board under authority of this chapter.

19305. Money received for the sale of food or for any services performed by the cafeterias may be paid into the county treasury to the credit of the "cafeteria fund" of the particular school district.

19306. The cafeteria fund shall be used only for such expenditures as are necessary for the operation of school cafeterias.

19311. Food shall not be sold at any cafeteria operated by a school district to anyone except pupils and employees of any school district, members of the governing board thereof, and members or employees of the fund or association maintaining the cafeteria; provided, however, that nothing herein contained shall prohibit the use of the cafeteria facilities by any work or harvest camp maintained by or within the district, and by persons entitled to use the school under the Civic Center Act; and provided further, that the governing board of any school district operating a cafeteria may exempt by formal resolution of the board other individuals and organizations from the operation of this section.

19312. Perishable foodstuffs and seasonal commodities needed in the operation of cafeterias may be purchased by the school district in accordance with rules and regulations for such purchase adopted by the governing board of said district notwithstanding any provisions of this code in conflict with such rules and regulations.

RIGHTS AND DUTIES OF PUPILS

Recesses and Noon Intermission

R. & R. 21. No pupil shall be required to remain in school during the intermission at noon, or during any recess. All pupils shall be required to pass out of the school rooms at recess, unless it would occasion an exposure of health.

Prohibition of Fees and Deposits

R. & R. 25. No pupil enrolled in a public elementary or secondary school shall be required to pay any fee, deposit or other charge not specifically authorized by law.

Compliance With Regulations

R. & R. 62. Every pupil must attend school punctually and regularly; conform to the regulations of the school; obey promptly all the directions of his teacher and others in authority; observe good order and propriety of deportment; be diligent in study; respectful to his teacher and others in authority; kind and obliging to schoolmates; and refrain entirely from the use of profane and vulgar language.

Student Organizations

16141. The governing board of any school district may authorize any organization composed entirely of pupils attending the schools of the district to maintain such activities as may be approved by the governing board.

16142. Any group of students may organize a student body association within the public schools with the approval and subject to the control and regulation of the governing board of the school district. Any such organization shall have as its purpose the conduct of activities on behalf of the students approved by the school authorities and not in conflict with the authority and responsibility of the public school officials. Any student body organization may be granted the use of school premises and properties without charge subject to such regulations as may be established by the governing board of the school district.

16143. The governing board of any school district shall provide for the supervision and auditing of all funds raised by any student body or student organization using the name of the school.

The cost of supervision and auditing may constitute a proper charge against the funds of the district.

16144. The funds of any student body organization shall be deposited in a bank approved by the governing board of the school district and shall be expended subject to such procedure as may be established by the student body organization subject to the approval of an employee or official of the school district designated by the governing board.

TRANSPORTATION OF PUPILS TO AND FROM SCHOOL ACTIVITIES

16271. The governing board of any school district may use school busses to transport pupils attending the schools of the district and teachers or other employees employed by the district to and from school athletic contests or other school activities or to and from fairs or expositions held in the State or in any adjoining state and in which the pupils participate actively or as spectators. The transportation may be provided on any day or days throughout the school year.

HEALTH SUPERVISION

Contracts for Health Supervision

16425. Contracts between any city and the governing board of any school district located wholly or partially within such city for the performance by the health officers or other employees of the health department of any city of any or all of the functions and duties set forth in Chapter 3 of Division 8 of the Education Code, relating to health supervision of school buildings and pupils are hereby authorized.

In any such contracts the consideration shall be such as may be agreed upon by the governing board and the city and shall be paid to the city by the governing board at such times as shall be specified in the contract. This section shall not apply to any district which is under the control of a governing board which has under its control a district or districts having a total average daily attendance of 100,000 or more pupils.

Health and Safety Code Section 485. The board of supervisors may contract with the county superintendent of schools of the county for the performance by health officers or other employees of county health departments of any or all of the functions and duties set forth in Chapter 3 of Division 8 of the Education Code, relating to the health supervision of school buildings and of pupils enrolled in the schools of any or all elementary and high school districts over which the county superintendent of schools has jurisdiction.

In the contract the consideration shall be such as may be agreed upon by the board of supervisors and the county superintendent of schools and shall be paid by the county superintendent of schools at such times as shall be specified in the contract to the county treasurer.

Health and Safety Code Section 486. A contract under this article, except contracts with county superintendents of schools, may provide for the care and support, including medical attendance, of indigent sick, and for compensation therefor.

Exclusion of Pupils With Contagious Diseases

Health and Safety Code Section 200. The State Department of Public Health shall examine into the causes of communicable disease in man and domestic animals occurring or likely to occur in this State.

Health and Safety Code Section 203. It shall examine and may prevent the pollution of sources of public domestic water and ice supply.

16032. The governing body of any school district may exclude children of filthy or vicious habits, or children suffering from contagious or infectious diseases.

R. & R. 65. No pupils while infected with any contagious or infectious disease shall be allowed to remain in any of the public schools.

Vaccination

16401. The control of smallpox is under the direction of the State Board of Health, and no rule or regulation on the subject of vaccination shall be adopted by school or local health authorities.

Healthful Environment

18221. If the supervisor of health of any school district notes any defect in plumbing, lighting, or heating, or any other defect in the school building which tends to make the building unfit for the proper housing of the children, he shall at once make a detailed report to the governing board of the school district.

If within 15 days after he has filed this report, he finds that the board has made no provision for the correction of the defect, he shall at once report the defect to the county superintendent of schools who shall under the provisions of Article 2 of Chapter I of this division, proceed to have the defect corrected.

Qualifications of Supervisors of Health

13053. The qualifications of supervisors of health shall be as provided in Sections 13054 to 13059, inclusive.

13054. The qualifications for a physician shall be an unrevoked certificate to practice medicine and surgery issued by this State and a health and development certificate.

13055. The qualifications for a teacher shall be a life diploma of this State or a special credential in physical education, and a health and development certificate.

13056. The qualifications for an oculist shall be a certificate to practice medicine and surgery in this State and a health and development certificate.

13057. The qualifications for a dentist or a dental hygienist shall be a certificate issued by the Board of Dental Examiners of California and a health and development certificate.

13058. The qualifications for a nurse shall be a certificate of registration issued by the Board of Nurse Examiners of the State of California and a health and development certificate.

13059. The qualifications for an optometrist shall be a certificate issued by the State Board of Optometry and a health and development certificate.

13059.1. The qualifications for an otologist shall be a physician's and surgeon's certificate and a health and development certificate.

13059.2. The qualifications for school audiometrist shall be a certificate of registration as a school audiometrist issued by the State Board of Public Health and a health and development certificate.

Health Supervisors

16416. The governing board of any school district shall give diligent care to the health and physical development of pupils, and where sufficient funds are provided by district taxation, shall employ properly certified persons for the work.

16417. The governing board of any school district may provide for proper health supervision of the school buildings and pupils enrolled in the public schools under its jurisdiction.

16441. The governing board of any school district may appoint a supervisor of health, or supervisors of health, consisting of a physician, teacher, nurse, oculist, dentist, optometrist, otologist, chiropodist, school audiometrist, or any one or more of such persons. In case of the appointment of more than one supervisor of health the supervisors may, in the discretion of the board, all be chosen from any one of the classes designated. The board may also appoint such number of nurses and dental hygienists as it may deem necessary to work under the direction of the supervisor of health and may provide for the compensation of such employees. No money set aside for the payment of teachers' salaries or for library purposes shall be used for this purpose.

16442. The governing boards of two or more school districts in the same county may join in the employment of a supervisor of health, or supervisors of health, and may use funds not set aside for the payment of teachers' salaries or for library purposes for the expenses of the work. The boards may employ a nurse or nurses under the direction of a supervisor of health to examine the schools under their jurisdiction.

16443. No physician, oculist, dentist, dental hygienist, optometrist, otologist, chiropodist, school audiometrist, or nurse, not employed in such capacity by the State Department of Public Health, shall be, nor shall any other person be, employed or permitted to supervise the health and physical development of pupils unless he holds a health and development certificate.

Health and Safety Code Section 935. A local health district may exercise the powers in this chapter granted or necessarily implied.

Health and Safety Code Section 936. A district may do any or all of the following:

    *   *   *   *   *   *   *

(d) Acquire, construct, maintain, and operate all works and equipment necessary for the inspection of water, milk, meat, and other foods.

    *   *   *   *   *   *   *

(g) Employ public health nurses and health visitors and cooperate with educational authorities in health inspection in public or private schools in the district.

    *   *   *   *   *   *   *

(1) Exercise all other needful powers for the preservation of the health of the inhabitants of the district, whether the powers are expressly enumerated in this chapter or not.

The powers granted in this chapter shall be liberally construed for the purpose of securing the well-being of the inhabitants of the district.

16461. The county superintendent of schools of each county may employ one or more supervisors of health as defined in Section 16441, to supervise the health of pupils enrolled in the schools of elementary and high school districts over which he has jurisdiction, or may contract with the board of supervisors of the county in which he holds office for the performance by employees of the county health department of any or all of the functions relating to proper health supervision of the school buildings and of pupils enrolled in the schools of such elementary and high school districts. All rules governing health supervision in the schools shall be made by the county superintendent of schools. No supervisor of health shall be employed, and no county employees shall perform duties under any contract, who does not possess a health and development credential.

16462. A supervisor of health employed by the county superintendent of schools shall perform such duties in connection with the supervision of the health of pupils as are prescribed by the county superintendent of schools.

A parent or guardian having control or charge of any child enrolled in the public schools may file annually with the principal of the school in which he is enrolled a statement in writing, signed by the parent or guardian, stating that he will not consent to the physical examination of his child. Thereupon the child shall be exempt from any physical examination, but whenever there is a good reason to believe that the child is suffering from a recognized contagious or infectious disease, he shall be sent home and shall not be permitted to return until the school authorities are satisfied that any contagious or infectious disease does not exist.

16463. The salary and necessary traveling and other expenses of any supervisor of health employed pursuant to this article or the contract price agreed upon between the board of supervisors and the county superintendent of schools shall be paid by the county superintendent of schools from the county school service fund.

Health and Safety Code Section 252.6. The governing body of a city, county, city and county or school district may employ one or more school audiometrists, each of whom shall be registered with the State Board of Public Health and possess such qualifications as may at the date of registration be prescribed by the said State board.

The school audiometrist shall give audiometer tests with instruments accepted by the Council on Physical Therapy of the American Medical Association. Subject to Section 16483 of the Education Code, and Section 252.5 of this code, such tests may be administered to school and preschool children in school buildings and other places as are or may be used by schools for otologic examinations, and in official public health otological diagnostic clinics.

PHYSICAL EXAMINATION OF PUPILS

16481. The governing board of any school district shall make such rules for the examination of the pupils in the public schools under its jurisdiction as will insure proper care of the pupils and proper secrecy in connection with any defect noted by the supervisor of health or his assistant and may tend to the correction of the physical defect.

16482. The governing board of any school district shall, subject to Section 16483, provide for the testing of the sight and hearing of each pupil enrolled in the schools of the district. The test shall be adequate in nature and shall be given only by duly qualified supervisors of health employed by the district, or by contract with a duly authorized agency. The records of the tests shall serve as evidence of the need of the pupils for the educational facilities provided physically handicapped individuals. The equipment necessary to conduct the tests may be purchased or rented by governing boards of school districts. The State, any agency, or political subdivision thereof may sell or rent any such equipment owned by it to the governing board of any school district upon such terms as may be mutually agreeable.

16482.1. A person employed by a school district in a position requiring certification qualifications who holds a valid special credential for, teaching lip reading may, subject to Section 16483, test the hearing of pupils of the district through the use of an audiometer for the purpose of detecting pupils with impaired hearing.

16483. A parent or guardian having control or charge of any child enrolled in the public schools may file annually with the principal of the school in which he is enrolled a statement in writing, signed by the parent or guardian, stating that he will not consent to the physical examination of his child. Thereupon the child shall be exempt from any physical examination, but whenever there is good reason to believe that the child is suffering from a recognized contagious or infectious disease, he shall be sent home and shall not be permitted to return until the school authorities are satisfied that any contagious or infectious disease does not exist.

16484. When a defect has been noted by the supervisor of health or his assistant, a report shall be made to the parent or guardian of the child, asking the parent or guardian to take such action as will cure or correct the defect. Such report, if made in writing, must be made on a form prescribed or approved by the Superintendent of Public Instruction and shall not include therein any recommendation suggesting or directing the pupil to a designated individual or class of practitioner for the purpose of curing or correcting any defect referred to in the report.

The provisions of this section do not prevent a supervisor of health from recommending in a written report that the child be taken to a public clinic or diagnostic and treatment center operated by a public hospital or by the State, county, or city department of public health.

16485. The supervisor of health shall make such reports from time to time as he deems best to the governing board of the school district, or as the board may call for, showing the number of defective children in the schools of the district and the effort made to correct the defects.

17252. Every attending or consulting physician who examines any child under 20 years of age found to be totally deaf, or with impaired hearing, as defined by the State Board of Education, shall report at once to the Department of Education the name, age, residence, and the name of the parent or guardian of the minor.

Health and Safety Code Section 252.5. The State Department of Public Health shall seek out children with impaired sense of hearing, especially in the primary and grammar grades of all schools and in its conferences and diagnostic clinics it shall employ for such diagnostic investigation trained otologists.

This section does not give the department power to require medical or physical examination of children without consent of parent or guardian.

Provision of Meals for Pupils

16418. The governing board of any school district may provide, without charge, breakfasts and lunches, or either, for pupils within the district who do not otherwise receive proper nourishment.

16419. The governing board of any school district may establish rules by which to determine which pupils are entitled to meals without charge.

16420. For the purpose of providing funds with which to obtain breakfasts or lunches, or both, for needy pupils, the governing board of any school district may levy and collect a district tax over and above the maximum elsewhere specified in this code.

16421. District funds may also be used for the purchase of breakfasts or lunches, or both, for needy pupils.

16422. Each official and department of the State having charge of the administering of funds for the relief of indigents may contribute and pay any of the funds subject to his disposal to any school district within the State, to be used by the district for the purchase of breakfasts or lunches, or both, for needy pupils. Every county, city and county, and city within the State may pay any of its funds available for the relief of indigents to any school district, within or partly within the county, city and county, and city for this purpose.

Absence Due to Illness or for Dental, Optometrical, or Medical Service

6803. The total days of attendance of a pupil upon a regular full-time day kindergarten, elementary school, high school, or junior college during the fiscal year shall be the number of days school was actually taught for not less than the minimum school day during the fiscal year, less the sum of his absences due to causes other than his illness. Absence due to illness must be verified by the district in such manner as the Superintendent of Public Instruction shall require.

16486. Any absence of a pupil from school for the purpose of having optometrical or medical service rendered which does not exceed one day or fraction thereof during each school month of four weeks shall not be deemed an absence in computing average daily attendance.

16486a. No absence of a pupil from school for the purpose of having dental service rendered shall be deemed an absence in computing average daily attendance.

Medical and Hospital Service for Athletes and Other Pupils

16423. The governing board of any school district may provide medical or hospital service, or both, through nonprofit membership corporations defraying the cost of medical service or hospital service, or both, or accident insurance, for pupils of the district injured while participating in athletic activities under the jurisdiction of, or sponsored or controlled by, the district or the authorities of any school of the district. The cost of the insurance or membership may be paid from the funds of the district.

The insurance may be purchased from, or the membership may be taken in, only such companies or corporations as are authorized to do business in this State.

16424. The governing board of any school district which does not employ at least five physicians as full time supervisors of health, or the equivalent thereof, may provide medical or hospital service, or both, through nonprofit membership corporations defraying the cost of medical service or hospital service, or both, or through accident or liability insurance, for injuries to pupils of the district arising out of accidents occurring while in or on buildings or other premises of the district during the time such pupils are required to be therein or thereon by reason of their attendance upon a regular day school of such district or while being transported by the district to and from such school or other place of instruction. No pupil shall be compelled to accept such service without the consent of his parent or guardian.

Such insurance may be purchased from, or such membership may be taken in, only such companies or corporations as are authorized to do business in California.

LIABILITY OF MEMBERS OF GOVERNING BOARDS

1026. No member of the governing board of any school district shall be held personally liable for accidents to children going to or returning from school, or on the playgrounds, or in connection with school work.

1027. No member of the governing board of any school district shall be held personally liable for the death of, or injury to, any pupil enrolled in any school of the district, resulting from his participation in any classroom or other activity to which he has been lawfully assigned as a pupil in the school unless negligence on the part of the member of the governing board is the proximate cause of the injury or death.

1028. If suit is brought against any member of the governing board of any school district as an individual, for any act, or omission, in the line of his official duty as member of the board, or if suit is brought against any employee of any school district for any act performed in the course of his employment, the district attorney of the county shall defend the member of the board or the individual employee upon request of the governing board of the school district, without fee or other charge.

1029. The governing board of any school district may insure against the liability (other than a liability which may be insured against under the provisions of Divisions 4 and 5 of the Labor Code) of the district and against the personal liability of the members of the board and of the officers, agents, and employees of the board, for damages by reason of death, or injury to person or property, as the result of any negligent act by the district, or by a member of the board, or any officer, agent, or employee when acting within the scope of his office, agency, or employment. The insurance may be written in any insurance company authorized to transact the business of insurance in the State.

INSTRUCTION IN HEALTH AND PHYSICAL EDUCATION

Prescribed Courses in Elementary Schools

10302. The course of study in the elementary schools shall include instruction in the following prescribed branches in the several grades in which each is required pursuant to this article: (a) reading, (b) writing, (c) spelling, (d) language study, (e) arithmetic, (f) geography, (g) history of the United States and of California, (h) civics including a study of the Declaration of Independence and of the Constitution of the United States, (i) music, (j) art, (k) training for healthful living, (*l*) morals and manners, and such other studies not to exceed three as may be prescribed by the board of education of the city, county, or city and county; provided, however, that whenever any part of "training for healthful living" conflicts with the religious beliefs of the parent or guardian of any pupil, then on written request of the parent or guardian the pupil may be excused from the part of the training which conflicts with such religious beliefs.

Instruction on Alcohol and Narcotics

8253. Instruction shall be given in all grades of school and in all classes during the entire school course, in manners and morals, and upon the nature of alcohol and narcotics and their effects upon the human system, as determined by science.

8254. All persons responsible for the preparation or enforcement of courses of study shall provide for instruction on the subjects of alcohol and narcotics.

Courses in Physical Education

8252. Attention shall be given to such physical exercises for the pupils as may be conducive to health and to vigor of body, as well as mind, and to the ventilation and temperature of schoolrooms.

10116. The Department of Education shall:

(a) Adopt such rules and regulations as it deems necessary and proper to secure the establishment of courses in physical education in the elementary and secondary schools.

(b) Compile or cause to be compiled and printed a manual in physical education for distribution to teachers in the public schools of the State.

10117. The Department of Education may:

(a) Employ the necessary expert and clerical assistants in order to carry out the provisions of this article.

10118. The Department of Education shall exercise general supervision over the courses of physical instruction in elementary and secondary schools of the State; exercise general control over all athletic activities of the public schools; advise school officials, school boards, and teachers in matters of physical education; and investigate the work in physical education in the public schools.

10119. The aims and purposes of the courses of physical education established shall be as follows:

(a) To develop organic vigor.

(b) To provide neuro-muscular training.

(c) To promote bodily and mental poise.

(d) To correct postural defects.

(e) To secure the more advanced forms of coordination, strength, and endurance.

(f) To promote such desirable moral and social qualities as appreciation of the value of cooperation, self-subordination, and obedience to authority, and higher ideals, courage, and wholesome interest in truly recreational activities.

(g) To promote a hygienic school and home life.

(h) To secure scientific supervision of the sanitation and safety of school buildings, playgrounds, and athletic fields, and the equipment thereof.

10120. The board of education of each county, city and county, and city, whose duty it is to prescribe the course of study for the elementary schools of the county, city and county, or city, shall prescribe suitable courses of physical education for all pupils enrolled in the day elementary schools, except pupils who may be excused in accordance with the provisions of this article.

10121. The governing board of each school district maintaining a secondary school shall prescribe suitable courses of physical education for all pupils enrolled in the day secondary schools of the district, except pupils who may be excused.

10122. The superintendent of schools of every county, city and county, or city, and the governing board of every school district shall enforce the courses of physical education prescribed by the proper authority, and require that such physical education be given in the day schools under their jurisdiction or control.

10123. All pupils enrolled in the elementary schools, except pupils excused, shall be required to attend upon the courses of physical education for an instructional period in each school day which shall be not less than 20 minutes, exclusive of recesses and the lunch period.

10124. All pupils enrolled in the junior or senior high schools, except pupils excused, shall be required to attend upon the courses of physical education for an instructional period in each school day which shall be not less than the length of the regular academic periods of the school.

10125. All pupils enrolled in the junior colleges, except pupils excused, shall be required to attend upon the courses of physical education for a minimum of 120 minutes per week. Where adequate facilities are available a daily program is recommended.

10126. The governing board of each district may grant temporary exemption to pupils who are ill or injured where a modified program to meet the needs of the pupils cannot be provided, and to pupils while enrolled for one-half, or less, of the work normally required of full time students. Permanent exemption may be granted a pupil who has reached, in the case of an elementary school or high school pupil, his twenty-first birthday, or in the case of a junior college pupil, his twenty-fifth birthday, or a pupil enrolled as a post-graduate student.

10127. When the number of pupils in any city, or city and county, or school district is sufficient, the governing board shall employ a competent supervisor and such special teachers, trained in physical education, as are necessary to obtain the aims and purposes set forth in this article.

10128. The governing boards of two or more contiguous school districts may, by a written agreement, join in the employment of competent supervisors and teachers trained in physical education for the districts, and the salary of the supervisors and teachers and the expenses incurred on account of the instruction shall be apportioned as the governing boards concerned may agree.

Education of Physically Handicapped Minors

9601. Subject to the provisions of this article the governing board of any school district may make such special provisions as in its judgment may be necessary for the education of physically handicapped minors. "Physically handicapped minor," as used in this article means a physically defective or handicapped person under the age of 21 years who is in need of education.

9601.1. Any school district furnishing education to physically handicapped minors pursuant to this article shall furnish such education to all such handicapped minors actually living within the district five or more days a week, although their legal residence may be outside the district.

9601.2. Any school district which does not maintain facilities for the education of physically handicapped minors shall enter into a contract with a school district in the same county maintaining such facilities. If there is no district in the same county maintaining such facilities, the governing board of the school district shall enter into a contract with a school district maintaining such facilities in any other county. If any question arises concerning the adequacy of the facilities provided for the education of physically handicapped minors by the school district in which the child is actually living, the parent or guardian of such child may appeal to the county superintendent of schools, and if the county superintendent of schools determines that the facilities offered are inadequate, he shall order the school district in which the child is actually living either to provide the facilities or enter into a contract with a school district maintaining adequate facilities.

Such contract shall provide for the payment of the cost of tuition by the district in which the physically handicapped minor actually lives. The cost of tuition shall not be greater than the difference between current expenditures per unit of average daily attendance, including transportation, for the education of a pupil in the particular category of physically handicapped minors to which the pupil belongs and the apportionment of state funds for the education of physically handicapped minors in that category.

The amount shall be determined not later than the last Monday in December and the last Monday in May of each year by the county superintendent of schools of the county in which the child attends schools and certified to the superintendent of schools having jurisdiction over the schools of the school district in which the child actually lives. The amount shall be forthwith paid from any funds of the school district available for that purpose.

9602. Any minor who, by reason of a physical impairment, cannot receive the full benefit of ordinary education facilities, shall be considered a physically handicapped individual for the purposes of this chapter. Minors with speech disorders or defects shall be considered as being physically handicapped.

9603. No minor shall be required to take advantage of the special provisions for the education of physically handicapped minors if the parent or guardian of the minor files a statement with the governing board of the school district showing that the minor is receiving adequate educational advantages.

9604. Physically handicapped minors may be instructed in special schools or special classes, in hospitals, sanatoriums, or preventoriums, in the home through the employment of home instructors, by cooperative arrangement with the Bureau of Vocational Rehabilitation of the State Department of Education, or by any other means approved by the State Department of Education.

9645. The Superintendent of Public Instruction shall determine the amount of the excess cost incurred by each county superintendent of schools for the education of physically handicapped pupils. "Excess cost" as employed in this section includes the total current expenditures incurred for remedial classes and for individual instruction of physically handicapped children, plus the excess amount of the current expenditures made for all other physically handicapped pupils instructed in special schools, in special classes, or in regular classes apportioned for the average daily attendance of these pupils under apportionment for basic state aid for pupils not classified as physically handicapped pupils. "Remedial classes" as herein employed includes special classes providing remedial instruction for physically handicapped pupils who are excused in small numbers for a portion of a class period from regular classes, without appreciable reduction in the costs of the regular classes.

Training in Athletics

10521. In addition to other subjects of instruction each high school course of study may include training in athletics, military drill and tactics, manual training, domestic science and art, agriculture, horticulture, dairying, or other vocational work, for which credit may be given as a part of the high school work. Instruction therein shall be given at such times and in such manner as the high school board shall determine.

Requirements for Graduation from Secondary School

R. & R. 102. The governing board of a school district maintaining a secondary school shall authorize to graduate from any secondary school maintained any pupil of good character and citizenship who satisfactorily completes the full curriculum prescribed for the school in which the pupil is regularly enrolled and in attendance at the time of completion of his work, including instruction in the Constitution of the United States and the successful passing of an examination thereon.

(a) The governing board of a school district maintaining a four-year or senior high school shall grant a diploma of high school graduation for the completion of a course of study or curriculum which includes not less than 190 semester periods and not more than 240 semester periods of classroom instruction and supervised learning, including work experience.

(1) A semester period is defined as one period of 40 to 60 minutes per week throughout one semester of not less than 17 weeks. When a school is operating on a minimum school day (four clock hours) adjustments in length of period or number of periods per week may be made without reduction of the number of semester periods which would otherwise be credited.

(b) The governing board of a school district maintaining a junior college shall confer the degree of Associate in Arts upon the satisfactory completion in grades 13 and 14 of 60 credit hours of work which shall include the following:

*   *   *   *   *   *   *

(3) Two credit hours of community and personal hygiene; except that a junior college student, whose parents or guardian state in writing that the course in community and personal hygiene is contrary to the religious beliefs of the student, may be excused from such course and permitted to substitute a two-hour course in a field or fields specifically designated by the governing board of the district in lieu of the required two-hour course in community and personal hygiene.

(4) Two credit hours in physical education earned at the rate of one-half credit per semester for a minimum of 120 minutes per week in directed physical education activities, except as a pupil may be exempted in accordance with Section 10126, Education Code; and.

*   *   *   *   *   *   *

Requirement for State College Graduation

20459. The State Board of Education in standardizing the courses of instruction offered in the several State colleges shall prescribe a course in physical education and shall make the completion of the course a requirement for graduation.

INSTRUCTION IN PUBLIC SAFETY AND ACCIDENT PREVENTION

R. & R. 17. Except where the governing board of the school district has arranged for the conducting of fire drills at least once each school month by a fire department, the principal of each school shall hold at least once each school month a fire drill in which all pupils, teachers and other employees shall be required to leave the building. A record shall be kept in the principal's office of the date and hour of each fire drill.

10171. Instruction shall be given in every elementary and secondary school in the State in the subjects of public safety and accident prevention primarily devoted to avoidance of the hazards upon streets and highways.

10172. The State Board of Education shall:

(a) Adopt such rules and regulations as it deems necessary and proper to secure instruction in public safety and accident prevention in the elementary and secondary schools of this State in accordance with the provisions of this article.

(b) Compile or cause to be compiled and printed a manual in public safety and accident prevention, primarily devoted to avoidance of hazards incident to the use of streets and highways for distribution to teachers in the public elementary and secondary schools of the State.

10173. The State Board of Education in standardizing the courses of instruction offered in the state colleges shall prescribe a course in public safety and shall make the completion of the course a requirement for graduation.

10174. The Superintendent of Public Instruction shall make arrangements for carrying out the provisions of this article, and the superintendent of schools of every county, city and county, or city, and the governing board of every school district shall require that instruction in public safety be given in the schools under its jurisdiction or control.

First Aid Equipment

24501. The governing board of any school district, superintendent of schools, or principal in whom is vested the administration or supervision of any public or private school in the State shall equip the school with a first aid kit containing the articles mentioned in Section 24503, whenever any pupils of the school are conducted or taken on field trips under the supervision or direction of any teacher in, or employee or agent of, the school.

24502. The teacher, agent, or employee shall have the first aid kit in his possession, or immediately available, while conducting the field trip.

24503. Every first aid kit shall include the following articles and such other equipment as the school officials charged with the duty of maintaining it may consider useful or necessary for the purposes of this chapter:

(a) Six standard packages each containing two (2) pieces of sterile gauze, one (1) ribbon bandage, one (1) triangular cambric picture bandage in antiseptic container.

(b) Written instructions for the use of the contents.

24504. Whenever a field trip is conducted into an area which is commonly known to be infested by poisonous snakes, the first aid kit shall include some form of antivenom medicine intended to counteract the effects of poisonous snake bites.

24505. Any member of the governing board of any school district and any superintendent of schools, principal, teacher, or agent who wilfully violates the provisions of this article is guilty of a misdemeanor.

PURCHASE OF ATHLETIC EQUIPMENT

18852. The governing board of each school district shall, except as otherwise provided in this code, purchase school furniture, including musical instruments, and apparatus, and such other articles as are necessary for the use of schools, and may, in its discretion, purchase uniforms and other regalia for the use of school bands or orchestras, and including uniforms and equipment necessary for the use of athletic teams. Any such articles purchased shall always remain the property of the school district purchasing them. Only such books, apparatus, uniforms, and equipment shall be purchased by the governing board of an elementary school district, if the board is not a city board of education, as have been adopted by the county board of education having jurisdiction over the district.

USE OF SCHOOL PROPERTY FOR PUBLIC PURPOSES

Use for Meetings

19401. The governing board of any school district may grant the use of school buildings or grounds for public, literary, scientific, recreational, or educational meetings, or for the discussion of matters of general or public interest upon such terms and conditions as the board deems proper, and subject to the limitations, requirements, and restrictions set forth in this chapter.

19402. No use shall be inconsistent with the use of the buildings or grounds for school purposes, or interfere with the regular conduct of school work.

19403. No use shall be granted in such a manner as to constitute a monopoly for the benefit of any person or organization.

19404. No privilege of using the buildings or grounds shall be granted for a period exceeding one year. The privilege is renewable and revocable in the discretion of the board at any time.

Use as Civic Centers

19431. There is a civic center at each and every public school building and grounds within the State where the citizens, parent-teachers' associations, Campfire Girls, Boy Scout troops, farmers' organizations, clubs, and associations formed for recreational, educational, political, economic, artistic, or moral activities of the public school districts may engage in supervised recreational activities, and where they may meet and discuss, from time to time, as they may desire, any subjects and questions which in their judgment appertain to the educational, political, economic, artistic, and moral interests of the citizens of the communities in which they reside. Governing boards of the school districts may authorize the use, by such citizens and organizations of any other properties under their control, for supervised recreational activities.

19432. Any use, by any individual, society, group, or organization which has as its object or as one of its objects, or is affiliated with any group, society, or organization which has as its object or one of its objects the overthrow or the advocacy of the overthrow of the present form of government of the United States or of the State by force, violence, or other unlawful means shall not be granted, permitted, or suffered.

    *   *   *   *   *   *   *

19433. The use of any public schoolhouse and grounds for any meeting is subject to such reasonable rules and regulations as the governing board of the district prescribes and shall in nowise interfere with the use and occupancy of the public schoolhouse and grounds, as is required for the purposes of the public schools of the State.

19434. The management, direction, and control of the civic center is vested in the governing board of the school district.

19435. The governing board of the school district shall make all needful rules and regulations for conducting the civic meetings and for such recreational activities as are provided for in this chapter and which aid, assist, and lend encouragement to the activities.

19436. The governing board of any school district may appoint a person who shall have charge of the grounds, preserve order, protect the school property, plan, promote, and supervise recreational activities, and do all things necessary in the capacity of a representative of the board. He shall have the power of a peace officer, to carry out the provisions and the intents and purposes of this chapter.

19437. The use of schoolhouses, property, and grounds pursuant to this chapter shall be granted free.

19438. In the case of entertainments or meetings where admission fees are charged or contributions are solicited and the net receipts of the admission fees or contributions are not expended for the welfare of the pupils of the district or for charitable purposes a charge shall be made for the use of the schoolhouses, property, and grounds.

The governing board may, however, permit such use, without charge, by organizations, clubs, or associations organized for general character building or welfare purposes, when membership dues or contributions solely for the support of the organization, club, or association, or the advancement of its character building or welfare work, are accepted.

19439. Lighting, heating, janitor service, and the services of the person when needed, and other necessary expenses, in connection with the use of public school buildings and grounds pursuant to this chapter, shall be provided for out of the county or special school funds of the respective school districts in the same manner and by the same authority as similar services are provided for.

Community Recreation

24401. The purposes of this chapter are:

(a) To promote and preserve the health and general welfare of the people of the State and to cultivate the development of good citizenship by provision for adequate programs of community recreation.

(b) To authorize cities, counties, cities and counties, and public school districts to organize, promote, and conduct such programs of community recreation as will contribute to the attainment of general educational and recreation objectives for children and adults of the State.

24402. The following terms, wherever used or referred to in this chapter have the following meanings, respectively, unless a different meaning clearly appears from the context:

(a) "Public authority" means any city of any class, city and county, county of any class, any recreation districts organized under and pursuant to the provisions of Chapter 3 of Division 5 of the Public Resources Code, or school district in the State.

(b) "Governing body" means, in the case of a city, the city council, municipal council, or common council; in the case of a county or city and county, the board of supervisors; in the case of a recreation district, the governing board of the recreation district; and in the case of a school district, the governing board of the school district.

(c) "Recreation" means any activity, voluntarily engaged in, which contributes to the physical, mental, or moral development of the individual or group participating therein, and includes any activity in the fields of music, drama, art, handicraft, science, literature, nature study, nature contacting, aquatic sports, and athletics, or any of them, and any informal play incorporating any such activity.

(d) "Community recreation" and "public recreation" mean such recreation as may be engaged in under direct control of a public authority.

(e) "Recreation center" means a place, structure, area, or other facility under the jurisdiction of a governing body of a public authority used for community recreation whether or not it may be used also for other purposes, playgrounds, playing fields or courts, beaches, lakes, rivers, swimming pools, gymnasiums, auditoriums, rooms for arts and crafts, camps, and meeting places.

24403. The governing body of every public authority may (a) organize, promote, and conduct programs of community recreation, (b) establish systems of playgrounds and recreation, and (c) acquire, improve, maintain, and operate recreation centers within or without the territorial limits of the public authority.

No events for which an admission price is charged shall be held pursuant to this chapter, except amateur athletic contests, demonstrations, or exhibits and other educational and noncommercial events.

24404. The governing bodies of any two or more public authorities may cooperate with each other or with the Federal Government or any department thereof to carry out the purposes of this chapter, and to that end may enter into agreements with each other, and may do any and all things necessary or convenient to aid and cooperate in carrying out the purposes of this chapter.

The governing bodies of any two or more public auhorities having jurisdiction over any of the same territory or over contiguous territories may jointly establish a system or systems of recreation, and may jointly do any act which either is authorized to do under Section 24403. Nothing in this chapter shall be construed to prohibit any joint or cooperative action authorized by this section.

24405. The governing body of any public authority other than a school district may designate any already existing board, officer, or employee of the public authority to exercise the powers granted by this chapter to carry out the purposes of this chapter, or may provide for the appointment of a board of recreation commissioners to exercise such powers. A school district may appoint one or more members of the board of trustees, officers or employees, to represent the district on a board of recreation commissioners.

24406. The board of recreation commissioners shall consist of five members, who shall serve without compensation.

24407. The board of recreation commissioners in each public authority, or the board, officer, or employee of the authority designated to exercise the powers, shall exercise such powers and perform such duties, pursuant to this chapter, as the governing body of the public authority may prescribe.

24408. The governing body of any school district may use the buildings, grounds, and equipment of the school district, or any of them, to carry out the purposes of this chapter, or may grant the use of any building, grounds, or equipment of the district to any other public authority for the purposes, whenever the use of the buildings, grounds, or equipment for community recreational purposes will not interfere with use of the buildings, grounds, and equipment for any other purpose of the public school system. Nothing in this section is intended to repeal any provision of, or to restrict or otherwise affect the use of school buildings under Chapter 9 of Division 9 of this code.

24409. Every public authority may appoint, prescribe the duties of, and provide for the compensation and necessary expenses of such recreational directors, supervisors, custodians, assistants, deputies, and other employees as it deems reasonably necessary for carrying out the provisions and purposes of this chapter. Only persons employed in positions requiring certification qualifications shall be paid out of the funds set aside for the payment of teachers' salaries.

24409.1. The governing body of a school district may require persons, other than students, or organizations desiring to use the recreational facilities on school grounds or belonging to a school or the facilities provided by the district at a community recreation center maintained solely by the district to pay such fees for such use as the said governing body may prescribe.

24410. All necessary expenses incurred by the governing body of any school district in carrying out the purposes of this chapter are a charge against the funds of the district from whatever source the funds have been received. All such expenditures shall be made in the same manner as funds are expended for other school purposes.

Nothing in this chapter shall be construed to change in any way existing laws regarding the use of school grounds or school buildings by governing boards of school districts, except as specifically provided in this chapter.

24411. The Department of Education may advise and assist public school authorities, and upon request any public authority other than school districts, in establishing, developing, and maintaining a system or systems of recreation in accordance with this chapter.

Appendix B

REFERENCE MATERIALS

I. BOOKS AND PAMPHLETS

ALLEN, BETTY, AND BRIGGS, MITCHELL PIRIE. *Behave Yourself!* Chicago: J. B. Lippincott, 1937, 1945 (rev. ed.).

————. *If You Please!* Chicago: J. B. Lippincott, 1942.

AMERICAN CAMPING ASSOCIATION. *Marks of Good Camping*. New York: Association Press, 1941.

ANNIS, ELSIE K., AND MATTHEWS, JANET. *Rhythmic Activities*. New York: Ginn & Co., 1944.

ARMSTRONG, LUCILE. *Dances of Portugal*. New York: Chanticleer Press, 1949.

BACON, FRANCIS L. *Outwitting the Hazards*. New York: Silver Burdett Co., 1941.

BAKER, GERTRUDE M. *The Modern Teacher of Physical Education*. New York: F. S. Crofts & Co., 1940.

BALCH, ERNEST. *Amateur Circus Life*. New York: Macmillan Co., 1916, 1924.

BALLWEBBER, EDITH. *Group Instruction in Social Dancing*. New York: A. S. Barnes & Co., 1938.

BANCROFT, JESSIE H. *Games*. New York: Macmillan Co., 1937.

————. *The Posture of School Children*. New York: Macmillan Co., 1913, 1919.

BARNETT, CECILLE JEAN. *Games, Rhythms, Dances*. Oshkosh, Wis.: J. O. Frank & Sons, 1941.

BAUMGARTNER, A. J. *Posture Training and Remedial Gymnastics*. Minneapolis, Minn.: Burgess Publ. Co., 1941.

BELIAJUS, FINADAR VYTAUTAS. *Dance and Be Merry*. Chicago: Clayton F. Summy Co., Vols. I, II, 1941, 1942.

BENSEL, ELSIE VAN DER VON-TEN. *Dances of the Netherlands*. New York: Chanticleer Press, 1949.

BENTLEY, BERENICE BENSON, AND MATHEWSON, SOPHIE B. *Music in Playtime*. Chicago: Clayton F. Summy Co., 1948.

BLANCHARD, VAUGHN S., AND COLLINS, LAURENTINE. *A Modern Physical Education Program for Boys and Girls*. New York: A. S. Barnes & Co., 1940.

BOWERS, ETHEL. *Parties Plus: Fun for Threesomes*. New York: National Recreation Association, 1943.

BOVARD, J. F.; COZENS, F. W.; AND HAGMAN, E. P. *Tests and Measurements in Physical Education*. Philadelphia: W. B. Saunders Co., 1938, 1945, 1949.

BOYKIN, ELEANOR. *This Way, Please: A Book of Manners*. New York: Macmillan Co., 1940.

BRADY, MARNA VENABLE. *Tumbling for Girls*. Philadelphia: Lea & Febiger, 1936.

BRECKENRIDGE, MARIAN E., AND VINCENT, E. LEE. *Child Development*. Philadelphia: W. B. Saunders Co., 1943.

BREUER, KATHARINA. *Dances of Austria*. New York: Chanticleer Press, 1949.

BROWN, CORA L., AND OTHERS. *Outdoor Cooking*. New York: The Greystone Press, 1940.

BURCHENAL, ELIZABETH. *American Country-Dances*. New York: G. Schirmer, Inc., 1918.

————. *Dances of the People*. New York: G. Schirmer, Inc., 1913, 1934.

————. *Folk-Dances and Singing Games*. New York: G. Schirmer, Inc., 1909-22, 1933.

————. *Folk Dances from Old Homelands*. New York: G. Schirmer, Inc., 1922.

————. *Folk Dances of Germany*. New York: G. Schirmer, Inc., 1938.

Camping and Outdoor Experiences in the School Program. Washington 25, D. C.: U. S. Office of Education, Federal Security Agency, 1947.

COLESTOCK, CLAIRE, AND LOWMAN, CHARLES LEROY. *Fundamental Exercises for Physical Fitness*. New York: A. S. Barnes & Co., 1943.

COLLAN, ANNI, AND HEIKEL, YNGVAR. *Dances of Finland*. New York: Chanticleer Press, 1949.

COTTERAL, B. AND D. *The Teaching of Stunts and Tumbling*. New York: A. S. Barnes & Co., 1936.

————. *Tumbling, Pyramid Building, and Stunts for Girls and Women*. New York: A. S. Barnes & Co., 1926.

CRAINE, HENRY C. *Teaching Athletic Skills in Physical Education*. New York: Inor Publishing Co., 1942.

CRAMPTON, C. WARD. *The Folk Dance Book*. New York: A. S. Barnes & Co., 1909.

————. *The Second Folk Dance Book*. New York: A. S. Barnes & Co., 1916.

CRAMPTON, C. WARD, AND WOLLASTON, M. A. *The Song Play Book*. New York: A. S. Barnes & Co., 1917.

CRAWFORD, CAROLINE. *Dramatic Games and Dances*. New York: A. S. Barnes & Co., 1914.

————. *Folk Dances and Games*. New York: A. S. Barnes & Co., 1908.

CROSFIELD, DOMINI. *Dances of Greece*. New York: Chanticleer Press, 1949.

CURTISS, MARY L., AND CURTISS, ADELAIDE B. *Physical Education for Elementary Schools*. Milwaukee: Bruce Publishing Co., 1945.

CZARNOWSKI, LUCILE. *Dances of Early California Days*. Palo Alto: Pacific Books, 1950.

DICK, WILLIAM BRISBANE. *Dick's Quadrille Call-Book*. New York: Fitzgerald Publishing Corp.

DIXON, CLARICE MADELINE. *The Power of Dance: The Dance and Related Arts for Children*. New York: John Day Co., 1939.

DREW, LILLIAN CURTIS. *Individual Gymnastics. A Handbook of Corrective and Remedial Gymnastics*. Philadelphia: Lea & Febiger, 1945 (5th ed.).

DROUGHT, ROSE ALICE. *A Camping Manual*. New York: A. S. Barnes & Co., 1943.

DUGGAN, ANNE SCHLEY; MONTAGUE, MARY ELLA; AND RUTLEDGE, ABBIE. *Conditioning Exercises for Girls and Women*. New York: A. S. Barnes & Co., 1945.

DUGGAN, ANNE SCHLEY; SCHLOTTMAN, JEANETTE; AND RUTLEDGE, ABBIE. *The Folk Dance Library* (5 volumes). New York: A. S. Barnes & Co., 1948.

DUGGAN, ANNE SCHLEY. *Tap Dances for School and Recreation*. New York: A. S. Barnes & Co., 1935.

DUNBAR, FLANDERS. *Emotions and Bodily Changes*. New York: Columbia University Press, 1946 (3d ed.).

DURLACHER, E. *Honor Your Partner.* New York: Devin-Adair Co., 1949.

––––––. *The Play Party Book. Singing Games for Children.* New York: Devin-Adair Co., 1945.

––––––. *Square Dances.* New York: Mills Music, Inc. (1619 Broadway, New York 19), 1946.

DYKEMA, PETER. *Twice 55 Games with Music.* Boston: C. C. Birchard & Co., 1924.

ELSOM, J. C., AND TRILLING, BLANCHE M. *Social Games and Group Dances.* Philadelphia: J. B. Lippincott Co., 1919, 1927 (2d ed.).

Extending Education through Camping. New York City Board of Education Report of School Camp Experiment. New York: Life Camps, Inc. (369 Lexington Avenue, New York 17, N. Y.), 1948.

EVANS, BESSIE. *American Indian Dance Steps.* New York: A. S. Barnes & Co., 1931.

Folk Dances from Near and Far. Berkeley, California: Folk Dance Federation of California. Vols. I, II, III, IV, 1945, 1946, 1947, 1948.

Folk Festival Handbook. Prepared by the Evening Folk Festival Association. Philadelphia 5, Pa.: The Philadelphia Bulletin.

FOOTE, DOREEN. *Modified Activities in Physical Education.* New York: Inor Publishing Co., 1945.

The Foster Way, Square Dances, Part II. Foster's Folkway Features, Publishers. Smith-Brooks Printing Co., printers, P. O. Box 540, Denver, Colorado, 1940. *Cards giving calls for 29 easy dances and directions for squares, circles, and couple dances.*

FRYMIR, ALICE W. *Basket Ball for Women: How to Coach and Play the Game.* New York: A. S. Barnes & Co., 1928.

GATES, ARTHUR I., AND OTHERS. *Educational Psychology.* New York: Macmillan Co., 1948 (3d ed.).

GESELL, ARNOLD L., AND OTHERS. *The Child from Five to Ten.* New York: Harper & Bros., 1946.

"Good Morning." Music, Calls, and Directions for Old-time Dancing as Revived by Mr. and Mrs. Henry Ford. Compiled by Benjamin B. Lovett. Dearborn, Mich., 1943 (4th ed.).

GOODRICH, LAURENCE B. *Living with Others.* New York: American Book Co., 1939.

GROMBACH, JOHN V. *Touch Football.* New York: A. S. Barnes & Co., 1942.

GROVER, EDWIN D. *The Nature Lover's Knapsack. An Anthology of Poems.* New York: Thomas Y. Crowell Co., 1927, 1947 (enlarged ed.).

Guide for Planning Facilities for Athletics, Recreation and Physical and Health Education. Chicago: Published for National Facilities Conference by the Athletic Institute (209 S. State St., Republic Bldg.), 1947.

Guide for Planning School Plants. Published by the National Council on Schoolhouse Construction, n.p., 1949. (Previously published by the Council with the Proceedings of the Annual Meeting, 1946.)

HALL, A. NEELY. *Home-Made Games and Game Equipment.* Boston: Lothrop, Lee & Shepard, 1923.

HAMLIN, ALICE P., AND GUESSFORD, MARGARET G. *Singing Games for Children.* Cincinnati: Willis Music Co., 1941.

Handy I and *Handy II* (2 volumes). Edited by Lynn Rohrbough. Delaware, Ohio: Co-operative Recreation Service. *Kits containing loose-leaf pamphlets of songs and games.*

HARBY, SAMUEL F. *Tumbling for Students and Teachers.* Philadelphia: W. B. Saunders & Co., 1932.

Health Education: A Guide for Teachers in Elementary and Secondary Schools and Institutions for Teacher Education. A Report of the Joint Committee on Health Problems in Education of the National Education Association and the American Medical Association. Fourth Revision. Washington, D. C.: National Education Association, 1948.

Health in Schools. Twentieth Yearbook of the American Association of School Administrators. Washington: American Association of School Administrators, National Education Association, 1942.

HERMAN, MICHAEL. *Folk Dances for All. Community Dances from Fifteen Countries.* New York: Barnes & Noble, Inc., 1947.

HISS, JOHN MARTIN. *New Feet for Old.* New York: Doubleday, Doran & Co., 1933, 1934, 1937.

HOFER, MARI RUEF. *Children's Singing Games, Old & New.* Chicago: A. Flanagan Co., 1901, 1938.

————. *Popular Folk Games and Dances.* Chicago: A. Flanagan Co., 1907, 1914 (revised ed.).

HORNE, VIRGINIA LEE. *Stunts and Tumbling.* New York: A. S. Barnes & Co., 1944.

————. *Stunts and Tumbling for Girls.* New York: A. S. Barnes & Co., 1943.

HOSTETLER, LAWRENCE. *The Art of Social Dancing.* New York: A. S. Barnes & Co., 1934.

HOWLAND, IVALCLARE SPROW. *The Teaching of Body Mechanics in Elementary and Secondary Schools.* New York: A. S. Barnes & Co., 1936.

HUGHES, WILLIAM LEONARD, AND WILLIAMS, JESSE FEIRING. *Sports, Their Organization and Administration.* New York: A. S. Barnes & Co., 1944.

HUPPRICH, FLORENCE L. *Soccer and Speedball for Girls.* New York: A. S. Barnes & Co., 1942.

HUNT, BEATRICE A., AND WILSON, HARRY ROBERT. *Sing and Dance. Folk Songs and Dances, Including American Play-Party Games.* Chicago: Hall & McCreary Co., 1945.

JACOBS, A. GERTRUDE. *The Chinese-American Song and Game Book.* New York: A. S. Barnes & Co., 1946.

JAMES, PHOEBE. *Accompaniments for Rhythmic Expressions. Children's Music for Children.* Pacific Palisades, Calif.: Phoebe James (Box 134), 1946.

————. *Harbor Rhythms.* Pacific Palisades, Calif.: Phoebe James, 1948.

————. *Songs for Rhythmic Expressions.* Pacific Palisades, Calif.: Phoebe James, 1944.

JAMEYSON, ALICE. *Old Time Ballroom Dances that are Fun to Dance Today.* Berkeley: The Professional Press, 1941.

JOHNSTON, EDITH. *Regional Dances of Mexico.* Dallas, Texas: Banks, Upshaw & Co., 1935.

KELLY, ELLEN DAVIS. *Teaching Posture and Body Mechanics.* New York: A. S. Barnes & Co., 1949.

KIRKELL, MIRIAM H., AND SHAFFNIT, IRMA K. *Partners All—Places All!* New York: E. P. Dutton & Co., Inc., 1949.

KOZMAN, HILDA CLUTE. *Character Dances for School Programs.* New York: A. S. Barnes & Co., 1935.

LAMBERT, CLARA, AND SHOEMAKER, ROWENA. *Let Them Play: A Primer to Help Children Grow Up.* New York: Play Schools Association, 1943.

LAMBERT, CLARA. *Play: A Yardstick of Growth.* New York: Summer Play Schools Committee of the Child Study Association of America, 1938.

LANE, JANET. *Your Carriage, Madam! A Guide to Good Posture.* New York: John Wiley & Sons, 1934, 1947 (2d ed.).

LA PORTE, WILLIAM RALPH. *The Physical Education Curriculum.* Los Angeles: University of Southern California Press, 1949 (4th ed.).

LA PORTE, WILLIAM RALPH, AND RENNER, A. G. *The Tumbler's Manual.* New York: Prentice-Hall, Inc., 1938.

LA SALLE, DOROTHY. *Guidance of Children through Physical Education.* New York: A. S. Barnes & Co., 1946.

————. *Physical Education for the Classroom Teacher.* New York: A. S. Barnes & Co., 1937.

————. *Play Activities for Elementary Schools.* New York: A. S. Barnes & Co., 1926.

————. *Rhythms and Dances for Elementary Schools.* New York: A. S. Barnes & Co., 1926.

LEONARD, FRED EUGENE, AND AFFLECK, GEORGE B. *A Guide to the History of Physical Education.* Philadelphia: Lea & Febiger, 1947 (3d ed.).

LINDERMAN, WANDA T., *The Outdoor Book.* New York: Camp Fire Girls, Inc., 1947.

LINSON, ELLEN, AND SMITH, JACQUELINE. *All Join Hands: First Steps for Recreation Leaders.* Chicago, Ill.: The Co-operative League of the United States (343 S. Dearborn Street), 1946.

LOWMAN, CHARLES LEROY; COLESTOCK, CLAIRE; AND COOPER, HAZEL. *Corrective Physical Education for Groups: A Text Book of Organization, Theory and Practice.* New York: A. S. Barnes & Co., 1928.

LUBINOVA, MILA. *Dances of Czechoslovakia.* New York: Chanticleer Press, 1949.

McCRADY, M. E. F., AND WHEELER, B. *Manners for Moderns.* New York: E. P. Dutton & Co., 1942.

MACHEREY, MATHIAS H., AND RICHARDS, JOHN N. *Pyramids Illustrated.* New York: A. S. Barnes & Co., 1932.

MANNERS, ZEKE. *American Square Dances.* New York: Robbins Music Corp., 1948.

McCLOW, L. L., AND ANDERSON, D. N. *Tumbling Illustrated.* New York: A. S. Barnes & Co., 1931.

McCLOY, CHARLES HAROLD. *Philosophical Bases for Physical Education.* New York: F. S. Crofts, 1940.

————. *Tests and Measurements in Health and Physical Education.* New York: F. S. Crofts, 1939, 1942 (2d ed.).

MARRAN, RAY J. *Table Games—How to Make and How to Play Them.* New York: A. S. Barnes & Co., 1939.

MASON, BERNARD S., AND MITCHELL, ELMER D. *Active Games and Contests.* New York: A. S. Barnes & Co., 1935.

MASON, BERNARD S. *Dances and Stories of the American Indian.* New York: A. S. Barnes & Co., 1944.

MASON, BERNARD S., AND MITCHELL, ELMER D. *Party Games for All.* New York: Barnes & Noble, Inc., 1946.

MASON, JOHN LEONARD. *Sand Craft.* Boston: J. L. Hammett Co., 1937 (2d ed.).

Mental Hygiene in the Classroom: How Would You Help a Child Like This?
Report of the Joint Committee on Health Problems in Education of the National
Education Association and the American Medical Association. Washington, D. C.:
Committee for Mental Hygiene, National Education Association, 1939.

MITCHELL, ELMER D. *Sports for Recreation and How to Play Them.* New York:
A. S. Barnes & Co., 1936.

MITCHELL, ELMER D., AND MASON, BERNARD S. *The Theory of Play.* New York:
A. S. Barnes & Co., 1934, 1939, 1948 (revised ed.).

MORTON, DUDLEY JOY. *Oh Doctor! My Feet!* New York: D. A. Appleton-Century
Co., 1939.

NASH, JAY B. *Physical Education: Interpretations and Objectives.* New York: A. S.
Barnes & Co., 1948.

NATIONAL RECREATION ASSOCIATION. *Community Sports and Athletics.* New York:
A. S. Barnes & Co., 1949.

————. *Recreation Areas: Their Design and Equipment.* Prepared by George D.
Butler. New York: A. S. Barnes & Co., 1947.

————. *Athletic Badge Tests for Boys and Girls* (1931). *Nature in Recreation*
(1938). *Games for Quiet Hours and Small Spaces* (1938). *Home Play* (1945). *Homemade Play Apparatus.* New York: National Recreation Association (315 Fourth
Avenue), U. S. Office of Education.

NATIONAL SECTION ON WOMEN'S ATHLETICS. Official Sports Library for Women.
*Official Basketball Guide. Official Tennis-Badminton Guide. Official Individual
Sports Guide with Archery, Bowling, Fencing, Golf and Riding. Official Recrea-
tional Games—Volley Ball Guide. Official Softball-Track and Field Guide. Official
Soccer-Speedball Guide.* Washington: National Section on Women's Athletics,
American Association for Health, Physical Education and Recreation (1201 Six-
teenth St., N.W., Washington 6, D. C.). Published annually or at approximately
annual intervals.

NEILSON, N. P., AND COZENS, FREDERICK W. *Achievement Scales in Physical Education
Activities.* Sacramento: California State Department of Education, 1934.

NIXON, EUGENE W., AND COZENS, FREDERICK W. *An Introduction to Physical Education.* Philadelphia: W. B. Saunders Co., 1947 (3d ed.).

OBERTEUFFER, DELBERT. *School Health Education.* New York: Harper & Bros., 1949.

OLTZ, CARLE. *Rhythm Time. Music for the Rhythmic Development of Children of
the Kindergarten and Primary Grades.* Chicago: Clayton F. Summy Co., 1946.

OSGOOD, GEORGIA; ANDERSON, VIRGINIA; AND HOHOEISAL, GRACE. *Dancin' a Round.*
Los Angeles: "Sets in Order" (152 N. Small Drive, Los Angeles 48), 1950.

PARSONS, THOMAS E. *Popular Ballroom Dances for All.* New York: Barnes & Noble,
Inc., 1947.

*The Physically Below-Par Child. Changing Concepts Regarding His Care and Edu-
cation.* New York: National Tuberculosis Association, 1940.

POWDERMAKER, THERESE. *Visual Aids for Teaching Sports.* New York: A. S. Barnes
& Co., 1940.

PRICE, M. KATHERINE. *The Source Book of Play Party Games.* Minneapolis: Burgess
Co., 1949.

RADIR, RUTH. *Modern Dance for the Youth of America.* New York: A. S. Barnes
& Co., 1944.

RATHBONE, JOSEPHINE LANGWORTHY. *Corrective Physical Education.* Philadelphia:
W. B. Saunders Co., 1934.

RENSTROM, MOISELLE. *Rhythm Fun for Little Folks.* Salt Lake City: Pioneer Music Press, 1944.

REYES, FRANCISCA S., AND RAMOS, PETRONA. *Philippine Folk Dances and Games.* New York: Silver, Burdett & Co., 1935.

RICHARDSON, HAZEL. *Games for the Elementary School Grades.* Minneapolis: Burgess Co., 1936.
A card file of games.

RODGERS, MARTIN. *A Handbook of Stunts.* New York: Macmillan Co., 1940.

ROGERS, JAMES F. *What Every Teacher Should Know about the Physical Conditions of Her Pupils.* Pamphlet No. 68. Washington, D. C.: U. S. Office of Education, Federal Security Agency, 1945 (revised ed.).

ROGERS, JULIA ANNE. *Parties and Programs for Parents' Days.* New York: National Recreation Association, 1939.

ROSSMAN, FLOY ADELE. *Singing All the Way. Songs and Games for Little Folks.* New York: Paull-Pioneer Music Co., 1931.

RYAN, GRACE L. *Dances of Our Pioneers.* New York: A. S. Barnes & Co., 1939.

SALT, ELLIS BENTON, AND OTHERS. *Teaching Physical Education in the Elementary School.* New York: A. S. Barnes & Co., 1942.

SALVEN, ERIC. *Dances of Sweden.* New York: Chanticleer Press, 1949.

SCHMIDT, ANNA, AND ASHTON, DUDLEY. *Characteristic Rhythms for Children.* New York: A. S. Barnes & Co., 1931.

SCHWENDENER, NORMA. *A History of Physical Education in the United States.* New York: A. S. Barnes & Co., 1942.

SCHWENDENER, NORMA, AND TIBBELS, AVERIL. *Legends & Dances of Old Mexico.* New York: A. S. Barnes & Co., 1934.

SEEFELD, ELMER A. *Physical Education for Elementary Grades.* St. Louis: Concordia Publishing House, 1944.

SEHON, ELIZABETH, AND OTHERS. *Physical Education Methods for Elementary Schools.* Philadelphia: W. B. Saunders Co., 1948.

SELDEN, ELIZABETH. *Elements of the Free Dance.* New York: A. S. Barnes & Co., 1930.

SHAFER, MARY S., AND MOSHER, MARY MORGAN. *Rhythms for Children.* New York: A. S. Barnes & Co., 1938.

SHAW, LLOYD. *Cowboy Dances.* Caldwell, Idaho: The Caxton Printers, 1939.

————. *The Round Dance Book.* Caldwell, Idaho: The Caxton Printers, 1948.

SHEEHY, EMMA DICKSON. *There's Music in Children.* New York: Henry Holt & Co., 1946.

Singing Games and Folk Dances. Brasstown, N. C.: John C. Campbell Folk School, 1941.

SMITH, ANNE M. *Play for Convalescent Children in Hospitals and at Home.* New York: A. S. Barnes & Co., 1941.

Solving School Health Problems. The Astoria Demonstration Study, Sponsored by the Department of Health and the Board of Education of New York City, directed by Dorothy Nyswander. New York: Commonwealth Fund, 1942.

The Spanish-American Song and Game Book. Compiled by Workers of the Writers' Program, Music Program, and Art Program of the Work Projects Administration in the State of New Mexico. New York: A. S. Barnes & Co., 1945.

Special Activities in Physical Education for High School and Adult Groups. California State Board of Education Bulletin No. 14 (July 15, 1934). Sacramento: California State Board of Education, 1934.

STAFFORD, GEORGE. *Sports for the Handicapped.* New York: Prentice-Hall, 1947.

STALEY, SEWARD C. *Games, Contests, and Relays.* New York: A. S. Barnes & Co., 1924.

SUTTON, RHODA REYNOLDS; AND BROOKS, ELIZABETH. *Creative Rhythms.* New York: A. S. Barnes & Co., 1941.

TERRY, WALTER. *Invitation to Dance.* New York: A. S. Barnes & Co., 1942.

TOBITT, JANET E. *Promenade All.* New York: Janet E. Tobitt (228 E. 43d St.), 1947.

TODD, MABEL E. *The Thinking Body.* New York: P. B. Hoeber, Inc., 1937.

WATERMAN, ELIZABETH. *The Rhythm Book.* New York: A. S. Barnes & Co., 1936.

WILLIAMS, JESSE FEIRING, AND BROWNELL, C. L. *The Administration of Health and Physical Education.* Philadelphia: W. B. Saunders Co., 1946 (3d ed.).

WILLIAMS, JESSE FEIRING. *Personal Hygiene Applied.* Philadelphia: W. B. Saunders Co., 1950 (9th ed.).

————. *The Principles of Physical Education.* Philadelphia: W. B. Saunders Co., 1948 (5th ed.).

WILSON, HARRY ROBERT. *Songs of the Hills and Plains.* Chicago: Hall & McCreary Co., 1943.

WISSLER, CLARK. *Indians of the United States.* New York: Doubleday, Doran & Co., 1940.

WITZIG, LOUISE. *Dances of Switzerland.* New York: Chanticleer Press, 1949.

II. MAGAZINES

American Lawn Tennis. Monthly. Jacobs Sports Magazines, Inc., 35 W. 53d St., New York 16, N. Y.

American Squares. Monthly. American Folk Dancing. Published by Charley Thomas, 121 Delaware Street, Woodbury, New Jersey.

Beach and Pool. Monthly. Published by Hoffman-Harris, Inc., 425 Fourth Avenue, New York 16, N. Y.

The Folk Dancer. Monthly. Edited and Published by Michael Herman, Community Folk Dance Center, P. O. Box 201, Flushing, New York.

The Journal of Health and Physical Education. Monthly through academic year. American Association for Health, Physical Education and Recreation, National Education Association, 1201 Sixteenth St., N.W., Washington 6, D. C.

Let's Dance. Monthly. The Magazine of the California Folk Dance Federation, 262 O'Farrell St., San Francisco 2, California.

Recreation. Monthly. National Recreation Association, 315 Fourth Avenue, New York 10, N. Y.

Sets in Order. Monthly. A California magazine for square dances. 152 North Swall Drive, Los Angeles 48, California.

Viltis. Monthly. Published by V. F. Beliajus, 1028 East 63d Street, Chicago 37, Ill.

Appendix C

PHONOGRAPH RECORDS FOR RHYTHMICAL ACTIVITIES

I. RHYTHM RECORDS

Albums and Series

RUTH EVANS SERIES

Childhood Rhythms, Series I. Album of three unbreakable records
101-102 Fundamental Rhythms. Walk, Run, Skip I; March, Jump, Gallop, Skip II
103-104 Animal and Toy Rhythms. Ducks, Camels, Horses, Elephants; Trains, Tops, Soldiers, Airplanes
105-106 Play and Character Rhythms. Swings, See-saws, Bicycles, Rowboats; Fairies, Witches, Giants, Dwarfs

Childhood Rhythms, Series II. Album of three unbreakable records
201-202 Rhythm Combinations. Up and down, Round and round, Fast and slow; Walk, walk, hop, hop; Run, hop, hop, stop; Walk and skip
203-204. Bouncing Balls, Jumping Rope. Bounce and catch; Bounce, bounce, bounce, and hold; Bounce, hold, bounce, hold; Bounce and bounce and bounce and hold; Jump in place, Jump fast, Skip
205-206 Interpretative and Dance Rhythms. Elevators, Clocks, Jumping Jacks; Step and point, Heel and toe, Walk and bow

SALLY TOBIN DIETRICH RECORDS

Rhythmic Play. Album of four 10-inch unbreakable records
Skip, Walk, Glide; Hop, Jump, Gallop, Swing
Run, Bounce, Skip and turn; Run and jump, Stretch and bend, Walk and bounce, Skip and jump
Giants, Trains, Ringing chimes; Elephants, Airplane, Hallowe'en goblins
Pushing a swing, Fairies, Grandfather clock, Swaying trees; Curling smoke, Mechanical doll, Lullaby

PHOEBE JAMES SERIES (unbreakable records)

AED-1. *Animal Rhythms.* Five little ponies (song), Work-horse (song), Rabbits, Frogs, Lions or tigers, Bears
AED-2. *Free Rhythms.* Skip, Run, Gallop, Tip-toe walk, Jump, Hop, Skip and whirl, Run and fall down, Walk and run, Run and jump
AED-3. *Animal Rhythms and Sound Effects.* Rabbits, Frogs, Airplanes, Lions, Dogs, Elephants
AED-4. *Garden Varieties.* Bees, Butterflies, Small birds, large birds, Wind, Rain, Sun, Growing plants
AED-5. *Fundamental Rhythms.* 2 skips, 2 runs, 2 gallops (3 distinct modes)

R. C. A. VICTOR RECORD LIBRARY FOR ELEMENTARY SCHOOLS. Albums of unbreakable records, with teaching suggestions

Basic Rhythmic Activities for Primary Grades, Volume 1. Album E-71. Four records
Gnomes, Dwarfs, Fairies, Clowns
Sparks, Etude joyeuse, Barcarolle, Valsette, Valse serenade, Love's dream
March in F major, Theme for skipping, Flying birds, Wheel barrow motive, Plain skip, Tip-toe march, Military march, Galloping horses, Running horses, High stepping horses, Skipping theme
Gigue in A, Jaglied, Sicilienne, Ballet, Adagio

Basic Rhythmic Activities for Primary Grades, Volume 2. Album E-72. Four records
Soldiers' march, March in D-flat, March ("Nutcracker Suite"), March ("Alceste")
Boating on the lake, Skating, Walzer, March, La Bergonette, Waltz, Scherzo, L'Arabesque, Tarantelle
Run, run, run, Jumping, Running game, Air de ballet, Waltzes Nos. 1, 2, and 9
Praeludium, Les Pifferari, Happy and light of heart, Tarantelle

Basic Rhythmic Activities for Primary Grades, Volume 3. Album E-73. Four records
Northern song, Song of the shepherdess, March, Papillons No. 8, Dance of the Moorish slaves, Slavonic dance No. 1, Siciliana
Polly, put the kettle on, Lavender's blue, Waltz, Come lasses and lads, John Peel, Marche militaire
Cradle song, The blacksmith, Dolly's funeral, Tarantelle, Berceuse, Silhouette, Valse gracieuse
Mirror dance, Elfenspiel, The witch, March of the tin soldiers, Knight of the hobby-horse, The clock, Postillion, Peasants' dance

Basic Rhythmic Activities for Upper Grades, Volume 4. Album E-74. Four records. For intermediate grades
The skaters waltz, Minuet from third movement, Amaryllis, Waltzes
Snow drops, Allegro in G, Playtime No. 4, Passepied, Silhouette
Playtime No. 10, Country dance (Weber), Country dance (Beethoven), Gavotte, Gigue in B-flat, Second gavotte
March "Aida," March of the three kings, Soldiers' chorus, Toreador song, Street boys' parade

Basic Rhythmic Activities for Upper Grades, Volume 5. Album E-75. Four records. For intermediate grades
Shepherd's dance, Masquerade, Norwegian dance, The Swiss maid
The Irish washerwoman, Turkey in the straw
March ("Carnival"), War song, March ("Iphigenia in Aulis"), March ("Miniatures"), March (Grotesque), March of the priests
Minuet in F, Minuet ("Don Giovanni"), Gavotte ("Les Petits Riens"), Gavotte in D minor

Basic Rhythmic Activities for Upper Grades, Volume 6. Album E-76. Four records. For intermediate grades
Shepherd's hey, Country gardens
March ("Love for Three Oranges"), March of pilgrims, Procession of the Sardar
La Czarine, Spanish serenade
The Juba dance, From the canebrake

Indian Album. Album E-89. Four records
Chant of the eagle dance, Winnebago love song, Love with tears, Pueblo lullaby, Omaha ceremonial
The sunrise call, Dance song, Butterfly dance, Shuffling feet
From an Indian lodge, Love song
Shawnee Indian hunting dance, War dance

Separate Records

ALLEGRO JUNIOR UNBREAKABLES, aj13 The Nutcracker Suite for dancing (age 5 to 8)
ALLEGRO JUNIOR UNBREAKABLES, aj21 The Peer Gynt Suite for dancing (age 5 to 8)
HELENE ALLEN, Students' march, Record 1. Unbreakable. One side of record is tempo suitable for primary children and the other side a slower tempo.

R. C. A. Victor, 20736 Motive for Skipping, B-flat major, Theme for Skipping in F major, Camp of gypsies

R. C. A. Victor, 22765 Skipping—Phrasing

II. RECORDS FOR SINGING GAMES AND SIMPLE FOLK DANCES

Albums

Decca Album A-278. *Play Party Games*. Three records
  18222 Brown jug, Oh Susanna, Shoo-fly, Captain Jinks
  18223 Jolly miller, I've been to Harlem, Weevily wheat, Jubilee
  18224 Old Dan Tucker, Skip to my Lou, Pig in the parlor

R. C. A. Victor Record Library for Elementary Schools. Albums of unbreakable records with instructions
  Singing Games. Album E-87. Four records. For primary grades
    The big gray cat, Hippity hop to the barber shop, Ten little Indians, Yankee Doodle; The snail, Sally go round the moon, A-Hunting we will go, The thread follows the needle
    London Bridge, Here we go 'round the mulberry bush; Soldier boy, The muffin man
    Way down in the paw paw patch, Old Pompey, Skip to my Lou; The farmer in the dell, Did you ever see a lassie?
    Looby Loo, Oats, peas, beans, and barley grow; The needle's eye, Jolly is the miller

Separate Records

Allegro Junior Unbreakables, aj3 Ring-a-round the rosy
Allegro Junior Unbreakables, aj5 Skip to my Lou
Allegro Junior Unbreakables, aj6 All around the mulberry bush
Allegro Intermediate Unbreakables, ak58 Picking up paw paws, Shoo fly, Take a little peek
Solo, 12006 Looby Loo, Shoo-fly, Browneyed Mary (singing) (unbreakable)
R. C. A. Victor, 22759 The snail, Sally go 'round, A-Hunting we will go, Baa, baa, black sheep, The big gray cat, Hippity hop to the barber shop, Pussy cat, pussy cat
R. C. A. Victor, 22760 Hickory Dickory Dock, Ride a cock horse, Yankee Doodle, Sing a song of sixpence, The thread follows the needle
R. C. A. Victor, 21618 Hopp Mor Annika, The chimes of Dunkirk, The farmer in the dell, Did you ever see a lassie?

III. FOLK DANCE RECORDS

Albums and Series

Columbia Album C-26, *Popular American Waltzes*
  Memories, Naughty waltz
  Missouri waltz, Beautiful Ohio
  'Til we meet again, Let me call you sweetheart
  The waltz you saved for me, Three o'clock in the morning

Columbia Album C-136, *Waltz Time*. Recorded by Abe Lyman and his orchestra.
  Charmaine, La Golondrina
  Down by the old mill stream, Meet me tonight in dreamland
  Jeannie, Missouri waltz
  I'm falling in love, Valse Huguette

Folk Dance Records (arranged and recorded by Burns, Evans, & Wheeler). Albums of unbreakable records, with instruction on the records

Album I (for lower grades). Four records
  121-122 Bleking (Swedish), Bow Belinda (American)
  123-124 Donkey dance (Mexican), Children's polka (German)
  125-126 Seven steps (German), Danish dance of greeting (Danish)
  127-128 Chimes of Dunkirk (Belgian), Carousel (Swedish)

Album II (for intermediate groups). Four records
  221-222 Put your little foot (American), Kolos (Serbian)
  223-224 Oh! Susanna (American), Csebogar (Hungarian)
  225-226 Heel and toe polka (American), Swedish clap dance (Swedish)
  227-228 Corsican, Parts 1 and 2 (French)

Album A. Four 12-inch records (By Burns and Wheeler)
  331-332 Minuet (American), Lassie dance (Swedish)
  333-334 Dutch couples (Dutch), Swiss May dance (Swiss)
  335-336 Tantoli (Swedish), Good night ladies (American)
  337-338 Come, let us be joyful (German), Shoemaker's dance (Danish)

Album B. Four 12-inch records (By Burns and Wheeler)
  341-342 Highland schottische (Scotch), Tarantella (Italian)
  343-344 Ace of diamonds (Danish), Csardas (Hungarian)
  345-346 Norwegian mountain march (Norwegian), Crested hen (Danish)
  347-348 Gustaf's skoal (Swedish), Irish lilt (Irish)

FOLKCRAFT Album F-6, *Texas Couple Dances and Singing Quadrilles.* Four 10-inch
records, without calls
  F1034 Put your little foot (Varsovienne), Good night waltz
  F1035 Oklahoma mixer (Rustic schottische), Cotton eyed Joe
  F1036 My little girl, Ten pretty girls
  F1037 Hot time in the old town, Oh Johnny, oh!

FOLKCRAFT Album F-9, *Lithuanian Folk Dances.* Four 10-inch records, with instruc-
tions
  F1049 Mikita, Sustas, Koja-koja
  F1050 Kubilas, Suktinis, Noriu Miego
  F1051 Kalvelis, Vedaras
  F1052 Malunas, Ziogelis, Greiz-Greicius

4-STAR Album FS-107, *Couple Dances.* Four 10-inch unbreakable records. Carl Journell
with Grady Hester and his Texsons
  1365 Little brown jug, Glow worm
  1366 Put your little foot, Starlight schottische
  1367 Oxford minuet, Golden slippers
  1368 Red wing, Cotton eyed Joe

IMPERIAL Album FD-9, *American Folk Dances.* Played by Harley Luse and his
orchestra. Four records with directions
  1043 Under the bamboo tree, Spanish circle
  1044 Glowworm, Rye waltz
  1045 Veleta waltz, Cotton eyed Joe
  1046 Moon winks, California schottische

IMPERIAL Album FD-13, *Mexican Folk Dances.* Played by Manuel S. Acuña and his
orchestra. Instructions on album cover. Four records
  1081 El Chote, Las Altenitas
  1082 La Jesusita, La Cucaracha
  1083 La Bamba, La Mesticita
  1084 La Joaquinita, La Raspa

IMPERIAL Album FD-22, *American Old Time Dances.* Eva Decker and her Old
Timers. Four records
  1092 Virginia reel, Trilby

1093 Spanish waltz, Boston two-step
1094 Oxford minuet, Rosemary schottische
1095 Waltz quadrille, Fireman's dance

IMPERIAL Album FD-37, *Philippine Folk Dances*. Instructions on album cover. Four records
1184 Esperanza, Mazurka
1185 Cariñosa, La Jota Ilacano
1186 Aetana, Polka Sala
1187 Chotis, Ba-O

METHODIST RECORDS. *The World of Fun Series*. Unbreakable records, with directions
M101 Cshebogar, Kalvelis, Hol-di-ri-di-a, Seven steps
M102 Galway Piper, Ace of diamonds, Come, let us be joyful, Danish schottische
M103 Irish washerwoman, Captain Jinks
M104 Red River Valley, Pop goes the weasel, Sicilian circle, Camptown races
M105 Troika, Spanish circle, Chimes of Dunkirk, Danish weaving dance
M106 La Raspa, Green sleeves, Trip to Helsinki, Trallen
M107 Little Brown jug, Put your little foot, The fireman's dance
M108 Seven jumps, Korobushka, Gustav's skoal, Crested hen
M109 Cumberland Square eight, Good humor, Christ Church bells, Black nag

PIONEER RECORDS. Made for Houston, Texas, elementary schools. Relatively expensive
First Grade
  3001 Let your feet go tramp, The gallant ship, Let us wash our dolly's clothes; This is the way the lady rides, Round and round the village, Ducks
High First Grade
  3002 Little pony, The swing; Rig-a-jig, Three funny old men
  3012 How do you do my partner, A-Hunting we will go; Did you ever see a lassie? Oats, peas, beans
Second Grade
  3003 Water sprite; Skip to my Lou
  3004 Soldier boy, Carousel; Children's polka, Circle dance
  3013 With even step, The snail; Draw a bucket of water, Jump Jim Crow
  3014 Ladita (Lott ist Todt), Miller boy; Our little girls, Dance of greeting
Third Grade
  3005 Stole my partner, Herr Schmidt; Turn Simlin, Tidy-o
  3006 Amelosche Kermisse, Pop goes the weasel; La Raspa, One, two, three, four, five
  3015 The wheat, Flip; Csebogar, The thread follows the needle
  3016 Ten little Indians, Javornik; Turn around me, Bleking
Fourth Grade
  1007 Red River Valley, Sent my brown jug to town; Garden walk, O Susanna
  3008 Manchester, Little foot; Turning dance, Go from me
  3017 Gooseberry girl, Kaca; Paw paw patch, Rise sugar rise
  3018 Paterka, When I rode to Prague; Lotte Gik, Comin' round the mountain
Fifth Grade
  3009 Brass wagon, Ain't gonna rain no more; Puttjentar, Tancuj
  3019 Coffee grows on white oak trees, Jibi-di-jiba-da; Sekerecka, Weggis dance
Sixth Grade
  3010 Roxy Ann, Schottische; Reznicka, Badger gavotte
  3011 Kanafaska, Polka, Little brown jug
  3020 Dixie mixer, Palpankili; Veleta, Tovacov

SCANDINAVIAN Album S-2, *Scandinavian Folk Dances*. Instructions on album cover
1. Danish Hatter
2. Finnish Raatiko

3. Danish Ace of diamonds
4. Finnish Potku Masurkka
5. Swedish Varsovienne
6. Norwegian Feiar
7. Swedish Tantoli
8. Norwegian Ruggen

SONART Album M-8, *Folk Dances*. Instructions by Michael Herman
   M301 "Mexican Waltz," Kalvelis
   M302 Meitschi putz di, Tancuj
   M303 Eide Ratas, To Ting, Cherkessia
   M304 Masquerade, Kujawiak

Separate Records

CAPITOL, 20102 Golden slippers (two-step)
DECCA, 25061 Spanish waltz (slow)
DECCA, 25062 Military schottische
FOLKCRAFT, F1046 Black hawk waltz, Waltz quadrille (without calls)
FOLKCRAFT, F1047 Spanish circle waltz, Laces and graces
FOLKCRAFT, F1016 Spanish cavaliero, Get along, Cindy (used for American gavotte; instructions)
FOLKCRAFT, F1018 Buffalo gals (used for Patty-cake polka; instructions), Old Joe Clark
IMPERIAL, 1005 Road to the isles, Dashing white sergeant
IMPERIAL, 1006 Black hawk waltz, Laces and graces
IMPERIAL, 1007 Wooden shoes, Eide Ratas
IMPERIAL, 1008 Meitschi putz di, Weggis
IMPERIAL, 1009 Redwing, Rainbow (two-step)
LINDEN, 29 Balen I Karlstad (schottische), Styrmans valsen (waltz)
MACGREGOR, 400 Heel & toe polka, Schottische (fast)
R. C. A. VICTOR, 25-1002A Hot clarinet (polka, slow)
SIMMEL-MESERVEY MUSIC APPRECIATION SERIES. Dance steps with explanation on unbreakable record
   A. Minuet, Waltz, Polka, Jig, Mazurka
   B. Schottische, Country dance, Bolero, Moroccan

IV.   SQUARE DANCE RECORDS

NOTE: Unless otherwise indicated, records include calls

Albums

CAPITOL Album BD-44, *Square Dances*. Cliffie Stone. Four 10-inch records. Instructions included. No calls

Instruction record	Soldiers joy
Cripple Creek	Sally Gooden
Gal I left behind me	Bake them hoecakes brown
Golden slippers	Ragtime Annie

COLUMBIA Album C-47, Square Dances. Four 10-inch records

The first two ladies cross over	Darling Nellie Gray
Oh Susanna	Buffalo boy
Dive for the oyster (2 sides)	Possum in the 'simmon tree
Little brown jug (without calls)	(without calls)

DECCA Album DU-720, *Cowboy Dances* (American Folk Music Series). Called by Lloyd Shaw. Fast tempo. Includes instruction booklet and colored illustrations. Four 10-inch unbreakable records. Relatively expensive
Star by right

Slit ring hash
Docey Doe hoedown
Practice sides 1-2-3-4-5, music without calls

FOLKCRAFT Album F-2, *County Fair Square Dances* (without calls). Four 10-inch records. Pamphlet with instructions and written calls included

Ten little Indians, Life on the ocean wave
White cockade, Old log cabin
Angleworm wiggle, Wabash cannonball
Nellie Gray, Pop goes the weasel

MACGREGOR Album 1. Les Gotcher, caller. Music by Jack Rivers Boys. Four 12-inch, unbreakable records, with instructions

Hot time in the old town   Right hand over
Lady round the lady   Take a peek
Inside arch   Swing old Adam
I'll swing yours   Texas star

MACGREGOR Album 2. Les Gotcher, caller. Music by Jack Rivers Boys. Four 10-inch, unbreakable records, with instructions

Round dances, without calls: Varsovienna, Schottische, Heel and toe polka, Rye waltz, Sally Gooden
Square dances with calls: Cage the bird, Swing in the center, Dive for the oyster

MACGREGOR Album 3. Les Gotcher, caller. Music by Circle 8 Ranch Boys. Four 10-inch, unbreakable records, instructions included. Except for the last, these squares are more advanced

Two little sisters   Four in line
Forward eight and chain around   Double bow knot
Whirl away and resashay   Ocean wave
Gents bow under   Oh, Johnny (circle mixer)

MACGREGOR Album 4. Singing calls by Fenton ("Jonesy") Jones. Four 10-inch unbreakable records

Pine tree   Parle vous
Pop goes the weasel   Indian style
Comin' round the mountain   Marchin' through Georgia
Hot time   Pistol packin' mama

NOTE: MacGregor Albums 5, 6 and 7, square dances, are also available.

R. C. A. VICTOR Album C-36, *Square Dances*. Called by Floyd C. Woodhull. Four 12-inch records

Oh Susanna   The girl I left behind me
Pop goes the weasel   Triple right and left four
Captain Jinks   Blackberry quadrille (without calls)
The wearing of the green   Soldier's joy (without calls)

SQUARE DANCE ASSOCIATES Album 1, *Honor Your Partner*. Three 12-inch, unbreakable records, directions and calls on each record. A good beginning square dance album

Susanna, Formation of a set and heads and sides dance
Honolulu baby, Do-si-do and swing
Around the outside and swing, Two head ladies cross over

SQUARE DANCE ASSOCIATES Album 2, *Honor Your Partner*. Three 12-inch, unbreakable records. Directions with calls

Yankee Doodle, Sweet Alice waltz quadrille
Duck for the oyster, Ladies chain
Darling Nellie Gray, Push her away

SQUARE DANCE ASSOCIATES Album 3, *Honor Your Partner.* Three 12-inch, unbreakable records. Directions with calls

Loch Lomond, Ladies grand chain
Texas Star, Left hand lady pass under
My little girl, The basket
NOTE: Square Dance Associates Albums 4 and 5 are also available.

SUGGESTIONS FOR RECORD PURCHASES

Most four-record albums of the breakable type sell for under $5.00. The unbreakable records are more expensive but more satisfactory for school use. Many companies provide instruction booklets, instruction records, or directions on album covers for folk dances and singing games.

The records listed above were selected because they are particularly suitable for rhythmical activities in the elementary school. Many other rhythm and folk dance records are available and new recordings are being made constantly. Reviews of new records appear in periodicals devoted to folk dancing.

Most of the records listed may be purchased from local music dealers. The headquarters of the Folk Dance Federation of California, Ed Kremer's Folk Shop, 262 O'Farrell Street, San Francisco 2, California, has a large stock of rhythm and dance records. Some of the manufacturers of records who sell their records direct are the following:

HELENE ALLEN, Woodpecker Records Company, 4925 E. Broadway, Long Beach 3, California

JOSEPH BURNS, RUTH EVANS, AND EDITH WHEELER, Folk Dance Records, Joseph V. Burns, 573 Connecticut Avenue, Bridgeport 7, Connecticut, or Ruth Evans, 326 Forest Park Avenue, Springfield 8, Massachusetts

RUTH EVANS, Childhood Rhythm Records, 326 Forest Park Avenue, Springfield 8, Massachusetts

PHOEBE JAMES PRODUCTS, Box 134, Pacific Palisades, California

METHODIST RECORDS, World of Fun Series, Methodist Publishing House, 85 McAllister Street, San Francisco 2, California

PIONEER RECORDS, Sound Sales and Engineering, 1614 Fannin Street, Houston 2, Texas

Appendix D

FILMS AND FILMSTRIPS

I. BIBLIOGRAPHY

Catalogue of 16 MM Educational Motion Pictures Available for Loan to Schools, Industries, Organizations, Individuals. Department of Visual Instruction, University Extension, University of California, Berkeley and Los Angeles. Published annually.

Educational Film Guide. H. W. Wilson Company, 950-972 University Avenue, New York 52, N. Y. Published monthly, with annual compilation. Includes all current 16 mm. motion pictures of educational type. Orders should be sent to individual producers.

Educational Films in Sports. National Section on Women's Athletics, American Association for Health, Physical Education, and Recreation (1201 Sixteenth St., N.W., Washington 6, D. C.), 1945. An annotated list of films on sports. (Out of print; new edition in preparation, 1950.)

Educational Screen. Department of Visual Instruction of the National Education Association, published by Educational Screen, Inc., 64 East Lake St., Chicago, Ill. Monthly digest of literature on visual education, teachers' evaluation of films, and latest classroom tools in visual teaching.

FALCONER, VERA M. *Filmstrips, A Descriptive Index and Users' Guide.* New York: McGraw-Hill Book Company, 1948. A compilation describing filmstrips suitable for instructional use, with practical suggestions for use.

Filmstrip Guide. H. W. Wilson Co., 950-972 University Avenue, New York 52, N. Y. Published monthly.

"1000 and One." The Blue Book of Non-Theatrical Films. Published by the Educational Screen, 64 East Lake Street, Chicago, Ill. Published yearly.

See and Hear. The Journal of Audio-Visual Learning. E. M. Hale, Eau Claire, Wisconsin.

II. SELECTED FILMS

A. Films available from the UNIVERSITY EXTENSION, UNIVERSITY OF CALIFORNIA.[1] *The number following the title is the order number. Rental prices are given.*

Ball Handling in Basketball, 3689, sound, 10 minutes, $1.50. Encyclopedia Britannica. Stance, "feel" of ball, catching, passing, slow motion.

Ball Handling in Football, 3692, sound, 10 min., $1.50. Encyclopedia Britannica. Grip, stance, fingertip control. Action pictures.

Bowling Fundamentals, 3866, sound, 20 min., $3.00. Teaching Films, Inc. Posture, method of holding ball, approach, delivery, "spot" bowling.

Care of the Feet, 3371, sound, 10 min., $1.50. Encyclopedia Britannica. Weight-support, walking, foot ailments, and proper fitting of shoes.

Children of China, 2996, sound, 10 min., $1.50. Encyclopedia Britannica. Family play and recreation.

Children of Holland, 2811, sound, 10 min., $1.50. Encyclopedia Britannica. Normal day of play, school, games, and chores.

---

[1] Consult the *Catalogue* for instructions on ordering films. Orders should be sent to the Department of Visual Instruction, University Extension Bldg., Berkeley 4, California, unless they are from the southern counties—Imperial, Inyo, Kern, Kings, Los Angeles, Orange, Riverside, San Bernardino, San Diego, San Luis Obispo, Santa Barbara, Tulare, and Ventura—who order from the Southern Film Center, Room 6, Administration Bldg., 405 Hilgard Avenue, Los Angeles 24. California.

Children of Japan, 2987, sound, 10 min., $1.50. Encyclopedia Britannica.
Life at home, at school; playing baseball.
Children of Russia, 3826, sound, 13 min., $1.50. International Film Foundation, Inc.
School, play, pioneer camp.
Ice Carnival, 2895, sound, 10 min., $1.50. Castle Films.
Skating, stunts, solo and duo skating.
Navajo Children, 2691, sound, 10 min., $1.50. Encyclopedia Britannica.
Winter life, spring morning, use of bows and arrows, little play.
Play in the Snow, 3603, sound, 10 min., $1.50. Encyclopedia Britannica.
Three children play at making a snow man, playing fox and geese; stresses
safety in snow.
Shooting in Basketball, 3687, sound, 10 min., $1.50. Encyclopedia Britannica.
Set-shot, stance, co-ordination of body; slow motion and close-ups.
Soccer for Girls, 3879, sound, 10 min., $1.50. Coronet Films.
Teaches basic skill; slow motion; shows game.
Softball for Girls, 4002, sound, 10 min., $1.50. Coronet Films.
Shows fundamental skills of game: throwing, catching, batting, and fielding.
The Story of Menstruation, 3811, sound, color, 10 min., free. International Cellucot-
ton Products Co.
Animated drawings show what happens during menstrual period and health care.
Swimming for Beginners, 3559, sound, color, 10 min., $2.00. Visual Educational
Films.
How to overcome fear; leg action, breathing, arms.
The Technique of Tennis, 3051, sound, 10 min., $1.00. Teaching Films.
Lloyd Budge outlines tennis fundamentals.
Volleyball for Boys, 2637, sound, 10 min., $1.50. Coronet Films.
Serve, volleying the ball, spiking the ball.

B. *Films available from* CORONET INSTRUCTIONAL FILMS, IDEAL PICTURES CORPORATION,
2408 W. 7th St., Los Angeles 5, California. Purchase price is quoted.

Basketball for Girls—Fundamental Techniques, sound, 10 min., $45.
Demonstrates fundamental techniques of ball handling, passing, and shooting.
Basketball Fundamentals, sound, 13½ min., $56.25.
Shows fundamentals of shooting, passing, dribbling, defensive and offensive
footwork.
Matt Mann's Swimming Techniques for Boys, sound, 15 min., $78.75; color $157.50.
Demonstrates boys learning the crawl, breast stroke, back and butterfly.
Matt Mann's Swimming Techniques for Girls, sound, 10 min., $45; color $90.
Shows a beginning class learning swimming skills.
Posture Habits, sound, 10 min., $45; color $90.
Discusses standing, walking, and sitting posture.
Playground Safety, sound, 10 min., $45; color $90.
Safety rules are explained to all ages of children.
Softball for Boys, sound, 10 min., $45; color $90.
Analysis of individual player skills, and of team play.
Speedball for Girls, sound, 11 min., $45; color $90.
Positions, techniques, skills, team play.

C. *Films available from* PORTAFILMS, *418 N. Glendale Avenue, Glendale 6, California.
Purchase price is quoted.*

Let's Play Safe, sound, 10 min., $45; color $80.
Elementary safety series, intermediate grade level; produced with co-operation
of La Canada elementary school and Los Angeles County and City of Los
Angeles Board of Education; playground incidents dramatized.

D. *Films available from* CRAIG VISUAL AID SERVICE, *Los Angeles and San Francisco (rental basis).*

American Square Dances, sound, 10 min., Coronet Films.
    Boys and girls demonstrate simple square dances.
Social Dancing, sound, 10 min., Coronet Films.
    Instruction in positions and steps.

III. SELECTED FILMSTRIPS

A. *Filmstrips available from* ASSOCIATION FILMS (Y. M. C. A.), *351 Turk St., San Francisco 2, California.*

Play Softball, 86 frames, with script, $3.50.
    Illustrates basic skills and team play; produced with *Look* magazine.

B. *Filmstrips available from* ENCYCLOPEDIA BRITANNICA FILMS, INC., *1150 Wilmette Ave., Wilmette, Illinois.*

Care of the Feet and Human Body, 85 frames, $3.00.
    For classroom use.

C. *Filmstrips available from* SIMMEL-MESERVEY, INC., *321 S. Beverly Drive, Beverly Hills, California.*

Share the Ball, 32 frames, with text, $2.50.
    Shows distinction between "mine" and "ours."
Share the Sandpile, 26 frames, with text, $2.50.
    Two schoolboys build in a sandbox, quarrel, and solve the quarrel.

D. *Filmstrips available from* YOUNG AMERICA FILMS, INC., *18 E. 41st Street, New York 17, N. Y.*

Straight and Tall, 39 frames, with text, $3.50.
    Shows good posture and why it is desirable; proper food, exercise, rest gives strong, straight bodies.
Your Posture—Good or Bad, 46 frames, with text, $3.50.
    Shows importance of good posture—points to remember.

Appendix E

CATALOGUES OF TEACHING AIDS

Elementary Teachers Guide to Free Curriculum Materials. Edited by J. G. Fowlkes and Donald A. Morgan. Educators Progress Service, Randolph, Wis.

An annotated classified list of all free materials suitable to use in elementary schools—pamphlets, charts, maps, exhibits, etc. Much health education but, with exception of posture, first aid, and field diagrams, no physical education material.

Lantern Slides Any Teacher Can Make Free. Turtox Service Dept., General Biological Supply House, 761-763 East 69th Place, Chicago 37, Ill.

MILLER, BRUCE. *Sources of Free and Inexpensive Teaching Aids.* Revised edition, 1948. Bruce Miller, Box 222, Ontario, Calif.

A selected, annotated, classified list of materials suitable as teaching aids in schools.

NATIONAL RECREATION ASSOCIATION. Publications on Play and Recreation. National Recreation Association, 315 Fourth Avenue, New York 10, N. Y.

A catalogue of inexpensive pamphlets and books on every phase of play and recreation.

Nystrom Visual Aids to Learning and Teaching. Issued yearly by A. J. Nystrom & Co., 3333 Elston Ave., Chicago 18, Ill.

A catalogue of all types of charts for walls or tripods. There are a few on posture and safety suitable for elementary school use.

INDEX

INDEX

[995]

o

printed in CALIFORNIA STATE PRINTING OFFICE